RESIDENTIAL & LIGHT COMMERCIAL CONSTRUCTION STANDARDS

Third Edition, Updated

The All-in-One, Authoritative Reference Compiled from:

- Major Building Codes
- Recognized Trade Customs
- Industry Standards

RSMeans

RESIDENTIAL & LIGHT COMMERCIAL CONSTRUCTION STANDARDS

Third Edition, Updated

The All-in-One, Authoritative Reference Compiled from:

- Major Building Codes
- Recognized Trade Customs
- Industry Standards

RSMeans

Copyright © 2008
Reed Construction Data, Inc.
Construction Publishers & Consultants
63 Smiths Lane
Kingston, MA 02364-3008
781-422-5000
www.rsmeans.com
RSMeans is a product line of Reed Construction Data.

Managing Editor: Mary Greene. Editorial Supervisor: Andrea Sillah.
Editorial Assistant: Jessica deMartin. Production Manager: Michael Kokernak.
Production Coordinator: Jill Goodman. Composition: Sheryl Rose.
Proofreaders: Jill Goodman/Mary Lou Geary. Book and cover design: Sheryl Rose.

Printed in the United States of America

SKY10041692_012323

Library of Congress Cataloging in Publication Data

ISBN 978-0-87629-012-5

TABLE OF CONTENTS

PREFACE

This book began with a group of California construction defect analysts who, in the course of their work in claims litigation, collected a tremendous amount of data to help define construction quality standards. Their ongoing efforts to compile and maintain a current library of information from a range of authoritative sources convinced them that having this kind of data collected in one convenient resource would be a boon not only to defect analysts and insurance personnel, but for contractors and subcontractors, engineers, architects, and owners. Having quick access to reliable standards would enable users to answer questions directly and avoid costly errors, delays, and disputes. The result is fewer sources of conflict among all the parties involved in a project, and a much better chance for a job that meets code, quality, and schedule expectations.

At the National Association of Home Builders 1997 Builders Show, a group of contractors, leaders in their industry and within NAHB, first came together to help outline the book's contents. These individuals, listed in "Acknowledgments" and "About the Editors," provided the direction the book needed to ensure its usefulness to contractors and other members of the project team. Some of these NAHB members, many of them Trustees of the Commercial Builders Council, went on to play a major role in the book's development as editors. RSMeans editors brought their own practical experience as contractors and engineers to this project and directed and organized much of the research.

This third edition of *Residential & Light Commercial Construction Standards* has been updated over the years to the latest building codes and standards. It also includes new material from green building practices for nearly all areas of construction, to earthquake and hurricane construction. The Introduction explains these new features and how to find the information you need in the various parts of the book. It also includes some examples of common problems this book can solve.

DISCLAIMER

This book is a collection of information from a variety of published sources, both print and electronic, together with comments from the editors based on their own experience in the construction industry. Sources include building code organizations, related testing and standards organizations, trade associations, commercial publishers, government agencies, and some product manufacturers. Presentation of this information is not intended to suggest that there are no other sources, nor that these are the legal requirement or standard for every location. Other accepted standards may be found on any of these topics. Product manufacturers can provide additional information and instructions, and other publications may provide more detail or a different perspective on some installations. Manufacturers' warranty requirements should always be followed. In all cases, users of the book should consult their local codes and building practices. The editors have made their best effort to ensure that the information from the building codes, standards organizations, government agencies, and professional associations is current as of this book's printing. Users are urged to check with these organizations to ensure that they are referring to the latest available information at any given time.

Users of the book should apply their own judgment based on professional experience with the construction installations described, or obtain guidance from a professional with expertise on the subject(s). Users are also advised to refer, as necessary, to the excerpted sources in their entirety for a more complete understanding of a topic, and to consult the organizations listed at the beginning of each chapter for further information.

Many of the construction systems covered in the book are addressed by excerpts from several sources. The focus, coverage, and specific recommendations may overlap and may differ from one source to another. The purpose of including these different versions is to provide as complete a perspective as possible. Note that building code requirements throughout this publication have been paraphrased from the code text. Users are advised to refer to the codes for complete coverage and specific wording.

Note that the editors' comments (printed in blue boxes throughout the book) represent these individuals' own experience in the field and are not intended to signify building code requirements or other standards. The editors have applied diligence and judgment in locating and using reliable sources for the information included in the book.

However, neither RSMeans nor the editors make any express or implied warranty or guarantee in connection with the content of the information contained in this book, including the accuracy, correctness, value, sufficiency, or completeness of the data, methods, and other information contained herein. RSMeans makes no express or implied warranty of merchantability or fitness for a particular purpose, nor does it have any liability to any customer or third party for any loss, expense, or damage including consequential, incidental, special or punitive damages, including lost profits or lost revenue, caused directly or indirectly by any error or omission, or arising out of, or in connection with, the information contained herein.

Illustrations shown in the book are provided to assist users in understanding the construction systems. These graphics may not include all requirements for a system, product, or unit, and may not represent the only acceptable method.

Note that a few pages of published material from manufacturers are included in order to demonstrate installation methods. These references are not intended as an endorsement of any product or manufacturer.

ACKNOWLEDGMENTS

Assembling this book required the input, efforts, and cooperation of a team of experts, including a number of organizations. The editors selected the materials that have been excerpted from other sources and added their own "Comments" based on years of experience in the field and as instructors. The editors—contractors, engineers, an architect, construction defect analyst, and a former building inspection official among them—are listed in the "About the Editors" section of these acknowledgments.

Several other individuals who contributed their time and efforts in reviewing and helping to shape the book in its initial stages are listed below. The earliest drafts of the first edition were reviewed by Ray Caruso, Wayne DelPico, and Buzz Artiano. Mr. DelPico also reviewed the new third edition, along with Robert F. Cox, PhD, Roy Gilley, AIA, Martin Joyce, and Kenneth Humphreys, PE, CCE.

Key input in the development of the book came from a number of members of the National Association of Home Builders Commercial Builders Council: Cliff Schilling, George Goudreau, Jr., Dale Gruber, Robert Ross, Fred Dallenbach, and Jim Quinly.

We are grateful to the building code organizations, professional trade associations, product manufacturer institutes, and publishers who allowed us to reproduce their materials. Each source is identified where it is quoted in the book.

About the Editors

Editors of this third edition and previous editions of this book include:

Don Reynolds, commercial builder and construction defects analyst, has more than 30 years' experience in the industry. A licensed contractor and insurance adjuster, Don is senior estimator at Ninteman Construction Company, a firm that specializes in medium- and high-rise buildings, condominiums, and concrete parking structures. Don is also president of

Inland Property Consultants in San Diego, California, a firm that performs construction defect analysis, interprets building code, and provides expert witness testimony in litigation. Don has been a speaker at the National Association of Home Builders' annual Builders Show on the topic of defining and achieving quality in construction and avoiding defects.

Dale Peterson was the owner of Peterson Construction Company in Little Falls, Minnesota, for over 25 years. In addition to performing new and remodeling construction jobs, both residential and commercial, Mr. Peterson served as a "construction expert" in mediation and arbitration cases. He was an active member of the National Association of Home Builders, and a trustee of that organization's Commercial Builders Council. He also served as the director of the Builders Association of Minnesota.

Jim Watanabe is President of JW Inc., a construction and construction management company in Honolulu, Hawaii. His work focuses on light commercial, new residential, and remodeling projects. Mr. Watanabe has served as chairman of the National Association of Home Builders Commercial Builders Council and was area vice president and an Executive Committee member. He is a former president of the Building Industry Association of Hawaii, and has been honored by that organization as "Builder of the Year" three times.

Dennis Fong is a general contractor in California, with over 25 years of experience in residential and commercial construction. Mr. Fong also performs construction analysis for insurance companies for litigation claims.

Howard Chandler, executive director of the Builders Association of Greater Boston (BAGB), is a former senior engineer/editor at RSMeans. He was the editor of Means' *Residential Cost Data* and *Repair & Remodeling Cost Data* and instructor for Means' estimating seminar series. Mr. Chandler spent more than 30 years in the construction industry as the owner of a residential construction company and manager of field operations for a firm specializing in commercial, industrial, and institutional construction. He has taught construction technology and management as director of education for the Massachusetts/Rhode Island Associated Builders and Contractors and at the Wentworth Institute of Technology, and has presented programs for the Appraisal Institute, the National Association of Home Builders, and the National Association for Women in Construction, among other organizations.

Andrew Fleming, a licensed master plumber, journeyman plumber, and gas fitter, has more than 25 years experience in plumbing, as a practitioner, inspector, and instructor. Mr. Fleming performed all phases of plumbing, heating, and gas fitting in residential, commercial and industrial locations. He is a former plumbing and gas inspector for the city of Medford, Massachusetts, and has taught plumbing and gas fitting to apprentices and journeymen studying to obtain state licensure. He provides training, technical support, and quality control and ensures code compliance of work performed by trade partners with his firm, ServiceEdge Partners, Inc., in Burlington, Massachusetts. Mr. Fleming has served as former vice president on the Board of Directors of the New England Association of Plumbing, Gas, and Mechanical Inspectors.

Keith Everhart is a construction analyst for Golden Eagle Insurance Corporation. He performs investigations of residential construction defect allegations throughout California and Arizona; reviews building code interpretations, plans, and specifications; and determines "duty owed" based on industry standards and trade custom. Keith has over 30 years' experience as a general contractor, building homes, and managing commercial projects including schools and libraries, malls, parking garages, movie theaters, and hospital remodels. Keith is a past president of the Builders Association of Greater Nevada, a chapter of the National Association of Home Builders.

Raymond Arms, PE, is a registered professional engineer with over 30 years' experience in design, construction, contracting and failure analysis. He is registered in seven states, including California and Florida, where he designs electrical and HVAC systems for commercial and institutional buildings and performs failure analysis and construction defect analysis. He is a member of NFPA and ASHRAE.

Keith J. Reynolds is a general contractor who has built projects throughout the states of California, Arizona, and Texas. Mr. Reynolds performs both remodeling and new construction work—residential and commercial—including shopping centers, multi-family condominiums, and apartment buildings, specializing in concrete, masonry, and multi-family rehabs.

William Jorgensen is a contractor, construction analyst, and estimator with over 20 years experience in residential, commercial, and institutional construction, and a specialty in concrete, framing, and detailing in earthquake zones. As a construction analyst, he has sought fairness in identifying legitimate deficiencies by researching and presenting industry standards for items that are often not defined in the building codes. Mr. Jorgensen is vice president of quality and loss control for CAN Commercial Insurance Company's Building Assurance Center.

William H. Rowe III, AIA, PE, principal of Rowe Design Group, Inc. in Arlington, Massachusetts, has been involved in a range of new and retrofit construction projects, including residential, institutional, and commercial buildings. Mr. Rowe has also been a lecturer at universities, including Harvard and the Rhode Island School of Design, and a presenter of professional seminars.

INTRODUCTION

Purpose of the Book

This book is a resource for anyone concerned with quality in residential or light commercial building construction projects. It is a compilation of current standards that define quality in construction. Its purpose is to give contractors and others one-stop access to information that will help resolve or avoid disputes, set a quality level for subcontractors or employees, and answer client questions with authority. It is based on building code requirements and the educational materials developed by leading professional associations, product manufacturer institutes, and other recognized experts.

Virtually every aspect of the construction process is covered: paving; concrete and masonry; wood and metal framing; finish carpentry and cabinetry; insulation, ventilation, and vapor retarders; roofing, siding, and moisture protection; doors and windows; plaster, drywall, and ceramic tile; ceilings and floor coverings; painting and wall coverings; specialties; plumbing; HVAC; and electrical.

This edition also features new coverage of green building, seismic, hurricane, and mold-resistant construction. Throughout the book, you will find icons to alert you to standards and guidance relating to these topics. Several chapters include an introductory page identifying green approaches to that particular area of construction.

There are several ways to assess and interpret quality in building construction—including meeting safety and warranty requirements, aesthetic criteria, and other details of craftsmanship that contribute to the integrity and longevity of the structure.

A fundamental measure of quality is adherence to the standards established by building codes, whose purpose is to protect life and property. Another definition of quality is the recommendations of institutes representing building product manufacturers. Their guidelines are distributed through publications and electronic products, on the Internet, and in training sessions and videos. These recommendations, based on field and laboratory research, are often linked to warranties on the materials used.

Quality standards are also set forth by professional associations that serve as advocates for contractors and design professionals. One of the ways these organizations serve their members is by developing and distributing educational materials on current and correct construction methods.

Finally, there are the respected and experienced craftsmen, many of whom have taught courses and contributed to or authored books that convey quality in construction. The books they have written are often used in college-level and vocational schools to set a standard for the practice of residential and light commercial building construction.

To provide the most complete and balanced picture, the editors have drawn on as many of the above sources as practical in this book. In the process, they have reviewed scores of the most current publications, websites, and other materials. They have excerpted, with permission, key definitions of standards to create a one-stop overview of what contractors, owners, architects, building officials, and insurers should expect in the houses and light commercial structures they build, inhabit, design, inspect, and insure.

How the Book Is Organized

There are 16 chapters in this book, each covering a specialty within the construction industry—from paving to electrical. The table of contents lists the major topics within each chapter. Each chapter has its own individual table of contents, as well, with a more detailed breakdown of sub-topics. Throughout the book, notes from the editors will refer you to related information in other chapters.

Each chapter contains:

- *Common Defect Allegations:* Items to watch out for that are frequent targets of claims and disputes. (See the blue box at the beginning of each chapter.)

- *Introduction & Professional Associations:* Background on the topic and a list of authoritative resources to contact if you need more detailed information that exceeds the scope of this book. (We have made every effort to ensure that this information is current at the time of the book's printing. However, changes are inevitable, within organizations and particularly on the Internet. These contacts are, at the least, a reliable starting point.)

- *International Building Code and International Residential Code:* Always in blue lettering, these excerpts have been selected to give an overview of code requirements for various construction installations. The *International Building Code, International Residential Code* and other trade-specific codes are referenced to show how a construction installation is addressed, but users of the book will want to consult their own local codes for specific requirements in their own localities. Code excerpts in the chapters are always introduced by name, publication year, and code section number. In some cases, code sections may include references to further details or exceptions within the code book that we have not included in this publication due to space limitations and our goal of providing an overview. We have tried, in these cases, to summarize or note the topic of such references so you will know whether it is likely to be relevant to your question or problem. See "Understanding Building Codes" later in this section for an explanation of how the building codes apply (and relate to one another) in different parts of the country.

- *Industry Standards:* Recommendations, requirements, and tolerances for construction installations from professional associations, product manufacturers' institutes, and respected published references. Often these resources provide more specific requirements for quality and finished appearance than do building codes, since codes are focused primarily on ensuring the safety of the building occupants.

  In some cases, the recommendations of one industry standard authority may differ from another. Some may put forth more explicit, detailed, or stringent requirements or tolerances than others. Our purpose is to provide users with as complete a perspective as possible, based on reliable information from the leading authoritative sources.

- *Comments:* Always appearing in blue-colored boxes, "Comments" are practical observations from the editors, respected construction professionals, based on their own experience and knowledge of various regions. A few items are covered primarily in the form of comments. This occurs when there are no building code requirements on that topic and/or there are few available published standards for that type of installation.

Applying the Information

Following are a few examples of the many ways this resource can be applied to resolve or prevent a problem. Having readily available, authoritative information answers questions directly, so that disputes and costly errors can be avoided. This helps reduce adversarial relations among all the parties involved in a project, and fosters a job that meets code, quality, and schedule expectations.

Example # 1

The building codes that apply to various regions of the country are very similar in their basic requirements. (See "Understanding Building Codes" later in this section.) This book, with its building code excerpts (primarily from the *IBC* and *IRC*), allows you to quickly and easily identify the aspects of a construction system that are addressed by building codes, and shows you the format and language in which you are likely to find that item in your own local code. For example, a question arises on correct standards for installation of a roofing system. Finding the answer in a code book may require prior knowledge of the subject as well as familiarity with the code format and organization. Chapter 8 of this book shows the main issues and requirements addressed by the codes and other experts for the roof system in question. This information is easy to find, as it is clearly organized by type of roof installation.

While you must still comply with your local building code and the project documents, this book gives you a start on the basic requirements and some tools to help you navigate building codes.

Chapter 8 is also full of supporting information including the recommendations of authorities like the National Roofing Contractors Association, guidance from respected construction publications, and practical comments from experienced contractors. If you require very detailed information beyond what is covered in the book, the chapter provides contact information, including website addresses and phone numbers, to contact your preferred source.

Example #2

A residential contractor has to hire subcontractors to perform specialty concrete work for a light commercial job. While the contractor is confident in his firm's ability to build the project per plans and specifications, neither he nor his superintendent are experienced in this type of construction. Using Chapter 2 of this book as a reference enables the contractor and his superintendent to resolve any quality issues that come up, and to head off problems such as cracking, puddling, and cold joints. Not only is this information a helpful tool for preconstruction meetings with subcontractors, but it will be used during construction to clearly communicate quality standards and expectations.

Example #3

The owners of a new home complain to the contractor that they can hear the sound of plumbing in the bathrooms from the adjoining rooms. The contractor explains how he installed insulation in the interior partition walls to reduce sound transmission, but that it is impossible to completely muffle the sound. In Chapter 7, "Insulation and Vapor Retarders," the section on soundproofing states that while "you cannot expect to make any walls in the house truly soundproof, you can effectively cut down the transmission of sound ... (using) a number of approaches (including) filling the interior partition wall with batts of R-11 unfaced fiberglass insulation or rigid foam rated at around R-11. If you want to make the wall even more soundproof, double the drywall on each side of the wall." While these are indicated as acceptable solutions, the reference also notes that the "best" technique uses 2x6 top and bottom plates, with staggered 2x4 wall studs, weaving insulation between the studs, then installing double layers of drywall on each side of the wall. In the example scenario, the contractor has used what industry standards would consider a reasonable approach to reduce sound transmission. Contractors might want to offer homeowners a choice of these options up front, spelling out differences in their associated costs. (Note: The "Common Defect Allegations" at the beginning of Chapter 14 offer a plumbing solution to the noise problem.)

Example #4

A general contractor has been hired to perform interior build-out work for a corporate library. Based on previous experience with similar projects, the contractor has submitted an estimate based on shelving and units that are more costly than the client had anticipated. Using wider units and thinner shelving material would decrease the cost significantly, but increase the likelihood of shelf deflection (bowing and sagging) and, consequently, customer dissatisfaction. Using the American Woodwork Institute reference table on shelf deflection in Chapter 6, the contractor can provide the owner with a clear and authoritative explanation of his recommendation.

These examples are a small sampling of the many uses contractors, engineers, architects, owners, and others have described for this book. The primary intent of this publication is to make key information available for quick reference, thereby reducing errors and disputes and increasing project quality.

UNDERSTANDING BUILDING CODES & OTHER STANDARDS

As many as three levels of building code requirements—federal, state, and local—may apply to a project, depending on where it is located.

Federal codes address issues such as land use and environmental requirements. This category may include protection of historic properties or wetlands. Federal codes are not involved in most residential and light commercial projects.

State codes, enforced by local building officials, address life safety issues in areas such as fire protection and mechanical and electrical requirements. State codes may also cover environmental issues.

Local codes are based on regional or national codes established by national code organizations, such as the International Code Council. For example, local codes may specify setback and drainage requirements, maximum roof height, and minimum lot size. Local codes are typically enforced by the town or city building inspector and county zoning board.

Although there may be local modifications, most building codes are based on what is referred to as a "model" code. In 1994, the International Code Council (ICC) was formed in response to the request by many in the building trades for a single building code in the U.S. The ICC published the first edition of the *International Building Code®* (*IBC*) in 2000. The *IBC* has since been adopted by all 50 states, plus Washington, DC.

The *IBC* is an all-inclusive building code that covers all aspects of construction—from roofing, wall construction, and finishes, to fire protection, occupancy, and accessibility requirements. The *IBC* incorporates elements of each of the model codes, and applies to all new construction and alteration of existing structures.

The *IBC* does not apply to residential structures unless they are more than three stories, however. Residential structures are instead covered by the *International Residential Code®* (*IRC*), excerpted in this book along with *IBC* requirements. The *IRC*, which applies to residential construction only, replaced the 1998 *International One- and Two-Family Dwelling Code* (*IOTFDC*), which was maintained until 1997 by the Council of American

Building Officials (CABO). The 1998 *IOTFDC* was maintained by the ICC, and subsequently replaced by the *IRC*. To date, the *IRC* has been adopted by the majority of states, with just a few that have not yet adopted it.

Both the *IBC* and *IRC* often reference additional building codes in the International Code family, including the *ICC Electrical Code*, *International Mechanical Code*, *International Plumbing Code*, and *International Fuel Gas Code*.

In this book, summaries of *IBC* and *IRC* requirements are included wherever applicable, in blue print, to provide coverage of both residential and light commercial projects. Please note that code requirements have been summarized in this book. Please consult the *IBC* and *IRC*.

Code-Related Standards

Building codes often reference standards, such as NFPA and ASTM, which provide specific technical installation requirements for a particular system. For example, the *IBC* specifies where a fire suppression system must be installed within a building, and also specifies that the system must comply with the *National Electrical Code®* (published by NFPA).

The Americans with Disabilities Act (ADA), also referenced in building codes, is a federal civil rights law requiring building accessibility for people with disabilities. It applies to new construction for buildings with public accommodations or commercial use. Several states have adopted the *ADA Accessibility Guidelines* as a code requirement (some with amendments).

Factory Mutual, Underwriters Laboratories (UL), and the American National Standards Institute (ANSI) are also referenced in building codes. Factory Mutual is a property-loss prevention service. It offers testing and ratings for construction systems, such as fire-resistance ratings on doors and other components, and wind-resistance for roofing materials. Underwriters Laboratories also tests and rates construction systems and components for qualities such as fire- and wind-resistance. UL also rates electrical equipment and products. ANSI helps ensure consumer safety and the protection of the environment by establishing standards and guidelines for most industries, including construction and energy distribution.

The National Institute of Standards and Technology (NIST) conducts research on building materials which helps to provide guidance for building codes. The Federal Emergency Management Administration (FEMA) provides guidance related to flood management and disaster preparedness, and advises on related building code issues.

Contact Information

Following is a list of code and related organizations, with phone numbers and Internet websites.

International Code Council (ICC)
888-422-7233
www.iccsafe.org

American National Standards Institute (ANSI)
212-642-4900
www.ansi.org

American Society of Testing and Materials (ASTM)
610-832-9585
www.astm.org

Americans with Disabilities Act (ADA)
800-514-0301
www.ada.gov

Factory Mutual (FM)
www.fmglobal.com

Federal Emergency Management Administration (FEMA)
800-621-FEMA (3362)
www.fema.gov

National Fire Protection Association (NFPA)
617-770-3000
www.nfpa.org

National Institute of Standards and Technology (NIST)
301-975-NIST (6478)
www.nist.gov

Underwriters Laboratories, Inc. (UL)
847-272-8800
www.ul.com

CHAPTER 1

ASPHALT PAVING

Table of Contents

Text in blue type indicates excerpted summaries from the International Building Code® *(IBC) and* International Residential Code® *(IRC). Please consult the IBC and IRC for complete coverage and specific wording. "Comments" (in solid blue boxes) were written by the editors, based on their own experience.*

 This icon will appear with references to green building practices.

1

CHAPTER 1

ASPHALT PAVING

Common Defect Allegations

- Movement of the subgrade is the major cause of asphalt pavement failure. Water is the major cause of subgrade movement, beyond poor compaction. The cross slope should be such that there is no water ponding on the surface. Water should be directed away from buildings and paved surfaces.

- Ordinarily, defect claims on asphalt include cracking, settling, and alligatoring. Sometimes problems are caused by improper installation, but usually they result from lack of maintenance, or the system has simply run the length of its normal useful life. The insurance industry assigns the normal useful life of various products to establish depreciation schedules. The recognized industry normal useful life of asphalt paving is 10 years. Therefore, asphalt paving that shows deterioration at 9 years and 10 months, for example, is quite ordinary, and not a compensable claim. Traditional maintenance requires that the surface be recoated regularly with a slurry seal or fresh oil and sand to reduce the evaporation of resins from the integral adhesives within the product.

Introduction

Often there is no written residential standard that clarifies trade custom or defines deficiencies commonly found in defect claims. In the case of asphalt paving on private land (driveways rather than street paving), building codes typically do not address installation. There are, however, some industry standards that are helpful.

This chapter presents these industry standards, in addition to the editors' comments on good practice, which are based on experience in residential asphalt construction and light commercial paving.

The following checklist may be helpful as you review the site in preparation for starting an asphalt paving project.

- ☐ Site cleaning _____
- ☐ Soil type _____
- ☐ Subgrade moisture conditioning _____
- ☐ Subgrade compaction _____
- ☐ Drainage _____
- ☐ Vehicle weight _____
- ☐ Asphalt mix design _____
- ☐ Weather extremes _____
- ☐ Local code _____
- ☐ Local custom _____
- ☐ Edgings _____
- ☐ Special considerations _____

The following resources may be useful for locating additional information on asphalt paving.

Asphalt Paving Alliance (APA)
877-APA-0077
www.asphaltalliance.org

Asphalt Recycling and Reclaiming Association (ARRA)
410-267-0023
www.arra.org

International Society for Asphalt Pavements (ISAP)
651-293-9188
www.asphalt.org

National Center for Asphalt Technology (NCAT)
334-844-6228
www.eng.auburn.edu/center/ncat

National Asphalt Pavement Association (NAPA)
888-468-6499
www.hotmix.org

The Association of Asphalt Paving Technologists (AAPT)
651-293-9188
www.asphalttechnology.org

The Asphalt Handbook
Asphalt Institute
859-288-4960
www.asphaltinstitute.org

> The Asphalt Institute produces educational materials to help ensure the proper use of asphalt. The organization offers several publications, including "Model Specifications for Small Paving Jobs" (CL-2).
>
> See Chapter 2 for information on concrete slabs, finishes, and paving, including tolerances, defects, and deterioration.

Ed. Note: Comments and recommendations within this chapter are not intended as a definitive resource for construction activities. For building projects, contractors must rely on the project documents and any applicable code requirements pertaining to their own particular locations.

Green, or Sustainable, Paving Options

Consider permeable (porous) paving materials to reduce runoff where appropriate. Most types of permeable asphalt and concrete are not suitable for heavy traffic areas, where impervious asphalt and concrete paving are the best choices. Permeable paving can be used for parking areas, walkways, lightly used driveways, utility access roads, fire lanes, and highway shoulders. In addition to absorbing runoff, permeable paving helps reduce the "heat island" effect.

Permeable paving materials include gravel or reinforced grass paving for low-traffic areas, block, natural or concrete simulated stone, brick, permeable asphalt or concrete (that do not contain fine aggregate), and structural grid systems. These materials not only prevent runoff onto adjoining property and into storm drains, but can reduce the need to construct water detention and collection areas.

It's important that the property owner be informed of the need for regular surface cleaning of permeable paving to prevent pores from becoming clogged.

Recycled asphalt is another green paving option.

Subgrade Preparation

Comments

While there are no recognized national standards for residential driveway subgrade preparation, the following guidelines are recommended good practice.

Frequently, private asphalt driveways are placed on native soil. Consideration must be made as to soil type. Among the least desirable soil types is expansive clay, and preferable types include crushed stone. When expansive clay is encountered, an aggregate base material might be used to separate the subgrade and the asphalt.

Asphalt pavement is considered flexible. However, it will fail with subgrade movement. In simple terms, the best base is a granular material that will allow water to perk away from the asphalt without expanding or contracting. Design criteria should allow for a slope to divert water away from buildings and paved surfaces without ponding, usually requiring a horizontal surface slope of ¼" per foot or more.

Subgrade compaction helps support and strengthen the pavement. The thinner pavements commonly used on private driveways require that the subgrade be compact. While compaction and moisture testing is optimal, it is not usually performed on private driveways. Often, project specifications require that weed killer be applied on the subgrade prior to installing the base course.

One cause of bumps and dips in the pavement is lack of smoothness in the subgrade. The grade should be shaped to drain, and should be as smooth as the asphalt pavement that will be placed on it.

In colder climates, water can freeze under the asphalt and expand, causing heaving and cracking. Occasionally, wood 2x edge forms are used at the pavement edges to achieve proper thickness and maintain specified grade. The edge forms should have full bearing on the grade to prevent the roller from driving them down and changing planned grade.

Layers

Industry Standards

Means Graphic Construction Standards
(RSMeans)

Asphalt pavements transfer and distribute traffic loads to the subgrade. For commercial applications, the pavement is typically made up of two layers of material, the wearing course and the base course. The wearing course consists of two layers: the thin surface course and the thicker binder course that bonds the surface course to the heavy base layer underneath.

The base consists of one layer that varies in thickness, type of material, and design, according to the bearing value of the subgrade material. If the subgrade material has a low-bearing value, either the thickness or the flexural strength of the base must be increased to spread the load over a larger area. For residential driveways, typically only an asphalt wearing course, or asphalt with crushed stone base course, would be used.

Increasing the flexural strength of the base course can be accomplished by mixing asphalt with the base material. The addition of the asphalt doubles the load-distributing ability of a conventional granular base. For unstable soils, a layer of geotextile stabilization fabric can be added between the base and the subgrade. This fabric not only adds tensile strength to the base, it also prevents the subgrade material from pumping up and contaminating the base when the different layers are being installed. This method is sometimes used for light commercial projects. For commercial applications, granular base courses usually range from 6" to 18" in thickness. An alternate method is to install polypropylene stabilation fabric, which prevents water from infiltrating into the base course and causing freeze/thaw heaving in colder climates.

Asphalt Pavement for Commercial Applications

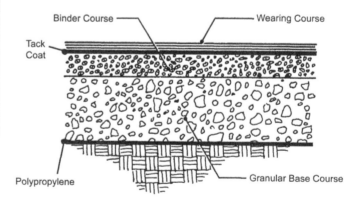

Binder Course   Wearing Course

Tack Coat

Polypropylene   Granular Base Course

Figure 1.1   RSMeans, *Means Graphic Construction Standards*

Asphalt Placement

Comments

There are no recognized national standards for asphalt placement. However, the following guidelines are recommended good practice.

Do not begin placing asphalt when the atmospheric temperature is below 40°F, and never place asphalt on frozen ground. Asphalt for paving is a mixture of various aggregate sizes and asphalt oil. This mixture is heated and hauled to the job site in open dump trucks.

The mix for private driveways and parking lots is usually finer (no coarse aggregates) than for streets. This makes the surface smoother, with a finer texture. Ideally, you should know what temperature the asphalt should be when it arrives at the site. This information can be obtained from the plant. It is best to check the load in the truck with a thermometer. Experience has shown that an excessive amount of blue smoke will rise from a too-hot mix. If the mix is too cold, it will appear too stiff, and the large aggregate will not be fully coated with asphalt. If the mix levels off in the truck, the contractor has a good indication that there is too much asphalt in the mix. Asphalt is stiff enough when it remains in a pile or heaped in the truck. When there is too little asphalt oil, the mixture will have a brownish color and appear dull. Watch for nonuniform mixture.

Prior to placing the asphalt, all concrete and asphalt edges should be coated with tack coat (emulsified asphalt diluted with water). The tack coat allows the pavement to bond with other materials, helping to seal out water.

Sometimes, residential driveways are too confined and too small to permit the use of a mechanical spreading machine. When this situation occurs, the asphalt mix is dumped on the grade in piles. The piles should be spotted, so workers who are spreading the mix by hand do not walk on the material. If they should step on it, the footprints should be raked out to the full depth of the course. The hand placing should not include casting or throwing the material. An asphalt or lute rake should be used to spread material placed in piles by shovels.

The mixture should be placed to the depth of the final thickness—plus ¼" per 1" of depth—to allow for compaction.

Use a ride-on smooth wheel roller for compaction. Small, inaccessible areas can be compacted by a smooth plate vibrating compactor. Initial rolling should occur as soon as possible. This first roller pass will provide the greatest compaction on the pavement. The drive wheel of the roller should always be forward in the direction of the paving. On very steep grades, this position may have to be reversed. Work from low side to high side for the initial and second passes. Finish rolling (to achieve a smooth surface) should occur when the mix is hot but can barely be touched with the hand.

It is a common practice to use diesel oil to coat lute rakes, shovels, and compactors to keep them clean. This should be minimized as much as possible, because the distillate will damage the asphalt. Heating the shovels and lutes will work well to keep them clean.

If you should run short of paving mix and only need a small quantity to complete a job, you still have to order a ton of mix to keep it warm in transit. Long distances from the plant will require a larger quantity to keep warm. The plant dispatcher should be able to provide guidance on these issues.

Design

Industry Standards

Means Graphic Construction Standards
(RSMeans)

The thicknesses of the courses within the pavement vary with each layer, according to the intended use of the pavement and, as noted earlier for the base course, the bearing value of the subgrade. For example, pavement may contain a 1" surface course, a 2"–3" binder course, and a 5" or more base course. Standard commercial parking lot pavement may consist of 2½" of wearing surface and 8" of granular base, while a residential driveway may consist of two 2½"–3" wearing course with no binder course.

Bituminous Sidewalk or Driveway

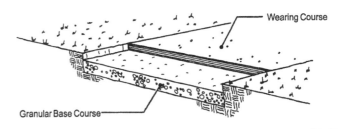

Wearing Course

Granular Base Course

Figure 1.2

RSMeans, *Means Graphic Construction Standards*

Recommendations

National Asphalt Pavement Association (NAPA)
(www.hotmix.org)

Hot mix asphalt is a mixture of aggregate and liquid asphalt cement, combined at a hot mix plant. The advantages of hot mix asphalt include:

- Availability for use immediately after being placed and rolled, with no curing time
- Durability
- Ease of maintenance
- Conformance to varying terrain
- Flexibility (resistance to damage from freeze–thaw)

Asphalt can be mixed in different formulas for different textures and purposes, such as a driveway that also functions as a play area or basketball court.

Full-depth hot mix driveways (constructed of hot mix from the subgrade up, as compared to a stone base with an asphalt layer on top) are more resistant to freeze–thaw and drainage problems, since they provide greater uniform pavement strength and keep water out of the driveway base.

Correct drainage must be figured before installing a new driveway and any low or soft spots corrected. A soil sterilizer should be applied to prevent grass or weeds from germinating and growing up through the pavement at a later date.

When overlaying an existing asphalt driveway with a new one, it is important to first patch and correctly compact all holes and trouble spots. If the driveway has a gate, the gate may need to be rehung to adjust for the increased thickness. If there are surface boxes (for example, water valves) or drainage gratings in the driveway, they may need to be releveled. These items may or may not be covered by the asphalt contractor.

Facilities Operations & Engineering Reference
(RSMeans)

The major issues in pavement design are drainage and the size and amount of traffic that will be operating on the asphalt surface. If it is a parking lot with no anticipated traffic heavier than passenger vehicles, a basic design with 6" of base and 3"–4" of asphalt will be sufficient. If heavy trucks will be operating on the pavement, then a base up to 12", with 6" of asphalt, may be needed. For loading docks, a concrete apron may be appropriate where the trailers will be parked. If a truck is parked for a considerable amount of time, it can depress the pavement underneath. The pavement surface must be strong enough to withstand distortion, resist wear from traffic, and provide both a smooth ride and skid-resistance. The pavement must also be well bonded to the course below.

A well-designed pavement should be free of water after a rain shower. The site should drain out and away from the pavement. Large paved areas should have an elevation plan showing the proposed grades on a grid. The base and sub-base of the pavement system are important to its structural effectiveness. These two elements, with the asphalt surface above, distribute traffic wheel loads and must offer internal strength properties. Full depth asphalt pavements have both tensile and compressive strength to resist internal stresses. Asphalt bases spread the wheel load over broader areas than untreated granular bases. Consequently, full depth asphalt pavements require less total pavement structure in terms of thickness.

Placement Considerations

Facilities Operations & Engineering Reference
(RSMeans)

Contract documents should specify the aggregate mixture, gradation, quality, grade of the asphalt, and the heat ranges at which the aggregate is to be mixed and placed. An engineer designs the project and prepares the plans and specifications, then works with the contractors who will supervise the construction. The engineer inspects the work. The engineer and his or her inspector should discuss the operation before starting the work with the contractor's superintendents and foremen, and should plan the operation together. The *Asphalt Handbook* (published by the Asphalt Institute) recommends discussing these important details:

1. Continuity and sequence of operations
2. Number of pavers needed for the project
3. Number and types of rollers needed
4. Number of trucks required
5. Chain of command for giving and receiving instructions
6. Reasons for possible rejection of the mix
7. Weather and temperature requirements
8. Traffic control

Asphalt concrete is usually placed on a base course. The base course should be well-graded material that is compacted to at least 98% optimum moisture (based on a modified Proctor test). The base course soils are classified in general terms by the predominate particle size or grading of particle sizes. These are usually gravel, course sand, medium sand, fine sand, silt, clay, and colloids. Well-graded soils contain a mixture of particle sizes and are generally free from organic matter.

The base course should be checked for thickness, elevation, and proper grading, and should be free of loose materials. Prior to placing the asphaltic concrete and before the binder course is installed, a tack coat of asphalt may be sprayed on. The binder course is placed first and contains larger stone sizes and sometimes stone chips. The wearing course, or top course, is made with coarse and fine sand. In cases such as the patching of a driveway or other use of only a small portion of paving material, only the wearing course is put down to save time. Asphaltic concrete is usually placed with a paving machine. Again, it is recommended that tack course be applied between existing or new pavement layers for good binding. The top course is usually hand-raked on the edges.

Truckloads of material should be inspected as they arrive, and the mix temperature checked on a regular basis. The paving inspector may reject loads that do not meet tolerance criteria. The paving crew must stay in close touch with the asphalt plant to communicate any changes needed in the mixture for subsequent truckloads. Records should be kept of loads placed, as well as any that are rejected.

The temperature of the mix is crucial. If too low, it will not compact properly. Too high and the curb may slough off. Temperatures generally range from 120–140 degrees Celsius (250–285 degrees Fahrenheit).

Compaction is accomplished with rolling equipment, as soon as possible after the hot asphalt mix has been spread. Rolling is usually done in three passes: first, the breakdown to compact the material; second, the intermediate rolling to create further density and seal the surface; and lastly, finish rolling to remove roller marks from previous passes.

Once rolling is complete, the surface should be checked to ensure there are no defects. Those that can be corrected by additional rolling should be addressed by placing fresh, hot asphalt and compacting it before the surrounding area cools (below 85 degrees). Tolerances for smoothness must be ensured. Most specifications provide for a transverse variation no greater than 6mm in 3m, or ¼" in 10'. Variations from the tolerance levels in any layer should be corrected before placing the next layer.

Sampling & Testing

Facilities Operations & Engineering Reference
(RSMeans)

First the subgrade is tested for compaction. This can be done with a modified Proctor test or a nuclear density test. The modified Proctor test involves taking an in-place sample of the subgrade, then utilizing a lab test to determine the moisture content of the soil at which maximum compaction can be obtained. Nuclear density tests have become more common now because results can be obtained instantly and they are nondestructive. Sampling allows the contractor to correct any areas that are not adequately compacted.

Testing asphaltic concrete generally involves temperature monitoring during the installation and sampling of the material in place. Sampling can be done by core-drilling a sample and having a lab test it. Nuclear density testing can also be performed on in-place asphalt. The average of the densities from the samples obtained must meet targets based on percentages set by the lab, by maximum possible (theoretical) density, and by control strip density.

Resurfacing Existing Roadways

Facilities Operations & Engineering Reference
(RSMeans)

The surface of an existing road should be examined before beginning any resurfacing work. Scarifying, recompacting, or repair of the old surface may be necessary before placing new material. If there are any soft spots or irregularities, these should be addressed. It may be necessary to patch or remove excess asphalt. Application of tack coat before any new asphalt layers are placed is highly recommended. Adequate time must be allowed for consolidation of patches before performing final surface preparations. Correction of drainage problems is extremely important.

These kinds of repairs often fall into the category of maintenance. In some cases, maintenance repairs may be addressed as temporary measures. Asphalt concrete and other types of hot mixes offer a more durable and lasting solution, and should be used when practical. Alternatives, including cold-plant and road mix materials that contain medium curing or emulsified asphalt, can be used right away or stored for a short time. Materials with slow-curing asphalt or a solvent emulsion can be stored for a longer time for patching. Patching should be done before cracks lead to larger problem areas by allowing water to enter the subgrade.

Full-Depth Asphalt Pavements for Private Driveways

Industry Standards

Asphalt Institute (AI)

(www.asphaltinstitute.org)

Drainage

Good drainage is important for pavement durability. It is desirable to blend the surface of the pavement to the contour of the existing ground so that the surface water runs over it or away from it in its natural course. In flat areas, the driveway should be sloped or crowned not less that 1/4 in./ft. (2 cm/m) so all surface water will drain off. Roof drainage from downspouts should, if feasible, be piped well away from the edge of the driveway. In some cases, pipe cross drains may be needed to take the water under the driveway. Water should not be allowed to stand at the edges.

Generally, an underdrain system is not required when the pavement is constructed by the full-depth asphalt method, even over poor soil or in certain other undesirable drainage conditions. However, an underdrain system may be required if the driveway pavement is constructed using an untreated gravel or crushed rock base.

Pavement Width

Primary consideration should be given to building a driveway of proper width. It should be no less than 8 ft (2.4 m), but 10 ft (3 m) is a more practical minimum width. If the driveway will be used for both pedestrians and automobiles a 12 ft (3.7 m) width should be considered.

It usually is desirable to preserve aesthetic objects such as trees and rocks. Also, to avoid unsightly cuts in hilly areas, driveways should conform to the terrain. Therefore, where the property will accommodate it, a curving driveway will be more attractive. A curved driveway needs to be wider in sharp curves.

Pavement Thickness

Full-depth asphalt pavements for residential driveways should have a minimum of 4 in. (10 cm) compacted thickness on a properly prepared subgrade (see Subgrade Preparation, below). This minimum is sufficient for many years of service (automobiles and an occasional truck) if the driveway is properly constructed. However, if there is concern about foundation conditions, such as soft subgrade or an exceptional number of heavy vehicles using the pavement, it may be desirable to increase the thickness to 5 in. (13 cm), or under extreme conditions, 6 in. (15 cm).

Ed. Note: The Asphalt Institute offers further information on thickness design in two reports, "Full-Depth Asphalt Pavements for Parking Lots" and "Service Stations and Driveways."

Subgrade Preparation

Before construction begins, buried utility lines in the vicinity of the driveway should be located. If they are likely to be damaged during construction, they should be relocated or protected. The subgrade soil must serve as a working platform to support construction equipment, and it also must serve as the foundation for the pavement structure. Because it must be capable of carrying the loads transmitted to it from the pavement structure, it is most important that the subgrade be properly graded and adequately compacted.

After grading and compacting with a roller, the subgrade should be tested to determine if it will support the construction equipment. This is done by driving a heavily loaded truck over it and noting the deflections. If part of the subgrade shows pronounced deflection, this indicates that the soil has not been sufficiently rolled or that the soil-moisture content of the subgrade is too high. If additional rolling fails to correct the unstable condition, the soft areas should be removed and replaced with 2 or 3 in. (5–8 cm) of hot-mix asphalt. In some cases of extremely poor subgrade, it may be necessary to remove the upper portion of the subgrade and replace it with better material.

Where it is possible that weeds may grow in the subgrade soil, the subgrade should be treated with a non-toxic commercial sterilant prior to paving.

Composition of Paving Mixture

It is recommended that the asphalt paving mixture to be used be of a type locally and readily available. Typically this would be a state highway department mix used for residential streets. Because they are used extensively, these mixes are usually the least expensive. If such locally specified mixes are not available, it is advisable to use the American Society for Testing and Materials Standard Specification D351 5, "Hot-Mixed, Hot-Laid Asphalt Paving Mixtures." Mix Designations and Nominal Maximum Size of Aggregate, 1/2 in. (12.5 mm) or 3/8 in. (9.5 mm) are recommended.

Spreading the Mixture

The thick lift technique (placing in lifts of 4 or more in. [10 or more cm]) is in most instances satisfactory. However, if subgrade conditions or traffic loads necessitate thicknesses greater than 4 in. (10 cm), it is suggested that the asphalt be placed in two layers. In some cases it may also be necessary to place the mix in more than one layer to achieve desired smoothness. Three in. (8 cm) of base and 2 in. (5 cm) of surface mix or 4 in. (10 cm) of base and 2 in. (5 cm) of surface are suggested thickness combinations for 5 and 6 in. (13 and 15 cm) total thicknesses.

Small pavers are available but most asphalt paving machines in use today place widths ranging from 8 to 12 ft (2.4 to 3.7 m). Relatively sophisticated self-propelled pavers as well as simpler towed equipment have been successfully used for residential driveway construction.

Whenever possible, hand placement of the mixture should be avoided. However, where access to the driveway site is limited, hand placement may be the only feasible construction method. When the asphalt mixture is placed by hand, it is essential that forms be set at the edge of the driveway. These will ensure a neat edge and will minimize surface imperfections when used as a reference for a strikeoff board.

Weather Conditions
Weather conditions affect asphalt construction. To obtain the best results asphalt paving should be done in warm and dry weather.

Compaction
Compaction of asphalt pavement mixtures is one of the most important construction operations contributing to the proper performance of the completed pavement. That is why it is so important to have a properly prepared subgrade against which to compact the overlying pavement. A steel-wheeled tandem roller is generally used for this type of work. However, many other types of rollers, including small self-propelled vibrating rollers, can be used to obtain the required compaction.

Maintenance
It is not necessary to seal the surface of a newly-constructed asphalt concrete driveway. When the pavement is properly constructed, the driveway should afford many years of service before a thin application of asphalt emulsion driveway sealer containing mineral grit (available at hardware stores) becomes desirable to improve the surface texture and seal small cracks. But, if the pavement is not properly compacted during construction a surface sealer may be needed within two to four years.

CHAPTER 2 CONCRETE

Table of Contents

Text in blue type indicates excerpted summaries from the International Building Code® (IBC) *and* International Residential Code® (IRC). *Please consult the* IBC *and* IRC *for complete coverage and specific wording. "Comments" (in solid blue boxes) were written by the editors, based on their own experience.*

 This icon will appear with references to green building practices.

CHAPTER 2

CONCRETE

- Cold joints are a defect caused when too much time elapses between placement of batches of concrete. The first batch begins to harden before the next load is placed on top of it, and the two batches do not completely merge. A cold joint could allow moisture to penetrate the foundation wall.

- Flatwork surface pitting from shale is another defect. Shale, found in some quarries where aggregate is mined, is a hard sandstone. Small pieces often go through the separators and get batched into the concrete. Pops in the surface tend to occur about a week after the concrete has been poured as the shale gradually absorbs moisture and expands, breaking out a small portion of the slab above it.

- Another common claim is structure soil settlement, which causes foundation cracking and vertical dislocation. Claims can involve post-tensioned slabs (slabs with steel rods and threaded ends tightened after the concrete setting) tilting, but not cracking. This happens along the crown of a slope, especially on expansive soil from slope creep. Slope creep usually results from the cycle of drying and wetting of the soil, with gravity creating a dynamic that results in all movement, expansion and contraction, down slope. The bank starts shifting downhill.

- Placing concrete in very hot or very cold weather can create structural problems. To avoid this, ready-mix plants can add ice or hot water to maintain the proper temperature during placement. Concrete placement in extreme temperature conditions should be avoided if possible.

- Exposed reinforcing steel is another concrete foundation complaint. Steel ties should be broken off and the wall patched with appropriate mortar where the ties were broken off.

- We address the allowable tolerances for concrete installations in other parts of this chapter. However, the acceptable tolerances for a structure following exposure to natural disasters is a much broader interpretation. For example, immediately after the Northridge, California, earthquake, when many buildings were being condemned, some building officials adpoted a standard of ±1" in 20 feet as straight line livable level. This became a common criterion of acceptability.

Introduction

Concrete has long been thought of as a relatively simple product that is permanent, needs no maintenance, and generally only fails due to an outside, unexpected force. New research and advanced testing has shown that concrete is, in fact, sensitive to many ordinary conditions, such as the effect of sulfates, chlorides, and salts that exist in soils and are transported through water migration. In some cases, a quarry will sell unwashed sands or crusher run (rock manufacturing by-products) at reduced prices for fine grading under slab. Often these materials carry corrosives that will not show up in the soils report, but will become harmful if water migration develops. These chemicals can attack the cement paste and/or reinforcing, resulting in early concrete failure.

Most of the leading forensic engineers in the construction industry will agree that methods to prevent concrete failure are relatively inexpensive compared to the cost and complexity of remedial cures. Prevention is usually as simple as raising the cement quantity in the mix to create a more dense product, placing at a lower slump (less water), and installing surface grading and subsurface drainage so that all accumulated water will perk or drain away from the concrete structure.

Another form of prevention, especially in clay soils, is to keep copper water lines overhead in the building or completely wrapped underground to prevent the accelerated effects of galvanic action when acids or corrosives are present, especially on recirculating lines.

Note: *The International Building Code's* requirements for concrete are based on the American Concrete Institute's *ACI 318*. The code requirements provided in this chapter are IBC summaries; please consult the *IBC* or *ACI 318* for full coverage. *The International Residential Code* does not specifically address concrete. Chapter 4 of the *IRC* covers foundation requirements, some of which address concrete placement.

For more detailed information on various concrete installation procedures and standards, contact:

American Concrete Institute (ACI)
248-848-3700
www.concrete.org
ACI offers many publications on the details of correct concrete design and construction.

NAHB Research Center
800-638-8556
www.nahbrc.org
The NAHB Research Center, a subsidiary of NAHB, conducts research on home design and construction. Its programs cover topics such as green building, affordable housing, and building technology. NAHBRC offers many publications through its website.

Portland Cement Association
847-966-6200
www.portcement.org
The Portland Cement Association publishes many books on mix design, placement, and testing.

Other organizations that offer technical information on concrete construction are:

Concrete Reinforcing Steel Institute
847-517-1200
www.crsi.org

(continued)

National Concrete Masonry Association (NCMA)
703-713-1900
www.ncma.org
NCMA offers publications that provide information on building code requirements for masonry structures, software, and educational programs for contractors, designers, and homeowners.

Ed. Note: Comments and recommendations within this chapter are not intended as a definitive resource for construction activities. For building projects, contractors must rely on a copy of the project documents and applicable codes pertaining to their own particular locations.

 # A Greener Approach to Concrete Use
Green Building: Project Planning & Cost Estimating, **Second Edition**
(RSMeans)

To minimize the environmental problems with concrete, the following measures should be taken:

- Reduce concrete waste by recycling crushed concrete for fill material or road base, or grinding it up for aggregate. (Currently only 5% of concrete is recycled. By weight, it represents up to 67% of construction and demolition waste.)

- Carefully estimate the amount of concrete required to avoid ordering excess amounts that become waste.

- Consider less material-intensive alternates to poured-in-place concrete, such as insulation-form walls and autoclaved cellular concrete block. Precast concrete is factory-made to order, which, due to controlled production processes, also reduces concrete waste.

- Use insulated shallow foundations in northern climates; consider pier-and-beam foundations instead of slabs on grade.

- Protect aquatic ecosystems by washing forms and equipment where runoff will not contaminate waterways.

- Use the maximum amount of fly ash or other SCM appropriate to the construction application, location, and material quality.

See the LEED® for Homes rating system, developed by the U.S. Green Building Council for more information. (**www.usgbc.org**).

Green Concrete Products

DIVISION 03 – CONCRETE
- ☐ Permanent insulating concrete formwork
- ☐ Reusable concrete formwork
- ☐ Rebar supports fabricated from recycled steel
- ☐ Rebar supports fabricated from recycled plastic
- ☐ Cellular concrete
- ☐ Recycled aggregate in concrete mix
- ☐ Coal fly ash or ground granulated furnace slag in concrete mix
- ☐ Low-VOC concrete hardening compounds

Planning Concrete Construction

Comments

The concrete requirements for a project are found on the structural drawings, specifically the foundation plan and sections showing details of footings, walls, piers, and slabs. Concrete items may be indicated on other drawings as well, such as mechanical/electrical, which may specify box-outs for piping and conduit or equipment. Architectural drawings should indicate surface finish treatments. The specifications and drawings should provide information on the strength of the mix and any admixtures that might be required.

Residential concrete is often ordered and handled based on industry and regional standards. Seldom is a design mix requested. Rather, the contractor may be required to submit the strength of the mix, specified as the concrete's **compressive strength per inch** after curing (e.g., 3,000 psi, 3,500 psi). Contractors engaged in light commercial, commercial, and heavy construction often work with design mixes and are required to submit specific documentation to the architect or engineer from the ready-mix supplier identifying the characteristics of the cement, aggregate, or any admixtures used in the mix to conform to the specification. In these circumstances, site testing and certification of proper placing and curing procedures may also be required.

Most cast-in-place concrete used on construction projects is ready-mixed, delivered to the construction site by special trucks, and then placed in the forms by one of several methods: by a chute directly into formwork, into a hopper for distribution by wheelbarrows and mechanical buggies, into buckets to be hoisted by a crane, or into a concrete pump and pushed through a portable pipeline.

IRC 2006

The International Residential Code does not specifically address concrete. Chapter 4 of the IRC covers foundation requirements, some of which address concrete placement.

R402.2 The 2006 IRC calls for: concrete to have a specified compressive strength at 28 days psi (f'$_c$) of at least 2,500 for basement walls, foundations, garage floors, carport slabs, porches, and steps. In some cases, 3,000 or 3,500 is required for concrete that is exposed to foul weather conditions.

Industry Standards

Plan Reading & Material Takeoff
(RSMeans)

While concrete has many applications in construction, its main function is as a structural component. Concrete has an extremely high *compressive strength*; that is, the ability to resist a crushing force, usually imposed by the weight of the structure it supports.

With water as a main ingredient, mixed concrete is greatly affected by temperature and weather extremes. When placing concrete in cold weather, the poured concrete must be protected against freezing. Concrete that freezes prior to curing will never achieve its full strength. Similarly, pouring concrete on hot, dry days may evaporate essential water used for the curing process before it has a chance to set. Both conditions should be avoided.

The following factors should be considered in planning concrete construction:

1. The strength of the mix, specified as the concrete's *compressive strength per square inch* after curing (e.g., 3,000 psi, 4,000 psi).

2. The use of additives that accelerate the time for reaching full strength. For example, High Early Strength Portland cement will achieve the same strength in 72 hours that other types normally achieve in 7 days.

3. The size and type of the coarse aggregate used in the batching; for example, gravel, peastone, stone, and/or local aggregates such as slag.

4. The percentage of air incorporated into the mix, in the form of tiny air bubbles. This is known as *air entrainment*. Air entrainment increases the concrete's workability and resistance to weathering and salts. The standard air entrainment is between 3% and 5% and is accomplished by the use of an additive included in the mix.

5. Chemicals added to the mix, such as calcium chloride, which acts as a drying agent and decreases setting time for pouring in cold weather. Other chemicals are available that increase the curing time.

6. The use of lightweight aggregates to reduce weight per CY. Materials such as perlite and vermiculite are the most common and add considerable cost per CY. They are used to reduce the weight of the concrete, thereby reducing the overall structural load.

Other considerations for planning, such as a requirement for hot water (common practice in cold climates during the winter months), may be related to localized batching practices, and should be reviewed on an individual basis.

As a result of significantly better quality control, the use of ready-mixed concrete has all but eliminated the job-site batching of concrete in any large quantity. *Ready-mixed concrete* refers to concrete that is batched at an off-site location, then transported to the site in mixers.

Freezing & Thawing Exposures

IBC 2006

IBC 1904.2 The 2006 IBC calls for: air entrainment that complies with *ACI 318* for concrete exposed to freezing, deicing, and thawing. Consult *ACI 318* for specifics on the maximum water-cementitious materials ratios and minimum specified concrete compressive strength requirements.

Comments

Pozzolans, which are ground organic materials, can be used as additives to increase the workability of the mixture or as a water retainer.

ACI offers publications on cold and hot weather concreting. (See the Introduction for more on ACI.)

Deterioration, Damage, & Defects

Industry Standards

Concrete Repair and Maintenance Illustrated
(RSMeans)

Concrete does not always behave as we would like; some of the undesirable behavior can be seen as disintegration, spalling, cracking, leakage, wear, deflection, or settlement.

A variety of factors influence concrete behavior. These factors include: design, materials, construction, service loads, service conditions, and exposure conditions. Most of the observed behaviors are a combination of these factors working together.

Causes & Effects of Concrete Problems

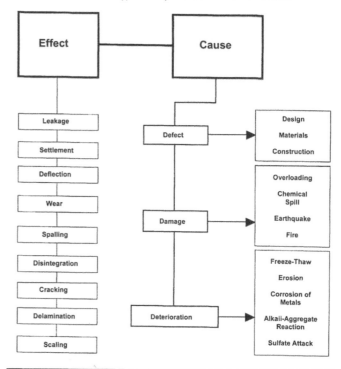

Figure 2.1 RSMeans, *Concrete Repair and Maintenance Illustrated*

Industry Standards

Building Materials Technology, Structural Performance & Environmental Impact
(The McGraw-Hill Companies)

3.16 Building Problems Related to Concrete

In general it is true that the most dense and impermeable concrete is more durable and more resistant to a hostile environment. Quality concrete requires carefully graded sizes of aggregate, adequate proportion of cement, selection of the appropriate type of cement for the intended application, and proper curing.

Some of the common building problems related to concrete are listed here with their causes and suggestions for correction.

1. Sulfate deterioration of concrete is caused by moisture and sulfate salts in the soil that is in contact with concrete foundations, floor slabs, and walls. Type V sulfate-resisting cement is made for this purpose. To correct the problem (if the soil cannot be kept away from the concrete), better drainage might keep the soil dry and the salts in solid, not solution, form.

2. Efflorescence is the appearance of an unsightly, fluffy white crust on the surface of walls. It is caused by salts in solution (in the concrete,

the stone, or the bricks) moving to the surface of an interior or exterior wall. As the water evaporates from the salt solution in dry weather, a loose mass of white, powdery salts remains. The process of efflorescence slowly continues as the soluble salts are leached from the concrete by heavy rain entering the wall through joints or cracks. These soluble salts can come from admixtures, but most likely will come from poorly washed aggregates. Some relief from efflorescence can be gained by treating the surface of the wall with a water repellent and sealing all cracks and joints to keep out rain. If no cracks or pin holes are in the coating, these soluble salts should no longer be able to reach the surface.

3. Freeze-thaw cracks (forming in concrete in subfreezing weather) can be caused by concrete with a water/cement ratio that is too large. This can produce tiny crevices and voids around the aggregates, allowing penetration of water into the concrete by wind-driven rain. Tremendous forces, produced by the expansion of water as it freezes to form ice, cause spalls and cracks in the concrete. Prevention requires a better water/cement ratio and an examination of the admixtures, if any were used.

    Correction requires waterproofing the surface of the concrete with a polymer-modified cement-based surface coating. Further protection could be gained by applying a protective coat of paint.

4. Corrosion of steel rebars can cause cracks and rust stains to appear in the concrete.

5. Leaks in concrete roofs or parking decks are due to water penetrating the surface. Although these surfaces should have been level, slightly raised in the middle, or slightly tilted toward the edge, rainwater often stands in pools. This water eventually penetrates into the concrete. Other cracks form from freezing and thawing or from heavy traffic on decks. Perhaps the parking deck is subjected to overloads and should have had better reinforcement. Perhaps expansion joints should have been used. Water leaks eventually form in the ceiling, with efflorescent salts showing in the cracks. A waterproof coating alone rarely works because the cracks continue to grow. A solution is to use epoxy in the clean cracks and to fill them with a flexible sealant material.

Cracks: Acceptable Tolerances & Effects of Chlorides

Industry Standards

Concrete Repair and Maintenance Illustrated
(RSMeans)

Cracks and construction joints in concrete permit corrosive chemicals such as deicing salts to enter the concrete and access embedded reinforcing steel. (See **Figure 2.2.**)

Steel corrosion may take place even in a high alkaline environment if chlorides are present. Chlorides are not consumed in the corrosion process, but instead act as catalysts to the process and remain in the concrete.

ACI 224R–90 presents the following table of tolerable crack widths in reinforced concrete:

Exposure Condition	Tolerance Crack Width	
	(In.)	(mm)
Dry air, protective	0.016	0.41
Humidity, moist air, soil	0.012	0.30
De-icing chemicals	0.007	0.18
Seawater and seawater spray; wetting and drying	0.006	0.15
Water-retaining structures*	0.004	0.10

*Excluding non-pressure pipes.

Note: 0.004 inches is equal to the width of a human hair. A crack of this width is almost unnoticeable unless the surface is wetted and allowed to dry.

The Corrosive Process

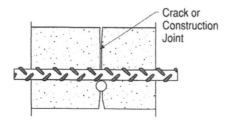

Crack or Construction Joint

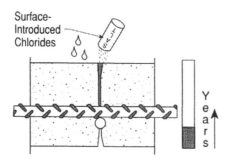

Surface-Introduced Chlorides

Years

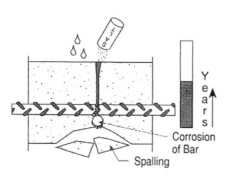

Years

Corrosion of Bar

Spalling

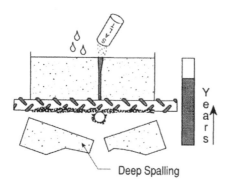

Years

Deep Spalling

The corrosion process is progressive, beginning at the intersection of the crack with the reinforcing bar, then progressing along the bar.

Figure 2.2   RSMeans, *Concrete Repair and Maintenance Illustrated*

Sulfate Exposure

Industry Standards

Concrete Repair and Maintenance Illustrated
(RSMeans)

Sodium and calcium are the most common sulfates in soils, water, and industrial processes. Magnesium sulfates are less common, but more destructive. Soils or waters containing these sulfates are often called "alkali" soils or waters.

All sulfates are potentially harmful to concrete. They react chemically with cement paste's hydrated lime and hydrated calcium aluminate. As a result of this reaction, solid products with volume greater than the products entering the reaction are formed. (See **Figure 2.3.**)

The formation of gypsum and ettringite expands, pressurizes, and disrupts the paste. As a result, surface scaling and disintegration set in, followed by mass deterioration.

Sulfate resistance of the concrete is improved by a reduction in water-cement ratio and an adequate cement factor, with a low tricalcium aluminate and with proper air entrainment. With proper proportioning, silica fume (microsilica), fly ash, and ground slag generally improve the resistance of concrete to sulfate attack, primarily by reducing the amount of reactive elements (such as calcium) needed for expansive sulfate reactions.

Effects of Sulfate on Concrete

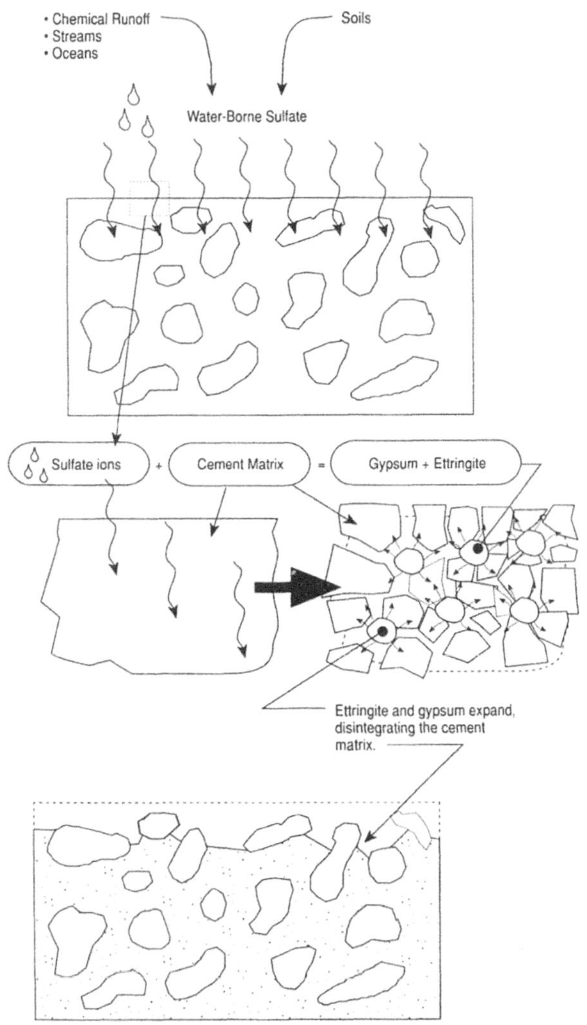

Figure 2.3

Corrosion Protection of Reinforcement

IBC 2006

1904.4 The 2006 IBC calls for: reinforcement to comply with the American Concrete Institute's *ACI 318*, section 4.4 for protection from corrosion and chloride exposure.

Industry Standards

Concrete Repair and Maintenance Illustrated
(RSMeans)

Concrete is a high-alkalinity material. The pH of newly produced concrete is usually between 12 and 13. In this range of alkalinity, embedded steel is protected from corrosion by a passivating film bonded to the reinforcing bar surface. However, when the passivating film is disrupted, corrosion may take place.

Corrosion is an electrochemical process requiring an anode, a cathode, and an electrolyte. A moist concrete matrix forms an acceptable electrolyte, and the steel reinforcement provides the anode and cathode. Electrical current flows between the cathode and anode, and the reaction results in an increase in metal volume as the Fe (Iron) is oxidized into $Fe(OH)_2$ and $Fe(OH)_3$ and precipitates as FeO OH (rust color). Water and oxygen must be present for the reaction to take place. In good quality concrete, the corrosion rate will be very slow. Accelerated corrosion will take place if the pH (alkalinity) is lowered (carbonation) or if aggressive chemicals or dissimilar metals are introduced into the concrete. Other causes include stray electrical currents and concentration cells caused by an uneven chemical environment. (Clifton, J.R. *Predicting the Remaining Service Life of Concrete,* National Institute of Standards and Technology Report NISTIR 4712).

Industry Standards

Building Materials Technology, Structural Performance & Environmental Impact
(The McGraw-Hill Companies)

3.15.3 Rusting of Rebars in Concrete

As concrete ages, faulty design or improper curing results in inadequate drainage and in crack formation. Additional cracks result from the stresses of thermal expansion and contraction of the concrete.

Seepage of water into these cracks, half a millimeter in size or larger, carries dissolved oxygen and carbon dioxide into the concrete. This dissolved oxygen and the carbon dioxide are active in promoting corrosion. For example, oxygen maintains the alkalinity of the cathodic electrodes by its conversion to the hydroxide ion. This reaction keeps the pH at the cathodes at a high alkaline value. Dissolved carbon dioxide destroys the passivity of steel at the anodes by neutralizing the alkali in the hydrated cement and by releasing free chloride ions from calcium-chloride-containing cement (carbonation). Also, as water seeps through the cracks, it leaches out the soluble alkali from the concrete. As the pH of the concrete adjacent to the steel drops below 9, the protective film of ferrous oxide deteriorates and the passivity it once provided the steel surface is lost.

Pitting occurs at the anodes as iron dissolves to form ferrous ions. At the cathodes, oxygen and water are converted to hydroxide ions, which further increases the corrosion voltage. Thus the corrosion process is accelerated and serious structural deterioration occurs if further environmental exposure is not prevented.

Protecting Finishes from Chemical Damage

Industry Standards

Concrete Repair and Maintenance Illustrated
(RSMeans)

Aggressive chemical attack (liquid or gas) on concrete surfaces can be controlled by using chemically resistant materials in the concrete mix, or using surface-applied barrier coatings, membranes, or surfacing systems. Typical protection systems are listed in **Figure 2.4**.

Preventing Surface Defects

Comments

There are many causes for concrete surface defects. Some of the major defects, their causes, and the construction techniques that should be used to prevent them are described here. Many defects result from improper curing or errors in mixing or finishing.

Selecting Appropriate Surface Protection

Type of Surface Protection	Maximum Service Temperature °F/°C	Alkalies		Acids				Solvents		
		Strong	Weak	Inorganic	Organic Weak	Organic Moderate	Organic Strong	Organic	Inorganic	Bleach
Epoxies	150/66	✔	✔		✔	✔		(1)	(1)	✔
Epoxy—Novolac	180/80	✔	✔	✔				✔(2)	✔(2)	
Furans	360/180	✔	✔	✔	✔	✔	✔	✔	✔	
Methacrylates (MMA)			✔		✔			✔(2)	✔(2)	
Polyesters	230/107		✔		✔	✔				✔
Potassium Silicates	2000/1093			✔(3)	✔	✔	✔	(1)	(1)	
Sulfur Cement	190/88			✔(4)	✔	✔				
Urethanes	150–250 / 66–122	✔	✔	✔(4)	✔	✔				✔
Vinyl Esters	220–250 / 104–127		✔	✔	✔	✔		✔	✔	
PVC		✔	✔	✔	✔	✔	✔			
Acid Brick	High			✔(3)	✔	✔	✔			
Carbon Brick		✔	✔	✔	✔	✔	✔			

(1) Resistant only to some solvents
(2) Moderate resistance to solvents
(3) Not resistant to Hydrofluoric Acid (HF)
(4) Moderate resistance to acids

Note: This table should be used as a guide only. Actual performance may differ depending on formulation.

Figure 2.4

RSMeans, *Concrete Repair and Maintenance Illustrated*

Industry Standards

Concrete Repair and Maintenance Illustrated
(RSMeans)

Plastic Settlement (Subsidence) Cracking

Plastic settlements cracking is caused by the settlement of plastic concrete around fixed reinforcement, leaving a plastic tear above the bar and a possible void beneath the bar. The probability of cracking is a function of:

1. Cover
2. Slump
3. Bar size

Settlement of plastic concrete is caused by:

1. Low sand content and high water content
2. Large bars
3. Poor thermal insulation
4. Restraining settlement due to irregular shape
5. Excessive, uneven absorbency
6. Low humidity
7. Insufficient time between top-out of columns and placement of slab and beam
8. Insufficient vibration
9. Movement of formwork

(See **Figure 2.5**.)

Plastic Shrinkage Cracking

Plastic shrinkage is caused by the rapid evaporation of mix water (not *bleed water*) while the concrete is in its plastic state and in the early stages of initial set. Shrinkage results in cracking when it produces tension stress greater than the stress capacity of the newly placed concrete. Plastic shrinkage cracking rarely fractures aggregate, but separates around the aggregate. Plastic shrinkage cracks may lead to points of thermal and dry shrinkage movement, intensifying the cracking. (See **Figure 2.6**.)

Industry Standards

Construction Principles, Materials, and Methods
(John Wiley & Sons, Inc.)

3.9.6.1 Scaling

Scaling is the breaking away of the hardened concrete surface of a slab to a depth of about $\frac{1}{16}$ to $\frac{3}{16}$ in. It usually occurs at an early age of the slab.

Scaling of a slab might occur if it is subjected to cycles of freezing and thawing soon after the slab has been placed. A favorable temperature must be maintained long enough to prevent injury. Cycles of freezing and thawing and applications of de-icing salts on non-air-entrained concrete can also cause scaling. This is why air-entrained concrete is recommended for all severe exposure conditions.

Performing a finishing operation while free excess water or bleed water is on the surface causes segregation of the surface fines (sand and portland cement) and also brings a thin layer of neat portland cement, clay, and silt to the surface, leaving another layer of nearly clean, washed sand that is not bonded to the concrete under it. To prevent scaling from this cause, water should be allowed to evaporate from the surface or be forced to evaporate by fans or blower-type heaters, or it should be removed by dragging a

Settlement (or Subsidence) Cracking

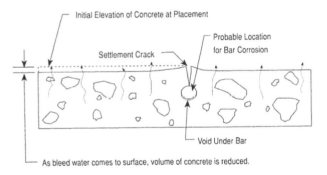

As bleed water comes to surface, volume of concrete is reduced.

Probability of Subsidence Cracking (%)*								
	2" Slump			3" Slump			4" Slump		
Cover	#4	#5	#6	#4	#5	#6	#4	#5	#6
¾"	80.4	87.8	92.5	91.9	98.7	100	100	100	100
1"	60	71	78.1	73	83.4	89.9	85.2	94.7	100
1½"	18.6	34.5	45.6	31.1	47.7	58.9	44.2	61.1	72
2"	0	1.8	14.1	4.9	12.7	26.3	5.1	24.7	39

Figure 2.5

RSMeans, *Concrete Repair and Maintenance Illustrated*

Shrinkage Cracking

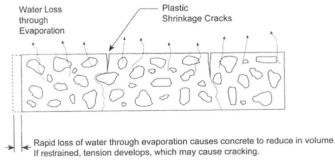

Rapid loss of water through evaporation causes concrete to reduce in volume. If restrained, tension develops, which may cause cracking.

Figure 2.6

RSMeans, *Concrete Repair and Maintenance Illustrated*

rubber garden hose over the surface before finishing operations begin.

3.9.6.3 Dusting

Dusting is the appearance of a powdery material on the surface of a newly hardened concrete slab.

An excess of harmful fines (clay or silt) in a concrete mix with the sand and portland cement at the surface can result in dusting. This condition emphasizes the need to use clean and well-graded coarse and fine aggregates.

Premature troweling and floating mix excess surface water with surface fines, weakening the portland cement paste. Troweling should be delayed until all free water and excess moisture have disappeared and concrete has started its initial set.

When carbon dioxide, as may be emitted from open portable fossil-fuel heaters and gasoline engines, comes into contact with the surface of plastic concrete, a reaction takes place that impairs proper hydration. Such fumes should be vented to the outside and sufficient fresh air ventilation provided.

Condensation sometimes occurs on a concrete surface before floating and troweling have been completed, usually in the spring and fall, when materials have become cold due to low night temperatures. If possible, this condition should be anticipated, and the concrete should be heated or at least hot water should be used for mixing. If this is impossible, blower type heaters should be used to lower the humidity directly over the slab, and fans should be used to increase air circulation. If heaters and fans are not available, windows and doors should be opened. When condensation is present, floating and initial troweling should be held to a minimum, and a concrete surface should not be given a second troweling.

Neat portland cement and mixtures of portland cement and fine sand should never be used as a dry-shake. Because condensation may occur for several hours while concrete is beginning to harden, emergency measures may have to be taken to finish a slab. A well-mixed dry mixture of 1 part portland cement and 1 part well-graded concrete sand may be evenly and lightly distributed over a concrete surface, if it is followed at once by troweling. There should be no second troweling, because additional condensation may take place after the first troweling.

Winter-protection heaters may lower the relative humidity around concrete excessively and inhibit proper hydration of the portland cement. Water jackets should be placed on heaters to increase the relative humidity by evaporation, and moist curing methods should be employed. Heaters should be moved periodically so that no area will be subjected to an extreme or harmful amount of heat.

Proper curing for the correct length of time is essential. Concrete that is not cured properly will often be weak, and its surface will be easily worn by foot traffic.

IRC 2006

IRC Concrete floors (on ground):

The 2006 IRC calls for: 3.5" of thickness for concrete slabs on ground floors. Fill: compacted to a depth no more than 24" (for clean sand/gravel) and 8" for earth. Base course, if required: 4" thick. Vapor retarder, where required: 6 mil polyethylene (or approved). Joints: lapped at least 6". Vapor retarder not needed, for example, for garages or unheated structures. Reinforcement required for upper third of the slab for entire concrete placement.

Segregation

Industry Standards

Concrete Repair and Maintenance Illustrated
(RSMeans)

Segregation of concrete results in nonuniform distribution of its constituents. High slump mixes, incorrect methods of handling concrete, and over-vibration are causes of this problem. Segregation causes upper surfaces to have excessive paste and fines, and may have excessive water-cement ratio. The resultant concrete may lack acceptable durability. (**Figure 2.7.**)

Segregation

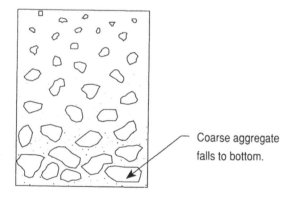

Coarse aggregate falls to bottom.

Figure 2.7   RSMeans, *Concrete Repair and Maintenance Illustrated*

Cold Joints

Industry Standards

Concrete Repair and Maintenance Illustrated
(RSMeans)

Cold joints are places of discontinuity within a member where concrete may not tightly bond to itself. Cold joints may form between planned placements and within a placement. Some construction placement procedures require multiple lifts. A dam is a good example, as are tall walls. To achieve proper bond and water-tightness, the surface of hardened concrete must be free of dirt, debris, and *laitance.*

Proper cleaning and placement procedures sometimes are not followed or are very difficult to achieve. The result is a weak connection between placements that could result in weakness or leakage at a later date.

The other type of cold joint may occur within a planned placement if a part of the concrete in one placement sets, and then the reset of the concrete is placed on it. During the set, laitances form, providing for a weakened plane. Leakage may occur when the structure is put into service. (**Figure 2.8.**)

Cold Joints

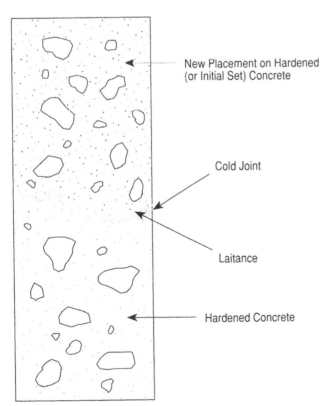

New Placement on Hardened (or Initial Set) Concrete

Cold Joint

Laitance

Hardened Concrete

Figure 2.8

RSMeans, *Concrete Repair and Maintenance Illustrated*

Honeycomb & Rock Pockets

Industry Standards

Concrete Repair and Maintenance Illustrated
(RSMeans)

Honeycomb is a void left in concrete due to failure of the mortar to effectively fill the spaces among coarse aggregate particles. Rock pockets are generally severe conditions of honeycomb where an excessive volume of aggregate is found. (See **Figure 2.9.**)

Primary Causes of Honeycomb

Design of Members

- highly congested reinforcement
- narrow section
- internal interference
- reinforcement splices

Forms

- leaking at joints
- severe grout loss

Construction Conditions

- reinforcement too close to forms
- high temperature
- accessibility

Properties of Fresh Concrete

- insufficient fines
- low workability
- early stiffening
- excessive mixing
- aggregate that is too large

Placement

- excessive free-fall
- excessive travel in forms
- lift that is too high
- improper *tremie* or *drop chute*
- segregation

Consolidation

- vibrator too small
- frequency too low
- amplitude too small
- short immersion time
- excessive spacing between insertion
- inadequate penetration

Honeycomb & Rock Pockets

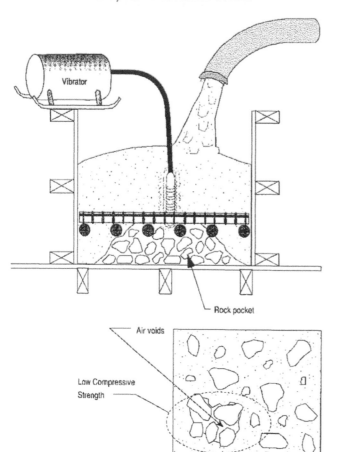

Figure 2.9   RSMeans, *Concrete Repair and Maintenance Illustrated*

Water Penetration Prevention Measures

Industry Standards

Construction Principles, Materials, and Methods
(John Wiley & Sons, Inc.)

Mix Ratios & Curing Time

3.7.1.3 For a concrete to be watertight and impervious, its portland cement paste must be formulated to produce this result. As with strength and durability, there is a direct link between a concrete's watertightness and its water-cement ratio.

Tests show that a portland cement concrete's permeability depends on the amount of mixing water in its water paste and the extent to which the chemical reactions between the portland cement and the water have progressed. The results of subjecting discs made with portland cement mortar, fine aggregate, and water to 20 psi (0.14 MPa) water pressure are shown in **Figure 2.10**.

In these tests, mortar cured moist for seven days had no leakage when made with a water-cement ratio of 0.50, but there was considerable leakage with mortars made with the higher water-cement ratios. Also, in each case, leakage became less as the length of the curing period was increased. Mortar discs with a

Concrete Curing Time & Watertightness

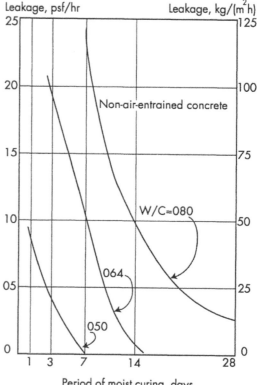

The effect of water-cement ratio on watertightness. Leakage is reduced as the water-cement ratio is decreased and the curing period is increased. Specimens were 1-in. x 6-in. (25-mm x 150-mm) mortar discs. Pressure was 20 psi (0.14 Mpa). Values are 48-hour averages.

Figure 2.10   Courtesy of Portland Cement Association

water-cement ratio of 0.80 leaked, even when moist-cured for a month.

Air entrainment improves watertightness by allowing reduction of the water-cement ratio. To be watertight, concrete must be free from cracks and honeycombing.

As a result of testing and experience in the field, definite recommendations can be made regarding the maximum amount of mixing water that should be used for various construction applications.

Vapor Barriers

3.8.1.2 Slabs on Grade Subgrades should be trimmed to specified elevations and uniformly compacted before concrete is placed. Except when a vapor retarder, waterproof membrane, or separator has been installed immediately below a slab, the subgrade should be moistened to prevent too rapid extraction of water from the concrete.

However, at the time of placing, there should be no mud, soft spots, or free water standing where concrete will be placed.

The Portland Cement Association (PCA) recommends that a vapor retarder be placed under every concrete slab on grade where an impervious floor finish will be installed and in every other location where the passage of water vapor through a slab on grade is undesirable. However, a vapor barrier placed in contact with the concrete will cause excess moisture in the concrete to bleed to the surface rather than downward, increasing the number of capillaries in the concrete and contributing to a weakening of the surface, more cracking, and higher permeability of the slab. Therefore, the PCA recommends that a vapor retarder not be placed directly beneath a slab, but rather covered by a 3-in.-thick layer of granular, self-draining material, such as sand.

When a vapor retarder is not used beneath a slab on grade, a separator of building paper or other material that will withstand handling and construction traffic is sometimes installed. When such separators are used, they are usually installed between the base course or fill and the slab to prevent the fines or paste of plastic concrete from seeping down into the base course or fill. However, if such a separator is complete and impervious, it should not be placed directly in contact with the slab. If it is, it could act in the same way a vapor retarder often acts and contribute to warping (curling) of the slab and exacerbate drying shrinkage cracking.

Steel reinforcing, ductwork, heating pipes, and other items embedded in a slab should be set and supported at the proper elevation before concrete is placed.

Industry Standards
Concrete Repair and Maintenance Illustrated
(RSMeans)

Proper Slab Grading
Slabs requiring drainage for proper runoff need special attention. Drains should be at low, not high, points. Proper slope-to-pitch for quick runoff is important to prevent deterioration and leakage within the structure. Standing water provides concrete with the potential for saturation, the worst condition for a freeze-thaw cycle. The quicker the water runs off the structure, the less leakage can occur through joints and cracks (**Figure 2.11**).

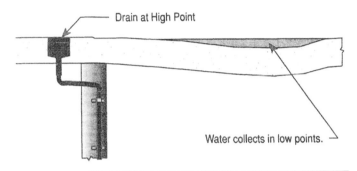

Incorrect Grading

RSMeans, *Concrete Repair and Maintenance Illustrated*

Figure 2.11

Waterproofing & Dampproofing Foundations

Waterproofing
Industry Standards
Plan Reading & Material Takeoff
(RSMeans)

The purpose of waterproofing is to prevent the penetration of water through the exterior surfaces of the structure. Waterproofing is most often done below grade at the foundation level to prevent the transmission of water through the foundation walls or slab. When reading a set of drawings, care should be taken to determine the limits of waterproofing materials.

There are three basic classifications for waterproofing. The *integral* method involves the use of special additives mixed with concrete for use in poured foundations. *Membrane waterproofing* is the application of a waterproof membrane to the surface of the protected area. Finally, *metallic waterproofing* involves the use of a fine iron powder mixed with oxidizing agents applied to the surface area to be protected. The compound fills the pores of the concrete or masonry and, as the iron particles rust, they expand to form an impervious barrier to the migration of water.

Again, the specifications should be thoroughly reviewed for methods and products to be used. **(Figure 2.12.)**

Comments

For more detailed information on concrete waterproofing, consult ACI's *Guide to the Use of Waterproofing, Dampproofing, Protective, and Barrier Systems for Concrete.*

Dampproofing Foundations

Dampproofing is typically applied to the foundation area below grade. It is not intended to resist water pressure and should not be confused with waterproofing. Dampproofing is used to prevent the penetration of moisture through the foundation wall in below-grade applications.

The most common methods of dampproofing include the application of a bituminous-based tar-like coating on the protected areas. The bituminous materials can be sprayed, painted, or troweled on, to provide a uniform coverage of the areas below grade. Another method involves the plastering of a cement-based mixture, called *parging*, over the surface area to be protected. Certain dampproofing products may require the application of a primer coat prior to the actual dampproofing application.

Foundation Waterproofing

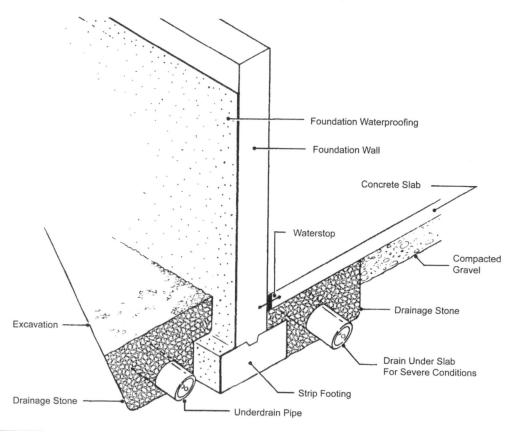

- Foundation Waterproofing
- Foundation Wall
- Concrete Slab
- Waterstop
- Compacted Gravel
- Drainage Stone
- Excavation
- Drain Under Slab For Severe Conditions
- Drainage Stone
- Strip Footing
- Underdrain Pipe

Figure 2.12

Industry Standards

Means Graphic Construction Standards
(RSMeans)

To be effective, foundation waterproofing requires a protective coating or covering on the exterior of the wall, a collecting underdrain, and porous backfill material to direct water to the underdrain. The protective coating may consist of bituminous coating applied by brush or spray, troweled on, asphalt protective board and mastic, or a membrane, an application of protective iron coating may also be used for waterproofing but requires an additional chipping of the concrete surface before installation.

The underdrain conduit should either be porous or contain openings to ensure collection of water. The conduit should be surrounded by coarse rock or gravel and laid with sufficient slope to direct the water to the collection area. The underdrain materials may be asbestos cement, bituminous fiber, corrugated metal (asphalt-coated), corrugated polyethylene corrugated tubing, porous concrete, vitrified clay, or PVC.

The porous backfill should extend up to a minimum depth below the final grade as required by site conditions. Where gravel or stone are uneconomical or unavailable, concrete block installed dry with spaced joints provides both protection for the waterproofing and a channel for excess water.

Comments

Normally the drain pipe is placed on the outside only of the foundation. In situations where the ground may become extremely wet, a drain pipe may also be placed on the inside of the foundation wall under the slab.

IBC 2006

IBC 1807 Dampproofing and Waterproofing

The 2006 IBC calls for: dampproofing and waterproofing for all portions of walls that retain earth and surround interior areas and floors below grade. All holes and recessed areas in the walls must be sealed prior to application.

IRC 2006

IRC R406 The 2006 IRC calls for: dampproofing from the top of the footing to the finish grade, using approved materials.

Testing Methods for Concrete Evaluation

Concrete Consistency/Slump Tests

Industry Standards

Construction Principles, Materials, and Methods
(John Wiley & Sons, Inc.)

3.5.3.1 Slump Test

A slump test conforming with the requirements of ASTM Standard C 143 may be used as a rough measure of the consistency of concrete. This test is not a measure of workability, and it should not be used to compare mixes of entirely different proportions or that contain different kinds of aggregate. Any change in slump on the job indicates that changes have been made in grading or proportioning the aggregate or in water content. The mix should be corrected immediately to get the proper consistency by adjusting amounts and proportions of sand and coarse aggregate, care being taken not to change the total specified water/cement ratio.

In a slump test, a test specimen is made in a mold called a slump cone, which is made of 16-gauge galvanized metal. The base and the top are open. The mold is provided with foot pieces and handles.

For a slump test, a concrete sample is taken just before its batch is placed in the forms. A slump cone is placed on a flat surface, such as a smooth plank or a slab of concrete, held firmly in place by the tester standing on the foot pieces, and filled with concrete to about one-third its volume. Then the concrete is puddled with 25 strokes of a 5/8-in.-diameter rod about 24 in. long and bullet-pointed at the lower end. The filling is completed in two more layers, each about one-third the volume of the cone. Each new layer is rodded 25 times, with the rod penetrating into the underlying layer on each stroke. After the top layer has been rodded, it is struck off with a trowel so that the cone is filled completely. The cone is removed, by gently raising it vertically, immediately after the top layer has been struck off.

The slump of the concrete is measured immediately after the cone is removed. If the top of the slump pile is, for example, 5 in. below the top of the cone, the slump for that concrete is 5 in.

Testing Methods for Concrete Evaluation

Mechanical Properties

- **Compressive Strength**
  - -Core testing (1)
  - -Windsor probe (3)
  - -Rebound hammer (2)
- **Quality of Concrete**
  - Ultrasonic pulse velocity(4)
- **Tensile Strength**
  - -Pull off testing
  - -Splitting tensile strength (5)
- **Flexural Strength**
  - (6) (7)
- **Abrasion resistance**
  - (8)
- **Bond Strength**
  - -Pull off testing

Chemical Make-up

- **Electro-chemical Activity**
  - -Half cell potential (9)
  - -Electrical resistivity (10)
- **Carbonation Depth**
  - -Acid based indicators (Phenolphthalein Solution)
  - -Petrographic analysis (11)
  - -X-ray diffraction
  - -Infrared spectroscopy
- **Alkali-Aggregate Reactions**
  - -Petrographic analysis (11)
  - -Uranyl (Uranium) Acetate fluorescence method
- **Chloride Content**
  - (12) (13) (14)

Physical Condition

- **Uniformity**
  - -Petrographic analysis (11)
  - -Pulse velocity (4)
  - -Windsor probe (3)
  - -Rebound hammer (2)
  - -Core testing (1)
- **Air-Void System**
  - (15)
- **Delaminations/voids**
  - -Hammer sounding
  - -Chain drag
  - -Impact echo
  - -Pulse velocity (4)
  - -Exploratory removal
  - -Remote viewing (TV, Borescope)
  - -Infrared thermography
- **Location/Condition of Embedded Metals**
  - -Pachometer
  - -Radiography
  - -Ground penetrating radar
  - -Exploratory removal
- **Water permeability**
- **Air permeability**
- **Water absorption**
  - (19)
- **Frost & freeze-thaw resistance**
  - (16) (17)
- **Resistance to deicing salts**
  - (18)

External Manifestation (behavior)

- **Cracks/spalls**
  - -Hammer sounding
  - -Infrared thermography
  - -Impact echo
  - -Pulse velocity (4)
  - -Remote viewing (TV, borescope)
  - -Exploratory removal
- **Deflections from Service Loads**
  - -Load testing (ACI 437R)
  - -Monitoring movements
- **Movements of Service/Exposure Conditions**
  - -Load testing (ACI 437R)
  - -Monitoring movements
- **Leakage**
  - -Visual observations
  - -Infrared thermgraphy
- **Temperature/moisture conditions**
  - -Thermocouple
  - -Thermometer
- **External Geometry**
  - -Visual observations

Note: Figures in parentheses denote number of standard test in Table A.

Figure 2.13

RSMeans, *Concrete Repair and Maintenance Illustrated*

Standard Test Methods for Evaluating Concrete

NO.	DESIGNATION	TITLE
1	ASTM C 42	Obtaining and Testing Drilled Cores and Sawed Beams of Concrete
2	ASTM C 805	Rebound Number of Hardened Concrete
3	ASTM C 803	Penetration Resistance of Hardened Concrete
4	ASTM C 597	Pulse Velocity Through Concrete
5	ASTM C 496	Splitting Tensile Strength of Cylindrical Concrete Specimens
6	ASTM C 78	Flexural Strength of Concrete (Using Simple Beam with Third-Point Loading)
7	ASTM C 293	Flexural Strength of Concrete (Using Simple Beam with Center-Point Loading)
8	ASTM C 418	Abrasion Resistance of Concrete by Sandblasting
9	ASTM C 876	Half-Cell Potentials of Uncoated Reinforcing Steel in Concrete
10	ASTM D 3633	Electrical Resistivity of Membrane-Pavement Systems
11	ASTM C 856	Standard Practice for Petrographic Examination of Hardened Concrete
12	AASHTO T 259	Resistance of Concrete to Chloride Ion Penetration
13	AASHTO T 260	Sampling and Testing for Total Chloride Ion in Concrete and Concrete Raw Materials
14	AASHTO T 277	Rapid Determination of the Chloride Permeability of Concrete
15	ASTM C 457	Microscopical Determination of Parameters of the Air-Void System in Hardened Concrete
16	ASTM C 666	Resistance of Concrete to Rapid Freezing and Thawing
17	ASTM C 671	Critical Dilation of Concrete Specimens Subjected to Freezing
18	ASTM C 672	Scaling Resistance of Concrete Surfaces Exposed to Deicing Chemicals
19	ASTM C 642	Specific Gravity, Absorption, and Voids in Hardened Concrete

RSMeans, Concrete Repair and Maintenance Illustrated [Table A]

Figure 2.14

Comments

The old rule of using a 4" slump and a minimum mix design of 2,000 psi or 5 sacks will not get it done anymore. The IBC follows the ACI code, which has very elaborate rules regarding pretesting of a mix design at varying slumps from the concrete ready mix producer.

Section 1910 of the IBC provides specific requirements for seismic design.

Concrete Admixtures

Comments

Admixtures are materials that are added to concrete to enhance certain properties for particular applications. Some types of admixtures include:

- fibrous reinforcing
- air entraining
- water reducing
- plasticizing
- quick setting
- corrosion inhibiting

Fibrous Reinforcing

Fibrous reinforcing is a synthetic fiber that promotes resistance in conditions in which high impact and abrasion are anticipated. It provides excellent secondary reinforcing and crack control. Fibrous reinforcing can be used in thin sections, pre-cast units, vaults, pipe, sidewalls, floor slabs, and similar applications. One and one-half pounds of fibrous reinforcing are used per cubic yard of concrete, and can be introduced with the aggregates or after all ingredients have been mixed.

Our experience with filament glass fiber strands added to the concrete or plaster mix has shown us, in a limited quantity of tests, that the fiber deteriorates from the Portland cement unless the material was chopped from a polypropylene source. Otherwise, the material leaves a hole in the concrete or plaster after three to five years. We do not yet have sufficient test results to determine the cause.

Air-Entraining Admixtures

Air entrainment can be achieved by adding an admixture to concrete or by using air-entraining Portland cement (see ASTM Standard C 150). Air-entraining admixtures introduce many air bubbles to the concrete, which results in better resistance to freezing and thawing in concrete slabs on grade. Air entrainment also enhances watertightness.

Water-Reducing Admixtures

This commonly used admixture is particularly appropriate when the mix design calls for a high-strength concrete.

Plasticizers

Plasticizers are used to create concrete that is extremely workable for high slump with the ability to flow for applications such as pumping. This admixture might be used for light commercial projects, for example, where concrete must be pumped to the second floor of a structure. Plasticizers are very useful for situations where a low-water cement ratio is desirable, along with a high degree of workability for ease of placement and consolidation. It is used for tremie concreting and other situations where high slumps are required.

Accelerators

This admixture promotes quick, high strength in concrete. It is available in chloride and non-chloride formula. (The non-chloride formula will not corrode reinforcing steel, metal decks, or other metal components.)

Accelerators speed up the chemical reaction between Portland cement and water, which accelerates the formation of gel—the binder that bonds concrete aggregates. Accelerated gel formation shortens the concrete's setting time, which in turn offsets the slow setting effects of cold weather, while helping to increase the strength of the concrete. Use of accelerators can also reduce concrete curing time, enabling forms to be removed earlier.

Retarders

This substance is used to prolong the time it takes concrete to set. It can be used in hot weather to prevent concrete from stiffening before it is properly placed. Retarders are occasionally used as part of the concrete finishing process. Retarders are sometimes applied to forms to allow the washing away of a fine layer of concrete for an exposed aggregate length.

Corrosion Inhibitors

Corrosion inhibitors added to the concrete during the batching process chemically inhibit the corrosive action of chlorides on reinforcing steel and other metals in concrete. The admixture is used in applications involving steel-reinforcement, and in post-tensioned and pre-stressed concrete that will come in contact with chlorides (such as near the ocean) or systems that are exposed to chemicals (such as parking garage decks and support structures).

ACI offers several publications with detailed information on admixtures. (See this chapter's introduction for more on ACI.)

Joints

Industry Standards

Construction Principles, Materials, and Methods
(John Wiley & Sons, Inc.)

3.6 It is not possible to entirely prevent cracks in concrete, but good jointing practice will help reduce their number and encourage them to occur in more acceptable locations. Joints in concrete work permit movement and volume changes; the handling, placement, and finishing of conveniently sized areas; and the separation of independent elements. The types of joints required in concrete include control joints, construction joints, isolation and separation joints, and building expansion joints.

The amount of thermal movement in concrete can be calculated by using its approximate coefficient of expansion (and contraction) of 0.0000055 in./in./°F. For example, a 100-ft.-length of unrestrained concrete would expand 0.66 in. in length for each 100°F in rise in temperature. If the temperature were to drop 100°F, the same amount of contraction would occur. Concrete would be exposed to a 100°F rise in temperature if it were placed in the spring when the temperature was 50°F and then in the summer the temperature rose to 150°F.

However, concrete shortens about 0.72 in./100 ft. while drying from its saturated condition at placing to an average hardened state, with a moisture content equilibrium with air at 50% relative humidity. This shrinkage slightly exceeds the expansion caused by such an extreme increase in temperature as 100°F. Furthermore, in most outdoor applications concrete reaches its maximum moisture content (and moisture expansion) during the season of low temperature (and thermal contraction). Thus, the volume changes resulting from moisture and temperature variations frequently tend to offset each other. Therefore, there is no need for expansion joints in most concrete associated with buildings. The common reference to *expansion* is misleading because it implies that an increase in size after placement must be allowed. There may be rare instances, in very large structures and in highways or other large, paved surfaces, where extensive surfaces of concrete are subject to large temperature variations and sufficient expansion may occur to justify expansion joints. In most instances, however, concrete is at its greatest mass when it is placed.

Nevertheless, some practitioners in warm regions insist that expansion joints are needed and include them as a safety factor, especially in concrete paving.

Control Joints

3.6.1 As concrete sets or hardens, its excess mixing water is lost through evaporation and through hydration. This initial loss of water produces shrinkage that is larger than subsequent increase in the size of the hardened mass resulting from an increase in temperature or moisture content.

Shrinkage as water dries from large areas of freshly placed concrete results in jagged, irregularly spaced cracks. By anticipating shrinkage and installing control joints to limit areas and control where cracking occurs, concrete work can be made more attractive, serviceable, and relatively free from unsightly random cracking. These joints provide a break or a reduction in slab thickness and thus create a weakened section that encourages cracking to occur at that location. When concrete shrinks, the cracks in these joints will open slightly, reducing the number of irregular and unsightly random cracks.

The maximum spacing between control joints depends on the concrete's thickness and shrinkage potential, the curing environment, and the absence or presence of distributed reinforcement.

Control joints in sidewalks should be spaced at intervals generally equal to the width of the slab, but should not be more than 6 ft. apart. Joints in driveways should be spaced generally equal to the width of the slab, but never more than 20 ft. apart.

In large slab areas that do not contain structural reinforcement, control joints should divide the slab into approximately square panels, with a maximum spacing of 20 ft. Actual spacings depend on slab thickness. A rule of thumb for plain concrete slabs is that joint spacing in feet should not exceed two slab thicknesses in inches for unreinforced concrete made with coarse ¾-in. maximum aggregate. Thus, a 4-in.-thick plain slab would require control joints at intervals not to exceed 8 ft. Additional control joints should be provided at the juncture of slab intersections.

Control joints are unnecessary in a slab that is to receive a floor finish, such as resilient flooring or carpeting, because the flooring will cover any unsightly cracks that result from shrinkage. Control joints are usually unnecessary in structurally reinforced slabs.

Control joints can be made by sawing a groove in the hardened, but not yet fully cured, concrete with a power saw or by installing a keyed joint. Sawed joints are approximately ⅛-in.-wide grooves cut in the concrete to a depth equal to one-fourth the total slab thickness, but not less than ¾ in., and at least equal to the maximum size of the aggregate. Tooled control joints should be of a similar minimum depth. However, grooves cut only for decorative purposes may be shallower.

On large concrete flat surfaces it may be more convenient to cut joints with an electric or gasoline-driven power saw fitted with an abrasive or diamond blade. Joints can be cut as soon as the concrete surface is firm enough not to be torn or damaged by the blade (within 4 to 12 hours) and before random shrinkage cracks can form in the slab.

Control Joint at Base of Column

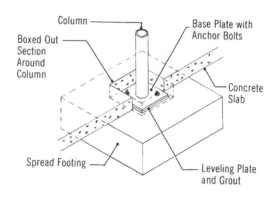

Figure 2.15   RSMeans, *Plan Reading & Material Takeoff*

Comments

Control joints are typically cut with a concrete saw on the day after the concrete is placed.

For more information on joints, it may be helpful to consult these ACI publications: *Joints in Concrete Construction* and *Building Movements and Joints.* (See this chapter's introduction for ACI contact information.)

Industry Standards

Plan Reading & Material Takeoff
(RSMeans)

It is not uncommon to have a combination of three different methods of creating control joints on the same project. The first, *tooled joints,* is accomplished by the use of a hand-held tool, and is typically used for walkways. The grooves are cut perpendicular to the length of the walk at intervals of approximately 5' during the finishing process. The second method, *saw cutting,* is done after the surface is hardened, but before final strength of the concrete has been achieved. Saw cutting is done with a diamond blade set to a specific depth. Saw cut control joints occur at column lines in large slabs. Finally, *formed control joints* are created by edge-forming areas to be poured at different times. (The slab is edge-formed in a checkerboard fashion and alternate squares are poured.) Formed joints are typically created at the intersection of a column's base and the surrounding slab. **Figure 2.15** shows a control joint at the base of a column.

Construction Joints

Industry Standards

Construction Principles, Materials, and Methods
(John Wiley & Sons, Inc.)

3.6.2 Construction joints are necessary in large construction work because it is not practicable to handle, place, and finish a large area in one operation. When construction joints are installed, concrete can be conveniently and practically placed in several operations with no loss in the appearance or performance of the complete job. Although they may double as control or isolation joints, construction joints must allow no vertical movement in the completed floor and are thus often keyed joints.

Plastic or rubber waterstops are inserted in construction joints below grade and in other locations to prevent water penetration through a concrete structural element.

Comments

Structural members such as steel beams may be embedded or cast into concrete to form a composite member. If a crack or construction joint intersects the top flange of the beam, corrosion may occur when moisture and corrosive salts are trapped against the beam. Corrosion on the top flange creates a jacking force on the concrete above. If the force is sufficient, delamination may occur, and the slab may separate from the beam.

Isolation & Separation Joints

Industry Standards

Construction Principles, Materials, and Methods
(John Wiley & Sons, Inc.)

3.12.3 Isolation and separation joints often are necessary to separate concrete sections and to prevent the bonding of one concrete section with another or to separate a concrete section from another material or structural part so that one can move independently of the other. Isolation joints are sometimes called expansion joints.

Isolation and separation joints are usually formed by installing ⅛-in.-thick (or slightly thicker) asphalt impregnated fiber sheets in floors at columns, footings, the junctures between floors and walls, and anywhere else that adjacent surfaces are required to move independently of each other.

Expansion Joints

Industry Standards

Plan Reading & Material Takeoff
(RSMeans)

Concrete, like other construction materials, expands and contracts with temperature changes. To allow for safe expansion and contraction without defects to the work, certain precautions must be taken during construction. For example, a pre-molded joint filler (which compresses as the concrete expands) allows room for expansion. These asphalt-impregnated fibrous boards come in a variety of widths, the most common of which are 4" and 6". Thicknesses are ⅜", ½", and ¾".

Expansion joints typically occur at the perimeter of a concrete slab where it terminates at a masonry or concrete wall. **Figure 2.16** shows the use of a pre-molded joint filler at the perimeter of a slab that meets a foundation wall.

Use of Pre-molded Joint Filler

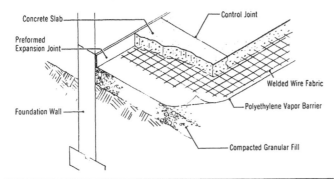

Figure 2.16

RSMeans, *Plan Reading & Material Takeoff*

Industry Standards

Construction Principles, Materials, and Methods
(John Wiley & Sons, Inc.)

3.6.4 While expansion of the concrete itself is seldom a problem, expansion of an entire structure often requires the insertion of *building expansion joints* that pass through both structural elements and finishes. Concrete that crosses a building expansion joint must be interrupted. Various types of joints have been developed to cover such joints.

In slabs and in walls, where water is likely to pass through a building expansion joint, waterstops are placed in the concrete.

Reinforcing Steel Placement

Industry Standards

Concrete Repair and Maintenance Illustrated
(RSMeans)

There are two important reasons to control the proper location of reinforcing steel in structures. First, reinforcing steel is placed in concrete to carry tensile loads, and if the steel is misplaced, the concrete may not be able to carry the tensile loads. Cantilevered slabs and negative moment areas near columns pose particular risk. Second, reinforcing steel requires adequate concrete cover to protect it from *corrosion*. The alkalinity of the concrete is a natural corrosive inhibitor. If the concrete cover is inadequate, it will not provide the necessary long-term protection. Shifted reinforcing bar cages in walls or beams may also cause the reinforcing steel to lose proper cover.

Welded Wire Reinforcement

Industry Standards

Wire Reinforcement Institute

Welded wire reinforcement is usually manufactured in 5' to 8' wide sheets and rolls. Sheets up to 14' wide are produced primarily for highway paving and precast components. Special widths can be furnished on request. Sheets can be provided up to 40' or more in length, but 12'-6", 15', 20' and 25' are the more common lengths for ease in shipping and placing. Pipe and standard building fabric are produced in roll form. Some standard building fabric is available in sheet form.

Wire sizes are available from W1.4–W45 and D4–D45. Other wire sizes are available and vary with individual manufacturers. The "W" for plan or "D" for deformed wire numbers are usually whole numbers. For a style designation of 12x12-D10xD10, the first set of numbers is the spacing of wires in inches for both the longitudinal and transverse directions, respectively. The second set is the cross-sectional areas of the respective wires in square inches multiplied by 100 (.10 sq. in. x 100 = 10, etc.). (See **Figure 2.17**.)

Spacings of longitudinal wires can vary from 2" to 18" (larger spacings are obtainable and vary with individual manufacturers). Transverse spacings are usually 4, 6, 8, 12, 16 or 18". Wires can be cut flush or have overhangs on the sides of the welded wire. The ends will generally have overhangs of ½ the transverse spacing unless other multiples of the transverse spacing are requested, i.e., for 12" transverse spacing, 6" & 6" or 8" & 4" or 10" & 2", etc.

Common Styles of Sheet[2] Welded Wire Reinforcement		
Style*	W[3] Numbers[4]	Weight (lbs/100 SF)
6x6	W1.4/W1.4[1]	21
6X6	W2.1/W2.1[1]	30
6X6	W2.9/W2.9[1]	42
6X6	W4/W4[1]	58
6X6	W5.4/W5.4	78
6X6	W7.4/W7.4	107
4X4	W2.9/W2.9[1]	62
4X4	W4/W4[1]	85
6X12	W7.4/W6.3	77

*Style numbers indicate spacing of wires in the reinforcement; 6x6, for example, has wires spaced at 6 inches on center both ways.

Notes:
1. Some styles may be obtained in roll form.
2. Standard sheet sizes are 4x8, 8x12, 8x15, 8x20, 7x20, and 7x25.
3. W prefix is for plain wire. Wires may be deformed using prefix D.
4. The number following the prefix W identifies the cross-sectional area of wire in hundredths of a square inch.

Figure 2.17 Courtesy of Wire Reinforcement Institute

The more common or standard WWR styles are designated: 6x6-W1.4xW1.4, 6x6-W2.1xW2.1, 6x6-W2.9xW2.9, and 6x6-W4xW4. Heavier WWR styles utilizing wire diameters up to ½" (some manufacturers can exceed ½" diameter) can be used for structural applications.

The size and area of reinforcement required is specified by the engineer and depends on the slab thickness, the spacing of the construction and control joints, the type and density of the sub base, a friction factor for the sub-grade, and the yield strength of the welded wire. There are a number of design methods used when the WWR is used for strength in the reinforced concrete slab or structure.

The ACI Building Code (*ACI-318*) assigns a minimum yield strength (f_y) value of 60,000 psi to most steel

reinforcing, but allows yield strengths up to 80,000 psi for many design applications. There is no cost difference for high strength WWR.

Welded wire reinforcement can be used as ties and stirrups for column, beam and joist cage (confinement) reinforcement. WWR cage reinforcement is also used for concrete encased columns. The WWR supplier uses a welded wire bending machine to shape the materials into required configurations. The placing drawings will identify the location and details of the cage assemblies.

Placing

WWR rolls are unrolled, cut to proper length and turned over to prevent ends from curling. Flattening the material is best accomplished mechanically with a "Mesh Runner," which will provide the necessary flatness to achieve proper positioning. All WWR should be placed on support accessories to maintain the required position and cover as specified by the engineer.

Splices or laps, either structural or temperature/shrinkage types, should be specified by the engineer and in conformance with the ACI Building Code. Typically, structural laps for welded wire fabric are a minimum length of 6"+ overhangs for plain wire and 8" including overhangs for deformed wires. The Code requires that one or two cross wires, depending on type of wire, occur in structural laps of WWR. Deformed wire structural laps, when no cross wires are included in the splice region, are a minimum of 12". In areas of low stress, splice lengths can be reduced.

Note: Generally, splices for slabs on grade only need to lap sufficient lengths to obtain a flat and stable layer of reinforcement, a minimum of 2".

For slab on grade construction: With slab thicknesses less than 5", a single layer of welded wire is placed in the middle of the slab. For slabs 6" and greater, the top cover is ⅓ the depth of the slab or a minumum of 2".

When two layers are specified (usually over 8" thick), the top cover will be minimum depending on saw cuts (WWR is placed below the saw cuts). The bottom cover will be 1½" min. on earth or 1" on vapor barriers. Support manufacturers produce concrete blocks or steel (coated and uncoated) and plastic chairs, bolsters, and WWR support accessories made specifically for either single layer or double layer reinforcing applications.

Placing WWR on appropriately spaced concrete blocks, steel or plastic supports with base plates and tying the WWR at laps is adequate to maintain its position during concrete placement. WWR should not be placed on the sub grade and pulled up during concrete placement. Following is a suggested guide for spacing support accessories:

Heavy WWR styles—W9 or D9 and larger 4'-6'*

Medium WWR styles—W5 or D5 to W8 or D8: 3'-4'

Light WWR styles—W4 or D4 or less 2'-3' or less*

* Spacing of supports for WWR with wires larger than W or D9 could possibly be increased over the spacings shown depending on the construction loads applied.

Consider using additional rows of supports when large deflections or deformations occur—also spacing of supports may be increased provided supports are placed and properly positioned as concrete is needed.

Refer to *ACI 318-95* for the ACI Building Code requirements for tension development lengths and tension lap splices of welded wire reinforcement. For additional information, see *Welded Wire Reinforcement Manual of Standard Practice* and *Structural Welded Wire Reinforcement Detailing Manual*, both published by the Wire Reinforcement Institute.

Accessories

Industry Standards

Construction Principles, Materials, and Methods
(John Wiley & Sons, Inc.)

3.4.3 Design and Replacement

The primary standards for reinforcing steel design, fabrication, and installation is the Concrete Reinforcing Steel Institute publication *Manual of Standard Practice* and the American Welding Society publications D1.4, "Structural Welding Code Reinforcing Steel," and "Connections in Reinforced Concrete Construction."

Reinforcing steel is usually fabricated in a mill or a shop according to shop drawings prepared by the fabricator from the structural engineer's drawings and approved by the structural engineer and the architect. The fabricated steel is bundled, tagged as to its location in the building, and delivered to the construction site. Details of *bends* and *hooks* are standard. Bundles are delivered to their place in the building by hand or crane. The reinforcement is then wired in place to maintain its location and alignment until the concrete has set. In some cases, sections of reinforcement, such as those for a column, are preassembled and delivered to the site in one piece. Such assemblies may also be made up at the site on the ground and lifted into place by crane.

Steel should be accurately positioned, secured to prevent its displacement during the placing of concrete, and cleaned of rust and foreign matter before concrete is placed against it. Steel should be protected from possible harm by fire and corrosion by a covering at least the thickness of concrete.

Welded wire fabric should be installed in the largest practicable length. Adjoining pieces should be lapped at least one full mesh and tied together with wire to prevent movement during concrete placement.

3.4.2.3 Accessories

Accessories are used to support structural steel and to make splices in it. Welded wire fabric in slabs on grade should be supported on similar devices having flat plates *(sand plates)* at their legs to prevent the legs from sinking into the slab base. The common practice of supporting reinforcement in slabs on grade using pieces of concrete or concrete bricks is discouraged because concrete often does not adhere to such materials. This produces cracks, which permit water to reach and rust the reinforcement, destroying its effectiveness. The plastic caps on the feet of the support devices are used when the underside of the slab will be exposed and in other locations to prevent the supports from rusting and transferring this rust to the reinforcement.

In beams, girders, walls, and slabs, when bar space is not at a premium, splices usually are made by overlapping the bars a prescribed number of bar diameters and tying them together with wire to keep them in place until the concrete has set. Sometimes, in columns when the space is limited, bars are butted end to end and connected with special devices made for the purpose or welded together.

Anchor Bolts

Comments

Anchor bolts are threaded, with right-angle bends embedded in poured concrete. They are provided for the future connection of steel columns, beams, or wood sill plates. They anchor that future work to the concrete. The size, quantity, spacing, and location of anchor bolts should be noted on the structural drawings. Often set by a surveying crew, anchor bolts are critical to the structure and must be located precisely.

Where exposed to "salt" air and high humidity, galvanized bolts, washers, and nuts are highly recommended.

For more information on anchor bolts, consult the ACI publication, *Guide to the Design of Anchor Bolts and other Steel Embedments*. (See this chapter's introduction for contact information.)

Post-Tensioning

Industry Standards

Construction Principles, Materials, and Methods
(John Wiley & Sons, Inc.)

3.13.3.5 Post-Tensioning

Tensile forces near the bottoms of loaded beams tend to pull the concrete apart, making it crack. Even when reinforcing steel is added, these cracks often are large enough to be seen. Such cracks can be eliminated altogether by placing the concrete in compression before an external load is applied. If enough compression is applied and held there, when a load is applied, the amount of compression will be lessened but will never disappear completely. Compressing the concrete in a beam will also permit it to carry the same loads with less concrete, making it lighter and less expensive.

Compression loads can be added to a beam by stretching the steel and locking it to the concrete at the ends. As the steel tries to return to its normal length, the resulting stress is transferred to the concrete. There are two procedures used to produce this result. *Prestressing* is done before concrete is placed around the steel. This process is best done under controlled conditions in a shop or a factory and is very expensive to do anywhere else. Therefore, it is used almost exclusively in precast concrete work.

A process called *post-tensioning* is used to add permanent tension to the reinforcing steel in cast-in-place concrete and subsequently to place the concrete under compression. Essentially, it is done using *tendons*, which are bundles of high strength, cold-drawn steel wire strands or steel bars. The tendons are coated with oil or placed in a steel tube to prevent bonding between the concrete and the tendons. The concrete is placed and permitted to cure. Generally, the tendons are fastened to one end of the beam and stretched from the other end using hydraulic jacks. When the desired amount of tension has been achieved, the jack end of the tendon is secured to the concrete, usually with a bearing plate of some sort. When the strands are very long, they must be stretched from both ends simultaneously to ensure uniform tensioning.

Tendons can be placed level, as conventional reinforcing bars are placed. Post-tensioned beams are more efficient, however, if the tendons are placed in a shape that approximates the lines of tensile force in the beam. This is near the bottom of the beam in the center and sloping upward toward the top of the beam at the ends in a V-shape.

Post-tensioned beams tend to shorten due to elastic compression, shrinkage, and creep. These movements must be accommodated in the building design and construction. Adjacent elements that would be affected by these changes should be built after the post-tensioning has been completed, or they should be isolated from the post-tensioned unit. In addition, the amount of tension to be applied can sometimes be adjusted slightly upward to at least partially compensate for these movements.

Formwork

Industry Standards

Plan Reading & Material Takeoff
(RSMeans)

Because of its fluid-like consistency during placement, all cast-in-place concrete must be contained in some type of formwork. Formwork varies in size and composition, but is most often constructed from a wood facing applied over a steel or wood frame. Simpler forms, such as those used in forming a footing, may be no more than a plank anchored by stakes and straps.

Comments

Forms must not be allowed to warp or sag, and must be assembled tightly enough so that mortar cannot leak out. The project specifications indicate the duration that forms should be left in place, typically 7 days for vertical forms, and 28 days for support forms. Premature removal of forms (before the concrete has reached its proper strength) may result in compression and tension stresses, which cause cracking, deflection, and possible collapse.

Concrete foundation walls should be plumb and not bowed. Variances should not be more than approximately one inch in eight feet.

Forms must have a smooth interior surface to provide a clean finish on the concrete. (If a textured finish is desired, forms may be lined with rubber—or other material—liners to achieve that effect.) Cracks between form sections should be avoided, as they will result in ridges, or "fins," on the surface of the concrete. Removing these ridges can create problems such as rough surfaces and exposure of aggregate. Another problem occurs when some of the chamfer strips are left off the corners. Sharp corners tend to break off, leaving exposed aggregate. There should be no cracks in the finished wall large enough to allow water to penetrate the structure from the outside, nor should there be any cracks that contribute to bowing of the wall.

When forms are reused, they are oiled with a light oil, with the excess wiped off so the concrete will not be stained.

ACI publishes *Formwork for Concrete*, a 500 page "bible" of the formwork industry. (See chapter introduction for ACI contact information.)

Footing Forms

There are two main types of footings: *continuous strip footings,* on which walls will be erected, and *isolated spread footings,* which are used for supporting interior columns.

Strip Footings

To better distribute the load imposed by the structure, strip footings are wider than the walls they support. Strip footings follow the shape and perimeter of the wall. They are typically formed on both sides and braced on the top with temporary wood braces at 2' to 3' intervals. Bottoms of the footing are braced with a perforated metal strap at approximately 2' to 4' intervals. The forms used for footings are rough planking, similar to staging planks approximately 2" x 12", in varying lengths. Common sizes for footings are 20" to 36" in width by 12" to 18" in depth. The forms materials, with the exception of the perforated straps, are reusable (see **Figure 2.18**). Most strip footings

Strip Footings

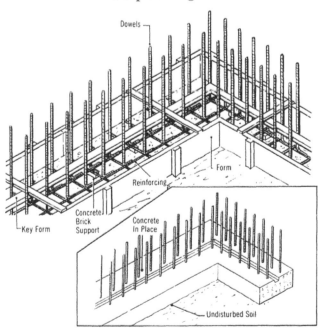

Figure 2.18

RSMeans, *Plan Reading & Material Takeoff*

remain constant in height. Because of the conditions of the soil after excavation, changes in elevation at the bottom of the footings may be required to ensure that the footing will rest on suitable soil. The contractor should note any changes in elevation that may require stepping the footings (see **Figure 2.19**).

Stepped Footings

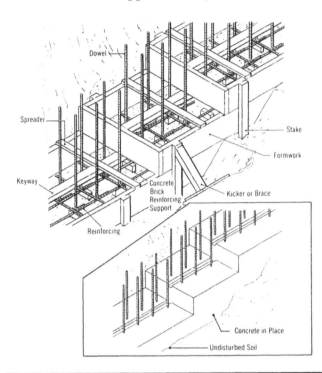

Figure 2.19

RSMeans, *Plan Reading & Material Takeoff*

To reduce the lateral movement of the wall to be placed on the continuous strip footing, a small trough, called a *keyway,* is formed by using a tapered 2" x 4" embedded in the top surface of the wet concrete in the footing. **Figure 2.20** illustrates the keyway form and the resulting trough after the forms have been stripped.

Spread Footings

Spread footings are isolated masses of concrete, often square or rectangular in shape, with thicknesses varying from 12" to 24". Their main purpose is to support point loads from the columns that rest on them. Their actual size is contingent upon the load carried and the soil's bearing capacity. A typical spread footing is shown in **Figure 2.21.**

The form material may be planks or panels, depending on the thickness of the footing. Footing forms are erected and braced in a manner similar to that used for

Keyway Detail

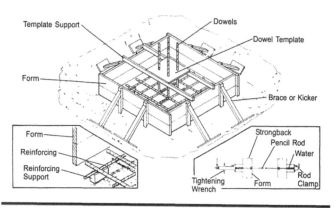

2" x 4" with Sloped Sides

Keyway

Foundation Forms

The keyway in the footing is formed with a tapered 2 x 4 in. member.

Figure 2.20　Courtesy of Home Planners, LLC

Spread Footings

Template Support

Dowels

Dowel Template

Form

Brace or Kicker

Form

Reinforcing

Reinforcing Support

Strongback
Pencil Rod
Water
Rod Clamp
Tightening Wrench
Form

Figure 2.21　RSMeans, *Plan Reading & Material Takeoff*

strip footings. Foundations with various-sized footings are typically listed in a footing schedule shown on the structural drawings. In addition, the spread footing may require the use of a template for embedded anchor bolts to support the column.

Walls & Piers

Concrete foundation walls are cast-in-place. Their function is to support the structure above. They are supported by footings and are mostly below grade. In a structure with a basement, foundation walls act to retain, or hold back, the outside soil.

A *pier* is a short column of plain or reinforced concrete used to support a concentrated load. Piers are used as components in foundation walls or as isolated, separate members.

Formwork for foundation walls is constructed of smooth wood sheathing applied to a 2" x 4" wood or steel frame. Formwork is built in modular sizes starting at approximately 8" in width and increasing to 16" widths in 2" increments. Larger panels for longer straight runs are in 24" and 48" widths. Standard panel heights are 48", 72", and 96".

Foundation walls are formed by erecting and fastening modular panels side by side on top of the strip footing. Foundation wall formwork requires the "doubling up" of panels to create a narrow box to hold the concrete until it has hardened. The panels are held apart at a predetermined space using metal ties. This space is ultimately the thickness of the wall. **Figure 2.22** illustrates formwork for a typical wall.

Ties are usually spaced at 24" on center both horizontally and vertically, though they may require closer spacing for greater loads imposed by the wet cast-in-place concrete. In addition, the panels are braced on the exterior (against the hydrostatic pressure caused by the wet concrete) by a series of horizontal wood or metal braces known as *walers*.

In addition, the contractor must make provisions for coating the forms with a release agent to break the bond between the wood and the concrete during the curing process.

Formwork for Grade Beams & Elevated Slabs

Grade beams are horizontal beams supported at the ends, as opposed to foundation walls that are supported by footings on the ground. The structure's

Foundation Wall

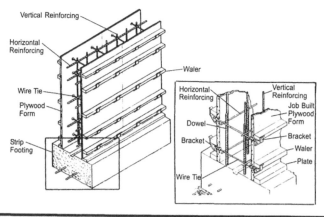

Vertical Reinforcing

Horizontal Reinforcing

Wire Tie

Plywood Form

Strip Footing

Waler

Horizontal Reinforcing

Vertical Reinforcing

Dowel

Bracket

Job Built Plywood Form

Bracket

Waler

Plate

Wire Tie

Figure 2.22　RSMeans, *Plan Reading & Material Takeoff*

load is carried along the grade beam and transmitted through the end supports (piers) to the soil below. Grade beams differ from wall formwork in that they sometimes require the forming of the bottom of the grade beam as well as the sides (**Figure 2.23**). Custom-made or one-time-use forms may be required for certain applications.

Elevated cast-in-place slabs are often integrated with concrete beams, similar to grade beams. Formed horizontal areas require considerably more bracing to support the weight of the concrete they contain. **Figure 2.24** is an illustration of an elevated cast-in-place slab. Another type of elevated slab involves placement of concrete on corrugated metal decking supported by bar joists.

Edge Forms

The simplest type of form, called the edge form, is most commonly used to contain shallow pours of concrete for slab-on-grade, walks, or pads. Edge form materials are typically rough-grade lumber in the dimension required by the depth of the pour, such as 2" x 4", 2" x 6", 1" x 4". The actual edge form is held in place by wood or metal stakes, driven into the ground at spacing as needed to support the work and prevent bowing.

Grade Beams

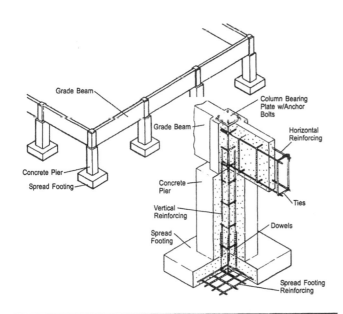

Figure 2.23   RSMeans, *Plan Reading & Material Takeoff*

Elevated Slab

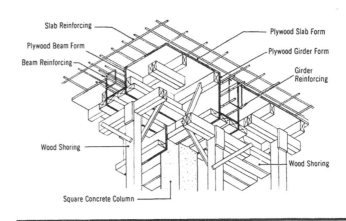

Figure 2.24   RSMeans, *Plan Reading & Material Takeoff*

Piles & Caissons

Industry Standards

Construction Principles, Materials, and Methods
(John Wiley & Sons, Inc.)

3.11.2.2 Piles and Caissons

Piles and caissons are used as foundation support for buildings when the soil is not capable of supporting the loads that will be imposed by a building on spread foundations.

Driven Piles

Driven piles are column-like units that transmit loads through poor soil to rock or lower levels of soil that have adequate bearing capacity. In some regions, short piles are called *piers*. Piles serve the same purpose as footings, in that they transmit loads to subbase strata capable of carrying the load. Piles usually are placed in clusters of two or more spaced from 30 to 48 in. on centers. This arrangement permits them to act together and produces a higher load-carrying capacity than can be achieved with isolated piles. The load capacities mentioned in this section are based on the piles being distributed in clusters. These load capacities are also the maximum permitted. Optimum load capacities are somewhat lower in each instance. Piles receive building loads from isolated columns and from grade beams by means of reinforced concrete pile caps. Pile caps are sometimes simply a widened section of a grade beam.

Pile foundations are either (1) *point bearing* types, which transmit loads to lower, stronger soil or rock through their points, or (2) *friction* types, which develop the necessary bearing capacity through surface friction between the pile and the ground.

Piles are driven with heavy *hammers* in large machines called *pile drivers*. *Drop hammers* are simply raised and dropped on a pile by force of gravity. *Differential-acting steam hammers* are rammed into the top of a pile by steam pressure or compressed air. Modern vibratory hammers and diesel-driven hammers are also used today.

Friction piles are driven to a predetermined depth or resistance based on soil boring analysis and field tests. To verify the design analysis, test piles are usually driven and loaded before the rest of the piles are driven. Point-bearing piles are driven until additional blows of the hammer produce very little movement in the pile (*refusal*).

Piles may be made of wood, concrete, steel, or a combination (composite) of these. Timber piles have been used for at least 2000 years and probably longer. Some below-water timber piles beneath bridges in Europe are known to have remained in continuous service for more than 1000 years. They are, however, suitable only for relatively light loads (40 tons maximum) and must be preservative-treated when they will extend above the water table. They are also limited in length to the effective height of the tree from which they are cut (45 to 65 ft.), because they cannot be spliced.

Steel piles may be either H-shaped sections or pipes. H-shaped piles are heavy wide-flange sections varying in size from 8 to 14 in. in both depth and flange width. They can carry loads of 50 to 200 tons each and may be as much as 150 ft. long. To produce such lengths, sections are welded together as they are being driven.

Steel-pipe piles are later filled with concrete. They are available in several types and shapes. These piles may be heavy-walled types, that can be driven directly, or thinner-walled types, that require a tight-fitting, heavy inner lining (*mandrel*) that is withdrawn before the concrete is placed. They may be smooth-walled or corrugated, round or fluted. Sizes range from 8 to 24 in. in diameter, and maximum load capacity ranges from 75 to 200 tons, depending on the type. Pipes with closed ends may be driven to as much as 120 ft. Other pipe piles are limited to about 80 ft.

Precast concrete piles are either solid concrete or open cylinders that are later filled solid with concrete. They may be square, round, or octagonal in cross section. All precast concrete piles are reinforced, and most are also prestressed. Solid precast concrete piles with simple reinforcement can be up to 80 ft. long. This increases to 150 ft. for cylinder piles and up to 200 ft. when they are prestressed. Maximum capacity ranges from 100 tons for simple reinforced piles to as much as 500 tons for prestressed cylinder piles. Sizes vary from 10 to 54 in. across.

Composite piles are constructed in several configurations. Some have timber or concrete-filled steel-pipe lower sections and concrete-filled shell with mandrel upper sections. Others have H-shaped steel lower sections and precast concrete upper sections. Composite piles sometimes permit less expensive applications. For example, the combination of timber and concrete-filled steel shell permits the use of relatively inexpensive timber piles at much lower depths than is ordinarily possible (up to 150 ft.). A disadvantage of using composite piles is that their load carrying potential is limited to that of the lower of the two elements. For example, a composite pile of timber and concrete filled steel shell is limited to 40 tons, instead of the 75 to 80 tons the concrete-filled steel piles can carry.

Caissons

Caissons are concrete columns placed in auger-drilled or excavated holes. They serve the same purpose as *piles*. While some caissons, sometimes called piers, are only 6 to 12 in. in diameter, most are much larger and capable of carrying much heavier loads. They can be as much as 6 ft. in diameter and carry 3500 tons or more. Caissons extend through unsatisfactory soil to a firm soil-bearing stratum or to bedrock. As a caisson hole is drilled or dug, a steel casing is lowered into it to keep the hole from caving in. This casing is raised and removed as the concrete is placed. Small, relatively short, and lightly loaded caissons, sometimes called piers, are frequently poured into cardboard or composition casings that are not removed as the concrete is placed.

Caissons come in four types: (1) *rock caissons* simply rest directly on solid rock; (2) *high-capacity rock caissons* rest in a socket cut into rock, thus supporting the load both by resting on the rock and by friction against the sides of the pocket these are sometimes called *socket caissons*; (3) *hardpan* or *clay caissons* rest on a soil bearing stratum, and (4) *friction caissons* are supported by the friction acting on the sides of the caisson, much as friction piles are supported. In fact, they are sometimes called *cast-in-place piles*.

Hardpan or clay caissons have either straight shafts or an enlarged base called a *bell*. Bells are produced by hand excavation or with a special device (*belling bucket*) on the auger.

Concrete Slabs

Ed. Note: See also "Elevated Slabs" on the previous page.

Industry Standards
Construction Principles, Materials, and Methods
(John Wiley & Sons, Inc.)

3.9.1.4 Edging
When all bleed water and water sheen have left the surface and the concrete has started to stiffen, other finishing operations such as *edging* may be started. Edging rounds off the formed edge of a slab to prevent chipping or other damage. An *edger* should be run back and forth until a finished edge is produced. All coarse aggregate particles should be covered, and the edger should not leave too deep an impression in the slab. If it does, the indentation may be difficult to remove with subsequent finishing operations.

Usually, edging is not required for most interior slabs on grade and is more commonly performed on sidewalks, driveways, and steps. An edger should not be used when a slab is to be finished with resilient flooring requiring a smooth, level subfloor. Edges at construction joints in the slab may be ground lightly with a silicon carbide stone to remove irregularities after the forms are stripped and before the adjacent slab is placed.

Comment
See also "Edge Forms" in the "Formwork" section earlier in this chapter.

3.9.1.5 Jointing
Except when joints will later be sawed, immediately following or during edging, premolded inserts are placed in concrete slabs to control cracking in the concrete as a result of shrinkage.

3.9.1.6 Floating
After edging and hand-jointing operations, a slab should be floated. Many variables, such as concrete temperature, air temperature, relative humidity, and wind, and other factors affect the process and make it difficult to set a definite time to begin floating. This knowledge comes only through job experience. In general, floating may be done when the water sheen has disappeared and the concrete will support the weight of the finisher.

The purpose of floating is to:

- Embed large aggregate just beneath the surface
- Remove slight imperfections, humps, and voids to produce a level or plane surface
- Consolidate mortar at the surface in preparation for other finishing operations
- Open the surface to permit excess moisture to escape.

Aluminum or magnesium floats should be used, especially on air-entrained concrete. This type of metal float greatly reduces the amount of work to be done by the finisher because the float slides more readily over the concrete surface, has a good floating action, and forms a smoother surface texture than a wood float. A wood float tends to stick to and "tear" the concrete surface.

The marks left by edgers and jointers should be removed by floating, unless such marks are desired for decorative purposes, in which case, the edger or jointer should be rerun after the floating operation.

3.9.1.7 Troweling
Troweling is done on slabs that are to be left exposed or to receive thin finishes, such as resilient flooring, carpet, tile, or paint. When troweling is required, the surface should be steel-troweled immediately after floating. It is customary for a cement mason using hand tools to float and then steel-trowel an area before moving the knee boards. If necessary, tooled joints and edges should be rerun before and after troweling to maintain true lines, proper depths, and uniformity and to remove kinks.

The purpose of troweling is to produce a smooth, hard surface. For the first troweling, whether by power or by hand, the trowel blade must be kept as flat against the surface as possible. If tilted or pitched at too great an angle, an objectionable *washboard* or *chatter* surface will result. For first troweling, a new trowel is not recommended. An older trowel that has been broken in can be worked quite flat without the edge digging into the concrete. The smoothness of a surface can be improved by timely additional trowelings. There should be a lapse of time between successive trowelings to permit the concrete to increase its set. As the surface stiffens, each successive troweling should be made by a smaller-sized trowel tipped at a progressively higher angle so that sufficient pressure can be applied for proper finishing.

For exposed slabs, additional troweling increases the compaction of fines at the surface, giving greater density and better wear resistance. A second troweling is recommended even if the slab is to be finished with resilient flooring, because it results in closer surface tolerances and a better surface to receive the flooring.

3.9.1.8 Broom Finish

Steel-troweled concrete surfaces are very smooth and can become quite slippery when wet. They can be slightly roughened to produce a nonslip surface by *brushing* or *brooming* them. A brushed surface is made by drawing a broom over the surface after steel troweling.

3.9.2 Finishing Air-Entrained Concrete Slabs

The microscopic air bubbles in air entrained concrete tend to hold the ingredients, including water, in suspension. This type of concrete requires less mixing water and still has good workability with the same slump. Since there is less water and it is held in suspension, little or no bleeding occurs. There is, therefore, no need to wait for the evaporation of free water from the surface, and floating and troweling can and should be started as soon as the slab can support the finisher and equipment. Many horizontal surface defects and failures are caused by performing finishing operations while bleed water or excess surface moisture is present. Therefore, better results are generally accomplished with air-entrained concrete.

As with regular concrete, if floating is done by hand, an aluminum or magnesium float should be used. A wood float drags and greatly increases the amount of work necessary to accomplish the same result. If floating is done with power equipment, the only major difference between the finishing procedures for air-entrained concrete and those for other concrete is that floating may be started sooner on air-entrained concrete.

3.9.3 Finishing Lightweight Structural Concrete Slabs

Finishing operations for slabs made with lightweight structural concrete containing coarse aggregates of expanded clay, shale, or slag vary somewhat from those used on slabs made with normal-weight concrete. When the surface of the concrete is worked, there is a tendency for the coarse lightweight aggregate rather than the mortar to rise to the surface. Lightweight concrete can be easily finished if the following precautions are observed: (1) the mix should be properly proportioned and not be over- or under-sanded in an attempt to meet unit weight requirements, and (2) finishing should not be started too early, and the concrete should not be overworked or over-vibrated. A well-proportioned mix can generally be placed, struck off, leveled, and floated with less effort than is necessary for normal-weight concrete. Excessive leveling and floating are principal causes of finishing problems, because the heavier mortar is driven down and the coarse aggregate brought to the surface.

3.9.4 Special Slab Finishes

Due to the plastic quality of concrete, many surface finishes can be applied. The surface may be scored or tooled with a jointer in decorative and geometric patterns. Some of the more common special finishes are discussed here.

3.9.4 1 Exposed Aggregate

An exposed-aggregate surface often is chosen for any area where a special textural effect is desired. A surface that is ground and polished is suitable, especially for such places as entrances, interior terraces, and courtyards.

Selection of aggregates is so important that test panels should be made before the job is started. Colorful gravel aggregate that is quite uniform in gradation and in sizes ranging from ½ to ¾ in. is recommended. Flat, sliver-shaped particles or aggregate less than ½ in. in diameter should be avoided, because they become dislodged during exposing operations. Exposing the aggregate used in ordinary concrete generally is unsatisfactory, as this will not necessarily reveal a high percentage of coarse aggregates.

Comments

Variations in slab thickness will generally promote cracking through the artificial creation of weakened planes. The building code specifies minimum thickness, but a slab should also have uniform thickness to give it a better chance of deforming under load without cracking.

It is recommended that a slab-on-grade be poured so that the tolerance remain at plus or minus ½" of the recommended design thickness, as there is no practical way to pour heavy concrete on grade and hold a fine tolerance. This is then the definition of nominal thickness.

Slab Thickness

Comments

The first process in concrete finishing is to place and consolidate the concrete. If it is a large rock mix (1" or larger), then tamping is required to move the rock away from the surface immediately after screeding and to raise the fine cement paste for later troweling.

ACI publishes several books on concrete slabs, including finishing, and surface defects (causes, prevention, repair). See this chapter's introduction for more on ACI.

Concrete Surfaces

Material Properties

Industry Standards

Concrete Repair and Maintenance Illustrated
(RSMeans)

Ed. Note: See **Figures 2.25** *and* **2.26** *on the following pages for desirable concrete properties and what to avoid. See also "Preventing Surface Defects," earlier in this chapter.*

Concrete Finishing

Industry Standards

Construction Principles, Materials, and Methods
(John Wiley & Sons, Inc.)

3.9.1.2 Screeding

The surface of newly placed concrete is struck off (*screeded*) by moving a straightedge back and forth with a saw-like motion across the top of the forms and screeds. If mechanical vibrating equipment is used in the striking-off process, the need for leveling may be eliminated. Whether boards, vibratory screeds, or roller screeds are used, a small amount of concrete always should be kept ahead of the straightedge to fill in low spots and maintain a plane surface.

Of all the placing and finishing operations, screeding the surface to a predetermined grade has the greatest effect on surface tolerances. Concrete should be struck off immediately after it is placed, and screed stakes used to establish surface elevation should be removed as the work progresses so that workers do not have to walk back into areas that have already been struck off.

3.9.1.3 Leveling

Leveling is the bringing of a concrete surface to true grade with enough mortar to produce the desired finish. After a concrete slab has been screeded, it should be immediately smoothed with a *darby* to level raised spots and fill depressions left after screeding. Long-handled floats, called *bull floats*, of either wood or metal are sometimes used instead of darbies to smooth and level concrete surfaces. Because it is hard to produce surfaces in plane near the edges of a slab using bull floats, darbies are sometimes needed after the bull floating has been done.

Leveling is sometimes called "darbying" or "bull floating", but this terminology requires that both terms be used or that the architect dictate which is to be used, which is inappropriate. In its literature, the PCA uses the broader term *leveling*.

The purpose of leveling is to eliminate the ridges and voids left by screeding. In addition, it should slightly embed the coarse aggregate, thus preparing the surface for the subsequent finishing operations of edging, jointing, floating, and troweling.

A slight stiffening of the concrete is necessary after leveling before further finishing operations are started. No subsequent operations should be performed until the concrete will sustain foot pressure with only about ¼-in. indentation.

Pipes & Conduits in Concrete

IBC 2006

1906.3 The IBC calls for: approval of a registered design professional for embedded conduit and pipes.

Buried Pipe

Industry Standards

Concrete Repair and Maintenance Illustrated
(RSMeans)

Buried pipes are loaded with surrounding backfill and overburden. Nonuniform loads surrounding the pipe may result in deformation of the pipe. Loads on top may exceed the load on the pipe's underside. The pipe is compressed in the vertical axis and bulges along the horizontal axis. Cracks may develop, forming hinges at three possible locations: the crown (top of pipe), and at the two spring line locations (side of pipe).

Allowable Tolerances

Industry Standards

Concrete Repair and Maintenance Illustrated
(RSMeans)

Structural members that are cast out of tolerance pose aesthetic and structural problems. Members cast out of tolerance may have improper concrete cover and cross section, which may produce eccentric loading. (See **Figures 2.27** and **2.28**.)

External Loads/Concrete Material Properties

Goal (performance requirements)	Results if the wrong material is selected (undesirable response)		Look for these properties	Avoid these!
Moving liquids	Erosion of surface 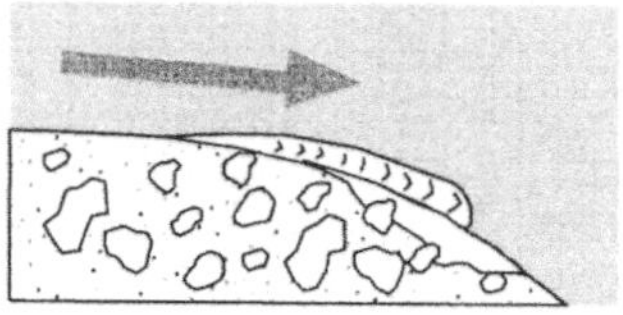		High density	Low density
			High compressive	Low compressive
			High tensile	Low tensile
Moving liquids and suspended solids			High density	Low density
			High compressive	Low compressive
	Erosion and abrasion of surfaces		High tensile	Low tensile
Vehicle wheels		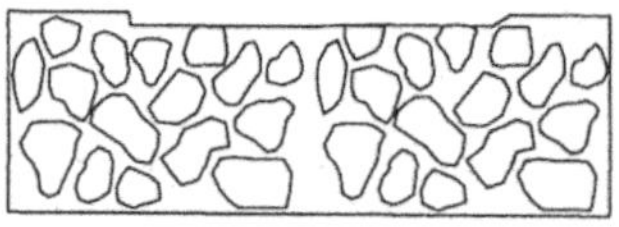 Abrasion damage to surface	High density, high compressive strength	Low density, low compressive strength
Impact		Edge spalling at joints	High compressive, tensile and bond strength, tensile anchorage into substrate	Low compressive, tensile and bond strength
		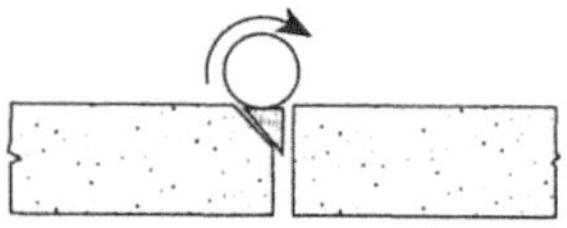 Spalling	High tensile strength, internal tensile reinforcement	Low tensile strength
			High compressive strength	Low compressive strength
			Low modulus of elasticity	High modulus of elasticity
		Loss of bond	High bond strength, tensile anchorage into substrate	Low bond strength

Figure 2.25

RSMeans, *Concrete Repair and Maintenance Illustrated*

Constructibility & Appearance Properties

	Goal (performance requirements)		Look for these properties	Avoid these!
Constructibility	Turn-around time 		Rapid strength gain	Slow strength gain
	Flowability 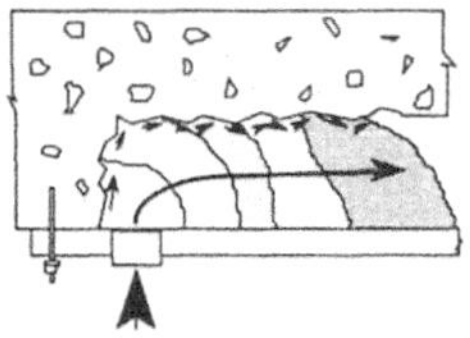		High slump	Low slump
			Small aggregate, fines, round shape	Large aggregate, angular shape, lack of fines
	Non sag 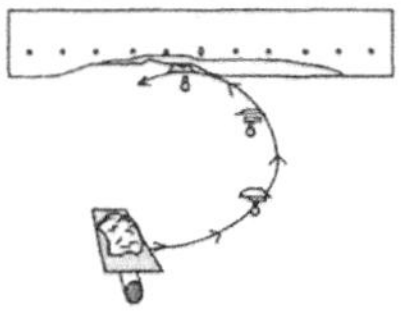		High internal cohesion, high adhesive grip	Low internal cohesion, low adhesive grip
	Forgiving "Murphy's Law"		Simple formulation, redundant	Complex formulation, dependent reactions

Goal (performance requirements)	Results if the wrong material is selected (undesirable response)		Look for these properties	Avoid these!
Appearance  **CRACKS**	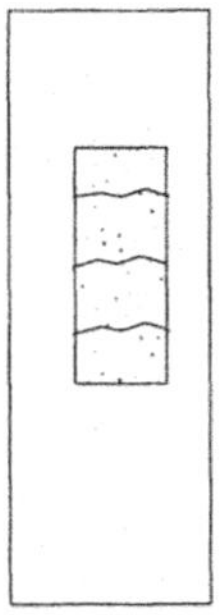	Cracking of surface from drying shrinkage*	Low drying shrinkage,* flexible surface membrane	High drying shrinkage*
		Cracking of surface in plastic stage	Low exotherm	High exotherm
			Low surface water loss during placement	High surface water loss during placement

*Refer to volume change affects included at the end of this section.

Figure 2.26

RSMeans, *Concrete Repair and Maintenance Illustrated*

Effects of Nonuniform or Excessive Loads

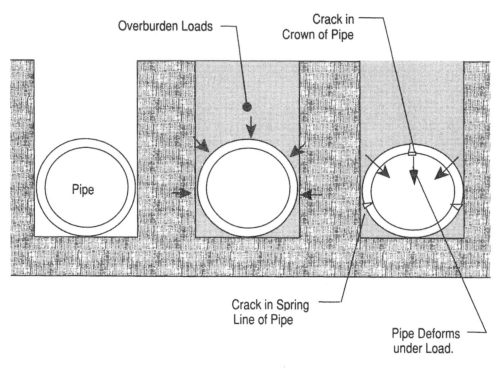

Figure 2.27

RSMeans, *Concrete Repair and Maintenance Illustrated*

Structural Members Out of Tolerance

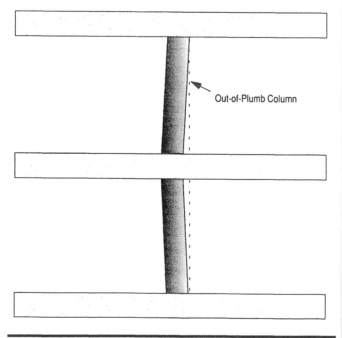

Figure 2.28

RSMeans, *Concrete Repair and Maintenance Illustrated*

Comments

Concrete Paving Tolerance

The *ACI Manual of Concrete Practice*, published by the American Concrete Institute, recommends a tolerance in concrete paving of ± ¼" in 10' in all sideways measurements, and ± ⅛" when measuring parallel to the centerline of the concrete paving.

Foundation Tolerances

The American Concrete Institute (ACI) and the American Society for Testing and Materials (ASTM) have developed a schedule to determine the flatness tolerances separately from a level tolerance. (The term **level** is a comparison above or below a theoretical elevation plane (benchmark), and the term **flatness** is the differential within a 10' straightedge.)

The allowance for level is ± ¾" against the benchmark. The maximum allowance for flatness is ± ³⁄₁₆" in 10'.

ACI publishes *Standard Tolerances for Concrete Construction*, which includes tolerances shown in ACI documents.

Ed. Note: See also "Cracks: Acceptable Tolerances and the Effects of Chlorides" earlier in this chapter.

Paving with Concrete: Green Approaches

Landscape Estimating Methods, Fifth Edition
(RSMeans)

Carefully selected materials, such as porous pavers that absorb runoff, can enhance a natural setting, and meet practical needs that might otherwise require a detention pond. Porous paving products include reinforced grass paving and gravel (for low-traffic areas), block interspersed with gravel for low-growing plantings, and porous asphalt, among others. *(See Chapter 1 for more on porous asphalt.)* Paving materials can also be green by virtue of their manufacture—from materials such as recycled asphalt or used brick from a deconstructed site.

Keep in mind that dark, asphalt-laden areas, especially in hot climates, typically absorb the sun's heat and can be several degrees hotter than the surrounding landscape. To reduce the effect of these "heat islands" where extensive paving is required in a landscape design, consider using concrete products manufactured with a combination of light-colored cements and aggregates. Concrete grid pavements with grass or other plantings also contribute some cooling benefits. White or light concrete masonry can also be used where walls are needed, further reducing this heat island effect.

Recycling Paving Materials: Recycling of pavement materials, particularly concrete and asphaltic concrete, is standard for material quantities weighing one ton or more. Disposal and storage of materials according to regulations are standard business practices routinely monitored within the profession.

See the LEED for Homes rating system, developed by the U.S. Green Building Council for more information. **www.usgbc.org**

Green Concrete Paving Products:

- Rebar fabricated from recycled steel
- Recycled aggregate in concrete mix
- Coal fly ash or ground granulated furnace slag in concrete mix
- Low-VOC concrete hardening compounds

Evaluating & Repairing Old Concrete

Historic Preservation: Project Planning & Estimating
(RSMeans)

Historic and modern concrete is subject to deterioration from a variety of causes, including environmental factors, inferior component materials, poor workmanship, design defects, and lack of proper maintenance. Environmental effects such as moisture absorption and freeze-thaw cycles produce internal stresses in concrete.

Repairs should be started only after the survey and analysis measures have been completed. If controllable, the cause of the deterioration, such as the overloading of structures or infiltration of water, must be corrected prior to performing repairs. Multiple repair techniques are used on historic concrete structures. In all cases, the materials and detailing should be as close to the original as possible to create a functional and visually acceptable solution.

Repair of spalling involves removal of loose or unsound material and installation of a compatible patch that dovetails into the existing sound concrete. Inactive cracks less than $1/16$" can be repaired with a mixture of cement and water. For larger cracks, sand should be added to the mixture. In cases where an inactive crack makes it necessary to reestablish the concrete's structural integrity, epoxy injection may be used. Active cracks may require the addition of expansion joints to the structure, and filling of the crack with sealant, to allow movement.

Where deflection has occurred in reinforced concrete members, repair involves in-situ strengthening or replacement. This work should be carried out under the direction of a certified professional engineer. Repair of eroded or weathered concrete surfaces requires the use of a compatible patching material and appropriate finishing techniques to match the historic finish.

Replacement of historic concrete structures or elements requires duplication of materials and detailing to match the original as closely as possible. Appropriate repairs, restoration techniques, and maintenance can extend the life of historic concrete structures indefinitely.

Table of Contents

Text in blue type indicates excerpted summaries from the International Building Code® (IBC) *and* International Residential Code® (IRC). *Please consult the IBC and IRC for complete coverage and specific wording. "Comments" (in solid blue boxes) were written by the editors, based on their own experience.*

 These icons will appear with references to green building practices and seismic regulations, respectively.

3 MASONRY

Common Defect Allegations

- Many defect claims include the allegation that a retaining wall has shifted. Ordinarily, there will be some observable deflection in a long, straight wall, even during backfill. Usually, high walls are required to be shored prior to the backfilling activities to reduce this distortion.

- Sometimes walls are improperly built. However, additional surcharges are often placed on the back of the wall in the form of either dead load improvements or the creation of an excessive live load where traffic of heavy vehicles impacts a previous design for a landscape wall. Sometimes a French drain is placed behind the wall with perforated pipe and crushed rock, and when the soil filters down through the gravel, it eventually fills the voids in the rock and plugs up the drainage, completely loading the wall with a new hydraulic static pressure. The proper method of creating a French drain is to use a filter fabric to filter out the silt, either around the perforated pipe with a sock, or preferably wrapping an envelope completely around the crushed rock. This is achieved by placing the filter fabric in the void before placing the gravel and the pipe, and then wrapping the fabric over the rock fill before the soil is placed.

- Occasionally, the "five foot to daylight" rule is violated. This rule basically states that the toe of the footing should be five feet from daylight (below ground) when the slope of the ground continues downward from the wall. First appearances are that the contractor built it wrong, although occasionally we find that the user of the property regraded the land in an attempt to create more usable pad area.

- Wall cracks are generally considered tolerable to $1/4$", as long as there is no dislocation of the plane of the wall and no vertical dislocation. Cracks should not be left open to the weather, but should be filled with an epoxy or expansive set grout and monitored for further movement with a crack gauge permanently mounted to either side of the crack and photographed for future analysis.

- Masonry-related claims for defects in construction often involve walls that are not laid up with precision. The basis of the disagreement

(continued)

usually lies in the contrast between hand-laid masonry and the exact measurement of synthetic panels, which actually can have an artificial appearance. In practical terms, building a wall involves a contractor's best judgment as well as variables between head joints, bed joints, and lead jambs. To the practitioner, the presence of variables among these elements is expected and adds to the attractiveness of hand-laid masonry. Determining the point at which an irregularity becomes a defect is a judgment that must be made by an experienced practitioner.

Introduction

The goal of this text is to clarify the standards of each trade, while noting deficiencies commonly stated in defect claims. We accomplish this by presenting building code information, along with the recommendations of industry leaders. This section covers common masonry installations, such as block and brick walls, fireplaces, and retaining walls. Code requirements are interspersed with installation standards from the Masonry Institute, ASTM, and other industry authorities.

International Building Code Development

The *International Building Code (IBC)* absorbs many of the masonry standards defined regionally or by the Masonry Institute. The result is a more comprehensive regulation that is much more definitive regarding applied methods of construction. The Masonry Alliance for Codes & Standards, a group of masonry industry representatives, followed the progress of the International Code Council to ensure proper incorporation of masonry provisions.

The following organizations may be helpful in providing more detailed information on masonry installations:

American Concrete Institute
248-848-3700
www.concrete.org

Brick Industry Association (BIA)
703-620-0010
www.bia.org

Marble Institute of America
440-250-9222
www.marble-institute.com

Masonry Institute of America (MIA)
800-221-4000
www.masonryinstitute.org

National Concrete Masonry Association (NCMA)
703-713-1900
www.ncma.org

Portland Cement Association
847-966-6200
www.cement.org

Ed. Note: Comments and recommendations within this chapter are not intended as a definitive resource for construction activities. For building projects, contractors must rely on the project documents and applicable codes for their own particular locations.

 A Green Approach to Masonry

Green Building: Project Planning & Cost Estimating, Second Edition

(RSMeans)

Factors used to evaluate the environmental friendliness of masonry units include the energy and pollution involved in producing or processing them, as well as delivering them to the construction site. Adobe is an especially green material, since its manufacture requires only a small fraction of the energy used to manufacture fired brick. Ideally, masonry products should be manufactured and obtained locally to meet green building goals.

Masonry units can also support sustainability goals by reducing energy costs if used as part of a thermal mass in south-facing walls.

Many types of masonry materials can be recycled. If a building is being deconstructed, the units should be salvaged and reused, if possible, on the same site for a new or remodeled structure, or as part of the landscaping. Otherwise, they can be turned over to a salvage company. See the "LEED® for Homes Rating System", developed by the U.S. Green Building Council. For more information, visit **www.usgbc.org**

Green Masonry Products

Division 04—Masonry

- Glass block fabricated from recycled plastics
- Glass bricks fabricated from recycled glass
- Simulated stone fabricated from recycled materials
- Concrete masonry units with integral insulation
- Concrete masonry units fabricated from recycled materials
- Autoclaved aerated concrete masonry units
- Salvaged brick reuse
- Rubber blocks fabricated from recycled materials
- Brick fabricated from recycled rubber
- Masonry cavity drainage material fabricated from recycled materials
- Locally-sourced stone

Installation

Comments

For instructions on the procedures for installing masonry walls, refer to the *Concrete Masonry Handbook*, which is available from the Portland Cement Association, 5420 Old Orchard Road, Skokie, Illinois 60077-1083 (Telephone: 1-847-966-6200).

CONSTRUCTION	MAXIMUM WALL LENGTH TO THICKNESS OR WALL HEIGHT TO THICKNESS
Bearing Walls	
Solid units or fully grouted	20
All others	18
Nonbearing Walls	
Exterior	18
Interior	36

Figure 3.1   Courtesy of ICC, *IBC-2006*

Construction of Mortar Joints

Note: The following are summaries of the basic code requirements of the *International Building Code* and *International Residential Code*. Please consult the *IBC* and *IRC* for complete coverage and specific wording.

Both the 2006 IBC and IRC call for: ³/₈" thickness for head and bed joints. Exception made for the bed joint of the starting course over foundations: must be between ¼" and ¾" (Section 2104.1.2.1 in IBC and R607.2.1 in IRC).

Lateral Support

IRC 2006

IBC 2006

Both the 2006 IBC and IRC call for: lateral support, either horizontally or vertically, for masonry walls. See **Figure 3.1**. (Section 2109.4 in IBC and 606.9 in IRC.) IRC also calls for an overlapping masonry bonding pattern.

Minimum Thickness

IBC 2006

IBC 2109.5.2 The 2006 IBC calls for 6" minimum for bearing walls in one-story buildings, and 8" for walls more than one story, shear walls, foundation walls, foundation piers, and parapet walls. 16" minimum required for rubble stone walls.

IRC 2006

IRC 606.2 The IRC 2006 calls for: 6" minimum for solid masonry walls and garages that are one story and 9' high or less, and 8" for bearing walls more than one story. Lateral or vertical support is also required.

Mortar Mixing

Comments

The Portland Cement Association recommends usage of Type N mortar for all general masonry work, including exterior load- and non-load-bearing walls, and parapet walls. It suggests that architects specify the weakest mortar that will meet the structural requirements of the building. For projects requiring higher flexural values, PCA recommends that Type S mortar can be used. ASTM C270, Standard Specification for Mortar for Unit Masonry, outlines mortar designations and specific applications.

Industry Standards

Portland Cement Association

Mix mortar materials in a mechanical mixer. With mixer running, add materials in following sequence:

- ²/₃–³/₄ of the required water
- ¹/₂ of the required sand
- Masonry cement or mortar cement or hydrated lime followed by Portland cement
- Remainder of sand
- Water required to reach workable consistency

Mix mortar for not less than 3 minutes and not more than 5 minutes after the last materials have been introduced into the mixer.

Evaluating & Repointing Mortar

Historic Preservation: Project Planning & Estimating
(RSMeans)

The decision to repoint is usually made based on signs of visual deterioration, such as disintegrating mortar (open joints), cracked joints, loose masonry units, damp walls, or damaged plasterwork. The source of deterioration should always be determined first and corrected. Examples include leaking roofs or drainage systems, differential settlement, rising damp, or extreme weather exposure. Without appropriate repairs, mortar deterioration will continue, and repointing will have been a waste of time and money. In many cases, it may be desirable to retain a professional consultant to analyze building conditions and make recommendations.

Mortars used for repointing should have compressive strength that is lower (softer) than the masonry units and the historic mortar, and a vapor permeability that is higher. If a higher strength mortar is used, stresses in the wall will likely cause permanent damage, such as cracks and spalling of the masonry units. Mortars with a greater permeability than the masonry units will allow moisture to evaporate, helping to prevent salt crystallization (or subflorescence) from causing damage to the internal brick structure. Ideally, the repointing mortar will match the historic mortar in strength, permeability, and appearance as closely as possible. If the new sand matches the original, then color and texture will usually match as well. The tooling of the joints should also match the original joints. Mortar analysis by a qualified laboratory can assist in the selection of an appropriate mortar.

Mortar specifications should include the mortar type according to ASTM standards. The ASTM-designated types represent a range of strengths from Type M (2500 PSI) to Type K (75 psi). The desired strength and appearance can be achieved by specifying the ASTM mortar by mix proportions. Other ingredients, such as crushed shells, pigments, or clays may be included in the mortar specifications.

Before the repointing project begins, the contractor should prepare test panels using the same techniques that will be used on the project. It may be necessary to create several panels to demonstrate the repointing of all the joints, masonry units, and mortar types included in the project. Cleaning tests should also be done in the same manner.

In the preparation of joints, the old mortar should be removed to a depth of two to two-and-a-half times the joint width. Any mortar that is loose or deteriorated beyond this depth should also be removed. Removal of old mortar with hand tools, such as chisels and mash hammers, causes the least damage to masonry. Small pneumatically powered chisels can be used, but only by careful, experienced masons. Power saws or grinders in the hands of unskilled masons will undoubtedly result in damage to masonry and are not recommended. New mortars should be applied in layers no thicker than ¼" each, allowing time for each layer to harden to allow for shrinkage of the mortar. The last layer should be tooled to match the historic joint. Improperly tooled or over-filled joints will significantly change the appearance of a historic building.

For historic restoration projects, it is important to allow time for evaluation, inspection, and the preparation of construction documents to obtain visually pleasing and durable results. If professional consultants are used, they should be knowledgeable in historic construction techniques and should determine the cause of deterioration and ensure its correction prior to repointing. Inspections can be expected to require more time than those performed for new construction.

IBC 2006

IBC 2103.8 The 2006 IBC calls for: Type S or N mortar for glass units, used within 1½ hours after mixing (2½ allowed for applications other than glass units). Mortar must comply with ASTM 270.

IBC 2104.1.2.5 The 2006 IBC call for: placing masonry units only when mortar is soft. Fresh mortar is required if units are disturbed/bond broken.

IRC 2006

IRC 607.1 The IRC 2006 calls for: Type M through S for foundation walls, and type M, S, or N for seismic design categories A, B, and C. Type M or S required for seismic design category D. Mortar must comply with ASTM 270.

Industry Standards

ASTM Material Specifications
(American Society of Testing and Materials)

Masonry Cement—ASTM C91 (Types M, S, or N)

Portland Cement—ASTM C150 (Types I, IA, II, IIA, III, or IIIA)

Blended hydraulic cement—ASTM C595 [Types IS, IS–A, IP, IP–A, I(PM)–A]*

Hydrated lime for masonry purposes—ASTM C207 (Types S, SA, N, or NA)**

Quicklime for structural uses (for lime putty)—ASTM C5

* Slag cement Types S or SA can also be used but only in property specifications.

** Types N and NA lime may be used only if tests or performance records show that these limes are not detrimental to the soundness of mortar.

Comments

The building code excerpts in the following sections demonstrate the importance of researching your area's requirements prior to construction. They are not intended to provide sufficient information for actual construction. Good construction supervision requires that a library of texts be present at the project site, including relevant code books, for handy reference when interpretation of proper construction techniques is necessary.

Anchorage for Shear

IBC 2006

IBC 2109.7 The 2006 IBC calls for: intersecting walls to be anchored by a bonding patterns, steel connectors, joint reinforcement, interior nonload-bearing walls, or ties/joint reinforcement or anchors. If wood floor joists bear on masonry walls, they must be anchored every 72" (or less) with metal straps. Steel floor joists need to be anchored with 3/8" round bars, not more than 72" on center.

Comments

The masonry reinforcement information outlined in the building code is so significant that it should appear on construction drawings as design criteria. In any case, during construction in seismic zones with high risk, the installer is bound by these rules. Often, defects occur at the corners in the placement of the vertical lap corner bars. These elements must be placed inside the corner bend of the horizontal bar when a single bar is placed in the bond beam block. This requires a machine bend that has a relatively sharp radius.

Similarly, retaining walls and restraining walls will differ as to the proper placement of the vertical bars, and the

construction plans should clearly reflect the requirements. A retaining wall is based on the footing that holds the vertical wall against the soil load; so the vertical steel rods should be placed at the back, or earth, side of the cell to stop rotation. A restraining wall is held at the bottom and the top by other structures. Therefore, the vertical rods should be placed away from the earth, or the front of the cell, where the wall may fail in the middle during tensile stress.

Masonry Walls

Concrete Block Walls

Industry Standards

Means Graphic Construction Standards
(RSMeans)

Concrete blocks are among the most frequently used materials for constructing masonry walls and partitions because of their strength, versatility, and economy. They may be used for many different types of bearing and nonbearing wall structures, including foundation walls, exterior and interior bearing walls, infill panels, interior partitions, and fire walls. They may also function effectively as backup walls for composite and cavity design wall structures with brick or other veneer facings.

Concrete blocks are manufactured in two types, solid and hollow, and in various strength ratings. If the cross-sectional area, exclusive of voids, is 75% or greater than the gross area of the block, then it is classified as "solid block." If the same area is below the 75% figure, then the block is classified as "hollow block." The strength of concrete block is determined by the compressive strength of the type of concrete used in its manufacture, or by the equivalent compressive strength, which is based on the gross area of the block, including voids.

There are several aggregates that can be used to manufacture lightweight blocks. These blocks can be identified by the weight of the concrete mixture used in their manufacture. **(Figure 3.2.)**

Regular weight block is made from 125 lb. per cubic foot concrete (PCF), and lightweight block from 105 to 85 PCF concrete. Care should be exercised when installing concrete block walls to prevent cracking caused by block shrinkage, temperature expansion and contraction, excessive stress in a particular area, or excessive moisture. The cracking can be controlled by selecting and installing blocks of the proper moisture content for the locality and by employing a sufficient

Concrete Block Wall

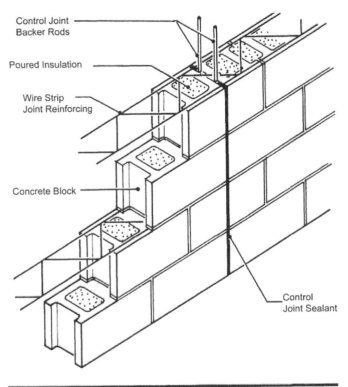

Control Joint
Backer Rods

Poured Insulation

Wire Strip
Joint Reinforcing

Concrete Block

Control
Joint Sealant

Figure 3.2

RSMeans, *Means Graphic Construction Standards*

amount of horizontal joint reinforcing. Cracking can also be controlled with vertical control joints, which are typically placed at intervals ranging from 20' to 40'. The spacing intervals of these control joints depend on the wall height and the amount of joint reinforcing used. Corners and openings generally require control joints as well. Mortar joints throughout the wall should be made weather tight (to restrict moisture invasion) by being tooled and compressed into a concave shape.

Joint reinforcing and individual ties serve as important components of the various types of concrete block walls. Two types of joint reinforcing are available: the truss type and the ladder type. Because the truss type provides better load distribution, it is normally used in bearing walls. The ladder type is usually installed in light-duty walls that serve nonbearing functions. Both types of joint reinforcing may also be used to tie together the inner and outer wythes of composite or cavity-design walls. Corrugated strips, as well as Z-type, rectangular, and adjustable wall ties, may also be used for this purpose. Generally, one metal wall tie should be installed for each 4½ square feet of veneer. Although both types of joint reinforcing may be used as ties, individual ties should not be used as joint reinforcing to control cracking.

Structural reinforcement is also commonly required in concrete block walls, especially in those that are load-bearing. Deformed steel bars may be used as vertical reinforcement when grouted into the block voids, and as horizontal reinforcement when installed above openings and in bond beams. Horizontal and vertical bars may be grouted into the void normally used as the collar joint in a composite wall. Lintels should be installed to carry the weight of the wall above openings. Steel angles, built-up steel members, bond beams filled with steel bars and grout, and precast shapes may function as lintels.

Various methods may be employed for insulating concrete block walls. Rigid foam inserts or loose perlite can be used to fill the voids in the blocks of single wythe structures. Composite and single wythe walls can also be insulated by installing the insulating material between the furring strips for the interior wall facing. For cavity walls, rigid-board insulation may be attached within the cavity to the surface of the inner wythe.

Aluminum Frames in Masonry Walls

Portland Cement Association

Architectural aluminum is widely used for window and door frames because it is attractive, durable, and requires little maintenance. However, unprotected aluminum interacts with cement-based materials, sometimes resulting in severe frame damage.

In fresh concrete, aluminum reacts principally with alkali hydroxides from cement. The pH of fresh mortar ranges from 12 to 13. Aluminum in contact with plain concrete can corrode, and the situation is worse if the concrete contains calcium chloride as an admixture or if the aluminum is in contact with a dissimilar metal.

Ensuring a good quality installation of aluminum-framed windows and doors includes proper material selection and correct construction practices.

Materials

The American Architectural Manufacturers Association recommends using only coated windows for installations involving any cement-based materials, including masonry. The coating materials may be either organic, such as paint, or inorganic, such as anodized aluminum. Currently, organic-type coatings are the most widely used finishes for architectural aluminum. For exterior use, the AAMA recommends high-performance coatings (fluorocarbons, siliconized acrylics, siliconized polyesters) that are capable of weathering outdoor exposure for at least 20 years.

Some coatings are only able to protect up to a pH of about 11. Fresh mortar can stain frames coated with these materials, and if allowed to rest on the frame, the mortar can also lead to corrosion or other surface damage. To prevent this, fresh mortar droppings should be removed as quickly as possible from aluminum frames.

Organic coatings on extruded aluminum window and door frames are categorized as pigmented, high performance, and superior performing coatings. For light commercial and residential applications, the "pigmented" category is acceptable. The coating should be at least 20 microns (0.8 mil) thick. Chemical resistance of the organic finishes is sufficient to withstand the mild cleaners (acid or alkaline) or other corrosives associated with the construction process or cleanup. AAMA Standards 2603, 2604, and 2605 provide test methods and performance criteria (including chemical resistance and corrosion resistance) for pigmented, high performance, and superior performing organic coatings, respectively.

Inorganic coatings, such as anodized finishes, convert the outer layer of aluminum to aluminum oxide, producing an extremely durable surface. Applying a clear (organic) coating can further protect the anodized surface. To prevent staining, alkaline building materials such as wet mortar, plaster, or concrete should be removed quickly from anodized surfaces.

Construction

Masonry walls should be built well in advance of inserting frames into the wall to protect aluminum. This allows time for the mortar to cure and dry, which reduces the movement of alkalies. The frame is then attached with screws at the bottom, top, and sides. A 13-mm (½-in.) gap should be left around the frame. When filled with caulk, this gap separates the inside of the building from the outside, reduces wall stresses acting on the frame, and creates a barrier between the mortar and the window/door frame material. Even so, (new) hardened mortar that is rewetted by precipitation can still be a source of alkalies. Good coatings should adequately protect aluminum from chemical attack. Two coats of bituminous paint or zinc chromate primer are often used in severe applications to provide separation of the aluminum from the cement-based products. A light coating of petroleum jelly painted onto the surface of the frame is another way to provide temporary protection to the finish during construction.

Anything that directs moisture away from the frame reduces alkali exposure. Therefore, if it is possible to separate the frame from direct contact with the mortar

by a sheet material (flashing), this can help reduce corrosion as well. Plastics, rubbers, and vinyl materials resistant to UV degradation and attack by alkalies are all acceptable.

If the masonry wall is to be cleaned following construction, the aluminum must not be subjected to harsh chemicals and must be rinsed thoroughly. Clear water should remove any products used to clean the wall and any alkalies washed off the building face.

For specifications and other information on aluminum coatings, visit: **www.aamanet.org**

Protecting aluminum frames in masonry walls:

- Choose coatings for resistance to high pH.
  - Thicker coatings are generally better.
  - Organics are usually more resistant than non-organics (anodized coatings).
  - Temporary coatings (plastic film, paper, cloth, or petroleum jelly) can provide protection during construction.
- Place aluminum frames into walls after mortar has cured.
- Separate frame and masonry with a caulk gap.
- Remove fresh mortar from aluminum frames as quickly as possible.
- Direct water away from the wall with drips and flashings.

Comments

In some regions, termite treatment inside the cells is recommended to prevent termites from entering the structure.

For concrete block wall tolerance, see the end of this chapter. Also refer to *Residential Construction Performance Guidelines*, published by the National Association of Home Builders (www.nahb.org).

Masonry Flashings
Portland Cement Association
(by Jake Ribar, reprinted with permission from PCA)

Modern masonry is thinner than its predecessors. It is often designed as a rain screen with cavities and flashings designed to expel water. Walls with properly designed and installed flashings provide weather resistant masonry construction, increase longevity, and minimize maintenance.

Investigation of masonry problems clearly reveals a lack of understanding by both designers and contractors as to the purpose of flashing. Properly installed flashings perform several functions necessary for satisfactory performance of masonry:

1. They create a slippage plane to accommodate differential movements between the masonry and the foundation.

2. They provide a path for water to be expelled from the masonry.

3. They prevent rising damp.

Flashing should be installed at the base of a masonry wall at finished grade, at all shelf angles and steel lintels, and where there is a change of materials in the horizontal plane (such as a change from a concrete masonry wall to a brick masonry wall). End dams are required wherever flashings terminate. For example, flashings over lintels require end dams.

Any mistakes in the installation of flashings will jeopardize the performance of the masonry. Repair of faulty flashing is expensive and disruptive for the building occupants. It pays to do it right the first time.

Brick Walls
Industry Standards
Means Graphic Construction Standards
(RSMeans)

Brick walls may function as bearing structures if the proper guidelines are followed for the type of brick, the type of mortar, and the reinforcement methods and materials. For example, brick units with a compressive strength between 2,000 and 14,000 psi, when installed with a mortar of commensurate compressive strength, produce a wall with a strength between 500 and 3,000 psi. Horizontal joint reinforcement can be placed within the wall to control shrinkage cracks and to tie the face wythe to the backup wythe in composite or cavity bearing wall systems. To provide resistance to lateral and flexural loads, bar reinforcement may be grouted vertically into the brick cores, or vertically and horizontally into the collar joint between two wythes of bearing wall.

Because brick walls are not waterproof, provisions must be made to limit the amount of water penetration through the exterior face. Flashing should be installed at the junction of walls and floors, as well as over and under openings. In cavity walls, the outside face of the backup wall or the insulation between the wythes should be waterproofed. Weep holes should be located above the flashing at brick shelves, relieving angles, and lintels to provide a means of escape for moisture that has penetrated the wall.

The most common size brick measures nominal 4" wide by 8" long, with heights of $2^2/_3$" (standard), $3^1/_5$" (engineer), 4" (economy), $5^1/_3$" (double), and 8" (square or panel). The next most commonly used size measures 4" in width by 12" in length, with heights of 2" (Roman), $2^2/_3$" (Norman), $3^1/_5$" (Norwegian), 4" (utility), $5^1/_3$" (triple), and 12" (square or panel). The heights of courses of brick may also vary slightly with the thickness requirements of mortar joints. For example, a $1/_2$" mortar joint requires a brick that is $1/_{16}$" thinner than does a $3/_8$" mortar joint to maintain the same modular coursing in the wall. Because the two apparent dimensions in any brick wall structure are its length and height, these two measurements are critical in determining the number of units of brick material to be used. Therefore, bricks with larger length and height dimensions are more economically installed because fewer of them have to be laid per square foot of wall area.

Comments

Oversized brick for veneer is available in 4" wide, 16" long pieces that are $2^1/_4$", $2^3/_4$", 4", or 8" high. For load bearing applications, sizes available are 6" or 8" wide x 16" long with 4" or 8" heights. For curtain wall or reinforced veneer, the same sizes as loadbearing are available.

The Brick Industry Association provides technical notes on proper design and installation of structural and veneer brick walls. (See chapter introduction for contact information.)

Flood Protection for Walls
Federal Emergency Management Agency (FEMA)
(www.fema.gov)

One way to protect a house from shallow flooding is to add a waterproof veneer to the exterior walls and seal all openings, including doors, to prevent the entry of water. As shown in the **Figure 3.3** the veneer can consist of a layer of brick backed by a waterproof membrane. Before the veneer is applied, the siding is removed and replaced with exterior grade plywood sheathing. If necessary, the existing foundation footing is extended to support the brick. Also, because the wall will be exposed to flood water, changes are made to the interior walls as well so that they will resist moisture damage. In the area below the flood level, standard batt insulation is replaced, and any wood blocking added inside the wall cavity is made of exterior grade lumber.

Waterproof Veneer

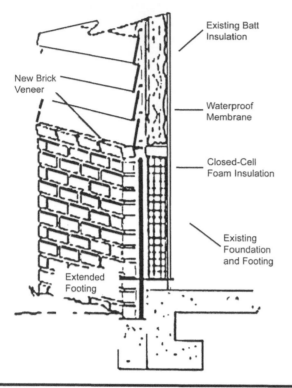

Figure 3.3

Courtesy of FEMA

Keep these points in mind if you plan to have a waterproof veneer added:

- Adding a waterproof veneer is appropriate in areas where the flood depth is less than 2 feet. When flood depths exceed 2 feet, the pressure on waterproofed walls increases greatly, usually beyond the strength of the walls. If greater flood depths are expected, consult with a licensed civil or structural engineer before using this method.

- Consider having the veneer added as part of remodeling or repair work.

- For structures with brick walls, the new brick veneer and waterproof membrane are added over the existing brick.

Evaluating, Repairing & Replacing Brick

Historic Preservation: Project Planning & Estimating
(RSMeans)

Deteriorated brickwork is repaired by removal and replacement of the affected units. Replacement units should match the original in color, dimension, physical characteristics, and texture. They should also meet current ASTM standards for absorption, strength, and saturations, and be of the proper grade for the local climate. Recycled bricks may be used, but should be tested and are not recommended for parapets, exterior paving, copings, sills, or any area exposed to extreme moisture, freezing, and thawing. New mortar to be used with old brickwork should generally be lime-based with the minimum amount of water added to achieve a workable consistency.

Stone

Grading Standards for Stone

Landscape Estimating Methods, Fifth Edition
(RSMeans)

Stone is nature's most enduring landscape material. Stone pavers are available as blocks and irregularly shaped modules. Because of its beauty and durability, stone is often used for stair treads, borders, and coping,

Types of Stonework

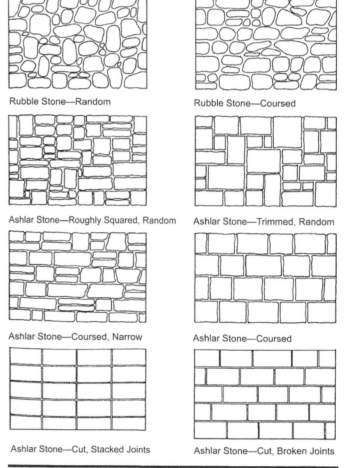

Rubble Stone—Random

Rubble Stone—Coursed

Ashlar Stone—Roughly Squared, Random

Ashlar Stone—Trimmed, Random

Ashlar Stone—Coursed, Narrow

Ashlar Stone—Coursed

Ashlar Stone—Cut, Stacked Joints

Ashlar Stone—Cut, Broken Joints

Figure 3.4

RSMeans, *Landscape Estimating Methods,* 5th Edition

as well as paving. It is well-suited to irregular floor patterns that can utilize "quarry run" irregular lines. Stone paving is graded by:

- **Hardness:** The comparative capacity of a substance to scratch or be scratched by another. The ASTM abrasion hardness standard for stone is graded from 6 minimum to 17 maximum. Stone preparation and installation details are particularly important in assuring appropriate hardness.

- **Porosity:** The ratio, expressed by a percentage, of the volume of pores or interstices to the total volume of its mass.

- **Abrasion resistance:** The ability to withstand scratching, scraping, rubbing, and erosion.

Stone Flooring

Kitchen & Bath Project Costs: Planning & Estimating Successful Projects
(RSMeans)

Stone floor tiles are rated by slip-resistance and glazing/porosity. Sealing is required to prevent stains. Maintenance is easier with a dark-colored grout. The subfloor must be able to support the weight of stone tiles.

Repairing & Replacing Stone

Historic Preservation: Project Planning & Estimating
(RSMeans)

Stone may deteriorate due to its inherent solubility in water or acid rain, or its exposure to runoff, which causes material dissolution. Salt crystals (sulfates, chlorides, nitrates, and phosphates) may form on the surface or stone as efflorescence. Corroded fasteners, especially those containing iron, may expand, stain, and eventually shatter stonework. Mortar joints may require repointing—in some cases because a previous repointing was done improperly, perhaps using mortar which was too hard.

For stone in historic structures, it may be appropriate to consult a professional architectural conservator, preservation architect, or knowledgeable masonry contractor. The selection of matching or similar replacement stone of the specified dimension may require traveling to the quarry. The stone should also meet appropriate ASTM standards for the specific use. Aesthetic factors to consider in restoring stone masonry include the visual graining pattern of the stone, the orientation of the bedding plane, and the size and manner in which units were placed.

If the original stone was not sufficiently durable, it may be necessary to select a different type to replace damaged or deteriorated stone. The replacement stone should not be of a type that may damage the adjacent masonry.

Glass Block

Repairing & Replacing Glass Block

Historic Preservation: Project Planning & Estimating
(RSMeans)

A durable material, glass block withstands weather conditions well. The maintenance requirements for glass block assemblies are similar to those for other types of masonry. Periodically the mortar joints may require repointing. Failure of the individual units due to traumatic impact or deformation from structural failure of the assembly may require removal and reassembly of the glass block wall. In this case, the original glass block should be carefully salvaged, and damaged units replaced with matching material. Cracked or fogged glass blocks can often be replaced with new versions of the same style. Standard glass block shapes and patterns are still manufactured. In the United States, they are most commonly 4" thick and 8" or 12" square, although other sizes are available. It is possible, though expensive, to have historic blocks duplicated. Where ongoing vandalism is a problem, replacement of the original hollow glass block with solid glass block may be warranted.

Glass block is a material of considerable weight. A structural evaluation may be necessary to ensure adequate support not only under the glass block wall itself, but also beneath any areas that may bear the weight of stockpiled materials during the restoration.

IBC 2006

IBC 2110.1 The 2006 IBC calls for: glass block to be installed with mortar and reinforcement (metal channel frames, embedded panel anchors, masonry or concrete recesses, or structural frames). Glass block is not allowed in load-bearing construction, fire walls/barriers, or party walls. However, glass block is allowed as opening protective if it has at least a 3/4 hour fire protection rating. Standard units: at least 3 7/8" thick each, maximum 144 SF for exterior panels, and maximum 250 SF for interior. Thin units: at least 3 1/8" thick each, maximum 85 SF for exterior panels, and maximum 150 SF for interior.

IRC 2006

IRC R610 The 2006 IRC calls for: hollow glass units to be partially evacuated, and their surface coated with latex-based paint of polyvinyl butyral where in contact with mortar. Standard units: at least $3\frac{7}{8}$" thick each, maximum 144 SF for exterior panels, and maximum 250 SF for interior. Thin units: at least $3\frac{1}{8}$" thick each for hollow (3" for solid), maximum 85 SF for exterior panels, and maximum 150 SF for interior. Type S or N mortar required, used within 1 $\frac{1}{2}$ hours of mix.

Fireplaces, Hearths & Chimneys

IBC 2006

IBC 2111.2 Footings and foundations: The minimum thickness for fireplace concrete or solid masonry footings is 12". Foundations must extend a minimum of 6" inches beyond the fireplace face or support wall. Footings must extend at least 12" below ground (in locations not subject to freezing).

IRC R1001.1 Same requirements.

IBC 2111.3 Seismic Reinforcing: The 2006 IBC calls for both masonry and concrete fireplaces to be properly reinforced, anchored, and supported in compliance with Chapter 21, with the exception of Seismic Design Categories A, B, or C, which do not require seismic anchorage or reinforcement.

IRC R1001.3 and **R1001.4** Same general requirements.

IBC 2111.7 Lintel and throat: Lintels supporting masonry over fireplace openings must be made of noncombustible material. Four inches is the minimum bearing length required on either end of the fireplace opening. Throats or dampers must be at least 8" inches above the lintel.

IRC R1001.7 Same requirements.

IBC 2111.9 Hearth and hearth extension: Hearths and hearth extensions for masonry fireplaces must be made of masonry or concrete. They must be reinforced and supported by noncombustible material to properly support loads.

IRC R1001.8 Same requirements.

IBC 2111.10 Hearth extension dimensions: Hearths must extend at least 16" in front and 8" beyond each side of fireplace. If fireplace opening is 6 SF or larger, hearths must extend at least 20" in front and 12" beyond the sides.

IRC R1001.10 Same requirements.

IBC 2111.11 Fireplace clearance: Clearance to combustibles: at least 2" from sides and front faces, and at least 4" from back of masonry fireplaces. See code for list of exceptions.

IRC R1001.11 Same requirements.

IBC 2111.12 Fireplace fireblocking: Fireblocking made of noncombustible material is required in between the fireplaces and the surrounding floors and ceilings, securely fastened. Firebloacking must be 1" deep, and placed on metal strips when between wood beams, joists, or headers.

See also IBC 2113 for additional provisions for masonry chimneys.

IRC 2006

IRC R1001.12 and R602.8 Fireblocking required: Fireblocking is required to cut off concealed draft openings and form a fire barrier between each story and roof space. Wood-framed buildings require fireblocking in six specific locations.

Industry Standards

Means Graphic Construction Standards
(RSMeans)

Masonry fireplaces are typically constructed of brick and block masonry units. (See **Figure 3.5.**) Because of the weight of the fireplace and chimney, a foundation of concrete block and/or cast-in-place concrete is required for support. The fire box consists of fire-resistant brick, while the hearth and face are of standard brick. Stone and tile are also used for these exterior surfaces. Accessories, such as clean-out doors, air vents and dampers complete the typical system.

Chimney types fall into two basic categories: masonry and prefabricated metal. Besides their use with fireplaces, chimneys are also required to vent exhaust gases from water heaters, furnaces, boilers and incinerators. Chimneys can be constructed within the building, on an outside wall, or as a freestanding structure. Foundation and intermediate support requirements will vary accordingly.

Masonry chimneys typically consist of a flue constructed from heat-resistant, refractory material, surrounded by a brick-framed exterior. Fire bricks and clay tiles are commonly used as refractory material. The weight of masonry chimneys is such that foundation support structures are also necessary.

Masonry Fireplace—Interior

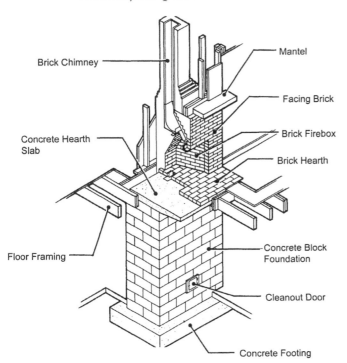

Brick Chimney
Mantel
Facing Brick
Brick Firebox
Concrete Hearth Slab
Brick Hearth
Floor Framing
Concrete Block Foundation
Cleanout Door
Concrete Footing

Prefabricated, Built-in Fireplace

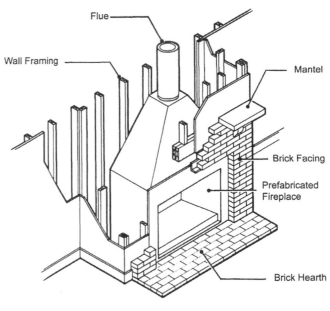

Flue
Wall Framing
Mantel
Brick Facing
Prefabricated Fireplace
Brick Hearth

Masonry Fireplace—Exterior

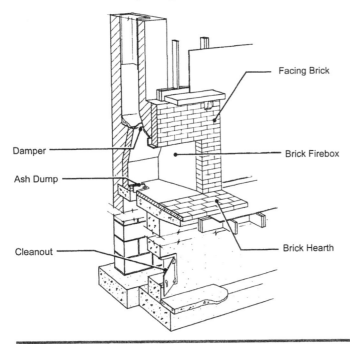

Facing Brick
Brick Firebox
Damper
Ash Dump
Brick Hearth
Cleanout

Masonry Chimney

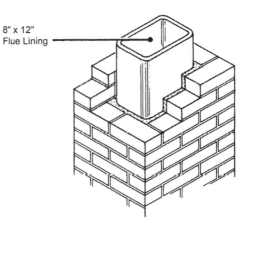

8" x 12" Flue Lining

RSMeans, *Means Graphic Construction Standards*

Figure 3.5

Both the chimney and the foundation should be sized according to the requirements of the specific installation.

Whether metal or masonry, all chimneys should extend at least 3' above the highest point at which they pass through or by the roof. Chimneys should also be at least 2' higher than any roof ridge within a 10' radius. For all chimney installations, it is important to use the appropriate material and to maintain the proper space requirements for installations.

Ed. Note: See Chapter 13, "Specialties," for information on prefabricated fireplaces.

Retaining Walls

Industry Standards

Means Graphic Construction Standards
(RSMeans)

Masonry retaining walls may be constructed of block, brick, or stone.

Brick or block walls are usually placed on a concrete footing that acts as a leveling pad and distributes imposed loads to the subsoil. Both the wall and the footing may be reinforced. Voids in the masonry are usually filled with mortar or grout, and the wall capped with a suitable material. Solid masonry walls should include porous backfill against the back of the wall and weep holes or drainage piping to eliminate hydrostatic head.

Stone retaining walls may be constructed dry or mortar set with or without a suitable concrete footing. All masonry retaining walls should be placed a sufficient depth below grade to eliminate the danger of frost heave. Mortar set walls should include an adequate drainage system.

Block Wall Tolerances

Industry Standards

ACI Manual of Concrete Practice
(American Concrete Institute)

Allowable Tolerances
American Concrete Institute (ACI) standards define both a total tolerance envelope within which the plane and edges of a wall must fall and relative alignment tolerances for adjacent elements and construction within a 10-ft (3-m) distance. For top of wall alignment, the tolerance depends on whether the wall is exposed and whether it is a bearing surface. These are

summarized below. All of the ACI tolerances apply to brick walls as well as concrete masonry walls and other types of masonry construction.

Top of Wall Alignment

    Exposed +/-½"

    Not exposed +/-1"

    Bearing surface +/-½"

    TOW Nonbearing +/-¾"

    Slope Alignment (Plumb) +/-¼" in 10'

    Vertical Alignment (Plumb) +/-¾" in total wall

    Horizontal Alignment +/-¼" in 10'

    Horizontal Alignment +/-½" in total wall

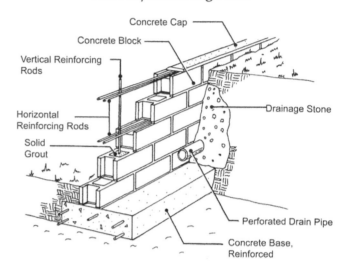

Masonry Retaining Wall

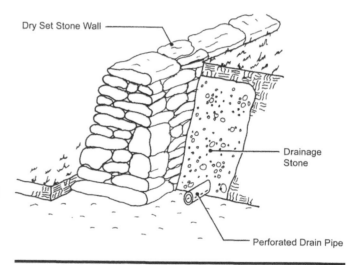

Stone Retaining Wall

Figure 3.6   RSMeans, *Means Graphic Construction Standards*

Comments

For more information on allowable tolerances in masonry construction, refer to *Residential Construction Performance Guidelines*, published by the National Association of Home Builders (**www.nahb.org**).

may be required in concrete beds that are large in area or subjected to heavy traffic.

Ed. Note: See Chapter 2 for concrete paving and Chapter 1 for asphalt paving.

Paving with Masonry Units

Industry Standards

Means Graphic Construction Standards
(RSMeans)

Both brick and stone may be set in a sand or concrete bed and grouted with mortar or watered and tamped sand. (See **Figure 3.7**.) Regardless of the type of bed material, the subbase must first be leveled and thoroughly compacted to prevent tracking and settling of the finished surface. Wire mesh reinforcing

Brick Sidewalk

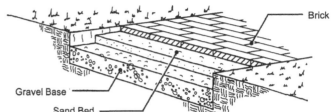

Plaza Brick Paving System

Brick Paving on Sand Bed

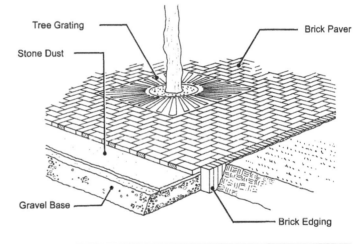

Figure 3.7

RSMeans, *Means Graphic Construction Standards*

Brick Paving on Concrete Bed

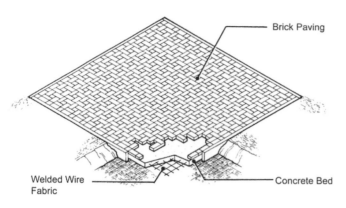

Brick Paving

Welded Wire Fabric

Concrete Bed

Stone Paving on Sand Bed

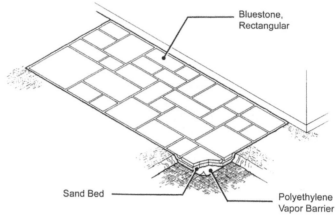

Bluestone, Rectangular

Sand Bed

Polyethylene Vapor Barrier

Stone Paving on Concrete Bed

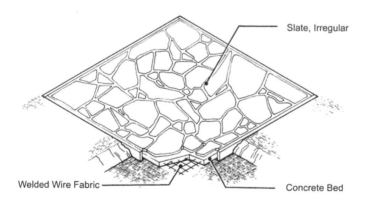

Slate, Irregular

Welded Wire Fabric

Concrete Bed

Figure 3.7 (continued)

RSMeans, *Means Graphic Construction Standards*

CHAPTER 4

METAL FRAMING

Table of Contents

Text in blue type indicates excerpted summaries from the International Building Code® (IBC) *and* International Residential Code® (IRC). *Please consult the IBC and IRC for complete coverage and specific wording. "Comments" (in solid blue boxes) were written by the editors, based on their own experience.*

 *These icons will appear with references to green building practices, seismic regulations, and hurricane-safe building requirements, respectively.*

CHAPTER 4

METAL FRAMING

Common Defect Allegations

Cold-formed metal framing is not as widely utilized in structural components as wood. As a result, there is less historic information available on alleged failures. One complaint that tends to emerge is lack of a tight fit between the stud and the track channel in a load-bearing condition. The problem is caused by the fact that the track channel has a slight radius at the 90° corners caused by the rolling process during manufacture. Since a cut stud C-Channel has a sharp end, the stud channel does not make complete contact with the track channel. After the building has been standing awhile, it settles slightly, showing wrinkles in drywall tape and on EIFS synthetic exterior plaster systems.

The solution is the same as in wood framing construction: load the building with roofing materials, and stock as much of the interior weight as possible before placing wall finishes. Also, hydraulic jigs can be used to compress the studs in a site prefabrication of the wall; then the assembled wall can be lifted to the erected location.

Introduction

Use of metal components in residential and light commercial construction is growing in the U.S., primarily due to its durability and ease and flexibility of design. Metal makes a good building material for several reasons: available scrap from recycled automobiles and construction activities makes it plentiful. The components do not warp after installation, and the materials are not flammable or affected by termites or fungal attack. Buildings with metal structural framing can, however, suffer rust from prolonged exposure to moisture. All steel framing members produced are coated with a galvanized zinc coating that protects it from corrosion. Just like other structural materials, steel framing should not be exposed to excessive moisture during construction.

Cold-formed steel framing, formerly known as light-gauge steel, is the most common form of metal framing found in residential and light commercial construction. Steel framing can be stick-built, panelized, or pre-engineered, and is readily available throughout the U.S. from major building material dealers. By virtue of its material characteristics and properties, steel offers significant advantages for building construction. Steel studs and joists are strong, lightweight, and made from uniform-quality material. In fact, steel has the highest strength-to-weight ratio of any building material, and it can be engineered to meet the strongest wind and seismic ratings specified by building codes.

While steel framing has been used for decades in the construction of non-load-bearing partition walls, it is only in the past several years that it has been adopted for use in load-bearing applications. In addition to both the *International Building Code* and the *International Residential Code*, cold-formed steel is also included in NFPA 5000.

Provisions cited in building codes were developed by the American Iron and Steel Institute. Below is information for this and other organizations that offer guidelines:

American Iron and Steel Institute (AISI)
202-452-7100
www.steel.org
The American Iron and Steel Institute's Specification for the Design of Cold-Formed Steel Framing Members (NASPEC) provides well-defined procedures for the design of load-carrying cold-formed steel in buildings. This document was developed through consensus committees, with representatives from steel mills, roll-formers, fabricators, framing contractors, educators, industry associations, researchers, and building code officials, from the United States, Canada, and Mexico and is intended for use throughout North America.

American Institute of Steel Construction, Inc.
312-670-2400
www.aisc.org

American Zinc Association
202-367-1151
www.zinc.org

Steel Framing Alliance
202-785-2022
www.steelframing.org
The Steel Framing Alliance (SFA) is a product development organization charged with expanding the use of steel framing in construction. Established in 1996, the SFA supports research and

development of best practices in steel design and installation techniques. The organization offers training and education programs for builders, framers, design professionals, sub-trades, building code jurisdictions and educators.

Ed. Note: Structural steel is also used in residential projects, such as girders to support floors. Structural steel and pre-engineered steel are occasionally used for light commercial applications, but require extensive training and specialized equipment. While the IBC covers structural steel in its Chapter 22, that material is not included in this chapter since it is comprised primarily of technical design criteria and formulas, typically interpreted by the engineer who designs the installation.

Since there are few standard techniques accepted by building officials, all metal buildings must be engineered. Several professional associations offer guidelines.

Green Building Attributes
(Steel Framing Alliance)

Designers and builders have long recognized steel for its strength, durability, and functionality. Increasingly, however, architects are recognizing steel's important environmental attributes—averaging 67 percent recycled content industry wide.

Steel is 100% recyclable and contains at a minimum 25% of scrap steel. For over 150 years, old steel that has seen its useful life has been returned to manufacturers' furnaces to be melted in the recipe to produce new steel products. Steel is the world's most recycled material. In the United States alone, almost 75 million tons of steel were recycled or exported for recycling in 2006. The use of cold-formed steel in a building helps contribute toward earning a "green" designation. Steel is recognized in green building programs and rating systems including the National Association of Home Builders Green Building Guidelines and Leadership in Energy and Environmental Design (LEED®).

Cold-Formed Steel Construction

Industry Standards

Means Graphic Construction Standards
(RSMeans)

Used for both light commercial and residential applications, cold-formed steel construction is a building system that utilizes galvanized steel studs for bearing walls and galvanized C joists (single or double) for support of the floor system. (See **Figures 4.1** and **4.2.**) Decking may consist of plywood, steel slab form and concrete, steel deck and concrete, or precast concrete. Studs are also used as a backup system for preformed fascia of various materials. They allow for easy attachment and bracing to resist wind or earthquake forces.

Fastening is accomplished by using self-drilling screws or by welding. Plywood decks are fastened using screws or spiral shank nails. Adhesives may also be used in conjunction with screws or nails. When welds are used with galvanized members, weld areas should be touched up with a suitable paint.

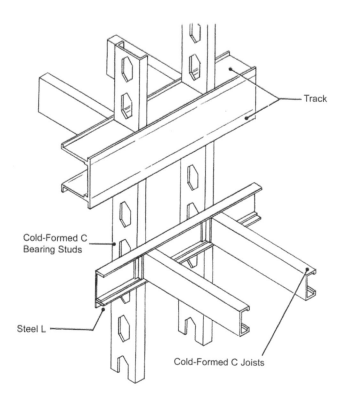

Cold-Formed Double Steel Joists

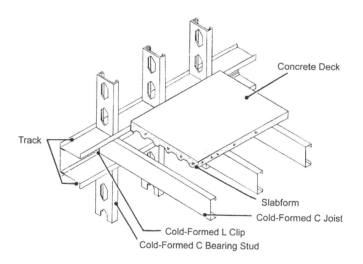

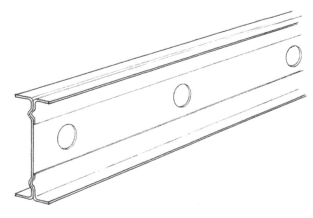

Figure 4.1

RSMeans, *Means Graphic Construction Standards*

76

Cold-Formed Metal Framing—Walls

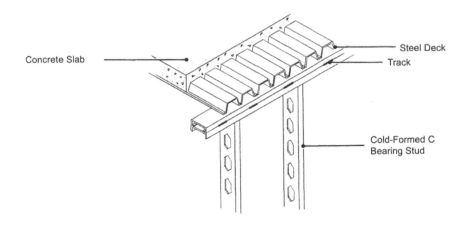

Concrete Slab

Steel Deck

Track

Cold-Formed C
Bearing Stud

Floors, on Steel Beam

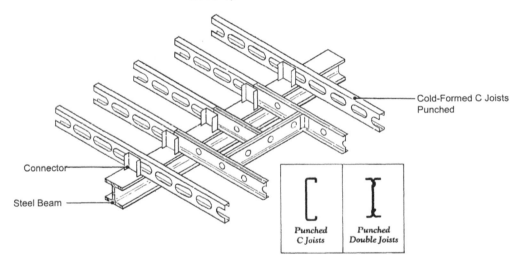

Cold-Formed C Joists
Punched

Connector

Steel Beam

Punched
C Joists

Punched
Double Joists

With Plywood Deck

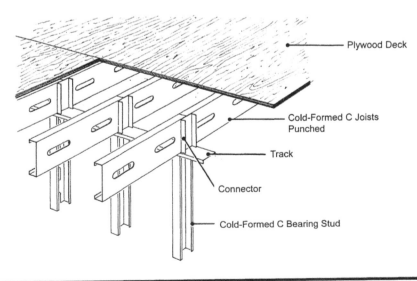

Plywood Deck

Cold-Formed C Joists
Punched

Track

Connector

Cold-Formed C Bearing Stud

Figure 4.2

Industry Standards
Gypsum Construction Handbook
(United States Gypsum Company)

Framing Components
It is important that cold-formed steel components such as steel studs and runners, furring channels and resilient channels be adequately protected against rusting in the warehouse and on the job site. In marine areas such as the Caribbean, Florida, and the Gulf Coast, where salt air conditions exist with high humidity, components that offer increased protection against corrosion should be used.

Steel Studs and Runners
Studs and runners should be channel-type, roll-formed from corrosion resistant steel, and designed for quick screw attachment of facing materials. They are used as strong, nonload bearing components of interior partitions, ceilings and column fireproofing and as framing for exterior curtain wall systems. Heavier thickness members are used in load-bearing construction. Limited chaseways for electrical and plumbing services are provided by punchouts in the stud web. Matching runners for each stud size align and secure studs to floors and ceilings, also functioning as headers.

Available in various styles and widths outlined below:

- **Efficient, low-cost 25-ga. members for framing non-load bearing interior assemblies.** Studs come in widths to match wood framing dimensions and are available in lengths up to 20-ft. Runners come in matching stud widths—10' lengths.

- **22-ga. studs and runners**—Heavier gauge, stronger studs in four widths—2½", 3⅝", 4", 6"—and cut-to-order lengths, up to 20'. Runners come in matching stud widths.

- **20-ga. studs and runners**—Heavier 20-ga. members used in framing interior assemblies requiring greater-strength studs and reinforcement for door frames. Also used in curtain wall assemblies. Studs available in 2½", 3⅝", 4", 6" widths—cut-to-order lengths up to 28'. Runners come in stud widths—0' lengths.

- **Stiffened flange studs and runners**—Used for framing load-bearing interior and exterior walls and non-load bearing curtain walls.

Partition Layout
Properly position partitions according to layout. Snap chalk lines at ceiling and floor. Be certain that partitions will be plumb. Where partitions occur parallel to and between joists, ladder blocking must be installed between ceiling joists.

Steel Framing
Steel stud framing for non-load bearing interior partitions is secured to floors and ceilings with runners fastened to the supporting structure.

Runner Installation
Securely attach runners:

1. To concrete and masonry—use stub nails, power-driven fasteners.
2. To foam-backed metal (max. 14-ga.) concrete inserts use ⅜" Type S-12 Pan Head Screws.
3. To suspended ceilings—use expandable hollow wall anchors, toggle bolts or other suitable fasteners.
4. To wood framing—use ¼" Type S Oval Head Screws or 12d nails.

To all substrates, secure runners with fasteners located 2" from each end and spaced max. 24" o.c. Attach runner ends at door frames with two anchors when 3-piece frames are used. (One piece frames should be supplied with welded-in-place floor anchor plates, pre-punched for two anchors into substrate.)

At partition corners, extend one runner to end of corner and butt or overlap other runner to it, allowing necessary clearance for gypsum panel thickness. Runners should not be mitered.

Stud Installation
Insert floor-to-ceiling steel studs between runners, twisting them into position. Position studs vertically, with open sides facing in same direction, engaging floor and ceiling runners and spaced 16" or 24" o.c. max., as required. Proper alignment will provide for proper bracing, utility runs and prevention of stepped or uneven joint surfaces. Anchor all studs adjacent to door and borrowed light frames, partition intersections and corners to floor and ceiling runners. Intermediate partition studs should not be anchored to runners.

Place studs in direct contact with all door frame jambs, abutting partitions, partition corners and existing construction elements. Grouting of door frames is always recommended and is required where heavy or oversize doors are used. Where a stud directly abuts an exterior wall and there is a possibility of condensation or water penetration through the wall, place a No. 15 asphalt felt strip between stud and wall surface.

Backing

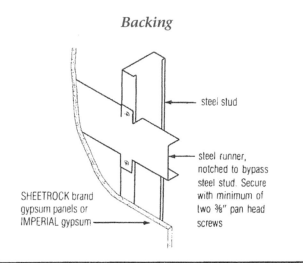

steel stud

steel runner, notched to bypass steel stud. Secure with minimum of two ⅜" pan head screws

SHEETROCK brand gypsum panels or IMPERIAL gypsum

Figure 4.3   Courtesy of United States Gypsum Company, *Gypsum Construction Handbook, Centennial Edition.*

Over metal doors and borrowed light frames, place a section of runner horizontally with a web-flange bent at each end. Secure runner to strut-studs with two screws in each bent web. At the location of vertical joints over the door frame header, position a cut-to-length stud extending to the ceiling runner.

Fasten together with two ⅜" Type S pan head screws in each flange or web. Locate each screw no more than 1" from ends of splice. Steel Studs may be conveniently spliced together when required. To splice two studs, nest one into the other forming a box section, to a depth of at least 8" and fasten with screws.

Curved Surfaces

Gypsum Panels and Gypsum Base can be formed to almost any cylindrically curved surface. Boards can be applied either dry or wet, depending on the radius of curvature desired. To prevent flat areas between framing, shorter bend radii require closer than normal stud and furring spacing.

Boards are horizontally applied, gently bent around the framing, and securely fastened to achieve the desired radius. When boards are applied dry, the minimum radius of curvature meets many applications. By thoroughly moistening the face or back paper prior to application, and replacing in the stack for at least one hour, the board may be bent to still shorter radii. When the board dries thoroughly, it will regain its original hardness.

Installation of Curved Surfaces

Framing—Cut one leg and web of top and bottom steel runner at 2" intervals for the length of the arc. Allow 12" of uncut steel runners at each end of arc. Bend runners to uniform curve of desired radius (90 max., arc). To support

the cut leg of runner, clinch a 1" x 25-ga. steel strip to inside of leg. Select the runner size to match the steel studs; for wood studs, use a 3½" steel runner. Attach steel runners to structural elements at floor and ceiling with suitable fasteners as previously described.

Position studs vertically, with open side facing in same direction and engaging floor and ceiling runners. Begin and end each with a stud, and space intermediate studs equally as measured on outside of arc. Secure steel studs to runners with ⅜" Type S pan head screws; secure wood studs with suitable fasteners. On tangents, place studs 6" o.c., leaving last stud freestanding. Follow directions previously described for erecting balance of studs.

Panel Preparation—Select length and cut board to allow one unbroken panel to cover the curved surface and 12" tangents at each end. Outside panel must be longer than inside panels to compensate for additional radius contributed by the studs. Cutouts for electrical boxes are not recommended in curved surfaces unless they can be made after boards are installed and thoroughly dry. When wet board is required, evenly spray water on the surface which will be compressed when board is hung. Apply water with a conventional garden sprayer. Carefully stack boards with wet surfaces facing each other and cover stack with plastic sheet (polyethylene). Allow boards to set at least one hour before application.

Panel Application—Apply panels horizontally with the wrapped edge perpendicular to the studs. On the convex side of the partition, begin installation at one end of the curved surface and fasten panel to studs as it is wrapped around the curve. On the concave side of the partition, start fastening panel to the stud at the center of the curve and work outward to the ends of the panel. For single-layer panels, space screws 12" o.c. Use 1" Type S screws for steel studs and 1¼" type W screws for wood studs.

For double-layer application, apply base layer horizontally and fasten to stud with screws spaced 16" o.c. Center face layer panels over joints in the base layer and secure to studs with screws spaced 12" o.c. Use 1" Type S screws for base level and 1⅝" Type S screws for face layer. Allow panels to dry completely (approx. 24 hrs under good drying conditions) before applying joint treatment.

Arches

Arches of any radii are easily faced with gypsum panels or base and finished with a joint system, or veneer plaster finish. Score or cut through back paper of panels at 1" intervals to make them flexible. The board should previously have been cut to desired width and length of arch.

Radius Walls

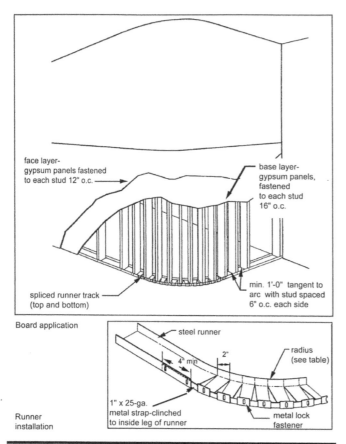

face layer-gypsum panels fastened to each stud 12" o.c.

base layer-gypsum panels, fastened to each stud 16" o.c.

spliced runner track (top and bottom)

min. 1'-0" tangent to arc with stud spaced 6" o.c. each side

Board application

steel runner

2"

4" min

radius (see table)

1" x 25-ga. metal strap-clinched to inside leg of runner

metal lock fastener

Runner installation

Figure 4.4

Courtesy of United States Gypsum Company, *Gypsum Construction Handbook, Centennial Edition.*

Screws

Identification on all screw heads (SDS¼ X 3 shown)

Titan hex head screw anchor for concrete

SDS ¼ x 3 US Patent 6,109,850

¼ x 3" Wood screw

SD8 X 1.25 ⁸/₃₂ x 1¼" wood screw

Figure 4.5

Courtesy of Simpson Strong-Tie Company, *Catalog on Wood Construction Connectors*

After board has been applied to arch framing with nails or screws, apply tape reinforcement (Joint Tape for drywall panels or Tape Type P or S for plaster base).

Allowable Tolerances

Industry Standards

Handbook of Construction Tolerances
(John Wiley & Sons)

The recommended tolerances from several sources are shown in **Figure 4.7**. Both the Metal Lath/Steel Framing Association (ML/SFA) and ASTM C1007 recommend that the plumbness and level of studs be within 1/960 of the span, or 1/8 in. in 10 ft (3.2 mm in 3048 mm). However, ASTM C1007 is for loadbearing studs only, while the ML/SFA specifications are for all metal studs. The 1/8 in. per 10 ft tolerance is consistent with the substrate requirements for other finish materials, such as some types of ceramic tile systems.

The Gypsum Association states that adjacent fastening surfaces of framing or furring should not vary by more than 1/8 in. (3.2 mm).

ASTM C754 requires that the spacing of studs and other framing members not vary by more than 1/8 in. (3.2 mm) from the required spacing and that the cumulative error not exceed the requirements of the gypsum wallboard. This is to ensure that the edge of a piece of gypsum board has sufficient bearing on half of a stud for fastening.

If the tolerances shown here are not required and specified, it is more likely that a +/- 1/4 in. (6-mm) tolerance will be observed in actual construction.

Metal Framing Connections

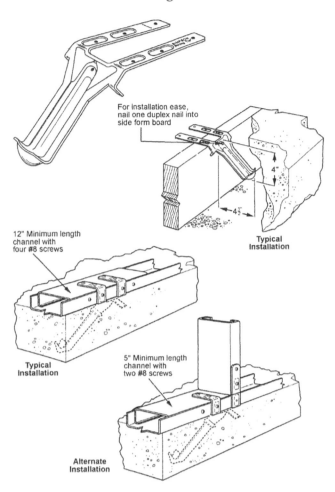

For installation ease, nail one duplex nail into side form board

4"

4½"

Typical Installation

12" Minimum length channel with four #8 screws

Typical Installation

5" Minimum length channel with two #8 screws

Alternate Installation

Figure 4.6

Courtesy of Simpson Strong-Tie Company, *Simpson Catalog on Light Gauge Steel Construction, Catalog C-LGS01*

Tolerances

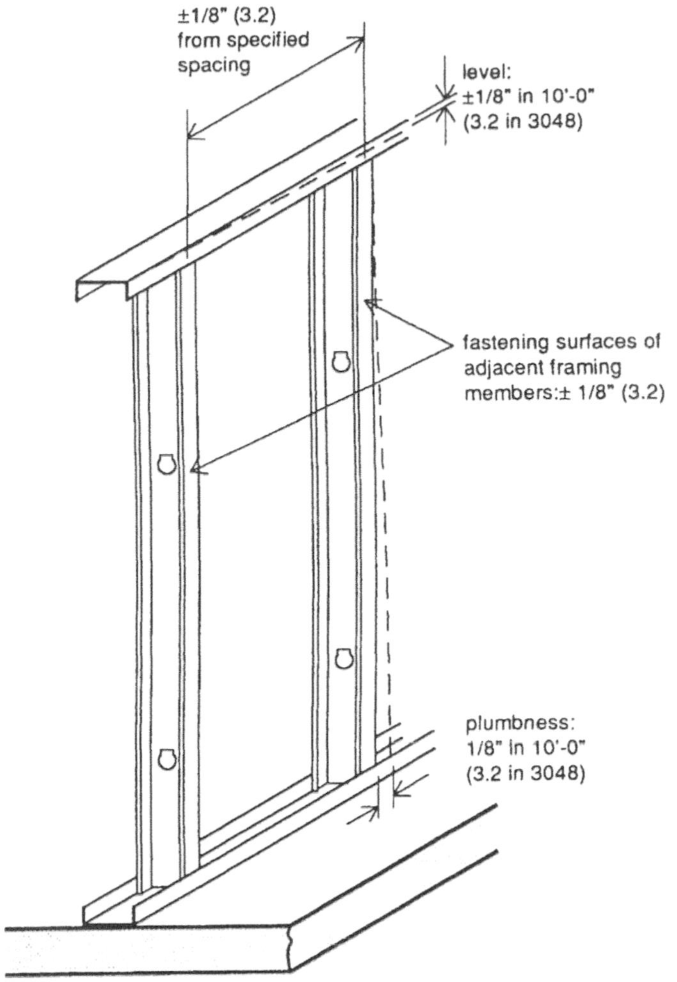

±1/8" (3.2) from specified spacing

level:
±1/8" in 10'-0"
(3.2 in 3048)

fastening surfaces of adjacent framing members:± 1/8" (3.2)

plumbness:
1/8" in 10'-0"
(3.2 in 3048)

Figure 4.7

Courtesy of John Wiley & Sons,
Handbook of Construction Tolerances

Comments

The Simpson hardware in this chapter is shown only as an example of metal framing connections. A competent designer or architect must incorporate the hardware into the drawings as part of the overall design.

Seismic and Hurricane Ties

Designed to provide wind and seismic ties for trusses and rafters, this versatile line may be used for general tie purposes, strongback attachments, and as all-purpose ties where one member crosses another.

MATERIAL: 18 gauge.

FINISH: Galvanized. Selected products available in stainless steel or Z-MAX coating; see Corrosion-Resistant Connectors, page 4.

INSTALLATION: • Use all specified fasteners.

- The S/H1 can be installed with flanges facing outwards (reverse of illustration #1). When installed inside a wall for truss applications.
- Ties are shipped in equal quantities of separate rights and lefts. S/H1 does not replace solid blocking.
- Reference section R603.8.3.2 of the International Residential Code (IRC).

CODE: ICBO ER-5275

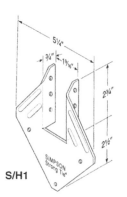

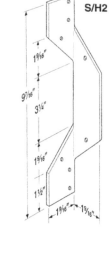

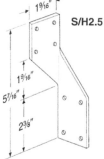

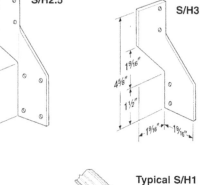

Model No.	Fasteners			Max Allowable Loads		
	To Rafters	To Plates	To Studs	Uplift (133)	Lateral F₁(133)	F₂(133)
S/H1	3- #10	2- #10	1- #10	275	100	115
S/H2	3- #10	–	3- #10	330	–	–
S/H2.5	4- #10	–	4- #10	415	75	105
S/H3	2- #10	2- #10	–	355	90	125

1. Loads have been increased 33% for wind or earthquake loading; no further increase allowed.
2. Multiply the loads shown by 0.75 when a 33% increase for wind or earthquake loading is not allowed by the design standard being used or when the 0.75 load combination factor in A.I.S.I. Section 5.1.3 (1996 edition) is not allowed, see page 4.

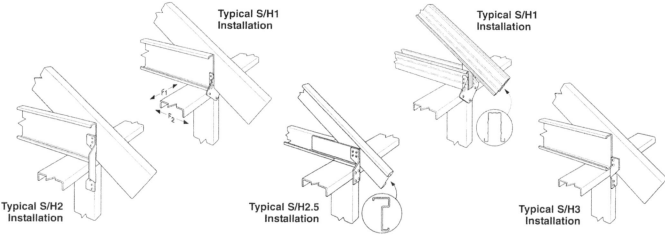

Typical S/H1 Installation

Typical S/H1 Installation

Typical S/H2 Installation

Typical S/H2.5 Installation

Typical S/H3 Installation

Figure 4.8

Courtesy of Simpson Strong-Tie Company, Inc., *Simpson Catalog on Cold-Formed Steel Construction, Catalog C-S96-R*

Cold-Formed Steel Framing Members & Material

Comments

The IBC requires compliance with standards from the American Institute of Steel Construction, and the American Iron and Steel Institute, and requires test records provided to demonstrate such conformity. IBC requirements, not included in this section, are comprised primarily of technical design criteria and formulas typically interpreted by the engineer who designs the steel framing.

Some important considerations and requirements include stipulations for "no field fabrications" (cutting or drilling of specified members), shop drawing requirements, and painting/moisture protection requirements.

Steel Designations & Terminology

Industry Standards

(Steel Framing Alliance)

Since 2001, a standard designator has been used to identify framing members used in cold-formed steel construction. The designator consists of four sequential codes:

The first is a three or four-digit numeral indicating the member web depth (D) in 1/100 inch. The second is a single letter indicating the type of member:

    S = stud or joist framing member with lips
    T = track section
    U = channel or stud framing section which do not have lips
    F = furring channels
    L = angle or L-header

The third is a three-digit numeral indicating flange width (B) in 1/100 inch, followed by a dash. The fourth is a two or three-digit numeral indicating the base steel thickness in 1/1000 inch (mils).

Types of Framing Members

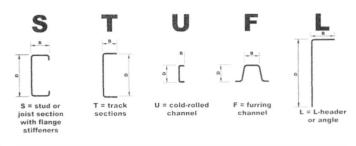

S = stud or joist section with flange stiffeners
T = track sections
U = cold-rolled channel
F = furring channel
L = L-header or angle

Figure 4.9

Steel Framing Alliance

The designator system for an 8"–16 Gauge C-shape with 1⅝" flanges is **800S162-54**:

    800 = 8" member depth expressed in 1/100th inches (outside to outside dimension)

    S = Stud or joist with flange stiffeners

    162 = 1⅝" flange in 1/100th inches
        and

    54 = Minimum Base steel thickness in mils
        (.054 in.
        = 54 mils)

All industry standards and building codes have adopted this method of identifying the most commonly used cold-formed steel framing members.

The system has made steel framing products easier to use and has accelerated their acceptance into markets.

Cold-formed steel members are coated to protect the steel from corrosion during the storage and transportation phases of construction, as well as for the life of the product. Hot-dipped zinc galvanizing is most commonly used to protect the steel because of its effectiveness in preventing corrosion. Depending on the thickness of zinc applied to the steel and the environment in which the steel is placed, zinc coatings can protect the steel as long as 250 years. It is important to realize that for bare metal to zinc to corrode, water contact must occur in the form of rain, condensation, fog or immersion. Without water present, corrosion will not occur. Therefore, even if the zinc is exhausted or removed during the construction process, once the steel is enclosed in a wall indoors, it should reduce the potential of corrosion as long as moisture does not collect in the wall cavity. This is true for the steel at fastener penetrations, edge cuts, or scratches on the steel itself.

Minimum Base Steel Thickness of Cold-Formed Steel Members

Designation (thickness in mils)	Minimum Base Steel Thickness Inches (mm)[1]	Old Reference Gauge Number[2]
18	0.0179 (0.455)	25
27	0.0269 (0.683)	22
30	0.0296 (0.752)	20 - Drywall[3]
33	0.0329 (0.836)	20 - Structural[3]
43	0.0428 (1.09)	18
54	0.0538 (1.37)	16
68	0.0677 (1.72)	14
97	0.0966 (2.45)	12
118	0.1180 (3.00)	10

[1] *Design thickness* shall be the minimum *base steel thickness* divided by 0.95.

[2] Gauge thickness is an obsolete method of specifying sheet and strip steel thickness. Gauge numbers are only a very rough approximation of steel thickness and shall not be used to order, design or specify any sheet or strip steel product.

[3] Historically, 20 gauge material has been furnished in two different thicknesses for structural and drywall (non-structural) applications.

Figure 4.10 Steel Framing Alliance

Structural and non-structural framing members used in steel construction shall have a minimum metallic coating complying with ASTM A1003/A1003M.

Structural members—G60 minimum

Non-Structural Members—G40 or equivalent minimum

Framing members shall be located within the building envelope and adequately shielded from direct contact with moisture from the ground or the outdoor climate unless additional corrosion protection is provided.

Dissimilar metals, like copper, cannot be used in direct contact with steel framing members without the use of appropriate grommets, plastic bushings, or other materials designed to separate the materials.

Cold-formed steel framing members used in construction must be identified with a legible sticker, stamp, stencil, or embossment, spaced a minimum of

96 inches on the framing member in accordance with one of the following standards:

ASTM C645 (Non-structural framing members only)

ASTM C955 (Structural framing members only)

ASTM A1003/A1003M (Framing members not described in ASTM C645 or C955)

The identification includes the manufacturer's identification, minimum uncoated steel designation thickness (mils), the level of corrosion protection if other than the minimum G40 for non-structural or G60 for structural, and the minimum yield strength if other than Grade 33.

Modern steel production relies on two technologies. The mills, also known as steel producers and suppliers, produce the sheet using either the basic oxygen furnace (BOF) or electric arc furnace (EAF) approach. The BOF process uses 25 to 35 percent old steel to make new steel. It produces sheet for products whose major required characteristic is drawability – products like automotive fenders, steel framing members, encasements of refrigerators, and packaging like food cans. The EAF process uses 95 to 100 percent old steel to make new. It is primarily used to manufacture products such as structural beams, steel plates, and reinforcement bars whose major required characteristic is strength.

No matter which process is used, the steel product produced has a minimum of 25 percent recycled content. Industry-wide, steel's recycled content averages 67 percent. During production, molten steel is poured into an ingot mold or a continuous caster, where it solidifies into large rectangular shapes known as slabs. The slabs are then passed through a machine with a series of rolls that reduce the steel into thin sheets at desired thicknesses, strength, and other physical properties. The sheets are sent through a hot-dipped galvanizing process that applies a metallic zinc coating to protect steel from corrosion, and are then rolled into coils that weigh approximately 13 tons.

Fasteners

While it may seem daunting, understanding how to select the right fastener for your steel-framing project will make all the difference. Fasteners include screws, pins, clinches, and welds; as well as anchor bolts, rivets, powder actuated fasteners, and expansion bolts. While screws are the primary fastener type used in steel construction today, the *Standard for Cold-Formed Steel*

Framing—General Provisions does not preclude the use of other connection methods. Proprietary fasteners must be designed and installed in accordance with the manufacturers' requirements.

Major tool manufacturers have fastening systems with evaluation reports to speed steel framing applications. It is important to note that much of the guesswork for fastener selection has been minimized by provisions in the *International Codes* and the *Standard for Cold-Formed Steel Framing—General Provisions*.

Fastening steel to steel is accomplished several different ways. Screws, pins, clinching, and welding are four of the most common methods available. Of these, the screw is most prevalent. The tool that applies this fastener is the "screwgun." The screwgun is the primary tool used on almost every framing jobsite.

Screwguns drive screws to connect steel members and attach sheathing material such as plywood and gypsum board to steel. A screwgun is an electric screwdriver, not a drill. Use of this tool is beneficial because the screw will spin only when pressure is applied against the screw tip. This permits the next screw to be positioned on the bit tip while the screwgun is running, improving installation efficiency at the job site. Because screwguns run at variable speeds, the user can adjust the speed to suit the work conditions. This feature is important to prevent the screw driller point from becoming dull or burned before it penetrates the steel.

The preferred screwgun for steel to steel connections should have an adjustable clutch and torque setting with a speed range of 0-2,500 rpm. An operating speed of 1,800 rpm is recommended by screw manufacturers for ¼ inch diameter screws.

Typically, one would use an adjustable clutch screwgun to attach 33-mil and thicker steel material, while a drywall screwgun would be used for 18-, 27-, and 30-mil material.

Using the correct screw for the application is essential to keeping the costs of fasteners and labor down. The correct type is specified in the codes and *The Standard for Cold-Formed Steel Framing*, by a design professional and/or in the manufacturer recommendations. If the wrong screw is used, the proper connection may not be made, or the screw may break off or not penetrate the steel, wasting fasteners and labor. Becoming more familiar with the different types and terminology of screws will aid in fastener selection, making framing easier.

Because holes are not pre-drilled in steel framing, steel-framing screws must have the ability to make their own holes before they engage. Given this feature, steel screws—also known as self-tapping screws—form their own threads when driven into steel. The "pullout" capacity of a screw (the ability to resist being pulled out of the connection) is based on the number of threads penetrating the steel, not by friction as it is for nails. Accordingly, it is very important to select the correct screw to prevent it from stripping the hole.

The point at the end of a screw must be sharp enough to cut steel. The point pre-drills the hole and allows the threads to engage in the steel. The most common points used in steel framing are self-drilling and self-piercing.

Self-drilling screws drill through layers of steel before any of the screw threads engage. If the drill point is too short, a screw "jacking" occurs in which the first layer of steel climbs up the threads of the screw while attempting to penetrate the second layer. In most instances, the screw will break off, frustrating the framer.

Self-piercing screws, on the other hand, have sharp points that can typically penetrate 18- to 30-mil material with ease. They are commonly used to attached plywood and gypsum board to these thinner layers of steel.

An example of each is shown in **Figure 4.11**.

Self-Drilling Screw   *Self-Piercing Screw*

Figure 4.11   Steel Framing Alliance

Minimum fastener types and installation requirements are referenced in fastener schedules throughout codes and *The Standard for Cold-Formed Steel Framing* by a design professional and/or in the manufacturer recommendations.

Cutting Cold-Formed Steel

Production Cutting—In the production environment, the steel is pre-cut by the roll former with hydraulic shears on a roll forming line, or by the framer with shears and saws.

Field Cutting—With the advent of prefabrication, the amount of field cutting is minimized but may still be necessary. Several options exist for cutting steel in the field:

Chop Saws: Chop saws are most commonly used for field cutting, employing an abrasive blade that cuts quickly through the steel. While chop saws are very effective for square cuts and for cutting bundled studs, they are very noisy in operation and give off hot flying metal filings. The edge produced by a chop saw is very rough with sharp burrs left on the steel.

Swivel-Head Shears

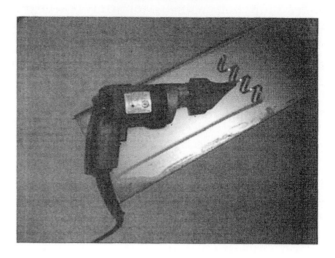

Figure 4.13 Steel Framing Alliance

Plasma Cutters: Plasma cutters produce an electric arc that melts through the steel, producing a jagged, burned edge. Plasma cutters are popular with framers.

Chop Saw

Figure 4.12 Steel Framing Alliance

Swivel Head Shears: Shears are now manufactured in both electric and battery operated models that can cut thickness up to 68 mil. While originally designed to cut sheet metal, they can be found on most cold-formed steel construction sites given their easy portability and ability to make smooth cuts with no abrasive edges. Shears may be difficult to use in cutting tight radii on C-Shapes, and blades are expensive to replace.

Plasma Cutter

Figure 4.14 Steel Framing Alliance

Circular Saws/Dry Cut Metal Cutting Saws: A new generation of metal cutting saws are appearing with blades made of titanium and aluminum that produce a smooth edge. One manufacturer produces a dry-cut saw that collects the metal filings right in the tool.

Aviation Snips: Aviation snips are hand tools that can cut cold-formed steel up to 43-mil material. They are useful when cutting and coping steel, for snipping flanges and for making small cuts. Some brands of snips are color coded for left, right, and straight.

Holes in webs of studs, joists and tracks must be in conformance with an approved design or a recognized design standard. Webs with holes not conforming to the above must be reinforced or patched in accordance with an approved design or a recognized design standard.

Hole Punches: For small holes, up to approximately 1 to 10½ inch in diameter, a hole punch can be used to punch holes in steel members up to 33 mils in thickness. Grommets are made to fit these holes, as needed, to protect wiring from sharp edges as it's pulled through walls. They may also be used to isolate copper or other dissimilar metals from the steel.

Hole Saws: For larger holes up to 6-inches in diameter, and through material thicknesses greater than 33 mils, hole saws and bits are manufactured. The saws are used on a drill motor to cut through the steel. Bits, while more costly, tend to cut through the steel faster.

Manufacturers have continued to develop additional hand tools and other accessories to use with cold-formed steel framing.

Locking C-clamps and bar clamps are used to hold the steel members together during fastening. C-Clamps prevent separation, also known as screw "jacking," when the first layer of steel climbs the threads of the screw. Bar clamps are used extensively to hold steel wall members together until permanent fastenings are applied. They are also used to hold headers in place until they are fitted into the top track. All clamps used in steel framing should have regular tips on ends without pads to reach around the steel flanges.

Prohibited Methods—Coping, cutting or notching of flanges and edge stiffeners is not permitted for load bearing members without an approved design.

Torch cutting is **not** acceptable.

C-Clamp

Figure 4.15

Steel Framed Walls

Ed. Note: The following section refers to the International Residential Code. *See your local building department for the latest information.*

Industry Standards

Constructing Cold-Formed Steel Walls
(Steel Framing Alliance)

Thanks to the development of the *Prescriptive Method for One and Two Family Buildings* and its adoption in to the building codes architects, builders and framers are now afforded the opportunity to design and select the steel framing members for their projects without the assistance of an engineer. This puts steel framing on a competitive path with conventional framing methods. The following is a step-by-step procedure for designing and selecting steel framed walls and floors using the *2006 International Residential Code*:

Step 1: Know the local requirements. Throughout the country local jurisdictions have specific design requirements based on the conditions in their local community. If you are a first-time steel builder, or are designing in a new territory, make sure to check with all building agencies that may have jurisdiction. Find out exactly what drawings and documents they need, what building code they use and what loads they require for design.

It will also be important to find out if they have any experience with conducting a plan review or inspection for steel framing. If they do not have much experience with steel framing, it is in your best interest to help them by leading them to resources that will help them become better informed. The SFA and other construction related organizations have developed a training series for building jurisdictions know as "Design and Inspection for Cold-Formed Steel Structures." This program is available nationwide and reviews the most important aspects of steel framing according to the latest standards and codes. Additionally, the SFA operates 1-800-79-STEEL hotline for questions regarding the proper design and inspection of steel structures. Making the building department's job easier can save you both time and money.

Step 2: Know the Loads and the Codes. Most likely, your county or city has adopted a version of the *International Residential Code*. Based on national standards, the local municipality will have the following parameters for you to consider as you design your project:

- Wind speed
- Wind exposure category
- Seismic zone
- Ground snow load

You will need some or all of these values to complete your design.

Step 3: Design within the Code Limits. *Standard for Cold-Formed Steel Framing—Prescriptive Method for One and Two Family Dwellings* refers to the 2001 Edition with Supplement 2, printed September 2006, (AISI Publication #SG02-4-PN). This Prescriptive Method covers increased wind loads for residential framing up to 150 mph. Limits of applicability can be found in Table A1-1 of this Prescriptive Method on page 11, or if you are using the *IRC 2006 Code* it is available in Sections 505.1 Steel Framed Floors, Section 603.1.1 for Steel Framed Walls, and Section 804.1.1 for Roofs.

Steps 4 through 6 focus on the design and construction of the steel framed walls for a two story structure in a 85 mph wind zone, exposure B, using 350S162, (3½" steel stud with a 1⅝" flange) and 33

ksi (kips per square inch) yield strength. The ground snow load is 30 psf (pounds per square feet), and the structure is 27.9 feet wide. The design calls for using 8 foot studs on the second floor and 10 foot studs on the first with 24 inch on center spacing.

Step 4: Design from the Top Down. The second floor walls will be designed first. In the *IRC 2006*, you will select the thickness of the steel studs using the information provided in step 3 above and Table R603.3.2 (4). If you use the prescriptive method it is Table E3-2a. As you will notice at the top of each table the parameters are included relative to the building width yield strength and what it supports. In the instance of the second floor walls they are supporting the roof and ceiling only.

Using the information already provided the thickness of the studs on the second floor is required to be a minimum of 33 mils.

Step 5: First Floor Walls. The process for selecting the first floor walls is the same; however, different tables are used because you are supporting one floor, roof and ceiling. If you use the *IRC 2006,* you use Table R603.3.2 (14). In the prescriptive method it is Table E3-7a. Following the same loads and spacing for the building the correct thickness for the first floor studs is 43 mils.

Step 6: Connections and Bracing. While screws are the predominant method for attaching studs to track, advancements have been made in other connection methods including pneumatic pins and clinching. The most critical issue in load-bearing applications is to make sure that the stud is seated inside the track with no more than ⅛th of an inch gap between the web of the stud and the web of the track. Specific bracing instructions and options are included throughout the IRC and Prescriptive Method for floors, walls and roofs and can include steel sheet, strapping, blocking, and other structural sheathing methods.

In addition, provisions included in the IRC 2006 and the prescriptive method there is a wealth of information on design and construction techniques for cold-formed steel available from the Steel Framing Alliance, **www.steelframing.org**, and the Steel Stud Manufacturers Association at **www.ssma.com**.

The Steel Framing Alliance maintains a hotline for any questions about cold-formed steel 1-800-79-STEEL.

TABLE R603.3.2(2)
24-FOOT-WIDE BUILDING SUPPORTING ROOF AND CEILING ONLY[a, b, c]
33 ksi STEEL

WIND SPEED Exp. A/B	Exp. C	MEMBER SIZE	STUD SPACING (inches)	8-Foot Studs				9-Foot Studs				10-Foot Studs			
				Ground Snow Load (psf)											
				20	30	50	70	20	30	50	70	20	30	50	70
85 mph	—	350S162	16	33	33	33	33	33	33	33	33	33	33	33	33
			24	33	33	33	33	33	33	33	33	33	33	33	43
		550S162	16	33	33	33	33	33	33	33	33	33	33	33	33
			24	33	33	33	33	33	33	33	33	33	33	33	33
90 mph	—	350S162	16	33	33	33	33	33	33	33	33	33	33	33	33
			24	33	33	33	33	33	33	33	33	33	33	33	43
		550S162	16	33	33	33	33	33	33	33	33	33	33	33	33
			24	33	33	33	33	33	33	33	33	33	33	33	33
100 mph	85 mph	350S162	16	33	33	33	33	33	33	33	33	33	33	33	33
			24	33	33	33	33	33	33	33	33	33	33	33	43
		550S162	16	33	33	33	33	33	33	33	33	33	33	33	33
			24	33	33	33	33	33	33	33	33	33	33	33	33
110 mph	90 mph	350S162	16	33	33	33	33	33	33	33	33	33	33	33	33
			24	33	33	33	33	33	33	33	43	33	33	33	43
		550S162	16	33	33	33	33	33	33	33	33	33	33	33	33
			24	33	33	33	33	33	33	33	33	33	33	33	33
—	100 mph	350S162	16	33	33	33	33	33	33	33	33	33	33	33	33
			24	33	33	33	43	33	33	33	43	43	43	43	43
		550S162	16	33	33	33	33	33	33	33	33	33	33	33	33
			24	33	33	33	33	33	33	33	33	33	33	33	33
—	110 mph	350S162	16	33	33	33	33	33	33	33	33	33	33	33	33
			24	33	33	33	43	43	43	43	43	54	54	54	54
		550S162	16	33	33	33	33	33	33	33	33	33	33	33	33
			24	33	33	33	33	33	33	33	33	33	33	33	33

For SI: 1 inch = 25.4 mm, 1 foot = 304.8 mm, 1 mil = 0.0254 mm, 1 mile per hour = 0.447 m/s, 1 pound per square foot = 0.0479 kPa, 1 ksi = 1000 psi = 6.895 MPa.

a. Deflection criterion: $L/240$.
b. Design load assumptions:
   Roof/ceiling dead load is 12 psf.
   Attic live load is 10 psf.
c. Building width is in the direction of horizontal framing members supported by the wall studs.

Courtesy of ICC, IRC-2006, Copyright 2006, International Code Council, Inc., Falls Church, Virginia

Figure 4.16

Construction Guidelines

Steel Floor Framing

IRC R505 Steel Floor Framing

R505.1 Cold-formed steel floor framing: All steel elements must be defect-free and straight, so as not to impact structural stability.

R505.1.1 Applicability limits: The IRC requirements apply to one- or two- story residential construction 60 feet in length or less perpendicular to joist span, and no greater than 40' in width parallel to joist span. Wind design speed on site must not exceed 100 MPH. Exposure must be A, B, or C. Ground snow load must not exceed 70 psf.

R505.1.2 In-line framing: Floor joists must be in direct line with load-bearing studs below the joists with tolerance not exceeding ¾ inch between the center lines of the stud and joist.

R505.1.3 Floor trusses: Trusses may not be cut or altered without approved design. They must also comply with AISI "Standard for Cold-Formed Steel Framing-Truss Design."

R505.2 Structural framing: This section of the IRC addresses specific requirements for joist web holes,

TABLE R603.3.2(3)
COLD-FORMED STEEL STUD THICKNESS FOR 8-FOOT WALLS
Studs supporting one floor, roof and ceiling (first story of a two-story building) 33 ksi steel

WIND SPEED		MEMBER SIZE[c]	MEMBER SPACING (inches)	STUD THICKNESS (mils)[a,b]															
				Building width (feet)[d]															
				24				28				32				36			
Exp. A/B	Exp. C			Ground snow load (psf)				Ground snow load (psf)				Ground snow load (psf)				Ground snow load (psf)			
				20	30	50	70	20	30	50	70	20	30	50	70	20	30	50	70
85 mph	—	350S162	16	33	33	33	33	33	33	33	33	33	33	33	43	33	33	33	43
			24	43	43	43	43	43	43	43	43	43	43	43	54	43	43	54	54
		550S162	16	33	33	33	33	33	33	33	33	33	33	33	33	33	33	33	33
			24	33	33	33	33	33	33	33	43	33	33	43	43	33	43	43	54
100 mph	85 mph	350S162	16	33	33	33	33	33	33	33	33	33	33	33	43	33	33	43	43
			24	43	43	43	54	43	43	54	54	54	54	54	54	54	54	54	54
		550S162	16	33	33	33	33	33	33	33	33	33	33	33	33	33	33	33	43
			24	33	33	33	33	33	33	33	43	33	33	43	43	43	43	43	54
110 mph	100 mph	350S162	16	33	33	33	33	33	33	43	43	43	43	43	43	43	43	43	43
			24	54	54	54	54	54	54	54	54	54	54	54	68	54	54	68	68
		550S162	16	33	33	33	33	33	33	33	33	33	33	33	33	33	33	33	33
			24	33	33	33	33	33	33	43	43	43	43	43	43	43	43	43	54
120 mph	110 mph	350S162	16	43	43	43	43	43	43	43	43	43	43	43	43	43	43	43	54
			24	54	54	54	68	54	68	68	68	68	68	68	68	68	68	68	68
		550S162	16	33	33	33	33	33	33	33	33	33	33	33	33	33	33	33	33
			24	33	43	43	43	43	43	43	43	43	43	43	43	43	43	43	54
130 mph	120 mph	350S162	16	43	43	43	54	43	54	54	54	54	54	54	54	54	54	54	54
			24	68	68	68	68	68	68	(d)	(d)	(d)	(d)	(d)	(d)	(d)	(d)	(d)	(d)
		550S162	16	33	33	33	33	33	33	33	33	33	33	33	33	33	33	33	43
			24	43	43	43	43	43	43	43	54	43	43	54	54	54	54	54	54
—	130 mph	350S162	16	54	54	54	54	54	54	54	54	54	54	54	68	54	54	68	68
			24	(d)	(d)	(d)	(d)	(d)	(d)	(d)	(d)	(d)	(d)	(d)	(d)	(d)	(d)	(d)	(d)
		550S162	16	33	33	33	33	33	33	33	43	33	33	43	43	43	43	43	43
			24	43	43	54	54	54	54	54	54	54	54	54	54	54	54	54	54

For SI: 1 inch = 25.4 mm, 1 foot = 304.8 mm, 1 mil = 0.0254 mm, 1 mile per hour = 1.609 km/h, 1 pound per square foot = 0.0479 kN/m², 1 kilogram per square inch = 6.895 MPa.

a. Deflection criteria: L/240.

b. Building width is in the direction of horizontal framing members supported by the wall studs.

c. Design load assumptions:
   Roof dead load is 12 psf.
   Attic live load is 10 psf.

d. 68-mil-thick stud is allowed used if wall is fully sheathed per Section R603.3.2.

Figure 4.17

ASTM standards and labeling, corrosion protection, and fasteners.

R505.3 addresses floor to foundation or bearing wall connections, allowable joist spans, joist bracing, bearing stiffeners, cutting and notching, hole patching, cantilevers, splicing, and openings.

Industry Standards

Low-Rise Construction Details and Guidelines
(Steel Framing Alliance & Cold Formed Steel Engineers Institute)

.1 FRAMING SYSTEM

.1.1 Axial load bearing members, including jamb studs and all members in built-up sections, should be installed seated squarely against the web portion of the top and bottom tracks.

.1.1.1 The maximum gap between the end of the stud and the web of the track should not exceed 0.063 inches (1.5mm).

.1.1.2 Cripple (or less than full-height) studs that are installed between an opening header and the bearing elevation of members above should be designed to transfer all axial loads from the members above to the header. These less than full-height members should also be seated squarely against the webs of the track.

.1.2 Bearing surfaces for joists, rafters, trusses, and the bottom track of axial load bearing walls should be uniform and level to assure full contact of the bearing flange or track web on the support over the required bearing and anchorage area.

Exception: Forces may be transferred through clip angles on sloped members such as roof rafters.

.1.2.1 A bearing material (i.e., building paper, shims or grout) should be provided between the underside of the bottom steel track and the top of the foundation to provide a uniform bearing surface for the steel members.

.1.3 All axial load bearing members should be aligned vertically and transfer all loads to structural supports or foundations. This vertical alignment should also be maintained at floor/wall intersections.

Exception:

1. Where load carrying members do not align a load distribution member should be provided to transfer loads from joist bearing to axial load bearing studs.

2. Members may be added between the members at the specified spacing, to support members that are not in alignment. These added members should transfer loads into a continuous load path to a foundation or structural support.

.1.3.1 Where through continuity of axial load bearing walls cannot be maintained, due to an interruption by floor joists that are not aligned, short sections of joists, studs, track or added joist members, capable of transferring the loads, should be placed in alignment with the stud above. As an alternate, a small section of stud (a filler), with an axial capacity at least equal to the capacity of the stud above, is permitted to be used to transfer the loads.

.1.4 All framing members should be horizontally aligned, plumb and level, except where required to slope.

.1.5 Both flanges of studs should be attached to the top and bottom track with screws or an approved fastener.

Exception: Where slip joints are specified at the top track follow the detailing requirements for the slip joint.

.1.6 Splices in framing members should not be permitted.

Exception: Track members or tension members with designed slice connections.

.1.7 Additional framing members (i.e., multiple studs or joists) may be needed as follows:

.1.7.1 Adjacent to openings as required by design. In lieu of additional members, an alternate member may be provided, with the required capacity, by increasing the steel thickness and/or flange width.

.1.7.2 At wall intersections and corners.

.1.7.3 Under joist supported partitions, parallel to the direction of the floor framing, where partition length exceeds one half of the joist span.

.1.8 The use of members with standard manufacturer's web punch-outs is usually acceptable. The location of these punch-outs should be coordinated with load, bracing and utility requirements.

.1.8.1 Web punch-outs or web openings should not be located at bearing points for studs, joists, rafters, and trusses without special reinforcement.

.1.8.2 Web openings should not exceed the dimension of the manufacturer's standard punch-out or the provisions in the AISI Specification without design analysis or reinforcement.

.2 Connections

.2.1 Utilize fasteners and fastener heads that are designed for the requirements of the connection. The substitution of screws, welds, bolts, powder actuated fasteners or pneumatically driven fasteners for the specified fastener in many cases can be considered acceptable. Each substitution should provide an equal or greater performance, and be approved by the designer.

.2.1.1 Penetration of screws through joined materials should not be less than 3 exposed threads.

.2.1.2 All weld should be completed by AWS D1.3 qualified welders experienced in welding sheet steel. Touch-up coatings damaged by the welding of exterior framing, and framing that separates rooms with large temperature or humidity differentials.

Comments

Touch-up is necessary because such conditions can cause moisture accumulation and rusting of exposed steel.

.2.1.3 Fasteners should be installed in accordance with manufacturer's recommendations.

.2.2 Multiple steel members designed as noncomposite can be connected together with one row of #10 screws at 16 inches (400mm) o.c. along the length of the member. Locate each row within 1 inch (25mm) from an adjacent flange. The fastener spacing for non-composite members less than 4 inches in depth may be revised to 24 inches (600mm) o.c.

.2.3 When approved by the designer, end connections for members 0.04 inches (1mm) or less in steel thickness, used for headers, sills, bracing, or blocking, may utilize the member web for the connection. Flanges can be coped or cut allowing bending of the web, as required, to form an angle for connection to supporting members.

.3 Bracing and Stiffeners

.3.1 Adequate bracing should be provided for all building systems until lateral stability systems (i.e., shear walls or braced frames) have been installed and anchorage is complete.

.3.1.1 Adequate bracing is recommended for both chords or flanges of members until sheathing has been installed. Where Sheathing is applied to one side only, the required bracing should be permanently installed on the unsheathed face.

.3.1.2 Temporary bracing should be provided and left in place until work is permanently stabilized.

.3.2 Blocking may be a section of stud, joist or track which is the full depth of the framing member that

is being blocked and should fit tightly between the members. Blocking should be anchored at each end.

.3.3 Bridging may consist of blocking, flat strapping, channel stock, or a proprietary bridging system. Bridging should be placed diagonally between opposite flanges of framing members or run flange to flange along the same face of the framing members.

.3.3.1 Bridging shall be anchored to each framing member.

.3.3.2 Wire tied bridging should not be permitted.

.3.3.3 Floor joist bridging may be spaced as follows, except where member design requires or will accommodate an alternate spacing:

Recommended Minimum Number of Rows of Bridging for Floor Joists	
Span, ft. (m)	Number of Rows
up to 14 (4.3)	1 row at mid-span
14 (4.3) to 20 (6.1)	2 rows at 1/3 points
20 (6.1) to 26 (7.9)	3 rows at 1/4 points

.3.4 End blocking or bridging for joists, rafters, and trusses is recommended over supports when bearing ends are not otherwise restrained from rotation.

.3.5 Web stiffeners should be provided, as determined by design, at bearing points and at points of concentrated loads.

.3.5.1 Web stiffeners can be a small stud, track or angle section designed to carry axial loads and cut to seat squarely against supports.

.3.5.2 Solid blocking or continuous track may be used in lieu of web stiffeners, when approved by the designer.

.4 MISCELLANEOUS

.4.1 All steel components and accessories in exterior walls, roofs, floors over crawl spaces, or in high humidity areas should be hot-dipped galvanized or aluminum-zinc coated. Co-polymer or cadmium coatings can also be used for fasteners.

.4.2 Back blocking for wall mounted assemblies should be made from flat stock or track or stud sections with flanges notched at the location of studs to allow for connections to the studs.

.4.3 It is recommended that steel framing members be cut with a saw or shear. Torch cutting of the ends of compression members in axial bearing connections is not recommended.

.4.4 Sheathing materials for shear walls or diaphragms should extend and be connected to chord members (i.e., top and bottom wall track).

Design and Detailing: General Considerations

Industry Standards

Low-Rise Construction Details and Guidelines
(Steel Framing Alliance & Cold Formed Steel Engineers Institute)

.A GENERAL

.A.1 The design of structural members and connections should be in accordance with the latest edition of the AISI Specification for the Design of Cold-Formed Steel Structural members or the Load and Resistance Factor Design Specification for Cold-Formed Steel Structural Members.

Exceptions:

1. The capacity and spacing of screws should be in accordance with the Center for Cold-Formed Steel Structures Technical Bulletin Vol. 2, No. 1 dated February 1993 or manufacturer's recommendations.

2. Pneumatically driven fasteners, powder actuated fasteners and expansion anchors should rely on manufacturer's or independent test data for design capacities and proper installation.

.A.2 Shear wall/diaphragm designs should be based on AISI Research Report CF 92-2 on the Shear Resistance of Walls with Steel Studs, American Plywood Report 154 dated July 1990, approved test results or rational engineering analysis.

.A.3 Refer to the **Residential Construction Guidelines** for additional guidelines that should be considered during design and detailing of cold-formed steel framing.

.B FRAMING

.B.1 All framing members should be spaced as required by design and as limited by the capabilities of the facing material.

.B.2 Material thickness for track or runners should be at least equal to the framing member thickness used for that framing assembly.

.B.3 Wall track should not be used to support any load, unless specifically designed for that purpose.

.B.4 Allowable tolerances for vertical alignment of webs supported on a track or track assembly should be based on the shear and bending capacity of the track or track assembly.

.B.5 Interior non-bearing partitions located under horizontal load carrying members (i.e., joists, rafters, and trusses) should be evaluated for possible loads induced due to the deflection (dead and live load) of the horizontal members.

.B.6 Generally one member can be provided along the edge of openings for each member that is interrupted by the opening. As an alternative, members of greater thickness can be used to reduce the number of additional members.

.B.7 Construction adhesive or a gasket material between the top flange of floor joists and plywood flooring is recommended to reduce sound transmission.

.B.8 Solid blocking or continuous track may be used in lieu of web stiffeners, and should be designed to reinforce the member that is intended to support concentrated loads.

.C CONNECTIONS

.C.1 Material thickness and dimensions of clip angles or flat plates used for connections should be as required by design, but the thickness should be less than the supported member material thickness.

.C.2 Truss connections should be evaluated for shear, moment and axial forces due to the eccentricities of the connected members.

.C.3 Connections between multiple, ganged or built-up members and design of these members for composite action should be in accordance with the AISI Specification.

.C.4 The projection of screw heads used to connect steel framing members together under plywood, portland cement board or other rigid or brittle materials, may require back drilling of the board to allow a flush installation.

.D INSULATION AND MOISTURE PROTECTION

.D.1 A moisture barrier (i.e., building paper), sealer and/or bearing material should be provided between the underside of the bottom track and the top of the foundation to create a thermal break, to prevent the migration of moisture through the joint, and to provide a uniform bearing surface.

.D.2 Insulation should fill the full dimension between member webs. In addition to providing insulation between framing members located in assemblies that separate climate controlled spaces from the exterior or nonclimate controlled spaces, the required insulation should be placed in all jambs, headers, doubled, and built-up members.

.D.3 The use of a thermal break or rigid insulation on the exterior face of framing can result in a significantly better thermal performance of the envelope, over adding additional insulation between the framing members. When a specific thermal performance is required, contact an engineer experienced in the evaluation of thermal building envelopes.

Hurricane Bracing

Hurricane Construction Guidebook
(Building Media Inc.)

Codes require a certain percentage of wood and steel framed walls to be sheathed or otherwise braced depending on wind design conditions and home dimensions. Items to consider include:

- Metal straps and let-in braces are acceptable under certain wind conditions.
- Structural sheathing provides improved performance while using materials that even novice carpenters are familiar with.
- IBHS recommends the "code-plus" practice of fully sheathing 100% of exterior walls with OSB or plywood. This also improves the axial load capacity of walls.
- With any bracing method, it is critical to follow blacking and fastener schedules.
- Structural insulated panels (SIPS) provide a continuously braced wall that can eliminate most of the blocking, bracing, and fastener requirements. Check with local jurisdiction for code approvals.

Steel Siding Support

Industry Standards

Means Graphic Construction Standards
(RSMeans)

Steel siding support can be used as an alternate superstructure system in light commercial projects. Girts used to support aluminum, steel, or composition siding are usually channels with the stronger axis oriented horizontally to resist wind load. Bending or sagging is generally resisted by sag rods threaded at each end for connections and adjustment. When column spacing is greater than the allowable channel span, wind columns, or vertical members used to resist lateral loads, may be introduced. (See **Figure 4.18** and **Figure 4.19**).

Pre-Engineered Steel Buildings

Industry Standards

Means Graphic Construction Standards
(RSMeans)

Pre-engineered buildings, relatively low in construction cost, are used extensively for industrial, commercial, institutional, and recreational facilities. (See **Figure 4.19**.)

Pre-engineered steel buildings are manufactured by many companies and are normally erected by franchised dealers. They are manufactured of pre-engineered components, which allow flexibility in the choice of configuration for one- or two-story buildings. Some systems are available with provisions for cranes, balconies, and mezzanines. There are four basic types: rigid frame, truss type, post and beam, and sloped beam. Roof pitches vary, but the most popular type is a low pitch of 1" in 12". Eave heights are available in increments from 10' to 24'.

Rigid-frame, clear-span buildings are manufactured in widths of 30' to 130', and tapered-beam, clear-span buildings in widths of 30' to 80'. Post and beam building widths, with one post at center, measure from 80' to 120'; with two posts, from 120' to 180', and with three posts, from 160' to 240'. Bay sizes are usually 20' to 24', but may be extended to 30'.

Roofs and sidewalls are normally covered with 26-gauge colored steel siding with various insulation options. Some manufacturers offer precast concrete and masonry siding options. Other options include eave overhangs, entrance canopies, end-wall overhangs, doors and windows, gutters and leaders, skylights, and roof vents.

Steel Siding Support System

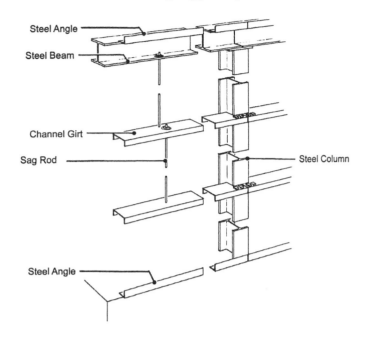

Steel Angle
Steel Beam
Channel Girt
Sag Rod
Steel Column
Steel Angle

Steel Siding Zee Girt Connection

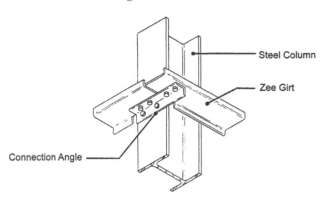

Steel Column
Zee Girt
Connection Angle

Channel Girt Connection

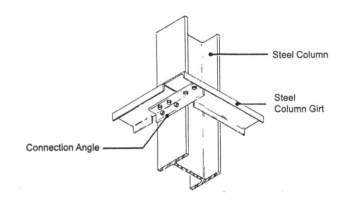

Steel Column
Steel Column Girt
Connection Angle

Steel Siding Girt Support

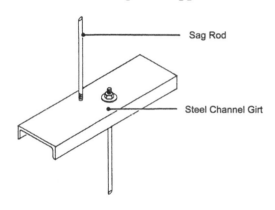

Sag Rod
Steel Channel Girt

Girt Connection

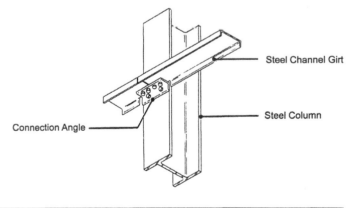

Steel Channel Girt
Steel Column
Connection Angle

Figure 4.18

RSMeans, *Means Graphic Construction Standards*

Pre-Engineered Building

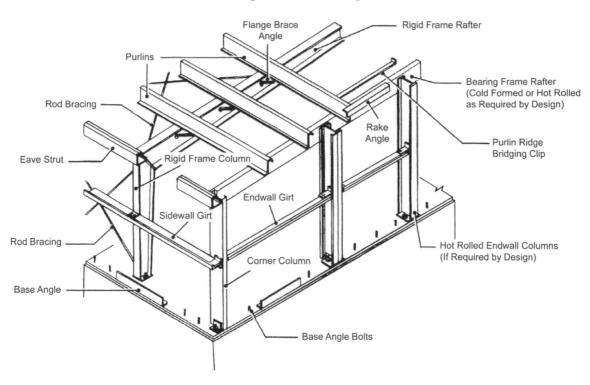

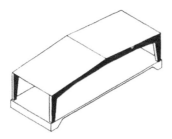

Low Profile Rigid Frame

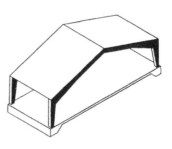

High Profile Rigid Frame

RSMeans, *Means Graphic Construction Standards*

Figure 4.19

CHAPTER 5 WOOD FRAMING

Table of Contents

Text in blue type indicates excerpted summaries from the International Building Code® (IBC) *and* International Residential Code® (IRC). *Please consult the IBC and IRC for complete coverage and specific wording. "Comments" (in solid blue boxes) were written by the editors, based on their own experience.*

   These icons will appear with references to green building practices, seismic regulations, and hurricane-safe building requirements, respectively.

WOOD FRAMING

Common Defect Allegations

Wood structural framing defects are a common and expensive claim on multiple- and single-family developments and custom homes. Framing is the basic skeleton of the structure, and repairs to the framing nearly always require removing finish materials. The destructive investigation of a less-than-10-year-old structure will frequently result in the discovery of major framing deficiencies.

- *A common complaint (particularly in multiple housing) is the lack of draft stops both in attics and, horizontally, in stacked party walls that are separated intentionally to prevent sound transmission. The lack of draft stops is commonly missed, very expensive to correct after the construction is complete, and is critical in stopping the advance of a ground-floor fire.*

- *The most critical deficiency (and unfortunately one of the most frequent) is the missing connectors to hold roof framing to the bearing walls. In zones with no seismic requirements and no wind load, it is not as critical a mistake. Because of the life safety issues and the extreme property damage caused by neglecting this attachment, we will address the following comments in terms of Seismic Zone 4 and hurricane design elements.*

- *Starting at the mudsill, there is a tendency for the framed wall to pull from the bolted plate when the connection is strictly end nails spiked into the stud. Seismic and hurricane forces can simply pull the structure right off the wood plate. The positive connection that is usually called out on the plans involves clips or hold-downs that transfer the connection from the bolted sill plate through the framing to the top plate. Plywood shear is also called out on many walls. The code requires that when edge nailing is less than 3" on center, all edges must be supported by 3x dimensional lumber. The reason for this is that the adjoining panel also must be nailed to the same member, and as the edge nailing gets closer than 3" on each of the two panels, the 2x framing member will split and lose its nail-holding strength. For example, at $2^1/_2$" OC, both the adjoining sheets of plywood will be nailed into the same stud, spiking the*

(continued)

wood on an average of every 1¹/₄". This means that for any member, the edge-nailed studs, boundary blocking, sill plate or the top plate that will support two panel edges must all be 3 x 4 or 3 x 6. Caution: studs nailed through 3x material require a 20d nail due to the thickness of the plate.

- Mudsills with anchor bolts at close pattern will split the framing member under stress. Investigations of failures after the Northridge Earthquake in California revealed that 2x sill plates with anchor bolts at 16" OC often split right down the center.

- The plate line for the second story has the same potential pull-out of the spiked-end nails. The shear panel plywood often covers the floor joist of the second floor and stop. The upper wall shear starts at the second story plate. Therefore, the only connections between the two shear assemblies are spiked nails from the bottom plate to the floor joist. If this condition exists, it is imperative that metal straps are added to the exterior, or hold-downs are through-bolted, or some other code-approved metal clips are added to transfer a positive connection continuously through the joint.

- Roof-to-wall connections face the same dilemma. In ordinary framing, the roof rafter and joist or truss is simply toenailed onto the top plate. A positive blocking with metal clips all the way to the roof sheathing is required to resist high-wind load. In seismic or wind areas, check with your local building official for the minimum requirement.

- A common problem stems from the isolation of stair stringers from the wall to provide acoustic transfer. When the return air plenum uses a framed void in the vicinity of the stair assembly, the edges of the carpet can turn a black color (more noticeable on lighter shades of carpet). The black edge is from the return air being drawn through the carpet at the edges, which causes the carpet to act as a filter at that location. The solution is to pack backer rod foam or to caulk it solid with a nonhardening material such as silicone or PVC.

- Gypsum board installed in the stairwell will often develop a bead projecting out from the wall. This is due to lumber shrinkage with the tape joint beading out as the drywall closes the gap.

- Overdriven plywood nailing (driving the nail beyond the outer skin) is a common problem. Care should be taken to set the nail gun to just dimple the skin. Remember that nail pops result from lumber shrinkage; the nail itself usually does not move. Occasionally, when water leaks occur, the plywood will swell, lifting nails. However, most nail pops occur from lumber drying out.

- It is imperative that the framer read and understand the plywood grade stamp. Carefully check the building plans for the required plywood grades. As noted in the text, some plywood panels now include a reference to "sized for spacing," which means the sheet is ¹/₈" shorter and ¹/₈" narrower to allow the edges and ends to be spaced in the event of reaction to moisture changes. We frequently see plywood panels that have expanded against each other so tightly that the edges actually swell and push out enough to crack stucco plaster. These panels were originally installed tight to each other, and a moisture increase caused them to swell and grow in size.

- Good framing practice requires that joists, beams, and headers be crowned up. We repeatedly see these members crowned down, and in some cases floor joists are crowned up and down alternately, making the floor roll like a roller coaster. Wall studs should also be crowned so that the wall will have a more uniform appearance, with all the crowns in one direction.

The rules for midspan joist and rafter blocking changed with the 1997 UBC, which was later incorporated into the IBC. Prior codes required midspan blocking on joists and rafters at intervals not exceeding 8', to stop rotation (collapse by folding over). With study and testing, those guidelines were modified to a system that determines blocking requirements based on the width-to-height ratio of the joist, rafter, or beam, with consideration as to whether the top and/or bottom edges are held in line. The code changes allow for the installation of joists, rafters, and beams without midspan blocks, if the ends are held in place and all of the supports that the joists or rafters bear upon are blocked. When we investigate allegations of framing errors, we frequently see blocks missing, improperly nailed, or some other variance with the code. Most structural engineers specify midspan blocking and/or alternate methods to prevent a "deck of cards" type collapse from rotation of the joist.

Introduction

Quality standards for wood framing can be defined to include not only individual framing components, but the ways in which components are tied together to form sound, aesthetically acceptable structures. A quality product must meet not only safety (building code) requirements and design specifications set forth in the project plans, but also standards of acceptable workmanship. Quality also means properly addressing regional issues, such as hurricane and seismic considerations, and other climate factors, such as provisions for special types of insulation.

This chapter is assembled in the order a house or light commercial project would be framed. Quality begins with the selection of the overall framing system and materials and understanding the effect and management of moisture, continues through the assembly of framing members, and ends with the supervision of work by other trades that may affect the soundness of the structure. A variety of sources have been referenced to convey accepted practices of workmanship, as well as guidelines for code requirements. While we have not covered every possible framing condition, we do address the components that are most commonly alleged in defect claims.

The following professional associations may be helpful in locating more information about wood framing standards:

APA—The Engineered Wood Association
253-565-6600
www.apawood.org

American Forest & Paper Association (AFPA)
800-878-8878
www.afandpa.org

American Wood Council
202-463-2766
www.awc.org

American Society for Testing and Materials (ASTM)
800-262-1373
www.astm.org

NAHB Research Center
800-638-8556
www.nahbrc.org

National Frame Building Association (NFBA)
800-557-6957
www.nfba.org

Northeastern Lumber Manufacturers Association (NELMA)
207-829-6901
www.nelma.org

Southern Forest Products Association
504-443-4464
www.sfpa.org

Truss Plate Institute, Inc. (TPI)
703-683-1010
www.tpinst.org

Western Wood Products Association
503-224-3930
www.wwpa.org

Wood Truss Council of America (WTCA)
608-274-4849
www.sbcindustry.com

Ed. Note: Comments and recommendations within this chapter are not intended as a definitive resource for construction activities. For building projects, contractors must rely on the project documents and any applicable code requirements pertaining to their own particular locations.

General Considerations

Lumber Grade Stamps

Comments

The grade stamp allows you to verify that the wood selected is appropriate for its intended use. Since grade stamps are usually located at one end of the product, experienced carpenters have learned to cut the opposite end, leaving the grade stamp intact for the building official to check.

The components of the Western Wood Products Association lumber grade stamp are defined in the graphic on this page. Other agencies that designate standards for lumber include the Northeastern Lumber Manufacturers Association, the Southern Pine Inspection Bureau, the Northern Hardwood and Pine Manufacturers Association, the National Lumber Grades Authority, the Redwood Inspection Service, and the West Coast Lumber Inspection Bureau. The grading rules of these agencies have been approved by the Board of Review of the American Lumber Standards Committee and certified for conformance with U.S. Department of Commerce Voluntary Product Standard PS 20-99 ("American Softwood Lumber Standard").

Refer to the "Structural Sheathing" section later in this chapter for information on plywood stamp designations from APA—the Engineered Wood Association (formerly the American Plywood Association).

Industry Standards

Guide to Understanding WWPA Grade Stamps and Quality Control Identification
(Western Wood Products Association)

Integrity of the Grade Stamp

Western Wood Products Association (WWPA) is one of the largest associations of lumber manufacturers in the United States, representing sawmills in the 12 western states. The Association's Quality Services Division supervises lumber grading by maintaining a staff of lumber inspectors who regularly check the quality of mill production, including visual grade requirements of glued products and machine stress-rated lumber. (See **Figure 5.1**.)

The Association's *Grading Rules for Western Lumber* establishes standards of size and levels of quality in conformance with the American Softwood Lumber Standard PS 2099. The association is certified as a rules writing and inspection agency by the Board of Review, American Lumber Standard Committee. The association is approved to provide mill supervisory services under its rules and the rules of the West Coast Lumber Inspection Bureau, the Redwood Inspection Service, the National Lumber Grades Authority for Canadian Lumber, and the NGR portion of the Southern Pine Inspection Bureau Rules. In addition, WWPA is approved to supervise finger-jointed and machine stress-rated lumber.

Interpreting Grade Marks

Western Wood Products Association uses a set of marks to identify lumber graded under its supervision. The grade marks are stamped on the lumber and appear near the ends of the product. Most grade stamps, except those for rough lumber or heavy timbers, contain five basic elements. Lumber carrying the WWPA grade stamp will meet or exceed the performance and aesthetic standards set for each grade.

WWPA Grade Stamp

WWPA Certification Mark

(a) This symbol certifies association standards and is a registered trademark.

Mill Identification Firm

(b) **12** Identifies the name brand, or assigned mill number. WWPA can be contacted to identify an individual mill whenever necessary.

Grade Designation

(c) **STAND** Provides grade name, number, or abbreviation.

Species Identification

(d) Indicates species by individual species or species combination.

Condition of Seasoning

(e) **S-DRY** Indicates condition of seasoning at the time of surfacing: MC-15, KD-15 15% maximum moisture content; S-DRY, KD 19% maximum moisture content; S-GRN Over 19% moisture content (unseasoned).

Figure 5.1

Courtesy of Western Wood Products Association

Certified Wood Products

Industry Standards
Green Building: Project Planning & Cost Estimating, Second Edition
(RSMeans)

Certified wood should be used for any wood application for which it is available. Certified wood comes from well-managed forests that seek to balance the sometimes competing economic, community, and environmental concerns associated with lumber harvesting and production. Certified wood suppliers can be found by using the interactive website **www.certifiedwood.org** and clicking on Certification Resource Center.

Forest Stewardship Council

The FSC logo identifies products that contain wood from well-managed forests certified in accordance with the rules of the Forest Stewardship Council.

Formed in 1993, the Forest Stewardship Council is concerned with ecological, social, and economic aspects of the forest management practices used to produce wood products. These products are tracked from the logging sites through to the end-user. The council has adopted criteria that a company must follow in order for its products to be certified. The company harvesting the product must:

- Meet all applicable laws
- Have legally established rights to the harvest
- Respect indigenous rights
- Maintain community well-being
- Conserve economic resources
- Protect biological diversity
- Have a written management plan
- Engage in regular monitoring
- Maintain high conservation value forests
- Manage plantations to alleviate pressures on natural forests

Generally, the forest must be managed to maintain ecological productivity. Management must minimize waste and avoid damage to other forest resources. A complete environmental assessment must be performed before the start of any site-disturbing activities. Safeguards must be in place to protect endangered species. Environmentally friendly pest control should be used, and chemical pesticides avoided.

Engineered Wood Products

Comments

OSB (oriented strand board) beams, joists, and sheathing are commonly used in residential and light commercial construction and are referred to as "engineered wood products." They can be used in place of (or in conjunction with) typical framing lumber. The advantages of this material include: superior tensile and compressive strength, stability, the same workability as wood, and longer available lengths. Engineered wood products have structural qualities different than those of traditional wood, so they must be used within the specification set by the manufacturer.

See also "Wood Shrinkage," "Bored Holes & Notching," and "Wood Roof Trusses" later in this chapter for further comments on engineered wood products.

Industry Standards
Green Building: Project Planning & Cost Estimating, Second Edition
(RSMeans)

Years ago, the dwindling supply of old growth timber spurred the wood industry to manufacture structural products that can be made with smaller diameter, lower-strength, faster-growing tree species. Engineered wood products include glu-lam beams, I-joists, and oriented strand board. These products enhance quality control while reducing pressure on natural forests. They can make use of up to 80% of each log, as compared to solid-sawn lumber, which only uses about 50%.

Glu-lam beams are composed of wood boards glued together to create high-strength beams with depths ranging from 5" to 4' or more (depths and spans are limited only by shipping concerns). Similarly, prefabricated I-joists are more structurally efficient than solid joists, thus they require less wood. Engineered trusses are also an excellent option for creating predictable strength while reducing the amount and size/quality of materials required.

A potential downside of engineered wood is that it may contain toxic adhesives. Off-gassing of these toxins, such as formaldehyde, is particularly hazardous during curing in the factory (unless protective measures are taken), but still can be an issue after curing, especially for chemically sensitive people. These products may also release deadly gases in a fire. Fortunately, substitute products are now available.

Industry Standards

Builder's Essentials: Advanced Framing Methods
(RSMeans)

Engineered Wood Products (EWP) fit into two general categories, **Engineered Panel Products (EPP)** and **Engineered Lumber Products (ELP)**. The first group includes plywood, oriented strand board **(OSB)**, waferboard, and composite and structural particleboard.

The second group includes I-joists, composite beams, metal-plate-connected wood trusses, and structural composite lumber (LVLs, PSLs, and LSLs).

Engineered Panel Products

Engineered Panel Products: Plywood, oriented strand board and waferboard, and particleboard are so common that their uses are defined in the building codes. Specific applications vary from job to job and from manufacturer to manufacturer. Use of these products requires a design for each job.

Oriented Strand Board and Waferboard

Most building codes recognize oriented strand board and waferboard for the same uses as plywood, as long as the thicknesses match.

Working with Engineered Panel Products

When working with any engineered panel products, keep the following guidelines in mind:

1. On the floors and roofs, run the face grain perpendicular to the supports (except with particleboard, which has no grain). (See **Figure 5.3**.)

2. Do not use any piece that does not span at least two supports for floors and roofs.

3. Allow a gap of at least ⅛" on all edges, and a gap of more than ⅛" if the piece will be exposed to moisture. Note that this also applies to walls. These materials tend to expand more than plywood panels in both thickness and length when exposed to moisture. In extreme damp or nonventilated areas, particular care should be taken to maintain consistent gapping.

4. Follow manufacturer's recommended installation directions.

Engineered Panel Products

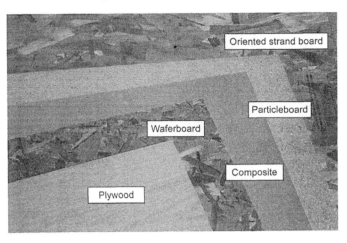

Figure 5.2

RSMeans *Complete Book of Framing*

Engineered Lumber Products

Complete Book of Framing
(RSMeans)

I-Joists

I-Joists were introduced in 1968 by the Trus Joist Corporation. Although use of this product has grown rapidly over the years, there is still no industry standard for its manufacture and installation. And while The Engineered Wood Association (APA) has established a standard for its members, not all manufacturers are members of APA. Because there is no universal standard, it's important to use the installation instructions that come in the I-joist package. The I-joist package is generally prepared by the manufacturer's representative working with the architect or designer.

I-Joist construction is substituted for more traditional stick framing. The I-joist package should include installation plans for the building. These plans will be specific to the building you are working on, and will include a material list and accessories. Accessories can include web stiffeners, blocking panels, joist hangers, rim boards, and beams. The plans typically include a sheet of standard details.

Below is a list of elements you'll find in most I-joists packages, and some items to consider when installing them:

1. **Minimum bearing** is 1¾". (See **Figure 5.4**.)

2. **Closure** is required at the end of an I-joist by rim board, rim joists, or blocking. This closure also serves to transfer vertical and lateral loads, as well as providing for deck attachment

Using Engineered Panel Products

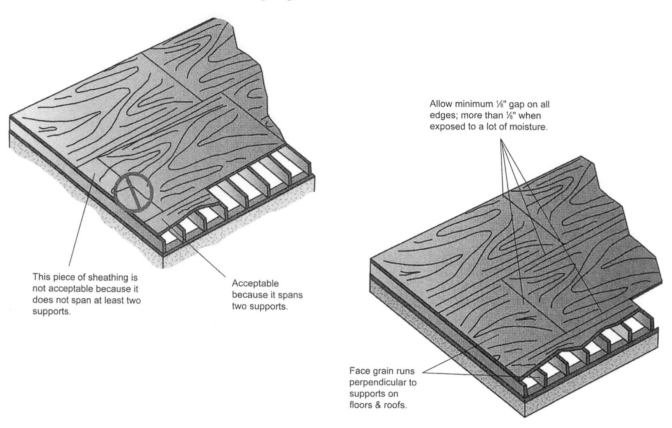

Allow minimum ⅛" gap on all edges; more than ⅛" when exposed to a lot of moisture.

This piece of sheathing is not acceptable because it does not span at least two supports.

Acceptable because it spans two supports.

Face grain runs perpendicular to supports on floors & roofs.

Figure 5.3

RSMeans, *Complete Book of Framing*

and fireblocking, if required. Do not use dimensional lumber such as a 2 x 10, because it is typically 9¼" instead of 9½". It shrinks much more than the I-joists do and will leave the I-joists supporting the load.

3. **Interior bearing walls** below I-joists require blocking panels or squash blocks when load-bearing walls are above.

4. **Rim boards** are required to be a minimum 1¼" thick in thickness.

5. Make sure **squash blocks,** which are used to support point loads (like the load created by a post) are ¹⁄₁₆" taller than the joists, so that they will properly support the load. (See **Figure 5.5.**)

6. **Web stiffeners,** which are sometimes required at bearing and/or point loads, should be at least ⅛" shorter than the web. Install web stiffeners tight against the flange that supports the load. If the load comes from a wall above, install the web stiffener tight against the top of the flange. If the load comes from a wall below, the stiffener should be installed tight against the bottom. (See **Figure 5.6.**)

7. Use **filler blocking** between the webs of adjacent I-joists to provide load sharing between the joists.

8. Use **backer blocking** on one side of the web to provide a surface for attachment of items like face-mount hangers. (See **Figure 5.7.**)

9. I-joists are permitted to **cantilever** with very specific limitations and additional reinforcement. If the I-joists are supporting a bearing wall, the maximum cantilever distance with additional reinforcement is 2'. If the I-joists are not supporting a bearing wall, the maximum cantilever is 4'. Check plans for specifics on the cantilever.

10. **Top-flange hangers** are most commonly used for I-joists. They come in the I-joist package, but you can also get them from a construction supply store. When installing top flange hangers, make sure that the bottom of the hanger is tight against the backer block or the header. When nailing the hanger into the bottom of the joist, be sure to use the correct length nails. Nails that are too long can go through the bottom flange and force the joist up. When installing hangers on wood plates that rest on steel beams, the hanger should not touch the steel. The distance it can be held away from the steel depends on the plate thickness. Note that hangers rubbing against the steel can cause squeaks.

11. **Face mount hangers** can be used. Make sure that the hangers are tall enough to support the top flanges of the hangers. Otherwise use web stiffeners. (See **Figure 5.8**.) Be sure to use the correct length and diameter of nail.

12. The **bottom flange** cannot be cut or notched except for a bird's mouth. At a bird's mouth, the flange cut should not overhang the edge of the top plate. (See **Figure 5.9**.)

13. Leave a ¹⁄₁₆" gap between I-joists and the supporting member when I-joists are placed in hangers. (See **Figure 5.10**.)

14. The **top flange** can be notched or cut only over the top of the bearing and should not extend beyond the width of the bearing. (See **Figure 5.11**.)

15. The **web** can have round or square holes. Check the information provided with the I-joist package. Typically the center of the span requires the least strength and can have the biggest holes. The closer to the bearing point, the smaller the hole should be.

16. **When I-joists are used on sloped roofs,** they must be supported at the peak by a beam. This is different from dimensional lumber where rafters do not require such a beam.

In working with residential I-joists, you should be aware that the APA has developed a standard for this purpose called "Performance Rated I-joists" (PRI). This standard shows the span and spacing for various uses for marked I-joists.

Glu-lam Beams

Glu-lam beams are used when extra strength and greater spans are needed. They are usually big, heavy, and expensive, and require hoisting equipment to set them in place. Most often glu-lam beams are engineered for particular jobs. Glu-lam beams are produced by gluing certain grades of dimensional lumber together in a specific order. Many times the pieces are glued together to create a specific shape or camber. If a camber is created, the top of the beam will be marked. Make sure your crew installs it right-side-up.

Notching and Drilling

The general rule for glu-lam beams is no notching or drilling without an engineer's direction. The engineer who determined the strength needed for the glu-lams is the person who will know how a notch or hole will affect the integrity of the glu-lam beam.

The way glu-lam beam connections are made can affect the strength and integrity of the beams. Following are examples of correct and incorrect ways to connect glu-lam beams, and some tips for easy installation.

Tips for Installing Glu-lam Beams

- For glu-lam beams installed at a pitch and need the bottom cut to be level, make sure the end of the bottom cut closest to the bearing edge receives full bearing. (**See Figure 5.12**.)
- Ends of beams should not be notched unless approved by the engineer.
- Glu-lam beams will shrink as they dry out. If the top of the beam is connected in a way that doesn't allow for shrinkage, the beam will split.
- When a lateral support plate is used to connect two glu-lam beams, the holes should be slotted horizontally to prevent splitting.
- Glu-lams are also used for posts. Keep them away from concrete, which contributes to their decay. Placing a steel shim under the beam will keep it from touching the concrete. (**See Figure 5.13**.)
- Hinge connectors should be installed so that they don't cause splitting of the composite beams. This can be done by using a strap that is independent of the hinge connector, or by slotting the holes in a strap that is connected to the hinge connector. (See **Figures 5.14** and **5.15**.)

Solid Blocking and I-Joist Minimum Bearing

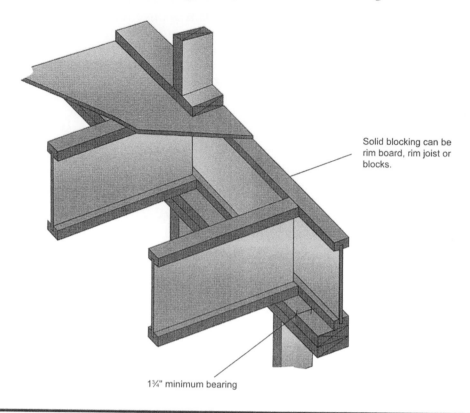

Solid blocking can be rim board, rim joist or blocks.

1¾" minimum bearing

Figure 5.4

Squash Blocks

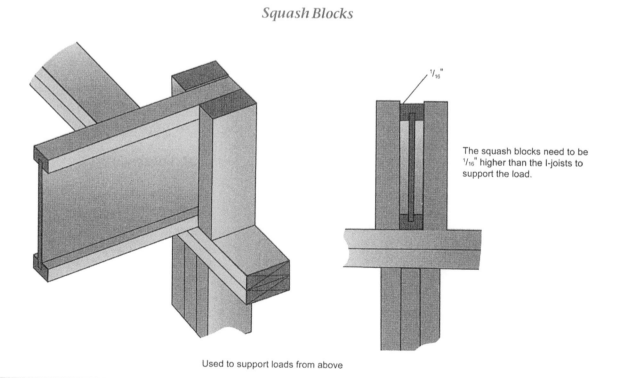

¹/₁₆"

The squash blocks need to be ¹/₁₆" higher than the I-joists to support the load.

Used to support loads from above

Figure 5.5

Web Stiffener

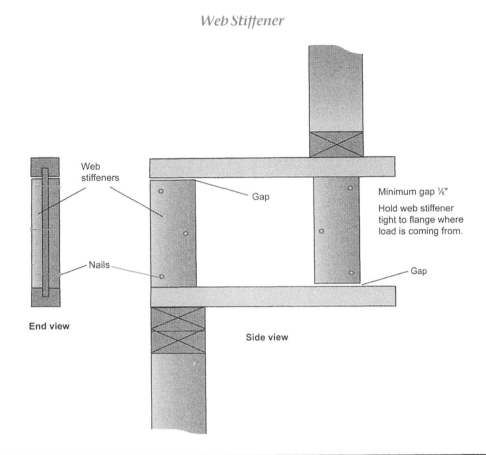

Web stiffeners

Gap

Minimum gap ⅛"

Hold web stiffener tight to flange where load is coming from.

Nails

Gap

End view

Side view

Figure 5.6

Filler Blocking and Backer Blocking

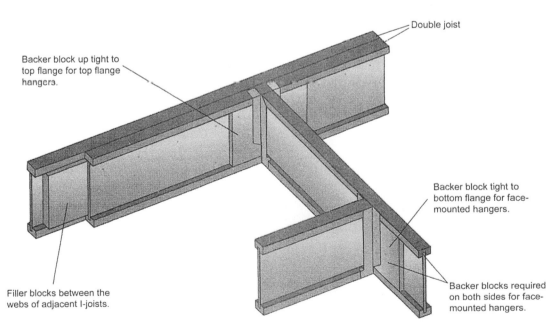

Double joist

Backer block up tight to top flange for top flange hangers.

Backer block tight to bottom flange for face-mounted hangers.

Filler blocks between the webs of adjacent I-joists.

Backer blocks required on both sides for face-mounted hangers.

Figure 5.7

Face-Mount Hangers

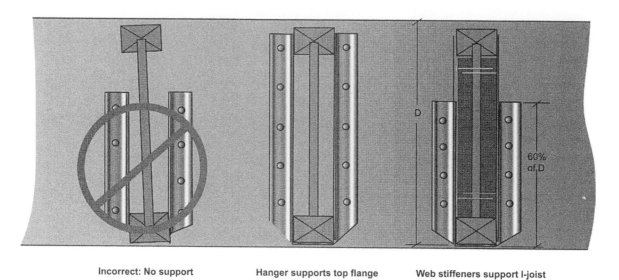

Incorrect: No support   **Hanger supports top flange**   **Web stiffeners support I-joist**

Figure 5.8   RSMeans, *Complete Book of Framing*

Bottom Flange I-Joist

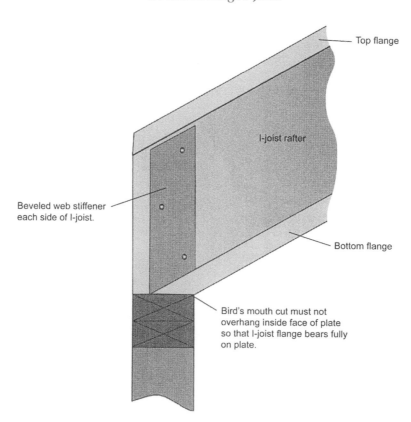

Top flange

I-joist rafter

Beveled web stiffener each side of I-joist.

Bottom flange

Bird's mouth cut must not overhang inside face of plate so that I-joist flange bears fully on plate.

Figure 5.9   RSMeans, *Complete Book of Framing*

110

Gap Between I-Joist and Support

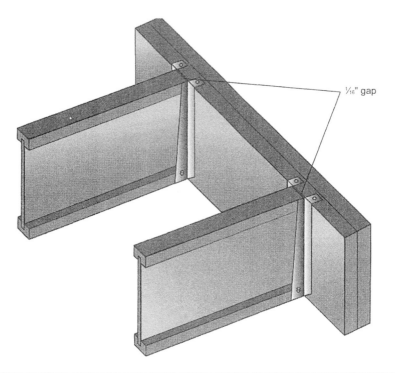

¹⁄₁₆" gap

Figure 5.10

Top Flange I-Joists

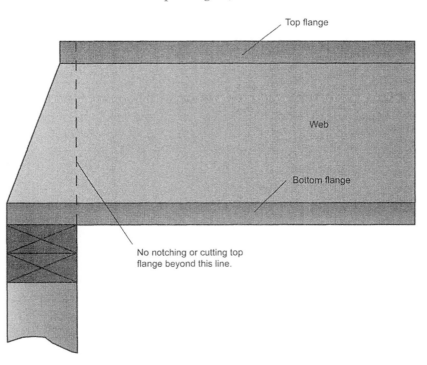

Top flange

Web

Bottom flange

No notching or cutting top
flange beyond this line.

Figure 5.11

Metal Plate-Connected Wood Trusses

Metal Plate-Connected (MPC) Wood Trusses were first used in the early 1950s. Today they are used in more than 75% of all new residential roofs. Basically they are dimension lumber engineered and connected with metal plates. Less expensive than alternative roof systems, these trusses can also span longer distances. The "Pitched Truss Parts" illustration (**Figure 5.16**) shows the parts of a simple pitched truss.

Because MCP trusses are engineered products, they should never be cut, notched, spliced, or drilled without first checking with the designing engineer.

When flying trusses, you should attach the cables around the panel points. When the trusses are greater than 30', a spreader bar should be used. The cables should toe inward to prevent the truss from buckling. If the truss is longer than 60', you will need a strongback temporarily attached to the truss to stabilize it. (**See Figure 5.17.**)

If you have multiple trusses, you can build a subassembly of several trusses on the ground with cross braces and sheathing, then erect them together.

When trusses sit on the ground, on the building, or in place for any length of time, keep them as straight as possible. They are more difficult to set in place and to straighten if they have not been stored properly on site.

Cut Edge Full Bearing

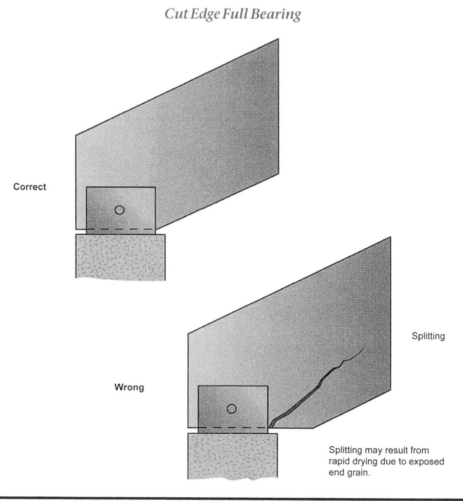

Correct

Wrong

Splitting

Splitting may result from rapid drying due to exposed end grain.

Figure 5.12

RSMeans, *Complete Book of Framing*

Decay Prevention Next to Concrete

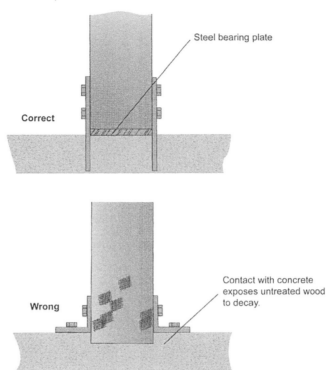

Correct

Steel bearing plate

Wrong

Contact with concrete exposes untreated wood to decay.

Figure 5.13

Hinge Connector Slotted Holes

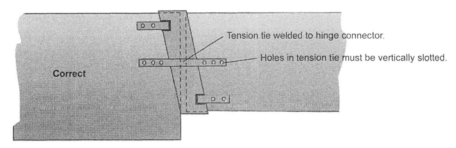

Correct

Tension tie welded to hinge connector.

Holes in tension tie must be vertically slotted.

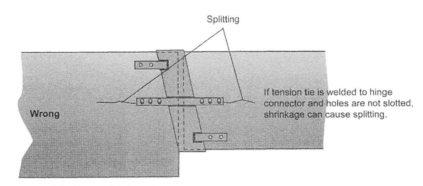

Splitting

Wrong

If tension tie is welded to hinge connector and holes are not slotted, shrinkage can cause splitting.

Figure 5.14

Hinge Connectors

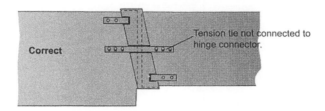

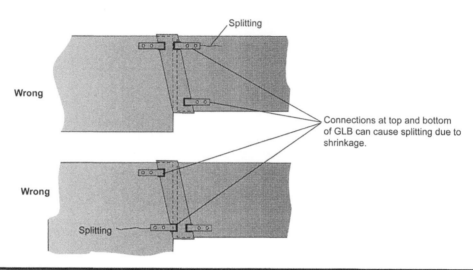

Figure 5.15

RSMeans, *Complete Book of Framing*

Pitched Truss Parts

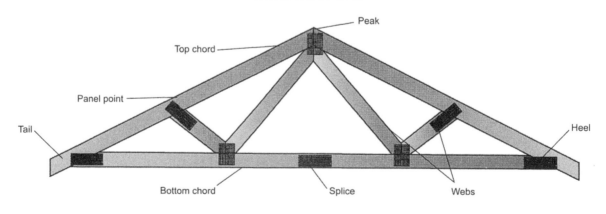

Figure 5.16

RSMeans, *Complete Book of Framing*

Flying Trusses

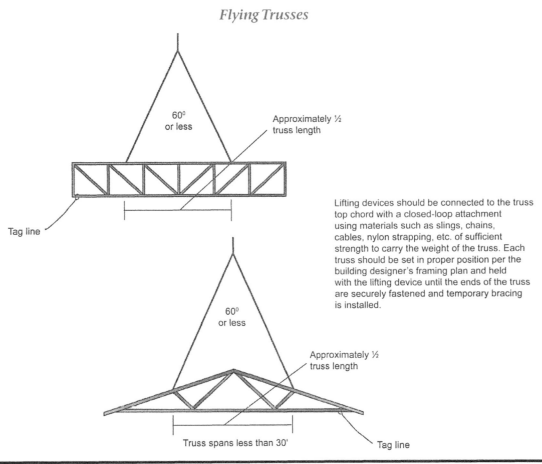

60°
or less

Approximately ½
truss length

Tag line

Lifting devices should be connected to the truss
top chord with a closed-loop attachment
using materials such as slings, chains,
cables, nylon strapping, etc. of sufficient
strength to carry the weight of the truss. Each
truss should be set in proper position per the
building designer's framing plan and held
with the lifting device until the ends of the truss
are securely fastened and temporary bracing
is installed.

60°
or less

Approximately ½
truss length

Truss spans less than 30'

Tag line

Figure 5.17

RSMeans, *Advanced Framing Methods*

Structural Composite Lumber (SCL)

Structural composite lumber is an engineered wood product that combines veneer sheets, strands, or small wood elements with exterior structural adhesives. The most common of these products are laminated veneer lumber (LVL), parallel strand lumber (PSL), and laminated strand lumber (LSL).

Like other engineered products, structural composite lumber requires that you follow the engineered specifications which will appear on the plans. Sometimes the specifications simply indicate the use of a particular piece of SCL in a particular location. For larger jobs, you will find the SCL requirements called out in the shop drawings or the structural plans. Because these are engineered products, you must consult the design engineer before you can drill or notch. Some manufacturers provide guidelines for drilling and notching, but this is not typical.

SCL has the advantages of dimensional consistency, stability, and availability of various sizes. It is important to note, however, that where dimensional lumber (4 x 10s, 4x12s, etc.) can shrink significantly, SCLs have minimal

shrinkage. The engineer should allow for this in the design so that you will not have to consider this factor when using SCLs as the plans specify.

Wood Shrinkage

Note: The following are summaries of the basic code requirements of the International Building Code *and* International Residential Code. *Please consult the IBC and IRC for complete coverage and specific wording.*

IBC–2006

2304.3 Wall Framing: Wall framing must comply with Section 2308 or a submitted design.

2304.3.1 Bottom plates: Studs are expected to have full bearing on a 2-by (actual 1½") or larger plate or sill. The plate or sill should be at least equal to the width of the studs.

2304.3.2 Framing over openings: Approved assemblies, including headers, double joists, and trusses that are large enough to transfer loads to vertical members, will be provided over door and window openings in load-bearing partitions and walls.

Comments

Often architects and builders will introduce different-sized members of the same material as components of a building system. Materials that are known to shrink noticeably should be avoided in these situations, as they can cause uneven settlement. This condition may cause a variety of building defects, including uneven and/or squeaking floors, stress cracks, and other defects in interior floor and wall finishes. For the same reasons, care should be taken when selecting structural members composed of different materials or different grades of the same material.

Composite building materials—including wood and steel open-web trusses; laminated veneer lumber; parallel strand lumber beams, headers, columns, and posts; and laminated strand lumber—are manufactured to approximately equal moisture content, and they generally do not shrink, warp, or change shape after installation. This quality should be taken into consideration when composite members are used in conjunction with conventional framing systems.

Effects of Moisture Content

Industry Standards

Timber Construction Manual
(John Wiley & Sons, Inc.)

Between zero moisture content and the fiber-saturation point, wood shrinks as it loses moisture and swells as it absorbs moisture. Above the fiber saturation point there is no dimensional change with variation in moisture content. The amount of shrinkage and swelling differs in the tangential, radial, and longitudinal dimensions of the piece. Engineering design should consider shrinkage and swelling in the detailing and use of lumber.

Comments

Wood expands or shrinks in relation to its moisture content. Wood with 19% or more moisture content is commonly used in new construction. As the wood dries to equilibrium (around 8%), the wood shrinks.

Wood shrinkage can have a dramatic effect on the height of a building. It is reported that a four-story building shrank four inches because of the change in moisture content of the framing lumber. The shrinkage was detected because the building had an internal stucco cement-lined shaft that raised at the roof line as the building shrank. Even though most single-family homes have three or less stories, the effect of lumber shrinkage must be addressed. At one extreme is a production multi-story home that is built fast with green lumber and at the other extreme is a slowly-built, single-level home constructed with kiln-dried lumber.

Temperature changes can also cause wood to expand and contract, but the effect is usually not significant. In fact, other common building materials expand three to ten times the amount for the same change in temperature. Consideration should be given to the other materials used in conjunction with wood and the differential in thermal expansion and contraction.

Shrinkage occurs when the moisture content (MC) is reduced to a value below the fiber saturation point (for purposes of dimensional change, commonly assumed to be 30% MC) and is proportional to the amount of moisture lost below this point. Swelling occurs when the moisture content is increased until the fiber saturation point is reached; then the increase ceases.

For each 1% decrease in moisture content below the fiber saturation point, wood shrinks about $1/30$th of the total possible shrinkage, and, for each 1% increase in moisture content, the piece swells about $1/30$th of the total possible swelling. The total swelling is equal numerically to the total shrinkage. Shrinking and swelling are expressed as percentages based on the green dimensions of the wood. Wood shrinks most in a direction tangent to the annual growth rings, and somewhat less in the radial direction, or across these rings. (See **Figure 5.18.**) In general, shrinkage is greater in heavier pieces than in lighter pieces of the same species, and greater in hardwoods than in softwoods.

As a piece of green or wet wood dries, the outer parts are reduced to a moisture content below the fiber saturation point much sooner than are the inner parts. Thus the whole piece may show some shrinkage before the average moisture content reaches the fiber saturation point.

The Three Principal Axes of Wood

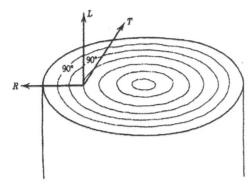

L. Longitudinal (parallel to grain); *R*, radial (perpendicular to grain, radial to annual rings); *T*, tangential (perpendicular to grain, tangential to annual rings).

Figure 5.18   Courtesy of John Wiley & Son, Inc., *Timber Constructional Manual*

Comments

Each species of wood has its own value of shrinkage. For example, as Douglas fir, Interior West, passes from fiber saturation of 30% to oven dry (0%), it shrinks 4.8% across radial growth rings and 7.5% tangential to growth rings.

The moisture content of materials such as wood, soil, masonry units, or roofing materials is expressed as a percentage of the total dry weight. At 70° and 50% humidity, the equilibrium moisture content of wood is 9.1%.

The information about wood shrinkage and moisture content can be usefully applied to a typical two-story house built on a raised foundation. At the foundation there is a 2x plate with a 2x10 rim joist, then ply and a 2x bottom plate, a stud and double top plate with a 2x12 rim joist with ply above, and a 2x plate and stud with a double 2x top plate on which 2x8 rafter tails rest.

The foundation plate (1¹⁄₂"), first floor joist (9¹⁄₂"), bottom plate (1¹⁄₂") and two top plates (3") and second floor joist (11¹⁄₂") with a bottom plate (1¹⁄₂") and two top plates (3") and rafter (8") add to a total wood thickness of 39¹⁄₂".

(continued)

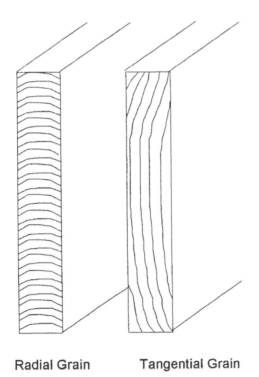

Radial Grain   Tangential Grain

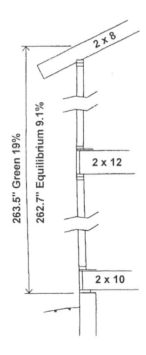

Figure 5.19   Drawings by Keith Everhart

These portions of the wall height are either tangential or radial grain and will shrink or swell with moisture change.

Averaging the tangential and radial percentages, we find that we can expect the noted framing to shrink 6.2% from fiber saturation to oven dry. If the wood in our example is at saturation and reduced to oven dry, it will shrink 6.2%, or 2$^7/_{16}$" (39½" x .062). However, the moisture content in our example only moves from 19% green to 9.1% equilibrium. This is a reduction of 9.9%, which is about $^1/_3$ of the total 30% possible. If 30% reduction will give us 2$^7/_{16}$" shrinkage, 9.9% will result in shrinkage of .80", or just over $^3/_4$". The reduction in height occurs after ply shear wall, sheet siding, or plaster is already attached.

There is a possibility that the exterior siding or shear wall will show signs of compression stress as the weight of the house comes to bear on it. Ripples or bulges in the siding, or cracking and bulges in the plaster finish can occur. These effects are often observed where narrow sections of walls are carrying heavy loads. It is often thought to be a structural defect, but is usually caused by framing shrinkage.

The effects of wood shrinkage on building construction may be noticed in other parts of the structure as well. Plumbing pipes, particularly ABS plastic plumbing drainpipes, have been known to fail because of framing shrinkage. This situation is most frequently manifested in fittings that split at floor level. Similarly, nail pops are the direct result of lumber shrinkage. The best procedure for reducing nail pops is using the smallest legal nail allowed, which gives the nail a chance to move with the lumber.

Protecting Wood from Moisture & Decay

IBC–2006

2304.11 Protection against decay and termites: Wood must be naturally durable or preservative-treated to prevent decay and/or termite infestation. Provides specific construction requirements for wood used above ground and for joists, girders, subfloors, walls supported by exterior foundation walls, exterior walls below grade, sleepers and sills, girder ends, wood siding, posts, and columns. Also provides requirements for laminated timbers, wood in contact with fresh water or the ground, and supporting members for permanent building appurtenaces.

IRC–2006

R320.1 Subterranean termite control: In areas likely to have termite damage, as established in IRC Table R301.2(1), protection methods will include chemical soil treatment, a properly installed and maintained termite baiting system, pressure-treated wood that conforms with AWPA standards, wood that is naturally termite-resistant, physical barriers, or a combination of these.

R402.1 Wood foundations: These must be designed and installed to comply with provisions of the IRC.

R402.1.2 Wood treatment: All wood and plywood must be pressure-treated, then dried, according to AWPA U1 and must carry the label of an accrediting agency. After it is cut, lumber or plywood must have its treated surface field treated with copper naphthenate (containing a minimum of 2% copper metal). The wood or plywood must be treated by repeated brushing, dipping, or soaking until it absorbs no more preservative.

IBC–2006

2304.11.2 Wood used above ground: Wood must be naturally durable or preservative-treated wood that uses water-borne preservatives, and will be treated according to AWPA U1 standards.

2304.11.2.1 Joists, girders, and subfloor: Where joists or subfloor without joists are closer than 18" or wood girders are closer than 12" to exposed ground within the foundation perimeter, the floor assembly (including subfloor, posts, joists, and girders) must be made of naturally durable or preservative-treated wood.

2304.11.2.2 Wood supported by exterior foundation walls: Wood framing members that sit on exterior foundation walls and are less than 8" from the ground must be made of naturally durable or preservative-treated wood.

2304.11.2.3 Exterior walls below grade: Wood framing members attached to the exterior masonry or conrete walls below grade must be made of approved naturally durable or preservative-treated wood.

2304.11.2.4 Sleepers and sills: These on a concrete or masonry slab in direct contact with earth must be made of naturally durable or preservative-treated wood.

2304.11.2.5 Girder ends: Unless made out of naturally durable or preservative-treated wood, wood girder ends that enter exterior masonry or concrete walls must have a ½" air space on top, sides, and end.

2304.11.2.6 Wood siding: Except where siding, sheathing, and wall framing are made of naturally durable or preservative-treated wood, clearance between earth and wood siding on the outside of a building must not be less than 6".

2304.11.2.7 Posts or columns: Posts or columns that support permanent structures and are supported by a concrete or masonry slab or footing that is in direct contact with the earth must be made of naturally durable or preservative-treated wood.

Exceptions: Posts or columns that are located in basements or cellars, or that are exposed to weather in ways outlined by code, and as a result separated by an impervious moisture barrier. Also, posts or columns in unexcavated areas or enclosed crawl space within a building's periphery.

Comments

In this section, we have combined information concerning wood products embedded in the earth, placed close to or in contact with the earth, or in contact with concrete slabs placed on earth. The use of pressure-treated lumber is common in all areas of the country. While some of these code sections may apply, this section is not intended to cover wood foundations. For wood foundations, see IBC–2006 Chapter 18, Section 1807.2.

Dryrot, which is really wet rot, and advanced fungal growth are common factors in defect claims. Water should not be allowed to come into prolonged contact with structural wood components. However, when it occurs, the best defense is use of the proper wood products.

Any discussion of wood in contact with the earth should begin with a reminder that all construction wood debris and concrete forms must be removed from the site. This

wood material is an attraction to termites and encourages infestation in the building lumber.

The IBC–2006 **Section 2303.1.8.1 Quality and Identification** requires all preservative-treated wood to be identified by the quality mark of an inspection agency that has been accredited by an accreditation body complying with the requirements of the American Lumber Standard Committee Treated Wood Program, or its equivalent. **Figure 5.21** denotes the typical quality mark for waterborne preservatives for pressure-treated lumber. Waterborne preservatives are the only type of preservative commonly used to treat wood for residential and commercial construction. This information may help in selection of the proper products for an intended application.

2302 Definitions: The following terms are defined and used in this way in Chapter 23 of the IBC.

Naturally durable wood: Defined as the heartwood of the species listed below. Occasionally pieces of corner sapwood are allowed if 90% or more of the width of each side on which it occurs is heartwood.

Decay resistant: Redwood, black locust, cedar, and black walnut.

Termite resistant: Redwood and Eastern red cedar.

Typical Quality Mark for Pressure-Treated Lumber

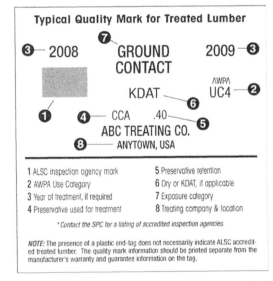

Figure 5.21

Courtesy of Southern Forest Products Association

Pressure-Treated Wood Application

RETENTION (IBS/FT³)	PRODUCTION APPLICATION
0.25	Above Ground
0.40	Ground Contact
0.60	Permanent Wood Foundation
2.50	Salt Water

Figure 5.20

American Wood Preservers Institute, www.awpi.org

Comments

1. Damage from rot (fungal decay) may be prevented or controlled by providing roof overhangs and gutters that will keep water off the building. Insect damage may be prevented by using properly seasoned wood that is well-ventilated, in conjunction with properly installed vapor barriers. In some areas of the country, codes specify use of pressure-treated or other specially treated materials.

2. Good drainage is very important for any structure. Care should be taken to eliminate puddling and ponding adjacent to the foundation. Check the ground slope requirements in your building code.

3. Shrub beds and planting areas next to a structure should be checked from time to time to ensure that they are draining properly and that mulch and organic material are not building up against wood members and/or siding materials.

Ventilation

IBC–2006

1203 Ventilation: Requirements established for attic spaces, under-floor, natural ventilation, and other ventilation and exhaust systems; refers to IMC, IFC, and IECC.

1203.2 Attic spaces: Enclosed attics and rafter spaces where ceilings are applied directly to underside of roof framing members will have cross ventilation for separate spaces by ventilating openings protected against entrance of snow and rain. Blocking and bridging must conform to code, and air space must be provided between insulation and roof sheathing.

1203.3 Under-floor ventilation: The space between bottom of floor joists and earth beneath any structure, except spaces occupied by a basement, must have ventilation openings through foundation walls or exterior walls.

1203.3.1 Openings for under-floor ventilation: The minimum net area of ventilation openings cannot be less than 1 square foot for each 150 feet of crawl space area. Openings must be covered for their height and width using materials that meet specific criteria listed in code (these include perforated sheet metal, cast iron grille or gratings, extruded load bearing vents, hardware cloth, and corrosion resistant wire mesh). Note that there are exceptions.

1203.4 Natural ventilation: Natural ventilation of an occupied space will be through windows, doors, louvers, and other openings to the exterior. The

operating mechanisms for these openings must be readily accessible for building occupants.

1209 Access to unoccupied spaces: Provides requirements for minimum access for crawl spaces, attics, and mechanical appliances. Refers to the IMC.

Comments

It is important to stay abreast of code updates on ventilation, as well as other framing requirements.

Nails, Fasteners & Bolts

Industry Standards

Complete Book of Framing
(RSMeans)

Connectors can refer to beams or other construction elements, but in most cases, connectors are hardware specifically designed for common framing connections. As part of the load path, connections have to be strong enough to transfer the forces of nature.

Important Points for Connection Framing

- Install all connectors per catalog instructions.
- Drill holes no more than $1/16$" bigger than bolts.
- Use washers next to wood.
- Fill all nail holes unless using catalog specifications.
- Know that the connection is only as strong as the weakest side. Make sure to space and nail each side the same.
- Be aware that some connectors have different-shaped nail holes. The different-shaped holes have different meanings.

Nails and Fasteners

IBC–2006

2304.9 Connections and fasteners

2304.9.1 Fastener requirements: Fasteners for wood members must comply with IBC–2006 Section 2301.2. Fastener dimensions and quantities must comply with IBC–2006 Table 2304.9.1.

2304.9.2 Sheathing fasteners: Sheathing nails or other approved connectors must be driven so that their crown or head is flush with the sheathing surface.

2304.9.3 Joist hangers and framing anchors: Connections depending on joist hangers or framing anchors, and other mechanical fastenings not otherwise covered will be allowed under code.

2303.9.4 Other fasteners: Clips, staples, glues, and other methods of fastening are allowed where approved by code.

2304.9.5 Fasteners in preservative-treated and fire-retardant-treated wood: These fasteners must be made of hot-dipped zinc coated galvanized steel, stainless steel, silicon, bronze, or copper. Fastenings for wood foundations must conform to requirements listed in AF&PA Technical Report No. 7.

Comments

Nails are the most numerous and common component in the construction of a new home. Using the wrong nail, having the wrong spacing between nails, and improperly installing nails has been the cause of considerable property damage, and the subject of many construction defect lawsuits. For example, in high-wind areas, buildings have lost their roofs and/or siding; and in areas prone to earthquakes, buildings have collapsed—partially due to the improper use of the nails and other fasteners.

Note that the 2006 *IBC* stipulates that pressure-preservative treated and fire-retardant treated wood require hot dipped galvanized or one of the other designated fasteners. Treated sill plates require hot-dipped galvanized, stainless steel, silicon bronze, or copper fasteners.

Pneumatic nailers and staplers may be used to connect a variety of materials to both concrete and steel, in addition to wood. Manufacturers should be consulted for correct selection of fasteners, as well as for appropriate pressure settings. If the power nailer is not set correctly, fasteners may penetrate too deeply, or not deeply enough, jeopardizing their holding performance. For more information on nail selection (how nail diameter, length, shape, and surface affect holding power), contact the National Frame Building Association. For staples and nails for pneumatic fasteners, refer to the Industrial Stapling and Nailing Technical Association and HUD-FHA Bulletin No. UM–25d.

Nails are available in different sizes and with various holding capacities. Common nails, with a broad head and thick shank, are used for rough framing. Ring shank nails, with ridges to increase their holding capacity, are used for subflooring (underlayment). Roofing nails, with broad heads, hold shingles, building paper, and vapor barrier materials in place. Galvanized steel nails are suitable for exterior work, such as siding that will be exposed. Their

zinc coating prevents marks and stains on the wood materials they contact.

For detailed technical data on seismic, hurricane, or high-wind areas, consult the 2006 *IBC*, Chapter 16.

Comments

Green Vinyl Sinkers

For the last three decades on the West Coast, green vinyl sinkers have been used almost exclusively for residential construction. The 16d green vinyl sinker used for framing, for the most part, meets the requirement of the code, which allows either 16d box or 16d common nails to be interchanged. The sinker nail is mid-point between box and common on shank diameter and has the same head diameter as a common nail. The sinker is 3$\frac{1}{4}$" long, which is $\frac{1}{4}$" shorter than either the box or common.

This shorter length does not violate the specifications if used for 2x material, which is 1$\frac{1}{2}$" thick. The 16d green vinyl sinker is out of spec on 3x lumber.

Another area in which the green vinyl sinker fails to comply with code is in nailing structural panels, subfloor, or wall sheathing, to framing. In some cases, this can be corrected by using a larger sinker as described below. Code specifically requires common nails or, in some cases, deformed shank (screw or ring) nails for structural panels. Smooth shank green vinyl sinkers cannot be substituted for deformed shank nails.

The 8d sinker is $\frac{3}{8}$" longer, but otherwise identical to the 6d common nail. The 8d sinker can be substituted for the 6d common to attach $\frac{1}{2}$" or thinner structural panels, subfloor, or wall sheathing to framing.

The 16d sinker has the same diameter shaft as the 10d common, but has a larger diameter head and is $\frac{1}{4}$" longer. The 16d sinker can be substituted for the 10d common for nailing 1$\frac{1}{8}$"–1$\frac{1}{4}$" structural panels, subfloor, subfloor-underlayment, or wall sheathing to framing.

Anchor Bolts

Industry Standards
Complete Book of Framing
(RSMeans)

Where braced wall lines rest on concrete or masonry foundations, they must have anchor bolts that are not less than $\frac{1}{2}$" in diameter or a code-approved anchor strap. The anchor bolts or straps should be spaced not more than 6' apart (or not more than 4' if the building is over two stories).

Each piece of wall plate must contain at least two bolts or straps. There must be one between 4" and 12" from each end of each piece. A nut and washer must be tightened on each bolt. In IRC seismic design categories D, E, and F, engineered shear walls require 0.229" x 3" x 3" plate washers. In IRC seismic design categories D0, D1, D2, and E, braced walls require 0.229" x 3" x 3" plate washers. These requirements also apply to townhouses in seismic design category C.

Comments

Hangers, Ties, and Anchors

Metal hangers, ties, and anchors are required in some geographic areas to protect structures from hurricane strength winds. Local codes, in areas where hurricane damage is most common, have specific guidelines for these items. Hangers and ties are generally required for the following connections:

- bottom to sill plates
- ceiling or floor joists to headers or rim joists
- rafters to top plates (of walls)

(Refer to the "Roof Framing" section later in this chapter for more on hurricane anchors.)

Seismic fastener requirements are described in local codes for earthquake-prone areas such as California.

Joist hangers are intended for use with specific sizes of framing members. If the hanger is too big for the member, it will not perform properly.

Load Resistance Values

Comments

Manufacturers of construction hardware generally set standards or load resistance values based on the American Forest and Paper Association's National Design Specification (NDS®).

Load resistance values may change from time to time; it is important to be aware of current values.

Manufacturers' catalogs and product information may be used as a general reference for the selection of standard or typical connectors. To achieve allowable loads, all specified fasteners must be used and proper installation procedures observed. This includes verifying that support members' dimensions are sufficient to receive the specified fasteners. If products are modified without the written permission of the manufacturer, the

manufacturer will not be liable for building failure. In most cases, products are sized for standard surfaced lumber or manufactured wood products.

Custom or special hardware is available for composite wood members. Nails are generally 8d, 10d, 16d, 20d common wire and bolts that conform to ASTM A 307–89 standards or better. All structural-rated products should meet ASTM–D1761, the testing standard recognized by all model agencies.

Construction hardware manufacturers offer custom design services and have the capability to produce connectors to meet all common and many unusual framing needs. (Due to regional builder preferences, code listings, or other factors, products may be offered in both Western Region and Eastern Region versions.)

Wood Joists & Plywood Decks

Industry Standards

Means Graphic Construction Standards
(RSMeans)

Wood joists may be used with all types of bearing wall or support systems. They may also be used in conjunction with various deck materials to provide economical floor and roof systems with moderate spans and loadings. The spacing of the wood joists may be varied to suit deck span or loading requirements.

Joists

IBC–2006

2308.8 Floor joists: Floor joist spans must comply with IBC–2006 Table 2308.8(1) or Table 2308.8(2). Provides specific design and construction requirements including those for bearing, framing, and lateral support.

IRC–2006

R502.3 Allowable joist spans: Spans for floor joists must be in accordance to IRC Tables R502.3.1(1) and R502.3.1(2). For other species, grades, and for loading conditions, see the AF&PA Span Tables for Joists and Rafters.

IBC–2006

2308.8.1 Bearing: The ends of joists should not have less than 1½" of bearing on wood or metal, or less than 3" on masonry. The exception is where ends of joists are supported on a 1" x 4" ribbon strip and nailed to the adjoining stud.

IRC–2006

R502.4 Joists under bearing partitions: Joists beneath parallel bearing partitions must be of a size that supports the load. Double joists that are separated to allow the installation of piping or vents must be solid blocked with lumber of at least 2" thick and spaced 4' on center. Unless the joists are of sufficient size to carry additional load, bearing partitions perpendicular to joists must not be offset from supporting girders, walls, or partitions more than the joist depth.

IBC–2006

2308.10.4.3 Framing around openings: Trimmer and header joists shall be doubled, or of lumber of equivalent cross section, when the span of the header exceeds 4'. The ends of header rafters more than 6' long must be supported by rafter hangers or framing anchors unless bearing on a beam, partition, or wall.

IRC–2006

R502.10 Framing of openings: Similar requirement.

IBC–2006

2308.9.2 Framing details: Wide dimension of stud must be perpendicular to the wall. No fewer than three studs can be installed at each corner of an exterior wall. There are a few exceptions: Two studs are allowed at corners provided that wood spacers or back-up cleats, or other devices that conform to code, are used as backing for the attachment of facing materials.

Comments

Joists are part of the floor framing system, along with the girder, sill plates, sill sealer, and subfloor sheathing. Joists provide the support for the floor. They are usually spaced at 12", 16", and 24" on center, between the girder and the sill on the foundation wall. A band or box joist (also called a "rim" or "perimeter" joist) is attached at the ends of the joists at the perimeter of the subfloor system.

Most codes require that joists adjacent to floor openings be doubled. Joists must also be doubled under partitions that run parallel to the joists. Joist hangers should be used to support joists whose ends do not bear on anything.

Joists must be stabilized by blocking (blocks installed square between joists) or bridging ("x-" shaped components made of 5/4 x 3s, angled at 45°). Bridging is installed along the length of the joist at 6' intervals. Prefabricated metal bridging can also be used.

Tapered Joists

Industry Standards

Western Lumber Framing Basics
(Western Wood Products Association)

It is sometimes necessary (or at least convenient) to taper the ends of ceiling joists or beams to keep them under the plane of the roof, as in **Figure 5.26**. But by reducing the depth of the joist or beam, you reduce its load carrying capacity.

If you must taper-cut the ends of ceiling joists, make sure the length of the taper cut does not exceed three times the depth of the member, and that the end of the joist or beam is at least one-half the member's original depth.

With taper-cut beams, you should also check the shear rating. If you can't meet this criteria, you'll probably have to lower the beam into a pocket so that enough cross-section can be left, after taper-cutting, to carry the applied load.

Bored Holes & Notching

IBC–2006

2308.9.8 Pipes in walls: Stud partitions that contain plumbing, heating, or other pipes must be framed, and the joists underneath spaced, as to give proper clearance for piping. When a partition that contains such piping runs parallel to the floor joists, the joists underneath such partitions must be doubled and spaced to allow the passage of pipes, and must be bridged. Where plumbing, heating, or other pipes are placed in or partly in a partition, necessitating the cutting of the soles or plates, metal tie not less than 0.058" and 1½" wide must be fastened to each plate across and to each side of the opening with no fewer than six 16d nails.

Timber Connectors

Post Base

Floor Systems

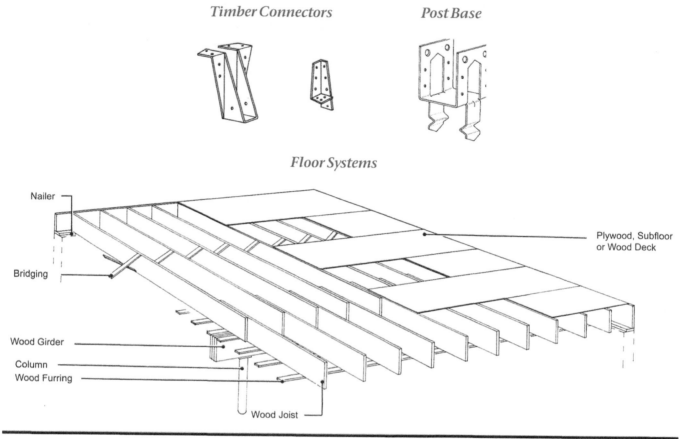

Nailer

Bridging

Wood Girder

Column

Wood Furring

Wood Joist

Plywood, Subfloor
or Wood Deck

Figure 5.22

RSMeans, *Means Graphic Construction Standards*

Headers & Trimmers

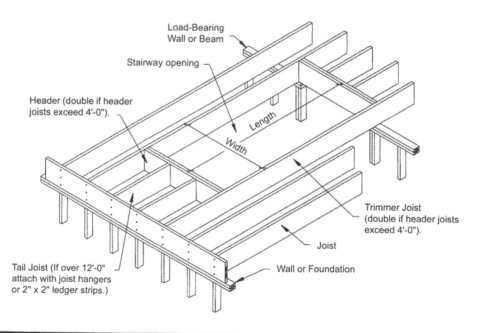

Load-Bearing
Wall or Beam

Stairway opening

Header (double if header
joists exceed 4'-0").

Length

Width

Tail Joist (If over 12'-0"
attach with joist hangers
or 2" x 2" ledger strips.)

Trimmer Joist
(double if header joists
exceed 4'-0").

Joist

Wall or Foundation

Figure 5.23

Courtesy of Western Wood Products Association, *Western Lumber Framing Basics*

2308.9.10 Cutting and notching: In exterior walls and bearing partitions, wood studs may be cut or notched to a depth not beyond 25% of their width. Cutting or notching of studs to a depth not greater than 40% of the width of the stud is allowable in nonbearing partitions supporting no loads other than the weight of the partition.

2308.9.11 Bored holes: A hole not greater in diameter than 40% of the stud width may be bored in any wood stud. Bored holes not greater than 60% of the width of the stud are permitted in nonbearing partitions or in any wall where each bored stud is doubled, provided not more than two such successive doubled studs are so bored.

In no case should the edge of the bored hole be nearer than ⅝" (15.9 mm) to the edge of the stud. Bored holes should not be located at the same section of stud as a cut or notch.

Comments

For engineered or manufactured building components such as wooden I-joists; composite wood and steel open-web trusses; laminated veneer lumber; parallel strand lumber beams, headers, columns and posts, refer to the manufacturers' installation standards.

Load conditions and hole sizes should be obtained from manufacturers' hole charts. Do not cut or notch flanges without approved engineered or manufacturers' drawings. If an improper cut or notch is made, the integrity of the member is compromised and the manufacturer may not be liable for related construction defects or failure.

Bridging

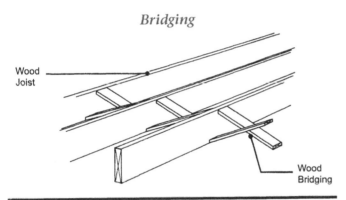

Wood Joist

Wood Bridging

RSMeans, *Means Graphic Construction Standards*

Figure 5.24

Tapered Joist Ends

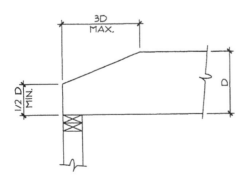

3D MAX.

½ D MIN.

D

Overtapering joists to fit beneath roofs creates inadequate joist depth at the plate. A proper cut leaves at least half the depth of the joist.

Courtesy of Western Wood Products Association, *Western Lumber Framing Basics*

Figure 5.25

Walls

Wall Partition/Framing Assembly

Industry Standards

Plan Reading & Material Takeoff
(RSMeans)

The wall and partition framing consists of the exterior walls and sheathing, the interior load-bearing walls, and the interior nonload-bearing partitions. *Load-bearing* walls carry live and dead loads from a part of the structure above, such as a floor, roof, or ceiling. A major component of a load-bearing wall is the *header*. Headers span the openings in load-bearing walls above windows and doors. They are structural members that transmit the load from above the opening to the framing on either side of the opening. Typical header construction consists of 2" x 6", 8", 10", or 12" (nominal) framing lumber nailed together with ½" plywood spacers to equal the thickness of the wall. **Figure 5.30** illustrates a typical wood header.

The vertical members that support the header are called *trimmers* or *jack studs*. The jack studs are nailed to full studs at each side of the header, sometimes referred to as *king studs*.

All partitions and walls have horizontal members that hold the *studs*, or vertical members at the desired spacing. These horizontal members are called *plates*. The plate at the top of the wall is referred to as the *top plate*, and the one at the bottom is called the *sill plate* or *sole plate*. Most load-bearing wall construction requires that the top plate be doubled. The horizontal

Drilling and Notching Studs, Exterior and Bearing Walls

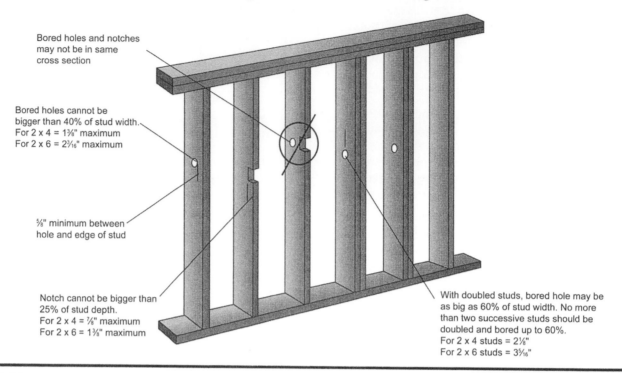

Bored holes and notches may not be in same cross section

Bored holes cannot be bigger than 40% of stud width.
For 2 x 4 = 1⅜" maximum
For 2 x 6 = 2³⁄₁₆" maximum

⅝" minimum between hole and edge of stud

Notch cannot be bigger than 25% of stud depth.
For 2 x 4 = ⅞" maximum
For 2 x 6 = 1⅜" maximum

With doubled studs, bored hole may be as big as 60% of stud width. No more than two successive studs should be doubled and bored up to 60%.
For 2 x 4 studs = 2⅛"
For 2 x 6 studs = 3⁵⁄₁₆"

Figure 5.26

Drilling and Notching, Studs, Interior Non-Bearing Walls

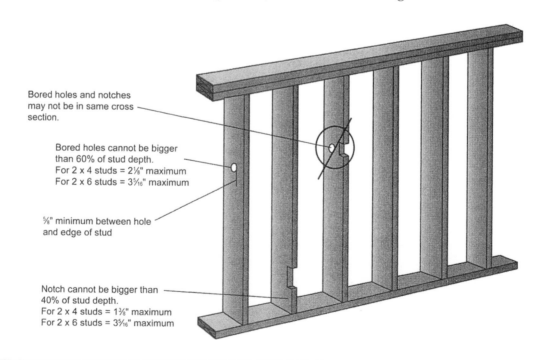

Bored holes and notches may not be in same cross section.

Bored holes cannot be bigger than 60% of stud depth.
For 2 x 4 studs = 2⅛" maximum
For 2 x 6 studs = 3⁵⁄₁₆" maximum

⅝" minimum between hole and edge of stud

Notch cannot be bigger than 40% of stud depth.
For 2 x 4 studs = 1⅜" maximum
For 2 x 6 studs = 3⁵⁄₁₆" maximum

Figure 5.27

Guide for Cutting, Notching, and Boring Joists

Table 1: Maximum Sizes for Cuts in Floor Joists

Joist Size	Max. Hole	Max. Notch Depth	Max. End Notch
2x4	none	none	none
2x6	1-1/2"	7/8"	1-3/8"
2x8	2-3/8"	1-1/4"	1-7/8"
2x10	3"	1-1/2"	2-3/8"
2x12	3-3/4"	1-7/8"	2-7/8"

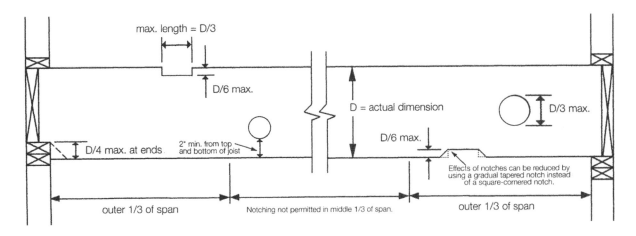

Figure 5.28

Courtesy of Western Wood Products Association, *Notching & Boring Guide*

Holes & Notches in Framing Members

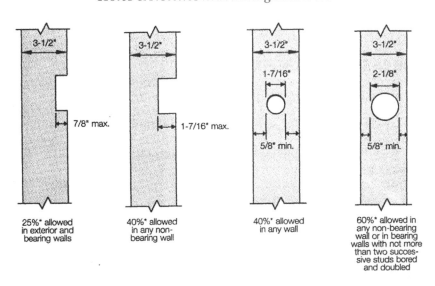

Figure 5.29

Courtesy of Western Wood Products Association, *Notching & Boring Guide*

Wood Header

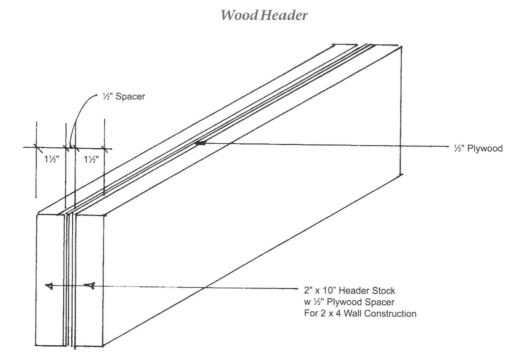

½" Spacer

½" Plywood

1½" 1½"

2" x 10" Header Stock
w ½" Plywood Spacer
For 2 x 4 Wall Construction

Figure 5.30

RSMeans, *Plan Reading & Material Takeoff*

member that runs parallel to the header at the window sill height is called the *sill*. The short studs that fill in under the window sill or above the header are called *cripples*. **Figure 5.31** illustrates typical load-bearing wall framing.

To complete the exterior wall system, plywood or similarly rated sheathing is installed over the framed wall. This helps give the wall rigidity and bracing against the wind. Just as in floor framing, wall sheathing is nailed with the 8' length perpendicular to the studs.

IBC–2006

2308.1 General: Conventional light-frame construction: This section outlines the requirements for conventional light-framing construction. It also states that other methods can be used as long as a satisfactory design is submitted that shows compliance with other provisions of IBC code. Not subject to the limitations of this section are: interior load-bearing partitions, ceilings and conventional light-frame construction curtain walls. Compliance with AF&PA WFCM will be permitted subject to limitations of it and this code. *International Residential Code* shall apply to detached

one- and two-family and multiple single-family dwellings not more than three stories and with a separate means of egress.

2308.2 Limitations: Conventional light-frame construction may be used if meeting specific requirements of this section for maximum number of stories, wall heights, loads, wind speed, and roof truss and rafter span.

Comments

A diaphragm is a horizontal or almost horizontal system that transmits lateral forces to vertical-resisting elements. The definition of diaphragm also applies to horizontal bracing systems.

Bearing Walls

Industry Standards

Western Lumber Framing Basics
(Western Wood Products Association)

Loads carried by bearing walls or posts must be transferred through floor systems. If the bearing wall or post above doesn't line up closely enough with a bearing wall, post, or beam below, the floor joists in

Load-Bearing Wall Framing

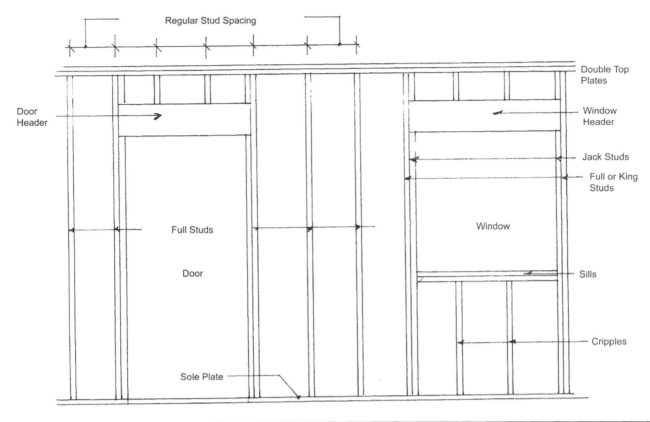

Figure 5.31

RSMeans, *Plan Reading & Material Takeoff*

between can be overstressed, causing severe deflection. This can eventually split the joists, as well as cause finish cracking problems.

Bearing walls supported by floor joists must be within the depth of the joist from their bearing support below (just as with cantilevers), as in **Figure 5.32.**

This code requirement applies only to solid-sawn wood joists. Engineered products such as wood I-beams are required to have the loads line up directly over each other, and special blocking is required. Special engineering of either dimensional or engineered lumber may allow placing loads at other locations, but you shouldn't try it without consulting an engineer first.

Bearing Walls on Cantilevers

Industry Standards

Western Lumber Framing Basics
(Western Wood Products Association)

How far can a conventionally framed cantilever extend and still support a bearing wall?

Most of the confusion about how far a cantilever can extend beyond its support stems from an old rule of thumb used by builders and code officials alike: the rule of "one-to three."

This states that a joist should extend back inside the building at least three times the length of the cantilevered section—if the cantilevered section hangs 2' out, the joists should extend at least 6' in.

This rule works fine for nonbearing situations. But it does not apply to a cantilever that supports a bearing wall. In this situation, the maximum distance that joists can be cantilevered without engineering them is a distance equal to the depth of the joists, as in **Figure 5.32.** So if you are using 2 x 10 floor joists, the maximum cantilever for those joists supporting a bearing wall is 9¼". Beyond this distance, shear becomes a serious factor, as does the bending moment at the support. This combination could eventually cause splitting of the cantilevered joists. The only way to work around this problem is to have it engineered.

Cantilevers

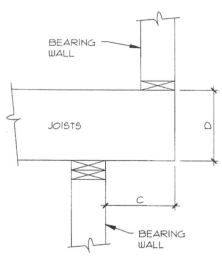

When a cantilever supports a bearing wall, the distance it extends beyond its support (C) should not exceed the depth of the joist (D).

Figure 5.32

Courtesy of Western Wood Products Association, *Western Lumber Framing Basics*

Comments

Composite joists may be cantilevered up to a maximum of 2'-0" when supporting roof load, but may require reinforcement. Manufacturers' loading tables should be consulted to determine the required reinforcement.

Composite joists may be cantilevered up to $1/3$ of the adjacent span if not supporting concentrated loads on the cantilever. Cantilevers exceeding 4' may require special construction. Manufacturers should be contacted for assistance.

Bracing Framing

IBC–2006

2308.3 Braced wall lines: Buildings must have exterior and interior braced wall lines in compliance with this section. Spacing, connection, anchorage, and support requirements are provided.

2308.6 Foundation plates or sills: Foundations and footings must comply with Chapter 18 of IBC–2006, and plates or sills must comply with Section 2304.3.1 and meet anchorage requirements provided.

2304.11.2.4 Sleepers and sills: Sills and sleepers on a concrete or masonry slab that directly contacts the earth must be of naturally durable or preservative-treated wood.

1805.6 Foundation plates or sills: Wood plates or sills must be bolted to the foundation or foundation wall as specified in Chapter 23.

Aligning Bearing Walls

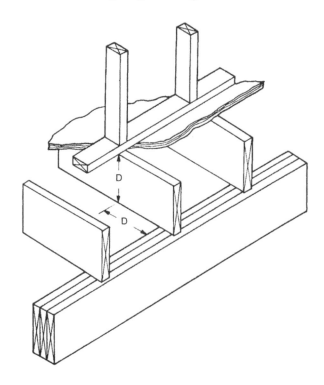

If a bearing wall doesn't line up with the support below, it should lie no farther than the depth of the joists (D). If the joists are engineered lumber, the walls and support must align exactly.

Figure 5.33

Courtesy of Western Wood Products Association, *Western Lumber Framing Basics*

Comments

See "Nails, Fasteners & Bolts" for information on hurricane and seismic requirements.

Shear Walls

Industry Standards

Complete Book of Framing
(RSMeans)

Shear Wall Construction
The factors that affect the strength of any shear wall are:

- The size and type of material used for the plates and studs
- The size and type of material used for the sheathing

- Whether one side or both sides have sheathing
- The nail sizes and patterns
- Whether or not there is blocking for all the edges of the sheathing

Engineers and architects are free to use any system they prefer, as long as they can prove that it meets the minimum strength requirements. The easiest and most common method is using the code book tables that provide accepted values for walls with given resistance capabilities. (IBC-2006 Table 2306.4.1 shows these values.)

Important Points for Shear Wall Construction

1. Stud sizes—Specified nailing patterns may require changes in the stud sizes. There are three conditions where 3x studs are required for nailing adjoining sheathing edges:

   If the edge nailing is 2" OC or less.

   If there is sheathing on both sides of the wall, the adjoining sheathing edges fall on the same stud on both sides of the wall, and the nailing pattern is less then 6" OC.

   If 10d (3" x 0.148") nails are used with more than 1½" penetration, and they are spaced 3" or less OC.

2. Penetration—It is very important that the nail does not penetrate the outside veneer of the sheathing. A pressure regulator or nail-depth gage can be used to make sure this doesn't happen. The top of the nail should be flush with the surface of the sheathing.

3. Nail size—The nail size may change from wall to wall. Check the specified thickness and length of the nails.

Columns

Industry Standards
Western Lumber Framing Basics
(Western Wood Products Association)

Bringing Columns to Foundation Properly
If you use a column to support a beam or other member, make sure it bears on something that can, in turn, support it. A common mistake is to rest one on the floor, without extra blocking or support beneath. Doing this can crush the underlying joists. Columns shouldn't rest on unsupported floor joists; they should run continuously to the foundation, or (if you must have a clear space beneath) to an engineered beam or header to transfer the load out to other columns or bearing members.

Columns shouldn't rest on rim (perimeter) joists either, for similar reasons. If you need to rest a column at the rim, add full-depth vertical blocking inside the rim joist the full depth and width of the column base, so that the load is transferred through the blocking to the foundation.

Wood Columns, Girders, Beams & Wood Decks
Industry Standards
Means Graphic Construction Standards
(RSMeans)

Wood columns, girders, and beams may be used with wood deck, or joists and plywood deck, to provide a floor or roof-framing system. The system is sometimes called "post and beam construction." This system is primarily used in situations where the floor or roof loading is relatively moderate, and where clear spans are not excessive.

Laminated Columns, Girders, Beams & Wood Decks
Industry Standards
Means Graphic Construction Standards
(RSMeans)

Laminated wood members and decking (or plywood) may be used to frame floors and roofs with varied spans and loadings. Both the framing members and decking may be left unfinished or supplied factory-stained. The connectors are usually fabricator-designed and supplied.

Wood Girder Supported by Square Tube Column

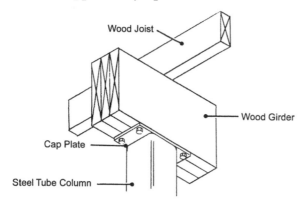

- Wood Joist
- Wood Girder
- Cap Plate
- Steel Tube Column

Wood Girder Supported by Pipe Column

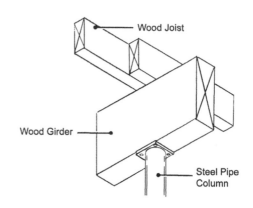

- Wood Joist
- Wood Girder
- Steel Pipe Column

Wood Column Girder and Joist

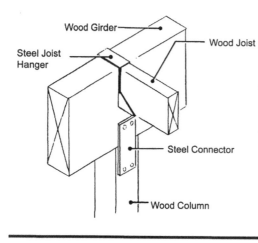

- Wood Girder
- Wood Joist
- Steel Joist Hanger
- Steel Connector
- Wood Column

Wood Girder Supported by Masonry Wall

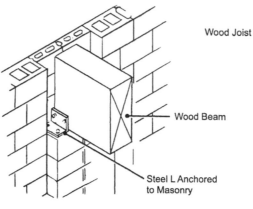

- Wood Beam
- Steel L Anchored to Masonry

Wood Column with Laminated Haunches

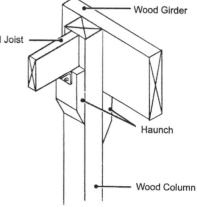

- Wood Girder
- Wood Joist
- Haunch
- Wood Column

Figure 5.34

RSMeans, *Means Graphic Construction Standards*

Laminated Wood Floor Beams

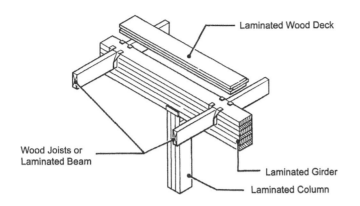

Laminated Wood Deck

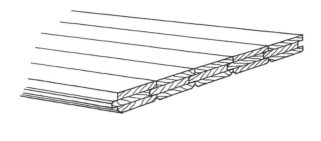

Laminated Girders & Beams With Wood Deck

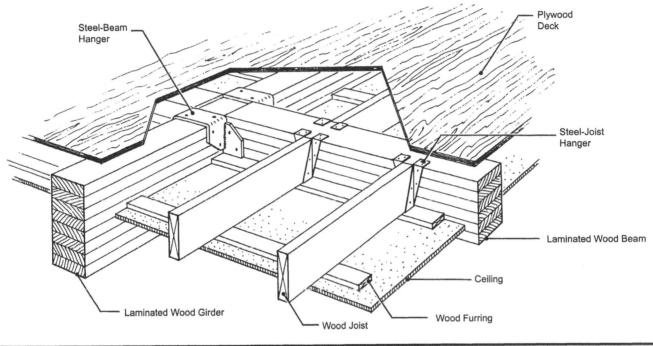

Figure 5.35

RSMeans, *Means Graphic Construction Standards*

Roof Framing

Industry Standards

Plan Reading & Material Takeoff
(RSMeans)

The rafters are supported at the base by the top plate at the top of the exterior wall. In the same way that floor joists are spaced along the pressure-treated sills, rafters are spaced along the top plate. Common spacing is 12", 16", or 24" on center. The part of the rafter that extends beyond the face of the exterior wall is called the *rafter tail*, or *tail*. It provides the nailing for the fascia and soffit (discussed later in this chapter), and constitutes the roof's overhang. The highest point of the rafter terminates at a perpendicular member in the horizontal plane called the *ridge*, or *ridgeboard*. To complete the triangular shape of the roof frame, horizontal members called *ceiling joists* provide the floor of the attic space or ceiling of the floor below.

Ceiling joists extend from the top plates of bearing walls and span the space, much like floor joists that span from sill to girder or sill. Ceiling joists for gable-end roofs run parallel to rafters. *Strapping* (called furring when applied to walls) is typically comprised of 1" x 3" (nominal) boards nailed to the ceiling side of the ceiling joists. Strapping runs at right angles to the ceiling joists in the same horizontal plane. Strapping is used to maintain the spacing of ceiling joists between bearing points and to provide furring for the ceiling finish. Strapping is commonly spaced at 12" or 16" on center.

To increase the rigidity of the roof frame, horizontal members called *collar ties* are installed from rafter to rafter on opposite sides of the ridge. Collar ties are typically located in the top third of the imaginary triangle created by the roof frame.

The *roof sheathing* extends from the rafter tail to the ridge board along the top surface of the rafter and provides a substrate for the application of the roofing. **Figure 5.37** shows a typical roof frame as viewed in a building cross section.

IBC-2006

2308.10 Roof and ceiling framing: Framing requirements of this section apply to roofs with slope greater than 25%. Provides requirements for roof and ceiling joists and includes span tables and wind uplift provisions.

IRC-2006

Section R802 Wood roof framing: Covers framing details, design and construction, and identification and grade of lumber used.

Comments

 For seismic, hurricane, or high-wind areas, reference the 2006 *IBC*, Chapter 16.

Wood Rafters

Industry Standards

Means Graphic Construction Standards
(RSMeans)

Wood roof rafters are fabricated in the field from dimensional lumber, for high or low pitched roofs, hipped roofs, mansard roofs, and flat roofs. They are typically used in conjunction with plywood decking to provide a roof structure compatible with many types of bearing wall systems. The spacing and slope of wood rafter systems may be varied to suit the loading span and aesthetic requirements of the installation.

Comments

Based on regional differences in load (wind, snow) placed on the roof structure, code may require different structural members.

Roof Support Structures

The roof frame furnishes the base to which the roofing material is attached. The frame must be made strong and rigid to withstand imposed, live, and dead loads. Rafters are structural in nature and are arranged, at equal intervals, along walls and extending up from the top of the wall to the ridge.

All lumber should be inspected for compliance with the specification. Grade stamps should be checked to ensure proper type and structural properties. Members that are damaged or have gross defects should never be used.

Lumber should be stored on blocking off the ground, covered to protect it from moisture, in properly drained areas.

Framing members should not be cut or notched without leaving sufficient strength to carry the load. (See "Bored Holes & Notching" earlier in this chapter.)

Rafters

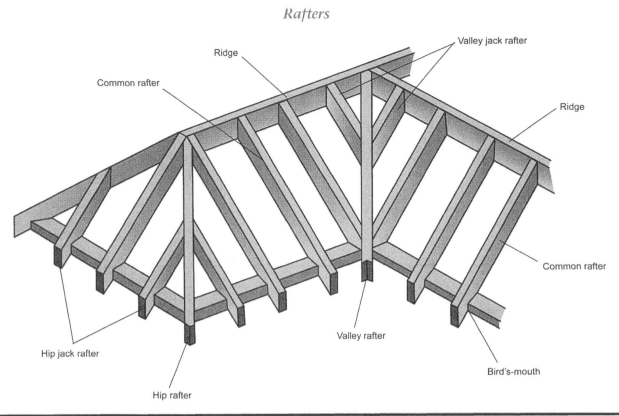

Valley jack rafter

Ridge

Common rafter

Ridge

Common rafter

Hip jack rafter

Valley rafter

Hip rafter

Bird's-mouth

RSMeans, *Complete Book of Framing*

Figure 5.36

Section at Roof Frame

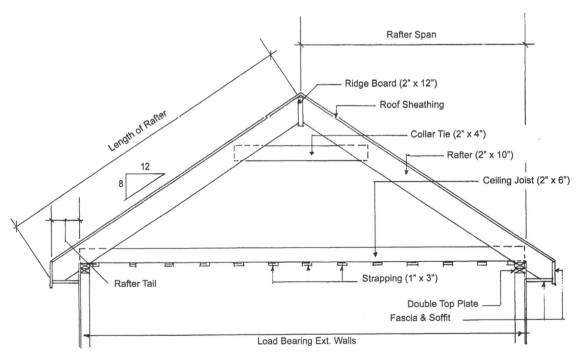

Rafter Span

Length of Rafter

Ridge Board (2" x 12")

Roof Sheathing

Collar Tie (2" x 4")

Rafter (2" x 10")

Ceiling Joist (2" x 6")

12
8

Rafter Tail

Strapping (1" x 3")

Double Top Plate

Fascia & Soffit

Load Bearing Ext. Walls

RSMeans, *Plan Reading & Material Takeoff*

Figure 5.37

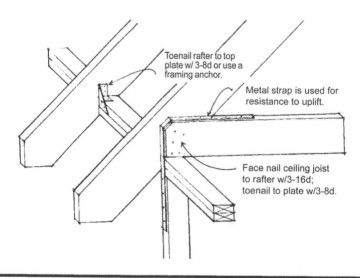

Toenail rafter to top plate w/ 3-8d or use a framing anchor.

Metal strap is used for resistance to uplift.

Face nail ceiling joist to rafter w/3-16d; toenail to plate w/3-8d.

Figure 5.38

Courtesy of Western Wood Products Association, *Western Lumber Framing Basics*

Gable End Roof

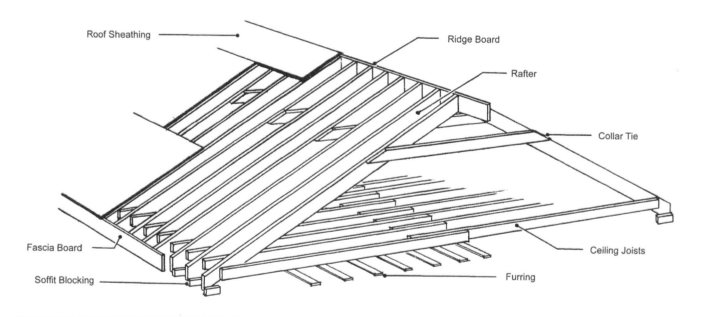

Roof Sheathing

Ridge Board

Rafter

Collar Tie

Fascia Board

Ceiling Joists

Soffit Blocking

Furring

Figure 5.39

RSMeans, *Means Graphic Construction Standards*

Mansard Roof

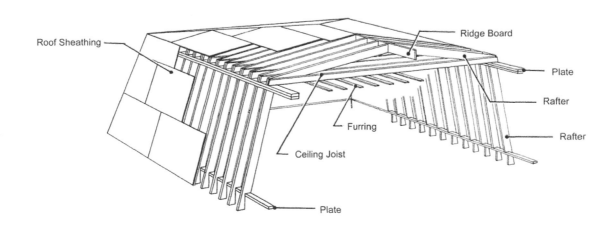

Shed Roof

Hip Roof

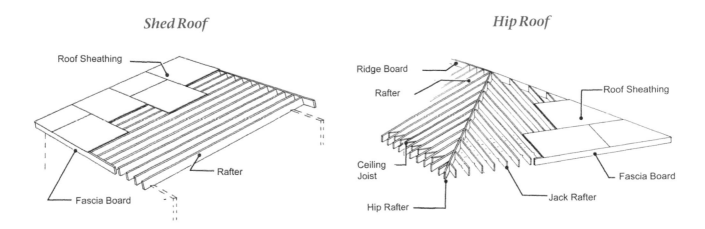

Gambrel Roof

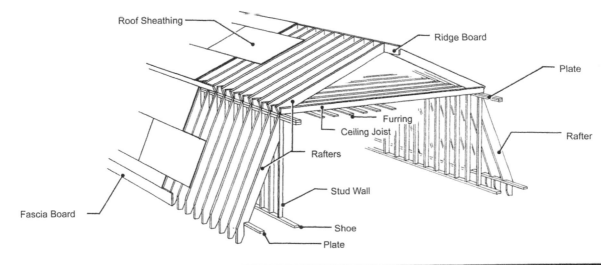

RSMeans, *Means Graphic Construction Standards*

Figure 5.39 (continued)

Rafter Bearing

Industry Standards

Western Lumber Framing Basics
(Western Wood Products Association)

Another area that inspires excessive cutting is the level cut of the seat of a rafter. Many times, especially on low slope rafters, this level cut becomes a long taper cut on the tension (lower) side of the rafter, as in **Figure 5.40**. If the bearing point on the rafter is at the heel (interior side) of the cut, there is no problem. But usually these long cuts put the bearing point near the toe. This reduces the effective size of the rafter, producing stresses that can create splits at the bearing point, and eventually a sagging rafter.

To prevent this, cut your rafters so that the heel rests on the plate. This will mean using a slightly longer rafter. It will also give you a few extra inches between the top of the exterior wall and the roof sheathing. This translates into more room for attic insulation to extend over your outside wall, reducing those cold spots that can cause condensation or ice dam problems at the eaves.

Rafter-to-Wall Connection

Industry Standards

Western Lumber Framing Basics
(Western Wood Products Association)

Conventional construction leaves too little connection between rafters and walls. Nails connect rafter to plate and plate to stud, but do nothing to connect the rafters to the wall itself. Such structures are subject to damage from the high, near-hurricane force winds that sooner or later blow across virtually every roof.

As a result, the building codes have gotten more restrictive about how rafters and trusses are tied to the rest of the building. Now, often rafters or trusses must be tied not just to the top plate, but to the studs below at 4-foot intervals. This means using some kind of metal connector to provide a positive tie to the studs.

Heel & Toe

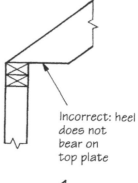

Incorrect: heel does not bear on top plate

Correct: heel bears on plate

Setting a rafter's toe on the top plate (top) risks splitting the rafter and causing the roof to sag. The inside edge of the level cut, or heel, should rest on the plate (bottom).

Figure 5.40   Courtesy of Western Wood Products Association, *Western Lumber Framing Basics*

Rafter Bearing

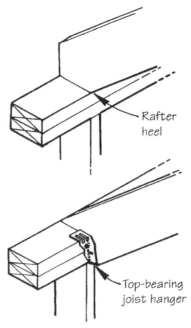

Rafter heel

Top-bearing joist hanger

It's best to have the rafter heel on the plate (top). Where this isn't possible, you can sometimes support it with a joist hanger (above). The joist hanger also keeps the rafter from rotating, a job that normally requires ceiling joists or solid blocking.

Figure 5.41   Courtesy of Western Wood Products Association, *Western Lumber Framing Basics*

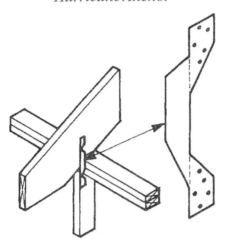

Hurricane Anchor

Nailing rafters to plates, and plates to studs, is not always enough to resist high winds. Hurricane anchors at 4-foot intervals will securely tie rafters to studs.

Figure 5.42

Courtesy of Western Wood Products Association,
Western Lumber Framing Basics

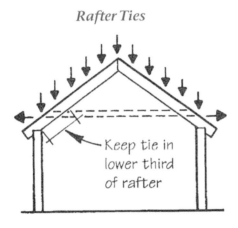

Rafter Ties

Keep tie in lower third of rafter

As rafters settle, their outward thrust pushes out on exterior walls. Rafter ties should be placed in the lower third of the rafter span so they have enough leverage to resist this thrust.

Figure 5.43

Courtesy of Western Wood Products Association,
Western Lumber Framing Basics

The answer is the hurricane anchor (see **Figure 5.42**). You don't need to face a hurricane to need it—winds of roof-damaging gale force blow in most parts of the country. If you build in an area subject to high winds (or seismic conditions), you should consider using these or other hold-downs.

Wood Roof Trusses

Industry Standards

Means Graphic Construction Standards
(RSMeans)

Wood roof trusses are factory fabricated of dimension or engineered lumber for high- or low-pitched roofs, hipped roofs, mansard roofs, and flat roofs. They are available from manufacturers in many different configurations. Members are connected with wood or metal gussets and are glued and/or power nailed in a jig to ensure uniformity.

The clear span characteristics of trusses provide flexibility for interior planning and partition layout. A considerable cost savings results from the fact that ceilings or decking can be applied directly to the truss chords. Truss spacing is dictated by maximum allowable span of the sheathing material. Normal span wood trusses can be erected by hand, due to their light weight, but are also efficiently erected utilizing a boom truck or crane and a small erection crew.

Fire Blocks & Draft Stops

IBC–2006

717.2 Fireblocking: Required between floors, top of story, and roof or attic in combustible construction per IBC–2006 Sections 717.2.2–2.7.

717.2.1 Fireblocking materials: Fireblocking materials may be 2" lumber or other approved materials securely installed.

717.3 Draftstopping in floors: Draftstopping must subdivide floor-ceiling assemblies in compliance with this section.

Truss Roof

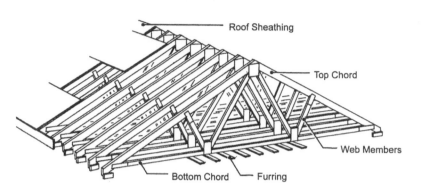

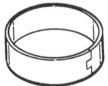

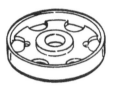

Split Ring Connector

2⅝" Shear Plate Connector

4" Shear Plate Connector

Flat Spiked Grid Connector

Figure 5.44

RSMeans, *Means Graphic Construction Standards*

717.3.1 Draftstopping materials: Draftstopping materials must be gypsum, wood structural panel, particleboard, nominal lumber, cement fiberboard, mineral wool, glass fiber, or other approved materials meeting width requirements.

717.3.2 Groups R-1, R-2, R-3, and R-4: Draftstopping required in floor/ceiling spaces, except for buildings sprinklered per NFPA 13 or NFPA 13R and sprinklered in combustible concealed spaces.

717.3.3 Other groups: Draftstopping required to limit horizontal floor spaces to 1,000 square feet except for sprinklered buildings per NFPA 13.

717.4 Draftstopping in attics: Draftstopping required to divide attic and concealed spaces.

717.4.1 Draftstopping materials: Per Section 717.3.1.

Comments

Installed fireblocks and draft stops should be checked after all wall penetrations have been made (for piping electrical, and ductwork) and prior to installation of insulation materials. Subtrades may remove fireblocks and draft stops, not realizing that these elements are essential to code compliance.

For more information on fireblocking, refer to *House Framing*, published by Creative Homeowner®.

Structural Sheathing

IBC–2006

2304 General construction requirements

2304.1 General: Applies to all three design methods listed in Section 2301.2.

2304.2 Size of structural members: Net dimensions, not nominal, must be used in calculating required sizes of wood members.

Comments

Sheathing Nailed to Composite Joist Flanges and Engineered Wood

Refer to manufacturers' tables for maximum spacing of nails related to specific flange size. If more than one row of nails is used, rows should be offset and nails staggered. If staples or pneumatic nails are substituted for common nails, consult manufacturer recommendations for gauge and wire size.

Roof Sheathing

IBC–2006

2304.4 Floor and roof framing: Floor and roof framing must comply with IBC-2006 Section 2308 or a submitted design.

2304.7 Floor and roof sheathing: Floor and roof sheathing must comply with this section and IBC-2006 Tables 2304.7(1)–2304.7(5).

Industry Standards
Framing & Rough Carpentry, Second Edition
(RSMeans)

Roof Sheathing

1. Make sure the first piece goes on square.

2. Chalk a line from one end of the roof to the other. When measuring for the chalk line, make sure you consider how the plywood intersects with the fascia. The plywood may cover the fascia, or the fascia may hide it.

3. If the sheathing overhang is exposed, the sheathing could take a special finish.

   If the exposed sheathing material is more expensive than the unexposed sheathing, then often the exposed sheathing is cut to fit only the exposed area. In this situation, cut the sheathing so that it breaks in the middle of the truss or rafter blocking.

Nailing Sheathing

1. Read the information on the stamp on each piece of plywood. Make sure you are using the right grade. Sometimes the stamp will tell which side should be up.

2. There should be at least a ⅛" gap between sheets for expansion.

3. The heads of the nails must be at least ⅜" from the edge of the sheathing.

4. Make sure that the nail head does not go so deep that it breaks the top veneer of the sheathing. Control nail gun pressure with a pressure gage or depth gage.

5. Angle the nails slightly so that they won't miss the joist, stud, or rafter.

6. Use the building code pattern for walls, floors, and roofs. Always check the plans for special nailing patterns. (Most shear walls have special patterns.)

Moisture changes in plywood make it expand or contract. It is very important to install the panels with a 1/8" gap at the edges and the ends.

1/8" space required at panel edges and ends unless otherwise directed by panel

Figure 5.45   Drawing by Keith Everhart

Exterior Wall Coverings

IBC–2006

Section 1402–Definitions

Exterior Wall Covering: The material or materials used on the exterior of the outside wall for reasons of providing weather-resisting barriers, insulation, or aesthetics includes veneers, siding, exterior insulation and finish systems, architectural trim and embellishments such as soffits, cornices, facias, gutters, and leaders.

IRC–2006

Section R703: Exterior Covering

R703.1 General: Exterior walls must provide the building with weather-resistant exterior wall envelope that must include flashing as described in IRC–2006 Section R703.8. The exterior wall envelope must be designed and constructed in a way as to avoid the accumulation of water within the wall assembly by providing a water-resistive barrier behind the outside veneer as required by Section R703.2.

IBC–2006

2304. 6 Wall sheathing: Minimum thickness of wall sheathing is set forth in Table 2304.6, which covers requirements for wood boards, fiberboard, wood structural panels, M-S and M-2 Particleboard, gypsum sheathing, gypsum wallboard, and reinforced cement mortar.

Comments

Plywood is available in two basic types: exterior, which has a 100% waterproof glueline, and interior, which has a moisture-resistant glueline. Exposure 1 panels (produced with exterior glue) can be used where the materials must resist moisture while construction is delayed or where there is some exposure of the installed material. For long-term exposure to moisture and weather conditions, only exterior-type plywood should be used.

The Engineered Wood Association (APA) has rated plywood performance as follows:

Exterior—For use in areas subject to continuous weather/moisture exposure (comparable to PS 1 as "Exterior").

Exposure 1—For use in protected situations requiring resistance to moisture for limited periods of time (e.g., construction delays); comparable to PS 1 as "Exposure 1" or "Interior" with exterior glue.

> **Exposure 2**—For use in protected situations where there may be limited exposure to moisture, water leakage, or high humidity; (comparable to PS 1 "Interior"-type with intermediate glue).

instances stairs are designed to conform to the structural framing system: concrete stairs with a concrete-framed building; steel stairs with a steel-framed building; and wood stairs with a wood-framed building.

Subfloor

IRC–2006

R502.1.2 Blocking and subflooring: Blocking must be a minimum of utility grade lumber. Subflooring can be of No. 4 common grade boards or a minimum of utility grade lumber.

Comments

See "Egress" later in this chapter for code information on stair construction. See the section titled "Wood Stairs & Railings" in Chapter 6, "Finish Carpentry & Cabinetry," for more information on stair installations, including *IBC* requirements.

Industry Standards

Complete Book of Framing
(RSMeans)

Subfloor Sheathing
Six Steps for Setting First Sheet of Sheathing

1. Snap a chalk line 4¼" in from one rim to its opposite, perpendicular to the joists.
2. Apply glue to joists, if called for. Be sure to nail sheathing before glue dries.
3. Center first piece of sheathing to last joist on the chalk line and nail each end.
4. Pull joist layout from corner of sheathing and mark sheathing.
5. Nail sheathing to joist next to rim joist along chalk line and layout marks.
6. Set remaining joists to layout marks and nail.

Setting Second Sheet

1. Set to chalk line and layout mark.

Setting Second Row and Remaining Sheets

1. Set to existing sheets, allowing ⅛" gaps.
2. Stagger sheet ends on joists.
3. Ensure rim joists are straight before nailing. (See "Allowable Tolerances" at the end of the chapter for more on subfloors.)

Stair Framing

Industry Standards

Means Graphic Construction Standards
(RSMeans)

Stairs may be prefabricated or built in place from aluminum, concrete, cast iron, steel, or wood. In many

Industry Standards

Builder's Essentials: Framing & Rough Carpentry
(RSMeans)

The three main dimensions in stair building are those for risers, treads, and headroom. The riser height and the tread width are usually given on the plans. You can generally use the tread width given on the plans. The riser height, however, is often not accurate enough to use.

Standard Riser and Tread Dimensions

If the riser and tread dimensions are not given on the plan, you need to calculate them. To do this, you should consider the following points:

- You want the steps to feel comfortable.
- When walking up steps, a person determines the height of the riser based on the first step. Make sure all risers and treads are equal, so the stairs will not cause people to fall.
- When walking up steps, a person determines the height of the riser based on the first step.
- The lower the riser, the longer the tread needs to be to feel comfortable.
- Common dimensions for riser and tread are 7" rise and 10½" tread.
- Use the following three rules to check to see if your stair dimensions are in the comfortable range.

  Rule 1: Two risers and one tread added should equal 24" to 25".

  Rule 2: One riser and one tread added should equal 17" to 18".

  Rule 3: Multiply one riser by one tread, and the result should equal 71" to 75".

Wood Stair

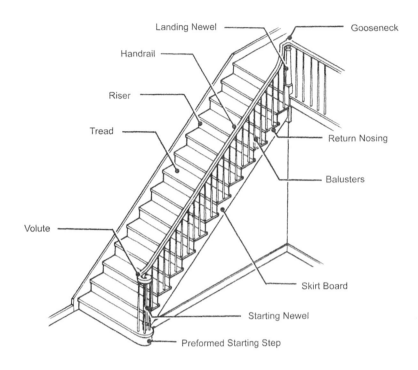

Landing Newel — Gooseneck

Handrail

Riser

Tread — Return Nosing

— Balusters

Volute

— Skirt Board

— Starting Newel

— Preformed Starting Step

Steel Pan Stair

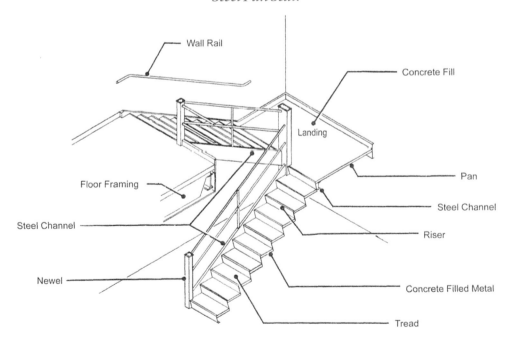

— Wall Rail — Concrete Fill

Landing

Floor Framing — Pan

Steel Channel — Steel Channel

— Riser

Newel

— Concrete Filled Metal

— Tread

RSMeans, *Means Graphic Construction Standards*

Figure 5.46

Headroom Calculations for Stairs

Checking Headroom Height for Stairs
1. Plumb down from lowest headroom point.
2. Count the number of full risers from the end of the stair to the headroom plumb line.
3. Find the partial riser height by multiplying the partial tread length by the riser percent.
4. Height at lowest headroom location equals full riser heights plus partial riser height.

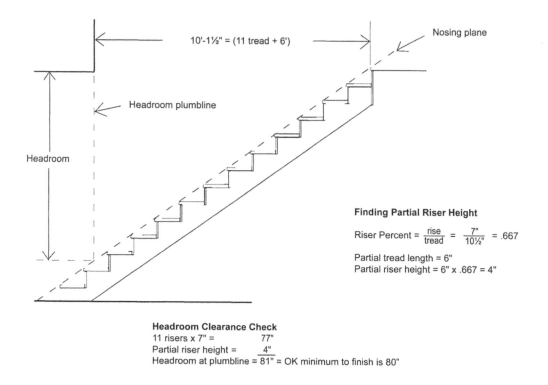

Finding Partial Riser Height

Riser Percent = $\dfrac{\text{rise}}{\text{tread}}$ = $\dfrac{7"}{10\frac{1}{2}"}$ = .667

Partial tread length = 6"
Partial riser height = 6" x .667 = 4"

Headroom Clearance Check
11 risers x 7" =   77"
Partial riser height =   4"
Headroom at plumbline = 81" = OK minimum to finish is 80"

Figure 5.47

RSMeans, *Advanced Framing Methods*

Egress (Stairs, Ramps & Guardrails)

Comments

There are many elements to consider in providing safe access to and egress from residences. We have not included comprehensive information here on accessibility for the physically and sensorially disabled. The code and regulations vary from state to state and even from jurisdiction to jurisdiction. See IBC Chapter 11, "Accessibility," and the Americans with Disabilities Act for more information. Your local building official will provide local regulations and code requirements for your project.

IBC-2006

1013 Guards: Required at open-sided walking surfaces, mezzanines, stairways, ramps, and landings that are more than 30" above the below floor or grade. Strength and means of attachment must comply with Section 1607.7. Exceptions include loading docks, stages and platforms, vehicle service pits, and (when in accordance with Section 1025.14) assembly seating.

IRC-2006

R312.1 Guards: Porches, balconies, ramps, or raised floor surfaces that are more than 30" above the floor or grade below must have guards not less than 36" in height. Open sides of stairs with a rise of more than 30" above the floor or grade should not have guards less than 34" vertically from nosing of the tread.

IBC-2006

1013.2 Height: Guards must be at least 42" in height. Exceptions for R-3 and individual dwelling units of R-2 that allow the guard to be a minimum of 34 and maximum of 38" high when it is also used as a handrail.

1013.3 Opening limitations: Openings between balusters must be small enough to prevent a 4" sphere from passing through for guard heights 34" or less and an 8" sphere for guards over 34" high. Exceptions: openings at the joint of risers and treads must be no larger than 6"; guards serving access to mechanical equipment and I-3, F, H, and S occupancies must have openings no larger than 21"; guards in assembly seating must have openings no larger than 4" or 8" (depending on location and height); and guards on the sides of stair treads within individual dwelling units in Group R-2 and R-3 occupancies must have openings no larger than 4.375".

IRC-2006

R312.2 Guard opening limitations: Required guards on raised floor areas, open sides of stairways, balconies, and porches must have intermediate rails or closures that do not allow passage of a sphere 4" in diameter.

Exceptions: Triangular openings formed by the riser, bottom rail, and tread of a guard at the open side of a stairway can't allow a 6" sphere to pass through, and openings on the sides of stair treads can't allow a $4\frac{3}{8}$" sphere to pass through.

IBC-2006

1009.3 Stair treads and risers: Riser height limited to between 4" and 7". Treads must be at least 11" deep. Provides guidance to measuring tread depth and riser height. Exceptions included for spiral stairways, alternating tread devices, stairs in assembly seating (in accordance with IBC-2006 Section 1025.11.2), and Group R-3 occupancies and in dwelling units in Group R-2 and Group U occupancies.

IRC-2006

R311.5.3 Stair treads and risers: The maximum riser height must be $7\frac{3}{4}$" and the minimum tread depth must be 10", and handrails must conform to code as described. Winder treads must have a minimum tread depth of 6" at any point. The largest tread depth and riser height within any flight of stairs shall not exceed the smallest by more than $\frac{3}{8}$".

IBC-2006

1009.3.2 Dimensional uniformity: Treads and risers are required to be uniform in size and shape (maximum difference in dimension from largest to smallest tread or riser is 0.375" within any flight of stairs). Exceptions apply to riser dimensions of aisle stairs and winders meeting IBC-2006 Section 1025.11.2 and also to winder treads of consistent shape differing from rectangular treads within a stair case. Also addresses treatment of top and bottom risers adjoining sloping surfaces at grade that form landings. Limitation is placed on the slope, and slip-resistant marking stripes are required.

1009.3.3 Profile: Leading edges must not project more than 1.25" and must be uniform on entire stairway. Provides criteria for the shape of the leading edge of treads, angle of risers, and openness of risers (solid if required to be an accessible means of egress or limited to maximum 4" openings).

IRC–2006

R311.5.3.5 Profile: The radius of curvature at the leading edge of the tread must be $9/16$" or smaller. A nosing that is no smaller than $3/4$" but no bigger than $1\frac{1}{4}$" must be provided on stairways with solid risers. Provides criteria for nosing projection, and riser angle, as well as exceptions.

IBC–2006

1009.4 Stairway landings: Requires landings at the top and bottom of stairway. Landings must not be less than the width of the stairway, except in straight runs where the landing does not need to exceed 48". Aisle stairs complying with Section 1025 are exempt. Doors cannot obstruct the landing by more than 50% of the required width at any point in swing and cannot project into a landing more than seven inches when open.

1009.5 Stairway construction: Material must be consistent with those permitted for type of construction of the building. Wood handrails are permitted in any type of construction.

1009.7 Curved stairways: Must have treads and risers comply with Section IBC–2006 1009.3. The smallest radius must not be less then twice the width required of the stairway. Provides exemptions for Group R-3 and R-2 occupancies.

1009.8 Spiral stairs: Only allowed in means of egress system within dwelling units or from spaces less than 250 SF in area serving five people or less. Exception allows their use for galleries, catwalks, and gridirons that comply with Section 1015.6. Provides requirements for tread and riser measurements, headroom, and stairway width.

IRC–2006

R311.5.8.1 Spiral stairs: These are allowed, as long as they have a minimum width of 26", with each tread having a $7\frac{1}{2}$" minimum tread width at 12" from the narrow edge. All treads must be identical, and rise must not be more than $9\frac{1}{2}$". Minimum headroom is 6'-6".

Access

IBC–2006

1014.1 General: Requires compliance with IBC-2006 Sections 1014–1017, and applicable provisions in Sections 1003–1013.

1015.1 Exit or exit access doorways required: Two exits are required from a space if occupant load exceeds Table 1015.1, if the common egress path exceeds limitations of IBC–2006 Section 1014.3, or if required by Sections 1015.3–1015.5.

IRC–2006

R311.4.1 Exit door required: Requires at least one door per dwelling unit provide direct access from the habitable portions of the dwelling to the outside without requiring travel through a garage. Any habitable levels not having such an exit require access by ramp (according to IRC–2006 R311.6) or stairway (according to IRC–2006 R311.5).

IBC–2006

1024.5 Egress courts: Must meet requirements of this section.

1024.5.1 Width: Width of egress courts must be at least 44" (or 36" for Group R-3 and Group U occupancies). Width must be unobstructed to a height of 7', unless by handrails or an open door (neither of which can reduce the width by more than 7"). Doors in any position can't reduce the width by more than half, and other objects, such as trim, must not project more than 1.5".

508.1 Mixed use and occupancy: When a building or portion of a building contains two or more occupancies or uses, it shall comply with the applicable provisions of IBC-2006 Section 508.

Garages

IBC–2006

Section 312 Requirements for Group U occupancies: Accessory-type buildings and structures, or those not classified as having a specific kind of residency will be built, equipped, and maintained according to code most having to do with the fire and life hazard incidental to their occupancy.

406.1.1 and 406.1.2 Classification and area: Group U Buildings limited to 1,000 SF and one story. Area may be increased to 3,000 SF if no repair work is done and no fuel is dispensed there, as long as provisions are met. Buildings may have more than one Group U in a building if separated by fire walls.

Hurricane & Earthquake Resistance

Comments

See "Nails, Fasteners & Bolts" and "Seismic Bracing" earlier in this chapter for more information on framing in seismic and hurricane-prone areas.

Industry Recommendations

Building Strong Walls with Plywood and OSB
(APA—The Engineered Wood Association)

When a high wind or earthquake strikes a house, the brunt of the forces hit the walls and roof. That's why the construction of the walls and roof is particularly important to a building's overall strength.

Industry Recommendations

Introduction to Lateral Design
(APA—The Engineered Wood Association)

Lateral loads are those that act in a direction parallel to the ground. The two major contributors to lateral load are high winds, such as those from a hurricane, and seismic (earthquake) forces.

The structure must be designed to withstand lateral loads in two directions at right angles to each other. As a result, three separate load designs must be calculated for every building: one vertical load design and two lateral load designs (one for each direction). Then, the load capacity of all major building elements and *every* connection between each element must be calculated to make sure each has the capacity to resist all three loads and transfer lateral and vertical forces between them.

Correct lateral design is essential. A building that has not been specifically designed and built to resist lateral loads will likely collapse when subjected to these forces.

The elements of a wood-framed building that enable it to withstand lateral forces are *shear walls* and

diaphragms. These elements must be designed to resist the lateral loads applied, and connections between elements must be strong enough to transfer the loads between elements.

Shear Walls and Diaphragms

Wind and seismic forces are resisted by *shear walls* that are composed of wood structural sheathing fastened to wood framing, properly connected to the foundation below and the roof above. Similarly, the installation of wood structural panels over a roof or floor supports creates a *diaphragm*, a flat structural unit that acts like a deep, thin beam that resists lateral forces.

Shear walls and diaphragms are building elements necessary for proper lateral design. Aside from the fact that a shear wall is vertical and the diaphragm is horizontal (or nearly horizontal), they are essentially the same kind of structural element.

A diaphragm is designed as a simply supported beam while the shear wall is designed like a vertical, cantilevered diaphragm. A diaphragm acts in a manner similar to a deep I-beam or girder, where the panels act as a "web" resisting shear, while the diaphragm edge members perform the function of flanges, resisting bending stresses. These edge members are commonly called *chords* in diaphragm design, and may be joists, ledgers, double top plates, etc.

Engineered versus Prescriptive Requirements

Current model building codes allow the designer to use either of two methods to design light frame wood structures. Both are appropriate for detached one- and two-family dwellings as well as many other wood structures. These two methods are by the use of *engineering design* or *prescriptive* requirements.

Chapter 16 of all three major model building codes and the *International Building Code* is the chapter that provides the information required to *engineer* a structure, the design-based requirements. This chapter provides all of the vertical and horizontal design loads (gravity, snow, wind, seismic, impact, construction, live and dead loads, etc.) that must be considered when doing an engineering design of *any type* of structure covered by the building codes.

This data must be interpreted by a designer or engineer whose responsibility it is to provide all of the details necessary to resist the applied loads and build the structure.

The wood chapter of the IBC (Chapter 23) contains *prescriptive requirements* for the design of wood structures. Prescriptive requirements provide a "cookbook" method for the design of wood structures within certain limitations. They tell the designer what size and grade lumber to use for the different applications, what anchor bolt spacing to use, what size joists to use for various floor spans, the fastening schedule for all applications, etc. Because prescriptive requirements ignore specific factors, such as the actual geometry of the structure, actual loads seen by the structure, and their location, this design method is limited for use in locations with low wind and minimal risk of seismic activity.

Bracing versus Shear Walls

The design method chosen, engineered or prescriptive, will determine whether shear walls or wall bracing are used to provide lateral bracing and resistance in the structure.

In the process of *designing* a "box-type" structure, the engineer/designer will find that he or she must provide a number of vertical wall elements designed to resist the horizontal forces acting on the building (earthquake, wind, or both). The elements used in a box-type structure to resist lateral loads are *shear walls*. These shear walls also act as interior and exterior walls, load bearing, and non-load bearing walls required to meet the architectural goals of the building as well as the requirements of other design loads.

While shear walls may look similar to other walls, they often contain a number of important differences, including:

- Additional base shear anchor bolts in the bottom plate (the size and number may be different from the prescriptive requirements of the code).
- Hold-down anchors at each end of the shear wall.
- Tighter-than-conventional nailing of the sheathing/siding.
- Thicker-than-conventional sheathing/siding.
- Different framing grades, species, and sizes.
- Limitations on the placement of the shear wall segments (e.g., shear walls on upper floors must be placed directly over shear walls below).
- Special fastening requirements at the top of the shear wall elements to insure load transfer from the roof/floor diaphragm into the shear wall.

When the building is designed using *prescriptive requirements*, lateral forces are resisted by *wall bracing* instead of by shear walls. This wall bracing must be placed at prescribed locations throughout the structure: e.g., "located at each corner and at every 25 ft (7620 mm) of each exterior wall." While these bracing panels serve the same function as the

engineered shear wall—provide resistance to the lateral forces acting on the structure—they have few elements in common with the shear walls described above. Their lack of detailing severely limits the strength and stiffness of the wall bracing when compared with an engineered shear wall. For this reason, wall bracing is relegated to low-load situations.

What Is Wall Bracing?

The codes give various options. Most commonly used: one "unit" of wall bracing could be 4 lineal feet of studs sheathed with wood structural panels, 8 lineal feet of studs sheathed with gypsum board on one side, 8 lineal feet of wall containing a let-in brace at 45 degrees (limited to single story or second story of a two-story building), etc.

> ## Comments
>
> See the "Roof Framing," "Fasteners" and "Structural Sheathing" sections of this chapter for more information on hurricane and seismic framing requirements. For detailed technical data on seismic, hurricane, and high-wind areas, consult the 2006 *IBC*, Chapter 16.

Allowable Tolerances

Industry Standards

Handbook of Construction Tolerances
(John Wiley & Sons)

Wall Framing
6-6. Rough Lumber Framing

Description

Rough lumber framing includes posts, beams, joists, rafters, studs, and other wood framing for residential or commercial construction. It also includes glued laminated timber and heavy timber construction.

Allowable Tolerances

There is not a single, fixed standard for rough lumber framing tolerances. Various documents and industry practices refer to a variety of measurements. In most cases, positional tolerances of framing members of dimensional lumber (less than 5" [127 mm] in nominal dimension) are not critical for the application of finish materials. A tolerance of +/- ¼" (6 mm) is frequently used and is acceptable. For heavy timber construction a tolerance of +/- ½" (13 mm) is often used. However, plumbness tolerance is important because out-of-plumb walls and partitions can be noticeable and can affect the successful application of many finish materials. The *Quality Standards for the Professional Remodeler* and the Insurance/Warranty Documents require that walls be plumb to within ¼" (6 mm) in any 32" (813-mm) vertical measurement. However, a smaller tolerance of ¼" in 10' (6 mm in 3 050 mm) is often recommended for gypsum wallboard and plaster applications. For gypsum wallboard application, the maximum misalignment of adjacent framing members must not exceed ⅛" (3.2 mm).

A tolerance of ¼" in 10' provides a reasonable tolerance for carpenters while allowing gypsum wallboard to be installed without excessive shimming when tighter tolerances of the wallboard surface are required. For example, if a ⅛" in 8' (3.2 mm in 2 440 mm) plumbness is required for a thin-set mortar application of ceramic tile, the gypsum board can be shimmed from a ¼" tolerance to the ⅛" tolerance. However, most wallboard contractors prefer not to shim, so the specifier may want to require that the smaller tolerance be built into the framing specifications.

Floor Framing

6-7. Wood Floor Framing and Subflooring

Description

This section includes wood floors framed with standard wood joists and covered with sub-flooring of plywood, particleboard, or other sheet material as a base for underlayment and other finish flooring.

Allowable Tolerances

As with rough framing, there is no single accepted tolerance for flatness of wood subfloors. In most cases, the required level depends on the type of finish surface used and other considerations, such as whether factory built cabinets will be placed on an uneven floor, requiring shimming. In general, a level tolerance of +/-¼" in 10' (6 mm in 3 050 mm) for new construction is a reasonable expectation and is less than the maximum allowable deflection (L/240 for dead and live load) stated by the IBC. It also allows for slight misalignments of supporting members. However, the *Quality Standards for the Professional Remodeler* and Insurance/Warranty Documents state a more generous maximum out-of-level tolerance of ¼" in 32" (0 mm in 813 mm) measured parallel to the joists. For total variation in a floor surface of a room, the *Quality Standards for the Professional Remodeler* state a tolerance of +/-½" in 20' (13 mm in 6100 mm) while the recommended specification of the Spectext® master specifications is ½" in 30' (13 mm in 9144 mm).

If the floor framing is also supporting a gypsum wallboard ceiling below, the Gypsum Association requires that deflection not exceed L/240 of the span at full design load, where L is the span. In addition, the fastening surface of adjacent joists should not vary by more than ⅛" (3mm).

As with other rough framing, if a smaller tolerance than those mentioned above is required for finish materials, such as ceramic tile or wood flooring, it should be specified.

Comments

Structural Insulated Panels

Structural insulated panels (SIPs) provide a structural/insulation system. They're comprised of a core of rigid foam plastic insulation between two structural skins of oriented strand board (OSB). SIPs are used for walls, roofs, and floors for residential and light commercial structures. SIPs are produced in factories under controlled conditions. Their attributes include structural strength, energy-efficiency and quick installation on-site.

SIPs are more expensive than conventional lumber, but save time on framing, insulating, and sheathing as separate operations. Panels can include electrical chases within their core, which avoids drilling through wall studs. (SIP panels are manufactured according to the home's electrical design.) Window openings can be precut. For some windows, a header may not be required. Panels are manufactured in different sizes, up to 8' x 24'.

The smaller 8' x 4' SIPs can be erected by hand, but large 8' x 24' panels require equipment for unloading at the site and setting in place. SIPs are fastened using staples, nails, or screws. Joints are sealed with SIP mastic, low-expanding foam sealant, and/or SIP tape. Low-expanding foam is used to seal voids between panels and unused electrical chases. SIP wall panels can rest on poured concrete, block, or insulated concrete form foundations.

SIPs are sized to accept dimensional lumber, for example, using SIPs for walls with a conventional truss roof, or conventionally framed walls with an SIP roof. (Consult roofing manufacturers for instructions for installation of their product to SIP panels.)

Modification can be made on site with SIP tools—for example, panels can be cut and the foam core recessed for splines or dimensional lumber with a hot wire foam scoop or special angle grinder attachment.

Crews need some training and education in SIP installation. The Structural Insulated Panel Association (SIPA), a non-profit trade association representing

(continued)

manufacturers, suppliers, fabricators/distributors, design professionals, and builders, provides information on their website and by phone.

Green Attributes

The R value of SIPs results in significant energy savings that may enable the building's HVAC system to be downsized. SIPs are also more airtight than conventionally framed homes. Reducing energy use translates to a cleaner environment.

Since SIP homes are more airtight, incoming air and humidity can be better controlled, which can make a home more comfortable and less prone to mold and other allergens.

The production of SIP insulation does require some petroleum, but its insulation, a rigid foam plastic, is comprised of 98% air, according to SIPA. SIPs should result in less material waste going to the landfill, since panels are prefabricated.

Structural Strength

SIPA compares the structural characteristics of SIPs to those of steel I-Beams, with the OSB skin acting as the flange, and the rigid foam core as the web—an advantage in handling in plane compressive loads. Detailed information on the structural performance of SIPs is available from SIPA member manufacturers.

For more information about SIPs, as well as technical support, visit **www.sips.org**

Framing Tolerances

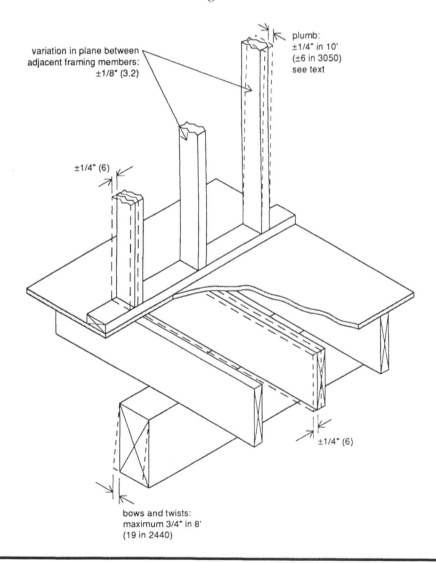

Figure 5.48

Courtesy of John Wiley & Sons, *Handbook of Construction Tolerances*

CHAPTER 6

FINISH CARPENTRY & CABINETRY

Table of Contents

Text in blue type indicates excerpted summaries from the International Building Code® *(IBC)* and International Residential Code® *(IRC). Please consult the IBC and IRC for complete coverage and specific wording. "Comments" (in solid blue boxes) were written by the editors, based on their own experience.*

These icons will appear with references to green building practices and seismic regulations, respectively.

CHAPTER 6

FINISH CARPENTRY & CABINETRY

Common Defect Allegations

Generally, there is a statute of limitations on patent defects of between two and five years for cabinetry and finish carpentry, depending on the nature of the failure. Patent defects are observable, as opposed to latent defects, which are concealed. Since patent defects are generally conspicuous, they tend to be handled as part of the punch list after initial occupancy. Claims are often associated with water or flooding and are related to particleboard expansion. Particleboard is, in fact, an acceptable material in all grades of cabinetry, contrary to some opinions.

Other claims may involve gaps at mitered or non-mitered trim and moulding joints, visible nails or nail holes (usually considered a defect in painting and finishing), and visible hammer marks on interior trim.

Cabinet installation defects include gaps between cabinets and walls, and failure of doors or drawers to operate properly. Countertop issues include scratched surfaces, delamination, and installation out of level.

Introduction

Finish carpentry and wood cabinetry are categorized under Finishes and Furnishings and are not usually associated with the structural integrity of a building. Consequently, building codes have very little to address in these areas. Standards for these aspects of construction are therefore set primarily by professional associations and published textbooks.

This chapter provides standards primarily from those developed by the Architectural Woodwork Institute, the Woodwork Institute, and the National Kitchen & Bath Association. The Kitchen Cabinet Manufacturers Association also provides a standard for cabinet manufacture. The following page lists contact information for all these organizations.

Architectural Woodwork Institute
571-323-3636
www.awinet.org
AWI's mission is to improve industry standards, provide technical help for design professionals, and research new and better materials and methods for engineering, fabricating, finishing, and installing fine architectural woodwork. AWI has published *Architectural Woodwork Quality Standards Illustrated*, 8th Edition, Version 2.0, which includes specifications and specifically defines quality grades for architectural woodwork. The *AWI Quality Standards* have been used for over 45 years by owners' representatives for the specification of architectural woodwork.

The Architectural Woodwork Institute has established and defined three grades of quality for wood finishes and woodwork: economy, custom, and premium. (When AWI standards are referenced in the specifications, but no grade is specified, AWI Custom Grade Standards are considered the prevailing grade. Economy is defined as "areas out of public view, such as mechanical rooms;" custom as "high quality, appropriate for most jobs;" and premium as "special jobs with exceptional requirements.")

Woodwork Institute
916-372-9943
www.wicnet.org
Woodwork Institute (formerly the Woodwork Institute of California) also defines quality grades (materials and installation requirements) for architectural woodwork, with particular emphasis on cabinetry and millwork. Woodwork Institute's grades are included in this chapter.

National Kitchen & Bath Association (NKBA)
800-843-6522
www.nkba.org
The National Kitchen & Bath Association (NKBA) has a certification program to test minimum requirements of a kitchen and bath designer's or distributor's job. The exams are based primarily on the NKBA's installation and technical manuals and universal planning books. NKBA's *Kitchen & Bathroom Installation Manuals* detail methods of kitchen and bathroom installation.

Kitchen Cabinet Manufacturers Association (KCMA)
703-264-1690
www.kcma.org

Ed. Note: Comments and recommendations within this chapter are not intended as a definitive resource for construction activities. For building projects, contractors must rely on the project documents and applicable code requirements pertaining to their own particular locations.

Green Material Alternatives

Green Building: Project Planning & Cost Estimating,
Second Edition

(RSMeans)

Architectural Woodwork

Use of reclaimed timbers, where available, helps preserve old-growth forests while making use of, rather than discarding, a valuable existing resource.

Cabinetry

To improve indoor air quality, formaldehyde-free, low-VOC glues should be specified for both binders and laminate adhesives. Wheat-based fiberboard and other products from agricultural by-products are also excellent choices. If standard particleboard or fiberboard is used, it is important to ensure that the millwork is completely wrapped in laminate (including the edges) to reduce the off-gassing of VOCs (particularly urea-formaldehyde).

Natural finishing products such as resins, beeswax, shellac, and linseed and tung oils have lower toxicity and are better for air quality.

Green Home Improvement

Many cabinets, as well as bathroom vanities and shelving, are made from particleboard or medium density fiberboard (MDF). These materials consist of sawdust and wood shavings, both waste products from lumber mills and plywood production. The wood fibers are bonded together by a small amount of plastic resin, which contains the potentially toxic chemical, formaldehyde.

Particleboard is used as a core material for interior doors, cabinets, bookcases, desks, vanities, and furniture. Medium-density fiberboard is also used to make furniture and cabinets, as well as moulding. All of these products release tiny amounts of formaldehyde, a suspected carcinogen, into the air. In concentrations well below those we can detect through our sense of smell, formaldehyde can also cause a rare, but debilitating autoimmune disease, known as multiple chemical sensitivity (MCS).

MCS is marked by allergy like and other physical reactions to several types of air pollutants, such as out-gassed chemicals from plastics, paints, carpeting, and so forth. Once exposed, people with MCS become highly sensitive to numerous other chemicals, including conventional paints, stains, and finishes. Many who suffer from MCS must strip their homes of all offending products. Unfortunately, breathing even small amounts of formaldehyde may also increase risk for nasal and lung cancer.

To avoid formaldehyde, you can custom-order cabinets made from solid wood or PrimeBoard, an MDF substitute made from wheat straw and a non-formaldehyde-producing resin. (There is also low-VOC cabinetry, as well as high-recycled-content cabinetry, made from MDF board [Norbord].) Request that cabinets be stained and finished with no-VOC products, made from FSC-certified solid wood or wheat straw material, formaldehyde-free agriboard case/drawer material, and low-VOC glues, adhesives, and finishes.

An alternative to custom-made cabinets is used cabinetry from local building supply salvage outlets. In a garage or pantry, where aesthetics are not as much of a concern, metal cabinets might be a solution.

Finish Carpentry

Comments

Finish carpentry involves the installation of finish woods (and trim made of plastic or molded polyurethane materials) to provide a finished appearance to installed doors, windows, stairs, and other features of a structure's interior. Elements include **casing** (the trim around window perimeters and the sides and head of doors), **baseboard** (the trim around the base perimeter of rooms) and (for stairs) **railings, newel posts, balusters, skirt boards,** and **cheek boards.** Interior trim installations also include **cornice moulding, chair rails, columns, mantels, grilles, louvers, paneling,** and **shelving.**

Contractors should find information on the location, size, type, and proposed arrangement of interior finish carpentry items on the project drawings—particularly the interior elevations and wall sections. Details are often provided to clarify a section of work.

Ed. Note: "Cabinetry, Millwork & Countertops," the second section of this chapter, contains an excerpt from the Woodwork Institute. To maintain its continuity, we have left this WIC text intact, rather than breaking out references such as "Trim" and "Shelving" and combining them with information presented under those headings in the first section. We recommend referring to both "Finish Carpentry" and "Cabinetry, Millwork, & Countertops" for the most complete perspective on architectural woodwork items.

Storage of Materials & Timing of Installation

Ed. Note: See also "Cabinetry, Millwork & Countertops" later in this chapter, which provides the Woodwork Institute's guidelines for delivery and storage of casework and countertops.

Comments

In regions with high humidity, wood trim, paneling, and doors should be allowed 24 hours to acclimate to the ambient humidity before installation.

No interior finish work should begin before the structure has been closed in and protected by a waterproof roof. Windows and doors should be in place (or openings at least temporarily closed) in order to control humidity and

temperature. Wood materials intended for use as trim should not be stored in an excessively moist environment. If job conditions are damp, materials should be delivered close to the time they will be installed. Prefinished materials require extra care in storage and handling.

Following is the order in which finish carpentry items are typically performed:

- Install trim window openings, mouldings (except base), stair rails, and stairs.
- Install cabinets, interior doors and trim, and wood flooring. (Wood flooring may be installed before or after the cabinets.)
- Install hardware. (If painting will follow, hardware may be fit, then removed for painting, then permanently installed.)

Standing & Running Trim

Comments

Interior trim (finish) is generally broken into two categories:

Standing trim, such as window and door casings, which can be created using single lengths of wood.

Running trim, trim of continuing length, such as baseboard, cornices, chair rail, and shoe moulding.

The applications of trim are not structural in nature, but proper installation may contribute to the integrity of the building element they serve to enhance. A door or window casing, when correctly applied, becomes an integral part of the assembly and can extend the utility of the unit.

AWI's publication *Architectural Woodwork Quality Standards Illustrated* provides standards for sawing and planing, and also recommends methods of cutting that will not only make cost-effective use of materials, but also reduce stress on the finished component, thereby reducing the chance of twisting, warping, and bowing. AWI's standards also describe their recommended methods for creating radius mouldings.

Figures 6.1–6.2 are tables showing AWI's standards for material and workmanship for moulding installation.

Standing & Running Trim: Standards for Material & Workmanship

300-T-2
Materials

Hardwood members exceeding dimensions defined in Section 100 may be glued for width and thickness.

If total length exceeds the available length of the species as defined in Section 100, members can have plant-prepared joints for field assembly. Unless otherwise specified or detailed, the following standards shall apply:

	Premium		Custom		Economy	
	Transparent	Opaque	Transparent	Opaque	Transparent	Opaque
Lumber Grade	I	II	II	II	II	II
Cut of Lumber	Plain sawn	Plain sawn or MDF	Plain sawn	Plain sawn or MDF	Plain sawn	Plain sawn or MDF*

300-T-3
Workmanship

	Premium	Custom	Economy
Finger-jointed lengths	Not permitted	Not permitted	Permitted
Exposed End (Return)	Plant Made	Not Required	Not Required
With Non Exposed Ends*	Backed Out	Backed Out	Flat Back
Plant Assembly of Trim Members (Must be Specified)	Lemon Spline Butterfly, Scarf or Dowel	Clamp Nails or Lemon Spline, Butterfly, Scarf or Dowel	Not Required
Factory Manufactured Radius Mouldings	Factory shaped and glued to longest practical lengths, for installation with smooth transitions.		Not Required
Minimum Lengths	Lengths of trim pieces are governed by material availability. Consult Section 100 for data.		

*Note: Door and window trim with non-exposed ends shall be backed out in Premium and Custom Grades when the width exceeds 2 inches. Other trims are backed out at manufacturer option.

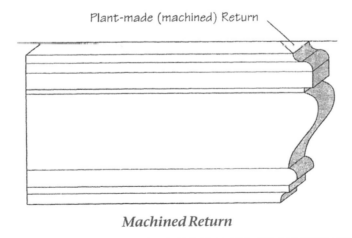

Plant-made (machined) Return

Machined Return

Courtesy of Architectural Woodwork Institute, *Architectural Woodwork Quality Standards Illustrated*, 8th version 2.0 [Tables 300-T-2 and 300 T-3]

Figure 6.1

Tables of Section Installation Standards

In the absence of specifications, the following standards will apply. Where more than one method or material is listed, AWI/AWMAC woodworkers will supply their choice from the alternatives.

Standards are separated by function: Required or Not required; Permitted or Not permitted, as appropriate.

- Items deemed Required shall be accomplished when practical.
- Items deemed Not required shall be accomplished when practical at the option of the installer.
- Items deemed Permitted shall be accomplished when practical at the option of the installer.
- Items deemed Not permitted shall not be performed in the absence of direct specification or bulletin.
- When the installer chooses to use a process of a higher grade than specified, it is permitted. Upon completion of the installation, shims and grounds shall not be visible, the installer shall clean all items of pencil or ink marks, excess adhesive, etc., and the area of his operations shall be broom clean, depositing debris in containers provided by the General Contractor.
- Open joint, visible machine marks, cross sanding, tears, nicks, chips, and/or scratches shall not be permitted unless part of the design aesthetic, such as hand carved, distressed, and/or rustic work.
- Installed solid lumber shall meet the Grades in Section 100-Lumber.
- Installed wood veneers shall meet the Grades in Section 200-Panel Products.
- Other installed products shall meet the material requirements of these standards.

The entire installation shall present Good Workmanship for the Grade specified.

Figure 6.2   Courtesy of Architectural Woodwork Institute, *Architectural Woodwork Quality Standards Illustrated*, [Table 1700-T-3]

Paneling

Comments

Paneling, generally produced in 4' x 8' sheets, is available in a wide range of wood materials and quality. Manufacturers' recommendations should be strictly adhered to, both for installation and for the proper storage and handling of the panels. Following are some general guidelines:

- Vertical panels should be installed in a plumb manner, and horizontal panels should be level.
- Panels may be fastened in a variety of ways including nailed, glued, mechanically fastened, or a combination of these methods.
- Paneling accessories include jointing devices, corner mouldings, and ceiling and base mouldings, which may be used to finish the applications. Or, panels may be "scribed," thereby eliminating the need for any type of finish moulding.
- For commercial applications, the installer must follow the installation instructions that are generally included within the specification. A specification usually requires the contractor to submit

manufacturers' literature regarding the quality, color, characteristics, and other information specific to the panel materials selected.

- Unless otherwise specified, panel joints should be tight and free of rough edges and defects.
- Unless otherwise specified, fasteners and adhesives should not be noticeable.
- Panels should be flat, without buckling or deformity of surfaces.

Wood Stairs & Railings

Comments

Building stairs is generally considered a specialty within the carpentry field. Stair components are often fabricated in a mill, and assembled by the carpenter on-site. Stairs must conform to rigid construction standards and adhere to building codes. Standard riser heights and tread widths have been established around ranges that may vary depending on tolerances developed by building code officials. Designers and builders should consult with local regulating authorities for their most current standards.

Interpretation of current code requirements is particularly important when designing and constructing special stairs, such as winders and curved stairways. Requirements for landing sizes and locations and door swings are also key factors.

Because finished stair tread, riser, and other dimensional requirements must be established before stairs are framed, excerpts from the building code requirements are included in Chapter 5, "Wood Framing." However, here are some rules of thumb according to the International Residential Code and International Building Code:

- Stairs should be at least 36" wide, for a building occupant load of 50 or fewer, and at least 44" for more than 50 occupants.
- Riser height (distance between finished treads) should be between 4" and 7^3/$_4$", depending on occupancy. All risers should be a consistent height.
- Tread depth (or "run") should also be consistent, between 10" and 11", depending on occupancy.
- Handrails should be installed between 34"–38" above the tread. A space of 1^1/$_2$" should be provided between wall and handrail.
- Balustrades on landings or balconies should be 36" above the finished landing, and 44" for commercial projects. A guardrail may also be necessary.

ADA-Compliant Stairs

Industry Standards

Means ADA Compliance Pricing Guide, **Second Edition**
(RSMeans)

Ed. Note: "ADAAG" stands for Americans with Disabilities Act Accessibility Guidelines. For further information, or to obtain copies of this material, call the ADA Technical Assistance Center at 800-514-0301 or visit their website **www.ada.gov**

ADAAG References:

210, Stairways

216.4, Signs at Egress Stairs

302, Floor or Ground Surfaces

307, Protruding Objects

504, Stairways

505, Handrails

Where Applicable

All stairs that are part of a means of egress. Local building codes, however, may require all stairs to meet ADAAG requirements. Also, all stairs must meet the handrail requirements.

Design Requirements

- Protection against bumping head below stairs for 80" height or less. If protection is a rail, maximum height of rail is 27".
- Minimum tread depth of 11"; minimum riser height of 4"; maximum riser of 7".
- Slip-resistant surface.
- A 2% slope is allowed for drainage. No pooling water allowed on exterior stairs and landings.
- No protrusion greater than $1\frac{1}{2}$" over the tread below. Underside of nosing sloped back at a 30° angle or less with the riser.
- Radius of the leading edge $\frac{1}{2}$" or less.
- No open risers.
- Rails on both sides, 34" to 38" above nosing, $1\frac{1}{2}$" exactly from the wall, with no rotation in fittings.
- Rails $1\frac{1}{4}$" to 2" diameter round, or, if not round, the perimeter between 4" and $6\frac{1}{4}$" and the maximum width $2\frac{1}{4}$".
- Continuous inside rail without interruption by newel posts or other construction. Brackets attached to bottom are acceptable if they drop $1\frac{1}{2}$" or more before returning to the wall.
- Rail extension: 12" minimum extension at the top parallel to the floor. Length of one tread, minimum, at the bottom, following the slope of the stair. Return to wall, post, or floor.

Ornamental Woodwork

Comments

This finish carpentry item includes decorative and functional components such as mantels, grilles, columns, corbels, and balusters.

Industry Standards

Architectural Woodwork Quality Standards Illustrated, **Eighth Edition, Version 2.0**
(Architectural Woodwork Institute)

700–G–4: Installation Recommendation (when specified)

While this section does not cover field installation of woodwork, the methods and skill involved in the installation of woodwork in large measure determine the final appearance of the project. The design, detailing, and fabrication should be directed toward achieving installation with a minimum of exposed face fastening. The use of interlocking wood cleats or metal hanging clips combined with accurate furring and shimming will accomplish this. Such hanging of woodwork has the additional advantage of permitting movement that results from humidity changes or building movement. Depending upon local practice, in many areas woodworkers will perform the wall preparation and installation of the woodwork.

700–G–5: Finishing Recommendation (when specified)

While this section does not cover finishing be aware that site conditions for finishing are rarely conducive to good results. Poor lighting, dust-laden air, and techniques available are limiting factors. Depending upon local practice, in many areas woodworkers will factory finish, yielding better results than can be achieved from field finishing.

Moulded Urethane

Comments

Moulded urethane products are designed for weather resistant exterior applications, and are suitable for most

(continued)

interior applications. Section 2605 of the IBC restricts plastic veneer attached to the exterior walls of a building to heights no more than 50' above grade. Local fire officials must be consulted to determine approval for the type of material and allowable height at which it may be applied. Most building codes address plastic interior trim and require specific information on smoke generation and flame test data. For interior use, it is suggested that applicable codes be consulted for compliance with flame-spread values.

Guidelines for Installation

- Urethane millwork (with the exception of balustrade systems and porch posts) should be used for decorative purposes only, not for structural support.
- For best results, noncorrosive fasteners should be used with the manufacturer's recommended adhesives.
- Materials should not be stored in extreme heat and humidity and should be acclimated to the site prior to installation.
- Cut surfaces should be primed and painted within a few days of installation.
- Urethane millwork should never be placed in an area subject to solar temperature buildups, such as behind a storm door.
- Joinery for urethane millwork should be to the same standard as for wood millwork—finishes should be better than or equal to wood.

Shelving

Comments

The designer of a project has no control over the weight of contents that may eventually be placed on shelving by the building user. The probability exists that shelves will be overloaded beyond their design strength. While the shelves may not break, they may deflect or sag severely enough to jeopardize the shelf support system, and become aesthetically unacceptable to the user.

The following information was developed for use primarily by manufacturers of custom casework. While it includes technical data such as the formula to compute deflection, it also provides information a contractor needs to answer these questions: How much weight will the proposed shelves hold? What material, thickness, span, and width will result in functional shelving that retains an acceptable appearance?

Industry Standards

Architectural Woodwork Quality Standards Illustrated, Eight Edition, Version 2.0
(Architectural Woodwork Institute)

Shelf Deflection Information

The Department of Wood Science in the Division of Forestry at West Virginia University conducted a study for the Architectural Woodwork Institute regarding the deflection of wood shelving materials under various amounts of stress. The following table represents their findings with the various products tested.

The table shows total uniformly distributed load requirements necessary to cause deflection of $1/4$" in shelves and 8" and 12" wide with spans (i.e., unfixed, supported at each end) of 30, 36, 42, and 48 inches. Load required to deflect shelves more or less than $1/4$" may be estimated by direct proportion. For example, the uniformly distributed load required to cause a deflection of $1/8$" is one-half that of the value in the table. For width different than 8" or 12" (the values used in the table), load required to cause a $1/4$" deflection may also be determined by direct proportion. A 6" wide shelf, for example, will deflect twice as much as a 12" wide shelf under the same load.

The following equation shows how deflection is related to shelf dimensions, width, thickness, span, load per inch of span and E-value, a material property which measures stiffness or resistance to deflection. The higher the E-value, the less the deflection. When a shelf is made with several materials, each with its own E-value, a composite E-value must be determined.

To compute deflection:

$$D = \frac{0.1563wl^4}{Ebh^3}$$

In which the values are:

D = deflection (in inches)

w = load per lineal inch of span

l = span (length)

E = modulus of elasticity

b = base (width)

h = depth (thickness)

Ed. Note: See "Finishing of Millwork," item III D "Library Shelving" later in this chapter for information on finishing shelves.

Shelf Deflection of 1/4" by Estimated Total Distributed Load in Pounds

Material	Thickness	Span	30"		36"		42"		48"	
		Width	8"	12"	8"	12"	8"	12"	8"	12"
Yellow-Poplar / Red Gum / Sweet Gum	lumber 3/4"		322 lbs.	483 lbs.	189 lbs.	284 lbs.	117 lbs.	175 lbs.	78 lbs.	117 lbs.
	1-1/16"		912	1368	538	807	332	498	221	332
Hard Maple / Pecan / Red Oak	lumber 3/4"		356	534	209	313	133	206	88	232
	1-1/16"		1011	1516	592	888	373	560	249	374
Birch / Hickory	lumber 3/4"		400	600	232	348	146	219	977	146
	1-1/16"		1134	1701	660	990	414	621	277	415
Medium Density Particleboard (raw or covered with "melamine")	3/4"		78	117	46	69	29	43	19	28
	1"		185	277	109	164	69	102	45	66
Medium Density Fiberboard (raw or covered with "melamine")	3/4"		100	150	58	87	36	54	25	38
	1"		237	356	137	206	85	128	59	90
Birch faced plywood, veneer core	3/4"		145	218	86	129	54	81	36	54
Birch faced plywood, medium density particleboard core	3/4"		125	188	72	109	46	68	31	46
Medium density particleboard covered two sides and one edge with nominal 0.028" high pressure decorative laminate	3/4" (core)		174	261	100	139	64	96	42	63
Medium density particleboard covered two sides and one edge with nominal 0.050" high pressure decorative laminate	3/4" (core)		234	350	137	205	86	129	58	87
Medium density particleboard with 1/8" solid lumber edge	3/4"		89	139	53	79	33	50	22	33
Medium density particleboard with 3/4" solid lumber edge	3/4"		100	150	60	90	42	63	25	38
Medium density particleboard with 3/4" x 1-1/2" solid lumber dropped edge	3/4"		384	435	216	241	132	152	92	107

NOTE: All medium density particle board is ANSI 208.1-1998 Type M-2.
The information and ratings stated here pertain to material currently offered and represent results of tests believed to be reliable. However, due to variation in handling and methods not known or under our control, neither the AWI nor the AWMAC can make any warranties or guarantees as to end result.

Figure 6.3

Courtesy of Architectural Woodwork Institute, *Architectural Woodwork Quality Standards Illustrated*

Cabinetry, Millwork & Countertops

Millwork

Industry Standards

Means Graphic Construction Standards
(RSMeans)

Millwork refers to finish material made of wood, plastic, and sometimes molded gypsum or polyurethane. Millwork can be custom designed and fabricated, or factory-fabricated or milled.

The millwork contractor will commonly furnish the following wood items: doors, windows, factory- and custom-fabricated cabinetry and casework, columns, mantels, grilles, louvers, mouldings, paneling, railings, shelving, siding and stairs.

Plastic materials include laminates, cabinets, mouldings, doors and windows.

Factory-molded gypsum and polyurethane, medallions, mantels, stair brackets, door and window features and mouldings may also be supplied under the millwork contract.

Comments

Solid surface items, such as countertops, may be included in millwork packages.

Delivery & Storage

Industry Standards

WIC Manual of Millwork (Effective 5/1/03)
(Woodwork Institute, www.wicnet.org)
Ed. Note: The following excerpts from the Woodwork Institute include only information that applies directly to finish carpentry and cabinetry.

Recommended Care and Storage of Architectural Woodwork
II. Delivery and Storage

A. The delivery of all items of architectural millwork shall be as required by a progress schedule furnished by the general contractor, and subject to conditions as follows:

1. Delivery of architectural millwork shall be made only when the area of operation is enclosed, all plaster and concrete work dry, and the area broom clean.

2. A clean storage area, well ventilated and protected from direct sunlight, excessive heat, rain or moisture, in which the relative humidity is between 45% and 65% at 60° to 90° F, and EMC (Equilibrium Moisture Content) conditions between 8% and 12%, shall be provided and maintained at the building site by the general contractor. The air conditioning or heating system shall be on and functioning, and the architectural millwork shall be acclimated to these conditions for 72 hours prior to installation.

3. Millwork should not be subjected to abnormal heat, extreme dryness, humid conditions, sudden changes in temperature, or direct sunlight.

4. If the above paragraphs are not adhered to, severe damage could result to the millwork. The fabricator of the work shall not be held responsible for any damage that might develop by not adhering to the above paragraphs.

E. Cabinets should be handled carefully and set or stored on a level floor. Care should be taken to protect the exposed finished portions from bumping, scratching, etc. Never use cabinets or counters for "work benches" or convenient places to store other materials.

F. Plastic tops should be stacked flat if possible, at least 4" off the floor, with a protective covering under the bottom unit, and covered on top to protect surfaces from scratching. Strips of wood or other suitable materials should be placed between tops. If tops are fully-formed or have splashes attached, extreme care must be taken to prevent breaking. Never stand or stack plastic tops on end against a wall where they can be broken or damaged by falling.

Wood Casework

Comments

Successful cabinetry begins with a complete set of shop drawings. These drawings should include the following:

- Cabinet Grade
- Door Schedule & Details
- Hardware Elevations and Profiles
- Finishes
- Drawer Assembly Details
- Floor & Wall Connections
- Countertop & Splash
- Overhang
- Laminate Selections
- Adhesive
- Selection
- Backpriming Treatments
- Method of Joining
- Sealant Specifications

The drawings should be issued first as a preliminary and reissued after approvals, so that corrections can be incorporated into the working set.

Cabinetry can generally be separated into three categories: Commercial, Industrial/Laboratory, and Residential. Classifying cabinets into one of the categories is one way to establish a grade standard for the product. As with many other trades, cabinet contractors or mill shops often specialize in either commercial/industrial fabrication or residential cabinetry.

Commercial and industrial cabinets require full design and specifications due to special requirements, finishes, or aesthetics of a project. Architects or designers are usually retained to provide specifications.

In recent years, the industry has moved toward "European" frameless construction and prefabricated modular cabinets built in a factory assembly line. Factory-built modular cabinets offer more standardized construction and incorporate the latest technology for cabinet finishes at a more economical price.

Some cabinet contractors build the cabinet boxes in their shops and purchase prefinished doors and drawer fronts from a supplier. This is because many states now prohibit the use of oil-based paint products and lacquers unless there are elaborate ventilating and hazardous waste systems installed at the shop. Now terms such as "conversion varnish" and "thermafoil" have replaced lacquer and sprayed polyurethane.

The cabinet industry is one of the fastest growing and evolving trades. A large contributor to this growth has been the dramatic increase in residential kitchen remodeling. We can expect that new standards will continue to be established and published in the near future.

Good planning will keep damage to millwork and cabinetry to a minimum. After fabrication, there should be only one more handling—the delivery to the job site and the installation.

I. Wood Casework—Scope

A. **Casework** shall be fabricated complete in the mill to field dimensions. At manufacturer's option one of the following will be supplied unless specified otherwise:

   a. Type I—multiple self-supporting units fastened together to form a larger unit.

   b. Type II—a single length section as required, or in such sections as access openings will permit.

II. Casework Grades

A. **Economy Grade** establishes a standard to meet the requirements of lower cost residential and commercial construction where economy is the principal factor, and for use in storage and utility areas.

B. **Custom Grade** includes all the requisites of high quality casework and is suitable for all normal uses in high grade construction, such as higher quality construction for residential, school, medical facilities, and commercial buildings.

C. **Premium Grade** as the name implies, is a superior quality of materials and craftsmanship, with a corresponding increase in cost. It is intended, primarily, for the best of natural hardwood construction; but any species of wood may be specified.

D. **Laboratory Grade** is intended for usage in chemistry or "hard acid" areas where exposed or semi-exposed portions of the cabinet require additional protection. This grade shall meet all the requirements of Premium Grade. Grades contain additional requirements. (Specifications shall indicate any special finishing requirements for exposed and semi-exposed surfaces.)

Special Note: All grades shall meet requirements for Economy Grade. Custom, Premium, and Laboratory Grades contain additional requirements.

Seismic Zones 3 & 4

 Seismic Forces Requirements: The WIC has had tests performed for several types of cabinet construction that meet the seismic forces requirements for Title 24. The types of construction are: Doweled, Confirmat Screws, Modeez®, Fully Plowed-in Back, and Backs Screwed on in rabbeted ends, tops, and bottoms. The exact method of cabinet construction for each of these tests would be available from organizations as the Woodwork Institute.

III. Casework Specification Requirements

For clarity of bid and fabrication, the job drawings and specifications should clearly indicate or specify the following:

A. **Grade Desired.** If the grade is not specified, it shall be Custom Grade.

C. **Construction Style and Type Desired.**

   1. Construction Style. At manufacturers' option, one of the following will be supplied, unless otherwise specified.

Plan View: Casework Construction Style & Type

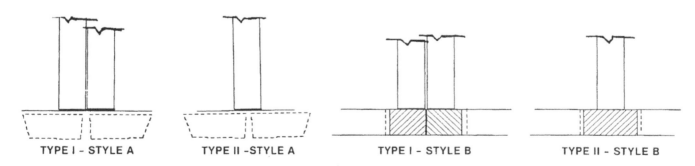

TYPE I - STYLE A   TYPE II - STYLE A   TYPE I - STYLE B   TYPE II - STYLE B

Courtesy of Woodwork Institute, *WIC Manual of Millwork*

Figure 6.4

a. Style A—Frameless

b. Style B—Face Frame

2. Construction Type. At manufacturers' option, one of the following will be supplied, unless otherwise specified.

a. Type I Construction. Multiple self-supporting units fastened together to form a larger unit.

Note: For Type I Construction, Custom and Premium Grades, joints are permitted where ends are flush with cabinet tops. In each unit, the exposed edges of the ends shall be banded with the same material as the exposed surfaces. If other construction is desired, it shall be so specified.

D. WIC Cabinet Design Series

1. Individual cabinets may be listed by a **Standard Design Number System.**

2. Cabinets shall be Type I frameless construction only and are limited to flush overlay or reveal overlay styles, unless otherwise specified.

3. Finished ends shall be either applied panels or integral members on the end cabinet. Gaps at wall-to-wall installations shall be closed by filler panels not to exceed 1½" in width.

4. Cabinets may be specified to be any desired dimensions. Industry standards indicate outside dimensions, unless otherwise specified.

E. Exposed Material. Indicate the following:

1. Intended finish, opaque or transparent.

2. Species and veneer cut. If veneer cut is not specified, Rotary Cut or Plain Sliced will be furnished at the option of the manufacturer.

3. Flame-Spread Class, if required.

F. Toe space will be considered concealed, unless otherwise specified.

G. Special Treatment of Semi-Exposed Surfaces

1. Interior surfaces of open cabinets or behind glass doors for WIC Economy and Custom Grades are considered semi-exposed. If it is desired that these open surfaces match the exposed, it shall be specified.

2. If it is desired that a particular portion of any semi-exposed surface be a material other

than minimum requirements of this section, it shall be specified.

H. Door and Drawer Front Style Desired

1. Flush overlay.

2. Reveal overlay (specify reveal dimension).

3. Lipped.

4. Flush.

J. If security or dust panels, tote trays, and levelers are desired, they shall be so specified.

K. Backs

1. If backs are desired for Economy Grade.

2. The thickness if other than 1¼" minimum for Custom and Premium Grade.

L. Shelves

1. If thicker shelves or center shelf supports are desired due to heavy loads, it shall be specified.

2. Thickness and type of glass for shelves shall be specified.

M. Cabinet Hardware Desired, Type, Manufacturer, and Finish

If not specified, selection shall be at the option of the manufacturer from Supplement 1, except in the case of pre-engineered drawer box systems whose use must be pre-approved in the specifications.

O. Cabinet installation by manufacturer, if desired, shall be specified.

P. Run and Match of Wood Grain

If it is desired that wood grain pattern is to run and match vertically, it shall be so specified, otherwise the drawer fronts may run horizontally at the option of manufacturer. For Premium Grade, vertical match is required.

Q. If provisions for the WIC Grade specified are in conflict with or modified by the drawings and specifications, the drawings and specifications shall govern.

R. Factory Finishing

1. If desired, it shall be specified.

2. Any special finish desired for Laboratory Grade exposed and semi-exposed portions.

Ed. Note: See "Finishing of Millwork" later in this chapter for more information on factory finishing.

S. For job site finishing, it is recommended that the following be included in the painting specifications:

"Before finishing the exposed surface of all millwork, the finishing contractor shall remove handling marks or effects of exposure to moisture with a thorough final sanding over all surfaces of the exposed portions, using at least 150 grit or finer sandpaper, and shall thoroughly clean all surfaces before applying sealer and finish."

IV. Casework Definitions

A. Exposed Portions

1. All surfaces visible when doors and drawers are closed, including knee spaces.

2. Underside of bottoms of cabinets over 4'-0" above finished floor, including bottoms behind light valances.

3. Cabinet tops under 6'-0" above finished floor or if 6'-0" and over and visible from an upper building level or floor.

4. Visible front edges of web frames, ends, divisions, tops, shelves, and hanging stiles.

5. Sloping tops of cabinets that are visible.

6. Visible surfaces in open cabinets or behind glass for Premium Grade.

7. Interior faces of hinged doors for Premium Grade.

8. Visible portions of bottoms, tops, and ends in front of sliding doors in Custom and Premium Grades only.

B. Semi-Exposed Portions

1. Shelves.

2. Divisions.

3. Interior face of ends, backs, and bottoms.

4. Drawer sides, sub-fronts, backs, and bottoms. Also included are the interior surfaces of cabinet top members when the top member is 36" or more above the finished floor.

5. The underside of bottoms of wall cabinets between 2'-0" and 4'-0" above the finished floor.

6. Interior faces of hinged doors, except Premium Grade.

7. Visible surfaces in open cabinets or behind glass for Economy and Custom Grades and all rooms designated as storage, janitor, closet, or utility.

8. Visible portion of bottoms, tops, and ends in front of sliding doors in Economy Grade only.

C. Concealed Portions

1. Toe space unless otherwise specified.

2. Sleepers.

3. Web frames, stretchers, and solid sub-tops.

4. Security panels.

5. Underside of bottoms of cabinets less than 2'-6" above the finished floor.

6. Flat tops of cabinets 6'-0" or more above the finished floor, except if visible from an upper building level.

7. The three non-visible edges of adjustable shelves.

8. The underside of countertops, knee spaces, and drawer aprons.

9. The faces of cabinet ends of adjoining units that butt together.

VI. Workmanship

A. **The assembled cabinet** shall present **First Class Workmanship**.

B. **Assembly.** Cabinets shall be assembled complete in the mill with doors, drawers, and hardware installed, unless otherwise specified.

C. **Rigidity.** Where essential to produce a rigid assembly, mechanical fasteners or glue shall be used.

D. **Casework Protection.** Casework shall be protected with skids, bracing, and corner guards or other protection as may be required to assure protection from rough handling.

E. **Casework** shall be free of adhesive overspray, fabrication marks, and shop accumulated dirt.

VIII. Material Requirements—Grade Rules

A. Exposed Portions

1. All wood grains shall be furnished as rotary cut or plain sliced at fabricator's option unless otherwise specified. Plywood grain and color do not match with grain and color of solid stock.

2. For transparent finish, if the species is not specified, the use of hardwood or softwood

(plywood or solid stock) of one species for the entire job is permitted, at the option of the manufacturer.

    a. For Custom Grade, solid stock and/or plywood shall be compatible in color and grain.

    b. For Premium Grade, solid stock shall be well matched for color and grain; plywood shall be compatible in color with solid stock; and adjacent plywood panels shall be well matched for color and grain.

    c. See Glossary for definition of compatible in color and well-matched for color and grain.

3. For Economy Grade, opaque finish, softwood plywood, particleboard, medium density fiberboard, medium density overlay, hardwood plywood, and solid stock are permitted.

4. For Custom Grade, opaque finish, particleboard, medium density fiberboard, medium density overlay, hardwood plywood, and solid stock are permitted.

5. For Premium Grade, opaque finish, softwood plywood is **not** permitted; medium density fiberboard, hardwood plywood are permitted. Hardwood plywood and solid stock shall be close grained only (i.e., birch and maple).

B. Semi-Exposed Portions

1. May be of species and grain other than exposed portions. When any surface is required to be the same species and grain as the exposed portion or if all materials are required to be one species and grain, it shall be so specified. For Premium Grade, all semi-exposed portions behind glass or in open cases shall be the same species, color, grain and grade as the exposed material.

2. For transparent finish, particleboard or medium density fiberboard is not permitted for open cabinets or behind glass doors.

3. May be of material other than exposed portions. Acceptable materials include any overlay material identified in Section 15, paragraph VIII, B, 1, a through g, or any mill option hardwood plywood. Color or species will be consistent throughout semi-exposed surfaces on entire job.

Casework Specification Requirements: Definitions

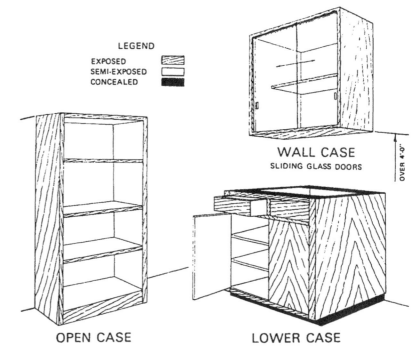

LEGEND

EXPOSED

SEMI-EXPOSED

CONCEALED

NOTE: Inside surfaces of open shelf cabinets and surfaces behind glass are considered exposed for **Premium Grade.** Tops of tall cabinets and upper cabinets 6' and over that are visible from upper levels are considered exposed.

WALL CASE

SLIDING GLASS DOORS

OVER 4'-0"

OPEN CASE

LOWER CASE

Figure 6.5

Courtesy of Woodwork Institute, *WIC Manual of Millwork*

C. Concealed Portions, Cores, and Substrates

4. Concealed portions shall be any species of sound, dry, solid stock, plywood, particleboard, medium density fiberboard, or a combination thereof.

D. Visible Edges, Exposed and Semi-Exposed, except door and drawer fronts. (See Paragraphs VIII. E. and VIII. F., respectively.)

1. Exposed or semi-exposed shall be treated as follows:

   a. For Economy Grade only, all voids filled and sanded.

   b. Banded with veneer or veneer tape. Finger joints are not permitted for Premium Grade.

   c. Banded with solid wood.

2. Only the front edge of adjustable shelves shall be considered visible.

3. Medium density fiberboard does not require edge filling.

4. Custom and Premium Grades shall be edge banded.

5. Premium Grade shall have concealed edge bands, except at shelves and bottoms.

6. For Custom and Premium Grades, the visible top edge of the end of cabinets 6'-0" or more from the floor does not require an edge band, but shall have all voids filled and sanded.

7. For Economy and Custom Grades Type II construction, the visible bottom edge of the end of upper cabinets does not require an edge band but shall have all voids filled and sanded. For Premium Grade, this edge shall be concealed, banded or shoulder mitered, and when specified to receive a transparent finish, edge bands shall be the same species, color and WIC Grade as the exposed material.

8. For all grades Type I construction, the visible bottom edge of the end of upper cabinets shall be edge banded.

E. Drawers

1. Drawer fronts.

   a. For Economy Grade, drawer fronts shall be a minimum of ¾" in thickness; all edges of plywood and particleboard are to be filled and sanded.

   b. For Economy and Custom Grade opaque finishes, medium density fiberboard does not require an edge band. Edge banding is required for Premium Grade.

   c. For transparent finish, banding shall be on all four edges.

   d. For transparent finish, edges visible after doors and drawers are closed are required to be the same species, color, grain, and grade as the exposed portions.

   e. For Custom and Premium Grades, banding shall be on all four edges. For Custom Grade, solid stock may be used and shall not require banding.

2. Sides, backs, and sub-fronts.

   a. For Economy Grade shall be a minimum of ⁷⁄₁₆" in thickness of any approved semi-exposed material except hardboard. Vinyl wrapped drawers are permitted. The same material shall be used for all parts of the drawer box.

   b. Hardwood or softwood plywood shall be filled and sanded on the top edges.

   c. For Custom Grade shall be a minimum of 12 mm and a maximum of ⅝" in thickness, and shall be one species of material and thickness for all parts for the entire job.

   d. Hardwood plywood shall be 7- or 9-ply with no core voids in the inner plies, or 5-ply edge banded.

> ## Comments
>
> Where available, lumber core ply panels are recommended, as they are very stable.

   e. Particleboard or medium density fiberboard shall have an overlay surface and be edge banded.

   f. For Premium Grade if solid stock, it shall be a minimum of 0.37 specific gravity hardwood. Hardwood shall be the same species of wood for the entire drawer box and job. If approved overlay material, the same material shall be used for the entire drawer box and job.

3. Drawer bottoms.

a. For Economy Grade, drawer bottoms shall be a minimum of $\frac{1}{8}$" in thickness, except if width exceeds 18", it shall be $\frac{1}{4}$" in thickness and shall be any of the approved semi-exposed materials.

b. For Custom Grade, drawer bottoms shall be a minimum of $\frac{1}{4}$" in thickness, except if width exceeds 30", it shall be a minimum of $\frac{3}{8}$" in thickness or reinforced with $\frac{1}{2}$" x $2\frac{1}{2}$" strip at center. Exposed particleboard or medium density fiberboard is not permitted.

c. For Premium Grade, drawer bottoms of Grade AD softwood plywood and hardboard is not permitted.

4. For Premium Grade only if solid stock, shall be a minimum of 0.37 specific gravity hardwood. Hardwood shall be the same species of wood for the entire drawer box and job. If overlay material, the same material shall be used for the entire drawer box and job.

F. **Cabinet Doors** (Maximum width shall be 24". Maximum height 80". Larger sizes are not recommended.)

1. Hinged.

a. Shall conform to the same thickness and banding requirements as drawer fronts (see Paragraph E, 1).

b. Interior faces for Economy and Custom Grades may be Economy Grade of the same species as exposed portion.

c. For Premium Grade, interior faces shall be the same species, color, grain, cut, and grade as the exposed portion of the cabinet. The faces of adjacent cabinet doors that are visible when closed shall be well matched for color and grain.

2. Sliding doors. (Bottom of upper cabinet may require reinforcement to prevent sagging.)

a. Shall be a minimum of $\frac{1}{4}$" in thickness, except when over 2'-0" high they shall be a minimum of $\frac{3}{4}$" in thickness.

b. Interior faces may be the same as exposed portion, or any balancing species.

c. Top and bottom edges are not required to be banded or filled.

d. Both vertical edges of sliding doors are considered visible.

3. Frameless glass doors shall be a minimum of $\frac{1}{4}$" thick clear safety glass with all exposed edges ground. For Premium Grade, all exposed edges shall be polished.

4. Stile and rail cabinet doors.

a. Solid lumber stile and rails shall be a minimum of $\frac{3}{4}$" in thickness and $2\frac{1}{4}$" in width. Stiles and rails consisting of MDF or particleboard cores shall be a minimum of $\frac{3}{4}$" in thickness and $3\frac{1}{2}$" in width.

b. Glass shall be a minimum of clear double strength, secured with removable stops of the same species of wood.

c. Panels shall be flat, unless otherwise specified.

d. For opaque finish, door components may be manufactured from solid stock of medium density fiberboard, at the mill's option.

I. **Face Frames**

Shall be solid stock, a minimum of $\frac{3}{4}$" in thickness.

J. **Ends and Divisions**

1. Shall be a minimum of $\frac{3}{4}$" in thickness, except for face frame construction, where Economy Grade permits a minimum of $\frac{1}{2}$" in thickness and Custom and Premium Grades permit a minimum of $\frac{5}{8}$" in thickness.

2. Paneled construction, stiles and rails shall be a minimum of $\frac{3}{4}$" in thickness and panels a minimum of $\frac{1}{4}$" in thickness. For Custom and Premium Grades for transparent finish, hardboard is not permitted.

K. **Shelves**

1. For Economy Grade, shelves shall be solid stock or particleboard a minimum of $\frac{3}{4}$" in thickness or may be veneer core plywood, a minimum of $\frac{5}{8}$" in thickness.

2. For Custom and Premium Grades, fixed shelves with spans in excess of 4'-0" are not recommended; if desired, a center support shall be specified. Shelves shall be solid stock, plywood or particleboard a minimum of $\frac{3}{4}$" in thickness. Fixed shelves 3'-6" in length with particleboard core between vertical members of the cabinet body shall be a minimum of 1" in thickness. If not

specified, the material shall be the option of the manufacturer subject to the 40 lb. load capacity, unless it is to be used in a school or hospital, which will require the 50 lb. load test.

3. If thicker shelves or center shelf supports are required due to heavy loads, they shall be so specified.

4. For Custom and Premium Grades, when hardboard is used for shelves, vertical or horizontal dividers, it must be smooth on two sides and tempered.

5. The grain of the face veneer of plywood shall run the length of the shelf.

L. Tops and Bottoms

1. For Economy Grade, tops and bottoms of cabinets shall conform to requirements of Paragraph J, 1.

2. For Custom and Premium Grades, tops and bottoms are required and shall be a minimum of $3/4$" in thickness.

3. Bottoms of upper cabinets (see Paragraph K, 2 and 3).

4. Wood tops, if an integral part of a cabinet, shall be a minimum of $3/4$" in thickness.

N. Backs

1. For Economy Grade when backs are used, backs shall be hardboard or plywood, a minimum of $1/8$" in thickness.

2. For Custom and Premium Grades, backs shall be hardboard, plywood, particleboard or medium density fiberboard, a minimum of $1/4$" in thickness.

3. Exposed backs shall be a minimum of $1/2$" in thickness.

4. If $1/2$" or thicker back is used, anchor strips are **not** required.

O. Breadboards and Pullout Boards

1. Breadboards

   a. Shall be solid stock, a minimum of $3/4$" in thickness, except for Economy Grade exterior grade plywood is permitted.

   b. When solid stock is glued for width, Type II adhesive shall be used.

2. Pullout Boards

   a. Shall be veneer core plywood, a minimum of $3/4$" in thickness.

IX. Construction Requirements—Grade Rules

A. Joinery

1. All cabinet members shall be securely fastened together using one or more acceptable joinery methods (see paragraph A, 5, a through e).

2. All joints shall be securely glued (see Glossary for definition).

3. Casework shall be assembled square and true, with a tolerance not to exceed $1/32$" difference in measurement at top versus bottom, and $1/16$" in diagonal measurement.

4. To assemble cabinet bodies and components, the use of finish nails is allowed. They shall be a maximum of 4" on center (except face frames—8" on center), with a minimum of 2 fasteners per joint for cabinet body and drawer construction. Staples, screws and T nails are not permitted for exposed surfaces.

5. For Custom and Premium Grades, at the option of the manufacturer, construction joinery shall be as follows:

   a. Dadoes or lock joints, plows or rabbets.

   b. Doweled Joints. The dowels shall be a minimum of 8 mm x 30 mm with a minimum of 2 dowels per joint. The first dowel shall be spaced a maximum of 37 mm from each edge or end, and the second dowel shall be a maximum of 32 mm on center from the first dowel. Subsequent dowels shall be spaced a maximum of 128 mm on center. All dowel construction shall be glued and clamped.

   c. Confirmat-Type Screws. Maximum of 37 mm from each end with subsequent screws being spaced 128 mm on center. Glue is **not** required with this system.

   d. Lamello-Type Jointing Plates. The plate shall be a maximum of 2 inches from each edge or end to the center of the plate. Subsequent plates shall be spaced a maximum of 6 inches on center. All joints shall be glued and clamped.

Typical Joints

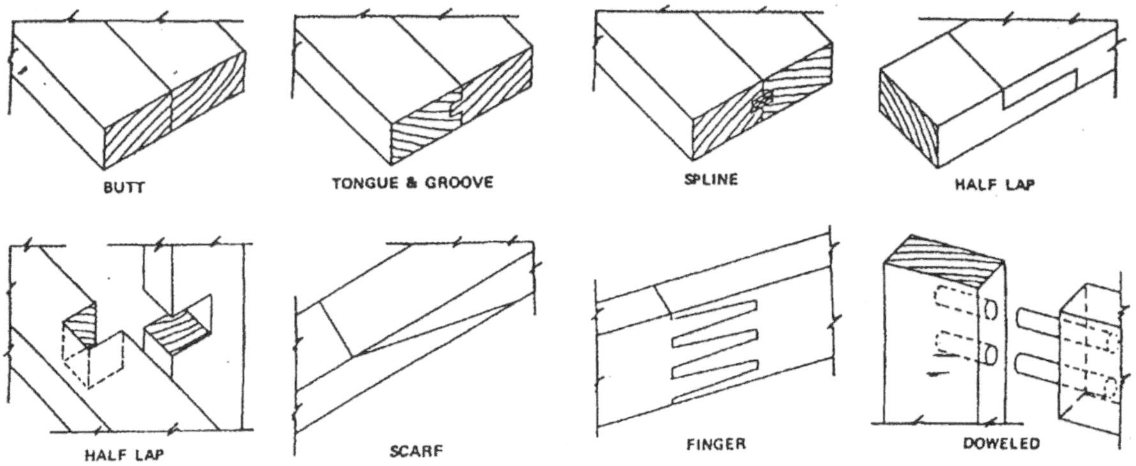

Figure 6.6

Courtesy of Woodwork Institute, *WIC Manual of Millwork*

e. Mod-eez Type Fastening Systems. The fasteners shall be a maximum of 16" on center and 4" from any edge or end. They shall be fastened with #10 full-thread sheet metal screws for cabinet body construction. Glue is not required with this system.

6. For Premium Grade, no exposed fastening is permitted except for access panels.

B. Edges of Exposed Portions

1. Blind or stop dadoes are not required for Economy Grade or for open shelving in rooms designated as janitor, closet, or utility.

2. For Custom Grade, when specified to receive a transparent finish, blind or stop dadoes are required. When lock joints are used, they shall not run through the edge band.

3. For Premium Grade, blind or stop dadoes are required.

C. Ends and Divisions

1. Cabinet ends are required.

2. Open ends or skeleton frames against walls are not permitted in any grade in any WIC Grade.

3. Exposed ends shall be rabbeted or plowed to receive backs if used.

4. For Custom and Premium Grades, drawer compartments shall be separated from shelf or open compartments by a solid vertical division unless design or usage prevents. A solid division shall occur behind all vertical face frame members or hanging stiles.

D. Face Frames

1. For cabinet doors flush with face frame, the use of a bottom member of the face frame is optional with the fabricator, unless otherwise specified.

2. Face frames shall be mortised and tenoned, doweled with wood or metal screw dowels, or Lamello type plates, and securely glued.

3. The grain shall run horizontally and vertically respectively.

4. For Economy and Custom Grades, frames shall be glued to cabinet bodies and may be face nailed.

5. For Premium Grade, all exposed corners shall be shoulder mitered, lock mitered, spline mitered, or mitered with a Lamello-type plate. Exposed nailing of face frames to cabinet bodies is not permitted.

E. Shelves

1. For Economy Grade, fixed shelves shall be nailed 4" or less on center to ends and divisions. Shelves in excess of 4'-0" shall be supported on cleats at the back or nailed through the back if a back is used.

2. Adjustable shelves shall be supported on metal shelf standards and metal shelf rests, or, in evenly spaced, cleanly bored holes

a maximum of 2" o.c. with metal shelf rests. Holes shall be bored from front and back edge of shelves a minimum of 1" to a maximum of 2¾". For shelves over 24" deep, there shall be three (3) supports at each end for Title 24—schools and hospitals. Cabinets over 30" deep shall have three (3) supports at each end of shelf.

3. For Custom and Premium Grades, if metal shelf standards are used, they shall be properly attached, recessed, and shall run continuous from top to bottom of plow. The particleboard edges shall not be visible.

4. The minimum length of adjustable shelves shall be ⅛" less than the inside dimension of the cabinet.

5. For cabinets over 72" high from the floor and that is not immediately abutting a structural wall or another cabinet, a fixed shelf is required at mid-height.

F. **Tops, Bottoms, Intermediate Horizontal Members, Web Frames, Sub-Tops, and Stretchers**

1. Design permitting, bottoms and tops are required.

2. All members shall be assembled with any of the approved methods under "Joinery Requirements."

3. At concealed ends, tops and bottoms may extend past the concealed end.

4. At exposed ends, horizontal members, except countertops, shall not extend beyond the exposed end.

5. Stretchers shall be provided at both front and back under countertops.

6. For sink compartments, stretchers may run front to back.

7. For Custom and Premium Grades, web frames shall be provided under drawers that operate on wood center guides. When banks of drawers operate on wood corner guides, side runner guides, metal side or bottom mount slides, front stretcher is only required when total drawer opening height exceeds 2'-6".

8. Wood countertops.

a. For Economy Grade, may be surface nailed.

b. For Custom and Premium Grades, all countertops shall be attached with concealed clips, screws, or other equivalent fastening.

9. Exposed tops.

a. For Economy and Custom Grades, tops which are flush with exposed ends do not require mitered joints. Exposed ends of the top shall be banded with the same material as other exposed surfaces.

Typical Joints

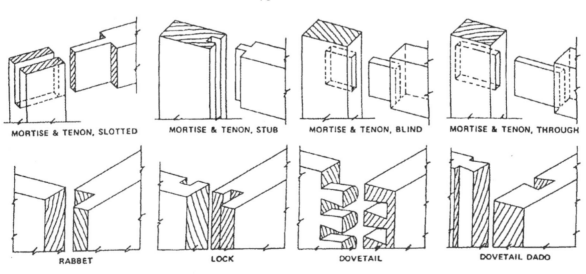

MORTISE & TENON, SLOTTED   MORTISE & TENON, STUB   MORTISE & TENON, BLIND   MORTISE & TENON, THROUGH

RABBET   LOCK   DOVETAIL   DOVETAIL DADO

Courtesy of Woodwork Institute, *WIC Manual of Millwork*

Figure 6.7

b. For Type I Construction (multiple self-supporting units fastened together to form a larger unit), Custom and Premium Grades, joints are permitted where ends are flush with tops. In each unit, the exposed edges of the ends shall be banded with the same material as the exposed surfaces.

c. For Type II Construction (a single length section as required, or in such sections as access openings will permit), Premium Grade tops (other than countertops) which are flush with exposed ends shall be shoulder mitered, lock mitered, spline mitered or mitered with a Lamello-type plate, or dowel mitered.

10. Sub-tops for tile shall be supplied with base cabinets.

11. Bottoms of upper cabinets.

a. For Economy Grade Type I and Type II construction, joints are permitted where ends are flush with bottoms in each unit. If ends extend below the bottom, the interior exposed surface of the end may be the same material as the semi-exposed surface.

b. For Custom and Premium Grades Type I and Type II construction, joints are

permitted where ends are flush with bottoms in each unit. The exposed edges of the ends shall be banded with the same material as the exposed surfaces. If ends extend below the bottom, the interior exposed surface of the end shall be the same material as the exposed surface.

12. Security and dust panels (if specified) shall be supplied above locked doors and drawers.

G. Backs

1. For Economy Grade, backs are required only when specified or where the cabinet will be set in an unfinished recess, or where the back would be exposed to view.

2. For Custom and Premium Grades, backs are required.

3. Shall be rabbeted or dadoed into exposed ends unless a plant-on end is used.

4. Shall be securely nailed, stapled, doweled or dadoed to the case body, divisions, or fixed shelves. Gluing is not required.

H. Breadboards and Pullout Boards

1. Shall operate smoothly in channels or other rigid guides.

2. Breadboards shall be provided with tongue and groove bands at each end, securely glued with Type II adhesive.

Typical Joints

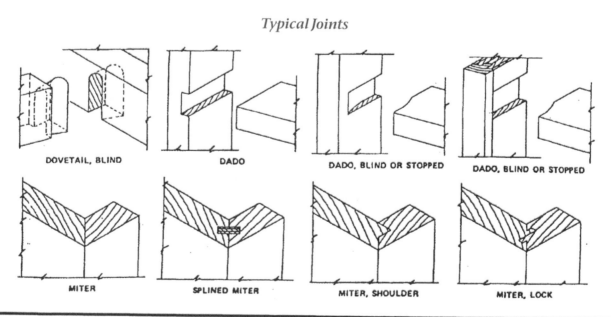

Figure 6.8

Courtesy of Woodwork Institute, *WIC Manual of Millwork*

3. Pullout Board shall be banded on three edges.

I. **Drawers**

1. All joints shall be securely glued.

2. Provision shall be made to prevent drawers from tipping when extended.

3. Hardwood guides of corner, center, side or side runner type, and all metal slides shall be as indicated in hardware supplement.

4. Drawers, trays, and sliding bins shall be properly fitted to the cabinet and operate smoothly without excessive play. Drawer boxes, trays and sliding bins must fill the cabinet opening, front to back, less than a maximum of 2", from top to bottom to the greatest extent possible, while remaining fully functional.

5. File drawers shall be provided with a follower mechanism or be of a size to allow use of pendaflex folders on a systems stand. All file drawers shall have full-extension slides. Direction of file is at the discretion of the designer. Legal-sized drawers with hanging file suspension bars must provide for both legal and letter-sized hanging files.

6. For Premium Grade, spring loaded tip-down stops shall be provided on all drawers (design permitting) unless a stop is built into a metal drawer slide.

7. For Style B face frame construction.

   a. For Economy Grade, the fronts or sub-fronts may be rabbeted to receive the sides. Backs may be butt jointed and nailed to the sides.

   b. For Custom and Premium Grades, drawer sides shall be multiple dovetailed (dovetail joints with exposed substrates are acceptable in all WIC Grades. Exposed particleboard and medium density fiberboard substrates must be painted to match the drawer box color), dovetail dadoed, doweled, lock jointed and nailed, fastened with Confirmat type screws, or rabbets with #8 screws, a minimum of 2 screws for each side, a maximum of 2" on center, to the fronts or sub-fronts and backs. Sides may be dadoed to receive backs. Nails shall be a maximum of 2" on center.

   c. For Premium Grade construction, top edges of side shall be stop shaped.

8. For flush overlay type construction.

   a. Drawer sides shall be blind dovetail dadoed, unless a sub-front is used.

   b. For Premium Grade, top edges of sides shall be stop shaped.

9. Sub-fronts.

   a. For Economy Grade, drawer sides may be nailed to sub-fronts and backs.

   b. For Custom and Premium Grades, drawer sides shall be multiple dovetailed or dovetail dado, doweled, lock jointed and nailed, fastened with Confirmat type screws, or rabbets with #8 screws, a minimum of 2 screws for each side, and a maximum of 2" on center to the fronts or sub-fronts and backs. Sides may be dadoed to receive backs. Nails shall be at a maximum of 2" on center.

   c. The finished front shall be securely attached to a sub-front with #8 x 1" pan head sheet metal screws a maximum of 1½" from inside corners of the finished front and a maximum of 12" on center.

   d. When a lock joint is used in the construction of a drawer box, attach the sub-front to the sides of the drawer, ⅛ of an inch of exposed particleboard and solid stock is permitted on the drawer sides.

10. Drawer bottoms.

    a. Shall be plowed into sides, fronts, or sub-fronts.

    b. Bottoms shall be securely attached to the backs either by plow or by nailing at a maximum of 4" on center if the bottom runs through, and shall be securely glued or glue blocked to form a rigid unit.

    c. The use of surface applied bottoms need not to be plowed or glued into sides, sub-fronts and backs is permitted in conjunction with approved metal bottom mounted side slides.

    d. Bottoms are not required to be plowed into drawer fronts or sub-fronts with the use of integral metal drawer side/slide systems if a minimum of ½" thickness bottom is used.

e. Wood trays, bins, and similar items shall be similarly constructed.

11. Drawer stops.

   a. For Custom and Premium Grades, to prevent drawer fronts from hitting the cabinet body, stops shall be provided at the back of both sides of all drawers unless a stop is built into a metal drawer slide and provision made to stop the drawer in both the in and out position without impact on the drawer front.

12. Unless otherwise specified, the following drawer box and drawer slide dynamic weight capacity standard will apply. Pencil drawers—50 lbs., general purpose drawers—75 lbs., file drawers—100 lbs., lateral file drawers longer than 24" in length—125 lbs., special weight requirements must be specified.

J. Doors

1. Sliding doors.

   a. For Economy Grade, sliding doors 3'-0" in height or less shall be equipped with adequate top and/or bottom guides or runs. Sliding doors in excess of 3'-0" in height shall be installed on hardware of a type optional with the manufacturer.

   b. For Custom and Premium Grades, doors over 2'-10" in height shall be installed on either overhead metal track with nylon roller hangers, or metal bottom track with sheaves and top guide.

   c. For Custom and Premium Grades, doors 2'-10" and under in height shall be installed on appropriate fiber or metal track, with top guide.

   d. For Custom and Premium Grades, for face frame type construction a continuous vertical filler strip shall be provided in the opening behind the face frame and in front of the rear sliding door.

   e. For Custom and Premium Grades, frameless sliding glass doors shall be installed on carriers with metal track and top guide. To prevent sagging, the bottoms of upper cabinets shall be increased in thickness or provided with a hardwood track member of sufficient thickness or a strongback screwed and glued to the underside.

2. Hinged doors.

   a. For all WIC Grades, doors shall stop against the body of the cabinet. Doors and door faces must overlap cabinet sides, top stretchers and bottoms, with the exception of handicapped units.

   b. For concealed European style hinges, doors less than 40" in height shall have a minimum of two hinges. Doors 40" to 60" in height shall have a minimum of three hinges. Doors more than 60" and up to 80" high shall have a minimum of four hinges. Doors over 80" in height shall have an additional hinge for every 18" of additional height.

   c. For wraparound style hinges, doors under 48" in height shall have a minimum of two hinges. Doors 48" to 84" high shall have a minimum of three hinges, and over 84" shall have a minimum of four hinges. Wraparound hinges shall be let into the edge of the door.

   d. Cabinet door hinges shall be installed by the cabinet fabricator unless otherwise specified. Installed doors shall operate properly without binding and shall be in proper alignment.

   e. For Custom and Premium Grades flush construction, a stop shall be provided at the top of hinged door openings. Hinges shall be either self closing or doors shall be provided with a catch.

   f. For Custom and Premium Grades, Style A construction, a stop-stretcher shall be provided at the top of pairs of hinged door openings.

   g. For Custom and Premium Grades, where drawers occur above pairs of doors, a stop-stretcher shall be required above the pairs of hinged door openings.

   h. For Premium Grade face frame flush construction, a stop shall be provided at both sides of the door opening.

   i. For Custom and Premium Grades, locking full height pairs of cabinet doors must be equipped with either two sliding bolts—one at top and one at bottom—or a single elbow catch at cabinets with fixed middle shelves.

K. Bases and Sleepers

1. Shall be fabricated of solid stock, plywood or particleboard, a minimum of ¾" in thickness and as either a separate unit or integral with the cabinet body at the manufacturers' option unless otherwise specified. Sleepers shall be provided at a maximum of 3'-0" on center.

L. Clothes Poles

1. Shall be wood a minimum of 1¼" in diameter or 1¹/₁₆" minimum diameter metal as approved in the hardware supplement at fabricator's option, unless otherwise specified.

2. Shall be supported a maximum of 4'-0" on center. Poles shall be supported at each end by rosettes or hook strips with bored holes. Nailing is not acceptable.

M. Wardrobes

1. Horizontal members at the top rail of sliding doors in wardrobes 5'-0" in width or over shall be rigidly supported with a vertical 1³/₈" round pole or two strips a minimum of ¾" x 1¼", forming a "T" member and securely positioned behind the door lap.

N. Anchor Strips

1. For Economy Grade, anchor strips are not required.

2. For Custom and Premium Grades, anchor strips of solid stock, plywood, particleboard, or medium density fiberboard shall be a minimum of ½" in thickness and a minimum of 2½" in width, and shall be provided at the wall side of the cabinet back on both top and bottom of wall hung cabinets and at top only of base cabinets. Anchor strips of semi-exposed material may be provided on the inside of the cabinet providing the back is flush with the top, bottom, and ends of the cabinet body and is attached to the cabinet body as well as the back. Base cabinets with integral base shall have anchor strips at top and bottom.

3. Cabinets over 5'-0" in height shall have an intermediate anchor strip.

4. Where ½" or thicker cabinet backs are used, anchor strips are not required.

5. Anchor strips shall be securely attached.

O. Sanding

1. For Economy Grade, all flat exposed and semi-exposed portions shall be machine sanded with all exposed edges and mouldings smoothly machined and clean.

2. For Custom and Premium Grades, the bottom edges of drawer fronts and aprons at knee spaces shall be smoothly sanded.

3. For Custom Grade, all exposed portions shall be smoothly sanded and all semi-exposed portions shall be machine sanded and free from tool marks and other blemishes.

4. For Premium Grade, all exposed portions shall be hand sanded and free from tool marks and other blemishes, scraped or otherwise completely smoothed, ready for finishing. All semi-exposed portions shall be smoothly sanded and free from tool marks or other blemishes.

P. Scribing

1. For Economy Grade, scribing is not required.

2. For Custom Grade, provision shall be made for scribing or scribe moulds furnished where cabinets contact finished walls or ceiling at the option of the manufacturer unless otherwise specified. End joints of scribe moulds shall be beveled and corners mitered.

3. For Custom and Premium Grades, the use of wood filler strips not to exceed 1½" in width, scribe strips, and cellulose sponge a minimum of ½" is permitted. Color compatible caulking is permitted not to exceed ¹/₁₆".

4. For Premium Grade, provisions shall be made for scribing unless otherwise specified.

5. For Custom and Premium Grades, closure panels and scribe moulds shall be provided at top and bottom of upper cabinets and at the top of tall cabinets requiring angle turns so that open spaces are not visible.

Q. Movable Cabinets

1. When metal glides are specified in lieu of casters, they shall be adjustable.

2. For casters see hardware supplement.

3. All lock joint corners of bottoms and top webs of movable cabinets shall be reinforced with a continuous 1" metal angle strip or a continuous wood reinforcing cleat securely

Table of Recommended Door and Drawer Tolerances

| GRADE | MAXIMUM CLEARANCE ALLOWED | | | | WARP[1] OR TWIST[1] TOLERANCE PER LINEAL FOOT | |
| | FLUSH OVERLAY TYPE | | FLUSH TYPE | | | |
	SINGLE UNIT	ADJACENT UNIT				
Premium	0.1250″ 4 mm	0.2500″ 8 mm	0.0938″	3/32″	0.0313″	1/32″
Custom	0.1250″ 4 mm	0.2500″ 8 mm	0.1250″	1/8″	0.0469″	3/64″
Economy	0.1563″ 5/32″	0.3125″ 5/16″	0.1563″	5/32″	0.0625″	1/16″

[1] Not to exceed 1/4″ in any size door.

Reveal overlay shall be as specified.

Figure 6.9   Courtesy of Woodwork Institute, *WIC Manual of Millwork*

screwed into the inside of both sides of the corner.

4. Movable cabinets with doors and without fixed stabilizing vertical or horizontal partitions shall be built with a diaphragm type double bottom.

R. Door and Drawer Tolerances

1. The recommended clearances allowed between any edge of doors or drawers, or between doors hung in pairs, or between flush face frames and doors and drawers, or any edge of doors and drawers and the surrounding border; and the warp and twist tolerances for doors less than 1⅜″ in thickness are indicated in the table above for all grades.

2. The test for warp and twist is made by placing a string, wire, or straight edge on the concave face of the door diagonally, horizontally, or vertically and measuring the maximum distance between the face of the door and the straight edge, wire, or string.

3. For reveal overlay construction, the maximum clearance allowed shall be as specified or indicated.

4. Doors and drawers shall align vertically and horizontally.

Plastic Laminate

Industry Standards

WIC Manual of Millwork (Effective 5/1/03)
(Woodwork Institute, www.wicnet.org)

Ed. Note: See also "Kitchen & Bathroom Countertops at the end of this chapter for more information on plastic laminates.

Laminated Plastic Countertops, Splashes and Wall Paneling

I. Scope of Classification.

All decorative high-pressure laminated plastic for facings, tops, splashes, wainscot, shelves, wall caps and window sills with plastic or metal trim applicable to these items.

A. Inclusions:

1. Decorative high-pressure laminated plastic, bonded to proper core.

2. WIC approved backing sheet.

3. Cutouts for sinks or other accessories.

4. Metal, wood, or self-edge trim.

5. Jobsite installation, if specified.

B. Excluded:

1. Stripping, furring, blocking, or grounds.

2. Furnishing or installation of sinks and sink rims.

II. Specification Requirements

A. The drawings and specifications should clearly indicate or specify the following:

1. WIC Grades.

   a. If the Grade is not specified, countertops of the same grade as specified for casework shall be furnished.

2. Type of edge covering; i.e., self-edged, rolled, no-drip bullnose, no-drip tilt edge, metal, wood, etc.

   a. If the above is not specified, self-edged will be furnished.

3. Type of back splash; i.e., square butt joint or integral cove.

   a. If the above is not specified, integral cove backsplash will be furnished.

4. Whether top of backsplash is to be waterfall or square with self-edge.

   a. If the above is not specified, top of splash will be square with self-edge.

5. Height of backsplash.

   a. If height is not indicated, splashes shall be a minimum of 4" in height above deck surface, unless job conditions do not permit.

   b. Unless specified otherwise, backsplashes are required at all countertops with sinks.

6. If solid colors, wood grains, or special finishes are desired.

   a. If the above is not specified, colors will be selected from non-premium priced standard patterns.

   b. If the brand, color and/or design numbers are not shown, the selection shall be based on sheet sizes available consistent with dimensions indicated on the drawings.

7. If Colorcore® or Solicor® are desired, they shall be specified. Colors selected by the architect/designer.

8. If other than textured-surfaced laminated plastic is desired for wall paneling, it must be specified, unless it is a part of a top.

9. Height of wainscot.

   a. If height is not indicated, the top of the wainscot shall be 4'-0" above the floor.

10. It is recommended that metal trim rims at sinks should overlap both countertop and sink by a minimum of 3/16". A self-rimming sink should overlap the countertop by a minimum of 3/16".

11. Cut-outs within countertops and paneling that are to be finished by the fabricator shall be so specified.

III. Grades

A. Economy: This grade establishes a standard to meet the requirements of lower cost residential and commercial construction wherein economy is the principal factor.

B. Custom: This grade includes all the requisites of a high-quality product and is suitable for all normal uses in high-grade construction, such as higher quality residential, school and commercial buildings.

C. Premium: This grade is a superior quality of workmanship and materials, with a corresponding increase in cost.

IV. Shop Drawings and Submittals

A. Shop drawings shall be submitted to the contractor, architect/designer, or owner for approval prior to fabrication.

C. Drawings shall show each typical plastic top or plastic wall panel with sufficient details to clearly indicate all unusual features in construction and shall conform to the requirements set forth in the WIC policy and procedures for Millwork Shop Drawings.

V. Workmanship

A. The assembled plastic top or plastic wall paneling shall present First Class Workmanship for Grade Specified.

VII. Material Standards

A. Surface material shall be high-pressure laminated plastic conforming to NEMA LD-3 latest edition.

   1. Tops, splashes, and shelves shall be faced with general purpose type laminated decorative sheets a minimum of .050" in thickness or .042" post forming grade if required.

B. Backing sheets shall be any one of the following for the entire job and WIC Grade indicated.

Premium Grade

1. A minimum of .020" thickness conforming to NEMA LD latest edition or Gator Ply® .028" thickness, is permitted for all grades and is required as the only backing sheet for Premium Grade.

Economy and Custom Grades

1. Man-made wood-fiber veneers that are impregnated with acrylic melamine fortified high load resin system, a minimum of .020". (Gator Ply®, produced by International Paper Co.) is permitted for Economy and Custom Grades only.

2. Synthetic polymer treated backing sheet .017"–.019" nominal thickness designed for use with decorative high pressure laminate known as Dynopregh-ply, thickness of .020" and .026" produced by Dyno Overlays, Inc., formerly Reichold Chemical Co., is permitted for Economy and Custom Grades only.

3. Dark brown colored .015" nominal thickness phenolic resin impregnated craft paper (Simpson Backing sheet #.015 produced by Simpson Timber Co.) is permitted for Economy and Custom Grades only.

4. Thermoset resin treated wood-fibered brown color 3-ply construction, a minimum thickness of .020", known as Resobak #184C produced by Pioneer Plastic Corporation is permitted for Economy and Custom Grades only.

Economy Grade Only

1. Hot melt coat brown colored .002" minimum thickness factory applied to particleboard core coat of blended wax petroleum, copolymer resins and anti-oxidants and swip controlling agents (HMC, produced by Willamette Industries) is required for Economy Grade only.

2. Low pressure polyester or melamine laminate (ALA 851) (to PB 1M-2) for Economy Grade only.

C. Core material for tops, splashes, and shelves shall be a minimum of ¾".

1. Unsupported spans should be reinforced to prevent deflection in excess of ¼" with a 50 lb. load.

D. Cove Stick.

1. For a ¾" radius, a moulded cove stick shall be used with no voids permitted between the plastic laminate and the cove stick. The cove stick shall be the same thickness as the core material, and no voids are permitted at either joint.

2. For a ¼" radius, a square stick is permitted with all voids filled with glue between laminate and cove stick, providing it is the same thickness as the core material.

E. Adhesives.

1. Contact adhesive laminations must pass the WIC Heat Resistance Test and must comply with Type II adhesive moisture resistance testing.

VIII. Grade Rules—Tops, Splashes, and Shelves

A. Economy Grade.

1. Core material shall be particleboard.

2. The laminated plastic shall be securely glued to the core with Type II adhesive applied as recommended by the adhesive manufacturer.

3. The underside of tops and the backside of splashes shall be covered with HMC backing sheet or any other approved backing sheet.

4. Exposed edges of core material shall be neatly and entirely covered by trim as shown or specified. Where tops are subject to excessive moisture, edges shall be sealed before the metal trim or sink rim is installed.

5. Holes for sinks will be cut, but the furnishing or installation of metal sink rims is not included.

6. All joints shall be neatly and carefully made. Care shall be taken to make all joints water tight. Waterproof sealant shall be used at all square butt joint splashes and shall be color matched. All connecting surfaces shall be flush within the manufacturing tolerance of the process used. Tops which require field joints shall be joined with bolt-up type fasteners, if practicable.

7. All exposed edges shall be eased.

8. Appropriate scribe allowance shall be provided.

9. Wood grained patterns for an L-shaped top shall have a diagonal joint approximately 45 degrees. A butt joint is not permitted.

10. Exposed fastening will not be allowed, except for access panels.

11. Maximum unsupported countertop spans shall not exceed 48", unless otherwise specified.

12. Sink cut-outs will not fall within 18" of discretionary field joints.

B. Custom Grade.

All requirements of Economy Grade are included herein, with additional requirements as follows:

1. Core material (1) shall be particleboard, rotary cut Lauan, or other hardwood plywood with "Sound" (2) Grade face veneer; and the crossband under the face veneer shall be Industrial (3) Grade or better.

2. The laminated plastic shall be securely glued to the core with Type II adhesive applied as recommended by the adhesive manufacturer. In addition to meeting the requirements of Type II, the adhesive shall meet WIC Heat Resistant Test Requirements.

3. The underside of tops and the backside of splashes shall be covered with an approved backing sheet.

4. Plastic tops requiring more than one sheet of laminate shall have the plastic prematched to minimize color variation within the scope of the manufacturer's guarantee, and shall be fabricated from the longest sheet lengths available.

5. Where self-edge trim is used, the top laminate may extend over the edge laminate, or the edge laminate may be face applied.

   a. Where self-edge front trim is used, the built-up member shall be particleboard, solid stock, plywood, or particleboard with backing sheet or liner. The bottom edge shall be free of dents, torn grain, glue, etc., and shall be smoothly sanded if a backing sheet is not used.

6. When backsplashes are required, square butt joint end splashes of a corresponding height shall be furnished at wall or closed end.

7. Exposed shelves (shelves not in cabinets) shall be covered on both sides with the same material. Shelves less than 4'-0" above the floor may have a backing sheet in lieu of exposed material securely glued to the underside of the core with identical adhesive and under identical circumstances as the face sheet.

   b. All visible edges shall be edge-banded with the same material as the face of the shelf, unless otherwise specified.

8. Exposed fastening will not be allowed, except for access panels.

9. Unless specified otherwise, an integral cove backsplash shall be provided.

C. Premium Grade. All requirements of Custom Grade are included herein, with additional requirements as follows:

1. The undersides of tops and the backside of splashes shall be covered with .020" thickness backing sheet conforming to NEMA LD 3.

2. Where self-edging trim is used, the top laminate shall extend over the edge laminate on the front edges of the top only.

3. Application of Colorcore® or Solicor® as set forth in manufacturer's literature. Strictly conform to manufacturer's recommendation for adhesives. A high pressure laminate backing sheet is required.

4. Exposed fastening will not be allowed except for access panels.

5. Raw core at joint between countertop deck and backsplash shall be sealed before assembly.

Finishing of Millwork

Industry Standards

WIC Manual of Millwork (Effective 5/1/03)
(Woodwork Institute, www.wic.net)

WIC has made no effort to determine whether any of these finishing systems complies with Air Quality Management District regulations in California or any other state. A firm that performs factory finishing should contact the local EPA or Air Quality Management District to determine what types of finish material are approved.

I. Scope of Classification

All Architectural Millwork that is to be factory finished prior to delivery and installation, shall be specified properly to attain the desired aesthetic effect, such as color, gloss, and thickness of finish. Also, serviceability, toughness, adhesion, good wearing characteristics, and moisture resistance.

(For obvious reasons it is very difficult to determine "how many coats" of each step in the system are needed. The desirable end result should be to provide a finish that adds beauty to the wood, and gives desirable color, tone, smoothness, and depth.)

A. Inclusions:

1. All architectural millwork specified to be prefinished, including wood doors with special finish systems.

2. All preparatory work.

3. Labor to apply materials.

4. Shop facility including spray room and equipment.

5. All materials as specified.

6. All related supplies needed.

B. Exclusions:

1. Any items not specified in architectural millwork contract.

2. All exterior or interior painting or priming of walls or surfaces not specified.

II. Specification Requirements

A. Drawings and specifications should clearly specify:

1. Indicate if factory or jobsite finishing is desired.

2. Architectural millwork including interior trim; miscellaneous interior millwork; interior wood jambs; interior wood stairwork; wood casework, counters, and fixtures; wood doors; wall paneling; wainscot; and other specialty wood items.

3. The type of finish required. Generic classifications are:

    System #1—Lacquers, Water reducible acrylic

    System #2—Varnish

    System #3—Polyurethane

    System #4—Epoxy

    System #5—Penetrating Oils

    System #6—Synthetic Enamels

    System #7—Fire-Retardant Coatings

4. If a Laboratory-Type finish is desired. Systems 1, 2, 3, or 4 must be specified as Catalyzed Lacquer, Catalyzed Conversion Varnish, Catalyzed Polyurethane, Catalyzed Vinyl Lacquer, or Epoxy for acid resistance.

5. If to be stained for transparent finish or opaque finish.

6. If back priming is to be done by manufacturer.

7. Whether Fire-Retardant Coatings are required.

III. Standards

A. General Information.

1. Finishing of Architectural Woodwork can be applied at the job site, provided there is no violation of local, state, or EPA codes or regulations.

2. If the Architect/Specifier requires a high-quality finish, then the factory controlled finishing environment offers a superior finished product.

3. The basic purpose of finishing woodwork is to protect it from potential damage caused by moisture in the atmosphere, from day-to-day usage, and to maintain good appearance for the life of the project.

    a. Each finish system should be selected to give the best performance results. Costs of each system vary considerably and should be weighed carefully to accomplish the results desired.

4. Before making the final selection of a finish system, there are some other considerations, namely:

5. Some species of wood contain a chemical (oak, particularly) which reacts unfavorably with certain finishes. Where possible, a test sample should be made to check for unfavorable reactions. Application of a sealer before finishing will usually prevent this difficulty.

6. Oil stain shall be wiped—small areas at a time. Non-grain raising dye stains can be sprayed.

7. Open grain wood and veneers shall be stained first, before applying sealer. If filler is specified, it shall be tinted to required color before finish is applied, unless an oil

finish is used. Where a dark stained finish is to be used, the wood surface shall be wash coat sealed. For finishing purposes, some hardwoods may be classified as follows:

Hardwoods with Open Grain	
Ash	Oak, Red
Butternut	Oak, White
Chestnut	Walnut
African Mahogany	Honduras Mahogany
Philippine Mahogany (Lauan)	

Hardwoods with Closed Grain	
Alder, Red	Gum
Beech	Maple*
Birch, Red*	
Birch, White*	
Cherry	

* Birch or Maple have pores large enough to take wood filler effectively when desired, but small enough as a rule to be finished without filler. Dark stains are not recommended; but if they are desired, it is recommended that Birch or Maple be filled and/or wash coat sealed before the stain is applied. It is very difficult to obtain a uniform dark color on Birch or Maple.

8. Panel products require special finishing consideration. A "balanced" panel product is specially constructed for stability. To remain free from warp, the panel should be finished with balanced coats of finishing material.

9. The Architect/Specifier after selecting the desired Finish System, should select the final color or sheen. If special colors or matching are required, the Architect/Specifier shall provide the woodworker/finisher with preferred color samples. This should be accomplished during the pricing stage, otherwise a price will be agreed upon for additional expense of a special finish match. In the event that grain and color of veneers vary widely the finisher may find it necessary to do substantial toning and color blending to arrive at the desired final color or sheen. It is mandatory that adequate finish samples be submitted.
(See IV, "Submittals")

10. Generally speaking the grade of finishing selected should be the same as the grade of woodwork fabrication. Exceptions to the above statement can occur when a fabrication grade is chosen to meet budget needs and perhaps a higher or lower grade of finishing will suffice. In any event, the specifications should clearly call for any such change in finishing grade.

11. The finishing of architectural woodwork is always critical to the final results. The Architect/Specifier is always free to modify suggested standards in any way he sees fit.

12. Standard door manufacturers will usually only produce their own standard finishes. If the specifier lists one or more acceptable door manufacturers in his or her specifications, this indicates that the door manufacturers standard finishes are acceptable. If special door finishes are required they must be so specified to be applied by the woodworker.

13. Glossary of Special Terms:

    Non-Grain Raising Stains contain no pigmented solids and are usually spray applied.

    Wiping Stains do contain color particles and many color variations are available. Can be applied by spray, brushing, or hand wiped.

    Bleaching lightens the base color of the wood to give a more uniform appearance.

    Fillers are used to close or fill the pores to give a smooth appearance. Apply by brush, roller, or spray. Wipe or squeeze off against the grain.

    Glazing is a specialty step to achieve color uniformity where the natural wood color may be too strong in contrast.

    Toning is the use of semi-transparent colors to block out or reduce the color of the wood.

    Sealers lock in the stain or fillers and provide a knit or base for the final top coat or coats. It contributes to the "build" and resists moisture penetration.

    Washcoats are thinned coats of sealer to act as a barrier against over penetration of stains which cause blotchiness.

    Hand Rubbing is performed to smooth, flatten or give a more uniform finished effect. Represents additional costs.

    High-Polished Finish involves several operations of wet sanding, buffing and final high gloss polishing. This also represents additional costs.

    Distressing of Aging gives the appearance of being older. Can be done by hand, mechanical, or chemical methods.

14. Color and light: Lighting can drastically affect the color of the finish system applied to the wood surface. The color we see is the result of the surrounding light reflected off the wood surface.

When a color is observed under more than one light source, such as fluorescent lighting, incandescent lighting, or natural sunlight, or when colors match under one of the light sources just mentioned but look different if all sources of light are in play, there undoubtedly will be a sharp contrast or difference in appearance. This phenomenon is known as "metamerism." Care must be taken to emphasize this to the Architect/Specifier to avoid conflict.

B. **Casework:** All items of casework shall include exposed, semi-exposed, and concealed areas as previously defined.

1. Both sides of cabinet doors and all edges shall receive the same number of coats to prevent warping and twisting.

C. **Running and Standing Trim and Wood Door Frames:** Normally include finishing of exposed faces and edges only. If back priming is desired, specifications should clearly state if it is to be done by the architectural millwork manufacturer.

D. **Library Shelving; Store and Bank Fixtures; Wall Paneling and Decorative Items:** These items shall be finished as specified with the materials and system selected to match approved color samples submitted. Before finishing, remove all handling marks or effects of exposure to moisture with a complete, thorough, and final block over all surfaces using at least 150 grit sandpaper, followed by 220 grit finishing paper, then carefully cleaned with dry brush or tack cloth before applying sealer or other coats. Deep scratches must be steamed out before sanding. Sharp edges shall be eased by sanding.

E. **Wood Doors:** Before finishing all hardware must be removed or properly masked. The entire surface of wood doors including faces, top and bottom edges, as well as hinge and lock edges, shall receive two coats of oil-base mixed paint, varnish, or lacquer immediately after fitting, cutting for closures, weatherstrips, and/or thresholds. Exterior wood doors shall be finished before exposure to weather. Adequate drying time must be allowed between coats. An equal number of finish coats shall be applied to each side, and the same system and material shall be used on each side. Pairs of doors and openings with sidelights and transoms shall be finished and toned together to achieve maximum uniformity of color.

IV. Submittals

A. Samples: Submit samples of sufficient size to clearly show grain and color variations with finish type specified. At least 16" x 24" for plywood; 6" x 10" long for solid stock. Each sample should bear a label identifying the job name, the Architect/Designer, the general contractor, and the Finish System number. The sample materials submitted shall be representative of that to be used for the project.

V. Delivery, Storage, and Handling

A. Provide adequate storage facilities.

Ed. Note: See the WIC excerpt, "Delivery & Storage," earlier in this chapter.

VI. Environmental Requirements

A. Measure moisture content of wall surfaces such as drywall, plaster, etc, using an electronic moisture meter. **Do not** apply finish unless moisture content of surfaces is below 12%.

B. Minimum application temperature for varnish and lacquer finishes is 65°F.

C. Provide adequate continuous ventilation and sufficient heating facilities to maintain temperatures above 65°F for 24 hours before, during, and 48 hours after application of finishes.

D. All waste materials must be properly disposed of to conform to all local, state, and federal requirements.

VII. Materials

A. Paint, varnish, stain, enamel, sealers, filters, and necessary thinners to apply finish system specified.

B. Provide all other materials not specifically indicated but necessary to achieve the finishes specified.

C. Coatings to have good flowing properties and capable of drying or curing free of streaks or sags.

VIII. Preparation

A. Examine carefully all surfaces to be finished before commencement of work. Report in writing to Architect/Designer/Engineer any condition that may affect proper application.

B. Remove handling marks or effects of exposure to moisture with a complete, thorough, and final sanding of all surfaces. The sanded surface shall be smooth and free from raised grain, cross-sanding, burnishing, machining, and manufacturing marks. Clean surfaces with dry brush or tack cloth before applying sealer, stain, or primer. Deep scratches must be steamed out before sanding. Ease sharp edges with light sanding. The finish sanding quality of unfinished woodwork will determine the quality of the final finished product. It is required that all sanding inconsistencies and defects be removed before the finish is applied.

C. As required for the finish system specified, open grain woods and veneers, if desired to have a paste wood filler prior to sealing, it shall be so specified. Tint the filler to approximate stain or grain color if transparent finishes are specified.

D. Opaque finishes require hard closed grain surfaces such as medium density fiberboard (MDF) or a closed grain hardwood such as Birch.

E. For transparent finish to prevent sharp color contrast from member to member, panel to panel, flitch to flitch, solid stock to adjacent veneers, toning or sap staining to obtain compatible and uniform color is required.

F. For transparent finish, if the species is not specified, the use of either hardwood or softwood (plywood or solid stock) of one species for the entire job is permitted, at the option of the manufacturer.

1. For Custom Grade, solid stock and/or plywood shall be compatible in color and grain.

2. For Premium Grade, solid stock shall be well matched for color and grain; plywood shall be compatible in color with solid stock; and adjacent plywood panels shall be well matched for color and grain.

IX. Protection

A. For factory finishing of cabinets, doors, trim, and specialty items, provide adequate protection to adjacent surfaces and items from overspray and damage. Repair damage as a result of inadequate or unsuitable protection.

B. Furnish sufficient drop cloths, shields, and protective equipment to prevent spray or droppings from fouling surfaces not being finished and, in particular, surfaces within storage and preparation area.

C. Place cotton waste, cloths, and material which may constitute a fire hazard in closed metal containers and remove daily from site. Be careful to avoid spraying near electric motors, compressors, or other spark inducing contact. Steel wool can be extremely dangerous on or near electrical outlets.

X. Application

A. Apply each coat at proper consistency, as recommended by the paint manufacturer.

B. Sand lightly between coats with an appropriate grit finishing paper to provide a smooth, scratch-free finish.

C. Do not sand or apply finishes to surfaces that are not dry.

D. Allow each coat to thoroughly dry before applying next coat.

E. In book matching plywood, every other leaf of veneer is turned over as the leaves are taken in sequence from the flitch, similar to turning or unfolding the pages of a book. Since one leaf will be loose side up and the next tight side up, book matching produces a color shading. In book matching, obtain a match for color and grain at the joints. The tight and loose faces alternating in adjacent leaves may refract light differently, and cause a noticeable color variation in some species. *Proper finishing techniques will minimize this variation.*

Adjacent panels, like pairs of doors, should be finished together to achieve maximum uniformity of color. If possible, entire elevations should be finished together.

F. First class workmanship shall be required for WIC Grade specified.

Where woodwork is to be factory-primed only, one coat of primer is to be applied to appropriate surfaces. Sanding of factory-primed only surfaces is not mandatory.

XI. Cleaning

A. Promptly remove all finish materials spilled, splashed, or spattered.

XII. Finishing Schedule

G. **Field Touch-Up:** Field touch-up after installation is important to the overall appearance expected. All scratches, dents, marks, screw and nail holes, raw or rough edges resulting from job installation, shall be properly sanded, puttied, stained, filled and coated to match the original finish. A final dusting of all exterior and interior surfaces, including drawers, shall be carefully done including the removal of fingerprints or other marks. Advised when items are ready for back priming, if specified. A quantity of touch-up materials shall be provided, after completed, to allow the owner to do minor touch-up. Materials must be properly labeled.

H. Back Priming

1. If back priming is not a part of the architectural millwork manufacturer's contract, the general contractor will be advised when items are ready for back priming, if specified.

2. Material requirements for back priming are based on the type of finish to be applied to exposed portions of installed millwork.

   a. Lacquer or Vinyl Finish—One Coat Lacquer or Vinyl Sanding Sealer.

   b. Varnish Finish—One Coat Semi-gloss Varnish.

   c. Opaque Finish—One Coat Primer or Undercoater.

   d. Plastic Laminate Faced Millwork—One Coat Primer, Sealer, or suitable Backing Sheet.

I. **Wood Finish Systems:** Several generic types of finishes are available to finish wood products. These systems vary in composition from alkyd clears to phenolic varnishes, polyurethane, epoxy, vinyls, epoxypolyesters, acrylic, polymeric oils, and lacquers. A finish system should be chosen that will perform properly for the end use required.

Kitchen Cabinets

Comments

Before kitchen cabinets can be installed, the job must be thoroughly planned, and the space prepared. Pre-planning includes sharing plan information with all involved subcontractors, and careful review of all their work to avoid potential conflicts. This is also the time to make sure that any structural issues have been identified and planned for, to ensure that the electrical service is adequate for equipment and proposed new outlets, and that proposed plumbing rough-ins are correctly located.

Prior to cabinet installation, all electrical, mechanical, and plumbing work should be roughed-in and preparation work for the walls, ceiling, and floor should be completed. Any finished surfaces should be protected with cardboard or tarps. Cabinets that have been removed from their boxes should be protected with padded coverings.

Since cabinets must be installed plumb and level, level floor and ceiling lines must be established, based on high (floor) and low (ceiling) points. Unevenness in walls should be identified and remedied.

Both imperial and metric dimensions are used by cabinet manufacturers, and many provide both units of measure for ease in integrating systems. Figure 6.10 shows the standard height and depth dimensions for base and wall cabinets, counter heights, and wall cabinet mounting heights. Note: On occasion, an owner may request or agree to a minor adjustment in these heights to accommodate factors such as wheelchair access or low ceilings.

Cabinet Performance Standards

Industry Standards

Kitchen & Bathroom Installation Manual, Volume 1
(National Kitchen & Bath Association)

The most recognized and specified standard for kitchen cabinets is ANSI/KCMA A.161.1.1990. This is a performance standard that measures the ability of cabinets to withstand various strict tests that replicate typical household usage and measures desirable construction and performance characteristics. The Kitchen Cabinet Manufacturers Association administers a nationally recognized testing and certification program. Companies that successfully pass this annual battery of tests, performed on randomly selected products, are able to display the blue and white seal. A directory of certified manufacturers and their approved lines is available from KCMA.

Ed. Note: See the Introduction to this chapter for NKBA and KCMA contact information.

Types of Cabinets

Framed Cabinets

In framed cabinet construction, thin component parts make up the sides, back, top, and bottom of the cabinet. These parts are then joined together and attached to a frame that is the primary support for the cabinet. Framed cabinets do not have the minimal clearance tolerances found in the frameless method of cabinet construction.

Comments

Three types of doors are used with framed cabinets: partial overlay (most frequently used), full overlay, and inset. Partial overlay doors can be adjusted fairly easily, so tolerances are not as crucial. Full overlay doors can also be adjusted vertically or horizontally, but the installer must be careful not to allow any obstructions between doors, drawers, or hardware.

Frameless Cabinets

With this method of construction, ⅝" to ¾" (1.59 cm to 1.91 cm) core material sides are connected, with either a mechanical fastening system or a dowel method of construction. Because of their thickness, these case parts form a box that does not need a front frame for stability or squareness. Whether the doors are full overlay or inset, the very tight tolerance for the reveal between doors or between doors and the cabinet box is critical. This reveal is usually ⅛" (3 mm) or less. The slightest misalignment is obvious with such tight tolerances, which is why the doors usually have (and need) 6-way adjustable hinges.

With full overlay doors, *scribing fillers* are required wherever a cabinet is being installed adjacent to a wall. This is necessary to allow for sufficient clearance for the door to hinge open. Scribing fillers are scribed or cut to follow the exact contour of the wall. Similar fillers may be required to allow for proper functioning of cabinets directly adjacent to appliances, when cabinets meet at right angles, or if the cabinet unit has roll-out drawers requiring the cabinet door to swing a little more than 90°. These fillers do not generally need to be scribed.

European Cabinets

European or *Euro-style* cabinets are frameless, and all the shelf supports and connecting hardware are inserted into pre-drilled holes a standard 32 mm (1¼") on center. European wall cabinets are hung on hanging rails that are generally furnished with the cabinet units. The wall cabinet units themselves are not permanently attached to the wall. The hanging rail is a length of steel approximately 1¼" wide. It has an offset channel that is designed to accept the adjustable hooks on the back of each wall cabinet unit. The rail length corresponds to the width of the wall cabinet being installed. The hanging rail is drilled and screwed to wall studs. Most manufacturers recommend that ¼" holes be pre-drilled in the rails for mounting. Use #14, 2½" pan head screws to attach the rails to the wall studs. European cabinet hinges are fully adjustable, allowing the typical full overlay doors to be easily adjusted.

Some cabinets are designed to have the hanging rail behind the wall cabinet units, while others use a rail that is run above the wall cabinets. When the rail is exposed, crown moulding or trim should be planned above the cabinets to conceal the hanging rail. If the hanging rail runs behind the wall cabinets, the backs of the cabinets should be notched so that the cabinets will sit tight against the back wall. However, do not notch the exposed end panel of a wall cabinet at the end of a run of cabinets. Instead, stop the rail at the inside of this end panel.

European base cabinets are not as deep as their North American counterparts, so standard-depth countertops will overhang these base cabinets too far. Some North American installers place blocking behind the cabinets to push them forward to the standard 24" (60.96 cm) depth. You will need special end panels on exposed cabinet ends to cover the gap between the wall and the base cabinets. Make sure you use washers or some other means of keeping the screws from pulling through the back of the cabinet if you choose to screw the base cabinets to the wall.

Cabinet Fasteners

All manufacturers agree that screws are the fastener of choice in almost all installation applications.

The fasteners most commonly used are #8 and #10 screws, with the recommended head types varying by cabinet manufacturer. Wall cabinets are generally attached to wood studs with #8 or #10 wood screws or drywall screws of sufficient length to pass through the cabinet and wall finish and penetrate the wall stud by at least ¾" (1.905 cm). A minimum of four (4) screws are mounted through the top and bottom horizontal mounting rails of each wall cabinet. Cabinets over 42" wide should have six (6) screws. This is somewhat dependent on the stud layout. If you were not able to locate a wall stud, or if a stud does not exist at the point where the cabinet is being mounted, install what you can and then use the next cabinet to add support.

Toggle bolts can be used in some cases in lieu of attaching to a stud, but in no case should a wall cabinet be installed without being secured to at least one wall stud.

Solid masonry walls offer an additional challenge, since there are no studs to screw into and no hollow walls to bolt through. Most manufacturers recommend the use of electrician rawls or some type of lag bolt system for mounting to masonry walls, with the quantity required being the same as for regular screw installations.

Typical Imperial and Metric Cabinet Dimensions

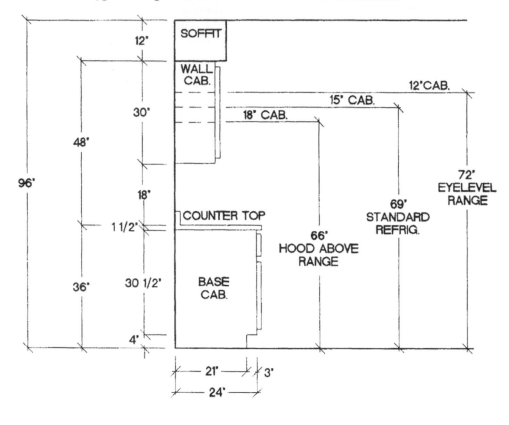

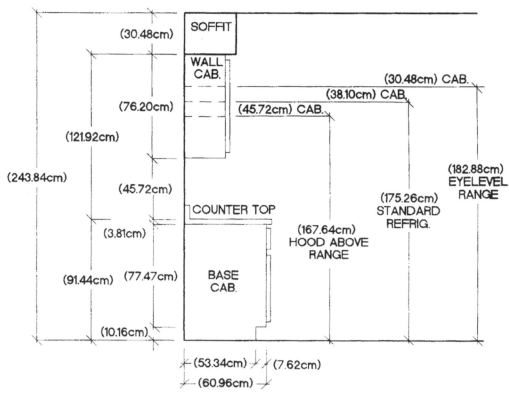

Figure 6.10

Alternatively, lag bolt a hanging rail to the masonry wall first, and then mount the cabinets to the rail. The hanging rail is usually a 1x4 (2.54 cm x 10.16 cm). Some installers will notch out the wall finish so that the rail can set directly against the masonry and thus reduce the gap between the back of the cabinets and the wall.

To attach adjacent wall cabinet units, #8 x 2¼" or 2½" (5.715 cm or 6.35 cm) wood screws or drywall screws should be fastened through the vertical stile of one cabinet into the vertical stile of the adjacent cabinet. The length is dependent on the thickness of the stiles, which varies from manufacturer to manufacturer. Two (2) screws per pair of wall cabinets being connected are generally sufficient for cabinets up to 36" (91.44 cm). Cabinets taller than this should have three (3) screws.

Fasteners for base cabinets are similar to those used for wall cabinets. However, because base cabinets are resting on the floor surface, fasteners are used basically to secure the unit in place once it has been leveled. If the base cabinet backs up to only one wall surface, two screws placed through the center of the mounting rail into wall studs are generally sufficient to stabilize the unit. Adjacent units are screwed together through the vertical stiles or through the adjoining cabinet side panel, depending on whether they are framed or frameless cabinets.

Brads or other suitable types of nails are recommended only for use with wood trim, panels, and other types of mouldings. Nails are not considered sufficient fasteners for either base or wall cabinets.

Professional Tips for Cabinet Installation

- When a wall cabinet is planned that is continuous from countertop to soffit or ceiling (a 48"- to 60"-high unit) (122–152 cm), consider special clearance. Reduce overall cabinet slightly. A countertop platform should be planned beneath the wall cabinet, finished either to match the cabinet with moulding, or the counter material, so doors will not rest on the countertop. Scribing room is built in. A ¾" to 1½" (2–4 cm) platform is recommended.

- When installing wall cabinets to the ceiling, make sure there are not recessed lights designed with the lamp below the edge of the diffuser (which is flush with the ceiling), nor any surface-mounted light closer than the dimension of the cabinet door when open. Ideally, the cabinet should be down from the ceiling an inch or so

and trimmed out with moulding to let doors open and close.

- If placing a drawer unit against a wall with a window or door opening, use a 1" to 1½" (2.5–4 cm) filler between cabinet and wall so drawer will miss casing. Do the same with a drawer unit in a corner so drawers at right angles will miss each other.

- (For roll-out shelves) make sure the door opens past 90° to allow the shelves to roll out.

- Corbel brackets support extended counters. Generally, an overhang more than 12" (30 cm) needs a support bracket every 36" (91 cm).

- Outside corner moulding is used to seal a joint between two panels at right angles. Scribe moulding is used to finish along an uneven ceiling. Batten moulding is used to cover joints between adjacent cabinets.

- Countertop edge mouldings and backsplash mouldings are used to finish the top with solid surface, ceramic tiles and laminates. These surfaces should be finished all the way around if used with tile. With solid surface, mouldings maybe installed unfinished so they can be sanded flush with the top, then finished. Or finished mouldings can be installed slightly offset from the solid surface edgings.

Comments

Cabinets should not be forced into position. Use of shims and scribes should be the rule. Forcing will only rack the cabinet out of square and make operation of drawers and doors sticky.

Kitchen & Bathroom Countertops

Industry Standards

Kitchen & Bathroom Installation Manual, Volume 1
(National Kitchen & Bath Association)

Kitchen and bathroom countertop surfaces must stand up to heavy use, and be very resilient. Typical surface materials for countertops include decorative laminates, cast polymers, solid surface composites, ceramic tile, marble, granite, wood, and stainless steel. These materials may be used alone or in combination.

Decorative Laminates

Decorative laminate surfacing materials are generally adhered to a substrate of ¾" (1.91 cm) plywood or particle board. A ¾" (1.91 cm) thick wood frame is attached to the bottom of the substrate material to give the countertop rigidity. The countertop is attached to the base cabinets by screwing into this wood frame. The wood frame is generally applied at the perimeter of the countertop and at all seams in the substrate material.

Solid-Surfacing

Solid surface materials are man-made composites, made of polymers and acrylics in combination with other materials that produce tough, rigid, high performance countertop surfaces. Installation tips for solid-surface countertops:

- A quality installation is largely dependent on the skill and experience of the fabricator. Most manufacturers of solid surface materials train and certify fabricators.

- When properly fabricated, the seam between two pieces of the solid-surfacing materials is almost imperceptible.

- All manufacturers recommend that unsupported overhangs should not exceed 12" (30.48 cm) with ¾" sheets or 6" (15.24 cm) with ½" sheets.

- All manufacturers recommend that the material "float" on the substrate. Most recommend perimeter frames and a web support system 18" on center rather than a full substrate.

- Because solid surface materials expand when heated, all manufacturers recommend at least ⅛" clearance on wall-to-wall installations.

- While only one manufacturer specifically requires the use of biscuit splines, some installers find that it is wise to use biscuits for most installations to allow for accurate alignment of the two sections being joined. Generally three biscuits are used for each joint: one set in about 3" from each outside edge and one in the middle.

Comments

Most manufacturers of solid surface countertops do not recommend their use for exterior applications. Exposure to temperature variations and sunlight can cause changes in color, and expansion and contraction of the material.

Cast Polymers

Cultured marble, cultured onyx, cultured granite and *solid-colored polymer-based materials* are all used for cast mineral-filled polymer fixtures. Although generally referred to as "cultured marble," a better term to use when describing all of these materials is *cast polymer.* Cast polymers are created by pouring a mixture of ground marble and polyester resin into a treated mold where curing takes place at room temperature or in a curing oven.

The best way to ensure that you will receive a quality cast polymer countertop is to use suppliers who are certified under the joint Cultured Marble Institute (CMI)—National Association of Home Builders Research Center (NAHB RC) Certification Program.

Ceramic Tile

Ed. Note: See also Chapter 10, "Drywall & Ceramic Tile," for more information on ceramic tile.

Comments

Ceramic tile used for kitchen and bath countertops is most likely to be **glazed tile** or **mosaic tile.** Glazed tile can show signs of wear over time, but mosaic stands up well to wear in these conditions. Quarry tile is better suited to flooring applications because it is porous and irregular in shape. Decorative tile works better for walls or backsplashes, where a painted or relief pattern will not be worn off or damaged.

Make certain that the type of ceramic tile specified for the installation project is manufactured with all the specially designed edge and trim pieces required to put together a countertop. Trim pieces are generally manufactured with a ¾" (1.91 cm) radius for conventional mortar installations and a ¼" (.64 cm) radius for organic adhesive installations.

Comments

Grouts

There are four categories of grout specified for kitchen and bathroom installations:

- **Epoxy:** used when superior strength and chemical resistance are necessary. Does not require sealers.

- **Silicone:** Provides elasticity and moisture resistance. Ideal for bathrooms, but not kitchen countertops, since it is unsuitable for food preparation areas.

- **Dry-set ("non-sanded"):** Suitable for joints that do not exceed $1/8$" (.32 cm). When mixed with a latex additive, dry-set is ideal for wet areas such as bathroom and kitchen countertops.
- **Sanded:** Used with joints up to $3/8$" (.96 cm). Used most often with ceramic mosaic tile and floor tile.

See the "Tile Grout" section in Chapter 10, "Drywall & Ceramic Tile" for more information on this topic.

Ceramic tile countertops are installed directly on a deck or substrate by one of three installation methods: *mastic* (organic adhesive), *conventional mortar bed* (mud), or *thin set* over a backerboard.

While plywood decking is the most common substrate material for countertops, some installers prefer traditional lumber decking. Traditional decking is often used to provide flexibility under the tile. Generally, grade-one or grade-two kiln dried Douglas fir, 1" x 4" (2.54 cm x 10.16 cm) or 1" x 6" (2.54 cm x 15.24 cm) spaced $1/4$" (.64 cm) apart, is used. It may be installed perpendicular to the backsplash (from the front of the counter to the back) or running parallel with the cabinet space.

The decking should be delivered to the project site several days before the installation to allow the wood to reach the relative humidity of the room. The decking should overhang the cabinets and be flush with the face of the drawers and doors.

Fixture cutouts are made during the tile decking installation. Whenever possible, any cutout should be a minimum of 2" (5.08 cm) away from a wallboard or plastered backsplash.

Elimination of stress is critical when countertop overhangs are planned. The tile must have a solid base. If any movement occurs when pressure is placed on the top, the tile and/or grout will crack. The underside of the decking should be finished to match the cabinets or correspond with other products used in the project.

Granite

Granite countertops are prefabricated and delivered to the job site ready for installation. Accurate field dimensions are a must, since modification of a granite countertop in the field is nearly impossible.

For most granite countertops, the optimum thickness is $1 1/4$" (3.18 cm). The difference in cost over the more fragile $3/4$" (1.91 cm) slabs is minimal and the added thickness gives more strength for extensions and cutouts, while reducing the risk of breakage during transport and installation. For example, a

$1 1/4$" (3.18 cm) granite slab can support 12" (30.48 cm) of overhang. Keep in mind the weight of these countertops as you plan your installation.

Granite slabs for countertops can measure up to 4'-6" (137.16 cm) wide and up to 9' (274.32 cm) long. This allows flexibility in countertop design. Should more than one piece be necessary, the slabs can be matched for color and grain consistency and then cut to butt squarely against each other. You want to plan seams at the most inconspicuous locations possible, such as around cutouts or back corners. However, avoid seams in the vicinity of the sink cutout due to the possibility of moisture infiltration.

Marble

Marble is extremely brittle, and must be handled like glass during installation. Marble is soft and porous. This means it will stain easily if it is not sealed with at least two coats of penetrating sealer. And it must be frequently resealed.

Wood

Countertops made from laminated wood products are commonly referred to as butcher block. In addition to full countertops, insert blocks are often installed in other types of kitchen countertops as cutting boards. The intended use of block should determine the finish selection. Unfinished wood is most desirable if the entire counter surface is wood and local fabrication of seams or miters is required. (Seams do not adhere properly with prefinished tops, and the wood must be refinished if any sanding is done.) For prefinished wood, the factory finish will include a penetrating sealer and nontoxic lacquer finish. This type of finish is appropriate for countertop sections, such as island tops or sandwich centers. Wood treated with varethane sealer is not appropriate for use as a chopping surface or in contact with food. The finish is, however, very good on countertops that will be exposed to moisture or liquids.

Clean-Up

Comments

When all kitchen components have been installed, all debris and temporary protective materials should be removed. All surfaces should be left "maid-clean." Scratches or nicks that may have occurred can usually be patched using a touch-up kit available from the manufacturer. In anticipation of these minor repairs, the kit can be ordered along with the cabinets.

CHAPTER 7

INSULATION & VAPOR RETARDERS

Table of Contents

Text in blue type indicates excerpted summaries from the International
Building Code® (IBC) *and* International Residential Code® (IRC).
*Please consult the IBC and IRC for complete coverage and specific
wording. "Comments" (in solid blue boxes) were written by the editors,
based on their own experience.*

 This icon will appear with references to green building practices.

CHAPTER 7

INSULATION & VAPOR RETARDERS

Common Defect Allegations

- *Insufficient filling of wall space with blown-in insulation: This situation usually results from obstructions inside the wall or because the installer did not keep the nozzle moving during installation. An opening that fills too quickly usually indicates an obstruction. A trained installer knows the average time and pressure required to fill a wall space. This type of claim is usually discovered at a later date when a wall is opened for repairs or remodeling.*

- *Blowout of interior walls on blown insulation: The pressure generated by the machine can cause interior nail pops and even entire walls to blow out. This type of complaint is usually directed toward the installer, but the situation can also be caused by incorrect nail size or insufficient nailing of the drywall during original construction.*

- *Failure to allow an air gap between the roof sheathing and the insulation space when installing insulation in ceiling joist spaces on vaulted ceiling: The gap is intended to allow condensation that forms against the sheathing to evaporate before saturating the insulation. Condensation forms when there are extreme differentials in temperature between the inside and outside air. Insulation that becomes wet will compress and lose its R-value. Additionally, wet insulation will hold water against a wood structure and promote mold, fungus, and subsequent dryrot.*

- *Blocked vents at the frieze blocks: This prevents the necessary air circulation required in that void. This condition can cause miscellaneous water intrusion to stay in the building, leading to some of the problems described above. Also, ceiling/wall cracking is prevalent when the vents are blocked due to expansion from excessive heat buildup.*

- *Insulation covering vented recessed light fixtures, such as heat lamps in violation of the 3" rule for clearance: Be sure to check with an electrician about which rough-ins may require special clearances, or read the label on the unit.*

(continued)

> • *Electrical and plumbing holes not properly filled: In cold climates, the insulator usually fills the holes (electrical and plumbing) in the top and bottom plates with expanding foam. This is an important task and should be watched and checked.*
>
> • *Foam roofing failures on commercial buildings where the roof slope has been achieved with sprayed foam under the roof membrane: When water enters this system, there is no way that we have found to save it. The remedy is to remove the entire system and reinstall. Building owners should be given instructions on maintaining this system when they purchase the building, and an aggressive maintenance program must be applied to keep out water intrusion.*

Introduction

Many defect claims, especially in cold climates, are related to moisture entrapment in insulation and unvented areas. While this chapter provides an overview of general requirements for the United States, it is important to understand the specific and proper procedures and requirements for installation of insulation and vapor barriers for your particular location.

The purpose of insulation is to reduce the transmission of heat, cold, or sound. Insulation materials are rated for thermal resistance, expressed as R-value. Insulation requirements for a particular project are typically specified on the plan cross section, wall sections, and details through the exterior building envelope. (See **Figure 7.1.**)

This chapter addresses common insulation applications in residential and light commercial construction. It is broken down into types and uses of various insulation materials, followed by requirements for building components that are commonly insulated.

Some types of housing may have to meet additional federal government requirements, such as H.U.D. (Housing and Urban Development).

The U.S. government created the *Model Energy Code* in 1992 to address the current energy shortage. It included minimum requirements for the use of energy in new building construction or additions to existing structures. Now called the *International Energy Conservation Code,* it is maintained by the International Code Council (ICC). In this chapter, we refer to the *Model Energy Code* only in a general way because it relates to energy calculations from an engineering approach. A builder applying for a permit conveys the proposed type and R-value of the insulation to be used. It is

Insulation Details

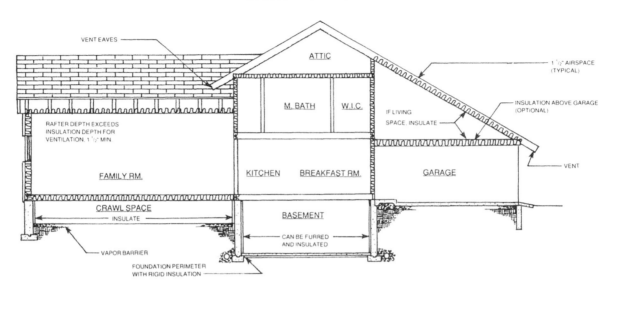

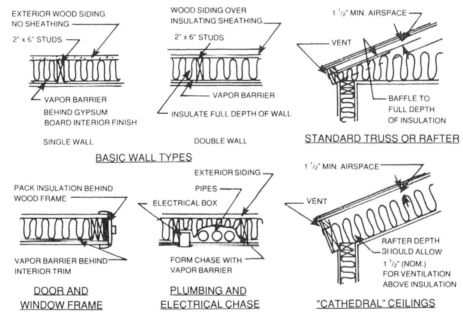

Figure 7.1

important to note that the contractor needs to determine the thickness and type of insulation required to meet the specified R-value. In some cases, such as cathedral ceilings, special high-density (and higher cost) batt insulation may be required due to space limitations.

The Consumer Update Bulletin #1, "Cellulose Insulation in the ICC International Codes," published by the Cellulose Insulation Manufacturers Association (CIMA), indicates that although R-value is an essential component in selecting the best insulation for a project, it is only one factor in the actual performance of insulated building assemblies. Other key factors include:

- Air infiltration from leaks through gaps in the system
- Permeability of system elements
- Convective flows within insulation systems
- Thermal bridging across the building envelope
- Thermal mass of building occupants

Note: Pipe and duct insulation are covered more fully in Chapter 15, "HVAC."

The following professional associations may be helpful in locating more information about insulation.

Association of the Wall and Ceiling Industry (AWCI)
703-538-1600
www.awci.org

Cellulose Insulation Manufacturers Association (CIMA)
888-881-2462
www.cellulose.org

Insulation Contractors Association of America (ICAA)
703-739-0356
www.insulate.org

National Insulation Association (NIA)
703-683-6422
www.insulation.org

North American Insulation Manufacturers Association (NAIMA)
703-684-0084
www.naima.org

Polyisocyanurate Insulation Manufacturers Association (PIMA)
301-654-0000
www.pima.org

Green Building & Insulation

Installing the recommended levels of insulation greatly improves a home's energy efficiency, reduces fuel use and energy bills, and increases comfort. It's one of the most cost-effective ways to save energy and money. And, like other energy-saving measures, it has huge environmental benefits. The less energy a home consumes, the less pollution will be produced by power plants, and the cleaner the skies and healthier the environment.

For attics, the current standard in most parts of the United States is around R-30 to R-38—which translates to 10" to 14" of insulation, depending on the material. Energy-smart builders often exceed these recommendations by at least 30%–50%. Log onto the EPA's Energy Star® website to check out recommendations for your area. The site provides a map of temperature zones with an accompanying table that lists recommended R-values for walls and ceilings. Or check out the Department of Energy-sponsored Zip Code Insulation Program website **www.ornl.gov**

Environmentally Friendly Insulation Options

For green homes, consider environment- and people-friendly products. Cellulose, for instance, is made from recycled newspaper and wood fiber. Some types of fiberglass insulation are made from recycled glass. And some fiberglass insulation batts are encapsulated to prevent workers from inhaling the fibers. Some manufacturers are using safer binders that replace formaldehyde resin in fiberglass batt insulation. Many of the rigid foam insulation products are no longer made with ozone-depleting chemicals.

There are also a number of new products to consider, including cotton batt insulation (made from waste from blue-jean factories) or loose-fill wool insulation and liquid foam insulation made from chemicals derived from soy.

Green Building: Project Planning & Cost Estimating, Second Edition
(RSMeans)

Insulation is a potential source of indoor pollutants, from fibers and chemicals in materials such as cellulose, fiberglass, and mineral wool (which uses phenol formaldehyde binders), polyurethane spray foam, and polystyrene. Safer choices include Perlite, Icynene, and Air Krete, as well as scrap cotton. Formaldehyde-free fiberglass insulation is available from the major insulation manufacturers.

During the 1970s, many properties had urea-formaldehyde foam insulation (UFFI) installed in the wall cavities as an energy conservation measure. However, many of these properties were found to have relatively high indoor concentrations of formaldehyde soon after the UFFI installation.

Use of this product has been declining. Studies show that formaldehyde emissions from UFFI decrease with time; therefore, homes in which UFFI was installed many years ago are unlikely to have high levels of formaldehyde now.

General Types & Forms of Insulation

Industry Standards

National Insulation Association

(NIA Internet Web Site: www.insulation.org)

Insulations will be discussed according to their generic types and forms. The type indicates composition (i.e., glass, plastic) and internal structure (i.e., cellular, fibrous). The form implies overall shape or application (i.e., board, blanket, pipe covering).

General Types of Insulation

Fibrous Insulation—Composed of small diameter fibers, which finely divide the air space. The fibers may be perpendicular or horizontal to the surface being insulated, and they may or may not be bonded together. Silica, rock wool, slag wool and alumina silica fibers are used. The most widely used insulations of this type are glass fiber and mineral wool.

Cellular Insulation—Composed of small individual cells separated from each other. The cellular material may be glass or foamed plastic, such as polystyrene (closed cell), polyurethane and elastomeric.

Granular Insulation—Composed of small nodules which contain voids or hollow spaces. It is not considered a true cellular material, since gas can be transferred between the individual spaces. This type may be produced as a loose or pourable material, or combined with a binder and fibers to make a rigid insulation. Examples of these insulations are calcium silicate, expanded vermiculite, perlite, cellulose, diatomaceous earth, and expanded polystyrene.

General Forms of Insulation

Insulations are produced in a variety of forms suitable for specific functions and applications. The combined form and type of insulation determine its proper method of installation. The forms most widely used are:

1. **Rigid boards, blocks, sheets, and pre-formed shapes such as pipe covering, curved segments, lagging, etc.** Cellular, granular, and fibrous insulations are produced in these forms.

2. **Flexible sheets and pre-formed shapes.** Cellular and fibrous insulations are produced in these forms.

3. **Flexible blankets.** Fibrous insulations are produced in flexible blankets.

4. **Cements (insulating and finishing).** Produced from fibrous and granular insulations and cement, they may be of the hydraulic setting or air drying type.

5. **Foams.** Poured or froth foam is used to fill irregular areas and voids. Spray is used for flat surfaces.

Uses of Insulation

Insulation materials have been developed for specific uses and are produced in many forms. Some of these are as follows:

- **Loose fill**—Used for pouring or blowing in attic or wall spaces of buildings.

- **Batts**—A loose, fluffy insulation material with little structural strength which must be placed in an enclosure or laid flat.

- **Blanket**—A flexible material used to wrap different shapes and forms. (Example: duct wrap)

- **Semi-Rigid Boards**—Sheets and pre-formed shapes with little "give." (Example: fiberglass boards and pipe insulation)

- **Flexible**—Plastic sheets and tubing insulation used in various applications such as refrigerant pipe on residential air conditioning systems. (Example: Armaflex)

- **Rigid Boards**—Block, sheets, and pre-formed shapes with little "give" used on straight sections of flat surfaces. May be fabricated for curved and irregular surfaces. (Example: Calcium silicate pipe and block insulation)

- **Tapes**—Used to wrap small diameter apparatus where other forms are not practical.

- **Cements**—Used for molding various shapes and surfaces.

- **Foam-in-Place Plastic Materials**—A liquid mixed at time of application which sets or hardens to insulate surfaces or cavities.

- **Spray-On-Fiber, Granular, or Cement Materials**—Used for building and equipment insulation in a wide temperature application range. (Example: spray-on fireproofing)

- **Reflective Insulation**—Layers of reflective stainless steel foil. It is used extensively in nuclear power plants. Another type is reflective glass or film for plate glass windows that reflect the heat from the sun.

Comments

Building Codes & Material Standards

Building codes are in one of two forms—a specification or a performance code. The specification code provides the technical description of the material, and the performance code describes how the product or system should perform. One must also be aware of any additional code or energy requirements as established by the local building authority that has actual jurisdiction over the structure.

Insulation materials must generally meet standards determined by the American Society for Testing and Materials (ASTM) and those set by the General Services Administration (GSA), which are known as Federal Specifications. Also, all material standards, tests, and codes are revised at various intervals, and it is important that architects and contractors are aware of the latest revisions. In addition to manufacturers' recommended standards, the following resources may be helpful in providing information on insulation requirements:

- *International Energy Conservation Code*
- HUD MPS (Minimum Property Standards)
- Farmers Home Administration (FMHA)
- State energy codes
- NAHB Research Center Certification and Labeling Program
- *International Building Code*
- *International Residential Code*

Rock & Slag Wool Insulation

North American Insulation Manufacturers Association
(NAIMA Internet Website: www.naima.org)

Rock and slag insulations, sometimes referred to as mineral wool, have been produced naturally for centuries. During volcanic eruptions, when a strong wind passes over a stream of molten lava, the lava is blown into fine silky threads that look like wool. From this natural inspiration sprung one of the most innovative and versatile insulation products on the market today. Today's rock and slag wool insulations are high-tech versions of their predecessors, produced from plentiful basalt and industrial slag. Their versatility allows them to be used in a wide variety of residential, commercial and industrial applications to provide sustainable thermal and acoustical comfort and, perhaps most uniquely, to serve as passive fire

protection. Although rock and slag wool are not as well known among North American consumers as other insulation products, these fiberized products have been used effectively in buildings around the world for more than a century and remain some of the most innovative and versatile insulations in use today.

Benefits

Rock and slag wool insulation offers a wide array of benefits for specifiers, designers, and builders interested in using materials offering environmentally responsible characteristics and demonstrating proven performance.

Outstanding Thermal Performance

Thermal performance is a critical determinant in choosing an insulation product and the product must be thoroughly tested and proven to perform at the same level as when installed for the life of the building. Rock and slag wool insulation is tested to all applicable industry standards to ensure its R-value does not deteriorate over time. Loose-fill rock and slag wool insulation resists settling, and batt products spring back after average compression so that installed thermal performance is maintained over the life of the product. The insulation also lends to the sustainable nature of the structure by protecting the building from moisture and fire damage. Further, the higher density of rock and slag wool insulation allows it to achieve higher R-values in a typical wall cavity than most other insulation products.

Excellent Fire Resistance

The performance of building materials in a fire is a key factor in protecting the occupants of the building and allowing them to escape safely. Rock and slag wool insulation is naturally non-combustible and remains so for the life of the product without the addition of harsh and potentially dangerous chemical fire retardants. The insulation can resist temperatures in excess of 2,000°F. Because these products have a high melting temperature, they can be used in a wide variety of applications that call for these unique properties. These products meet NFPA 220 and ASTM E 136 standards and test methods and are Class A product tested per ASTM E 84 and NFPA 101.

Rock and slag wool insulation is used as passive fire protection in many buildings. Manufacturers of these products encourage a balanced design, which includes a combination of active, detective and passive fire protection in building codes to ensure the safety of building occupants.

Excellent Sound Absorption

The fibrous structure and high density of rock and slag wool insulation offer excellent sound absorption properties, making these products an outstanding part of overall wall systems designed to reduce sound transmission.

Mold, Fungi and Bacteria Resistant

Rock and slag wool insulation resists the growth of mold, fungi and bacteria because it is inorganic. These products offer enhanced protection against damaging moisture infiltration that can rob insulation of R-value.

Composition

Rock wool and slag wool insulation is comprised of basically the same raw materials but in different proportions and is produced in the same way. Manufacturers use a mechanized process to spin a molten composition of rock and slag into high temperature-resistant fibers. Their similar properties also produce fairly similar performance attributes. The major difference is in the specific volumes of the various raw materials used to make each product.

Rock Wool Insulation

Rock wool insulation is composed principally of fibers manufactured from a combination of aluminosilicate rock (usually basalt), blast furnace slag and limestone or dolomite. Slag is a byproduct from steel production that would otherwise wind up in landfills. Binders may or may not be used, depending on the product. Typically, rock wool insulation is comprised of a minimum of 70–75 percent natural rock. The remaining volume of raw material is blast furnace slag.

Slag Wool Insulation

Slag wool insulation is composed principally of fibers manufactured by melting the primary component, blast furnace slag, with a combination of some natural rock, with or without binders, depending on the product. Typically, slag wool insulation uses approximately 70 percent blast furnace slag, with the remaining volume of raw materials being natural rock.

Spray Foam Insulation

Comments

Spray foam insulation is made of different materials, including polyurethane, latex, and natural products like soy. It is used in new and existing construction to provide a continuous air barrier around framing, joints, and other building support structures. It helps maximize loss of heated and cooled air, reducing heating and cooling costs by as much as 40%. Spray foam insulation is also used to reduce noise transmission between floors. It keeps insects and rodents out and is not a food source for them. Some types of "double-density" foam also offer some structural support. The product is recommended by FEMA for use in flood-prone areas.

 Spray foam insulation is available from several manufacturers in a "green" version made from soy beans, an annually renewable resource. Some products include a sugar cane material. Foam insulation helps seal a home or business from moisture, mold spores, pollen, and airborne pollutants, thereby improving air quality.

Loose-Fill Insulation

Comments

Loose-fill insulation can be applied by hand-pouring, machine-blowing, or spraying. Loose-fill is specified by R-value rather than inches of thickness because manufacturers can vary slightly in the R-value to thickness of insulation ratio. Information on coverage and the inches of thickness necessary to attain a specific R-value is provided by each manufacturer on the package. Cellulose R-values should always be stated at settled density. Insulation blown in the direction of joists, rather than across them, ensures complete filling of the joist spaces.

Loose-Fill Insulation Defect Claims

Loose fill insulation of existing walls usually involves two different types of defect claims.

1. Insufficient filling of wall space—This situation usually results from obstructions inside the wall or because the installer did not keep the nozzle moving during installation. An opening that fills too quickly usually indicates an obstruction.

The trained installer knows the average time and pressure required to fill a wall space. This type of claim is usually discovered at a later date when a wall is opened for repairs or remodeling.

2. Blowout or distortion of interior walls— The pressure generated by the machine can cause interior nail pops and even entire walls to blow out. This type of complaint is usually directed toward the installer, but the situation can also be caused by incorrect nail size or insufficient nailing of the drywall during original construction.

Note: The following are summaries of the basic code requirements of the International Building Code *and* International Residential Code. *Please consult the IBC and IRC for complete coverage and specific wording.*

IRC–2006

R316.2 Loose-fill insulation: Insulation that cannot mount in the required ASTM E 84 apparatus without artificial supports must have a flame-spread required of 25 or less and smoke-developed index of 450 or less. This applies to both concealed and exposed insulation. Cellulose loose-fill is only required to meet the smoke rating.

IBC–2006

719.4 Loose-fill insulation: Same requirements as IRC.

Cellulosic Fiber Insulation

Comments

Cellulosic fiber insulation is applied by blowing, pouring, and sometimes by combining with adhesives for spraying.

Cellulosic fiber insulation is primarily used for insulating walls and attic spaces. Rated materials can also be used in commercial applications.

Care must be taken to keep cellulosic insulations at least 3" away from light fixtures or any other heat-generating item. (See Chapter 16, "Lighting Outlets" and "Lighting Fixtures," for electrical code requirements.) Blown or pourable cellulosic insulations should not be installed in locations where temperatures will exceed 180°F.

Be sure to follow the cellulosic fiber installation methods exactly as stated on the manufacturing label. Chemicals that are mixed in cellulosic insulations have been known to cause chemical corrosion of electrical wiring and plumbing when blown-in products were improperly installed as a spray-on application.

Rigid & Blanket Insulation

Comments

Rigid insulation is fabricated in boards or sheets and is predominantly used in exterior walls, foundations, and roofs. The materials commonly used for rigid insulations include **polystyrene** (often called "beadboard"), **perlite, polyurethane, polyisocyanurate, phenolic, cellular glass block, organic fiber,** or **glass fiber.**

Polystyrene insulations are similar to other plastic foam insulations, but they generally have lower R-values.

Prolonged exposure to sunlight will cause polystyrene to deteriorate.

In industrial and commercial buildings, polystyrene is commonly used for foundations, floors, walls, and roofs. In residential construction, it is used for perimeter slabs, foundations, exterior sheathing, and siding backerboards.

Perlite does not burn, but has a tendency to absorb water, so it should be kept dry.

Polyisocyanurate foam, like other urethanes, will burn and must be protected from flame and damage. In industrial and commercial buildings, polyisocyanurate is commonly used in foundations, floors, walls, and roofs. In residential construction, it is principally used for sheathing, exterior foundations, and slab-on-grade.

Phenolic insulation is used for roofs and walls. It has a higher R-value than other foam plastic insulations, but it is fragile and must be handled carefully.

Cellular glass is used on roof and exterior decks, and as perimeter insulation for foundations and slabs. Cellular glass must be handled carefully and protected from freezing and thawing.

Organic fiber rigid insulation and rigid glass fiber insulation are primarily used for roofing systems in which the boards are tapered to provide positive drainage.

Mineral fiber insulation is resistant to fire, moisture, and vermin.

Semi-rigid boards, 1"–3" thick, are primarily used as curtain walls between exterior wall furring and in locations requiring a semi-rigid product.

Batts and blankets are primarily used for insulating walls and partitions, below floors, in crawl spaces, above ceilings, in attic spaces, and as a sound barrier. Batts or blankets can be manufactured with facings that can act either as a vapor barrier or as breather paper. Only one face on the batt or blanket is a vapor barrier. Any other facing is a breather paper, which is installed for easier handling or to provide flanges for stapling. Unfaced batts or blankets are designed to be friction fit and are held in place by pressure.

Flexible Piping Insulation

Comments

Hot water piping can be insulated with pre-formed lengths of insulation, which are made from fiberglass or closed cell foam. To ensure a snug fit, the insulation (which is usually in 4' lengths) is manufactured to fit a specific pipe type and size.

(continued)

A slit along the length of the insulation allows it to be slipped onto the pipe after the waterline is in place. Tape wrapped around the insulation secures it to the pipe.

See Chapter 14, "Plumbing," and Chapter 15, "HVAC," for more information on pipe insulation.

IBC–2006

719.7 Insulation and covering on pipe and tubing: A flame-spread of 25 or less, and a smoke-developed index of 450 or less, is required. Insulation installed in plenums must meet requirements of the *International Mechanical Code.*

Insulation Materials & R-Value

Comments

Energy standards list insulation products according to their ability to resist heat flow at a given thickness. This measurement is commonly known as the R-value or

U-factor. However, the following terms may sometimes be used: **thermal resistance** or **thermal conductivity (k-value)**.

R-value listings are preferred, because they can be added directly to calculate the overall thermal resistance of an assembly. The overall R-value is the reciprocal of the assembly's U-factor, which is used to calculate the heat loss through the assembly.

R-values of the same product may vary slightly with each manufacturer. In most cases, specific minimum R-values are dictated by building codes. Manufacturers then fabricate and package their finished products to meet the code.

Manufacturers of loose-fill and sprayed-on-foam list a specific thickness that must be installed for their product to meet the specified R-value.

R-values are not directly related to the thickness of the insulation product. Density determines an insulation's R-value. The more fibers per square inch of insulating material, the greater its density, and the higher its R-value.

Figure 7.2 shows the formulas for calculating heat transfer, using a masonry wall example to illustrate the changing R- and U-values when different insulating materials are applied. **Figure 7.3** is a chart listing the R-values of common building materials. **Figure 7.4** is a table listing the maximum R-values or various types of insulation.

"U" and "R" Factors

Table B2010-031   Example Using 14" Masonry Cavity Wall with 1" Plaster for the Exterior Closure

Total Heat Transfer is found using the equation

$Q = AU(T_2 - T_1)$ where:

Q = Heat flow, BTU per hour
A = Area, square feet
U = Overall heat transfer coefficient
$(T_2 - T_1)$ = Difference in temperature of the air on each side of the construction component in degrees Fahrenheit

Coefficients of Transmission ("U") are expressed in BTU per (hour) (square foot) (Fahrenheit degree difference in temperature between the air on two sides) and are based on 15 mph outside wind velocity.

The lower the U-value the higher the insulating value.

$U = 1/R$ where "R" is the summation of the resistances of air films, materials and air spaces that make up the assembly.

Figure B2010-031   Example Using 14" Masonry Cavity Wall with 1" Plaster for the Exterior Closure

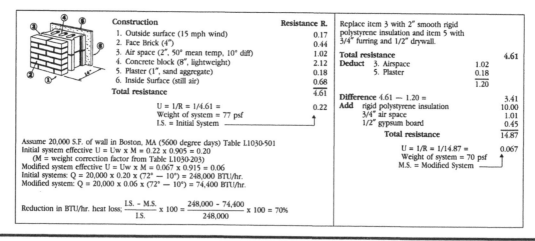

Construction	Resistance R.
1. Outside surface (15 mph wind)	0.17
2. Face Brick (4")	0.44
3. Air space (2", 50° mean temp, 10° diff)	1.02
4. Concrete block (8", lightweight)	2.12
5. Plaster (1", sand aggregate)	0.18
6. Inside Surface (still air)	0.68
Total resistance	**4.61**

$U = 1/R = 1/4.61 = 0.22$
Weight of system = 77 psf
I.S. = Initial System

Replace item 3 with 2" smooth rigid polystyrene insulation and item 5 with 3/4" furring and 1/2" drywall.

Total resistance		4.61
Deduct 3. Airspace	1.02	
5. Plaster	0.18	
		1.20

Difference 4.61 — 1.20 =	3.41
Add rigid polystyrene insulation	10.00
3/4" air space	1.01
1/2" gypsum board	0.45
Total resistance	**14.87**

$U = 1/R = 1/14.87 = 0.067$
Weight of system = 70 psf
M.S. = Modified System

Assume 20,000 S.F. of wall in Boston, MA (5600 degree days) Table L1030-501
Initial system effective U = Uw x M = 0.22 x 0.905 = 0.20
  (M = weight correction factor from Table L1030-203)
Modified system effective U = Uw x M = 0.067 x 0.915 = 0.06
Initial systems: Q = 20,000 x 0.20 x (72° — 10°) = 248,000 BTU/hr.
Modified system: Q = 20,000 x 0.06 x (72° — 10°) = 74,400 BTU/hr.

Reduction in BTU/hr. heat loss; $\dfrac{\text{I.S.} - \text{M.S.}}{\text{I.S.}} \times 100 = \dfrac{248,000 - 74,400}{248,000} \times 100 = 70\%$

Figure 7.2

"U" and "R" Factors

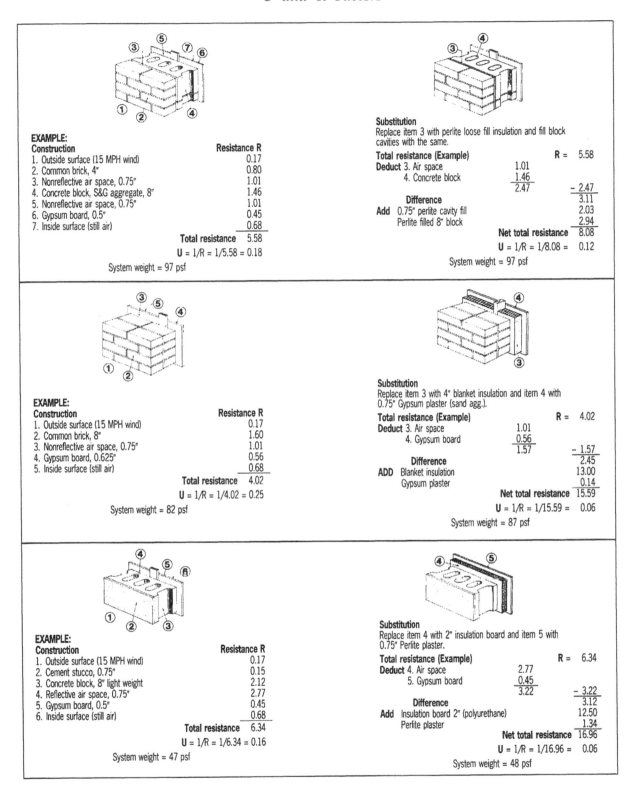

EXAMPLE:

Construction	Resistance R
1. Outside surface (15 MPH wind)	0.17
2. Common brick, 4"	0.80
3. Nonreflective air space, 0.75"	1.01
4. Concrete block, S&G aggregate, 8"	1.46
5. Nonreflective air space, 0.75"	1.01
6. Gypsum board, 0.5"	0.45
7. Inside surface (still air)	0.68
Total resistance	5.58

$U = 1/R = 1/5.58 = 0.18$

System weight = 97 psf

Substitution

Replace item 3 with perlite loose fill insulation and fill block cavities with the same.

Total resistance (Example)		R = 5.58
Deduct 3. Air space	1.01	
4. Concrete block	1.46	
	2.47	– 2.47
Difference		3.11
Add 0.75" perlite cavity fill		2.03
Perlite filled 8" block		2.94
Net total resistance		8.08

$U = 1/R = 1/8.08 = 0.12$

System weight = 97 psf

EXAMPLE:

Construction	Resistance R
1. Outside surface (15 MPH wind)	0.17
2. Common brick, 8"	1.60
3. Nonreflective air space, 0.75"	1.01
4. Gypsum board, 0.625"	0.56
5. Inside surface (still air)	0.68
Total resistance	4.02

$U = 1/R = 1/4.02 = 0.25$

System weight = 82 psf

Substitution

Replace item 3 with 4" blanket insulation and item 4 with 0.75" Gypsum plaster (sand agg.).

Total resistance (Example)		R = 4.02
Deduct 3. Air space	1.01	
4. Gypsum board	0.56	
	1.57	– 1.57
Difference		2.45
ADD Blanket insulation		13.00
Gypsum plaster		0.14
Net total resistance		15.59

$U = 1/R = 1/15.59 = 0.06$

System weight = 87 psf

EXAMPLE:

Construction	Resistance R
1. Outside surface (15 MPH wind)	0.17
2. Cement stucco, 0.75"	0.15
3. Concrete block, 8" light weight	2.12
4. Reflective air space, 0.75"	2.77
5. Gypsum board, 0.5"	0.45
6. Inside surface (still air)	0.68
Total resistance	6.34

$U = 1/R = 1/6.34 = 0.16$

System weight = 47 psf

Substitution

Replace item 4 with 2" insulation board and item 5 with 0.75" Perlite plaster.

Total resistance (Example)		R = 6.34
Deduct 4. Air space	2.77	
5. Gypsum board	0.45	
	3.22	– 3.22
Difference		3.12
Add Insulation board 2" (polyurethane)		12.50
Perlite plaster		1.34
Net total resistance		16.96

$U = 1/R = 1/16.96 = 0.06$

System weight = 48 psf

RSMeans, *Assemblies Cost Data*

Figure 7.2 (continued)

Thermal Properties of Materials

Table L1030-401 Resistances ("R") of Building and Insulating Materials

Material	Wt./Lbs. per C.F.	R per Inch	R Listed Size
Air Spaces and Surfaces			
Enclosed non-reflective spaces, E=0.82			
50° F mean temp., 30°/10° F diff.			
.5"			.90/.91
.75"			.94/1.01
1.50"			.90/1.02
3.50"			.91/1.01
Inside vert. surface (still air)			0.68
Outside vert. surface (15 mph wind)			0.17
Building Boards			
Asbestos cement, 0.25" thick	120		0.06
Gypsum or plaster, 0.5" thick	50		0.45
Hardboard regular	50	1.37	
Tempered	63	1.00	
Laminated paper	30	2.00	
Particle board	37	1.85	
	50	1.06	
	63	0.85	
Plywood (Douglas Fir), 0.5" thick	34		0.62
Shingle backer, .375" thick	18		0.94
Sound deadening board, 0.5" thick	15		1.35
Tile and lay-in panels, plain or			
acoustical, 0.5" thick	18		1.25
Vegetable fiber, 0.5" thick	18		1.32
	25		1.14
Wood, hardwoods	48	0.91	
Softwoods	32	1.25	
Flooring Carpet with fibrous pad			2.08
With rubber pad			1.23
Cork tile, 1/8" thick			0.28
Terrazzo			0.08
Tile, resilient			0.05
Wood, hardwood, 0.75" thick			0.68
Subfloor, 0.75" thick			0.94
Glass			
Insulation, 0.50" air space			2.04
Single glass			0.91
Insulation Blanket or Batt, mineral, glass			
or rock fiber, approximate thickness			
3.0" to 3.5" thick			11
3.5" to 4.0" thick			13
6.0" to 6.5" thick			19
6.5" to 7.0" thick			22
8.5" to 9.0" thick			30
Boards			
Cellular glass	8.5	2.63	
Fiberboard, wet felted			
Acoustical tile	21	2.70	
Roof insulation	17	2.94	
Fiberboard, wet molded			
Acoustical tile	23	2.38	
Mineral fiber with resin binder	15	3.45	
Polystyrene, extruded,			
cut cell surface	1.8	4.00	
smooth skin surface	2.2	5.00	
	3.5	5.26	
Bead boards	1.0	3.57	
Polyurethane	1.5	6.25	
Wood or cane fiberboard, 0.5" thick			1.25

Material	Wt./Lbs. per C.F.	R per Inch	R Listed Size
Insulation Loose Fill			
Cellulose	2.3	3.13	
	3.2	3.70	
Mineral fiber, 3.75" to 5" thick	2-5		11
6.5" to 8.75" thick			19
7.5" to 10" thick			22
10.25" to 13.75" thick			30
Perlite	5-8	2.70	
Vermiculite	4-6	2.27	
Wood fiber	2-3.5	3.33	
Masonry Brick, Common	120	0.20	
Face	130	0.11	
Cement mortar	116	0.20	
Clay tile, hollow			
1 cell wide, 3" width			0.80
4" width			1.11
2 cells wide, 6" width			1.52
8" width			1.85
10" width			2.22
3 cells wide, 12" width			2.50
Concrete, gypsum fiber	51	0.60	
Lightweight	120	0.19	
	80	0.40	
	40	0.86	
Perlite	40	1.08	
Sand and gravel or stone	140	0.08	
Concrete block, lightweight			
3 cell units, 4"-15 lbs. ea.			1.68
6"-23 lbs. ea.			1.83
8"-28 lbs. ea.			2.12
12"-40 lbs. ea.			2.62
Sand and gravel aggregates,			
4"-20 lbs. ea.			1.17
6"-33 lbs. ea.			1.29
8"-38 lbs. ea.			1.46
12"-56 lbs. ea.			1.81
Plastering Cement Plaster,			
Sand aggregate	116	0.20	
Gypsum plaster, Perlite aggregate	45	0.67	
Sand aggregate	105	0.18	
Vermiculite aggregate	45	0.59	
Roofing			
Asphalt, felt, 15 lb.			0.06
Rolled roofing	70		0.15
Shingles	70		0.44
Built-up roofing .375" thick	70		0.33
Cement shingles	120		0.21
Vapor-permeable felt			0.06
Vapor seal, 2 layers of			
mopped 15 lb. felt			0.12
Wood, shingles 16"-7.5" exposure			0.87
Siding			
Aluminum or steel (hollow backed)			
oversheathing			0.61
With .375" insulating backer board			1.82
Foil backed			2.96
Wood siding, beveled, ½" x 8"			0.81

Figure 7.3

Insulation Fact Sheet—Maximum R-Values

Type of Insulation	R-Value per Inch
Loose-fill:	
Cellulose	3.1-3.7
Fiberglass	2.2-4.2
Rock wool	2.2-2.9
Batts:	
Fiberglass	2.9-3.8
Cotton	3.0-3.7
Sprayed insulation:	
Polyurethane foam	5.6-6.2
Icynene foam	3.6-4.3
Wet-spray cellulose	2.9-3.4
Spray-in fiberglass	3.7-3.8
Foam board:	
Expanded Polystyrene	3.9-4.2
Extruded Polystyrene	5
Polyisocyanurate	5.6-7.0
Polyurethane	5.6-7.0
Phenolic (closed cell)	8.2
Phenolic (open cell)	4.4
Source: DOE Insulation Fact Sheet www.eere.energy.gov/buildings	

Figure 7.4   RSMeans, *Green Building: Project Planning & Cost Estimating*, 2nd Edition

Green Insulation Properties

Green Building: Project Planning & Cost Estimating, Second Edition
(RSMeans)

The following are considerations when choosing an insulation material.

- Does the insulation retard airflow? (Spray foams and rigid insulations with sealed joints do; loose-fill, batt, and cellulose products do not.) Even if no perceptible gaps in the insulation are present, air under pressure will travel through products that are not airflow retarders. If gaps are present, the issue becomes even more critical. Even small gaps in fiberglass insulation have been found to decrease its effectiveness by up to almost 50%.

- What type of insulation will provide the best R-value within a reasonable thickness for the particular application?

- Does the insulation pose potential health risks to installers or manufacturers, and if so, can proper precautions be used to prevent these risks?

- Does the insulation contain ozone-depleting chemicals?

- Does the insulation have the potential to release gaseous pollutants into the building interior?

- In a retrofit situation, what type of insulation is most practical? For instance, it may be possible to retrofit a conventionally framed structure by blowing insulation into the voids between studs (using holes drilled at the top and bottom of a wall and then resealing them). For a masonry building, however, unless there is a cavity between wall wythes, insulation must be added on either the inside or outside of the walls, which might impose space constraints or other considerations.

It should be noted that providing adequate insulation levels, even given the disadvantages of particular insulation products, is better than providing minimal insulation or none at all. The energy saved by the insulation will occur year after year, reducing the amount of heating and cooling required in the building and the burning of fossil fuels typically associated with that heating and cooling. That said, the best insulation for the job may depend on the circumstances. For instance, if space constraints are a critical issue, the high insulation value per inch of polyisocyanurate and high-density polyurethane foams (4" provides about R-30) may make them the best choices.

If chemical sensitivity is the most critical issue, the structure should be designed to accommodate adequate amounts of a product that does not off-gas harmful pollutants, such as cementitious foam insulation. Alternative building materials that provide high insulation value without toxicity (such as straw bale construction) may also be a good choice for chemically sensitive people.

Another general consideration is the reduction of insulation waste. Trimmings from insulation batts can be recycled into loose-fill insulation and cellulose excess can be reused during the installation process. Rigid foam roofing insulation can be salvaged during roofing retrofits if during the original installation a sheathing layer was installed between the insulation and the roof surface.

For **roof insulation**, loose-fill/blown or batt insulation can be added on top of the upper-story ceiling or, if the attic is to be used for storage, insulation can be installed between the rafters. In addition, a radiant barrier, which reflects radiant heat back (either into or out of a building, depending on the climate) can be attached to the underside of the rafters (or the underside of the insulation), with the shiny side facing down into the attic. It can also be attached on top of the ceiling joists (shiny side facing up into the attic). The radiant barrier must be adjacent to an air gap to work; otherwise heat will travel through the radiant barrier via conduction.

Foundation slabs should be insulated to the climatically appropriate degree by installing rigid insulation around the perimeter and underneath them before the concrete is poured. Pier and beam foundations can be insulated by filling the floor cavities over the crawl space with insulation. Thermal protection can also be achieved by installing a radiant barrier in the floor joist air space above an unheated basement or crawl space.

The R-value of a **radiant barrier** will vary greatly depending on its location (attic or basement) and whether it is the heating or cooling season. During the heating season, the radiant barrier will be effective in the floor joist air space above an unheated basement because the warm air above the basement will tend to stratify, eliminating convection and making radiation the prime mode of heat transfer. By contrast, in the attic space, during the heating season, convection will carry heat right past a radiant barrier. In the cooling season, however, a radiant barrier located in the attic will reflect the heat of a hot roof out of the cooler attic.

Comments

Some insulation is manufactured from materials that are flammable or produce toxic fumes when burned or subjected to extreme heat. Most building codes require these materials to be protected by fire-resistant finishes, such as gypsum wallboard.

Insulation materials containing polyurethane, polyisocyanurate, and polystrene should not be exposed to sunlight because they will be subject to ultraviolet deterioration. Molded polystyrene and expanded perlite boards must be protected from water, as they will absorb moisture.

Classifying Installation Work

Industry Standards

National Insulation Association
(NIA Internet Web Site: www.insulation.org)

Conventional building insulation is usually installed by laborers or carpenters and is not considered a skilled trade. Foam-in-place and spray-on materials are installed by those specializing in the specific materials and applications. Low temperature space insulation (cold storage rooms) is usually installed by carpenters, as it is part of the structure and requires room finishes similar to regular building construction.

Industrial contractors specialize in the installation of pipes, ducts, and equipment. They employ skilled insulation trade mechanics. Some industrial contractors also participate in specialized fields of insulation, especially in low temperature space insulation and foam-in-place applications.

Two broad classifications of insulation work are industrial and commercial. Industrial consists of pipe, duct, and equipment insulation applied in manufacturing plants, power plants, ships, refineries, chemical plants, and other industrial facilities.

Commercial work is performed in buildings other than industrial plants. For example, an office building would have plumbing which would consist of cold water, hot water, and drain pipes. It may also have a heating and air conditioning system on pipes and ducts. Pipe and duct would be insulated to hold heat in hot pipes and/or ducts, to prevent condensation (sweating) on cold pipes or ducts, and to keep them cold. These uses conserve energy.

In industrial work, pipe and equipment are insulated for many important reasons. These include:

- Energy conservation.
- Employee protection from hot pipe burns.
- Maintenance of consistent manufacturing processing temperatures.
- Prevention of fire hazards.
- Noise reduction (to meet legal or company requirements).
- Prevention of moisture condensation damage (sweating) from low-temperature lines or equipment.
- Increase in equipment working life as a result of reduced internal corrosion.
- Environmental protection due to reduced fuel consumption and the emission of air pollutants such as sulfur oxides.
- Reduced requirements for air-conditioning and heat generating systems.

Builder Compliance with Federal Consumer Law

Insulation Contractors Association of America

(ICAA Internet website: **www.insulate.org**)

There is a federal consumer law that requires specific information on insulation be included in a homebuilder's sales contract with home buyers.

If you are a homebuilder, federal consumer law (FTC Home Insulation Rule 460) requires that the R-value of any insulation installed in the homes you sell cannot be below the R-value shown in your sales contract. You must put the following information in every sales contract: the *type, thickness,* and *R-value* of the insulation that will be installed in each part of the house.

Builders are subject to a $11,000 fine each time the Rule is broken. FTC regulates the home insulation industry under its Rule 460, which covers builders who sell new homes.

For loose-fill insulation, you must also show the initial installed thickness and the minimum settled thickness.

Ventilation

Comments

Ventilation can be accomplished through a natural (static) or a power ventilation system. Static systems (simple vent openings) are most common in attics. Ridge, eave, and/or gable vents can be used. Insulation must not be allowed

to cover vent openings. Two or more vent openings allow air to flow through.

There should be one square foot of vent area for each 150 square feet of ceiling area if there is no vapor retarder in the ceiling. If there is a ceiling vapor retarder, allow one square foot for each 300 square feet of ceiling area. Optimally, vents located in the upper portion of the attic should accommodate 50% of the required ventilating area. The other 50% should be addressed by eave vents.

In cathedral ceilings, insulation is installed in rafter spaces, and the ceiling finish layer is fastened to the rafters. A vented air space between insulation and roof sheathing is desirable.

Figure 7.5 shows various types of gable vents.

Ed. Note: Refer to Chapters 5, 14, and 15 for more information on code requirements for ventilation. See also "Foundations, Basements, & Crawl Spaces" at the end of this chapter.

Roof Insulation

IBC–2006

719.5 Roof insulation: Roof insulation may be combustible in any type construction, provided that it is covered directly by roof coverings.

IRC–2006

R906.1 General: Above deck thermal insulation is allowed if it is covered by roof covering that complies with FM 4450 or UL 1256.

Gable Vents

Rectangular
Gable-End Vent

Pitched Triangular
Gable-End Vent

Half-Round
Gable-End Vent

Figure 7.5

RSMeans, *Exterior Home Improvement Costs*

Comments

The roof has a significant impact on a building's heat transmission. Heat transmission through a roof can be reduced by:

1. Use of shiny or light-colored roofing materials for heat reflection.
2. Use of optimum insulation quantities.
3. Increased ventilation in attic spaces.
4. Design of roof pitches and overhangs to increase the lag time of heat flow.
5. Use of building materials that reduce heat transmission.

Many building jurisdictions require roofs with a Class A rating, and will no longer allow installation of a wood shake roof. Composition residential roofs simulate the color of wood shakes. Popular colors for these roofs tend to be dark brown or gray, and the differences in roof colors affect heat transmission. The darker colors absorb more heat than lighter-colored roofs, creating hotter attic spaces. Proper attic ventilation—passive or active—will decrease the temperature of the attic space and, therefore, decrease the degree of heat transmission through the ceiling.

Flat roof systems should use a type of rigid board insulation that provides a base for the roofing as well as thermal resistance.

Industry Standards

Roofing: Design Criteria, Options, Selection
(RSMeans)

Roof insulation can serve a dual purpose: to reduce heat transfer, and to act as a stable, uniform substrate for the roof membrane. In most cases, roof insulation is installed *between the structural deck and the roof membrane*. **Figure 7.6** is an illustration of a conventional roof insulation system. One exception, the Inverted Roof Membrane Assembly (IRMA), is used in severely cold climates. In this arrangement, the insulation rests above the waterproofing membrane. This system, also known as Protected Membrane Roofing (PMR), is also shown in **Figure 7.6**.

There are many types and thicknesses of material available for roof insulation. **Figure 7.7** is a chart comparing the characteristics of various roof insulation materials. The most common are described in the following paragraphs.

Note: Composite board is a combination of two of the following boards, with a facing of a different material. The two boards are laminated in the factory to produce a product with the advantages of both materials.

Polyisocyanurate Foam Board

Polyisocyanurate board is a dimensionally stable, closed-cell foam which normally has a glass fiber facing bonded to it in order to receive hot moppings or adhesive. It has a high thermal efficiency (R = 7.2 per inch of thickness) and relatively low cost.

There have been some problems with polyisocyanurate board. The most publicized is thermal drift of the "R" value as the insulation ages. There have also been incidences of facer separation. It is best to use materials from the same supplier whenever practical, and to ensure that the board manufacturer also cross-references, or approves, the bitumen and adhesive(s) used.

Polyurethane Foam Board

Polyurethane and urethane foam boards have been in common use for a longer period than polyisocyanurate, and were the efficiency "leaders" before the advent of phenolic and polyisocyanurate. Urethane has had the same "thermal drift" problems as polyisocyanurate, but overall, it is still an efficient insulation board.

Polystyrene Foam Board

Expanded polystyrene: Expanded polystyrene (EPS) is a polymer (plastic) impregnated with a foaming agent, which—when exposed to heat—creates a uniform structure resistant to moisture penetration. Polystyrene has an "R" value of 3.85–4.76 per inch and a compressive strength of 21–27 psi (pounds per square inch) at 1.5 pounds per cubic foot of density. As a comparison, the compressive strength of mineral board (perlite) is 35 psi.

Most expanded polystyrene is used under loose-laid, ballasted single-ply systems. The type of expanded polystyrene often used in these cases is a material with a density of one pound per cubic foot, with an average "R" value of 4.2 per inch. This type of polystyrene is similar to that used in the manufacture of inexpensive picnic coolers.

Using mechanized gravel buggies for ballast installation tends to damage this lighter density EPS. The lighter material is also more likely to "shuffle" or crack under the membrane. The industry favors using a board with a minimum density of 1.5 pounds of the extruded material, which is far more durable.

Extruded polystyrene: Extruded polystyrene is a closed-cell foam with a low capacity for water absorption (.06% by volume), which makes it ideal for use in the insulated roof membrane assembly (IRMA). Its "R" value is approximately 4.8 per inch.

Conventional Roof Insulation System

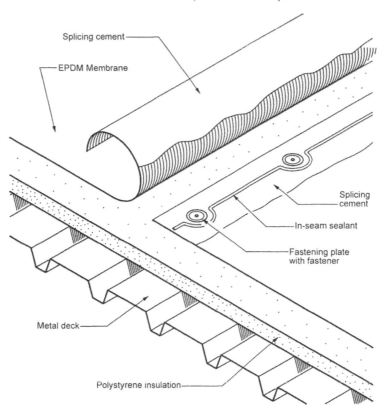

Splicing cement

EPDM Membrane

Splicing cement

In-seam sealant

Fastening plate with fastener

Metal deck

Polystyrene insulation

Protected Membrane Roofing

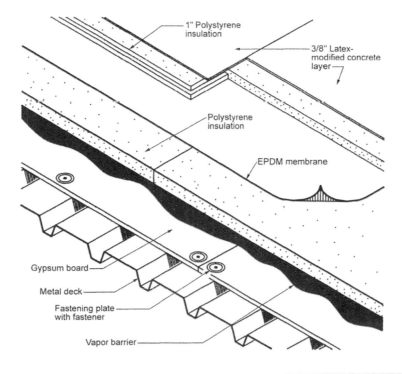

1" Polystyrene insulation

3/8" Latex-modified concrete layer

Polystyrene insulation

EPDM membrane

Gypsum board

Metal deck

Fastening plate with fastener

Vapor barrier

Figure 7.6

Characteristics of Various Roof Insulation Materials

Characteristics	TYPE OF INSULATING BOARD								
	Polyisocyanurate Foam	Polyurethane Foam	Extruded Polystyrene	Molded Polystyrene	Cellular Glass	Mineral Fiber	Phenolic Foam	Wood Fiber	Glass Fiber
Impact resistant	G	G	G	F	G	E	G	E	F
Moisture resistant	E	G	E	G	E	G	E		
Fire Resistant	E				E	E	E		E
Compatible with bitumens	E	G	F	F	E	E	E	E	G
Durable	E	E	E	E	E	G	F	E	E
Stable "k" value			E	E	E	E		E	E
Dimensionally stable	E	E	E	E	E	E	E	E	G
High thermal resistance	E	E	E	G	F	F	E	F	G
Available tapered slabs	Y	Y	Y	Y	Y	Y	Y	Y	Y
"R" value per in. thickness*	7.20	6.25	4.76	3.85-4.35	2.86	2.78	8.30	1.75-2.00	4.00
Thicknesses available	1"-3"	1"-4"	1"-3½"	½"-24"	1½"-4"	³/₄"-3"	1"-4"	1"-3"	¾"-2½"
Density (lb./ft.³)	2.0	1.5	1.8-3.5	1.0-2.0	8.5	16-17	1.5	22-27	49
Remarks	Prone to "thermal drift"	Prone to "thermal drift" Note "A": Should be overlaid with a thin layer of wood fiber, glass fiber or perlite board, with staggered joints.	Somewhat sensitive to hot bitumen & adhesive vapors Note "A": Should be overlaid with a thin layer of wood fiber, glass fiber or perlite board, with staggered joints.	Somewhat sensitive to hot bitumen & adhesive vapors Note "A": Should be overlaid with a thin layer of wood fiber, glass fiber or perlite board, with staggered joints.			Prone to "Thermal drift" relatively new & untested.	Expands with moisture —holds moisture.	Prone to damage from moisture infiltration.

E = EXCELLENT
G = GOOD
F = FAIR

*from ASHRAE 1985 Fundamentals Manual

Figure 7.7

RSMeans, *Roofing: Design Criteria, Options, Selection*

Installation: Most building codes require the installation of a ½ inch fire-rated gypsum board underlayment when polystyrene is used over a steel deck. The NRCA also recommends that, when using polystyrene board, a thin (minimum ¼ inch) layer of perlite of fiberboard "recover board" be overlaid, with joints staggered from the insulation board joints below. Polystyrene board must also be protected from ultraviolet light.

Cellular Glass Board

Cellular glass board is no longer used as often as it once was for roof insulation. Its lower "R" value per inch and relatively high density (thus, weight) has rendered it less popular than the newer materials. It is, however, a moisture-resistant, stable, and durable material.

Mineral Board

Mineral board is composed of expanded perlite, cellulose binders, and waterproofing agents. Low water absorption, stability, superior fire-resistance, and the best compressive resistance of all the insulations currently used, make this material extremely popular. The biggest drawback of mineral board is its relatively low "R" value (2.78 per inch). It becomes impractical and expensive to use 4" of this material to achieve an "R" value of 10 when the same value can be attained using only 1½" of foam insulation.

When mineral board is used as the base layer of a two-layer insulation system, it must be mechanically attached to the deck. A vapor retarder should then be installed or mopped over the mineral board, followed by a high performance insulation. This system ensures secure attachment to the deck and positive control of vapor, which would otherwise tend to be driven into the insulation during the winter months. By installing two separate layers of insulation with staggered joints, thermal bridging of the fasteners is eliminated, as is bridging at joints. Placing the vapor retarder above the fasteners and maintaining a temperature at the fasteners above the dew point reduces corrosion of the fasteners and the deck.

Phenolic Foam Board

Phenolic foam is popular with specifiers because of its "R" value of 8.3 per inch and its competitive pricing. It is a fire-resistant, dimensionally stable, foamed plastic. It is friable (subject to crumbling), and will fracture if abused. There have been instances where phenolic foam "dished" (raised at the corners) under single-ply membranes. If soaked, phenolic foam will absorb moisture and lose much of its thermal efficiency. Although not fully tested, it is reasonable to assume that phenolic foam is affected by thermal drift, as are the other foams that use fluorocarbon blowing agents. (Thermal drift is the reduction in "R" value that occurs when the fluorocarbon used as the foaming agent in manufacture vacates the material over time, and is replaced with atmospheric air, which has a lower "R" value.)

Wood Fiber Board

Wood fiber is used as a combination decking and insulation board for many roof systems. It is stronger and more durable than the other board insulation products, and makes a far better attachment substrate. However, these attributes are offset by its relatively low thermal resistance. Many specifiers use a composite board or a combination of wood fiber board and one of the high efficiency foams to create a solid, efficient system upon which to overlay a roof membrane.

Glass Fiber Board

Glass fiber insulation board is comprised of glass fibers, bound by a resinous binder and rolled into rigid board. A top surface (facing) of asphalt-adhered kraft paper or foil is applied as protection. This type of insulation is very efficient (R = 4 per inch) and has been tested by both Factory Mutual and Underwriters' Laboratory. This board is relatively soft and prone to moisture, which attacks the binder and causes the material to collapse.

Comments

While the preceding materials for roof insulation can be used for both commercial and residential buildings, the foam and fiberboard density requirements may differ depending on the application.

Associated Roofing Insulation Materials

Industry Standards

Roofing: Design Criteria, Options, Selection
(RSMeans)

Recover Boards

When installing single-ply membranes over hard-surfaced insulation board, fasteners or gravel can work their way up through the membrane, causing leaks that are very difficult to locate. Some specifications call for the use of *recover boards*, made of pressed fibers, over the insulation board. Recover boards are susceptible to moisture contamination and, therefore, should not be used over wet decks.

Vapor Retarders

Comments

Household activities such as cooking and bathing, as well as the presence of occupants, can generate 2 to 3 gallons of water vapor per day. If moisture vapor traveling into attics and exterior walls is not slowed by a vapor retarder or barrier, condensation can result when the vapor contacts cold surfaces. Prolonged condensation can lead to wood rot, mildew, and mold. Furthermore, damp insulation reduces thermal performance.

Vapor retarders are used to limit water vapor transmission. They are typically kraft or foil facings on building insulation. Polyethylene (4- or 6-mil) can also be used with unfaced insulation to provide a continuous, airtight vapor retarder.

Vapor retarders should generally be installed on the side of the insulation that is warmer in winter (usually toward the interior, but on the exterior in some warm, humid areas; check local practice and/or building codes).

In cold climate construction, 4- or 6-mil polyethylene must be installed on the interior side of the insulation. All seams and penetrations must be sealed with a nonhardening adhesive (butyl caulk or acoustical caulk).

Vapor retarders are not required in some dry, high temperature climates, such as parts of Arizona and California. Vapor retarders are not required if there is sufficient ventilation.

Industry Standards

Insulation Contractors Association of America
(Copyright ICAA *Technical Bulletin No. 6* "Use of Vapor Retarders")

What is a Vapor Retarder?

A vapor retarder is defined by ASTM Standard C 755 as a material or system that adequately retards the transmission of water vapor under specified conditions. The permeance of an adequate retarder for residential construction will not exceed 1 perm. A perm rating is a measure of the diffusion of water vapor through a material. Vapor diffusion accounts for only a small amount of the total moisture in a building. Therefore, other means should be utilized to reduce water vapor migration due to air infiltration.

An air retarder is different from a vapor retarder in that it blocks only air and liquid water, not water vapor.

Air retarders block drafts of hot or cold air caused by winds and pressure differences between the inside and outside of the house. A housewrap is one form of an air retarder. Typical exterior housewraps are not vapor retarders.

What Is the Purpose of a Vapor Retarder?

A vapor retarder slows the rate of water vapor diffusion but does not totally prevent its movement. Building occupants, certain appliances, and plumbing equipment generate moisture that is carried in the air as vapor. As water vapor moves from a warm interior through construction materials to a cooler surface, the water vapor may condense as liquid water that can damage the building. It is for this reason vapor retarders are installed in buildings.

Placement

The *International Residential Code* (IRC Section R322, N1102.5) states that frame walls, floors, and ceilings not ventilated to allow moisture to escape shall be provided with an approved vapor retarder. The IRC specifies that the vapor retarder shall be installed on the warm-in-winter side of the thermal insulation (see illustration) with the following exceptions:

Exception 1: In construction where moisture or its freezing will not damage the materials.

Exception 2: Frame walls, floors, and ceilings in jurisdictions in Zones 1 through 4.

Exception 3: Where other approved means to avoid condensation are provided.

Materials That Are Vapor Retarders

Many insulation products are faced with an asphalt-impregnated kraft paper or a foil laminate. Each of these facings is a vapor retarder. Other materials such as polyethylene sheet or aluminum foil backed gypsum board are also vapor retarders that are typically used with unfaced insulation.

Important: Many standard insulation facings will burn and must not be left exposed in an occupied building. Standard facings must be covered with gypsum board or another code-approved interior finish. Use only flame-resistant facings for exposed applications. Any material that has a perm rating of 1 or less is considered to be a vapor retarder. The following table shows the perm rating of some common building materials that are consistent with the ASHRAE Handbook of Fundamentals and other industry sources.

Vapor Retarders	Perm Rating
Insulation Facing, Kraft	1.0
¼ inch Plywood (Douglas fir, exterior glue)	0.7
Insulation Facing, Foil Kraft Laminate	0.5
Vapor Retarder Latex Paint, 0.0031 inch thick	0.45
0.002 inch Polyethylene Sheet	0.16
0.004 inch Polyethylene Sheet	0.08
0.006 inch Polyethylene Sheet	0.06
Aluminum Foil 0.00035 inch thick	0.05
Aluminum Foil 0.001 inch thick	0.01

Not Vapor Retarders	Perm Rating
³/₈ inch Gypsum Wall Board (plain)	50
4 inch Unfaced Mineral Wool	30
Typical Latex Paint, ~0.002 inch thickness	5.5 to 8.6
4.4 lb./100 ft.² Asphalt Saturated Sheathing Paper	3.3
¼ inch plywood (Douglas fir, interior glue)	1.9

Industry Standards

Insulation Contractors Association of America
(Copyright ICAA Technical Bulletin No. 6 "Use of Vapor Retarders")

Kraft Faced Insulation
Three accepted methods of installing faced insulation are inset stapling, face stapling, and pressure fit-no stapling. The vapor permeance of a wall is not affected by any one of these methods.

Polyethylene Sheet or Foil Vapor Retarders
Separate vapor retarders are used in some applications.

When required, a separate vapor retarder should be installed at the warm-in-winter side of the framing. In hot, humid climates, vapor retarders are sometimes omitted or installed outside the insulation.

Ground Covers
Where the floor of a crawl space is soil or gravel, a ground cover should be used to limit the movement of water from damp soil into the crawl space. It is recommended that a ground cover be 4 mil or thicker polyethylene sheet or 55 pound or heavier asphalt roll roofing, lay on the floor and approximately 6 inches up the walls.

Encapsulated Batts
Polyethylene facings that are "nonperforated" are vapor retarders and should be considered interchangeable with other faced batts. A perforated poly "backer" film on one or both sides of the batt should be considered interchangeable with unfaced batts; i.e., a non-vapor retarder.

Spray Foam Insulation
Check with manufacturers for recommendations regarding the installation of a vapor retarder with spray foam applications. The perm ratings of closed-cell polyurethane and spray foam products vary from 0.8 to 2.5. Therefore, some do qualify as a vapor retarder in general construction situations. Open-cell spray foam perm ratings vary from 16 to 25 perms or more and do not qualify as a vapor retarder. For those spray foam products not qualifying as a vapor retarder, the use of foil-backed gypsum board or a vapor retarder

Vapor Retarders

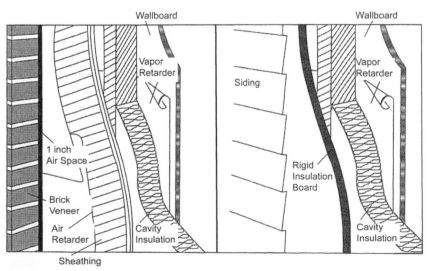

Figure 7.8

Courtesy of Insulation Contractors Association of America

paint applied to the interior wall surface is generally recommended.

Note: In all cases, consult with the project architect, engineer, or building code official prior to the use of vapor retarders. ICAA Technical Bulletins are provided for informational purposes only. ICAA and/or its members are not responsible for loss or damage caused by errors or omissions or any other cause.

Industry Standards

Roofing: Design Criteria, Options, Selection
(RSMeans)

Vapor retarders used to be referred to as "vapor barriers," until the industry conceded that no true "barrier" may be devised against moisture intrusion using readily available sheet materials or mopped membranes. Every vapor retarder allows *some* moisture to permeate. Moisture permeability through a vapor retarder is measured in *perms*.

A vapor retarder is strongly recommended when the average outside January temperature is below 40 degrees and the indoor relative humidity in winter is 45 percent or above. The NRCA recommends that when a vapor retarder is specified, moisture relief venting must be installed as a means of allowing any trapped moisture to escape from the system. There is, however, strong evidence that roof vents do not significantly contribute to moisture removal in insulation that is already wet. The primary source of moisture in roof insulation is breaks in the membrane. Therefore, it stands to reason that adding many roof vents in the system will only increase the chances for a leak.

Vapor retarders *should not be used* unless dew point vapor flow calculations clearly indicate that these devices are necessary, or unless the previously stated January temperature and humidity ranges prevail in that location. For most areas of the U.S., the "downward drying" that occurs in the building space during warm seasons of the year will far exceed the "upward wetting" which occurs in the colder periods. There is one clear exception to this rule: in wet-process applications, such as laundries, canneries, and swimming pools, the "upwardwetting" potential virtually demands a vapor retarder to restrict contamination of the insulation.

It is very important that vapor retarders, when used, be as homogeneous as possible, with as few seams or breaks as practical.

Vapor Barriers & Ceilings

Comments

Flexible insulation with vapor barriers should be installed in ceilings so that the vapor barriers are facing the living space. (See "Vapor Retarders" on previous page.) Loosefill, batt, or blanket insulation without a vapor barrier should have a separate polyethylene film placed below the insulation facing the living space. Batt or blanket insulation at the ceiling is usually installed at the same time as wall insulation, from underneath the ceiling joists.

For maximum effectiveness, the vapor barrier facing the insulation should overlap the faces of the framing members. The insulation should extend across the entire top plate to prevent heat loss at the joint. If necessary, the junction between the insulation and the plate should be stuffed with loose insulation.

Loose-fill insulation is installed over the top of the finished ceiling by pouring or blowing it in to fill the joist space. Since loose-fill is installed later in the construction process, the ceiling insulation is usually inspected as part of the final overall inspection.

When eave vents are used, the insulation should not block the air movement between the vent and the space above the insulation. Eave baffles should be installed to prevent loose-fill insulation from covering the vents.

Cellulose insulation should be kept from contact with potential heat sources, such as light fixtures. A minimum 3" clearance should be provided around each fixture. (Note: Some recessed light fixtures are now rated to allow direct contact with insulation. However, many local building jurisdictions still require the installation of a gypsum wallboard or plywood box around recessed light fixtures, prior to installation of insulation, to prevent contact.)

Cathedral Ceilings

If cathedral ceilings are insulated, they require both a vapor barrier and ventilation. Faced fiberglass insulation can be installed between ceiling rafters, or unfaced insulation can be used in combination with a 4- or 6-mil polyethylene vapor barrier stapled to ceiling rafters. (In areas such as Florida and the Gulf Coast, an interior vapor barrier may not be required.)

Insulation should be friction-fit (no inset stapling). Any stapling should be to the front-side of the rafters. Ventilation space of 1" should be provided between the roof sheathing and the insulation. Baffles and eave vents can be installed along the ceiling space to create air flow.

Finish materials, such as gypsum wallboard, should be installed when the insulation is in place. Faced insulation should never be left exposed. Kraft and foil-faced materials are flammable, and should be covered by approved wall, ceiling, or floor materials.

Vapor Retarders & Cathedral (Sloped Ceilings)

Industry Standards

Insulation Contractors Association of America

(Copyright ICAA Technical Bulletin No. 6 "Use of Vapor Retarders")

Since commonly used asphalt roof shingles have very low vapor permeance, cathedral ceilings perform like walls with very low permeance exterior skins. If there is no vented airspace between the insulation and the wood roof deck, moisture problems may occur in the wood deck, and ice dams may occur in cold climates. Most asphalt shingle manufacturers require a ventilated ceiling below their shingles. Otherwise the shingle warranty is often reduced to ten years. An airspace of approximately 1 inch should be provided between the insulation and the roof deck. This airspace, when coupled with eave and ridge vents, allows for the successful movement of moisture from the ceiling cavity. This airspace is usually maintained with a formed attic vent chute or baffle that is installed from eave to ridge. Since these baffles are sometimes made of a vapor retarder material, it is common to maintain an approximate 2 inch gap between the ends of adjacent baffles so that moisture may move into the vented airspace. Check codes for up-to-date regulations.

Airspaces without both eave and ridge vents will not add protection against moisture condensation in sloped ceilings; air won't move through a space unless it has a place to exit as well as a place to enter. Water vapor can move by diffusion through many materials, including fibrous insulation. Therefore, limited amounts of water vapor that get around or through a vapor retarder can exit a cathedral ceiling rafter bay through a vent opening even when an airspace does not exist. Moving air can carry lots of moisture, but air movement is not necessary for moisture to escape from buildings. However, without a vented airspace, one needs to be concerned if the moisture accumulation exceeds the ability of the ceiling to dissipate the moisture through diffusion alone.

The best strategy for cathedral ceilings in cold and mild climates is to use a vapor retarder below the insulation and, if recessed lights are used, air/vapor tight fixtures. A kraft-faced batt is sufficient in those areas requiring a vapor retarder. If blown insulation is used, a continuous 4 mil vapor retarder can be used in heating climates and a vapor retarder paint in mild climates.

Note: In all cases, consult with the project architect, engineer, or building code official prior to the use of vapor retarders. ICAA Technical Bulletins are provided for informational purposes only. ICAA and/or its members are not responsible for loss or damage caused by errors or omissions or any other cause.

IRC–2006

R808.1 Combustible insulation: Combustible insulation must have at least three inches of clearance from recessed lighting, fan motors, and other heat sources, except when reduced clearances are permitted.

Framed Walls

Comments

Insulation requirements for framed walls are usually similar to ceiling applications. The maximum R-value of material that can be installed in a framed wall is dictated by the thickness of the framing material. The stud cavity of a standard 2x4 framed wall permits 3$\frac{1}{2}$" of blanket insulation, with an R-value ranging from about 11 to 17, depending upon the insulation material and its density.

The insulation values recommended in many climate zones require a wall R-value of 19 or higher and are often difficult to accomplish using a single layer of insulation. Sometimes the other portions of the wall, such as interior and exterior finishes and sheathing, may contribute enough insulating value to provide sufficient total wall R-value. The only other means of increasing the R-value of the wall is to increase the thickness of the insulation. This can be accomplished by using 6" stud walls, which provides 5$\frac{1}{2}$" of stud cavity, or by adding additional layers of insulation to the interior or exterior surface of the wall.

The most common material used for framed wall insulation is fiberglass batts or blankets. Exterior walls are insulated with batts or blankets faced with kraft paper or foil as a vapor barrier.

Fiberglass batts or blankets are manufactured to fit between the standard stud spacing of 16" or 24" on center. The batts or blankets should fit snugly at all sides and at the top and bottom plates. The batts or blankets with a vapor barrier are held in place by "face" (on the edge of the room side of the stud) or "inset" (on the inside cavity space of the stud) stapling.

When adding batts or blankets to an existing condition, install a layer of batts or blankets between the joist spaces. Then, install a second, unfaced layer at a right angle across the joists. This installation method provides a higher insulating value because the wood joists are covered with insulation. (Note: This method cannot be effectively used with engineered trusses.)

(continued)

Loose-fill insulation can be applied to framed walls in new construction if the manufacturer has designed a system that will keep the insulation in place. One method is to install a vapor barrier material to the interior side of the wall to enclose the stud cavity. The loose-fill insulation is blown in through a hole in the vapor barrier near the top of the stud cavity.

Some manufacturers have a system of spraying the insulation into the stud cavities and then scraping off the excess material even with the interior edge face of the studs. This process involves a wetting agent that is mixed with the insulation at the spray nozzle, thus activating a binding action to keep the loose fill insulation in place. Loose-fill insulation can also be used to insulate existing sidewalls. Openings are drilled—usually from the exterior—at various intervals, and the insulation is pumped into the stud cavity. The exterior openings are then plugged and finished.

It is important to determine whether there are obstructions in the walls, such as fireblocking. Blowing loose-fill insulation through a single opening at the top of an 8' wall would leave much of the stud cavity without insulation. Most walls require two, if not three, openings per stud cavity. Openings should be located vertically at 4' to 5' intervals, depending upon any predetermined obstacles.

Generally, the lower holes are filled first to ensure that insulation has reached the lowest portion of the wall in the correct density. The blowing machine is equipped with a pop-off valve that will bleed off pressure as the wall cavity is filled, preventing the interior wall from blowing out. Pressures for drywall applications are considerably less than lath and plaster walls.

Exterior wall insulation is often installed when the exterior finish is remodeled. Rigid board insulation in foundation and basement applications is installed between the existing wall and new siding material.

important. A wall consisting of wood studs, kraft-faced insulation, and wood sheathing is more forgiving than a steel assembly with foil-faced insulating sheathing and continuous 4 mil polyethylene sheet over unfaced insulation, since the former assembly can store more moisture when needed and release it later as conditions permit.

In climates requiring a vapor retarder on the interior surface, a kraft-faced insulation is usually sufficient. When a loose-fill product such as fiberglass or cellulose is installed, a 4 mil continuous polyethylene sheet or a vapor retarder paint on the interior drywall should be used.

The poly is acceptable for heating climates and a vapor retarder paint for milder climates. In most cases, the use of a vapor retarder is not influenced by the type of cavity insulation used. Most manufacturers of sprayed cellulose advise contractors that a vapor retarder is not necessary or desired in a wall system. If the insulation is applied with water, manufacturers generally recommend waiting between 24 to 48 hours before installing drywall. Consult manufacturer's recommendations for details.

If you are reinsulating a home with blown insulation, installing a vapor retarder on the sidewalls if one has not been previously installed can be quite difficult. It may be necessary to paint the interior surfaces of exterior walls and ceilings with a vapor retarder paint.

Note: In all cases, consult with the project architect, engineer, or building code official prior to the use of vapor retarders. ICAA Technical Bulletins are provided for informational purposes only. ICAA and/or its members are not responsible for loss or damage caused by errors or omissions or any other cause.

Foundations, Basements & Crawl Spaces

Vapor Retarders & Insulated Walls

Industry Standards

Insulation Contractors Association of America
(Copyright ICAA Technical Bulletin No. 6 "Use of Vapor Retarders")

In general, the colder the climate, the greater the need for a vapor retarder. Heating climates are defined as climates with 4000 heating degree-days (HDD) or greater. Since the majority of moisture in the assembly is the result of water intrusion and air infiltration, the assembly should be designed so that excessive moisture can escape the assembly. In addition, the moisture storage capacity of the assembly is

Comments

In basements and heated crawl spaces, the foundation walls must be insulated and ventilated. Providing a minimum of two crawl space vents allows for a positive flow of air in and out of the crawl space.

The common insulation materials used for basements include polystyrene, polyurethane, polyisocyanurate, phenolic, and cellular glass block. The advantages and disadvantages of each are described in the material sections at the beginning of this chapter.

Crawl spaces that are unheated and/or have a dirt floor should be covered with a polyethylene vapor barrier.

Crawl spaces can be insulated by placing the insulation between the floor joists. Fiberglass batts are the common material used for this purpose. The vapor barrier should be facing towards the living space, just as it would for walls and ceilings.

Installing insulation in existing conditions can be very difficult when the crawl space is tight—sometimes only 18" to 24" high. Often plumbing, and electrical and HVAC ducts complicate the installation. In this case, the insulation can be installed from above, prior to the installation of the subfloor.

In new construction, mesh can be installed from the top of the joists before the subfloor is laid by rolling out the mesh and creating pockets at each joist space. The mesh is then stapled to the top edge of the joists. The batts or blankets are laid into the mesh pocket, and the subfloor is installed over the top of the insulation.

In existing construction, mesh can be stapled to the bottom face of the joists after the insulation has been installed.

Another option is wire lacing, which can be created by interweaving malleable wire and securing it to the bottom face of the joists by stapling or nailing.

Standard wall insulation has the stapling flange on the vapor barrier side. For new construction, we do not recommend relying on only staples applied from the top side of the wall insulation. The weight of the insulation may eventually cause the flange to tear from the staples, and the insulation will fall to the ground. Some method of support from the bottom of the insulation is needed.

Industry Standards

Construction Principles, Materials, and Methods
(John Wiley & Sons, Inc.)

Ventilation Requirements
In crawl space construction, adequate cross-ventilation should be provided under the floor. The total area of vent openings should equal 1.5% of the first floor area.

A groundcover of 4- to 6-mil polyethylene film is essential as a moisture retarder. Inadequate moisture control can harm any floor installation by contributing to warping or discoloration of the flooring.

Vapor Retarders & Insulated Basements

Industry Standards

Insulation Contractors Association of America
(Copyright ICAA Technical Bulletin No. 6 "Use of Vapor Retarders")

Below-grade basement walls differ from above-grade walls in that they are vulnerable to ground moisture wicking into the wall or basement floor. Because of this, it is important to maintain the drying potential of the wall since one never knows if the long-term moisture drive will be from the outside or the inside. A masonry wall is capable of absorbing large quantities of water due to the capillary action of concrete. If the masonry wall unit has hollow cores, air movements within the wall also increase the thermal and moisture movement. For this reason, it is recommended that a vapor retarder not be used in a wall that is partially or fully below grade. If a wall is above grade, such as in a walk-out basement, then that wall may use a vapor retarder, if the climate dictates a vapor retarder in above-grade walls.

If no stud wall is available, the insulation can be applied in blanket form with a perforated flame-resistant facing. Applied directly onto the wall, this is often used on the top half of the wall only, which may take it to the depth of the local frost line. If hollow core masonry units are used because of the air convection that takes place within the wall, the insulation should be applied on the entire wall.

While it is sometimes suggested that an airspace should be maintained between the masonry wall and the stud wall insulation in order to keep the wall dry, in actuality this may make matters worse. This vertical airspace can lead to a convective air loop, thereby increasing not only the thermal but also the moisture transfer within the wall. If a full height stud wall is used in addition to the masonry wall, this stud wall is often inset an inch or so, increasing the depth of the cavity to be insulated. The entire depth of this wall cavity should be insulated. This also insulates the back of the studs reducing thermal bridging.

If a stud wall is placed on a partially below-grade masonry wall, the stud wall should be insulated the same way as other above-grade walls in the house. When a vapor retarder is not desired, slashing a faced product's sheathing is not recommended, because narrow cuts are unlikely to significantly increase vapor transmission.

Vapor Retarders & Crawl Spaces

When the undersides of frame floors above crawl spaces are insulated with faced insulation, the vapor retarder facing, generally kraft facing, should be placed on the top side, and in substantial contact with the floor above. This prevents the kraft facing from being exposed and posing a fire hazard. The opportunity for air to infiltrate between the floor and facing and bypass the insulation is reduced. In many localities, it is standard practice to use unfaced insulation under floors, with the assumption that the flooring materials provide adequate vapor resistance to inside moisture. Please refer to the *IRC* exceptions as noted in Section IV of this bulletin.

When insulating perimeter walls, proceed the same as with a below grade masonry wall and use a perforated flame-resistant blanket that is attached to the top plate, extended down the wall and preferably extended two feet along the floor. Where the crawl space floor is bare earth, it is highly recommended that the entire area be covered with 4 mil polyethylene sheet (ground cover) to minimize the movement of underground moisture up into the structure. The latest thinking is that it is best to have non-vented crawlspaces and insulated walls, treating the crawlspace as conditioned space.

Note: In all cases, consult with the project architect, engineer, or building code official prior to the use of vapor retarders. ICAA Technical Bulletins are provided for informational purposes only. ICAA and/or its members are not responsible for loss or damage caused by errors or omissions or any other cause.

Sound Insulation

 Industry Standards
Green Building: Project Planning & Cost Estimating, Second Edition
(RSMeans)

Proper selection of wall insulation and wall framing and materials is essential to reducing noise from outside. Some sound-insulating materials, such as acoustic ceiling tile and straw-bale construction, can offer the advantages of recycling or using natural materials as an added green benefit. Walls constructed with insulated concrete forms can reduce noise from outside the building. Green, or "living roofs," can absorb sound, in addition to their other benefits.

Hard versus absorbent surfaces also have a major impact on noise level inside a space, as do interior wall framing and insulating techniques. Acoustic or sound-absorption panels are effective in mitigating the noise in gathering spaces. A preferred design approach is to reduce the number of parallel surfaces, using more curved and angled walls to diminish the acoustic bounce and the noise.

8 ROOFING, SIDING & MOISTURE PROTECTION

Table of Contents

(continued on next page)

Text in blue type indicates excerpted summaries from the International Building Code® (IBC) *and* International Residential Code® (IRC). *Please consult the* IBC *and* IRC *for complete coverage and specific wording. "Comments" (in solid blue boxes) were written by the editors, based on their own experience.*

 *These icons will appear with references to green building practices, seismic regulations, and hurricane-safe building requirements, respectively.*

ROOFING, SIDING & MOISTURE PROTECTION

Common Defect Allegations

Roofing

Roofing is a frequent defect allegation. Few roofs fully comply with building code and roofing manufacturers' recommendations. Claims often include one or more of the following:

- *Overexposure of roofing shingle or tile to weather. Production roofers usually make the field equal from eave to ridge without cutting, stretching the courses a little, if necessary, to make it even. Occasionally, the tiles or shingles are stretched to a point where the underlayment is exposed at the joints due to insufficient lap.*

- *Penetrations through flashing, or flashing that does not extend high enough.*

- *Water intrusion at plumbing and other utility penetrations.*

- *Improperly configured valleys. Open valleys are required to be larger at the bottom than at the top so that they will not have a tendency to trap debris.*

- *Shingles at the eaves failing to project beyond the edge of the roof framing. Many concrete shingles shave a drip lip to reduce the water curl as it is discharged from the roof. The more metal transition and drip flashing that can be incorporated in the installation, the better, including gutters. These are not mandatory; however, in defect investigation, wood damage is often seen from poor eave performance and is shown as the standard of care that the builder used in construction.*

- *Insufficient penetration of fasteners. In cement fiber shingle construction, many installations have not used a staple that fully penetrates the sheathing, or a minimum of $3/4$". The result is that high winds may lift off large sections of the shingles.*

- *Failure to install an upslope cricket in skylights over 30" in width. The skylight curb must be high enough to support this cricket with a minimum of $5^1/2$" curb height. The cricket rule also applies to chimneys over 30".*

(continued)

- *Failure to use pressure-treated wood for sleepers and nailers under roofing shingles. The sleepers and nailers should be in 4' lengths with spacing to allow water to drain off of the underlayment.*

Siding

- *Two of the most common siding defects are: (1) the wood material is not backprimed prior to installation, and (2) the siding does not terminate far enough above the surrounding grade. The absence of an air gap between the wood framing/siding assembly and paving or soil is the defect that causes the greatest damage. This is because it does not really show up until the wood fails, which takes about five years. Mold odor will occur in the living space, but the source is not easily detectable. The mold and fungal attack creates an unhealthy air quality inside the building. When the damage is discovered, it usually is a very expensive changeout.*

- *Failure of the shiplap siding due to improper maintenance. Shiplap siding has a distinct maintenance requirement. It is important that the builder deliver notice to the building owner that the siding and trim will require caulking and paint as frequently as every two years to maintain the structure.*

- *Failure to follow the manufacturers' recommended installation instructions for wood siding products in shingle and clapboard may result in unnecessary splitting and cracking, and uneven shrinkage. The result may be water penetration and exposure of fasteners that should not be visible.*

- *An EIFS building that is properly flashed and has watertight doors and windows is a durable and efficient building. The only drawback to this type of construction is the acoustic transmission. Acoustic problems are easily solved with additional layers of gypboard and sealants.*

Introduction

A tremendous number of construction claims involve defective roofing. Not only is the roof itself susceptible to defects and weather damage, but the building's interior finishes and contents can experience costly damage if the roof fails. Preventing roof leaks may be the single most important item in a strategy to prevent lawsuits and defect claims. Because this is such an important issue, we have included excerpts from publications that go beyond technical discussion to reflect opinions on failures and leaks. Material definitions and product ingredients/components are also covered to help clarify the discussion of proper application.

Flashing, the thin, impervious material used in construction to prevent water penetration or to direct the flow of water, has numerous applications—at roof hips and valleys, for roof penetrations, at joints between a roof and a vertical wall, and in masonry walls to direct the flow of water and moisture.

The requirements also vary with the different types of roofing materials. For these reasons, information on flashing will be found throughout the chapter rather than in one specific section. Valley requirements are also covered within the text on the different types of roofing.

The **National Roofing Contractors Association (NRCA)** has generously allowed us to reprint some construction details. While these definitions and designs may not reflect the minimum standards for every type of installation, they certainly do represent the correct way to build. We hope that this section, above all others, is used as a reference on every construction project you encounter.

Roofing designers, specifiers, consultants, inspectors, and installers should have the following resources at their disposal:

- The latest edition of the applicable building code(s)
- The Factory Mutual Research Corporation Approval Guide
- The UL Building Materials Directory
- The UL Fire Resistance Directory
- The ASTM Board of Standards, Vol. 04.04, *Roofing, Waterproofing, and Bituminous Materials*
- The *NRCA Roofing & Waterproofing Manual*

The following professional associations may be helpful in locating further information about roofing and moisture control:

American Society for Testing & Materials (ASTM)
610-832-9585
www.astm.org

Asphalt Roofing Manufacturers Association (ARMA)
202-207-0917
www.asphaltroofing.org

Factory Mutual Research Corporation
401-275-3000
www.fmglobal.com

Metal Building Manufacturers Association (MBMA)
216-241-7333
www.mbma.com

National Roofing Contractors Association (NRCA)
847-299-9070
www.nrca.net

Roof Tile Institute
541-689-0366
www.ntrma.org

(continued)

Roof Coatings Manufacturers Association (RCMA)
202-207-0919
www.roofcoatings.org

Rubber Manufacturers Association (RMA)
202-682-4800
www.rma.org

Single-Ply Roofing Institute (SPRI)
781-647-7026
www.spri.org

Underwriters Laboratories, Inc. (UL)
847-272-8800
www.ul.com

Siding is another area where defect claims frequently occur. Improper attachment of siding can lead to aesthetic problems and damage—to the structure, the interior finishes, and the building's contents.

The latter part of this chapter covers common exterior closure systems, from wood shingles and clapboards to brick, metal, stucco, and exterior insulation finish systems (EIFS).

The following associations provide information on siding and other exterior closure installations:

Brick Industry Association (BIA)
703-620-0010
www.bia.org

The Cedar Shake & Shingle Bureau
604-820-7700
www.cedarbureau.org

EIFS Industry Members Association (EIMA)
800-294-3462
www.eima.com

The Western Red Cedar Lumber Association (WRCLA)
604-684-0266
www.wrcla.org

The moisture protection section at the end of this chapter is concerned primarily with waterproofing and dampproofing of walls, floors, and substrates, and foundation drains. It also includes site grading and placement of backfill. For moisture protection for concrete foundation walls, see Chapter 2, "Concrete."

Ed. Note: Comments and recommendations within this chapter are not intended as a definitive resource for construction activities. For building projects, contractors must rely on the project documents and local building codes.

Green Roofing & Siding

Green Home Improvement
(RSMeans)

Green roofing products range from recycled plastic and rubber shingles, to recycled metal roofs, to sustainably harvested or recycled wood roofs. One of the "greenest" is shingles made from recycled waste, such as plastic, rubber, and wood. Some products are made from post-consumer waste, others from post-industrial (factory) waste. Using both types helps reduce landfill waste, energy use, and demand for natural resources. Some of these products are also recyclable. Several green roofing products come with 50-year warranties and Class A fire ratings.

Wood shingles and shakes, while natural in composition, are often made from old-growth western cedar. Although the energy it takes to produce this product is relatively low, the harvest of old-growth trees is often carried out in an unsustainable fashion. Where codes permit their use, look into products made from reclaimed lumber. Seek local sources to reduce transportation costs and energy use.

Slate is a natural, durable material that can last hundreds of years. Mining and transporting new slate shingles to market is an energy-intensive process, but several manufacturers offer salvaged slate shingles.

While most metal roofing products are not made from recycled materials, they offer exceptional durability and fire-resistance. They're also ideal for rainwater collection systems since they don't leach toxic chemicals like a conventional asphalt roof. Metal roofing can be recycled at the end of its life. Among the recycled metal roofing products are shingles made from recycled aluminum (mostly beverage cans) resembling wood shakes. Other products contain up to 50% recycled steel.

Another product that scores green points for durability and recycled content is fiber-cement—manufactured for both shingles and siding. They are made from cement, sand, clay, and recycled wood fiber, and some products are backed by a 50-year warranty. It comes in a variety of colors and styles resembling stucco, cedar shingles, and wood clapboards.

Reinforced rubber shingles, or shakes, are also recycled. They're made from the steel belts of old radial tires. The material is coated with ground slate for texture and a choice of colors. A big advantage is their long life and warranty, including hail and other extreme weather damage. Verify with your local building department that rubber roofs are permitted in your area.

Consider a lighter colored roofing material for hot, sunny climates. Lighter colors reflect, rather than absorb heat, which could reduce air conditioning costs. Keeping the roof surface cooler could extend the life of the shingles. Check with the local building department and/or neighborhood association for possible restrictions.

If you're removing old asphalt shingles, find out if they can be recycled locally. This is an emerging business—grinding asphalt shingles to create products for roadway maintenance and repair.

"Green" equipment may also be involved in the installation of a new or replacement roof. These include items like solar attic fans, solar panels, and energy-efficient HVAC equipment such as an evaporative cooler. Flashing requirements should be specified by the manufacturer.

Typical Roofing Problems & Correction

Comments

Following are some common roofing problems and solutions. For correct installation standards, see the individual sections on various types of roofs later in this chapter.

Industry Standards

Building Materials, Technology, Structural Performance & Environmental Impact
(The McGraw-Hill Companies)

The following questions are asked frequently:

1. **Why is water coming down the wall in a room on the top floor of a building?** Flashing against the parapet wall on the roof has probably pulled loose and the opening allowed rain to run down the wall to the floor below. The flashing at parapet walls is probably the most common source of roof leaks, and regular maintenance could prevent this complaint. Metal flashings should not exceed 3 to 4 meters (10 to 12 feet) in length because thermal expansion can cause them to buckle and pull away from the parapet walls. To repair, anchor the flashing securely to the wall and caulk the edge, touching the wall with a flexible caulking material. If the metal needs to be replaced, a flexible plastic flashing will be less apt to be a problem.

2. **Why does the attic ceiling have patches of mold covering it, but no sign of water leaks?** Evidently the temperature of the ceiling has been chilled below the dew point by the freezing temperature on the rooftop. The moisture condensed on the ceiling from the hot, humid air in the attic. The wet areas of the ceiling caused mold to form and thrive on the ceiling. Correction for this problem is to provide more or better insulation for the roof so that the extreme cold on the roof does not chill the ceiling below the dew point.

3. **What is the cause of most roof leaks?** Leakage at the parapet wall and the junctures of roofing materials with vent pipes and rooftop equipment are frequent causes of roof leaks. Regular maintenance could prevent this complaint. Drains should prevent water from standing in this area. Thermal expansion and contraction cause the metal flashing to pull away from the parapet wall, allowing rain to run down the wall to the floor below. The solution is to press the flashing into the wall—sometimes a groove is provided—and recaulk.

4. **What should be done about a large blister (bubble) on a built-up roof?** These are spectacular, but usually do not mean that there is a membrane failure and water leakage. They are inflated by the expansion of water vapor. Once the top layer of felt is raised, it stiffens and remains inflated. The bubble can be pierced, gently deflated, and the hole where it was pierced can be sealed with a covering of asphalt emulsion. However, if there is little danger of the bubble being torn open, it can be left undisturbed since it is not a source of leakage.

5. **What should be done if water is ponding around the drain on the edge of the roof, especially during heavy showers?** Evidently a scupper (a drain going into the wall) was overlooked. Scuppers in a parapet wall behind and above the level of the surface drain are usually supplied as an emergency overflow in case the surface drain is clogged. The drain should be unclogged and a scupper constructed in the wall.

6. **The ceiling is leaking near the center of the building, where the electrical and drainage facilities service the building.** The pipe connected to the roof drain is clogged with roof gravel and the extra weight of the gravel has pulled apart a pipe connection. Gravel is put on top of a built-up roof as a protective sun screen and to help hold down the membrane in order to keep it from blowing away during heavy winds. A low curb near the edge of the roof can keep the gravel from being carried off the roof by heavy rains, ice, and snow. Roof drains should be covered with a coarse grating to keep gravel from filling the drain pipes. Gravel is becoming scarce and is being replaced by a highly reflective aluminum paint to reflect the sun's rays and avoid excessive heating.

7. **What should be done about puddles of water standing on an asphalt built-up roofing membrane after a rain?** To ensure drainage, roof membranes should have a gentle slope toward the drains. Too often, perhaps due to poor design or construction or to repeated roof

coverings with one layer on top of the other, the layers of felt are lower in some regions and provide a depression for water to collect.

Although these are usually tolerated, they can be filled with a few patching layers of roofing felt carefully cemented down with an asphalt emulsion or cut-back asphalt.

8. **Water is leaking down the vent pipes that emerge from the roof.** Lead sheet flashing has pulled away from the pipe or is not tightly wrapped around the pipe. Lead is malleable and can be readily shaped to the pipe.

9. **There are ceiling water stains, but no leaks have been found around the edge of the roof or the drains.** There is some danger of a leak developing wherever the roof changes slope. The flashing may be too small and difficult to caulk because of insufficient overlapping of materials.

10. **Shingles (wood or asphalt) are ripped from the roof in a strong windstorm.** The shingles may have been installed with too much of the shingle showing (insufficient overlap). Also, the shingles may have been stapled in place mechanically with a varying depth of penetration into the roof. A better practice in regions of frequent strong winds is to hand nail the shingles and individually tab or cement them into place. In hurricane-force winds roof coverings are likely to be ripped loose. In this case even the hurricane straps holding the roof structure to the wall beams might loosen and let portions of the deck blow away.

Roofing Definitions

Comments

Section 1502 of IBC-2006 defines *built-up roof covering* as two or more layers of felt cemented together having a cap sheet, mineral aggregate, or similar surface. Refer to this section for more roofing terms and definitions.

Roof Drainage

Note: The following are summaries of the basic code requirements of the *International Building Code* and *International Residential Code*. Please consult the *IBC* and *IRC* for complete coverage and specific wording.

IBC-2006

1503.4 Roof drainage: Roof drainage systems must be in accordance with the *International Plumbing Code*.

1503.4.1 Gutters: Except in R-3, private garages, and Type V construction, gutters and leaders must be of noncombustible material or at least Schedule 40 plastic pipe.

IRC-2006

R903.4 Roof drainage: Roofs must have roof drains at all low points, unless the roof slopes enough to drain over the edge. Scuppers, when needed for drainage, must be installed in a wall or parapet and level with the surface of the roof.

R903.4.1 Overflow drains and scuppers: Overflow drains, leaders, and conductors must meet the requirements of the *International Plumbing Code*. When roof drains are necessary, overflow drains of the same size are required, and may not connect to roof drain lines. The inlet flow line must be 2" above the roof's low point. An alternative is to install overflow scuppers three times the size of roof drains in adjacent parapet walls.

Gutters & Downspouts

Industry Standards

Means Graphic Construction Standards
(RSMeans)

Gutter and downspout systems are used to collect and distribute water from roof edges. Metal gutters of aluminum, copper, lead-coated copper, galvanized steel, and stainless steel are available in stock lengths with accessories such as mounting brackets, connectors, corners, end caps, downspout connectors, and leaf guards. They may be box, round, or ogee in configuration and are often prepainted. Plastic or vinyl gutters in stock lengths and various cross-sectional shapes are manufactured with matching accessories. These types of gutters have the advantage that they deteriorate less from the effects of weather. Treated wood gutters are premilled in quarter round or ogee patterns. They may be job fabricated in box or V configurations. Downspouts, round or rectangular in cross section, are available with accessories to match the gutter systems. Pipe of black steel or cast iron may be used to provide a more durable downspout.

Industry Standards

Roofing: Design Criteria, Options, Selection
(RSMeans)

Gutters Versus Scuppers

Because of problems with maintenance, deterioration, and cleaning, it is best to avoid the use of gutters when possible on larger commercial structures, where they may be required to move the water a great distance, thereby increasing the chance of blockage by debris or ice. The best way to remove water from this type of roof is with interior ("field") drains. These drains should be installed along with tapered insulation, to ensure a positive slope and thus minimize ponding. Short lengths of gutter, *scuppers* or *heads,* and downspouts

are another solution. With this approach, water is directed away from the raised portion of the fascia by the use of *crickets* between the scuppers (see **Figure 8.2,** **"Downspout Scupper"**).

The most economical downspout is the 26-gauge corrugated rectangular type, readily available in most areas at sheet metal supply wholesalers. These downspouts are usually available in three sizes:

Area in Square Inches	Actual Size	Nominal Size
7.73	2⅜" x 3¼"	2" x 3"
11.70	2¾" x 4¼"	3" x 4"
18.75	3¾" x 5"	4" x 5"

Scuppers should be spaced no more than 50' on center; they should be closer if there are large areas to drain. The area to be drained by each downspout should be calculated. Then, using rainfall data derived from charts in the *SMACNA Architectural Manual, AIA Graphic Standards,* or a similar resource, the size of the downspouts can be determined, and the distance between the downspouts adjusted as necessary to produce practical spacing. If the downspouts are over 40' in length, relief valves or heads should be installed to admit air and prevent formation of a vacuum.

Ed. Note: See "Bituminous Roofing Products" later in this chapter for an illustration of a gutter system for that type of roof.

Flat Roof with Gutter

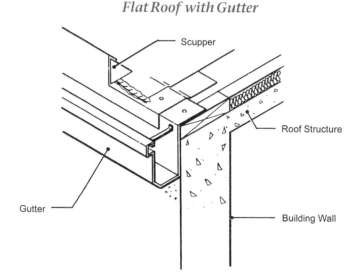

Scupper

Roof Structure

Gutter

Building Wall

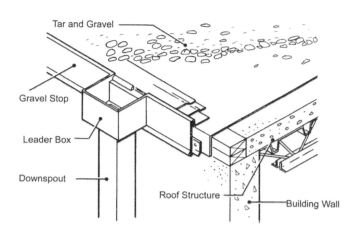

Flat Roof with Leader Box

Tar and Gravel

Gravel Stop

Leader Box

Downspout

Roof Structure

Building Wall

Wood Gutter

Metal or Vinyl Gutter

Figure 8.1

RSMeans, *Means Graphic Construction Standards*

Mechanical Equipment Support

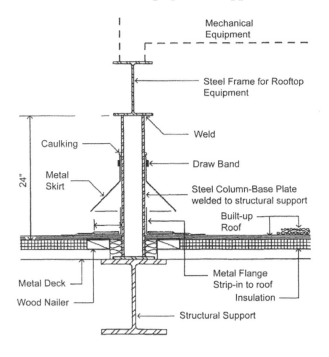

Gutter & Downspout

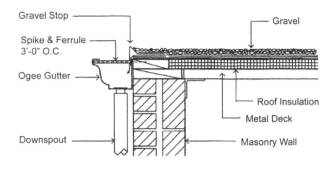

Downspout Scupper

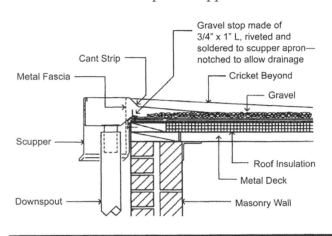

Figure 8.2   RSMeans, *Roofing: Design Criteria, Options, Selection*

Roofing Fire Safety & Wind Resistance

Industry Standards

Roofing Handbook
(The McGraw-Hill Companies)

Fire safety is an important consideration, especially since the roof is particularly vulnerable to fire from overhead or airborne sources.

The fire resistance of roofing materials is tested by the Underwriters' Laboratories, Inc. (UL), an independent, not-for-profit public safety testing laboratory. UL established the standard for the testing of roofing materials with the assistance of nationally recognized fire authorities.

Manufacturers voluntarily submit materials for testing. The materials then are classified and labeled according to the classes below. The American Society for Testing and Materials (ASTM) is a voluntary organization concerned with the development of consensus standards, testing procedures, and specifications.

Class A The highest fire-resistance rating for roofing as per ASTM E-108. This class rating indicates that the roofing material is able to withstand severe exposure to fire that originates from sources outside the building.

Class B This fire-resistance rating indicates that the roofing material is able to withstand moderate exposure to fire that originates from sources outside the building.

Class C This fire-resistance rating indicates that the roofing material is able to withstand light exposure to fire that originates from sources outside the building.

UL also tests shingle performance against high winds. To qualify for the UL wind-resistant label, shingles must withstand continuous test winds of at least 60 miles per hour for two hours without a shingle tab lifting.

Labeling of Roof Materials

IBC-2006

1506.4 Product identification: Roof covering materials must be packaged and labeled with the manufacturer's and approved testing agency's identifying information. For bulk shipments, this information may be in the form of a certificate or manufacturer's bill of lading.

IRC-2006

R904.4 Product identification: Same requirements.

Roof Structure

Industry Standards
Roofing: Design Criteria, Options, Selection
(RSMeans)

Structural Roof Deck

The structural roof deck is the foundation upon which the roofing system is built. The following basic principles should be kept in mind:

- In new design, provide a deck and its supporting structure with the strength and stability to accommodate loading for a variety of roofing systems, attachment of components, and temporary loading during construction. Re-roofing will inevitably be required in the future.

- Provide slope for positive drainage, using a minimum of $1/4$" per foot.

- Check special loading conditions, such as concentrated equipment loads, snow slides or banks at base of walls of high roof sections, and ponding behind potential ice dam locations.

- Check roof load bearing capacity for any roof that will have more dead load added by re-roofing. Steel and wood structures are more likely to be overloaded by the added weight, but do not overlook potential problems in reinforced or pre-stressed concrete. Long span "flat roof" members with perimeter drainage can be especially troublesome if they have lost their initial camber.

The structural roof deck is an integral part of the light commercial building structure. It supports not only the roofing system, consisting of insulation, membrane, and surfacing, but also live loads, such as wind and various forms of precipitation. In addition, economy of design often dictates that the deck perform beyond the simple function of carrying the roofing and gravity loading. The deck also acts as lateral bracing for compressive sections of slender framing, such as joists or purlins. Additionally, the structural deck may be used as a diaphragm to receive, distribute, and deliver lateral forces to walls or other buttressing elements of the building.

All roof decks must be compatible not only with their accompanying system components, but also with the service environment. To successfully support a roofing system, the deck must have the necessary strength, stiffness, dimensional stability, and durability to provide a good foundation for that system. If the building designer is not an expert on roofing technology, a professional should be consulted who can match the roofing system to the structure.

Comments

Roof Deck Classification

Decks are classified in a number of different ways, based on different criteria. Building codes or insurance-related agencies classify decks as *combustible* or *noncombustible*; built-up roofing manufacturers and their specifiers classify them as *nailable* or *nonnailable*. Structural engineers and architects usually classify decks by material, such as *concrete, cementitious wood fiber, steel,* or *wood*.

As some roof system components may be incompatible with certain deck types, the designer or roof specifier should be aware of potential problems with certain combinations in advance. This section covers characteristics of each of the various types of decks and potential problems these arrangements may present to the roof system. Such problems can be avoided through optimal system selection and design.

Steel Roof Decks

Industry Standards
Means Graphic Construction Standards
(RSMeans)

Steel roof decking (used in commercial structures) has the advantages of being a lightweight material that covers a large area and can be installed in a minimum amount of time. Decking is manufactured in depths ranging from $1^{1}/_{2}$" to $7^{1}/_{2}$", thicknesses from 18 gauge to 22 gauge, and various cover widths. Economy dictates that lengths cover a minimum of two supporting members. Roof deck measuring $1^{1}/_{2}$" thick is rolled in three configurations: narrow rib, intermediate rib, and wide rib. The interior finish may be galvanized or factory painted.

Steel deck stored on site should be blocked off the ground with one end higher than the other to provide drainage. They should be covered with ventilated waterproof material for protection from the elements. The deck may be welded to supporting members, including bearing walls, or fastened with screws. Welds are made from the top side of the deck with puddle welds at least $1/2$" diameter and fillet welds at least 1" long. Screws should be a minimum size No. 12.

Spacing of welds or screws are as follows for all widths of deck: all side laps plus a sufficient number of interior ribs to limit the spacing between adjacent points of attachment to 18". For spans greater than 5', side laps shall be fastened between supports, center-to-center, at a maximum spacing of 3'.

Comments

Steel deck surfaces that will remain exposed when the project is complete should be galvanized or painted on the underside to prevent rust and eventual staining.

Deck sheets should be placed in accordance with an approved erection-layout drawing supplied by the deck manufacturer and in accordance with the deck manufacturer's standards. Roofs having a slope of $\frac{1}{4}$" in 12" or more should be erected from the low side up to produce a shingle effect. The ends of the sheet should lap a minimum of 2" and be located over a support.

The deck erector normally cuts openings in the roof deck, which are shown on the erection drawings, and are less than 16 square feet in area, as well as skew cuts. Openings for stacks, conduits, vents, etc. should be cut (and reinforced if necessary) by trades requiring the openings.

Roof Deck System with Insulation

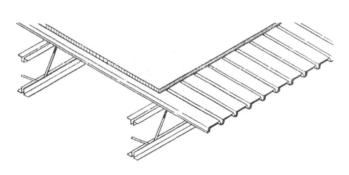

Acoustic Deck System

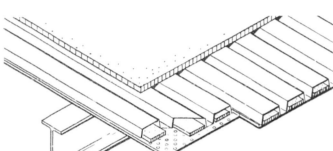

Composite Beam, Deck, and Slab

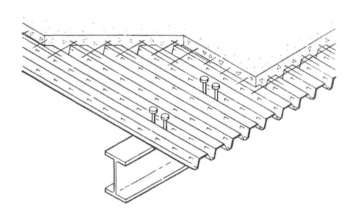

Cellular Deck System

Figure 8.3

RSMeans, *Means Graphic Construction Standards*

Steel Roof Deck

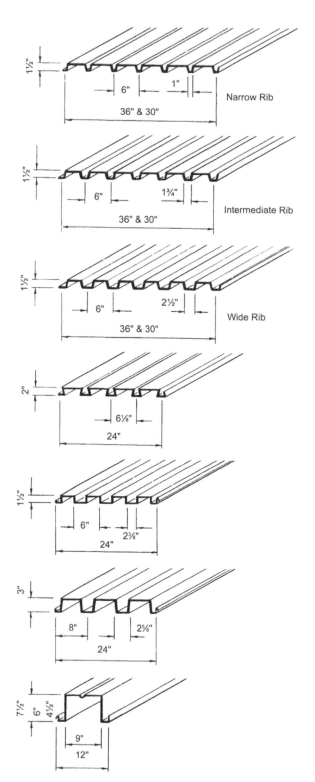

Acoustic Deck

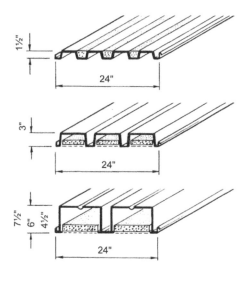

Cellular Deck

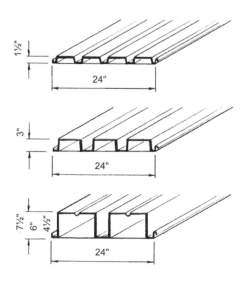

Figure 8.3 (continued)

RSMeans, *Means Graphic Construction Standards*

Metal Deck and Steel Joists on Beams

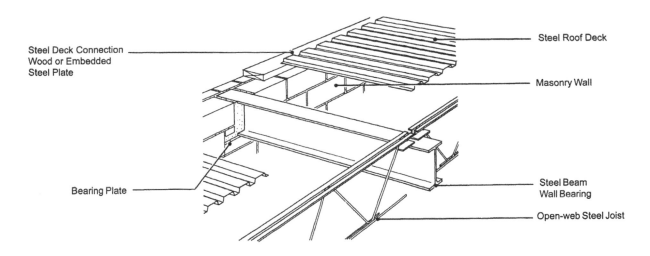

Steel Deck Connection
Wood or Embedded
Steel Plate

Steel Roof Deck

Masonry Wall

Bearing Plate

Steel Beam
Wall Bearing

Open-web Steel Joist

Metal Deck and Steel Joists on Walls

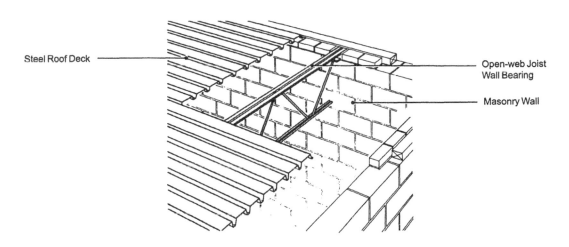

Steel Roof Deck

Open-web Joist
Wall Bearing

Masonry Wall

Formboard Deck, Bulb Ts, and Steel Joists

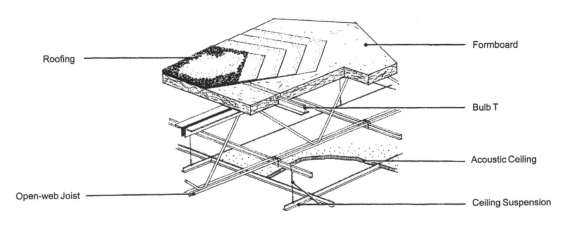

Roofing

Formboard

Bulb T

Acoustic Ceiling

Open-web Joist

Ceiling Suspension

Figure 8.4

Concrete Roof Decks

Industry Standards

Roofing: Design Criteria, Options, Selection
(RSMeans)

Structural Concrete

Structural concrete decks (also used for commercial applications) may be *cast-in-place* or *precast*. Cast-in-place concrete decks are either *conventionally reinforced* or *posttensioned*. Precast decks are also either conventionally reinforced (commonly designated "reinforced") or pre-stressed, but pre-stressed is by far more commonly used.

Concrete decks are superior to lightweight decks for ballasted roofing systems. For insulated or mechanically attached single-ply systems, however, the cost of attaching insulation to the deck becomes a factor. When not topped with cast-in-place concrete or underlayment, the insulation board may fracture or membranes may split. Adjacent deck sections must be properly attached structurally in order to prevent differential vertical movement. It is also necessary to level the butted ends of sections if they are out of level. If lateral movements are possible in the deck system, the roofing membrane must have adequate flexibility in order to prevent splitting.

Pre-stressed members deflect a greater distance than cast-in-place reinforced structural slabs under comparable loads. They also gain and lose camber from heating and cooling of the upper surface, if not well insulated. Considerable movement can also take place between the ends of members in multiple span arrangements; this movement must be addressed in the selection of the roofing system, its attachment, and flashings. Flashing along terminal (side) edges of long members must often accommodate several inches of vertical movement between the deck and the parapet.

In lightweight insulating concrete decks, venting is not provided beneath the concrete. Thus, efforts should be made to assure proper drying of the overlay prior to roofing. Attention should also be paid to lateral venting of moisture vapor between the concrete and the underside of a built-up roof (BUR) membrane. This may be accomplished with a *venting base sheet;* one-way *roof vents* may also be helpful.

Hot mopping of BUR membranes to lightweight fills is discouraged by roofing authorities. Instead, special fasteners are recommended to attach base sheets to this nailable substrate. Such fasteners usually have a two-piece shank and an oversized head. The shanks mechanically anchor into the media by expanding, deforming, or barbing as they are driven. The plain shanks of standard roofing nails do not offer sufficient resistance to withdrawal. To mechanically attach insulation boards to lightweight fill, special fasteners are available with large, coarse threads and integral, or two-piece, disc heads. Some also have internal "barbs" that are actuated from the top after setting the screw. These special screws are spaced more widely than nails (up to three times more widely spaced), for attaching a base sheet.

The larger value of uplift resistance required for the insulation fasteners is often beyond the pull-out strength of lightweight insulating concrete. Uplift tests should be run, using the planned fastener in the lightweight concrete on-site, to confirm that the required design values can be achieved. Otherwise, alternative methods of attachment must be used.

Wood Roof Decks

Ed. Note: For more information on wood framing, see Chapter 5.

Industry Standards

Roofing: Design Criteria, Options, Selection
(RSMeans)

Ventilation

Wood roof framing, if not pressure-treated against decay, *must be ventilated.* Air, wood, and decay-propagating organisms are ever present; suitable decay-producing temperatures are anywhere between

Truss Tees, Formboard, Mesh, and Poured Gypsum Deck

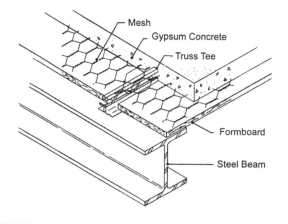

Mesh
Gypsum Concrete
Truss Tee
Formboard
Steel Beam

Figure 8.5   RSMeans, *Roofing: Design Criteria, Options, Selection*

45° and 110°F. To prevent decay, wood moisture content should be kept below 20 percent, or the wood should be pressure-treated to make it toxic, or unacceptable, to fungi or termites.

Cementitious Wood Fiber Decks

Cementitious wood fiber decks are often used in structures that do not have a suspended ceiling, such as gymnasiums and schools. The planks or panels are plant-produced, using treated wood fibers and a binder of Portland cement or gypsum. They are molded with controlled pressure and temperature to modular widths. When used with bulb tees, the planks have rabbeted edges to lay on bottom flanges of the tees (**Figure 8.6**). The tees are usually spaced at 2'-9" on center and the planks span transversely between them. When used to span longitudinally between joists or purlins, the planks are generally 8' long and have tongue and groove edges.

Bulb Ts and 3" Thick Deck

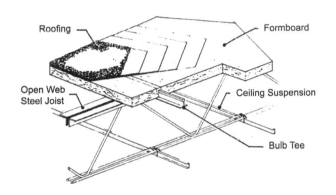

Roofing

Formboard

Open Web
Steel Joist

Ceiling Suspension

Bulb Tee

Figure 8.6   RSMeans, *Roofing: Design Criteria, Options, Selection*

Roof Shingles & Tiles: Definitions

Industry Standards

Plan Reading & Material Takeoff
(RSMeans)

Shingles and tiles are popular materials for covering sloped roofs. Both are *watershed* materials, which means they are designed to direct water away from the building by means of the slope or pitch of the roof. Shingles and tiles are used on roofs with a pitch of 3" or more per foot. Shingles are installed in layers with

staggered joints over roofing felt underlayment. Nails or fasteners are concealed by the course above. Shingle materials include wood, asphalt, fiberglass, metal, and masonry tiles. Asphalt and fiberglass are available in a variety of weights and styles, with three-tab being the most common. **Figure 8.7** illustrates an asphalt shingle roof system and its components.

Wood shingles may be either shingle or shake grade; cedar is the most common species of wood used. Metal shingles are either aluminum or steel and are generally available prefinished. Slate and clay tiles are available in a variety of shapes, sizes, colors, weights, and textures. These are typically heavier materials and therefore require specialized installation techniques, and a stronger structural roof system to support the added loads imposed by the extra weight.

In addition to the shingle or tile materials, special metal trim pieces are required to protect the edge of the roof deck and allow water to drip free of the roof edge. *Drip edge* (available in vented and nonvented) is a corrosion-resistant metal, typically aluminum; it may be omitted with wood shingles or slates when the edge of the shingle or slate projects beyond the roof edge. Metal flashings for the valleys of the shingled and tiled roofs may also be specified. Valley flashing can be lead-coated copper, copper, or zinc alloy.

To provide venting for the attic space, ridge vents are sometimes used. They allow the transfer of air from the attic or rafter space to the outside, to prevent the buildup of moisture along the underside of the roof sheathing. Ridge-venting materials are available in a variety of styles and compositions.

Shingles and tile roof systems require special shingles or tiles, called *cap shingles* at the ridge or hip of the roof. A cap shingle may be a regular three-tab shingle modified for use as a cap, as in the case of asphalt or fiberglass shingles, or a special prefabricated cap (as in the case of some clay tile or metal tile designs).

Special membrane material installed under the first couple of courses, and at the hips and valleys of the shingle or tile roof, is called an *ice/water barrier*. Most of these products are a bitumen-based self-adhering membrane for use in cold climates where ice and water may dam along the eaves and valleys and cause water to back up under the roof shingles.

Shingled Roof

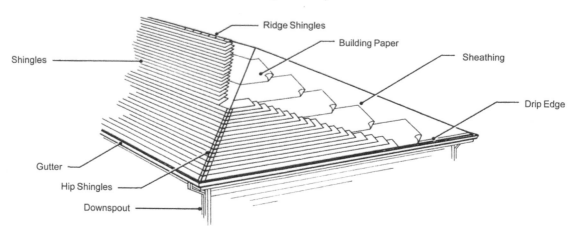

Figure 8.7

Asphalt Shingles

Industry Standards

Roofing Handbook
(The McGraw-Hill Companies)

Specifying Underlayments
When a single-layer underlayment is required, apply one layer of No. 15 asphalt-saturated, nonperforated felt horizontally. Heavier underlayment usually is not necessary, but might be required by local codes or area practice. Lap all felt sheets a minimum of 2 inches over the preceding felt sheet. Endlaps should be a minimum of 4 inches. Nail the felts under the lap only as necessary to hold the felts in place until the asphalt roofing material is applied. Laps can be sealed with plastic asphalt cement as required.

If specifications call for a double-layer underlayment, apply two layers of No. 15 (minimum) asphalt-saturated, nonperforated felt horizontally. Apply a 19-inch-wide starter sheet to the eaves. Cover the starter sheet with a full width sheet. Lap succeeding sheets 19 inches over the preceding sheets with a 17-inch exposure. Endlaps should be a minimum of 6". Backnail the felts under the laps only as necessary to hold tile felts in place until the asphalt roofing material is applied. Laps can be sealed with plastic asphalt cement as required.

In locations where the January mean temperature is 30°F or lower, apply two plies of No. 15 felt or one ply of No. 50 felt. Set in hot asphalt or mastic, or an adhered

bitumen membrane underlayment to roof decks with slopes less than 4 inches per foot, regardless of the slope. Work from the eaves to a point 24 inches inside the building's inside wall line to serve as an ice shield.

Comments

Kettle temperature must be monitored, because overheating asphalt causes a number of problems. When it is overheated, asphalt will apply too thin; when it is cool, it will become brittle. Overheated asphalt puddles at the bottom of slopes, resulting in future alligatoring, or checking, in the areas where the puddle thickens.

The National Roofing Contractors Association (NCRA) recommends the following mop application:

Type I	ASTM D 312	Level Asphalt	350°F ± 25°F
Type II	ASTM D 312	Flat Asphalt	400°F ± 25°F
Type III	ASTM D 312	Steep Asphalt	425°F ± 25°F

Refer to the manufacturer's recommendations for appropriate temperatures for a particular application. See also "Built-Up Roofing, Rule 5," later in this chapter.

The limitations imposed by the slope, or pitch, of the roof deck are factors that must be considered when the roof is designed and underlayments specified.

For instance, self-sealing strip shingles, with tabs, can be applied on roof decks that have a slope of 4 inches per 12 inches or more if at least one layer of No. 15 asphalt-saturated, nonperforated felt is applied horizontally to serve as the underlayment.

Self-sealing strip shingles, with tabs, also can be applied to roof decks with a slope of 3 inches per 12 inches or more if at least two layers of No. 15 asphalt-saturated, nonperforated felt is applied horizontally to serve as the underlayment.

Using Staples and Nails

Staples can be used in place of roofing nails on a one-for-one basis. If there is any doubt about the acceptability of staples in a particular application, consult the shingle manufacturer.

Selecting Nails

Use large-headed, sharp-pointed, hot-dipped, galvanized, or the equivalent, steel or aluminum nails with barbed or otherwise deformed shanks to apply asphalt shingles. The best roofing nails are made from 11- or 12-gauge wire, have heads that are $3/8$ or $7/16$ inch in diameter, and are long enough to penetrate the roofing materials. The nails should extend through plywood decks and at least $3/4''$ into wooden plank decks.

If a fastener does not penetrate the deck properly, remove the fastener and repair the hole in the shingle with asphalt plastic cement or replace the entire shingle. Then place another fastener nearby.

Do not nail into or above factory-applied adhesives. Carefully align each shingle. Whenever possible, make sure that no cutout or end joint is less than 2 inches from a nail in an underlaying course. To prevent buckling, start nailing from the end nearest the shingle just laid and proceed across. To prevent distortion, do not attempt to realign a shingle by shifting the free end after two nails are in place.

Place the fasteners according to the shingle manufacturer's specifications. Align the shingles properly to avoid exposing fasteners in the course below. Drive the nails straight and flush with the shingle surface. Do not sink the nail into or break the shingle's surface.

Applying 3-Tab Strip Shingles

In areas with normal weather conditions, fasten each of these shingles with 4 fasteners. When the shingles are applied with a 5-inch exposure, apply the fasteners on a line $5/8$ inch above the top of the cutouts, 1 inch from each end, and centered over each cutout.

For high wind areas, use six fasteners instead of four. The fastener locations should be on a line $5/8$ inch above the top of the cutouts, 1 inch from each end and 1 inch to the left and right of center of each cutout.

If a roof surface is broken by a dormer or valley, start applying the shingles from a rake and work toward the break. If the surface is unbroken, start at the rake that is most visible. If both rakes are equally visible, start at the center and work both ways. No matter where the application begins, apply the shingles across and diagonally up the roof. This ensures that each shingle is fastened properly.

Straight-up application or racking can result in less than the recommended number of nails being used because of the manner in which the shingles are applied.

Asphalt Roofing— 6-inch Pattern

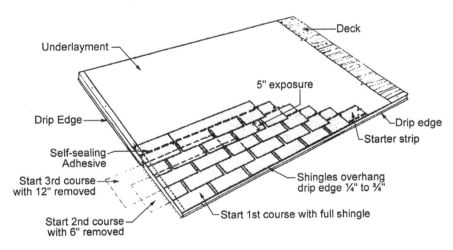

Courtesy of The McGraw-Hill Companies, *Roofing Handbook*

Figure 8.8

Comments

Improperly driven nails (**Figure 8.9**) can be addressed by removing and replacing the incorrect nail, or by adding another, correctly driven nail next to the original one. A small amount of roof cement can be applied over the nailhead or hole in the shingle.

Applying Successive Courses

The first course is the most crucial. Be sure it is laid perfectly straight. Check it regularly during application against a horizontal chalkline. A few vertical chalklines aligned with the ends of the shingles in the first course ensure the proper alignment of the cutouts.

If applying three-tab shingles or roll roofing for the starter strip, bond the tabs of each shingle in the first course to the starter strip by placing a spot of asphalt plastic cement about the size of a quarter on the starter strip beneath each tab. Then press the tabs firmly into the cement. Avoid excessive use of cement as this can cause blistering.

Comments

To adequately anchor asphalt roofing materials, special fasteners and/or details are required in certain deck materials, for example, gypsum concrete plank and tile, fiberboard, or similar nonwood deck materials. It is important to follow the manufacturers' instructions carefully when working with these types of materials, to ensure that responsibility for performance remains with the manufacturer.

Asphalt Shingles: Valleys & Flashing

Open Valleys

Open valleys can be formed by laying strips of at least 26-gauge galvanized metal, or an equivalent noncorrosive, nonstaining material in the valley angle and lapping the roofing material over the metal on either side. This leaves a space between the edges of the roofing material to channel the water down the valley.

Nailing Diagram

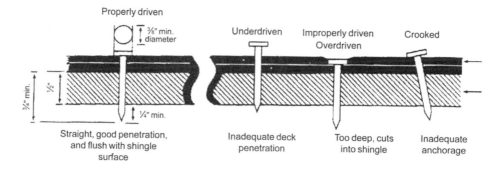

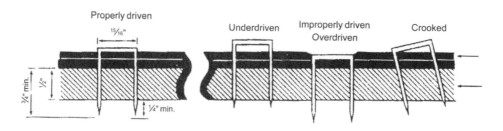

Figure 8.9   Courtesy of The McGraw-Hill Companies, *Roofing Handbook*

238

IBC–2006

1507.2 Asphalt shingles: Asphalt shingles must meet the requirements of IBC Table 1507.2. (See Figure 8.9)

1507.2.1 Deck requirements: Asphalt shingles must be attached to solidly sheathed decks.

IRC–2006

R905.2.1 Sheathing requirements: Same requirements as IBC.

IBC–2006

1507.2.2 Slope: Asphalt shingles may only be used for roofs with a slope of two units vertical in twelve units horizontal (17%) or greater. Double underlayment is required for roofs with a slope between 17% and 33%.

IRC–2006

R905.2.2 Slope: Same requirements as IBC.

IBC–2006

1507.2.5 Asphalt shingles: Asphalt shingles must be interlocking or have a self-seal strip. They must also meet the requirements of ASTM D 225 or ASTM D 3462.

IRC–2006

R905.2.4 Asphalt shingles: Same requirement as IBC.

IBC–2006

1507.2.9 Flashings: Flashing installation must meet the requirements of this section as well as manufacturers' instructions.

1507.2.9.2 Valleys: Installation of valley linings must meet manufacturer's requirements before asphalt shingles are applied. Only specific types of valley linings are permitted, including: (1) those that are at least 16" wide and of corrosion-resistant metal for open (exposed) valleys lined with metal, (2) those that comprise two plies of mineral roll roofing for open valleys (bottom layer must be 18" wide, and top layer at least 36" wide), and (3) those that consist of one ply of smooth roll roofing 36" wide and meet ASTM D 6380, Class S Type III, Class M Type II, or ASTM D 3909 for closed valleys (covered with shingles).

IRC–2006

R905.2.8.2 Valleys: Similar requirements. Permitted valley types: (1) those that are at least 24" wide and of corrosion-resistant metal for open (exposed) valleys lined with metals in Table IRC-2006 R905.2.8.2, (2) those that comprise two plies of mineral roll roofing for open valleys and meet ASTM D 3909 or ASTM D 6380 Class M. The bottom layer must be 18" wide, and top layer at least 36" wide, and (3) those that consist of one ply of smooth roll roofing 36" wide and meets ASTM D 6380 Class S Type III, Class M Type II, or ASTM D 3909 for closed valleys (covered with shingles).

Industry Standards

NRCA Roofing & Waterproofing Manual
(National Roofing Contractors Association)

NRCA recommends that valley metal, for use with asphalt shingles, be approximately 24 inches (610 mm) wide. This means that the NRCA recommends that the valley metal be formed with a "W"-shaped splash diverter, or rib, in the center. A center rib can be especially beneficial in valleys where adjoining roof areas are of unequal slope, as the rib helps to prevent "wash over" of runoff. The center rib should not be less than 1 inch (25 mm) high. For easier installation, and for controlling thermal expansion and contraction, NRCA suggests that metal valleys, used with asphalt shingle roofing, be no longer than 12 feet (4 m).

3.7.2 Woven Valleys

The woven valley method illustrated in **Figure 8.11** is preferred by some roofing professionals, but its use is generally limited to 3-tab strip shingles on roofs where the valley slope is at least 4 inches per foot (33%). However, in areas of the country where heavy accumulations of moss may grow between the shingle cutouts, a woven valley may hamper runoff. Therefore, as with all types of valleys, specifying a woven valley should be carefully considered to be sure it is beneficial for the particular project.

Some dimensional or architectural shingles can be difficult to use to create a rapidly draining woven valley. When dimensional shingles from opposite sides of the valley are woven, they can make for a relatively thick build-up of material, which can make the resultant valley irregularly sloped and slower draining. Individual locking-type shingles cannot be used with woven valley construction because nails are required for each tab, which would mean placing nails at or near the center of the valley.

Open Valley Using Metal Valley Flashing

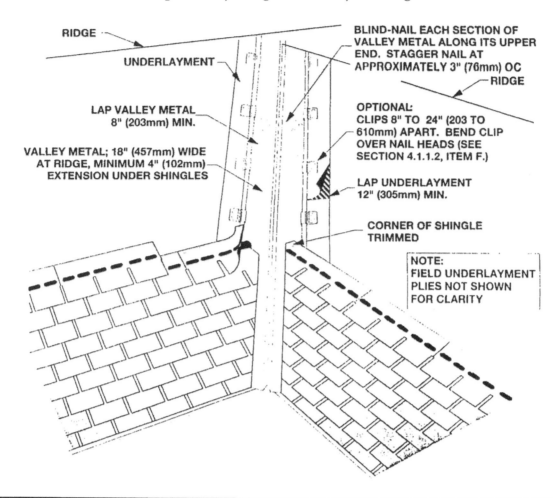

RIDGE

UNDERLAYMENT

LAP VALLEY METAL
8" (203mm) MIN.

VALLEY METAL; 18" (457mm) WIDE
AT RIDGE, MINIMUM 4" (102mm)
EXTENSION UNDER SHINGLES

BLIND-NAIL EACH SECTION OF
VALLEY METAL ALONG ITS UPPER
END. STAGGER NAIL AT
APPROXIMATELY 3" (76mm) OC

RIDGE

OPTIONAL:
CLIPS 8" TO 24" (203 TO
610mm) APART. BEND CLIP
OVER NAIL HEADS (SEE
SECTION 4.1.1.2, ITEM F.)

LAP UNDERLAYMENT
12" (305mm) MIN.

CORNER OF SHINGLE
TRIMMED

NOTE:
FIELD UNDERLAYMENT
PLIES NOT SHOWN
FOR CLARITY

Figure 8.10

Courtesy National Roofing Contractors Association, *NRCA Roofing & Waterproofing Manual*

Comments

While it is legal to construct the valley flashing from rolled roofing (both the *Roofing Handbook* and the *NRCA Roofing & Waterproofing Manual* address the acceptable methods), we exclude this method from this text as it does not reflect *common practice* for new construction.

Note: It is important, with all types of asphalt shingle valley construction, to keep from placing nails near the center of a valley. Nails should be kept away from the center of the valley to avoid leakage. Generally, nails should be kept back from the center of the valley by a minimum of 6" (152mm).

However, on relatively low-sloped roofs with valleys oriented into prevailing wind-driven rain, or in climates where freeze-thaw cycling may be regularly anticipated, holding nails back 6" to 8" (150 to 203 mm) or further from the center of the valley is not uncommon.

Industry Standards

Roofing Handbook
(The McGraw-Hill Companies)

Closed-Cut Valleys

This design can be used only with strip-type shingles and roll roofing materials. To install flashings at closed-cut valley locations, center a 36-inch-wide strip of No. 15 asphalt-saturated, nonperforated felt in the valley over the existing No. 15 asphalt-saturated felt underlayment. Use only enough nails to hold the sheet smoothly in place.

Lay the first course of shingles along the eaves of one roof area up to and over the valley. Extend it along the adjoining roof area for at least 12 inches. Continue to

Woven Valley

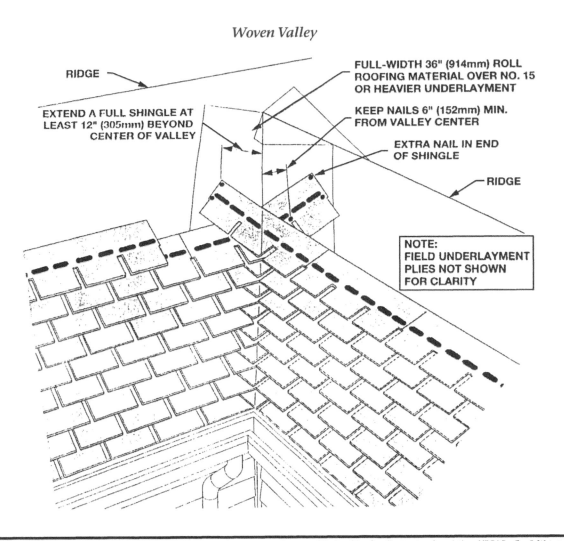

RIDGE

EXTEND A FULL SHINGLE AT
LEAST 12" (305mm) BEYOND
CENTER OF VALLEY

FULL-WIDTH 36" (914mm) ROLL
ROOFING MATERIAL OVER NO. 15
OR HEAVIER UNDERLAYMENT

KEEP NAILS 6" (152mm) MIN.
FROM VALLEY CENTER

EXTRA NAIL IN END
OF SHINGLE

RIDGE

NOTE:
FIELD UNDERLAYMENT
PLIES NOT SHOWN
FOR CLARITY

Figure 8.11

Courtesy of National Roofing Contractors Association, *NRCA Roofing & Waterproofing Manual*

apply the second and successive courses over the valley in the same manner as the first course. Tightly press the shingles into the valley and nail in place. Locate no nail closer than 6 inches to the valley's centerline. Locate two nails at the end of each terminal sheet.

Apply the first course of shingles along the eaves of the intersecting roof area and extend it over the previously applied shingles. Trim a minimum of 2 inches back from the centerline of the valley. Clip in place the upper corner of each end shingle to prevent water from penetrating under the courses and then embed it in a 3-inch-wide strip of plastic asphalt cement.

Flashing Against Chimneys

To avoid stresses and distortions due to the uneven settling of roofing materials, the chimney is usually built on a separate foundation from the building and normally is subject to some differential settling. Therefore, flashing at the point where the chimney projects through the roof requires a type of construction that allows for movement without damaging the water seal. To satisfy this requirement, use base flashings that are secured to the roof deck and counterflashings that are secured to masonry.

Before any flashings are installed, apply shingles over the roofing felt up to the front face of the chimney and construct a cricket or saddle between the back face of the chimney and the roof deck. Design the cricket to prevent the accumulation of snow and ice and to deflect water around the chimney.

Begin the flashing construction by installing at least 26-gauge galvanized metal, or an equivalent noncorrosive, nonstaining material, between the chimney and the roof deck on all sides. Apply the base flashing to the front first. Bend the base flashing so that the lower section extends at least 4 inches over the shingles and the upper section extends at least

Closed-Cut Valley

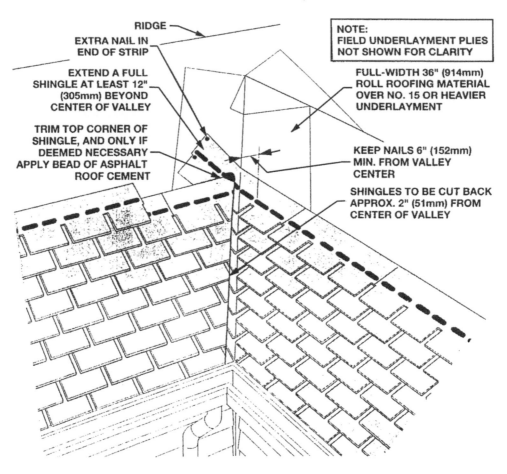

RIDGE

EXTRA NAIL IN
END OF STRIP

EXTEND A FULL
SHINGLE AT LEAST 12"
(305mm) BEYOND
CENTER OF VALLEY

TRIM TOP CORNER OF
SHINGLE, AND ONLY IF
DEEMED NECESSARY
APPLY BEAD OF ASPHALT
ROOF CEMENT

NOTE:
FIELD UNDERLAYMENT PLIES
NOT SHOWN FOR CLARITY

FULL-WIDTH 36" (914mm)
ROLL ROOFING MATERIAL
OVER NO. 15 OR HEAVIER
UNDERLAYMENT

KEEP NAILS 6" (152mm)
MIN. FROM VALLEY
CENTER

SHINGLES TO BE CUT BACK
APPROX. 2" (51mm) FROM
CENTER OF VALLEY

Figure 8.12   Courtesy National Roofing Contractors Association, *NRCA Roofing & Waterproofing Manual*

12 inches up the face of the chimney. Set both sections of the base flashing in plastic asphalt cement.

Use metal step flashing for the sides of the chimney. Position the pieces in the same manner as flashing for a vertical sidewall. Secure each piece to the masonry with plastic asphalt cement and use nails to secure to the roof deck. Embed the overlapping shingles in plastic asphalt cement.

Place the rear base flashing over the cricket and the back of the chimney. The metal base flashing should cover the cricket and extend onto the roof deck at least 6 inches. It should also extend 6 inches up the brickwork. Bring the asphalt shingles up to or over the cricket and cement in place.

Place counterflashings over all apron, cricket, and step flashings to keep water from the joint. Begin by setting the metal counterflashing into the brickwork. This is done by raking out the mortar joint to a depth of 1½ inches and inserting the bent edge of the flashing into

the cleared joint. Once it is in place and has a slight amount of spring tension, the flashing cannot be dislodged easily. Refill the joint with Portland cement mortar. Finally, bend the flashing down to cover the flashing and to lie snugly against the masonry.

Counterflashing

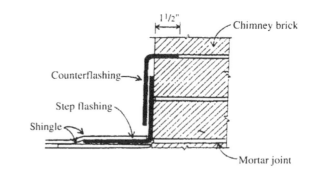

1½"

Chimney brick

Counterflashing

Step flashing

Shingle

Mortar joint

Figure 8.13   Courtesy of The McGraw-Hill Companies, *Roofing Handbook*

Step Flashing & Counterflashing Against Chimney

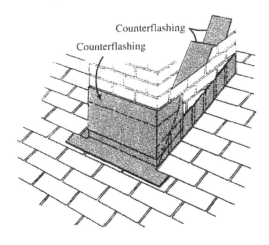

Counterflashing

Counterflashing

Figure 8.14   Courtesy of The McGraw-Hill Companies, *Roofing Handbook*

Drip Edges

Drip edges provide efficient watershedding at the eaves and rakes and keeps the underlying wood or plywood deck from rotting. Use 28-gauge galvanized metal, at a minimum, or an equivalent noncorrosive, nonstaining material to make drip edges along eaves and rakes and at edges of the deck. Provide an underlayment between the metal edge and the roof deck along the rake and over the metal edge along the eave.

Extend the drip edge back from the edge of the deck not more than 3 inches and secure with appropriate nails spaced 8 to 10 inches apart along the inner edge. In high-wind areas, space nails 4 inches on center.

Asphalt Shingles: Hips & Ridges

For hips and ridges, use individual shingles cut down to 12 x 12 inches from 12 x 36 inches three-tab shingles or to a minimum of 9 x 12 inches on two tab or no cutout asphalt shingles. Taper the lap portion of each cap shingle slightly so that it is narrower than the exposed portion. Some shingle manufacturers supply ready-cut hip and ridge shingles and specify how they should be applied.

To apply the cut ridge shingles, bend each shingle along its centerline so that it extends an equal distance on each side of the hip or ridge. Chalklines can assist in proper alignment. In cold weather, warm the shingle until it is pliable before bending. Apply the shingles with a 5-inch exposure, beginning at the bottom of the hip or from the end of the ridge opposite the direction

of the prevailing winds. Secure each shingle with one fastener on each side, placed 5½ inches back from the exposed end and 1 inch up from the edge. The fastener length for hip and ridge shingles should be ¼ inch longer than that recommended for shingles.

Asphalt Shingles: Shading & Discoloration

Shading

As a completed asphalt shingle roof is viewed from different angles, certain areas can appear darker or lighter. This difference in appearance is called shading. Shading also depends on the position of the sun and overall intensity of light. For example, slanting sun rays emphasize shading, while direct, overhead rays cause color shading to disappear.

Shading is a visual phenomenon that in no way affects the performance of the shingles. It occurs primarily as a result of normal manufacturing operations that produce slight differences in surface texture that cannot be detected during the production process. These unavoidable variations in texture simply affect the way the surface reflects light.

Algae Discoloration

A type of roof discoloration caused by algae and commonly referred to as fungus growth is a frequent problem throughout the country. It is often mistaken for soot, dirt, moss or tree droppings. The algae that cause this discoloration do not feed on the roofing material and, therefore, do not affect the service life of the roofing.

Fiber-Cement Shingles

Industry Standards

NRCA Roofing & Waterproofing Manual
(National Roofing Contractors Association)

Fiber cement products are generally a blend of a Portland cement, synthetic or natural fibers and, in some cases, lightweight aggregate that are manufactured to simulate natural slate, wood shakes or shingles, and tile. Others may be based on a cementitious resin or epoxy compound. With some of these products the coloring is created with mineral oxides or pigments. The resulting products can typically be fastened, and sawn or cut for use on steep-slope roofs. Currently, these products are cement-based, non-asbestos fiber reinforced.

2.2 Manufacturing Processes for Fiber Cement Roofing Products

Generally, the non-asbestos fibers, cement, and other ingredients are mixed together, then poured into a mold or formed for shape, and heated under pressure to form the shingles or roofing units. Some products are predrilled with fastener holes before packaging.

2.3 Some General Guidelines and Application Information Applicable to Various Fiber Cement Roofing Products

2.3.1 Roof Deck. With some products, both solid and spaced sheathing may be used. When solid sheathing is to be used, a minimum of 1-5/32 inch (12mm) plywood sheathing is recommended. However, with some products in certain climates more conservative roof deck and framing spacings are important to consider. Manufacturers' instructions and roof deck recommendations should be consulted.

NRCA recommends a minimum roof deck slope of 4 inches per foot (33%). Some manufacturers will allow application on lower slopes, such as 3 inches per foot (25%), if special precautions and underlayment configurations are followed (refer to Item 2.5.4, Slope Limitations).

2.3.2.1 Underlayment and Interlayments

Underlayments and interlayments are often essential components for use with fiber cement roof systems. With some systems, underlayments or interlayments are critical. NRCA suggests underlayments (and/or interlayments where applicable) be used with all fiber cement roof systems, particularly where wind-driven rain and snow are anticipated.

2.3.2.2 Additional Underlayment Requirements and Ice Dam Protection Membranes

A. When a single layer of underlayment is required, the non-perforated felt should be applied horizontally. NRCA recommends that the asphalt-saturated felt meet or exceed the standards set forth by ASTM D 226 or ASTM D 4869. In single layer applications, all felts should be lapped a minimum of 2 inches (51mm) over the preceding felt sheet. End laps should be a minimum of 4 inches (102mm). The underlayment should be fastened appropriately for the slope of the roof, as necessary to hold the felts in place until the installation of the primary roof covering materials.

B. When a double-layer underlayment is required, two layers of nonperforated felt should be applied horizontally. First, a 19-inch (483mm) wide starter sheet should be applied along the downslope roof edge (e.g., eave). A full-width sheet should then be applied, completely covering the starter sheet. Succeeding sheets should be lapped 19 inches (483mm) over the preceding sheets, leaving a 17-inch (432mm) exposure. End laps should be a minimum of 6" (152mm). It is suggested that the felts be nailed as necessary to hold the felts in place until the primary steep-slope roofing material is applied.

C. Regardless of the type of underlayment required, or the slope of the roof, in locations where the January mean temperature is 30°F (-1°C) or less, NRCA suggests installation of an ice dam protection membrane. An ice dam protection membrane may consist of:

- Two plies of No. 15 asphalt saturated organic felt, one nailed to the deck and the second set in hot, Type III (steep) or Type IV (special steep) asphalt or asphalt lap cement.

- A combination of heavyweight coated base sheet nailed to the deck, and another felt ply or ply sheet set in hot steep asphalt or asphalt lap cement.

- A self-adhering polymer-modified bitumen membrane, ASTM D 1970.

The ice dam protection membrane should be applied starting from the eaves and extending upslope a minimum of 24 inches (610 mm) from the inside of the exterior wall line of the building. Note: On slopes less than 4 inches per foot (250/4), NRCA recommends the ice dam protection membrane be extended a minimum of 36" upslope from the inside of the exterior wall line of the building.

Note: Ice dam protection membranes, by themselves, cannot be relied upon to keep leaks or moisture infiltration from occurring. Careful consideration of roof insulation, ventilation, and project specific detailing for the particular climatic conditions is vital. Also, self-adhering modified bitumen underlayment must not be left exposed for long periods of time. Self-adhering modified bitumen underlayments should be covered with the primary roofing material as soon as practical to prevent premature degradation of the modified bitumen material.

Fasteners

2.3.3.1 Nails, Screws, and Staples. Non-corroding copper, stainless steel, or galvanized fasteners are often required. Consult with the specific fiber cement product manufacturer for recommended fasteners.

2.3.3.1.2 Length. Fasteners should be long enough to penetrate through all layers of roofing materials and achieve secure anchorage into the roof deck. Fasteners should extend through the underside of plywood sheathing or other acceptable wood panel decks, and penetrate at least ¾ inch (19 mm) into wood plank decks.

2.3.3.2 Wind Clips. Wind clips (sometimes referred to as storm anchors) may be used with some products to secure the butt or downslope edge of the individual roofing unit. Generally, wind clips are made of stainless steel or copper wire, sometimes fashioned with an elongated shaft and disc base. Wind clips are recommended where wind uplift pressures may exceed the product's uplift resistance when through-fastened in the typical manner, or where required by code.

2.3.5 Hips and Ridges

Hips and ridges may be covered with a premanufactured hip and ridge unit supplied by the manufacturer, or a metal saddle ridge covering; with some products, a site-fabricated ridge covering may be made from field material.

In some cases, hip and ridge units are used in conjunction with an overlayment material covering the hip or ridge. With some fiber cement products, a site-fabricated unit made from field material that is cut to the proper size may be recommended by the manufacturer. Consult the fiber cement product manufacturer's recommendations for hip and ridge coverings.

2.4 Valleys and Other Flashings

2.4.1 Description. Because steep-slope roofs are frequently interrupted by the intersection of adjoining roof sections, adjacent walls, or penetrations such as chimneys and plumbing soil-pipe stacks, all of which create opportunities for leakage, special provisions for weather protection must be made at these locations. The components used to control water entry at these locations are commonly called flashings. Careful attention to flashing details is essential to successful long-term roof performance, regardless of the type of roof construction. Consult the fiber cement product manufacturer for recommendations regarding valley construction and various flashing details, and consider upgrading detail designs as necessary for the particular project, giving special attention to local climatic expectations.

2.5 Precautions

NRCA is concerned about potential problems that may be associated with some fiber cement products as they are exposed to severe, repetitive freeze-thaw and/or wet-dry cycling. NRCA suggests close examination of the manufacturer's test data before specifying a

particular material, to ensure that the material will withstand the climatic conditions it will be expected to endure.

Ed. Note: For building code requirements on valleys with asbestos-cement shingles, see the end of the "Slate Shingles" section later in this chapter.

Wood Shingles & Shakes

Comments

Although wood shakes and wood shingles are available in pressure-treated wood, enabling them to meet UL 790 fire-rated standards for Class A roofs, many areas of the country have outlawed their use because of fire proliferation.

Pressure treatment increases the cost of the product, and there is a possibility that, over time, some of the fire-retardant chemicals may leach out of the wood, reducing the effectiveness of the fire-resistant feature.

One other negative to the use of wood shingles on roofs is that skip sheathing (normally recommended to discourage fungal growth on wood shingles) makes a very poor shear diaphragm structurally.

Following are installation standards for those areas where wood shakes and wood shingles are still allowed.

IBC-2006

1507.8.7 Flashing: Flashing and counterflashing is required at the juncture of the roof and vertical surfaces and must meet manufacturer's installation guidelines. Metal flashing must be at least 0.019" and corrosion resistant. Valley flashing must extend at least 11" from the centerline. A splash diverter rib at least 1" high is also required. Roofs of 25% slope and greater must have valley flashing that has a 36"-wide underlayment of Type I. Additional requirements must be met for cold climates.

IRC-2006

R905.7.6 Valley flashing: Flashing must not be less than No. 26 gage corrossion-resistant metal. It must extent 10" from centerline for roofs with slopes less than 100%, and 7" from centerline for roofs with slopes 100% or greater.

Shingle Measurements

E   Exposure
TL   Toplap
HL   Headlap
SL   Sidelap
W   Width for Strip Shingles
     or Length for Individual Shingles

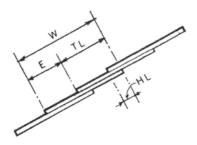

Figure 8.15   Courtesy of John Wiley & Sons, Inc., *Construction Principles, Materials, and Methods*

Industry Standards

NRCA Roofing & Waterproofing Manual
(National Roofing Contractors Association)

2.1.1 Perimeter Flashing and Downslope Underlayment

Depending upon climate severity, anticipated amounts of rainfall and freeze-thaw cycling, the use of perimeter drip-edge flashing may be considered for use with wood shakes. However, a metal drip-edge flashing may not be necessary with many types of steep-slope roof coverings that are rigid, and are capable of being extended beyond the edge of the roof without deformation to achieve a positive drip-edge. When perimeter flashings are specified, NRCA recommends the use of metal flashing with a formed drip-edge to allow water to drip off the edge of the roof without affecting the underlying construction. Where climate dictates the need for the use of perimeter flashing with wood roofing, NRCA recommends that a minimum of 26-gauge galvanized prepainted metal, or a non-corrosive flashing material of an expected longevity comparable to that of the shake roof, be specified for use along perimeter roof edges.

2.1.2 Starter Course for Shakes

In order for the shake roof to be two or three (whichever is specified) layers thick at all locations, including the downslope portion of the roof, a starter course is necessary. Generally, if the length of the shakes and the exposure specified will provide for a two layer thick wood roof, then the starter course may contain only one layer. If the length of the shakes and the exposure specified will provide for a three-layer-thick wood roof, then the starter course

should contain two layers. The starter course is applied directly over the underlayment or ice-dam protection membrane along the downslope portion of the roof. In addition to providing longevity to the finished roof, the primary purpose of the starter course is to shed water that may migrate through the gaps or joints between the shakes in the overlying first course.

The following procedures may be used to apply the starter course:

A. After the downslope underlayment or ice dam protection membrane has been installed, the starter course of wood roofing may be applied. Generally, the starter course may consist of 15 to 24" (380 to 610 mm) wood shakes or shingles as the exposure specified for the project allows.

B. The shakes in the starter course should be laid so that the butt ends extend a minimum of 1½ inches (38 mm) beyond the finished fascia board or outer sheathing board edge (if there is no fascia). When gutters or eaves troughs are used, the overhang may be reduced to approximately 1 inch (25 mm). Shakes should be laid to extend approximately 1½ inches (38 mm) beyond the rake edge.

C. Space the individual starter units approximately ¼ inch to ½ inch (6 to 13 mm) apart, and fasten each unit with two fasteners. Place the nails approximately ¾ to 1 inch (19 to 25 mm) from the sides.

D. If the starter course consists of two layers, offset the joints between neighboring shakes in the adjacent courses a minimum of 1½ inches (38 mm).

2.1.3 First Course of Shakes

A. After the starter course has been installed along the downslope portion of the roof, the first course of shakes is applied. The first course is installed directly over the starter course. The joints between shakes in neighboring courses should be offset by a minimum of 1½ inches (38 mm). In some roof layouts, shakes less than 4" (102 mm) wide should not be used.

B. The butt ends of the shakes in the first course should extend to approximately the same point as the butt ends of the starter course units, so that the downslope end of the first course is flush with the downslope end of the starter course.

C. Space the shakes in the first course approximately ¼ to ½ inch (6 to 13mm) apart, and fasten each shake with two fasteners (the type and size specified). Note: Non-corroding staples are considered acceptable by NRCA for attachment of wood shakes, as the varied grain structure of the wood and the manner in which it affects staple shank deformation generally provide for good withdrawal resistance. Place the fasteners approximately ¾ inch to 1 inch (19 to 25 mm) from the sides, and 1½ to 2 inches (38 to 51 mm) above the butt line that will be created by the next overlying course.

2.1.4 Interlayment

A. After the first course of shakes has been applied, an 18-inch (457mm) strip of No. 30 asphalt-saturated (non-perforated "shake felt") roofing felt meeting ASTM D 226 or ASTM D 4869 should be installed as an interlayment. This felt interlayment helps to serve as a shield to protect from wind-driven rain and snow entry, and sheds water. A No. 30 asphalt saturated roofing felt is the minimum felt recommended for use as interlayment.

B. The felt interlayment is laid over the top portion of the shakes in the first course, and should extend up slope so that it rests on top of the sheathing. The bottom edge of the interlayment felt should be set at a distance that is equal to twice the exposure dimension specified for the shakes. For example, if 24-inch (610 mm) shakes are specified to be applied at a 10-inch (254 mm) exposure, that would require the felt interlayment be set 20 inches (508 mm) above the shake butts in the first course. This would provide for coverage of the top 4 inches (102 mm) of the shakes.

C. The top edge of the felt interlayment must rest on the sheathing. Stagger fasten the interlayment along the upper portion to hold it in place until the next course of shakes is installed. Interlayment fasteners should be covered by the next consecutive course of interlayment.

2.1.5 Second and Succeeding Courses of Shakes

A. After the first course of shakes and the first layer of felt interlayment have been applied, the second and succeeding courses of shakes and their interlayment are applied.

B. Set the second course of shakes at the specified exposure.

C. Space the individual shakes approximately ¼ to ½ inch (6 to 13 mm) apart, and offset the shakes from the joints in the underlying course by a minimum of 1½ inches (38 mm).

D. Fasten each shake with two fasteners. Place the fasteners approximately ¾ to 1 inch (19 to 25 mm) from the sides, and approximately 1½ to 2 inches (38 to 51 mm) above the butt line that will be created by the next overlapping course of shakes.

E. The fasteners should be driven flush to the surface of the shake.

F. After fastening each course of shakes in place, the felt interlayment is applied prior to setting the next succeeding course of shakes.

2.3 Wood Shakes for Hip and Ridge Locations

To weatherproof the roof at hips and ridges, wood shakes may be used as hip and ridge coverings. Mills assemble bundles of premade hip and ridge units, or contractors may make their own. However, both types of hip and ridge units must have alternate overlaps, and the units must be blind nailed during application. Typically, the exposure for hip and ridge units is the same as is specified for the field of the roof, although the exposure can be shortened to create hip and ridge lines for visual accent.

After both roof areas have been roofed with shakes up to the adjoining hip or ridge intersection, and the shakes in each intersecting course have been cut to the apex of the hip or ridge, then the hip or ridge coverings may be applied. The following procedures may be used to apply shakes at hip and ridge locations.

A. Felt plies of interlayment can be wrapped and nailed over the hip or ridge centerline. Wrapping the hips and ridges with the field felts provides an additional layer of protection from wind-driven rain and snow. Note: At ventilating ridges, felt is not

Wood Shake Application

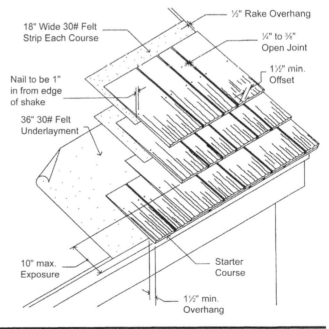

½" Rake Overhang

18" Wide 30# Felt Strip Each Course

¼" to ⅜" Open Joint

Nail to be 1" in from edge of shake

1½" min. Offset

36" 30# Felt Underlayment

10" max. Exposure

Starter Course

1½" min. Overhang

Figure 8.16

RSMeans, *Roofing: Design Criteria, Options, Selection*

wrapped over the ridge, as it would be closed off to ventilation.

B. For additional weather protection of the hip or ridge, a strip of asphalt-saturated felt may be fastened over the exposed juncture along the hip or ridge. This layer of felt should overlap the shakes on either side of the centerline by a minimum of 4 inches (102 mm). Note: At ventilating ridges, this extra strip of felt is not used.

C. Beginning at the downslope end of a hip or at the leeward end of a ridge, the shake hip or ridge units are applied in shingle fashion with each unit lapping over the previous unit. Note: Beginning the ridge shake application at the leeward end of the ridge orients each ridge shake's overlap away from the prevailing wind and weather. Applying ridge shakes with their laps facing away from the prevailing wind helps to keep wind-driven rain and snow from entering the roof and can help to minimize problems with wind blow-off.

D. Typically, hip and ridge shakes are made to provide a relatively uniform overlap of the hip or ridge centerline, covering the adjacent trimmed field shake by approximately 4 to 6 inches (102 to 152 mm). However, it is a good idea to chalk a straight line on one side of the hip or ridge, so that hip or ridge shakes can be set to the line for proper alignment.

E. Select and lay the hip or ridge units so the overlap along the top of each unit is alternated. One unit's overlap faces the roof area on one side of the hip or ridge; then the next sequential hip or ridge unit that is laid must face the opposite roof area.

F. Fasten each hip or ridge covering unit with two fasteners. Because hip and ridge fasteners must penetrate through more layers of roofing in order to securely attach the hip and ridge coverings to the underlying roof deck, the fasteners for hip and ridge units are recommended to be longer than those fasteners specified for the shakes covering the field of the roof. Place the fasteners approximately ¾ to 1 inch (19 to 25 mm) up from the sides, and approximately 1½ to 2 inches above the butt line that will be created by the next overlapping hip or ridge unit. The fasteners should be driven flush to the surface of the wood.

G. When reaching the upslope end of the hip or windward end of the ridge, the last unit is placed and fastened. These fasteners in the last hip or ridge unit will be exposed to the weather.

H. Sometimes hip and ridge boards are specified, in lieu of shakes, to cover hips or ridges, to enhance the aesthetic appeal of the wood roofing. Occasionally, the ridge boards are clad with sheet metal ridge covers.

Industry Standards

Roofing: Design Criteria, Options, Selections
(RSMeans)

A minimum of 4" in 12" slope is required to properly drain a wood roof. Two nails per shingle are required, as are baffles. Nails should always be galvanized or copper, placed 1" from each side and just high enough to be covered by the next course of shakes (see **Figure 8.16**). Nails should be driven flush to the surface and not into the fiber of the wood. The nails should penetrate the wood substrate by at least ½".

Sequence: The roof should be pre-loaded with bundles of wood shakes or shingles the day before application is to begin. Thirty-pound felt should then be applied to the entire deck. The installation should begin at the eave with an overlay of 1½". Chalk lines should always be struck to ensure uniformity and alignment. The 18" strips of 30 pound felt (the baffles) should be placed to overlap the shakes by 4". Cut shakes or shingles should be saved to use along the valleys. Proper planning should provide orderly coursing. Pre-manufactured

Wood Shingle & Shake Wall or Chimney Flashing

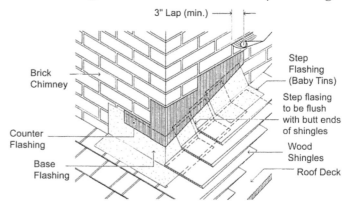

Baby Tin Step Flashing

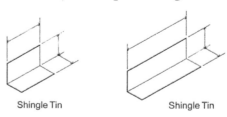

Figure 8.17   RSMeans, *Roofing: Design Criteria, Options, Selection*

hip and ridge units can be obtained from the supplier to ensure uniformity. It is recommended that a ³⁄₈" to ¹⁄₂" space be left between shakes to prevent buckling. Side lap should be 1¹⁄₂" for each succeeding course, as shown in **Figure 8.16**.

Slate Shingles

Industry Standards

Roofing: Design Criteria, Options, Selection
(RSMeans)

The most common thickness used for roofing slate is ³⁄₁₆". **Figure 8.18** shows the available sizes of standard slate, the minimum number of slates required per square, the exposures, and the quantity (by weight) of nails required per square of roof surface. Copper nails are the only suitable nails for use with slate. Nail length may be determined by adding 1" to twice the thickness of the slate. Nails should be large head, diamond-pointed, #10 gauge shank. Some basic guidelines for slate roof installation are as follows. (See **Figure 8.19** for an illustration of a slate roof system.)

- No through joints should occur from the roof surface to the felt.
- The overlapping slate should be joined as near the center of the underlying slate as possible, and not less than 3" from any underlying joint. A standard 3" *headlap* should be used. (Headlap is that portion of the slate which overlaps the lowest slate course beneath it.) The exposure (weathering surface) should be determined by subtracting 3" from the length of the slate and dividing by two.

Ridge Construction: Several methods may be used to construct the ridge on a slate roof, but the most common, shown in **Figure 8.19**, is called the *saddle ridge*. Using this method, the slates are brought together at the ridge so that the opposing slates will butt flush (see **Figure 8.19**). Wood lath is then nailed to the ridge so that the top row of slate will be properly aligned. To ensure that no moisture can be driven into the ridge, a strip of 60 mil. EPDM roof membrane is then placed over and along the ridge. The final *combing slate* is then placed over the top row of slate, with a 3" overlap. The ridge course should be run with the

Schedule for Standard Slate

Size of Slate (In.)	Slates Per Square	Exposure with 3" Lap	Nails Per Square (lbs.)	Nails Per Square (ozs.)	Size of Slate (In.)	Slates Per Square	Exposure with 3" Lap	Nails Per Square (lbs.)	Nails Per Square (ozs.)
26x14	89	11¹⁄₂"	1	0	16x14	160	6¹⁄₂"	1	13
					16x12	184	6¹⁄₂"	2	2
24x16	86	10¹⁄₂"	1	0	16x11	201	6¹⁄₂"	2	5
24x14	98	10¹⁄₂"	1	2	16x10	222	6¹⁄₂"	2	8
24x13	106	10¹⁄₂"	1	3	16x9	246	6¹⁄₂"	2	13
24x11	125	10¹⁄₂"	1	7	16x8	277	6¹⁄₂"	3	2
24x12	114	10¹⁄₂"	1	5					
					14x12	218	5¹⁄₂"	2	8
22x14	108	9¹⁄₂"	1	4	14x11	238	5¹⁄₂"	2	11
22x13	117	9¹⁄₂"	1	5	14x10	261	5¹⁄₂"	3	3
22x12	126	9¹⁄₂"	1	7	14x9	291	5¹⁄₂"	3	5
22x11	138	9¹⁄₂"	1	9	14x8	327	5¹⁄₂"	3	12
22x10	152	9¹⁄₂"	1	12	14x7	374	5¹⁄₂"	4	4
20x14	121	8¹⁄₂"	1	6	12x10	320	4¹⁄₂"	3	10
20x13	132	8¹⁄₂"	1	8	12x9	355	4¹⁄₂"	4	1
20x12	141	8¹⁄₂"	1	10	12x8	400	4¹⁄₂"	4	9
20x11	154	8¹⁄₂"	1	12	12x7	457	4¹⁄₂"	5	3
20x10	170	8¹⁄₂"	1	15	12x6	533	4¹⁄₂"	6	1
20x9	189	8¹⁄₂"	2	3					
					11x8	450	4"	5	2
18x14	137	7¹⁄₂"	1	9	11x7	515	4"	5	14
18x13	148	7¹⁄₂"	1	11					
18x12	160	7¹⁄₂"	1	13	10x8	515	3¹⁄₂"	5	14
18x11	175	7¹⁄₂"	2	0	10x7	588	3¹⁄₂"	7	4
18x10	192	7¹⁄₂"	2	3	10x6	686	3¹⁄₂"	7	13
18x9	213	7¹⁄₂"	2	7					

RSMeans, Roofing: Design Criteria, Options, Selection

Figure 8.18

Slate Roof System (Saddle Ridge)

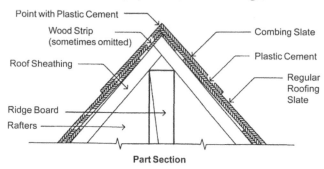

Part Section

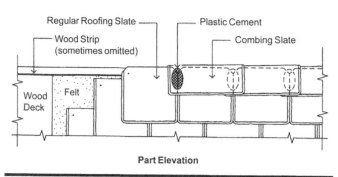

Part Elevation

Figure 8.19   RSMeans, *Roofing: Design Criteria, Options, Selection*

Saddle Hip

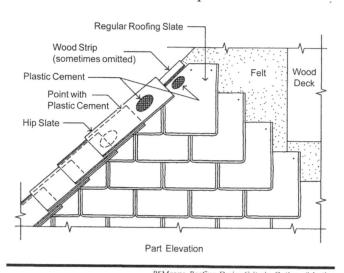

Part Elevation

Figure 8.20   RSMeans, *Roofing: Design Criteria, Options, Selection*

"grain" horizontal. The ridge slates are secured to the deck with two nails, which are then covered with plastic cement. All nails, except the last one on each side of the ridge, are concealed with a cover of cement.

Hip Construction: There are also several methods that can be used to form the hips. Again, the most common is the *saddle hip*, shown in **Figure 8.20.**

Here, as in the ridge, a wooden lath strip should be run along both sides of the hip. The ridge slate (of the same size as the exposure in the roof slates) should be attached with four nails per slate, with a strip of EPDM membrane underneath, as shown, to prevent moisture infiltration. All nail heads should be covered with plastic cement.

Valleys: Most valleys in slate roofs are "open," as shown in **Figure 8.21.** However, slate may also have

Open Valley

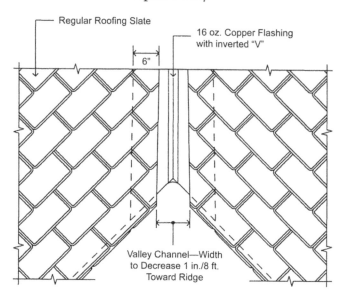

Closed Valley

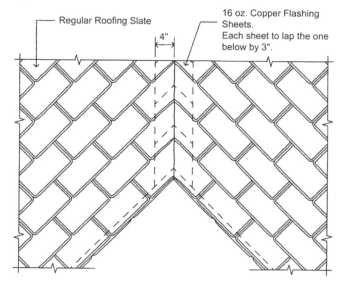

Figure 8.21   RSMeans, *Roofing: Design Criteria, Options, Selection*

closed valleys. (See **Figure 8.21**.) The valley is first lined with sheet metal (preferably 16 oz. cold-rolled copper sheet) so that water will be channeled between the slate on both sides. The width of this channel should uniformly increase down the valley toward the eave in order to carry the additional volume of water.

The slate application should begin 2" from the inverted "V" at the top and should taper away. The function of the inverted "V" in the valley is to "break up" the flow from each side and thereby prevent water from being driven up under the slate on the opposite side. The valley flashing should extend at least 6" under the slate and should be crimped back to intercept any moisture. The metal valley should be secured with cleats at 8" on center, along both sides of the valley.

Tile Roofing

Definitions & Considerations

Industry Standards

NRCA Roofing & Waterproofing Manual
(National Roofing Contractors Association)

1.3.1 Plain
Plain tiles are also referred to as flat slab or shingle tiles, as they are non-interlocking pieces. Plain tile is meant to be laid in a double thickness similar to asphalt shingles, and some wood shakes and slate.

With plain tile applications, an actual headlap is achieved, and the customary headlap dimensions are 2 or 3 inches (51 or 76 mm). Generally, plain tile thicknesses range from ¼ to ¾ inch (6 mm to 19 mm). Butts are usually square, but there are some with rounded and other cut-butt patterns. Some plain tiles have a roughened end that has a handmade appearance. A wide variety of surface treatments are applied during manufacture, including smooth, scored, grooved, sanded, ash coated, or others that create textures to achieve traditional appearances. In different parts of the world, plain tiles are also referred to as flat tiles, slab tiles, or shingle tiles.

1.3.2 Pan and Cover
Pan and cover tiles (also referred to as barrel tile or mission tile in some regions) are typically made in rounded pieces, half-circular pieces, or pairs. Pan and cover tiles are installed with one laid concave, the other laid convex. In some traditional styles, the pan is flatter, with side ribs or lips. Typically, depending on how the tile is specified to be installed, there is only one layer of tile throughout the field of the roof. Pan and cover tiles can be either straight or tapered. They are available with surface textures ranging from smooth and uniform to scored and rough surfaces.

Pans and covers are laid in a variety of ways. Pans can be laid tight to one another at the sides, or spaced apart (providing a minimum side lap by the covers). Straight barrel pans are sometimes used with tapered covers for added laying flexibility and aesthetics. Some covers have clipped-top corners that fit against clipped-bottom corners of the pans, which provides for a tight and relatively precise fit. Some pan and cover styles incorporate an interlocking feature to help keep out wind-driven rain and snow. Common styles are called Mission, Barrel, Straight Barrel Mission, and Tapered Barrel Mission.

1.3.3 Interlocking
Interlocking tile is laid in a single thickness with only a course-to-course overlap. The sides are channeled or ribbed so that neighboring tiles are lapped in an interlocking arrangement. The heads and butts may also interlock. Where there is no head-to-butt interlock, a simple overlap is used. With some styles the exposed surfaces are flat, and either smooth or textured. Many interlocking tiles are profiled, and the contours help direct runoff away from the interlocking side of the tile. Some contoured tiles are available that have the appearance of pan and cover tiles. Some molded-in contours add strength to the tile. Reinforcing ribs on the underside are used to add strength and reduce weight. The thickness at the butt, and, sometimes, the overall height of the flat styles range from ½ inch (13 mm) to 2 inches (51 mm).

1.3.4 S-Tile
S-tile refers to the profile of the tile. Sometimes S-tile is also referred to as one-piece pan and cover. S-tiles are laid in a single thickness with a course-to-course overlap. Thickness varies, but typical tile thickness is approximately ½ inch (13mm). Surfaces are available in smooth or a variety of textures. In some styles, the convex portion is slightly larger than the concave part. The concave portions may be rounded or flattened in contour. Common styles are referred to as S-tile.

Types of Tile

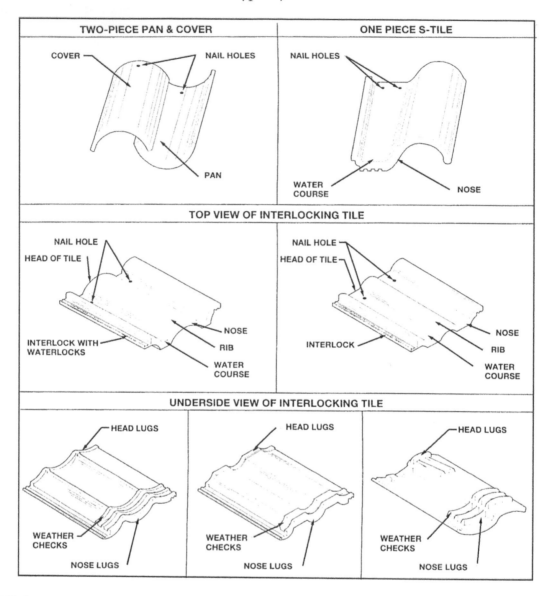

Figure 8.22

Courtesy of National Roofing Contractors Association, *NRCA Roofing & Waterproofing Manual*

Comments

Weight of roofing is an important part of the design and construction of any structure. An S-Tile roof can have a weight of 950 lbs per square (100 sq. ft.). A pan and cover can have 1,100 lbs per square, while an asphalt roof is 250 lbs per square. A square of roofing equals 100 square feet. Review the *NRCA Roofing & Waterproofing Manual* and the *Roofing Handbook* for further detail and comparison of options.

Installation Procedures

Industry Standards

Roofing: Design Criteria, Options, Selection
(RSMeans)

Decks: If plywood deck is used, the sheets should be separated by at least $\frac{1}{16}$". It should be exterior grade plywood of a thickness adequate to satisfy nailing requirements. If wood planking is used, it should be a minimum of 1 x 6 nominal lumber, spanning no more than 24" between rafters.

When the underlayment has been installed, vertical laths should then be nailed directly above all rafters, through the felt. Horizontal battens (stringers) are nailed across the lath, and spaced according to tile dimensions.

Stringers (Nailing strips): Hip and ridge stringers (see **Figure 8.23**) vary in height depending on the type of tile and the roof slope. It is best to lay out a few tiles at the ridge and determine the proper height for the ridge stringer.

Required Slopes for Tile Roof

The slope of a tile roof should be no less than four-in-twelve. For low-sloped roofs (3" to the foot), all configurations of clay tile may be installed *if* two layers of #43 base sheet are used; the first ply nailed and the second mopped in steep asphalt. Flat shingle tile without an interlocking feature should not be installed on roof decks having a slope of less than 5" per foot. A minimum of one layer of #30 roofing felt should be applied as an underlayment. Since the underlayment is the waterproofing course, it is best to use a #43 base sheet for this purpose. While a high density clay tile roof will last several hundred years, most underlayment will not.

Ice Shields

For installations where the January mean temperature is below 30 degrees Fahrenheit, an ice shield consisting of #43 felt mopped in steep asphalt should be installed. The ice shield should extend from the eave to the inside of the wall line.

Valleys

Special attention must be paid to the manner in which open valleys are installed in tile roofs. The requirements include an extra ply of dry-in felt installed before the metal valleys are fitted. The metal valleys should be "V" crimped in the middle in order to lessen the force of the water running down the slope and prevent it from driving up under the tiles on the opposite side.

At the valleys, tiles must be cut along a line to form an even edge, using a power saw and carborundum blade. Metal valleys and flashing should always be fabricated out of copper, stainless steel, or other noncorrosive metal.

Industry Standards

NRCA Roofing and Waterproofing Manual

(National Roofing Contractors Association)

With tile roofs, there are two basic types of valleys (*open and closed*).

2.9.3.1 Open Valleys

Open valleys are lined with sheet metal valley material. Note: The tiles are held back from the center of the valley so the valley flashing is exposed or open. Open valleys permit clear, unobstructed drainage, and are advantageous in locations where fallout from surrounding foliage (e.g., leaves, needles, and debris) settles on the roof and tends to accumulate in the valley. Open valleys constructed with durable heavy-gauge metal can be very long lasting.

Tiles from the adjoining roof areas are mitered to form a closed valley.

Generally, closed or mitered tile valleys are lined with sheet metal material. However, when metal flashing is used to line a closed tile valley, the metal is typically not exposed and lies under the courses of tile. With mitered tile valleys, the tiles are brought together over the metal liner at the valley centerline and mitered along the length of the valley to form a closed valley.

Note: With tile roofing, closed valleys are considered decorative because water can migrate through the layers of tile and it is the underlying metal valley that carries the runoff. Closed valleys are not recommended where surrounding foliage exists because fallout (e.g., leaves, needles, or debris) onto the roof can impede rapid runoff.

The two types of valleys described above are constructed only after the necessary layer(s) of underlayment, and any valley lining membrane material specified, have been applied to the roof deck.

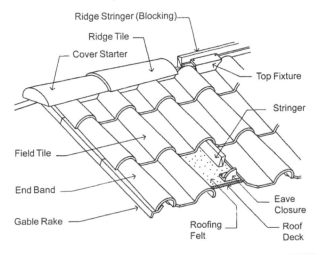

Clay Tile Application

Ridge Stringer (Blocking)
Ridge Tile
Cover Starter
Top Fixture
Stringer
Field Tile
End Band
Gable Rake
Eave Closure
Roofing Felt
Roof Deck

Figure 8.23

RSMeans, Roofing: Design Criteria, Options, Selection

Typically valley underlayment construction consists of a full width 36" sheet of No. 40 minimum asphalt-saturated felt, or an ice dam protection membrane. This valley underlayment is centered in the valley. Typically, valley underlayment sheets are secured with only enough roofing nails to hold them in place until the balance of valley materials are applied. The courses of underlayment from the fields of the two adjoining roof areas are extended so that each course overlaps the valley underlayment by at least 12" (305 mm). The valley is then lined with the balance of the valley flashing and tile roofing.

2.9.3.1.1 Open Valleys Using Valley Metal

Open valleys are usually constructed with sheet metal valley material. The metal valley is constructed by laying lengths (typically 8' or 10') of 24-gauge pre-painted galvanized steel or an equivalent non-corrosive metal through the valley. The tile (and with some area practices, the underlayment) is lapped onto the flange on either side of the valley metal, leaving a clear space between the roofing material to channel runoff water down the valley. The width of the valley, or the amount of space between the intersecting tile should increase uniformly, so the valley widens as it continues downslope. The difference in the width of the upper end of the valley and the lower end of the valley is referred to as the valley taper. In most climates, the amount of this valley taper is recommended to be 1/8" (3 mm) for every lineal foot (305 mm) of valley length. For example, in a valley 16' (5 m) long, the distance between tiles should be approximately 2" (51 mm) greater at the bottom of the valley than at the top. Note: Tapering valleys with tile roofing is not a common practice in all areas of the United States.

Tapering the valley has the following advantages:

- Allows tile to be laid closer to the valley at the upper end.
- Allows for increase in volume of runoff water to be received at the downslope end.
- Allows any ice that may form within the valley to free itself when melting, and slide down and exit the valley rather than lodging somewhere along the length of the valley.

2.9.3.2 Closed Valleys

Closed valley methods are preferred by some roofing professionals, but closed valley use with tile is generally limited to roofs where the valley slope is at least 8" per foot (67%). However, in areas of the country where heavy accumulations of foliage fallout are anticipated, or if moss can be expected to grow

between the tile roofing joints, a closed valley can hamper runoff. Therefore, specifying a closed valley should be carefully considered to be sure it is beneficial for the particular project.

Comments

Closed valleys should have a minimum gap of 2" at the bottom and 1/2" at the top to allow debris to self-clean during heavy rains.

IBC–2006

1507.3.9 Flashing: For clay and concrete tile, flashing and counterflashing is required at the juncture of the roof and vertical surfaces and must meet manufacturer's installation guidelines. Metal flashing must be at least 0.019" and corrosion resistant. Valley flashing must extend at least 11" from the centerline. A splash diverter rib at least 1" high is also required. Roofs of 25% slope and greater must have valley flashing that has a 36"-wide underlayment of Type I. Additional requirements must be met for cold climates.

IRC–2006

R905.3.8 Flashing: Same requirements.

Water Migration

Industry Standards

NRCA Roofing & Waterproofing Manual
(National Roofing Contractors Association)

1.4.1 Water Migration Potential

In steep roofing, water migration refers to the movement of water beyond the primary roof covering material. For example, water may migrate between the side-lap joints of tile and enter the roof system—this is one reason that underlayment materials can be so vital to the success of many types of tile roofs. Wind-driven rain and snow may migrate into some types of tile roofs. Also, the physical phenomenon of capillary action and surface tension, combined with wind, is a factor in the water migration characteristics of some types of tile. Different types of tile have different water migration potentials depending upon the tile's interlock (and waterlock) features, the headlap (if any) and the course-to-course overlap, the surface texture and finish, and the joint tolerances.

1.4.1.1 Water Migration Potential of Plain Tile

Plain tile functions as most other multiple layered watershedding roof coverings, in that there is an actual headlap. Wind, ice damming, and capillary action may cause water to migrate beyond the exposed portion of the overlying tile at the butt and the vertical or side joints. However, with plain tile, the width of the underlying tile, the location of its fastener holes, the slope of the roof, and the anti-capillary characteristics of the tile-to-tile surfaces, especially the headlap, all function to keep the roof weathertight. However, in extreme climates during harsh conditions (e.g., during hard wind-driven rains), water may migrate beyond the joints of plain tile. For the above reasons, underlayments are necessary with plain tile.

1.4.1.2 Water Migration Potential of Interlocking Tile

Interlocking types of tile function as a single layer, watershedding, primary roof covering, as there is just a course-to-course overlap, with individual interlocking tile shedding water downslope from one course to the next. Wind and capillary action can cause water to migrate beyond the exposed part of the tile at the edges. A wide variety of interlocking and waterlock configurations are used to limit water migration. Typical waterlocks include ribs and channels, although some have lips, angled diverters, and weeps to provide additional protection against water migration into the tile roof system. Different types of waterlock configurations function with different degrees of effectiveness. The width of the tile and the location of fastener holes, the slope of the roof, and the anti-capillary characteristics of the tile-to-tile surfaces are all important factors.

Therefore, on projects using interlocking tile, underlayments are necessary.

1.4.1.3 Water Migration Potential of Pan and Cover; and S-Tile

Two-piece pan and cover tile is applied so that the sides of the covers overlap the sides of the pan tile. The convex-shaped portions, or covers, shed water into the pans. The concave-shaped portion, or pans, channel the water downslope. The amount of overlap and the resistance to water migration vary with different styles, and with methods of laying pan and cover tile. Overlaps of both the pans and covers are typically 3 inches (76 mm). The dimensions of the laps, the location of fastener holes, and the slope of the roof are factors that affect the amount of water that may migrate beyond the tile edges. Therefore, on projects using pan and cover tile, underlayments are necessary.

One-piece S-tile functions as a single layer interlocking tile system where only a course-to-course overlap is achieved. With S-tile, both the sides and the head and butt overlap. The height of the pan side and point of overlap by the cover, play a large role in limiting the water that may migrate beyond the tiles edges.

Roof to Masonry Wall with Gutter Flashing

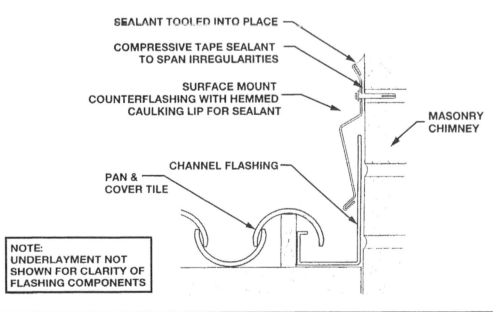

SEALANT TOOLED INTO PLACE

COMPRESSIVE TAPE SEALANT TO SPAN IRREGULARITIES

SURFACE MOUNT COUNTERFLASHING WITH HEMMED CAULKING LIP FOR SEALANT

MASONRY CHIMNEY

CHANNEL FLASHING

PAN & COVER TILE

NOTE: UNDERLAYMENT NOT SHOWN FOR CLARITY OF FLASHING COMPONENTS

Figure 8.24

Courtesy of National Roofing Contractors Association, *NRCA Roofing & Waterproofing Manual*

Overlaps are typically 3 inches (76 mm). With some styles, an interlock feature is added at the overlaps to restrict wind driven rain and capillary action. The dimensions of the lap, the type of interlock and waterlock configurations, the location of fastener holes, the slope of the roof, and surface conditions are all factors that affect the amount of water that may migrate beyond the tile. Therefore, on projects using S-tile, underlayments are necessary.

1.4.2 Wind and Seismic Considerations

Wind and seismic performance characteristics of tile roofs are being scrutinized more than in years past. The relatively regular occurrence of high wind events and seismic (earthquake) activities have caused designers to consider securing tile more conservatively than in the past. Different parts of the roof, such as the field, rakes, ridges, and downslope perimeters are subject to different wind-uplift pressures, and possibly different seismic loading forces.

Other factors affecting tile performance in wind and some seismic events include building height, eave overhang, tile size and weight, tile style and shape, the roof slope, and the securement method.

1.4.3.1 Water Absorption

The porosity of roof tile is an indication of its ability to endure freeze-thaw cycling. The lower the porosity the less water the material may hold, thus the less likely the tile is to be damaged (by crack, spall, etc.) when frozen. Porosity of some materials may indicate the possibility of increased decomposition of water soluble particles in the tile. Porosity is typically expressed as a percent of the weight of water that is absorbed by the tile. Dense well-baked clay tile may have porosity values under 2% when fully vitrified. The porosity values of some clay tiles range up to 10%. Concrete tiles have porosity values in the range of 3–20%. Sealers are sometimes used to reduce porosity. The service life of the sealers and some surfacings should be considered during the roof design phase, as should the possible need to reseal the tile's surface in the future.

Strength of the tile along the joints, where it is joined or lapped, is important because this is a likely location for cracking or breaking under loading.

Strength is typically measured as a breaking load. Generally, the breaking loads of roof tile range from 250 to 1,000 pounds (44 to 175 kN/m). Typical breaking loads are approximately 650 pounds (114 kN/m) for clay tile and approximately 400 pounds (70 kN/m) for concrete tile.

Fasteners

1.6.4 Types of Fasteners, and Fastening and Attachment Devices

Many different types and combinations of securement methods are used for the various types of roof tile. Early methods included setting the tile in a bed of mud or mortar; or loose-laying the tile, using gravity and friction to keep tile in place on lower slopes. Tapered tiles were used to help prevent slippage. Head lugs were used where open sheathing or battens were common, and at a time when metal fasteners were handmade and nearly as expensive as the tile. Wire-tie methods were used by the Romans for their tile roofs installed over concrete roof decks.

Recent developments in fastener and attachment technology have impacted the once simple methods of tile securement. The types of fasteners and various attachment methods must now be examined, along with the type of tile and roof deck, when securement is being considered during roof design.

1.6.4.1 Nails

Nailing is the most common method of fastening tile. The trend is toward more stringent nailing schedules along perimeters, especially in high wind and seismic areas. Designers should consult local code requirements. There are a wide variety of noncorrosive metal nail types, with differing mechanical and physical properties, depending upon the metal, nail shape, size, shank type, head type, and point type.

1.6.4.2 Screws

Screws are also used to fasten tile. There are a wide variety of noncorrosive metal screws, with differing mechanical and physical properties, depending upon the metal, screw shape, size, shank style, tread type, head type, and point type.

1.6.4.3 Wire

Hanging tile with wire is often used as a method of attachment on non-nailable or insulated decks, or in some areas where fastening through metal flashing needs to be avoided. Attaching entire tile roofs with wire is relatively common with concrete roof decks and other types of non-nailable substrates. For non-nailable roof decks, there is quite a variety of wire and strapping systems available. Wire-tying tile is also specified where penetrating the underlayment is undesirable, such as on low-slope applications. In strong earthquake zones, wire-tying tile (in some configurations) can allow for more movement of the tile than some rigid attachment methods, and can be an effective securement method. Nails, screws,

Roof to Wall Flashing

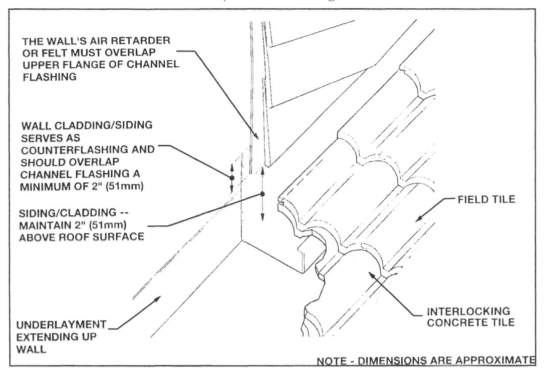

Figure 8.25

Courtesy of National Roofing Contractors Association, *NRCA Roofing & Waterproof Manual*

and expanding fasteners are commonly used in conjunction with wire-tie systems to affix the wire to certain substrates.

1.6.4.4 Clips
Nose or butt clips and side clips are sometimes used in conjunction with other attachment methods in high wind and seismic areas. Some tile clips are commonly referred to as wind clips or storm anchors. Clips can hold the tile in place and help reduce stress at the primary attachment point. Some types of clips may also hold the tile in place if the tile's primary nailing fails.

1.6.4.5 Lug-Hung Tile
When battens are used, many types of tile have lugs formed on the underside, near the head of the tile, on which the tile may be hung over the batten. In some areas, on roofs with shallow slopes, when tiles are loose laid they are simply hung over the battens. However, in most areas of the country, lug hanging of tile is usually used in combination with other securement methods, and some building codes require attachment of perimeter tile.

1.6.4.6 Bedding Tile
Laying tile in a full or partial bed of mortar is common in some areas of the United States (e.g., parts of the South) where freeze/thaw conditions are not encountered. Vertical-grade asphalt-based roof cements or cement mortars are commonly used to bed tile at hips and ridges. Tile laid along eaves, rakes and valleys, and some other flashing locations are sometimes bed in mortar. A variety of other roof cements, such as vertical-grade polymer-modified asphalt roof cement and slater's cement, are also used for bedding tile. Bedding is often used in combination with other securement methods.

2.7 Rakes
To weatherproof a tile roof along the rake edges, different details may be used depending upon the type and profile of the tile, the climate, and regional or area practices. Many of the clay tile rake details use specialty rake tile to complete the exterior edges of the roof. With plain tile, there is usually no rake tile or perimeter metal flashing used. A plain tile roof's rake edge may be detailed similar to the rake edge of a slate roof, where the perimeter tiles are simply extended beyond the

Rake Nailer

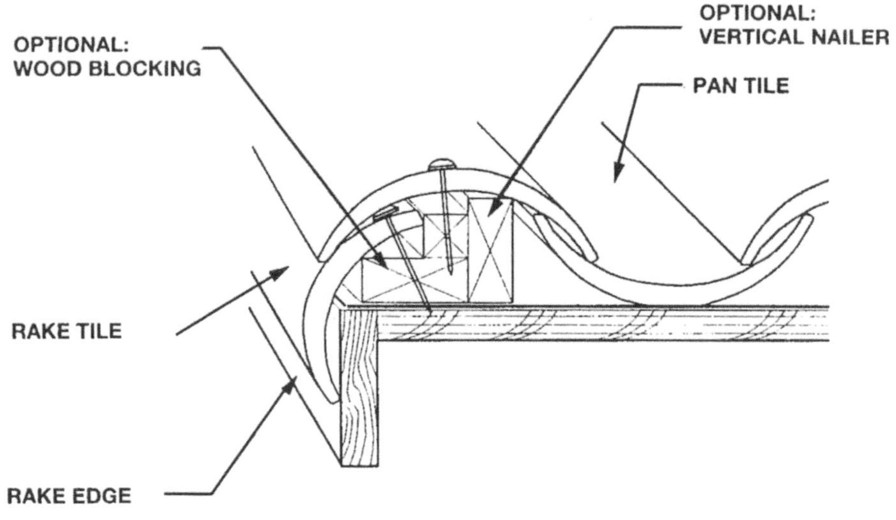

Figure 8.26

Courtesy of National Roofing Contractors Association, *NRCA Roofing & Waterproof Manual*

rake edge to provide a watershedding drip edge for runoff, and to help provide some weather protection for the underlying building components.

2.7.1 Rake Tile Attachment

Note: Where tiles are specified to be used along rake edges, the rake tiles should be fastened with two fasteners for prudent securement. However some types of tile are manufactured with only one fastener hole—which means that only one fastener can be used to attach the tile along the rake edge of the roof.

Hips & Ridges

2.8 Clay Tiles for Hip and Ridge Locations

To weatherproof the roof at hips and ridges, special hip and ridge tiles are used as hip and ridge coverings. Often, with pan and cover tiles, the covers are used for hip and ridge coverings. Typically, the exposure for hip and ridge tiles is the same as the field of the roof, although with some types of tile the exposure can be shortened to create different hip and ridge lines for visual accent and increased weather resistance.

After the field tile has been applied to both roof areas up to the adjoining hip or ridge intersection, and the tiles in each intersecting course have been cut to the apex of the hip or ridge, the hip or ridge coverings may be applied. The following procedures may be used to apply tiles at hip and ridge locations.

A. The plies of underlayment can be wrapped and nailed over the hip or ridge centerline. Wrapping the hips and ridges with the field underlayment provides an additional layer of protection from wind-driven rain and snow. Note: At ventilating ridges, felt should not be wrapped over the ridge as it would close off ventilation.

B. For additional weather protection with some types of tile roofs, the hip or ridge may be overlaid with a strip of heavyweight asphalt-saturated felt, or modified bitumen membrane material, secured over the exposed juncture along the hip or ridge. Note: At ventilating ridges, this extra strip of felt is not used.

C. Beginning at tile downslope end of a hip or at the leeward end of a ridge, the hip or ridge tiles are applied in shingle fashion with each unit lapping over the previous unit. Note: Beginning the ridge tile application at the leeward end of the ridge orients each ridge tile overlap away from the prevailing wind and weather. Applying ridge tile with their laps facing away from the prevailing wind helps to keep wind-driven rain and snow from entering the roof.

D. Typically, hip and ridge tiles are installed to provide a relatively uniform overlap of the hip or ridge centerline, covering the adjacent cut field tile by approximately 3 to 6 inches (76 to 152mm), depending upon the type of tile. However, it is a good idea to chalk a straight line on one side of the hip or ridge, so that hip or ridge tiles can be set to the line.

Ridge & Hip on Tile Roof

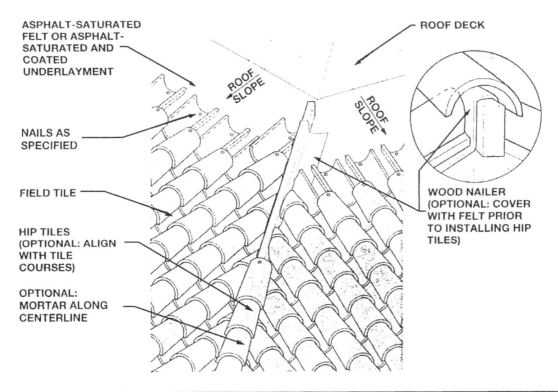

ASPHALT-SATURATED FELT OR ASPHALT-SATURATED AND COATED UNDERLAYMENT

ROOF DECK

ROOF SLOPE

ROOF SLOPE

NAILS AS SPECIFIED

FIELD TILE

HIP TILES (OPTIONAL: ALIGN WITH TILE COURSES)

OPTIONAL: MORTAR ALONG CENTERLINE

WOOD NAILER (OPTIONAL: COVER WITH FELT PRIOR TO INSTALLING HIP TILES)

Figure 8.27

Courtesy of National Roofing Contractors Association, *NRCA Roofing & Waterproof Manual*

Metal Roofs

Industry Standards

Roofing: Design Criteria, Options, Selection
(RSMeans)

Custom-fabricated
Custom metal roofs are the most visually appealing and versatile types of systems for use on custom designs or in achieving intricate details, such as barrel roofs and convex mansards. Commonly used materials are standing seam and batten seam terneplate, copper, or galvanized steel.

Terneplate: A terneplate roof should not be installed over structures with a slope of less than 3" to the foot. The deck should be stable and of a material capable of receiving and holding nails. Plywood is the preferred deck material and should be a minimum of ⅝" thick. Tongue-and-groove wood sheathing decks are also commonly used. The deck should be covered with a #30 asphalt felt. The felt should be covered with a red resin paper slip sheet to avoid bonding of the felt to the metal.

Preformed
Between the relatively inexpensive pre-engineered metal building systems and the custom-designed, site-formed metal system is the largest sector of the metal roofing market—preformed, pre-painted metal roofing.

There are two predominant methods of joining preformed metal roof panels: *snap-on seam clips,* and *automated seaming* using electric field-seaming machines. The seaming operation locks concealed, sliding clip fasteners into place, forms the seam. Joint sealant can be applied as a part of the operation.

Formed Metal Roofing
Formed metal roofing (copper, lead, and zinc alloy) is used on sloped roofs over a base of plywood or concrete. This material comes in flat sheets, which are joined with flat, batten or standing seams, followed by soldering or an application of adhesive.

Comments

Manufacturers recommend a minimum pitch when using preformed metal roofing on sloped roofs. Self-tapping screws with attached neoprene washers (to prevent leakage) are used to attach metal roofing to the supporting members. Lapped ends may be sealed with preformed sealant (available from the manufacturer) to match the deck configuration. Where self-tapping screws are used to attach the metal roofing, be sure the entire roof is swept to prevent the expelled metal chips and burrs from rusting and ruining the finish.

Metal Shingles

IBC–2006

1507.5.6 Flashing: Roof valley flashing must be of corrosion-resistant metal of the same material as the roof covering or comply with IBC-2006 Table 1507.4.3(1), and must extend at least 8" each way from the centerline. A splash diverter rib at least .75" high is also required. Additional requirements must be met for cold climates, including a 36"-wide underlayment.

IRC–2006

R905.4.6 Flashing: Same requirements.

Comments

Metal shingles are used for roofing or mansards on residential and commercial projects. They are available in decorative diamond shapes, in a standing seam, and in panels that simulate the look of wood-grained shingles. Metal shingles are very durable and virtually maintenance-free. A product with a quality finish should not fade, chalk, crack, peel, warp, or rot. Any surface residue can be cleaned with normal methods, and minor scratches touched up with matching paint from the manufacturer. Accessories are available from the manufacturers.

Metal shingles should be installed by roofers who are trained in the particular techniques required. Manufacturers provide installation manuals and seminars. (Contact their Technical Service Advisors for information.) The recommended slope is typically 3 in 12. Decorative, diamond-shaped metal shingles may be arranged in a design using different colors. The shingles have a turned-down front edge and turned up back edge for double-sealing protection. The fastening system is concealed. Standing seam metal shingles are installed vertically up the roof slope, interlocking for weathertightness. Panel seams are staggered for an attractive appearance. Simulated wood-grain panels, also interlocking, are installed horizontally from eave to ridge, with panel seams staggered.

Single-Ply Roofing

Comments

Single-ply roofing (SPR) systems originated as an alternative to built-up roofing (BUR). Manufacturer research, warranty programs, and incentives for quality installation have contributed to the success of SPR in the U.S. While the membrane for built-up roofing is constructed on the roof by the contractor from felts and asphalt, single-ply roofing is built from flexible sheets of compounded synthetic materials manufactured in a controlled environment.

SPRI, the Single-ply Roofing Institute, maintains that "primary among the physical and performance properties these materials provide are strength, flexibility, durability, versatility in their attachment methods, and broad applicability."

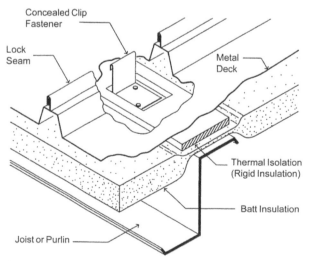

Standing Seam & Batten Seam: Custom-Fabricated

Concealed Clip Fastener

Lock Seam

Metal Deck

Thermal Isolation (Rigid Insulation)

Batt Insulation

Joist or Purlin

Figure 8.28   RSMeans, *Roofing: Design Criteria, Options, Selection*

Industry Standards

Roofing: Design Criteria, Options, Selection
(RSMeans)

Single-ply roofing is used in light commercial applications. Rolls of SPR membrane should be placed on the roof (over structural supports) as soon as the deck structure is in place. The SPR membrane should not be laid out on the ground. The rolls should not be concentrated in one area of the roof, but distributed immediately and evenly to avoid overloading the structure. Roof insulation should be placed on pallets not more than two tiers high, and covered with secured tarpaulins.

The roof area should be laid out in advance to utilize the largest sheets possible. This approach to layout

should be carried out in advance by all bidders, who should include in their submittals to the architect a roof sheet layout, showing seams and penetrations.

Before the membrane is unrolled, the roof surface should be checked to ensure that there are no sharp objects, such as gravel or bits of metal, that might pierce the membrane. After the sheets are unrolled and positioned, seam splicing begins. There is little margin for error in splicing seams, since SPR offers no second or third ply of membrane to back up the first in the event of a leak. A manufacturer's representative should be on site during this phase, at least initially, to ensure the quality of the splices. To make a field seam in an EPDM roof, the top sheet should be folded back 12", showing at least the same amount of membrane of the adjoining sheet. This 24" wide area should be

Ballasted

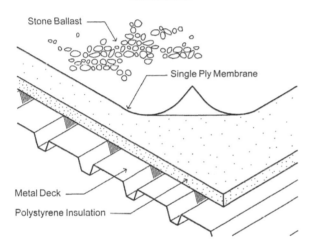

Fully Adhered

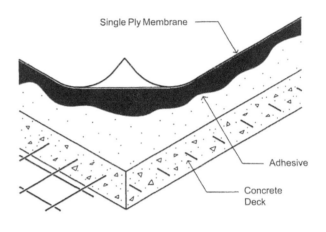

Partially Adhered

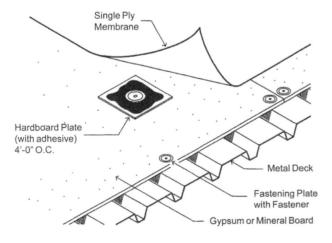

Mechanically Attached

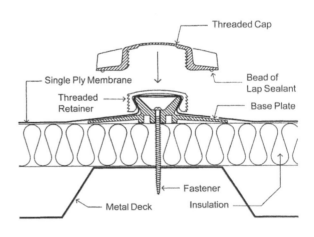

RSMeans, Roofing: Design Criteria, Options, Selection

Figure 8.29

261

wiped clean of talc and debris, using solvent or cleaner furnished by the manufacturer. Inadequately cleaned splices are a common cause of seam failure.

The splice cement should be labeled by the manufacturer of the membrane and thoroughly mixed using a drill-activated stirring device. Most manufacturers' specifications call for a 3" to 4" minimum splice. However, most professional roofing contractors generally require about 6". The extra cost of the materials is negligible, and the added splice area strengthens this critical juncture. One manufacturer specifies in-the-splice sealant for all of its mechanically attached systems. Most manufacturers specify that adhesive be brush-applied, but most roofing contractors prefer a 4" long-handled roller. The object is to achieve a thin, even film of adhesive on both mating surfaces; too much adhesive distorts the membrane. When the adhesive becomes tacky, but is not yet dry, the installer should carefully fold the top sheet over, and brush toward the seam with a roller or the palm of the hand, avoiding wrinkles or "fishmouths." If fishmouths do occur, they should not be "pressed down," but cut out. A patch should then be applied over the area of the cut-out, in accordance with the manufacturer's directions. The splice should then be rolled toward the seam with a heavy metal hand roller.

After the joint is cleaned, a bead of lap sealer should be applied along the exposed edge. It is important that this be done at the end of each day's work to prevent moisture from contaminating the seam adhesive overnight.

Attachment Methods

There are four methods of attaching the SPR membrane to the substrate or deck: using gravel slag ballast, mechanically fastening, partially adhering using "spots" or "lines" of adhesive, and fully adhering. As illustrated in **Figure 8.29**, many of the SPR products may utilize any of the attachment methods.

Bituminous Roofing Products

Industry Standards

Construction Principles, Materials, and Methods
(John Wiley & Sons, Inc.)

7.5.7 Four basic materials are used in the manufacture of bituminous roofing products: (1) a reinforcing base, which is either organic dry felt or glass fiber mat, (2) bitumen (asphalt or coal tar), (3) mineral stabilizers, and (4) either fine or coarse surfacings.

In general, the manufacture of organic felt bituminous roofing products includes processing cellulose fibers into dry felt, saturating and coating the felt with asphalt or coal tar, and then, depending on the type of finished product, surfacing the coated felt with selected mineral aggregates. When glass fiber mat is used as a reinforcing base instead of organic felt, the mat goes directly from a dry looper into a coater, bypassing the saturating process.

Dry Organic Felt

Dry organic felt, used as a base for making reinforcing felts for built-up roofing and waterproofing, underlayment, smooth and mineral-surfaced roll roofing, and asphalt shingles, is made from combinations of cellulose fibers such as those derived from rags, paper, and wood on a machine similar to the type used for making paper. The fibers are prepared by various pulping methods, then blended and proportioned to produce felt with the necessary weight, tensile strength, absorptive capacity, and flexibility required to make a suitable roofing product.

The felt must be able to absorb $1\frac{1}{2}$ to 2 times its weight in asphalt saturants and be strong and flexible enough to withstand strains placed on it during the manufacturing process.

As the felt comes off the end of the machine in a continuous sheet, it is cut into specified widths and wound into individual rolls from 4 to 6 ft. in diameter, weighing up to a ton or more.

Glass Fiber Mat

Dry glass fiber mats are used as a base for reinforcing felts for built-up roofing and waterproofing, coated smooth rolls and mineral-surfaced roll roofing, and asphalt shingles. To make glass fiber mats, sand, soda ash, and limestone are first combined to make chopped strand glass fibers. These fibers then are mixed with a binding agent and cured to produce a mat with the thickness, tensile strength, tear strength, weight, and flexibility required to produce roofing and waterproofing products.

Bitumens

The bitumens used in bituminous roofing products are asphalt and coal tar. They are used to saturate and coat dry organic felts and to coat glass fiber mats in the manufacture of roofing felt and to weld or fuse roofing or waterproofing felts together to form a built-up roof or waterproofing membrane. Both asphalt and coal tar bitumens are thermoplastic, which means that they become more fluid when heated and return to their former solid state when they cool.

A bitumen's equiviscous temperature (EVT) is the optimum temperature at which it should be used. Each asphalt and coal tar bitumen has its own EVT. The type with the lowest number has the lowest EVT.

Asphalt

Asphalt used to make roofing and waterproofing products, known as asphalt flux, is a petroleum product obtained from the fractional distillation of crude oil. Asphalt flux is processed to produce roofing grades of asphalt, called saturants or, when combined with mineral stabilizers, coating asphalts. Both forms combine with dry felt to make asphalt roofing or waterproofing membranes.

The preservative and waterproofing characteristics of asphalt reside largely in certain oily constituents. In making roofing products, the body of the highly absorbent felt sheet first is impregnated (saturated) to the greatest possible extent with saturants that are oil-rich asphalts. The saturant is then sealed in with an application of a harder, more viscous coating asphalt, which in turn can be further protected by a covering of opaque mineral granules. A primary difference between saturants and coating asphalts is the temperature at which they soften. The softening point of saturants varies from 100° to 160°F; that of coatings is as high as 260°F. Saturant asphalt is not used with glass fiber mat. The coating mixture is used to completely surround the glass fibers and to provide a layer of coating on both sides of the mat.

Asphalt flux is also the base material used to make asphalt plastic cement, quick-setting roof adhesives, asphalt primers, other roof coatings, and adhesives.

Coal Tar

Coal tar used to make roofing products is a distillation of bituminous coal. It is considered basically superior to asphalt for use in low-slope roofing. It is most effective at a slope of 1/4 in./ft. and can be used on slopes up to 1/2 in./ft., but cannot be used on slopes steeper than 1/2 in./ft.

The two types of coal tar recommended for use in built-up roofing are classified in ASTM D450 as Type I, *coal-tar pitch*, and Type III, *coal-tar bitumen*. Type III has a higher softening point than does Type I.

Mineral Stabilizers

Finely ground minerals, such as silica, slate dust, talc, micaceous materials, dolomite, and trap rock,which are called stabilizers, when combined with coating bitumens, control hardness, elasticity, adhesion, and weathering. Coated bitumens that contain stabilizers resist weather better, are more shatter and shockproof

in cold weather, and significantly increase roofing product life.

Built-up Roofing (BUR)

Types & Installation Guidelines

Industry Standards

Roofing Handbook
(The McGraw-Hill Companies)

There are three basic types of BUR systems.

Surfacing Smooth Systems

Smooth-surfaced inorganic BURs offer several advantages. For example, they are lightweight, generally less than 1/3 the approximate 400 to 700 pounds per square of gravel-surfaced roofs. They are easy to inspect and repair. The absence of gravel facilitates fast visual inspection of the smooth surface. If damaged, patching takes little time and there is no need to scrape away gravel. Because of these advantages, maintenance of smooth-surfaced roofs is simpler than other BUR roofs.

When reroofing is desired, or necessary, the job can often be done without removing the old smooth-surfaced membrane. If removal is necessary, there is less material to remove. In addition to all these, surfaced roofs often cost less than 3 gravel-surfaced roofs with the same design life.

Surfacing Gravel Systems

Gravel-surfaced, inorganic BUR systems are similar in construction to smooth-surfaced roofs, except in the final surfacing. Instead of the light mopping of asphalt or a light application of one of the other roof coatings used on smooth-surfaced roofs, a flood coat of approximately 60 pounds per square of hot bitumen is applied and followed by the appropriate aggregate.

Gravel-surfaced systems are typically more durable than smooth-surfaced BUR systems. The aggregate covering helps the asphalt flood coat resist the aging effects of the elements. The gravel also helps stabilize the flood-coat bitumen and permits heavier pours than typically are used in systems that do not employ gravel. This results in additional waterproofing material in the assembly.

Other, more obvious advantages are the improved fire resistance offered by the aggregate and added protection from penetrating forces, such as hail. Gravel-surfaced roofs generally are limited to slopes of 3" or less to minimize gravel loss and membrane slippage.

Comments

In high-wind areas, loose aggregates may become projectiles. Be sure all aggregates are fully embedded in bitumen.

There are differing opinions about how many layers of roofing can be applied over an existing roof before a tearoff is required. Section 1510 in the IBC states that, in general, new roof coverings should not be installed without removing the existing roof first. See the section on reroofing later in this chapter for more details.

Surfacing Mineral Systems

Mineral-surfaced cap sheets form the last visible ply in this type of BUR membrane. The inorganic mat is coated with weather-grade asphalt, into which is embedded opaque, noncombustible, ceramic-coated granules. The resulting sheet yields a roof that enhances the appearance of the building it protects.

Mineral-surfaced cap sheets provide BURs with several unique properties. Tile ceramic-coated granules on these products offer a uniform, factory-applied surfacing that helps the underlying bitumen resist weathering and aging. Unlike coatings, these granules are not typically a maintenance item. Many smooth-surfaced, coated roofs require periodic recoating. The cap sheet system also has improved fire resistance and reflective properties.

Industry Standards

Roofing: Design Criteria, Options, Selection
(RSMeans)

The following guidelines offer a good starting point for proper installation of built-up roofing.

Rule 1: Slope the Roof

Never design a flat or "dead level" roof! The design of near-level or dead-level roofs will eventually result in ponding and deterioration of flashing and roofing materials.

Rule 2: Inspect

Provide *continuous* inspection during the placement of roofing by a knowledgeable inspector. Carefully follow manufacturers' published specifications.

Rule 3: Restore Temporary Roofs

Always restore temporary roofing before applying the permanent built-up system. The practice of installing the first plies and one "mopping," then allowing other trades to use it as a staging area, and finally mopping in the additional plies and ballast, has become common as time becomes a crucial factor on construction projects. If a temporary roof is required, it should be properly restored before the permanent roof is installed.

All accessories, curbs, and penetrations through the roof should also be in place before the roof is installed.

Rule 4: Keep Materials Dry

Protect roofing and insulation materials from moisture *before,* as well as *during,* construction. The system is susceptible to moisture before, during, and after the roof installation. Prior to installation, roofing materials (especially insulation) must be protected from moisture infiltration. Simply covering these materials may not be sufficient. Some insulations have been found to absorb moisture while stored in a warehouse, to the extent that they are too "wet" to install. It is important to store material off the floor or ground on pallets, and cover it with tarpaulins. The lightweight plastic wrapping that the materials are shipped in is usually not a sufficient covering because it tends to tear easily.

Lightweight concrete decks must be properly vented. Most specifications call for the roofing contractor to "approve" the deck design before plans for proceeding with roof installation. The roof installer should perform a deck dryness test.

Rule 5: Avoid the Void

Prevent voids between plies in a BUR. The most prominent cause of failure in BURs, according to an NRCA survey, was interply blistering.

To prevent voids, an even bitumen application is essential; this can be obtained when the application temperature of the bitumen is in the equiviscous temperature range (EVT). The EVT is usually printed on the asphalt container. The roofing contractor must heat the bitumen in the kettle to a temperature above the EVT, but below the flash point, in order to allow for the chilling of the asphalt as it is transported and applied. The bitumen should "roll" (spread out) along the laps on application, and plies should be installed "shingle fashion," as shown in **Figure 8.30**.

Typical Built-up Roof

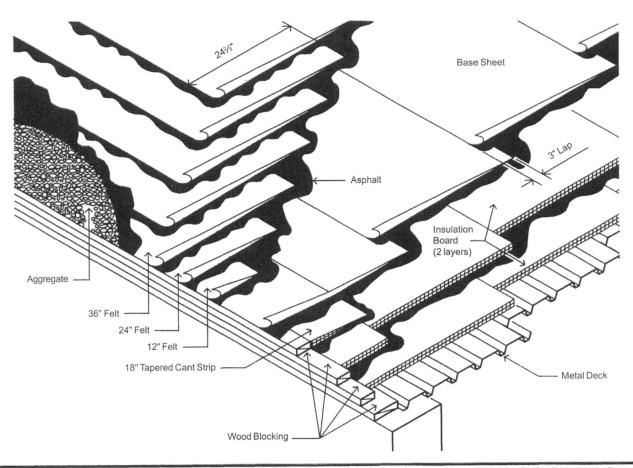

Figure 8.30

RSMeans, *Roofing: Design Criteria, Options, Selection*

Roof Drain—Built-up Roofing

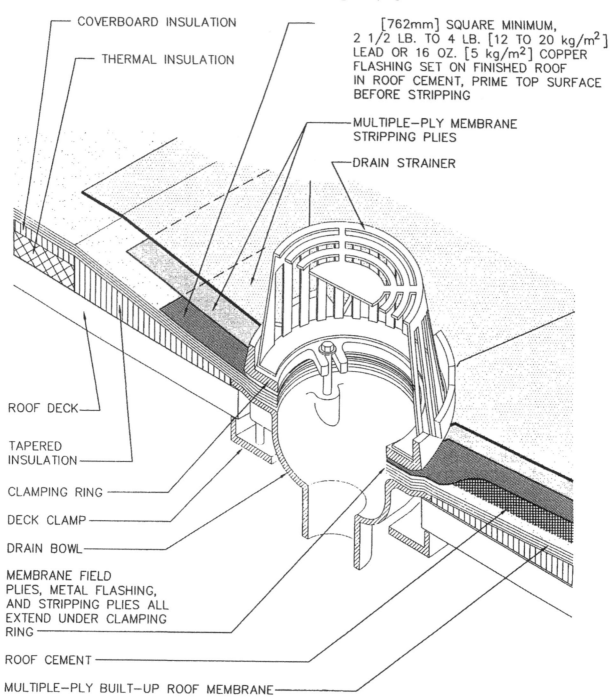

COVERBOARD INSULATION

THERMAL INSULATION

[762mm] SQUARE MINIMUM, 2 1/2 LB. TO 4 LB. [12 TO 20 kg/m²] LEAD OR 16 OZ. [5 kg/m²] COPPER FLASHING SET ON FINISHED ROOF IN ROOF CEMENT, PRIME TOP SURFACE BEFORE STRIPPING

MULTIPLE−PLY MEMBRANE STRIPPING PLIES

DRAIN STRAINER

ROOF DECK

TAPERED INSULATION

CLAMPING RING

DECK CLAMP

DRAIN BOWL

MEMBRANE FIELD PLIES, METAL FLASHING, AND STRIPPING PLIES ALL EXTEND UNDER CLAMPING RING

ROOF CEMENT

MULTIPLE−PLY BUILT−UP ROOF MEMBRANE

NOTES:

1. THE USE OF A METAL DECK SUMP PAN IS NOT RECOMMENDED. HOWEVER, DRAIN RECEIVER/BEARING PLATES ARE APPLICABLE WITH SOME PROJECTS.
2. DO NOT APPLY COAL TAR OR DEAD LEVEL ASPHALT INTO DRAIN SUMP.

Figure 8.31

Courtesy of National Roofing Contractors Association, *NRCA Roofing & Waterproofing Manual*

Skylights & Roof Accessories

Ed. Note: Skylights are considered roof accessories, along with roof hatches, pipes and conduits, and roof curbs for HVAC units. All of these items, though they may be installed by other trades, must be flashed into the roof.

Comments

Roof plans, sections, and elevations should contain information about roof accessories. These drawings should also show requirements and locations of gutters and downspouts. HVAC curbs, piping, and conduits should be indicated on the mechanical and electrical drawings.

IBC-2006

2405 Sloped glazing and skylights

2405.1 Scope: Applies to glass and other materials, such as skylights, roofs, and sloped walls, installed at a slope more than 15 degrees from the vertical plane.

IRC-2006

R308.6.1 Definition: Similar requirement. Also specifically applies to glazing materials in solariums and sun spaces.

IBC-2006

2405.2 Allowable glazing materials and limitations: Sloped glazing materials may consist of laminated glass, wired glass, light-transmitting plastic complying with Section 2607, heat-strengthened glass, or tempered glass. Laminated glass must have at least 30-mil polyvinyl butyral interlayer.

IRC-2006

R308.6.2 Permitted materials: Similar requirements. Laminated glass must have at least 0.015" (0.38) polyvinyl butyral interlayer for glass panes 16 square feet or less in area so that the highest point of the glass is no more than 12' above walking surface.

IBC-2006

2405.3 Screening: The use of heat-strengthened or tempered glass requires a screen beneath the glazing material, with specified requirements for supporting capacity, installation (fastening), and screen materials. Five exceptions are also provided.

IRC-2006

R308.6.3 Screens, general: Similar requirements. Provides exceptions for tempered glass used as single glazing or the inboard pane in multiple glazing under certain conditions.

IBC-2006

2405.4 Framing: Noncombustible framing is required in Type I and II construction and for sloped glazing and skylights. Buildings whose use involved metal-corroding acid fumes may use pressure-treated wood or other approved materials. Skylights set at an angle of less than 45 degrees from horizontal are required to be mounted on a curb a minimum of 4" above roof plane. Skylights are not permitted where the roof pitch is less than 45 degrees. The curb is not required in Use Group R-3 on roofs with a minimum slope of 1:4.

IBC-2006

2610.2 Mounting: Provides details for mounting of light-transmitting plastic glazing of skylight assemblies. Exceptions relate to roof slope and edge material.

2610.3 Slope: Flat or corrugated require 4:12 slope. Dome-shaped skylights require a minimum rise of 10% of the maximum span, but not less than 3", except skylights that pass Class B in ASTM E 108 or UL 790.

IRC-2006

R308.6.8 Curbs for skylights: Unit skylights installed in roofs flatter than 25% slope must be mounted on a curb that extends at least 4" above the plane of the roof (unless manufacturers' instructions specify otherwise).

IBC-2006

2610.4 Maximum area of skylights: 100 square feet unless building is sprinklered or has smoke and heat vents per Section 910.

IBC-2006

2610.5 Aggregate area of skylights: Maximum area is $1/3$ the area of the room or space below with some exceptions related to sprinkler systems and vents.

Industry Standards

Roofing: Design Criteria, Options, Selection
(RSMeans)

Skylights

Figure 8.33 is an illustration of the components and configuration of a skylight roof curb. It is imperative that curbs be built and located while the deck is being installed. If decks are not cut and curbs not installed until *after* the roof membrane is in place, there is a much greater chance of roofing failure at the point of curb installation.

Other Roof Curbs

Like skylights, other penetrations requiring curbs should also be coordinated early in the roof installation process. Items such as smoke vents and hatches should be detailed on construction documents. Without this information, field fabrication and setting of the curbs may result in damage to the roof membrane.

Skylights

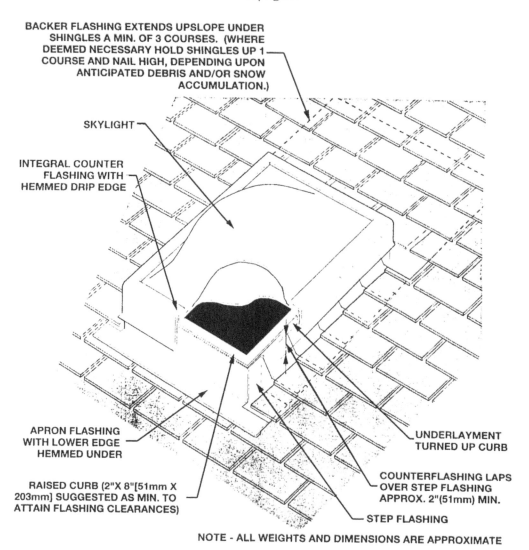

BACKER FLASHING EXTENDS UPSLOPE UNDER SHINGLES A MIN. OF 3 COURSES. (WHERE DEEMED NECESSARY HOLD SHINGLES UP 1 COURSE AND NAIL HIGH, DEPENDING UPON ANTICIPATED DEBRIS AND/OR SNOW ACCUMULATION.)

SKYLIGHT

INTEGRAL COUNTER FLASHING WITH HEMMED DRIP EDGE

APRON FLASHING WITH LOWER EDGE HEMMED UNDER

RAISED CURB (2"X 8"[51mm X 203mm] SUGGESTED AS MIN. TO ATTAIN FLASHING CLEARANCES)

UNDERLAYMENT TURNED UP CURB

COUNTERFLASHING LAPS OVER STEP FLASHING APPROX. 2"(51mm) MIN.

STEP FLASHING

NOTE - ALL WEIGHTS AND DIMENSIONS ARE APPROXIMATE

Figure 8.32

Courtesy of National Roofing Contractors Association, *NRCA Roofing & Waterproofing Manual*

Skylight Roof Curb

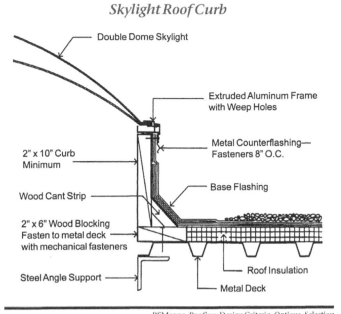

Double Dome Skylight

Extruded Aluminum Frame with Weep Holes

2" x 10" Curb Minimum

Metal Counterflashing— Fasteners 8" O.C.

Wood Cant Strip

Base Flashing

2" x 6" Wood Blocking Fasten to metal deck with mechanical fasteners

Steel Angle Support

Roof Insulation

Metal Deck

Figure 8.33

RSMeans, *Roofing: Design Criteria, Options, Selection*

Roof Penetrations & Flashing

Comments

Flashing is a thin, impervious sheet of material that is used in building construction to prevent water penetration or to direct the flow of water. Flashing is used especially at roof hips and valleys, roof penetrations, joints between a roof and a vertical wall, and in masonry walls. Refer to the information on different types of flashing and flashing materials throughout the chapter.

Pipe

Industry Standards

SMACNA Architectural Sheet Metal Manual
(Sheet Metal and Air Conditioning Contractors' National Association)

Figure 8.34, drawing A illustrates a method of flashing a roof opening where curb is not used. This method is recommended only if pipes are turned horizontally within 24 inches (610 mm) of the roof and the opening is not greater than 18 in. x 18 in. (460 mm x 460 mm).

The flashing is made in pieces with base portion being flanged 4 in. (102 mm) onto the roof. The flange is fastened through the roofing felts and is then stripped in by the roofer. Top section is notched to fit over the pipes and metal screwed to the base section. The closure is attached as shown in Closure Detail. Recommended minimum gage for flashing in **Figure 8.34, drawing A** is 16 oz. (.55 mm) copper, 26 ga (.477 mm) stainless steel, or 24 ga (.607 mm) galvanized steel.

Figure 8.34, drawing B illustrates two methods of flashing a vent pipe. The flange extends 4" (102 mm) on roof and is stripped in by roofer. The top of flashing is turned down inside the vent pipe. The flashing may be one piece or a two piece style. When a vent pipe extends above the roof so far that it is impractical to completely cover it with flashing (**Figure 8.34, drawing B**), it is recommended that it be flashed as shown in **Figure 8.34, drawing C** [minimum 2 in. (51 mm)].

Cants, Curbs, Nailers & Flashings

Ed. Note: Refer to the individual roof types (asphalt, fiber cement, wood, and tile) earlier in this chapter for more on flashing installations.

Industry Standards

Means Graphic Construction Standards
(RSMeans)

Flashings are required to ensure that discontinuities in the roofing system are protected from water penetration. Typical flashing locations include the roof perimeter, around penetrations such as vents, hatches, skylights, and equipment curbs, along roof expansion joints, and sometimes at changes in slope.

Typical flashing materials include aluminum, copper, lead-coated copper, lead, polyvinyl chloride, butyl rubber, copper-clad stainless steel, stainless steel, zinc and copper alloy, and galvanized metal. Flashing materials should be compatible with roofing system and all adjacent materials.

Roof Penetration Flashing—Pipes

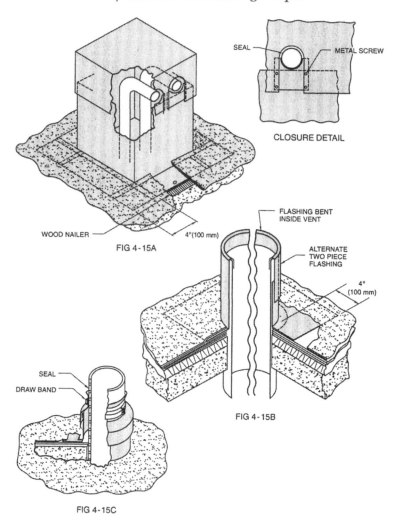

FIG 4-15A

CLOSURE DETAIL

FIG 4-15B

FIG 4-15C

Figure 8.34

Reprinted from the *SMACNA Architectural Sheet Metal Manual*, Sixth Edition.

Comments

Flashing can be formed on site, or preformed in the shop. Metal flashing should be a minimum of 26-gauge and corrosion-resistant.

Flashing is used not only on the roof, but over windows and doors, around skylights, and for some masonry installations.

Expansion joints are required to compensate for the change in dimensions or volume of building materials due to thermal variations, moisture, or other environmental conditions. In the roof structure, a joint or gap is placed at appropriate intervals to allow for expansion and contraction of the building parts. Expansion joints typically consist of job-built or prefabricated blocking material designed to raise the joint covering above the roofing material. The joint may be filled with a compressible material, such as felt, rubber, or neoprene to keep it clean and dry. A prefabricated protective covering of rubber, neoprene, or metal inhibits moisture penetration while allowing for movement. This covering, together with the necessary flashings, completes the joint system.

Gravel stop is used at the edges of flat or nearly flat roofs to contain the gravel on the roof, as a counterflashing, and as a decorative edge strip. It is usually used in conjunction with treated-lumber blocking and a cant strip to protect the flashing at the roof edge. The exposed face height varies from 4" to 12" or more and the flashing return is usually fabricated to suit the roof edge conditions.

Gravel stop may be fabricated from aluminum, copper, lead-coated copper, polyvinyl chloride, galvanized steel, or stainless steel. The finish may be natural or painted. A duranodic finish is commonly used with aluminum gravel stops.

Industry Standards

NRCA Roofing & Waterproofing Manual
(National Roofing Contractors Association)

15.1 Cants
The bending radius of bituminous roofing materials is generally limited to 45 degrees. To allow for this limited bending radius, cant strips must be provided at any 90-degree angle change, such as those created by roof-to-wall, roof-to-curb, or other roof-to-vertical surface intersections. Generally, the installation of cant strips to accommodate roof-to-wall or other horizontal-to-vertical plane change is consistent with good roofing practice.

15.2 Unit Curbs
Mechanical units using curbs that have built-in metal base flashing flanges can be difficult to seal for the long term and, therefore, are not recommended for use with bituminous roof membranes.

Some single-ply roof membranes may utilize prefabricated curbs with metal "self-flashing" flanges to be embedded in the roof membrane. However, the use of raised curbs that provide for proper application of the roof membrane, vertical extension, and proper termination of membrane base flashings, and installation of sheet metal counterflashing, promote good roofing and flashing practices with any membrane roof system.

15.3 Nailers
It is recommended that well-secured, decay-resistant (e.g., preservative pressure-treated) wood blocking/nailers be carefully designed and provided at all roof perimeters and penetrations for fastening membrane flashings and sheet metal components. Wood nailers should be provided on all prefabricated curbs and hatches for attachment of membrane base flashings.

15.4 Flashings
There are two types of flashings: membrane flashings and sheet metal flashings.

15.4.1 Membrane Base Flashing
Membrane base flashing is generally composed of strips of compatible membrane materials used to

Roof Vent Flashing

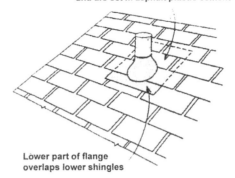

Upper and side shingles overlap flange and are set in asphalt plastic cement

Lower part of flange overlaps lower shingles

Figure 8.35   Courtesy of The McGraw-Hill Companies, *Roofing Handbook*

close-in or flash roof-to-vertical surface intersections or transitions. NRCA recommends the height of the membrane base flashing be not lower than (a nominal) 8 inches (203 mm), and generally not higher than (a nominal) 14 inches (356 mm) above the finished roof surface. Walls requiring flashings higher than 14 inches (356 mm) should receive special moisture-proofing, membrane wall flashing/waterproofing plies, or cladding. A wood nailer strip or suitable fixture allowing mechanical fastening of the membrane base flashing along its upper edge, must be provided. Membrane base flashings should be fastened to prevent displacement and/or slippage.

Depending upon the roof system, fastening may be accomplished with cap-head nails, securely fastened termination bars, or other appropriate mechanical fastening devices approved by the membrane manufacturer. Generally, membrane base flashing fasteners should be spaced 6 to 12 inches (152 to 305 mm) apart, depending upon the type of membrane and base flashing configuration being installed.

Sprayed polyurethane foam is said to be a self-flashing roofing system; however, NRCA recommends metal counterflashings be designed and installed to overlap and shield the foam and coating along points of termination. The polyurethane foam is sprayed to form a smooth transition between the horizontal roof structure and the vertical projection. The foam should be sprayed to a point at least 4 inches (102 mm) above the roof surface, and the protective coating should be carried 4 inches (102 mm) above the foam. Metal components should then be installed to the foam and coating points of termination.

For wall-supported roof decks scheduled to receive bituminous membrane systems, the vertical masonry or concrete surfaces scheduled for membrane

Base Flashing

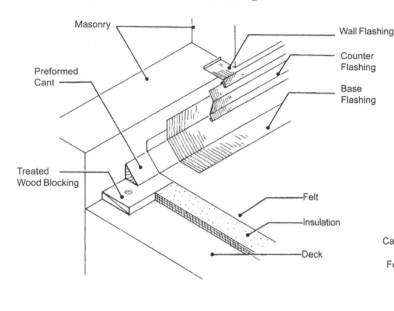

Masonry

Preformed Cant

Treated Wood Blocking

Wall Flashing

Counter Flashing

Base Flashing

Felt

Insulation

Deck

Structural Steel Flashing

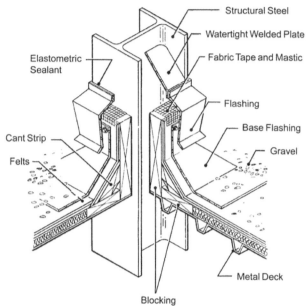

Structural Steel

Watertight Welded Plate

Fabric Tape and Mastic

Flashing

Base Flashing

Gravel

Metal Deck

Elastometric Sealant

Cant Strip

Felts

Blocking

Expansion Joint Flashing

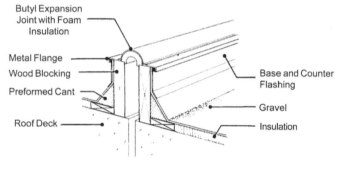

Butyl Expansion Joint with Foam Insulation

Metal Flange

Wood Blocking

Preformed Cant

Roof Deck

Base and Counter Flashing

Gravel

Insulation

Roof Edge Flashing

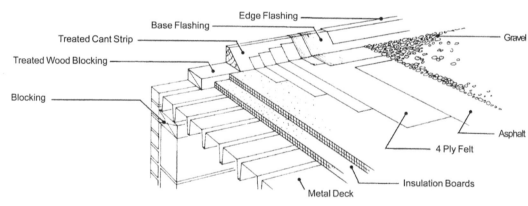

Edge Flashing

Base Flashing

Treated Cant Strip

Treated Wood Blocking

Blocking

Gravel

Asphalt

4 Ply Felt

Insulation Boards

Metal Deck

Figure 8.36

RSMeans, *Means Graphic Construction Standards*

Surface-Mount Counterflashing for Concrete Walls

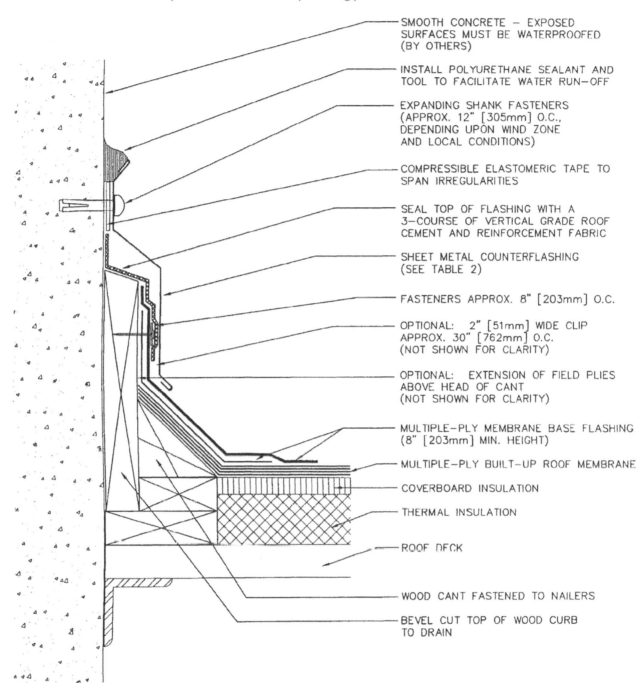

SMOOTH CONCRETE — EXPOSED SURFACES MUST BE WATERPROOFED (BY OTHERS)

INSTALL POLYURETHANE SEALANT AND TOOL TO FACILITATE WATER RUN—OFF

EXPANDING SHANK FASTENERS (APPROX. 12" [305mm] O.C., DEPENDING UPON WIND ZONE AND LOCAL CONDITIONS)

COMPRESSIBLE ELASTOMERIC TAPE TO SPAN IRREGULARITIES

SEAL TOP OF FLASHING WITH A 3—COURSE OF VERTICAL GRADE ROOF CEMENT AND REINFORCEMENT FABRIC

SHEET METAL COUNTERFLASHING (SEE TABLE 2)

FASTENERS APPROX. 8" [203mm] O.C.

OPTIONAL: 2" [51mm] WIDE CLIP APPROX. 30" [762mm] O.C. (NOT SHOWN FOR CLARITY)

OPTIONAL: EXTENSION OF FIELD PLIES ABOVE HEAD OF CANT (NOT SHOWN FOR CLARITY)

MULTIPLE—PLY MEMBRANE BASE FLASHING (8" [203mm] MIN. HEIGHT)

MULTIPLE—PLY BUILT—UP ROOF MEMBRANE

COVERBOARD INSULATION

THERMAL INSULATION

ROOF DECK

WOOD CANT FASTENED TO NAILERS

BEVEL CUT TOP OF WOOD CURB TO DRAIN

NOTES:

1. THIS DETAIL SHOULD BE USED ONLY WHERE THE DECK IS SUPPORTED BY THE WALL.
2. ATTACH NAILER TO DECK WITH SUITABLE FASTENERS.
3. OPTION: IF WOOD NAILERS ARE NOT USED, A FIBER CANT STRIP SET IN BITUMEN OR ADHESIVE MAY BE USED.
4. COUNTERFLASHING DETAIL MAY BE A TWO—PIECE REGLET AND COUNTERFLASHING (SEE TABLE 2.2, "C" FOR ALTERNATE SHEET METAL COUNTERFLASHING.)

Figure 8.37

Courtesy of National Roofing Contractors Association, *NRCA Roofing & Waterproofing Manual*

Flashing at Roof Parapet

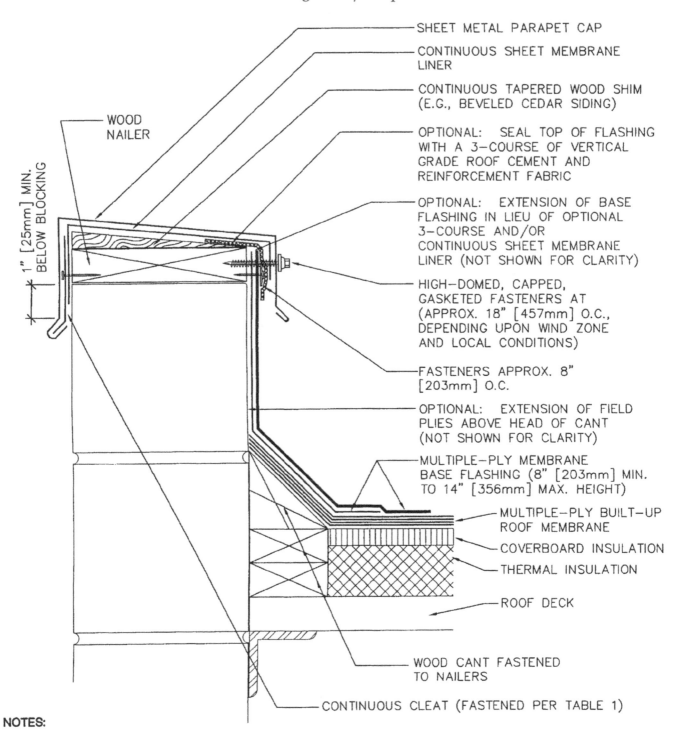

SHEET METAL PARAPET CAP

CONTINUOUS SHEET MEMBRANE LINER

CONTINUOUS TAPERED WOOD SHIM (E.G., BEVELED CEDAR SIDING)

OPTIONAL: SEAL TOP OF FLASHING WITH A 3-COURSE OF VERTICAL GRADE ROOF CEMENT AND REINFORCEMENT FABRIC

OPTIONAL: EXTENSION OF BASE FLASHING IN LIEU OF OPTIONAL 3-COURSE AND/OR CONTINUOUS SHEET MEMBRANE LINER (NOT SHOWN FOR CLARITY)

HIGH-DOMED, CAPPED, GASKETED FASTENERS AT (APPROX. 18" [457mm] O.C., DEPENDING UPON WIND ZONE AND LOCAL CONDITIONS)

FASTENERS APPROX. 8" [203mm] O.C.

OPTIONAL: EXTENSION OF FIELD PLIES ABOVE HEAD OF CANT (NOT SHOWN FOR CLARITY)

MULTIPLE-PLY MEMBRANE BASE FLASHING (8" [203mm] MIN. TO 14" [356mm] MAX. HEIGHT)

MULTIPLE-PLY BUILT-UP ROOF MEMBRANE

COVERBOARD INSULATION

THERMAL INSULATION

ROOF DECK

WOOD CANT FASTENED TO NAILERS

CONTINUOUS CLEAT (FASTENED PER TABLE 1)

WOOD NAILER

1" [25mm] MIN. BELOW BLOCKING

NOTES:

1. THIS DETAIL SHOULD BE USED ONLY WHEN THE ROOF DECK IS SUPPORTED BY THE WALL. DETAIL BUR-4 SHOULD BE USED FOR NON-WALL SUPPORTED DECK.
2. ATTACH NAILER TO DECK WITH SUITABLE FASTENERS.
3. OPTION: IF WOOD NAILERS ARE NOT USED, A FIBER CANT STRIP SET IN BITUMEN OR ADHESIVE MAY BE USED.
4. REFER TO BUR/MB TABLE 1 FOR METAL THICKNESS AND CLEAT REQUIREMENT.
5. SEE TABLE 3 FOR ALTERNATE SHEET METAL PARAPET CAP SECUREMENT AND LOCKS AND SEAMS FOR JOINTS IN SHEET METAL.

Figure 8.38   Courtesy of National Roofing Contractors Association, *NRCA Roofing & Waterproofing Manual*

Embedded Edge Metal Flashing—Thermoset Roofing

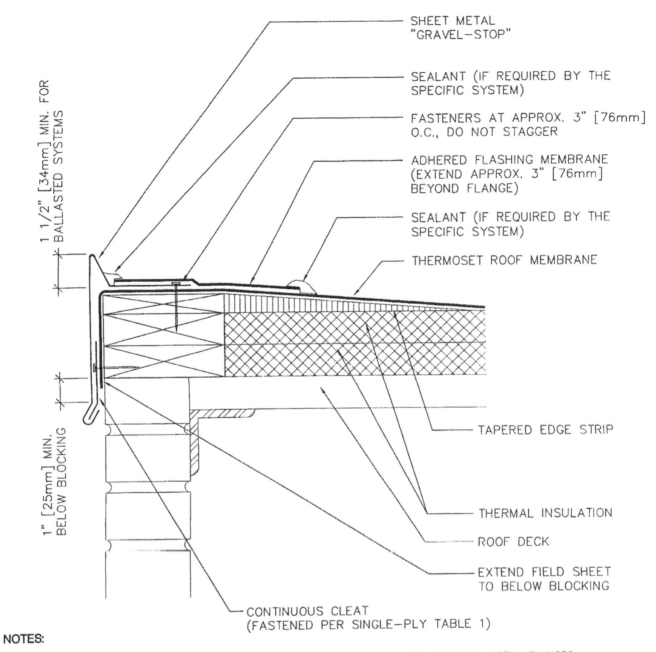

SHEET METAL "GRAVEL-STOP"

SEALANT (IF REQUIRED BY THE SPECIFIC SYSTEM)

FASTENERS AT APPROX. 3" [76mm] O.C., DO NOT STAGGER

ADHERED FLASHING MEMBRANE (EXTEND APPROX. 3" [76mm] BEYOND FLANGE)

SEALANT (IF REQUIRED BY THE SPECIFIC SYSTEM)

THERMOSET ROOF MEMBRANE

TAPERED EDGE STRIP

THERMAL INSULATION

ROOF DECK

EXTEND FIELD SHEET TO BELOW BLOCKING

1 1/2" [34mm] MIN. FOR BALLASTED SYSTEMS

1" [25mm] MIN. BELOW BLOCKING

CONTINUOUS CLEAT (FASTENED PER SINGLE-PLY TABLE 1)

NOTES:

1. NRCA SUGGESTS AVOIDING (WHERE POSSIBLE) FLASHING DETAILS THAT REQUIRE RIGID METAL FLANGES TO BE EMBEDDED OR SANDWICHED INTO THE ROOF MEMBRANE.
2. THIS DETAIL SHOULD BE USED ONLY WHERE THE DECK IS SUPPORTED BY THE OUTSIDE WALL.
3. ATTACH NAILER TO WALL WITH SUITABLE FASTENERS.
4. WOOD BLOCKING MAY BE SLOTTED FOR VENTING OF WET-FILL DECKS OR OTHER CONSTRUCTIONS WHERE APPLICABLE.
5. FREQUENT NAILING OF SHEET METAL FLANGE IS NECESSARY TO MINIMIZE THERMAL MOVEMENT.
6. REFER TO SINGLE-PLY TABLE 1 FOR METAL THICKNESS AND CLEAT REQUIREMENT.
7. TOP LAYER OF INSULATION CAN BE EITHER THERMAL INSULATION OR COVERBOARD INSULATION.

Figure 8.39

Courtesy of National Roofing Contractors Association, *NRCA Roofing & Waterproofing Manual*

Gutter Flashing—Modified Bitumen Roofing

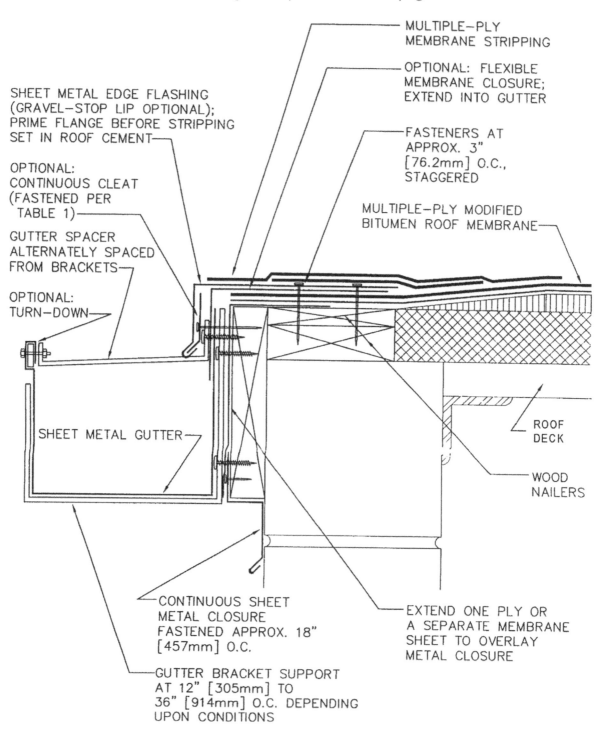

MULTIPLE–PLY MEMBRANE STRIPPING

OPTIONAL: FLEXIBLE MEMBRANE CLOSURE; EXTEND INTO GUTTER

FASTENERS AT APPROX. 3" [76.2mm] O.C., STAGGERED

MULTIPLE–PLY MODIFIED BITUMEN ROOF MEMBRANE

SHEET METAL EDGE FLASHING (GRAVEL–STOP LIP OPTIONAL); PRIME FLANGE BEFORE STRIPPING SET IN ROOF CEMENT

OPTIONAL: CONTINUOUS CLEAT (FASTENED PER TABLE 1)

GUTTER SPACER ALTERNATELY SPACED FROM BRACKETS

OPTIONAL: TURN–DOWN

SHEET METAL GUTTER

ROOF DECK

WOOD NAILERS

CONTINUOUS SHEET METAL CLOSURE FASTENED APPROX. 18" [457mm] O.C.

GUTTER BRACKET SUPPORT AT 12" [305mm] TO 36" [914mm] O.C. DEPENDING UPON CONDITIONS

EXTEND ONE PLY OR A SEPARATE MEMBRANE SHEET TO OVERLAY METAL CLOSURE

NOTES:

1. IN CLIMATES WHERE THE WINTER TEMPERATURE REMAINS BELOW FREEZING FOR EXTENDED PERIODS OF TIME, NRCA SUGGESTS USING BUR–1 AND INTERIOR DRAINS OR THROUGH–CURB SCUPPERS TO DRAIN THE ROOF.
2. GUTTER BRACKETS ARE RECOMMENDED TO BE AT LEAST ONE GAUGE HEAVIER THAN GUTTER STOCK.
3. ATTACH WOOD NAILER TO WALL/DECK WITH SUITABLE FASTENERS.
4. DESIGN GUTTER EXPANSION JOINTS PLACED AT APPROPRIATE INTERVALS COMMENSURATE WITH TYPE OF METAL

Figure 8.40

Courtesy of National Roofing Contractors Association, *NRCA Roofing & Waterproofing Manual*

Slope & Pitch

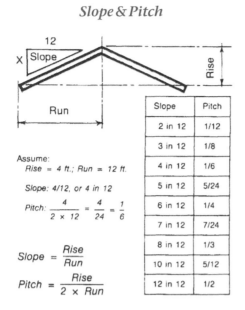

Assume:
Rise = 4 ft.; Run = 12 ft.

Slope: 4/12, or 4 in 12

Pitch: $\dfrac{4}{2 \times 12} = \dfrac{4}{24} = \dfrac{1}{6}$

Slope $= \dfrac{Rise}{Run}$

Pitch $= \dfrac{Rise}{2 \times Run}$

Slope	Pitch
2 in 12	1/12
3 in 12	1/8
4 in 12	1/6
5 in 12	5/24
6 in 12	1/4
7 in 12	7/24
8 in 12	1/3
10 in 12	5/12
12 in 12	1/2

Figure 8.41   Courtesy of John Wiley & Sons, Inc., *Construction Principles, Materials, and Methods*

base flashing should be primed with a compatible bituminous primer. Well-secured, decay-resistant (e.g., preservative pressure-treated) wood blocking/nailers should be designed and provided at all roof perimeters and penetrations for fastening membrane flashings and sheet metal components. Wood nailers should be provided on all prefabricated curbs and hatches for membrane base flashing attachment.

For non-wall-supported roof decks, raised wood blocking or curbing is recommended to isolate differential wall and roof assembly movement. The wood curbing that facilitates flashing application should be placed against the wall and secured only to the deck.

Membrane flashings on expansion joint curbs (allowing expansion and contraction) should be constructed, according to the NRCA Construction Details. The designer is cautioned to consider that building components are subjected to thermal movements at different rates and directions from the roof membrane. If the roof is to be tied into these components, special consideration should be given to the design of that juncture.

15.4.2 Metal Flashing (Counterflashing and Cap Flashing)

On mechanical units, and other raised curb equipment, sheet metal counterflashing should be installed to cover the top edge and overlap the upper portion of membrane base flashings. On units that will be frequently serviced, the counterflashings

may extend down over membrane flashings covering the cant and terminate near the roof surface so that membrane base flashings are protected.

On certain prefabricated metal roof hatches, skylight assemblies, and other roof-mounted curbed units, or on equipment that has a relatively short, built-in metal counterflashing flange, it may be necessary to attach an additional sheet metal counterflashing "skirt." In certain climates and geographic regions a sheet metal skirt is useful to extend the premanufactured counterflashing, so as to ensure adequate overlap of the membrane base flashing, thus restricting wind-driven rain and snow from entering the roof assembly.

Since metals generally have a high coefficient of expansion, metal flashing must be isolated from the roof membrane wherever possible to prevent metal movement from fatiguing and/or splitting the membrane. NRCA suggests avoiding (where possible), flashing details that require metal flanges to be embedded or sandwiched into the roof membrane.

For all walls that receive membrane base flashing, metal counterflashing should be installed in or on the wall above the base flashing. NRCA suggests the design of this counterflashing detail consist of separate reglet and counterflashing pieces, allowing installation of the sheet metal counterflashing after the membrane base flashing is complete on projects where single-piece counterflashing has been installed, it will be difficult to base flash properly during future reroofing, and when membrane flashing maintenance is necessary, without deforming the metal. Sheet metal is not recommended to be used as an embedded base flashing material with bituminous and certain other membrane roof designs where differential movement may attribute to fatiguing, cracking, or splitting of the aging, weathering membrane.

When precast walls are used, the designer should carefully consider the flashing provisions required to properly interface the roof to the precast wall units. Cast-in raggles (often mistakenly called reglets), frequently used for this purpose, are difficult to align. When they are not aligned, they hinder the proper installation of sheet metal reglets and counterflashing components. For this reason the use of cast-in raggles is not recommended. In all such flashing situations, consideration should be given to camber, creep, and the independent thermal movement of the walls, roof membrane, and flashings.

For non-wall-supported roof decks, the membrane base flashing should be fastened to a vertical wood upright whose horizontal base is attached to the deck only. After the membrane base flashing has been attached to the wood upright, the metal counterflashing can extend down over the top of the base flashing. This method allows independent movement of the wall and metal flashings without damage to the roof membrane and membrane base flashing.

Metal cap flashing or coping is often used to cover the top of a wall in lieu of masonry copings. In some cases (e.g., with intermediate-height parapet walls) metal counterflashing is attached to the inside face of metal cap flashing.

When used, metal gravel stops should be raised above the waterline or surface of the roof by using tapered wood blocking and edge strips. The metal flanges of metal gravel stops should be set on top of the completed roof membrane, and be fastened at approximately 3 inches (76 mm) on center to the perimeter wood nailer. The metal flange should then be stripped-in with membrane flashing plies or stripping plies.

Plumbing soil pipe stacks and all other pipe projections through the membrane require metal flashing collars or membrane pipe flashing "boots." Metal flashing flanges should be stripped-in with membrane flashing plies or strips.

Reroofing

IBC–2006

1510 Reroofing: Replacement roof coverings must meet IBC Chapter 15 requirements. Reroofing need not meet design slope requirement if roof has positive drainage. Remainder of section addresses structural requirements during installation, conditions that permit recovering vs. replacement, roof covering over combustible materials such as wood shingles, reinstallation conditions, and flashing requirements.

IRC–2006

R907 Reroofing: Must meet IRC Chapter 9 requirements, unless roof has positive drainage. Also addresses structural requirements during installation, recovering vs. replacement, recovering over combustible materials, reinstallation, and flashing requirements.

Chimney Flashing

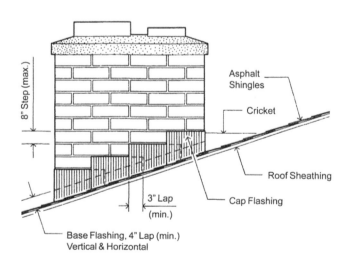

Ed. Note: For more information, see "Tile Roofing" earlier in this chapter.

Tile Roof Flashing

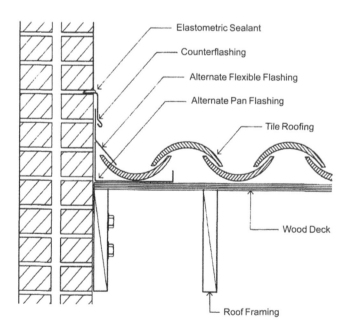

Figure 8.42

RSMeans, *Roofing: Design Criteria, Options, Selections*

Reflective Roofing

Industry Standards
Green Building: Project Planning & Cost Estimating, Second Edition
(RSMeans)

Research by energy service companies, product manufacturers, and organizations such as the Lawrence Berkeley National Laboratory (LBNL) are demonstrating the potential of reflective roofing to conserve energy, mitigate "urban heat islands," and improve air quality. Development in areas such as the U.S. Sunbelt has resulted in increased temperature and smog, as green areas and shade trees have been replaced with dark paving and roofs. Black roofs (such as EPDM, asphalt, and modified bitumen) have been shown to have a 6% reflectivity and temperatures 75°–100° hotter than the ambient temperature, while white, reflective roof membranes can reflect 80% of the heat, with roof temperatures only 15°–25° warmer than the ambient temperature.

Cooler reflecting roofs not only release less heat into the environment, but have a major effect on the building's interior temperature, thereby reducing cooling costs by as much as 30%. The net yearly impact depends on the building's particular location. (In extreme northern conditions, lower reflectivity may be preferred, as heat gain may be required for other reasons, including snow melting.) In addition to saving energy by reducing solar heat gain, cooler roofing materials can increase the longevity of the roof system itself.

A variety of coatings and materials can provide light colors and reflectivity. Like all products, selection of these systems should include evaluation of demonstrated life cycle and maintenance costs and a good warranty, supported by a reliable manufacturer. The Energy Star® program has established specifications for roofing products, including a solar reflectance of at least 65% for low-slope and steep-slope use, and 81% for low-slope only, when the product is initially installed. (See **www.energystar. gov** Click on *Roof Products*.) It should be noted that durability and maintenance influence reflectance, as the percentage can be reduced by surface weathering and dirt accumulation.

Appearance may be a factor in selection of reflective roofing, particularly in residential applications where sloped roofs are more visible than the low-slope roofs more common on commercial buildings. Houses may also have attics and radiant barriers to help reduce the effect of heat gain on air-cooling requirements.

Living Roof System

Industry Standards
Green Building: Project Planning & Cost Estimating, Second Edition
(RSMeans)

Living, or "green roofs," involve a waterproof membrane applied on a roof deck, covered with earth that will grow grass or other vegetation to collect the rain and minimize the impact of the site's impervious surfaces. Living roofs also provide thermal insulation and generate oxygen, causing a net reduction in a facility's CO_2 generation.

Green roof considerations include:

- Structural requirements (the sod and plantings can weigh as little as 2 lbs/SF in some systems to as much as 150 lbs/SF in others).
- Careful waterproofing (leaks being extremely difficult to pinpoint once the growing materials are in place).
- Maximum roof pitch of 17%.
- Best suited to wetter areas; can be a fire hazard in hot, dry climates.
- Maintenance requirements.
- Required certification by the contractor installing the membrane.

Green roofs can be as simple as 6" grass growing in sod (or grasses indigenous to the area, which require little water and no fertilizer), or as large and elaborate as a whole garden with seating areas. In addition to tremendous energy savings, green roofs provide aesthetic benefits, and, properly cared for, can last much longer than conventional roof decks, since the sod and plant materials protect the waterproof membrane from ultraviolet light. National and state green building organizations can be good sources of additional information.

Siding

Industry Standards
Plan Reading & Material Takeoff
(RSMeans)

Air Infiltration Barriers
Air infiltration barriers provide resistance to drafts caused by wind and water penetration. Barriers are installed at the exterior of the sidewall sheathing

under the exterior siding. There are a variety of products available, such as asphalt felt paper and synthetic wraps (such as TYVEK® Housewrap). The efficiency of the building insulation is influenced by humidity (moisture in the air) and the exterior temperature. The best possible scenario is to have a drywall cavity free from moisture; however, the building needs to "breathe."

The contractor should refer to the architectural wall sections for the location, and the exterior elevations for the limits of air infiltration barriers. Specifications should be reviewed for the particular product(s) required.

Comments

Air infiltration barriers should be in place and properly lapped before exterior windows, doors, and trim are installed. This is critical to ensure that the vertical joints created between the exterior window casing (or trim) and the sheathing are sealed. Otherwise, moisture may be driven into the sheathing. The air infiltration barrier should be lapped in the direction that water naturally flows.

Consult manufacturers' recommendations regarding allowable time between application of the air infiltration barrier and the application of siding. The integrity of air infiltration barrier materials can be compromised by prolonged exposure to sunlight.

Leaks or excess condensation may occur on the inside of the building in cases where the contractor failed to use an air infiltration barrier, or did not install this material behind the window casings.

See Chapter 9, "Windows & Doors," for more information on flashing.

Caulking and Sealants

Sealants and caulking compounds are used to provide a water, vapor, and air barrier between joints or gaps of adjacent but dissimilar materials. A classic example is the joint between a steel door frame and a masonry wall opening. Caulking and sealants are manufactured for a full range of applications, such as interior or exterior use, ability to expand and contract, service temperature range, paintability, and compatibility with the material to be sealed.

Joint sealants are normally applied over a backup material that controls the depth of the joint. They serve as bond breaks to allow free movement of the joint and prevent water penetration. The backup material, called *backer rod,* is available in a variety of compositions, such as butyl, neoprene, polyethylene, or rubber.

The contractor should refer to the architectural drawings, specifically elevations, wall sections, and details that show window and exterior door installations. Refer to the specifications for the appropriate location and type of caulking and sealants needed and their respective application.

Wood Siding

Industry Standards

Plan Reading & Material Takeoff
(RSMeans)

Wood siding is usually milled of wood species that can withstand extreme variations of weather. Redwood and cedar are two moisture-resistant woods used for board and sheet siding, as well as for shingles. Fir and pine are also used for board and sheet siding, but they must be finished with stain or paint after installation. Man-made material can also qualify for exterior applications. For example, hardboard and medium-density-overlay products can be used, but they also must be painted or stained. Plywood sheet siding is manufactured with waterproof glue to provide weather protection.

Watertight installation of siding is essential. Cedar and redwood clapboard siding are beveled in widths from 4" to 10". Proper installation dictates that upper boards should overlap the lower boards by a minimum of 1" and be nailed through plywood-sheathing backup to wall studs. Horizontal boards are butted and caulked into vertical corner boards at exterior and interior corners.

Vertical tongue-and-groove board siding is blind-nailed together through the sheathing to horizontal blocking spaced at 24" on center. It is manufactured in widths from 4" to 12" on center. Channel and shiplap board siding are also lapped, but are face-nailed to the blocking. Vertical boards are installed with a ½" joint between the boards and are held in place with a nailed batten strip. All vertical board siding should extend to the corners and be overlapped with corner boards. Vertical siding is usually interrupted at floors with a horizontal wood beltline and flashing strip, or flashing strip alone.

Plywood sheet siding can be installed directly to the stud wall, without sheathing, and nailed along all panel edges and intermediate stud supports. Vertical edges can be lapped, battened, or simply butted and caulked. Horizontal joints are usually flashed.

Clapboard siding comes in the better grades of cedar and redwood, i.e., B, A, and clear grade. Rough sawn and channel cedar are available in no. 3 grade and better.

Comments

Humidity can cause some buckling in installed clapboard siding. Refer to *Residential Construction Performance Guidelines*, published by the National Association of Home Builders, for an interpretation of allowable tolerances for bowing and buckling, end gaps, and straightness of siding.

Wood Shingles: Installation

Industry Standards

Cedar Shake & Shingle Bureau
(Cedar Bureau website: **www.cedarbureau.org**)

Ed. Note: The Cedar Shake & Shingle Bureau recommends a procedure summarized in the following paragraphs, for applying siding to a new exterior wall.

- **Preparation:** Be sure that the walls are smooth, without protuberances. Nail ends or points should be removed or pounded flush.

- **Building paper:** An approved paper should be applied over the sheathing. Apply it horizontally with a staple gun, starting at the base of the wall, with a 2" horizontal overlap with each succeeding course, and a 6" overlap vertically when starting a new roll. Wrap the paper 4" each way around both inside and outside corners.

- **Corner Boards:** Install corner boards at this time.

- **Flashing:** Install flashing and caulking over doors, windows, and other points of potential water entry.

- **Laying Out:** (Determining the number of courses and laying them out on all other walls.) Whenever possible, butt lines should align with tops or bottoms of windows or other openings, and for appearance the exposure of the final course at the top should match those below.

Single Coursing: Double the starting course at the base of the wall. Apply with ⅛" to ¼" vertical space between shingles allowing for expansion. Primed shingles can be butted close together. A natural shingle, if applied with tight joints, should be primed or stained soon after application to prevent buckling due to expansion caused by moisture absorption.

Double Coursing: The maximum weather exposures recommended for #1 grade shingles are 12" for 16"

shingles, 14" for 18" shingles, and 16" for 24" shingles. With shakes, the #1 grade 18" lengths can be laid at weather exposures up to 14" and 24", shakes up to 18".

Corners: It is standard practice to lace outside corners. On wide exposures this method requires small nails near the shingle butts to tighten and hold the lapped corners. Use only nails that are corrosion resistant. Corner boards also can be used to advantage by nailing 1" x 4" cedar board to a 1" x 3" cedar board, then attaching the preassembled corner to the building. It is good practice to use flashing behind shingles or shakes at the inside corners.

Clapboard Siding

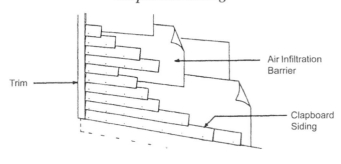

Figure 8.43   RSMeans, *Plan Reading & Material Takeoff*

Courses of Clapboard

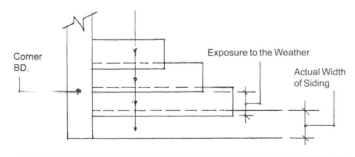

Figure 8.44   RSMeans, *Plan Reading & Material Takeoff*

Wood Shingle Siding

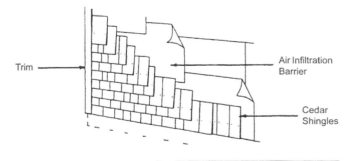

Figure 8.45   RSMeans, *Plan Reading & Material Takeoff*

Staggered Coursing: Apply the shingle irregularly at variable distances below (but not above) the horizontal line. Maximum distances are 1" for 16" and 18" shingles, and 1½" for 24" shingles.

Ribbon Coursing: A double shadow line effect can be obtained by raising the outer course shingles approximately 1" above the undercoursing. Use #1 grade for undercoursing when applying ribbon coursing.

Spacing Detail

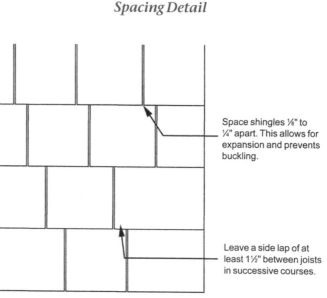

Space shingles ⅛" to ¼" apart. This allows for expansion and prevents buckling.

Leave a side lap of at least 1½" between joists in successive courses.

Figure 8.47

RSMeans, *Plan Reading & Material Takeoff*

Corner Details

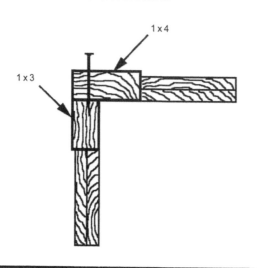

1 x 4

1 x 3

Figure 8.46

RSMeans, *Plan Reading & Material Takeoff*

Courses of Wood Shingles

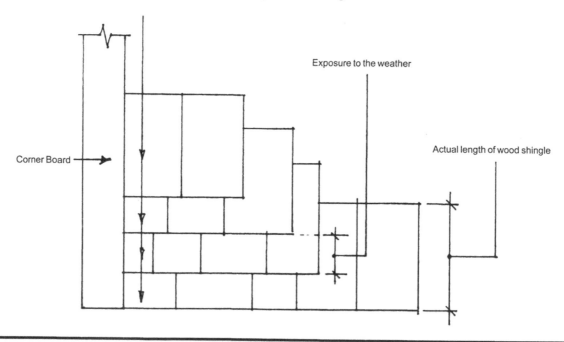

Corner Board

Exposure to the weather

Actual length of wood shingle

Figure 8.48

RSMeans, *Plan Reading & Material Takeoff*

Bevel Siding: Installation

Industry Standards

Western Red Cedar Lumber Association
(WRCLA website: **www.wrcla.org**)

Spacing for the siding should be laid out beforehand. The number of board spaces between the soffit and bottom of the lowest piece of siding at the foundation should be such that the minimum overlap is not less than 1". (See table below.)

Recommended Overlap for Bevel Siding	
Normal Width (in.)	Overlap (In.)
4	1
6	1
8	1–1–1/8
10	1–1–1/2
12	1–2 max*

*Use for unseasoned 10 in. bevel siding.

Notes: Do not exceed 2 in. overlap. Use the larger overlaps for unseasoned sidings to allow for shrinkage and expansion. Take care not to overdrive fasteners when using larger overlaps.

Start with the bottom course using a furring strip to support the lower edge. Each succeeding course overlaps the upper edge of the previous one by a minimum of 1". Rabbeted patterns are self-spacing, but leave ⅛ in. expansion clearance. Where possible, the bottom of the board that is placed across the top of the windows should coincide with the window cap.

Bevel siding should be face nailed to studs with 1½" penetration into solid wood using one nail per bearing spaced at a maximum of 24" on center. Place nail just above the 1" overlap. Take care not to nail through the overlap of two pieces.

Butt joints between boards should be staggered and made on studs. Fit snugly to other pieces and to trim and flashing. Ends should be caulked.

Bevel Siding Dimensions (Seasoned)		
Thickness (in.)	Nominal Width (in.)	Finished Width (in.)
1/2	4, 6, 8	3-1/2, 5-1/2, 7-1/2
5/8	6, 8	5-1/2, 7-1/2
3/4	6, 8, 10	5-1/2, 7-1/2, 9-1/2
7/8	10, 12	9-1/2, 11-1/2
5/4	8, 10, 12	7-1/2, 9-1/2, 11-1/2

Siding: Brick Veneer

Industry Standards

Means Graphic Construction Standards
(RSMeans)

Brick is among the most popular of wall materials because it is durable, economical to maintain, readily available in most areas, and varied in size and color. Also, brick can be installed rapidly with local labor and with a limited number of specialized tools and equipment. Brick can be used alone in single wythe walls or as the facing material in composite or cavity walls. Although the insulating value of a single wythe brick wall is a low 1.6R rating, it has the relatively high fire rating of one hour.

Because brick walls are not waterproof, provisions must be made to limit the amount of water penetration through the exterior face. Flashing should be installed at the junction of walls and floors, as well as over and under openings. In cavity walls, the outside face of the backup wall or the insulation between the wythes should be waterproofed. Weep holes should be located above the flashing at brick shelves, relieving angles, and lintels to provide a means of escape for moisture that has penetrated the wall.

Brick Veneer with Wood Frame Construction

Industry Standards

Technical Note 28—Anchored Brick Veneer, Wood Frame Construction
(Used with permission Brick Industry Association, Reston, VA. website: **www.bia.org**)

Ed. Note: The following excerpts from the Brick Industry Association's Technical Note 28 apply to new construction of buildings no more than three stories high. The excerpts describe the brick veneer/wood stud system, selection of materials, construction details, and workmanship techniques. For the complete Technical Note 28, contact the Brick Industry Association directly (see the Introduction to this chapter for the association's address, telephone number, and website).

According to the BIA, the minimum requirements given have proven successful for this type of wall construction.

Anchored brick veneer construction consists of a nominal 3" (75 mm) or 4" (100 mm) thick exterior brick wythe anchored to a backing system with metal ties in such a way that a clear air space is provided between the veneer and the backing system. The backing system may be wood frame, steel frame, concrete or masonry. By definition, a veneer wall is a wall having a facing of masonry units, or other weather-resisting, noncombustible materials, securely attached to the backing, but not so bonded as to intentionally exert common action under load. The brick veneer is designed to carry loads due to its own weight, no other loads are to be resisted by the veneer.

The minimum requirements given in this *Technical Notes* are based on successful past performance of brick veneer anchored to wood frame systems. The proper design, detailing and construction of anchored brick veneer walls ensure that these walls function as complete systems. It is important to understand that the failure of any part of the system, whether in design or construction, can result in improper performance of the entire system. Satisfactory performance of brick veneer wood frame systems is achieved with: (1) an adequate foundation, (2) a sufficiently strong, rigid, well-braced backing system, (3) proper attachment of the veneer to the backing system, (4) proper detailing, (5) the use of proper materials, and (6) good workmanship in construction.

DESIGN & DETAILS: Foundations for Brick Veneer

Brick veneer with wood frame backing must transfer the weight of the veneer through the veneer to the foundation. It is recommended that the foundation or foundation wall supporting the brick veneer should be at least equal to the total thickness of the brick veneer wall assembly. Many building codes permit a nominal 8" (200 mm) foundation wall under single-family dwellings constructed of brick veneer, provided the top of the foundation wall is corbeled. The total projection of the corbel should not exceed 2" (50 mm) with individual courses projecting beyond the course below, not more than one-third the thickness of the unit nor one-half the height of the unit. The top course of the corbel should not be higher than the bottom of the floor joist and shall be a full header course.

Foundations must extend beneath the frost line as required by the local building code. Design of the foundation should consider differential settlement and the effect of concentrated loads such as those from columns or fireplaces. Appropriate drainage must be provided in order to maintain soil bearing capacity and prevent washout.

Brick walls which enclose crawl spaces must have openings to provide adequate ventilation. Openings should be located to achieve cross ventilation.

DESIGN & DETAILS: Ties

There should be one tie for every $2^{2}/_3$ sq. ft. (0.25 m²) of wall area with a maximum spacing of 24 in. (600 mm) o.c. in either direction. The nail attaching a corrugated tie must be located within ⅝ in. (16 mm) of the bend in the tie. The best location of the nail is at the bend in the corrugated tie, and the bend should be 90°.

Wire ties must be embedded at least ⅝ in. (16 mm) into the bed joint from the air space and must have at least ⅝ in. (16 mm) cover of mortar to the exposed face. Corrugated ties must penetrate to at least half the veneer thickness and have at least ⅝ in. (16 mm) cover. Ties should be placed so that the portion within the bed joint is completely surrounded by the mortar.

DESIGN & DETAILS: Flashing and Weep Holes

Flashing and weep holes should be located above and as near to grade as possible at the bottom of the wall, above all openings, and beneath sills. Weep holes must be located in the head joints immediately above all flashing. Clear, open weep holes should be spaced no more than 24 in. (600 mm) o.c. Weep holes formed with wick materials or with tubes should be spaced at a maximum of 16 in. (400 mm) o.c. If the veneer continues below the flashing at the base of the wall, the space between the veneer and the backing should be grouted to the height of the flashing. Flashing should be securely fastened to the backing system and extend through the face of the brick veneer. The flashing should be turned up at least 8 in. (200 mm). Flashing should be carefully installed to prevent punctures or tears. Where several pieces of flashing are required to flash a section of the veneer, the ends of the flashing should be lapped a minimum of 6 in. (150 mm) and the joints properly sealed. Where the flashing is not continuous, such as over and under openings in the wall, the ends of the flashing should be turned up into the head joint at least 2 in. (50 mm) to form a dam.

DESIGN & DETAILS: Lintels, Sills and Jambs

Brick veneer backed by wood frame must always be supported by lintels over openings unless the masonry is self-supporting. Lintel design information may be found in *Technical Notes* 17H and 31B. Loose steel, stone or precast lintels should bear at least 4 in. (100 mm) at each jamb. All lintels should have space at the end of the lintel to allow for expansion. The clear span for ¼ in. (6.3 mm) thick steel angles varies between 5 ft. (1.5 m) and a maximum of 8 ft. (2.4 m), depending on the size of the angle selected. Steel lintels with spans greater than 8 ft. (2.4 m) may require lateral bracing for

Brick Veneer/Metal Stud Backup Wall System

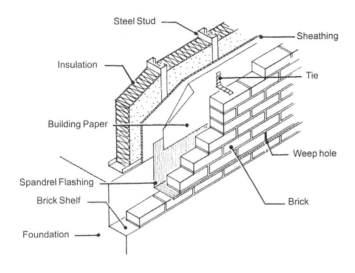

Brick Veneer/Wood Stud Backup System

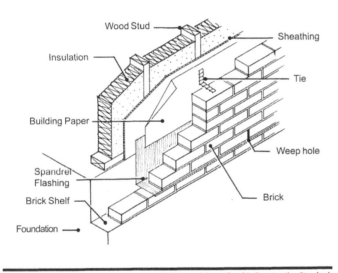

Figure 8.49   RSMeans, *Means Graphic Construction Standards*

stability. The maximum clear span may be restricted by the fire protection requirements of some building codes. Concrete, cast stone and stone lintels must be appropriately sized to carry the weight of the veneer.

Reinforced brick lintels are also a viable option. Some of the advantages of reinforced brick lintels are: more efficient use of materials; built-in fireproofing; elimination of differential movement which may occur with steel lintels and brick veneer; and no required painting or other maintenance.

DESIGN & DETAILS: Eave Details

Residential eave detail is suggested for the area at the top of the veneer. The air space between the top

of the brick veneer and wood framing is necessary to accommodate movement. Larger overhangs and gutters are helpful to keep water from contacting the wall below.

DESIGN & DETAILS: Movement Provisions

Design provisions for movement which include bond breaks, expansion joints, and joint reinforcement are not usually required in residential and low-rise brick veneer construction. However, they may be required in specific situations and the designer should analyze the project to determine such need.

Bond Breaks. Significant differential foundation settlement and horizontal movement may cause cracking in walls rigidly attached to the foundation. Bond breaks will help to relieve the stresses caused by these movements between the wall and the supporting foundation. Flashing at the base of the wall between the veneer and the foundation will provide sufficient break in the bond.

Expansion Joints. Expansion joints to allow for horizontal movement may be required in brick veneer when there are long walls, walls with returns, or large openings. The placement of expansion joints and the materials used should be in accordance with the information given in *Technical Notes* 18 Series.

DESIGN & DETAILS: Horizontal Joint Reinforcement

Masonry materials subject to shrinkage stresses, such as concrete masonry, require horizontal joint reinforcement for control of cracking from such movement. Brick is *not* subject to shrinkage, therefore horizontal joint reinforcement is never required in brick masonry for this purpose. It may be beneficial to use limited amounts of horizontal joint reinforcement in brick veneer for added strength at the corners of openings and at locations where running bond in the masonry is not maintained.

Horizontal joint reinforcement should be used to add integrity to veneer constructed in locations with intermediate and higher seismic activity or when the units are laid in stack bond. It may be either single- or double-wire joint reinforcement. In seismically active areas, the wire should engage the veneer ties. When using horizontal joint reinforcement, it *must* be discontinuous at *all* movement joints.

DESIGN & DETAILS: Sealant Joints

Exterior joints at the perimeter of exterior door and window frames to be filled with sealant should be formed by the adjacent materials or be a reservoir type joint. The joint should be no less than 1/4 in. (6.3

mm) nor more than ½ in. (12.7 mm) wide and ¼ in. (6.33 mm) deep. If wider joints are required, the sealant depth should be one-half of the joint width. A compressible backer rod or sealant bond break tape must be used. Fillet joints are not recommended, but if used, should be at least ½ in. (12.7 mm) across the diagonal. Sealant joints should be solidly filled with an elastic sealant forced into place with a pressure gun. All joints should be properly prepared before placing sealants. Appropriate primers should be applied as necessary. Expansion joints must be clear of all material for the thickness of the veneer wythe and closed with a backer rod and sealant.

MATERIALS: Flashing and Weep holes

There are many types of flashing available which are suitable for use in brick veneer walls. Sheet metals, plastics, laminates or combinations of these have been used successfully. Plastic flashing should be at least 30 mil thick. Asphalt impregnated felt (building paper) or air-infiltration barrier is *not* acceptable for use as flashing. These materials serve other purposes in the wall assembly. Building paper is applied as a moisture barrier to the sheathing. Air-infiltration barriers function as their name implies and may also serve as a moisture barrier.

Selection of flashing is often determined by cost; however, it is recommended that only superior materials be used, as replacement in the event of failure is exceedingly expensive.

Weep holes can be made in several ways. Some of the most common ways are leaving head joints open, using removable oiled ropes or rods, using plastic or metal tubes, or using rope wicks. There are also plastic or metal vents which are installed in lieu of mortar in a head joint. Clear openings without obstructions produce the best weep holes. For further discussion on flashing and weep holes see *Technical Notes* 7A.

MATERIALS: Horizontal Joint Reinforcement

Horizontal joint reinforcement should meet the requirements of ASTM A 951. It should have a corrosion-resistant coating which conforms to ASTM A 153, Class B-2.

MATERIALS: Lintel Materials

Lintels may be reinforced brick masonry, reinforced concrete, stone or steel angles. Reinforcement for reinforced brick masonry lintels should be steel bars manufactured in accordance with ASTM A 615, A 616 or A 617, Grades 40, 50, 60 and should be at least No. 3 bar size. Joint reinforcement can also be used in reinforced brick masonry lintels.

Steel for lintels should conform to ASTM A 36 Standard Specification for Structural Steel. Steel angle lintels should be at least ¼ in. (6.3 mm) thick with a horizontal leg of at least 3½ in. (89 mm) for use with nominal 4 in. (100 mm) thick brick veneer, and 3 in. (75 mm) for use with nominal 3 in. (75 mm) thick brick veneer. Steel lintels should be painted before installation.

MATERIALS: Sealants

There are numerous types of sealants available that are suitable for use with brick veneer. The material selected should be flexible and durable. Superior sealants may have a higher initial cost, but their high flexibility and increased durability result in savings of maintenance costs due to the reduced frequency of reapplication. Good grades of polysulfide, butyl or silicone rubber sealants are recommended. Oil-based caulking compounds are *not* recommended since most lack the desired flexibility and durability, see *Technical Notes* 7A. Regardless of the type of sealant chosen, proper primers and backer rods must be selected. Follow the recommendations of the sealant manufacturer.

CONSTRUCTION: Protection of Materials

Masonry. Prior to and during construction, all materials should be stored off of the ground to prevent contamination by mud, dust or other materials likely to cause stains or defects. The masonry materials should also be covered for protection against the elements.

To limit water absorption, it is recommended that all brick masonry be protected by covering at the end of each workday and for shutdown periods. The cover should be a strong, weather-resistant membrane securely attached to and overhanging the brickwork by at least 24 in. (600 mm). Partially completed masonry exposed to rain may become so saturated with water that it may require months after the completion of the building to dry out. This saturation may cause prolonged efflorescence. See *Technical Notes,* 23 Series, for more information.

Flashing. Flashing materials should be stored in places where they will not be punctured or damaged. Plastic and asphalt coated flashing materials should not be stored in areas exposed to sunlight. Ultraviolet rays from the sun break down these materials, causing them to become brittle with time. Plastic flashing exposed to the weather at the site for months before installation should not be used. During installation, flashing must be pliable so that no cracks occur at corners or bends.

CONSTRUCTION: Workmanship

Good workmanship is as essential in constructing brick veneer as it is in all types of brick masonry construction. All joints intended to receive mortar, including head joints with hollow brick, should be completely filled. Joints or spaces not intended to receive mortar should be kept clean and free of droppings. Courses of brick laid on foundations or lintels must have at least two-thirds of the brick thickness on the support.

The joints should be tooled with a jointer as soon as the mortar has become thumbprint hard. The types of joints recommended for exterior use with brick veneer are concave, "V" and grapevine. These joints firmly compact the mortar against the edges of the adjoining brick. Other joints are not recommended because they do not provide the necessary resistance to moisture penetration. See *Technical Notes,* 7B Revised, for further information.

It is essential when constructing brick veneer, to keep the 1 in. (25.4 mm) minimum air space between the veneer and the backing clean and free of all mortar droppings, so that the wall assembly will perform as a drainage wall. If mortar blocks the air space, it may provide a bridge for water to travel to the interior. In addition, all flashing, weep holes, ties and other accessories must be properly installed and kept clean.

Brick Veneer: Moisture Control

Industry Standards

Technical Note 28—Anchored Brick Veneer, Wood Frame Construction

(Used with permission Brick Industry Association, Reston, VA. website: **www.bia.org**)

Brick veneer wall assemblies are classified as drainage type walls. Walls of this type provide good resistance to rain penetration. It is essential to maintain the clear air space between the brick veneer and the backing to ensure proper drainage. Flashing and weep holes work with the air space to provide moisture penetration resistance. Refer to *Technical Notes,* 7 Series, for more information. Brick veneer with wood frame backing has historically been built with a 1 in. (25 mm) minimum air space. The protection provided by roof overhangs and the relatively low wall heights aid in reducing water penetration.

Industry Standards

Technical Note 13—Ceramic Glazed Brick Exterior Walls

(Used with permission Brick Industry Association, Reston, VA, website **www.bia.org**)

Wall Design System

Moisture Resistance

It is recommended that exterior glazed brick walls be designed to drain water that enters the wall system and to allow moisture from wind-driven rain or condensation to evaporate from behind the brickwork. Therefore, a vented drainage wall system is recommended. Drainage walls must be designed, detailed and constructed properly to accommodate the flow of water collected within the wall. Common examples of drainage walls include brick and block cavity walls, brick veneer, and rain screen walls.

In drainage wall design, penetrant water is intended to drain down the back of the brick, which is separated from interior wall elements by an air space. While a minimum 1 in. (25.4 mm) air space is required, 2 in. (51 mm) is recommended. Flashing and weeps are needed at horizontal interruptions in the air space to collect water and direct it out of the wall system. Refer to Figures 1a, 1b and 1c. They are typically provided above lintels and shelf angles, beneath sills, under copings and masonry or stone caps, and at the wall base. Discontinuous flashing, such as at window sills and loose lintels, should be constructed with end dams to ensure that collected water is directed out of the brickwork. End dams are also recommended where stepped flashings are used, such as at sloped grades, above arches, and above sloped roofs. Weeps must be provided in head joints directly above the flashing. Open head joint weeps are recommended with a spacing of no more than 24 in. (610 mm) on center. Spacing of wick and tube weeps is recommended at no more than 16 in. (406 mm) on center. Most building codes require weeps to have a minimum diameter of $3/16$ in. and permit weeps to be spaced up to 33 inches (838 mm) on center.

Mortar joints affect the moisture resistance of brickwork since they can account for up to 20 percent of the brickwork surface. Selecting mortar joint profiles that are most resistant to water penetration and cover the bed surface of the brick unit further minimize water intrusion and the possibility of water being trapped behind the glazed surface. Thus, concave, "V" and grapevine tooled mortar joints are recommended.

Glazed Brick Wall Sections

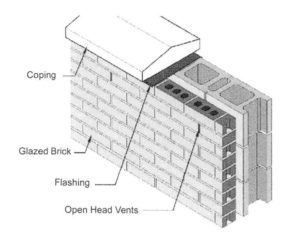

a) Glazed Brick at Top of Wall

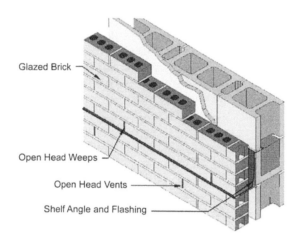

b) Glazed Brick at Shelf Angle

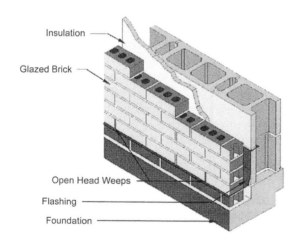

c) Glazed Brick at Foundation

Figure 8.50

Brick Industry Association

Brick Veneer: Methods of Thin Brick Installation

Industry Standards

Technical Note 28C—Thin Brick Veneer

(Used with permission Brick Industry Association, Reston, VA website: **www.bia.org**)

Adhered Veneer

Adhered veneer relies on a bonding agent between the thin brick units and the backup substrate. Adhered veneer construction may be classified as either thin bed set or thick bed set.

Thin Set. The thin bed set procedure typically utilizes an epoxy or organic adhesive, and is normally used on interior surfaces only. For areas subject to dampness, only clear and dry masonry surfaces or concrete surfaces should be used for backup. For dry locations, the backing material (substrate) may be wood, wallboard, masonry, etc.

Thick Set. The thick bed set procedure is used on interior and exterior surfaces. The backing material may be masonry, concrete, steel, or wood stud framing. The wire lath may be eliminated if the masonry wall is heavily scarified (sandblasted). (Williams, Griffith, Jr., "New Bricklike Tile Veneer," *Building Standards*, July-August, 1982). For applications over steel studs, procedures are similar to those used for concrete or masonry backup; however, wallboard and building felt must be installed over the studs before lath and mortar bed are placed.

Stucco & EIFS Systems

Industry Standards

Means Graphic Construction Standards
(RSMeans)

Stucco is a facing material applied like plaster to the exterior of buildings to provide a decorative and weather-resistant surface. Stucco is usually a mixture of sand, cement, lime, and water, but it may be composed of patented mixes with manufactured additives.

Stucco mixes differ from plaster mixes because Portland cement and lime are the basic ingredients in lieu of gypsum. Portland cement plasters are more difficult to trowel and finish, but are durable, relatively unaffected by water, and withstand repeated cycles of wetting, drying, freezing, and thawing.

The two common methods of applying stucco are the open-frame method and the direct-application system. In the open-frame method, the stucco is applied to galvanized metal lath attached directly to wood or steel studs. Three coats of stucco are normally required: (1) a scratch or first coat, (2) a brown or leveling coat, and (3) a finish coat.

The frame should be sufficiently braced to prevent movement. The flashings and drips should be carefully placed to prevent water penetration. Waterproof building paper applied over the studs or self-furring lath with integral waterproof paper are used for moisture protection. The system may also be waterproofed by backplastering or applying a coat of stucco on the interior side of the wall.

Directly applied stucco may be placed over sheathed wood or steel stud systems, or applied on concrete or masonry walls. One coat of stucco, with a bonding agent, or two coats of stucco may be used if the backing material possesses the surface characteristics required for adequate bonding. If the surface is not suitable for direct stucco application, the surface should first be covered with building paper and then furred with self-furring metal lath.

Exterior stucco is usually highly textured and coarse in appearance, to conceal staining and shrinkage cracks. Finish stucco coats may be tinted, painted, or treated with colorless coating materials to help prevent water penetration.

Comments

The plaster trade includes lath, the moisture barrier, and wire mesh. The moisture barrier is also referred to as "building wrap" because of the new high-performance materials now available that allow vapor transmission to exit the wall cavities. Moisture trapped in the wall cavity can result in mold and fungal growth, which could eventually lead to unhealthy air quality in the conditioned space. Climate is the determining factor on the correct moisture barrier to use, whether under plaster or siding.

Stucco

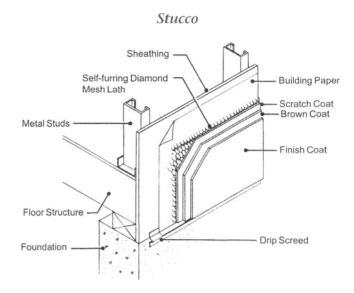

Stucco on Rib Lath

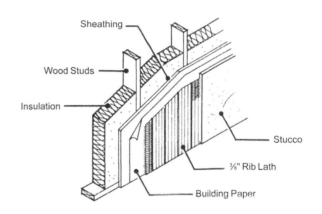

Stucco on Masonry

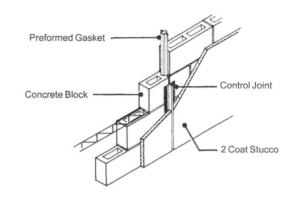

Figure 8.51

RSMeans, *Means Graphic Construction Standards*

289

Exterior Lath

IBC–2006

1403.2 Weather protection: Exterior walls must be water and weather resistant, use flashing, and must comply with the *International Energy Conservation Code* to prevent condensation buildup. Exceptions are made for concrete masonry walls and tested rain-resistant walls.

IRC–2006

R703.1 General: Similar requirements as IBC. However, does not specify compliance with *International Energy Conservation Code*, or give exceptions.

IBC–2006

2510.4 Corrosion resistance: Lath and attachments must be corrosion-resistant.

IBC–2006

2510.5 Backing: Backing must provide rigidity for plaster application. Solid backing support is required when lath on vertical surfaces extends between rafters or other members that project.

IBC–2006

2512 Exterior Plaster

2512.1 General: At least three coats are required over metal lath or wire; two coats over masonry, concrete, or gypsum board. Plaster surfaces to be covered or concealed by another wall or veneer require only two coats per ASTM C 926.

Comments

Horizontal Surfaces

Stucco can be used at the tops of walls and/or on patio and balcony railings. Good performance is dependent on plaster thickness and integrity, finishing, a proper weather barrier under the top, and adequate water control.

Moisture Barrier

To reduce the incidence of cracking, two layers of building paper are commonly used over the plywood sheathing. Moisture might enter the first layer, but the second layer tends to keep moisture from reaching the plywood, thereby minimizing expansion and contraction.

To maintain the integrity of the weather barrier, fasteners should not be installed on horizontal surfaces. Lath from the adjacent vertical surface should continue onto the horizontal surface. A weep screed is recommended where the vertical plaster ends on patio or balcony railings.

Plaster should be the same thickness over the cap as it is on the walls (generally $7/8$"). Corner reinforcement, when used, must be embedded in a minimum of $1/8$" of plaster to form a solid plaster corner. If nose wire is exposed, it can lead to corrosion and staining.

Application of acrylic polymer finish over the cap (the same color and texture as stucco) is recommended. This material is applied starting about 6" below the cap. It is applied across the horizontal surface, and should continue 6" down the other side.

Weep Screeds

Weep openings at the base of stucco walls are required by building codes to eliminate water that may inadvertently reach the back plane of the stucco. (Water could enter as a result of missing or improperly installed flashing, or where dissimilar elements meet, such as stucco abutting wood.)

Weep screeds must provide for free passage of water between the stucco termination and the "ground" (the part of the weep screed that extends outward from the vertical plane).

The weep screed ground (usually $3/4$" or $7/8$") provides a thickness gauge for plaster, as well as a place where the plaster can be leveled out.

Cement Plaster Cracking

Industry Standards

Cracking in Portland Cement Plaster
(Plastering Information Bureau)

Portland cement plaster, often referred to as stucco, as a 2- or 3-coat system is usually a $7/8$" to 1" thick inflexible membrane which most commonly provides the exterior skin for structures in Southern California and in some other parts of the country.

Structural penetrations such as windows, doors, plumbing, electric accessory outlets, light boxes, wall refrigeration units, vents, etc. pierce the thin plaster membrane. Such penetrations function as focus points or lines for stresses inherent in the supportive skeleton of the building.

Cracking in plaster occurs when the forces or stresses acting on it exceed the tensile strength of the plaster itself. Since Portland cement plaster gains strength gradually, it is most susceptible to cracking during its early, weaker stage.

There are two, and only two, factors that produce all cracking in portland cement plaster. One is that normal change in volume of portland cement plaster intrinsic to the hydration and curing of the cement binder and/or the loss of the mix water in excess of the moisture required for hydration. This process causes internal stresses. The other factor is stress transferred to the plaster membrane from external sources. It is classed as an external stress. Examples of transferred stresses are sonic resonance, seismic vibration, deflections of supporting members, thermal sock, wind loads, settlement and/or subsidence.

Portland cement plaster, like concrete, must be mixed with sufficient water to render it plastic and workable. Part of the water chemically combines with the cement for hydration. A significant amount of water is lost either by evaporation or by absorption. Accompanying the setting of portland cement plaster there is a natural shrinkage or loss of mass of its bulk. If the loss of moisture is not uniform throughout the thickness of the plaster, shrinkage will create internal stresses within the plaster membrane. Normally, contraction occurs towards the center of the portland cement area or panel. This is one of several possible factors which may affect shrinkage cracking.

Assuming that there are no deficiencies in either mix proportioning of the ingredients of the portland cement plaster or in the ensuing curing, the plaster will gain its largest percentage of ultimate strength during the first 7 days following its placement. This is the same period during which most shrinkage of the plaster takes place. The two natural, but counteractive, processes develop during a period of time when portland cement plaster should be expected to achieve its greatest gain in strength while at the same time, the greatest distortional stress from loss of volume occurs.

The second major factor in cracking, transferred stresses to the plaster membrane, is found in almost every structure built. The buildup of stresses is most pronounced in wood-framed construction. When framing, lumber loses the free moisture it contains, it is subject to volume change dimensionally through shrinkage, twisting, warping, bowing, bending, etc. Even kiln-dried lumber contains a considerable amount of water. Even when lumber is free of knots and is relatively straight-grained, it is subject to distortion to some degree.

In wood framing the natural deformation of supports and structural members may exert tremendous pressure perpendicularly to or in alignment with the plane of the plaster. Problems may be compounded if leaks occur and water is introduced into framing members after construction. Wet lumber swells and generates tremendous expansive forces.

In metal framing, a significant degree of transferred stressing often is generated in thermally-induced expansion and contraction of wall framing metal elements and of steel structural elements. The problem is worsened where the wall systems are welded in a unitized fashion without relief mechanisms.

Control joints in the lath-plaster areas should limit panel sizes.

Construction expansion joints should separate structural components into reasonable areas.

Other examples of transferred stresses are thermal shock, temperature-induced expansion and contraction, sonic vibrations, seismic temblors, concrete creep and sag, foundation settlement, structural subsidence, wind loads, live loading of floors, mechanical vibrations or other stress-producing impingements on the plaster membranes. Such transferred stresses are usually well within the range of accommodation by the building structure and pose little threat to serviceability, structural performance, weather resistivity or safety. These stresses are normally minimal in measurement or hardly measurable at all. However, they can sometimes reach a magnitude which exceeds the resistive strength of the nominal $7/8$" thickness of metal reinforced portland cement plaster. While minimal in detection, such stresses may react on the hard, brittle plaster skin to such a degree as to find relief in fractures in the cement membrane. Transferred stresses are of two types. One is a static force and the other a live or dynamic force. In the former the crack-induction potential is relieved once the stress has expended its energy in the fracture.

Weep Screed

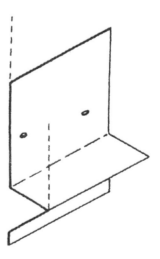

Figure 8.52   Courtesy of Western Wall & Ceiling Contractors Association, *Plaster & Drywall Systems Manual*

The other is the live crack which responds cyclically to recurrent stresses which may be reimposed on the plaster membrane in either a fixed or an uncertain periodicity. Where stress loads recur, live cracks may re-open, even if fractures have been repaired.

Some hairline cracking is almost always found in portland cement plaster and should be expected as normal. Movements in the supporting building structure most commonly cause cracks at the header and sill corners of windows and doors, over concentrations of large dimension wood framing members, and at focus points of stress buildup.

The use of control joints or other properly designed and installed stress relief mechanisms may reduce or prevent the focusing and concentration of both internal and external stresses. The building's designer and/or engineer should determine lines and points at which stresses may be expected and make relief provisions. Plaster panels should be limited in size to a maximum of 100 square feet and one dimension of the panel should not exceed 2½ times the other dimension.

Control joints which allow for some expansion and contraction movement are preferable to those which are rigid.

When unrelieved portland cement plaster panels exceed the recommended spacing of relief mechanisms, cracking is almost certain to occur in the plaster. While the use of relief joints is not an absolute guarantee of crack prevention, it minimizes stress fracturing. Where control joints are omitted in the design of a structure, the designer and/or owner, by default, must shoulder the major responsibility for cracking.

Portland cement plaster over solid wood shear panels, such as plywood sheathing, is subject to tremendous stress action. Even minutia amounts of water may cause swelling and buckling of the plywood. This is particularly true when plywood sheets are placed without a minimum ⅛" spacing between joints. Industry practice and building requirements dictate a double layer of Grade D weather barrier paper or its equivalent in asphalt-saturated felt, be placed over wood sheathing when in direct contact with the back face of the plaster membrane.

If the plywood is wet at the time of installation of the lath, cracking of the plaster is almost assured.

An application of a moisture barrier coating over plywood prior to lathing may reduce cracking problems. Over wood shear panelling, control joints

or other stress relief mechanisms are most urgently recommended.

Special relief provisions should be made at the juncture of dissimilar bases such as along the line of abutment of masonry and open framing construction. Relief should be designed at lines where wall membranes pass over concrete floors.

In some areas there is a strong opinion that the addition of short glass or polypropylene fibers added to portland cement plaster during the last stage of mixing provide considerable resistance to plaster fracture. Test results tend to confirm the theory that the plaster's ability to resist cracking is enhanced by the embedment of such reinforcing fibers in the plaster base coats.

Cracking is more apparent in certain stucco textures. Where the surface has been steel trowelled to a dense, smooth finish, cracking is almost always present. Sand float and to a lesser degree light machine dash textures highlight cracks more than skip-trowel or other coarse texture patterns which tend to absorb or conceal the cracks.

A plastering expert can usually tell from the location, dimension, state of spalling and pattern of the cracks whether the source of the stresses creating the fractures originate in the plaster membrane or were transferred to it.

Hairline surface cracking usually presents no leaking problems or other sub-standard performance of the plaster skin. It is usually a mere cosmetic or aesthetic consideration.

Most cracking ceases when the wooden skeleton of the building is in a condition of equilibrium, with the lumber set in its final configuration, as the building is occupied, loaded, stabilized and interior temperature brought to a fixed level. Because of the nature of the material, some hairline cracking in portland cement plaster is very normal and should be expected. Such cracks may easily be filled the first time the exterior is redecorated.

Penetration Flashing

Industry Standards

Plaster and Drywall Systems Manual
(Western Wall & Ceiling Contractors Association)

Penetration Flashing Material
Material for flashing shall be barrier-coated reinforced flashing material and shall provide for 4-hour minimum protection from water penetration when tested in accordance with ASTM D-779. Flashing

material shall carry continuous identification. Sealant shall be Butyl to comply with Fed. Spec. TT-S-1657.

Application

To flash penetrations, a strip of approved flashing material at least nine inches wide must be applied in weatherboard fashion around all openings. Apply the first strip horizontally immediately underneath the sill, cut it sufficiently long to extend past each side of the window, door, or vent, so that it projects beyond the vertical flashing to be applied. Fasten the top edge of the first segment to the wall, but do not secure the body and lower edge of the first horizontal strip, so the weather resistant building paper applied later may be slipped up and underneath the bottom flashing in weatherboard fashion. In the case of low-set windows, apply approved paper the full height from the bottom of the plate line to the bottom of the window sill when the window is flashed.

Next, apply the two vertical side sections of flashing. Cut the side sections sufficiently long to extend the width of the flashing above the top of the window and the same distance below the window. Apply the side sections over the bottom strip of flashing. *(Ed. Note: See Figure 9.1 in Chapter 9, "Windows & Doors," for an illustration of flashing placement.)*

The penetrating fixture then is installed by pressing the nailing flange positively into a continuous bead of sealant which extends around the bottom and vertical perimeter of the inserted fixture.

Ed. Note: The continuous head of sealant that is applied to the underneath side of the nailing flange of windows, doors, and vents is not to be construed as a substitute for flashing.

Apply the top horizontal section of flashing last, overlapping and sealed against the full height of the outer face of the top nailing flange with a continuous bead of sealant. Cut the top piece of flashing sufficiently long so that it will extend to the outer edge of both vertical strips of side flashing.

Installation of Exterior Plaster Weather-Resistant Paper Underlayment to Complete Acceptable Penetration Flashing

Commence at the bottom of the wall and overlapping the weep screed flange, lay the approved weather-resistant paper up the wall, overlapping 2" min. in weatherboard fashion. Be sure that the first layer is placed under the sill strip flashing.

Ed. Note: While the requirements for flashing and counterflashing are briefly addressed in the IBC and IRC, this area—along with roofing—is the focus of frequent complaints in construction litigation. The problems resulting from improper flashing (dryrot and fungal growth)

are easily visible. They not only weaken the structure, but spoil its appearance. Flashing and counterflashing claims are preventable by following the manufacturers' instructions, the project specifications, and any local building code requirements.

See Chapter 9, "Windows & Doors," for more information on flashing penetrations.

IBC–2006

2512.4 Cement plaster: Protect plaster coats from freezing for at least 24 hours after set. Apply plaster only when temperature is greater than 40°F during application and after 48 hours.

2512.5 Second coat application: Application and thickness must be suitable for finish cost bonding. Variation must be not more than ¼" under a straight edge of 5'.

2512.6 Curing and interval: First and second coats must be applied and moist-cured per ASTM C 926 and IBC Table 2512.6.

2512.7 Application to solid backings: Applied per IBC-2006 Section 2510.5 or directly on unit masonry. The second coat can be applied after first coat is sufficiently hard.

2512.8 Alternate method of application: Second coat may be applied when the first coat is rigid.

2512.8.1 Admixtures: May add calcium aluminate cement up to 15% of weight of Portland cement.

2512.8.2 Curing: First coat curing may be omitted. Second coat cured per ASTM C 926 and Table 2512.6.

2512.9 Finish coats: Must be applied over base coat when in place per ASTM C 926. Third or finish coat must be applied with adequate material and pressure to bond and over brown coat.

Exterior Insulation and Finish System (EIFS)

Industry Standards

Plan Reading & Material Takeoff
(RSMeans)

Exterior insulation and finish system (EIFS), sometimes referred to as *synthetic stucco,* is an exterior siding material that has the durability and thermal insulation value of stucco. It is composed of expanded polystyrene insulation board and cementitious base coat applied in varying thicknesses, with a synthetic woven mesh that acts as a reinforcement. The top or finish coat is an acrylic stucco, available in a variety of textures and colors. The insulation is adhered or mechanically fastened to the sidewall substrate of plywood, masonry, or gypsum sheathing. The base coat is troweled on, similar to a conventional stucco system, and the mesh reinforcing is embedded in the base coat. The finish coat is applied after the base coat has had sufficient time to dry.

The contractor should refer to the architectural drawings for sections and details of the system, with attention to the details at the abutting surfaces of dissimilar materials, door frames, windows, and wood surfaces. Control and expansion joints are required as per the manufacturer's recommendations to control expansion and contraction associated with the product. The specifications should indicate the individual product specified as well as the manufacturer's standard application and installation procedures.

Comments

EIFS systems, often referred to by the trade names "Dryvit" (Dryvit Systems, Inc.) and "Sto" (Sto Corporation), should be installed by a contractor approved and certified by the system manufacturer. Some projects may require that samples of finish coating (for color and texture) be submitted to and approved by the architect.

Following are some guidelines for the preparation and use of EIFS. Materials should be stored under cover in their original containers with manufacturers' seals and labels intact, and each production lot identified by batch number. Storage should be in a cool, dry location, at a temperature no less than 40°F. Installation should also be in conditions not less than 40°F. Adjacent areas need to be protected, and completed sections of the work must also be protected from moisture not only during the application, but until the coatings are dry.

Before EIFS installation can begin, it is important to make sure that the substrate is properly prepared. All areas should be even and free of surface irregularities. A substrate approved by the EIFS manufacturer should be in place. If exterior gypsum sheathing is to be used, it must meet the required standard, be clean, dry, and properly fastened with no deterioration or defects. The insulation board is installed in a running bond pattern with the long dimension applied horizontally. Board joints must be tightly butted. At least three fasteners per board should be used to tack the board to the substrate or framing. Boards should be interlocked at corners. (Rasp boards if necessary to ensure they are flush.) The installed insulated wall surface should be sound, flat, and level in all directions. Fiber mesh reinforcing should be applied mechanically over the insulation board with fasteners

spaced 12" on center vertically and 24" on center horizontally. Control joints should be installed as indicated by the manufacturer. When the base coat is applied over the reinforcing mesh, no mesh should be visible on the finished surface. The surface should be flat and even. The finish coat is then applied per manufacturer's instructions.

EIFS has not been around long enough to see performance over the life of the building (40 years). However, properly installed, EIFS has so far had excellent results. Detractors have claimed that the system has a low performance rating; but in reviewing numerous studies, we have not seen a single failure of the EIFS product itself. Problems typically stem from improper flashing and termination techniques.

EIFS Backwrapping, Flashing, Expansion Joints & Penetrations

An EIFS should not extend below grade. It should be a minimum of 8" above grade, held in place either by backwrapping with reinforcing mesh and base coat, or by returning the reinforcing mesh and base coat onto the foundation.

All terminations should be backwrapped, which means continuing the reinforced base coat from the face of the insulation board across the edge and onto the back side, which it should overlap by at least 2½".

When the system terminates at a dissimilar material such as wood or block, it should be held back ¾" to allow for an expansion joint and caulking. In wood frame construction, expansion joints are installed at each floor line as well as at areas where the substrate changes or significant structural movement is anticipated.

Where EIFS terminates at penetrations (light fixtures, hose bibs, dryer vents, wall receptacles, etc.) it requires backwrapping with reinforcing mesh and base coat. The insulation board must be held back from the opening a minimum of ³⁄₈"–½" for proper sealant application.

Flashing is installed between the plywood and the ledger board, with one piece turned onto the sleeper or nailer to prevent water from entering behind the deck or ledger boards. The EIFS should overlap the flashing where it is backwrapped and held up from the deck at least 2".

If a gap can be detected between the sill and jamb of a window, it should be caulked with the window manufacturer's recommended sealant. The heads of multiple openings (such as ganged windows) should have a continuous piece of drip flashing to prevent water entry.

Terminations at expansion joints, windows, and other openings must be caulked with sealants that are approved for use with the materials to which they must adhere. Use closed-cell backer rods and sealant primer.

(continued)

Components of an EIFS Wall

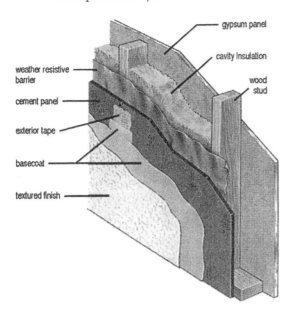

Figure 8.53
Courtesy of United States Gypsum Company

> Where the roof intersects a vertical wall, it is necessary to use a kickout or diverter flashing as the first piece of flashing. Diverter joints must be soldered. Step flashing should extend upward a minimum of 6". The step flashing and the diverter are intended to shed the water off the roof and away from the vertical wall below.

Glass Block

Industry Standards

Means Graphic Construction Standards
(RSMeans)

Glass block can be placed on a raised base, plate, or sill, provided that the surfaces to be mortared are primed with asphalt emulsion. Wall recesses and channel tract that receive the glass block should be lined with expansion strips prior to oakum filler and caulking. Horizontal joint reinforcing is specified for flexural as well as shrinkage control and is laid in the joints along with the mortar. End blocks are anchored to the adjacent construction with metal anchors, if no other provisions for attachment exist. If intermediate support is required, vertical I-shaped stiffeners can either be installed in the plane of the wall or adjacent to it, but the stiffeners should be tied to the wall with wire anchors. The top of the wall is supported between angles or in a channel track similar to the jambs.

Glass Blocks

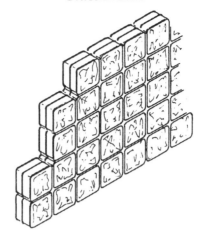

Glass Block Head Section

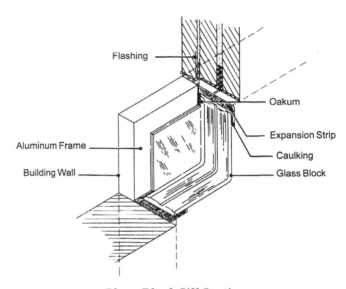

Glass Block Sill Section

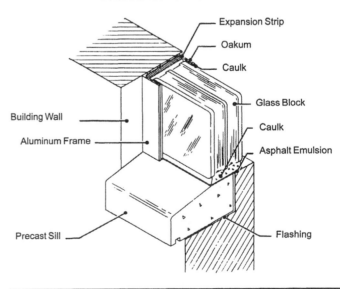

Figure 8.54
RSMeans, *Means Graphic Construction Standards*

Metal Siding

Industry Standards

Means Graphic Construction Standards
(RSMeans)

Formed metal panels are used for mansard roofing and building fascia, as well as for siding. The panels are made from sheet metal, aluminum, or steel and can span distances from 3' to 12'. The ability to transfer wind loads across these spans depends on the gauge of the sheet metal and the profile that is formed with the sheet during rolling. Where structural strength is not required, the corrugation can be regarded as merely an architectural feature.

Sheet metal can be finished with a variety of coatings for corrosion protection. Steel panels may be galvanized, aluminized, or stainless. Both aluminum and steel panels can have a baked enamel or porcelain finish.

Canopy fascia and mansard panels can be fastened or clipped to extruded or channel-shaped metal girts. They are placed horizontally at the required span distance and are supported on channel truss frames. Panels may also be fastened to solid backing (sheathing mounted on stud framing) directly or with metal clips. Where a backup wall exists, metal panels may simply be mounted on channel or stud furring. The top of the panels are supplied with matching coping or gravel stops, and the panel bottom with nose or sill trim. Conversion trim pieces are available for slope transitions. Inside and outside corners are finished with post or cap assemblies. Smooth or ventilated ceiling panels are used for soffits.

For a more custom installation, panel ribs and flat sheets can be supplied as separate components to be installed to a stud and sheathing backup system within the constraints of the field conditions. The exposed open ends of ribs can be closed with "plugs," should coping not be desirable. Ribs may also be field crimped at slope transitions. A very dramatic vertical rib effect can be obtained by mounting a standard 4" wide panel on horizontal carriers that will support the ribs in a variety of angles to the plane of the exterior wall, giving a "louvered" appearance.

A total siding system involves the metal panels fastened to a structural girt support, as mentioned above, with the addition of insulation and backup (liner) panels. In some metal siding systems, the liner panel and insulation are installed to the girt first. The face panel then interlocks with grooves in the liner panel. The thickness of the face and liner panels range from 24 to 20 gauge, and the span can reach 8'.

When the face and liner panels are stiffened by inserting a subgirt between them, the allowable span will increase to 15" for 22 gauge and to 30' for 18 gauge (and a deeper profile). The structural girt may be eliminated altogether if the liner panel is given a deeper profile or a structural stud is integrated into the liner design. This insulated panel and liner system can be factory assembled to save installation time in the field. The liner panel may be perforated to provide sound absorption. A multi-leaf gypsum wallboard layer can also be enclosed in a double-subgirt system with the face and liner panel to provide a fire-rated wall panel. Some factory assembled panels have a foamed-in-place insulation that is bonded to the face and liner sheet to provide composite structural action.

Vinyl Siding

IBC–2006

1405.13 Vinyl siding: Vinyl siding may be used on Type V construction up to 40' in height if compliance with IBC Chapter 16 is established. Must also meet ASTM D 3679 and manufacturer's guidelines.

1405.13.1 Application: Vinyl siding must be applied over approved sheathing or materials, and must comply with requirements for weather resistance. Installation must meet manufacturers requirements. Approved nails must resist corrosion and have a minimum .313" head diameter and .125" shank diameter. For horizontal installation, fastener spacing must be 16" horizontally or less and 12" vertically. Vertical installation requires spacing of 12" or less horizontally and 12" vertically.

Ed. Note: Refer to Residential Construction Performance Guidelines, *published by the National Association of Home Builders, for further information on tolerances for vinyl siding installation.*

Field Assembled Insulated Metal Wall

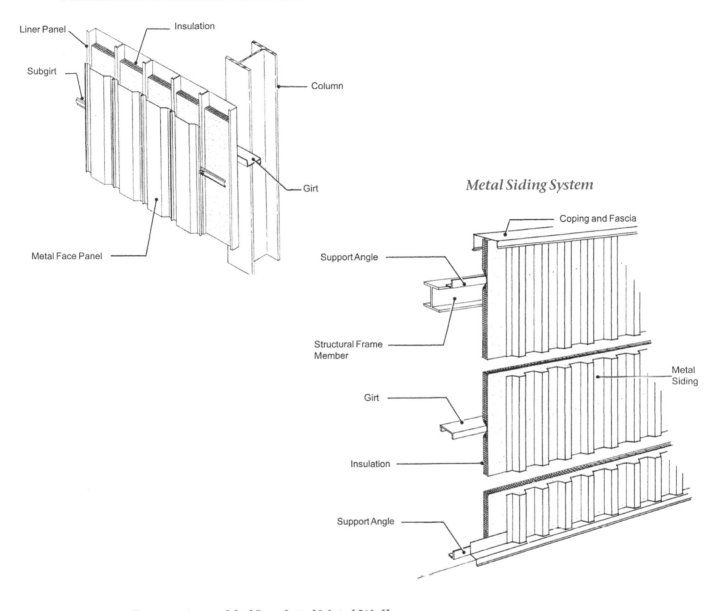

Liner Panel

Insulation

Subgirt

Column

Girt

Metal Face Panel

Metal Siding System

Coping and Fascia

Support Angle

Structural Frame Member

Girt

Metal Siding

Insulation

Support Angle

Factory Assembled Insulated Metal Wall

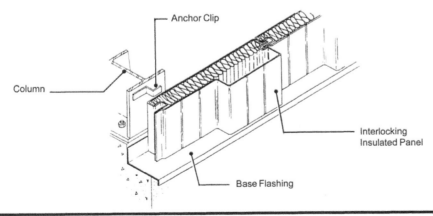

Anchor Clip

Column

Interlocking Insulated Panel

Base Flashing

RSMeans, *Means Graphic Construction Standards*

Figure 8.55

Fiber-Cement Siding

Green Home Improvement
(RSMeans)

Like conventional siding, fiber-cement siding is applied to the exterior of buildings to protect them from the elements. This product comes in a multitude of colors and styles that resemble conventional siding—notably, stucco, cedar shingles, and wood clapboards. What's different about this product is that it's made primarily from cement, ground sand, and wood fiber—often a recycled wood fiber waste product—a combination that results in an extremely durable, long-lasting material.

Fiber-cement siding typically costs a bit more than vinyl siding, but less than stucco and traditional wood siding, and much less than redwood siding. It also outlasts its competitors—often by decades—because it resists many common hazards, including fire, wind, insects, and rain. Fiber-cement siding is recommended in all climates, but is ideal for hot, humid regions. No matter how wet it gets, it won't rot.

Like conventional wood siding, fiber-cement siding can be applied to both wood and steel studs, but it's normally attached to exterior wall sheathing (OSB or plywood) on top of an appropriate weather-resistant barrier, such as Tyvek. Some fiber-cement products can be applied over rigid foam insulation. If you're installing the siding over concrete or concrete block walls, you'll first need to install vertical furring strips to which the siding is attached. Check the manufacturer's recommendations for spacing.

Fiber-cement is attached using corrosion-resistant galvanized or stainless steel nails or screws that penetrate into wall studs or exterior sheathing. Many fiber-cement siding planks can be blind-nailed onto exterior sheathing so that no nails show (an advantage over traditional wood clapboards). To do this, each plank is nailed about 1 inch down from the top edge. The next plank is placed so that it overlaps the nails, hiding them from view. Follow the manufacturer's instructions carefully, as there are some restrictions on blind-nailing wider planks to prevent wind uplift. (Wind can lift up wider planks if they're only attached at the top.)

Fiber-cement siding can also be face-nailed, but staples cannot be used due to the hardness of the material. Face-nailing will leave exposed nail heads. Do not under-drive nails or screws.

Waterproofing & Dampproofing

Industry Standards

NRCA Roofing & Waterproofing Manual
(National Roofing Contractors Association)

2.1.1 Waterproofing

Waterproofing is defined as the treatment of a surface or structure to prevent the passage of water under hydrostatic pressure. Water exerts a pressure of 62.4 pounds of force per foot (1000 kg per meter) of depth. Therefore, water lying against a barrier exerts a steadily increasing pressure as the depth increases. The waterproofing treatment must keep the water from penetrating into the building interior.

Waterproofing is used:

- To protect floors and walls below grade of buildings, tunnels, and similar structures from ground water.
- To protect spaces beneath roofs and plaza decks.
- To isolate wet spaces such as kitchens, showers, and mechanical equipment rooms from other areas of buildings.
- On bridge decks to protect against deterioration from de-icing salts and to help minimize the negative effects of thermal expansion of the structural elements and topping materials.
- To keep water from leaking from pools, planters, lagoons, irrigation trenches and dams, or into basements and other underground structures.

An understanding of the different loads and stresses placed upon the waterproofing material is important to the proper design of structures and facilities. Some of these forces are similar to those to which roofing membranes are exposed, but others are quite different. The following are some of the performance attributes required of waterproofing materials:

- Perform for an extended period of time, preferably for the life of the structure. It is usually quite costly, if not impossible, to excavate around the foundation walls or to remove a reinforced concrete floor slab to repair or replace the waterproofing material.

Consequently, unlike a roof membrane, a waterproofing membrane must perform completely trouble- and maintenance-free for an indefinite period of time.

- Perform successfully in a constantly wet environment. While there may be relatively dry periods depending on where the material is employed and the level of ground water, waterproofing is usually in continuous contact with ground water, or is retaining water, such as in a planter or pool.

- Resist environmental contaminants, such as acids or alkalis, and other contaminants. Soil chemistry varies from location to location, and sometimes from foot to foot of excavated depth. The material must be compatible with both the soil and the substrate to which it is applied. Some waterproofing materials are intolerant of certain soil salts, and others are affected by oils that could be spilled onto floors in mechanical equipment rooms. These contaminants are much different from those to which roof membranes are exposed.

- Withstand construction activity. The material must remain in place and intact until excavations can be backfilled or the protective wearing course can be applied. During backfill placement, rocks, construction debris, and other sharp objects may be dumped against the waterproofing material. However, the greatest threat to waterproofing often comes from other construction trades. Even though horizontal surfaces are usually covered with a protection course, other trades often use the waterproofed surface as a staging area or for access to adjacent work areas. Although this can also be a problem for roof membranes, it is more critical for waterproofing because once in use the waterproofing membrane is not readily accessible for repair.

- Accommodate anticipated structural movement in the substrate to which it has been applied. Below-grade concrete and masonry structures may experience settlement and/or shrinkage as the substrate materials cure. Horizontal plaza decks experience thermal movement and load deflection. These characteristics make it necessary for the waterproofing material to be able to bridge small cracks, and expand and contract to some degree without rupture or failure.

Waterproofing materials are generally concealed and often placed into more shielded environments than roof membranes. Therefore, materials used for waterproofing may not perform if used for roofing applications. The following are some conditions favorable to waterproofing membranes:

- Subjected to limited thermal stress. Below-grade waterproofing materials are usually kept at near constant temperatures because of their contact with earth backfill on the exterior and proximity to relatively constant interior temperatures. Further, the materials are usually directly adhered to thermally and dimensionally stable structural decks or wall surfaces.

- Not usually exposed to direct ultraviolet radiation because they are most often buried in the ground, covered with a plaza deck surface, or used inside the building. Sunlight and other environmental exposures cannot affect them once the building is completed.

- Most have the advantage of being adhered directly to structural substrates. Structural decks and walls are typically dimensionally stable. When the materials are fully adhered to the substrates, water penetrating the waterproofing cannot freely move laterally. Therefore, leaks tend to appear very close to the point of moisture penetration.

- Protected from physical abuse. After installation, waterproofing materials are usually covered with a protection course and backfill or with a permanent protection slab. People should not walk directly on the waterproofing membrane.

2.1.2 Dampproofing

Dampproofing is defined as the treatment of a surface or structure to resist the passage of water in the absence of hydrostatic pressure. Dampproofing methods will not work when hydrostatic pressures are present, and are generally employed above grade, or below grade in the absence of ground water. For this reason, many of the design factors that are critical to the performance of a waterproofing system are not as critical to the successful performance of dampproofing.

Dampproofing is employed to prevent moisture from wicking through the structure and damaging interior finishes. Some dampproofing materials are transparent and can be exposed above grade.

2.1.3 Hydrostatic Pressure Relief Systems

A hydrostatic pressure relief system is a system of perimeter and/or under-slab drains used to regulate the hydrostatic pressure in the earth surrounding a below-grade structure.

Clearly, the most effective way to waterproof walls and floors placed against earth is to remove the water from the earth prior to it reaching the wall or floor. Each of the waterproofing materials described in this manual will resist hydrostatic pressure to varying degrees. However, the waterproof integrity of any building can be greatly improved if the hydrostatic pressure against the waterproofing material can be reduced or eliminated entirely.

In below-grade structures, the determination of whether a hydrostatic pressure relief system can be used depends upon the quantity of water that must be handled and how it is to be handled or resisted. When gravity can be used to direct water from around the building foundation into a storm sewer, greater amounts of water can be handled than when pumping must be used to lower the water table. Operating the pumps can be costly if there is a great amount of water to handle, and there is always the threat of problems should the pumps fail.

If it is determined that a hydrostatic relief system cannot be economically employed, then the foundation floor slab must be designed with sufficient concrete mass and reinforcement to resist the uplift pressures of the anticipated water table, and the construction has to be carefully waterproofed, which can be an expensive construction process. If a hydrostatic pressure relief system can be employed, then the slab-on-grade can be designed with only surface load considerations, thereby greatly reducing construction costs. Furthermore, waterproofing of the floor slab may not be necessary.

The decision to use a hydrostatic pressure relief system depends upon a careful analysis of soil borings and water table level readings, and should be made with the input of an experienced soils or geotechnical engineer. A site with coarse, permeable soil that freely permits water percolation, combined with a water table level that is above the top of the foundation floor slab, is probably an unlikely candidate for a hydrostatic pressure relief system, particularly if the water table must be lowered by pumping. Conversely, a site with a dense clay soil resistant to water percolation could be an excellent candidate for a hydrostatic pressure relief system, even if the water table level is considerably higher than the foundation floor slab.

Hydrostatic pressure can be relieved from perimeter walls below grade by using a coarse aggregate backfill or a prefabricated drainage product known as a "geocomposite." These systems channel ground water traveling toward the building down to a perimeter drainage system located below the bottom of the foundation floor slab. The drain system may be installed either at the exterior or interior perimeter of the foundation walls or both, depending upon the specific type of hydrostatic pressure relief system being used. When aggregate is used to relieve hydrostatic pressure against wall surfaces, a separate protection course must be placed against the waterproofing membrane to protect the membrane from damage during aggregate placement.

Loose aggregate should not be placed directly against the waterproofing membrane. Alternatively, geocomposites relieve hydrostatic pressure and some also serve as protection for the waterproofing membrane during backfill operations.

Consideration should also be given to relieving water pressure from the surface of horizontal suspended structural slabs, such as a plaza deck slab. When water that permeates its way through upper layers down to the membrane surface can drain freely to deck drains, the horizontal waterproofing membrane will perform better. This drainage can be achieved by placing a suitable insulation board specially designed with drainage channels or grooves on its underside, or a protection course and a layer of aggregate, or a geocomposite directly above the waterproofing membrane surface.

2.1.4 Substrate Preparation

Most waterproofing materials are bonded or applied to surfaces that are installed by other trades. It is essential to the performance of the waterproofing material that these substrates be structurally sound and free from excessive cracks, holes or projections. Certain curing compounds and finishes may affect or interfere with the performance of the waterproofing material. The use of oils, waxes, and other surface contaminates should be avoided or the contaminates must be removed prior to waterproofing. The waterproofing contractor should visually inspect the substrate surfaces before the application of waterproofing materials, and report any deficiencies so that they may be corrected by the responsible trade.

Following are recommended surface preparation procedures acceptable for most waterproofing materials. Other procedures may be recommended or required by the waterproofing material manufacturer.

2.1.4.1 Masonry Substrates

Holes, joints, and voids in masonry substrates should be pointed flush with the surface. The masonry surface should be smooth and free from projections. Penetrations through the masonry surface should be grouted tightly. Irregular existing masonry surfaces that will be waterproofed with a membrane should receive an approximate ½ inch (13mm) thick parging, consisting of one part cement to three parts sand, finished to a smooth steel trowel surface. Block filler may be used in lieu of parging where conditions warrant.

2.1.4.2 Concrete Substrates

NRCA recommends that horizontal concrete decks cure a minimum of 28 days, or as specified by the material manufacturer, to allow moisture to dissipate from the top surface (forming systems typically prevent dissipation of moisture from the underside of horizontal decks) prior to applying waterproofing materials.

Form release agents and concrete curing compounds must be compatible with the waterproofing materials being used, or must be removed from the concrete surface by the responsible trade. Honeycombs, tie-wire holes, and other voids in the concrete substrate must be cut out and re-pointed with a non-shrinking concrete patching compound. Concrete fins or other projections should be removed to provide a smooth surface. Horizontal concrete slabs should be free from gouges, voids, depressions, ridges, and concrete droppings, and should preferably be sloped to drains.

ASTM D 5295, *Standard Guide for Preparation of Concrete Surfaces for Adhered (Bonded) Membrane Waterproofing System*, provides additional recommendations regarding the preparation of concrete deck surfaces prior to the installation of waterproofing.

2.1.4.3 Plywood Substrates

The grade of plywood utilized is critical to the performance of the waterproofing. NRCA suggests the use of marine grade plywood as a substrate for waterproofing applications.

The surface of plywood substrates must be smooth, and holes, open joints, or gaps between panels should be plugged or covered. Knot holes are not acceptable for waterproofing purposes. Plywood panel edges should bear on joists or blocking to reduce deflection from traffic. The thickness and deflection characteristics of plywood substrates are important design considerations. Plywood decks should be sloped for drainage.

Fasteners used for attaching plywood must be corrosion-resistant-type, either resin coated, ribbed, screw or ring shanked nails; or screws countersunk to prevent their backing out and puncturing the waterproofing membrane.

Waterproofing & Dampproofing Foundations

IBC–2006

1807 Dampproofing and waterproofing

1807.1 Where required: Waterproof or dampproof walls that enclose interior spaces below grade must comply with this section.

1807.1.1 Story above grade plane: Walls and floors must be dampproofed if the basement is considered a story above grade and the finished ground level next to the wall is below the basement floor elevation for 25% or more of the perimeter. The foundation drain must be installed around the perimeter of the basement where the floor in below ground level.

1807.1.2 Underfloor space: The finished ground level of a space under the floor (such as a crawl space) cannot be located below the bottom of the footings.

1807.1.2.1 Flood hazard areas: For structures in flood areas, the finished ground level of an under-floor space must be equal to or higher than the outside ground level, except for Group R-3 buildings that meet FEMA/FIA-TB-11 requirements.

1807.1.3 Ground-water control: Walls and floors must be dampproofed if ground-water table is lowered and kept at an elevation at least 6" below the bottom of the lowest floor.

1807.2 Dampproofing required: Dampproofing of floors and walls at areas where hydrostatic pressure does not occur (other than wood foundation systems) is required. Wood foundation systems must comply with AFPA TR7.

1807.2.1 Floors: Dampproofing materials must be installed between the floor and the base course required by Section 1807.4.1 (except where a separate floor is provided above concrete slab).

1807.2.2 Walls: Dampproofing materials must be of approved materials and be installed on the exterior surface of a wall, and extend above ground level from the top of the footing.

1807.2.2.1 Surface preparation of walls: Before dampproofing materials are applied to concrete walls, all holes and recesses in the concrete must be sealed according to approved methods.

1807.3 Waterproofing required: Floors and walls must be waterproofed in accordance with this section at areas where there is hydrostatic pressure and the design does not include a groundwater control system.

1806.3.1 Floors: Floors must be concrete and designed to withstand hydrostatic pressures. Provides specific requirements for acceptable waterproofing materials and installation methods.

1807.3.2 Walls: Walls must be concrete or masonry and designed to withstand hydrostatic pressure and other lateral loads. Provides specific requirements for acceptable waterproofing materials and installation methods.

1807.3.2.1 Surface preparation of walls: Prepare walls in accordance with Section 1807.2.2.1 (sealing holes with bituminous material) prior to applying waterproofing materials.

1807.3.3 Joints and penetrations: Joints and penetrations in walls and floors must be made watertight using approved methods.

1807.4 Subsoil drainage system: Dampproofing and a base course must be installed under the floor, with a drain around the foundation perimeter at areas where hydrostatic pressure does not occur.

1807.4.1 Floor base course: Basement floors must be placed over a 4"-thick base course consisting of gravel or crushed stone with no more than 10% passing through a No. 4 sieve. Exception made for well-drained sites meeting specific requirements.

1807.4.2 Foundation drain: Gravel or crushed stone drain must be installed around the foundation perimeter. Extend drain at least 12" beyond outside edge of footing. Provides additional requirements for materials and installation methods.

1807.4.3 Drainage discharge: Drain must lead to drainage system that complies with the *International Plumbing Code* (with exception of well-drained sites meeting specific requirements).

IRC–2006

R406: Foundation waterproofing and dampproofing

R406.1 Concrete and masonry foundation dampproofing: Foundation walls that retain earth and envelop usable space below grade must be dampproofed from the top of the footing to the finished grade. Masonry walls must have Portland cement on the exterior wall at least $3/8$" thick, which must be dampproofed in accordance with requirements of this section.

R406.2 Concrete and masonry foundation waterproofing: Exterior foundation walls must be waterproofed with a membrane that extends from the top of the footing to the finished grade. Waterproofing must be in accordance with requirements of this section.

R406.3 Dampproofing for wood foundations: Wood foundations must be dampproofed to meet the requirements of the following subsections if they enclose usable space below grade.

R406.3.1 Panel joint sealed: Plywood panel joints in foundation walls must be sealed with caulking that is consistently moisture-proof.

R406.3.2 Below grade moisture barrier: The portion on the exterior foundation that is below grade must have a polyethylene film six mils thick, applied before backfilling. Joints in the film must be lapped 6" and sealed and meet other specific requirements.

R406.3.3 Porous fill: The area between the excavation and foundation wall must be backfilled with the same material used for footings and covered with asphalt paper or polyethylene to allow for water seepage.

R406.3.4 Backfill: The rest of the excavated area must be backfilled with the same soil type as was originally removed.

CHAPTER

9

WINDOWS & DOORS

Table of Contents

Text in blue type indicates excerpted summaries from the International Building Code® (IBC) *and* International Residential Code® (IRC). *Please consult the IBC and IRC for complete coverage and specific wording. "Comments" (in solid blue boxes) were written by the editors, based on their own experience.*

 These icons will appear with references to green building practices and hurricane-safe building requirements, respectively.

Common Defect Allegations

Windows

- *When extensive or destructive inspections are required, construction analysts find that most windows and doors show evidence of some water intrusion. To avoid these kinds of claims, many builders have begun using a flexible, rubberized, self-adhesive flashing to create a positive watertight installation.*

- *Aluminum window frame assemblies are usually screwed together. The corners are metal to metal, with a dab of sealant, and many of these connections leak. It is good practice to apply extra high-grade flexible sealant in those corners. Another problem occurs when the frames are installed upside down, with the weepholes at the top of the window. Sometimes the windows are installed correctly, but plaster has filled the weepholes, which traps water in the track.*

- *Wood windows often deteriorate quickly. Problems can result from insufficient maintenance. Another factor is the use of paint with less durability in many areas where air quality regulations limit paint choices. In some conditions, windows will require repainting every two years. Failures can also result from the paint being cut back from the glass by the cleanup workers with a razor-type scraper that breaks the water seal.*

Along with roofing and HVAC/plumbing problems, improper flashing is one of the most frequent complaints in construction defect litigation. It creates significant visual defects due to the consequential dryrot and fungal growth. Flashing problems are among the most easily preventable defects. There are two sources of water intrusion from windows: the mechanical connection of the frame to the wall, and the interior of the window assembled by the manufacturer. We address only the frame wall connection.

The basic problem is that there is no standard method that can be enforced by the building official during the wrap of the building with

(continued)

regard to the integration of flashing materials, especially over radius windows or on windows that have a plant-on or reveal adjacent to the window frame itself.

The acceptable minimum standard flashing around residential windows is a sisal-type, reinforced paper flashing. This is considered to be a baffle system that is not caulked to the building paper, but is simply overlapped, assuming that gravity will take the water and shed it over the next layer before it travels horizontally and enters the interior of the wall cavity.

Doors

- Wood doors, like windows, often suffer from lack of maintenance. Very often, exterior doors are not painted on the top and bottom, which allows water to be absorbed into the wood assembly. Sometimes the door top and bottom are painted correctly, but a security system company drills a round magnet into the top of the door without sealing it.

- A very common problem is water intrusion under thresholds. The threshold must be caulked to the exterior building layer with a high grade flexible caulking. This includes shaping an end dam where the threshold ends at the wall.

- Exterior wood doors, especially French doors, are often scheduled to be stained with a clear finish. The finish will not stand up to extended exposure to weather, particularly on west- and south-facing walls. If it is a must to employ this finish, then clear instructions must be delivered to the owner that it will require annual refinishing, or use of a marine-grade finish to last longer.

(See also "Common Window & Door Problems & Corrective Measures" following the introduction to this chapter.)

Introduction

This chapter begins by listing common window and door problems (with corrective measures). It goes on to provide specific standards for window and then door installations, including basic installation requirements, finishing, flashing, trim application, testing, quality certifications, and tolerances. Chapter 5, "Wood Framing," contains information on building code requirements for egress.

Successful window and door installations begin with appropriate selection of the type of window or door for the particular application. Not only climate, but specific performance requirements should be considered. A perfect installation of a quality window or door could still fail if inappropriate materials are chosen for the site conditions and/or building use.

Windows and doors are built in a controlled environment, and defects in manufacture of the basic unit are generally attributed to the manufacturer, not the installer. Check the specifics of the product warranty. Typical warranty exclusions are cracked or broken glass; damage caused by improper installation, use, or maintenance; damage caused by improper finish-painting; and labor charges for repairs or replacements. Think "green" when purchasing doors and windows. Review to see if the components are made from sustainable materials.

Flashing is a common complaint in construction defect litigation and we address the topic in the section following "Selecting Environmentally Friendly Windows & Doors" toward the beginning of this chapter. We explore the options available according to the latest technologies recommended by restoration specialists and include comments on the plant-on cure.

Please note that there are several excerpts from different authoritative sources on door installation. Because each of these source organizations may have a somewhat different focus, their coverage of this subject may occur in a different order, may give more, or less, attention to certain aspects of the door installation process, and may overlap. We recommend checking all of these source references for the most complete understanding of what is required and/or desirable.

When choosing an exterior door or window, the following should be considered in addition to the above listed issues:

1. The energy rating of the unit.

2. Depending on geographic location, resistance to wind or flying-object damage.

3. The use of recycled or sustainable materials.

The following organizations may be helpful in providing additional information on window and door installation requirements.

National Fenestration Rating Council (NFRC)
301-589-1776
www.nfrc.org
The National Fenestration Rating Council (NFRC) has developed a window energy rating system based on whole-product performance. This system is designed to accurately account for the energy-related effects of all the products' component parts.

Window & Door Manufacturers Association (WDMA)
847-299-5200
www.wdma.com

(continued)

Steel Door Institute (SDI)
440-899-0010
www.steeldoor.org

California Association of Window Manufacturers (CAWM)
Although CAWM was dissolved in 1998, many of the association's publications are distributed as a courtesy by the American Architectural Manufacturers Association (AAMA). For information or to inquire about CAWM/AAMA publications, contact:
Architectural Manufacturers Association (AAMA)
847-303-5664
www.aamanet.org

Energy Star®, U.S. Department of Energy
888-782-7937
www.energystar.gov
The U.S. Department of Energy has announced it is considering revisions to the Energy Star requirements for windows, doors, and skylights, including updating its climate zones to match more closely with the 2006 *International Energy Conservation Code*. As of this printing, these new requirements were still being developed.

Ed. Note: Comments and recommendations within this chapter are not intended as a definitive resource for construction activities. For building projects, contractors must rely on a copy of the project documents and local building codes.

Common Window & Door Problems & Corrective Measures

Door Problems

Comments

- Temperature and/or humidity changes or improper finishing of one of a door's six sides can cause the door to warp and stick or to appear uneven. The Window & Door Manufacturers Association (WDMA) allows $1/4$" warpage, measured from corner to diagonal corner. If the warp exceeds this amount, or the sides have not been finished correctly, the door may have to be refit.

- There are gaps around the exterior edges of the door, the threshold, and the door jamb. The door can be repaired or adjusted to acceptable parameters. Note: See the NAHB's *Residential Construction Performance Guidelines* for suggested specific tolerances.

- Unpainted wood is exposed at the edge of a door panel. This condition may occur when wood door panels shrink and expand in accordance with humidity and temperature changes. This is considered to be a normal condition, rather than a defect. The door may require refinishing.

- A door panel splits, showing light through the crack. Depending on the severity of the split, the panel may be repaired and refinished as necessary, or the door may have to be replaced.

- Sliding glass or screen doors do not slide smoothly. A true malfunction resulting from improper installation can be corrected by carefully adjusting the track. While the doors should function properly when the job is completed, the project owner must maintain the doors to ensure continued smooth operation. This involves keeping the track clean, free of debris, and protected from damage.

Window Problems

Comments

- The thermal seal in a double- or triple-paned window yields, resulting in clouding of glass. One possible cause may be intense heat on one side of the window, or heat buildup between the panes. Another reason for thermal break problems is deterioration of the

original window, especially caulking and sealant, over time. Improvements in these materials have reduced the incidence of these problems. Check the manufacturer's warranty for specific coverage. Many window manufacturers include air seal failures in their warranties and will replace either the glass or the glass within the sash, depending on the type of window.

- The window glass breaks as a result of stress forces. Stress may be placed on the window frame if it was not installed plumb and level, if it is touching a structural member, or if uneven settlement occurs. All are situations that should be avoided in the installation. To correct the problem, remove the trim to discover the source of the stress, eliminate the source of stress, and then replace the window. Depending on the number of lights of glass and the severity of the damage, the contractor will generally opt for the most economical solution. In the case of a thermal glazed window, generally only the sash is replaced. These components are easily obtained from the distributor. In the case of small, single-glazed or multiple-pane custom windows, it may be less expensive to reglaze a single light.

Note: The window frame and sash act as a unit and serve to support the functionality of the window itself; they should never be considered part of the structural system, nor are they a source of any structural support.

- The window binds as a result of insulation packed too tightly around it, between the window frame and the rough opening frame. This situation also causes problems in the installation of the interior trim. To correct the problem, remove the trim and reinstall the insulation properly; then re-trim the window.

- The flashing is improperly installed, resulting in leaks around the window. A general rule: Flashing should be installed to allow moisture and water to flow away from and over joints. Follow manufacturer's specific instructions. Note: See the "Flashing" section later in this chapter.

- There are scratches on the window glass. Manufacturers' warranties generally exclude "minor" scratches or other imperfections as long as this condition is not visible from a distance of several feet, and does not obscure "normal visibility" or compromise the window's structural integrity.

- The window leaks at the point of glazing. This is a defect in a new window, and is usually covered by the manufacturer's warranty. Window glazing, unless of vinyl or similar material, should be painted according to the manufacturer's specification. The paint should seal to the glass. Sometimes on a construction job, the paint is scraped off of a window pane too aggressively, breaking the seal between the glazing, sash, glass, and finish.

(continued)

309

• Moisture buildup has occurred in the wall due to clogged or plugged weepholes. Some window manufacturers depend on the use of weepholes to relieve the accumulation of moisture in areas inside the wall frame. The idea is that any moisture that penetrates this space is drained to the exterior of the building. If weepholes become clogged, problems may ensue. Occasionally, owners and contractors intentionally plug weepholes in a misguided attempt to prevent leakage of air and moisture, not realizing that they are creating a moisture problem. The problem is solved by unplugging the weepholes and educating owners and others about the way these components function.

General Information

Industry Standards

Construction Principles, Materials, and Methods
(John Wiley & Sons, Inc.)

8.1.5 The finest door and frame design and the highest quality of manufacture will not compensate for poor installation. Weathertightness, although simple to achieve, can be ensured only if installation is made by an experienced worker following the guidelines and instructions supplied by the manufacturer and the appropriate industry standards. A rough opening should be prepared to receive each unit in such a manner that it can be installed, and will finish out square, plumb, level, straight, and true. The design of most assemblies provides for minor adjustments at the job site, but no unit will operate or weather properly if it is twisted and misaligned during installation.

A properly selected and manufactured door and frame will be weather resistant as a unit. Other things must be done, however, to finish with a completely weather-tight installation. For example, if the construction is insulated, the space between the rough opening and the unit should be filled with insulation. In addition, the joints between units and adjacent materials must be closed with a sealant, trim members, or both, to prevent the passage of air, dust, and water around the frame.

Door frames are seldom designed to support loads other than themselves. Therefore, unless the frame is specially reinforced to support other loads, a separate lintel or other support is usually required.

Door frames should be supported around the entire perimeter and anchored securely to the supporting construction in a firm and rigid position. They should

also be flashed at their heads and sills to provide a path back to the exterior for water that finds its way into the wall.

Some metals, such as aluminum and stainless steel, are compatible and can be used in contact with each other. Other metals, however, react with one another chemically or electrolytically and should be insulated from direct contact with each other by waterproof, nonconductive materials, such as neoprene, waxed paper, or coated felt. Such dissimilar metals located where water passing over them may contact another surface should be painted to prevent staining. Refer to Section 5.4 for a discussion about the effect of dissimilar metal materials.

Concealed aluminum in contact with concrete, masonry, or an absorbent material, such as wood, paper, or insulation, should be protected by coating either the aluminum or the adjacent materials with a bituminous or aluminum paint, or by coating the aluminum with a zinc chromate primer, to minimize the chance of chemical corrosion of the aluminum by acids, alkalies, and salts leached out of the adjacent materials. Creosote and tar coatings, which may damage the aluminum, should not be used.

Sealants should be used in locations where frames adjoin other materials to make the joints there airtight and watertight.

Window Sash Materials

Green Home Improvement
(RSMeans)

The sash is the part of the window that the glass is attached to. There are four basic choices: wood, metal, vinyl, and fiberglass.

By far the most popular is the wood-frame window. Wood windows are attractive, relatively inexpensive, and insulate well. They're also made from a renewable, natural resource. (Some manufacturers make windows from certified lumber. Ask the dealer about this greener option.) The most durable wood windows come with an exterior aluminum cladding that protects the wood sash from sunlight and weather. (Wood windows with vinyl cladding are also available, but vinyl production poses risks to workers and residents who live near factories. Vinyl chloride used to make vinyl is a carcinogen. When released from manufacturing plants, it pollutes the air in neighboring communities. Vinyl windows may also contain plasticizers, chemicals that outgas—that is, pollute indoor air in the homes in which they're installed.)

Insulated vinyl windows are also becoming popular and may perform better than wood windows. Vinyl is a durable material and never needs painting. However, as noted, they're not environmentally friendly.

Aluminum windows are also popular, but are extremely inefficient if the sashes are not insulated. If you purchase an aluminum-frame window, be sure it's insulated and comes with a high-quality thermal break—an insulated spacer placed between the layers of glass. Thermal breaks reduce heat loss around the edges of windows and dramatically improve the efficiency of windows. (Aluminum is also not a green choice because it takes a lot of energy to make it.)

Another option is an insulated fiberglass window. Fiberglass is a durable material like vinyl. Unfortunately, the manufacture of fiberglass windows exposes workers to some fairly toxic chemicals. (Fiberglass windows probably pose very little hazard to homeowners and families once installed.)

Window & Door Components Defined

Industry Standards

Nail-On Windows

(DTA, Inc.)

Windows once installed are part of the exterior wall assembly and should resist leakage as much as the principal wall construction. The main components of the window assembly can be identified as the supporting frame, the wall sheathing, the flashing, the window, and the surrounding exterior cladding. Each of these interrelated components can be analyzed as complete assemblies themselves.

Wall Frame

The frame provides the structural support around the window/door opening. The frame often supports the wall, too.

The frame type can be further categorized by the material used to construct the wall, e.g., wood-frame; masonry (includes brick and concrete block); light-gauge steel (steel studs), steel (as in high-rise construction); poured concrete and other material or structural systems.

The window or door opening in the wall frame must be properly constructed for size and support. The manufacturers of aluminum windows and doors have standard frame-to-rough opening sizes. Many also provide custom sizes. They recommend sizes for the framed opening to be slightly larger in order to fit the

window. The framed opening is typically called the "rough opening." Often the rough opening is 1/2 inch larger all around than the overall window dimensions. This dimension may change from manufacturer to manufacturer.

This part of the wall framing must be built square, with each corner at 90 degrees. The top and bottom of the opening must be parallel and level. The sides or jambs must be plumb, both in the plane of the wall as well as perpendicular to the wall plane. The top of the window is spanned by framing called a header. The header must be structurally adequate to support the weight of building materials and any occupants on floors above, the same as with a "bearing" wall. The building code and structural engineering practice determines the size of the header for window and sliding glass door openings.

Problems in framing which can affect the performance of the window or flashing include:

- Undersized header which sags or deflects to distort the window flashings or tears flashing from fasteners.
- Wood shrinkage or warping can cause wood framing to get out of alignment from being square, plumb or level.
- Severe framing distortion can affect window operation, leak resistance and distress flashings and sealants.
- Mechanical damage to the framing, installed window, flashing or exterior cladding can unexpectedly occur any time during construction where portions of buildings can be subject to physical abuse. Protection from environmental abuse may also be lacking during construction where building elements which are partially completed may be exposed to rain, wind or prolonged sunlight effects.

Wall Sheathing

Wall sheathing is usually a rigid paneling applied on the outside of the wall frame. It may be omitted in some construction, where the wall system would be termed "open framing."

Wall sheathing is provided for the purposes of structural strength improvement to the wall frame, fire resistive protection and insulation or energy conservation value. The wall sheathing provides a stable and uniform plane to support the easily damaged building papers and flashings. Wall sheathing also provides support for the exterior wall cladding.

Window/Sliding Glass Door

Window and sliding glass doors are manufactured products completely assembled in the factory or partially assembled in the field.

The components manufactured in the factory can vary in quality due to the stoutness of the aluminum extrusion, the type of joint connection used for corners, the sealants or gaskets used and the quality of the glazing components.

Product integrity is affected by the packing and shipping means used between the factory and the site or between the factory and a distributor. Transportation can cause stress to assembled windows and doors. Distributors, contractors, or installers receiving a product may not always recognize transportation damage which could influence later performance.

On-site storage precautions and the location on the construction site provides another period of risk for damage to the window/door units before installation.

Rough handling can damage glazing units during the process of installation, especially if a single mechanic is trying to maneuver a heavy glazed unit. This is a likely period where the nail-on flange corner can get distorted from being used as a pivot while being hauled around a construction site.

Exterior Wall Cladding

The wall covering providing weather protection is the exterior cladding of a building. The wall finish materials in common use today for residential construction with wood frame buildings include stucco (cement plaster), plywood siding, wood lap siding, hardboard siding, as well as different stucco systems (e.g., EIFS—Exterior Insulation Finish Systems).

Each of these different materials needs to be either integrated with the penetrations through the wall cladding with a concealed weather barrier or exclude moisture with an effective surface barrier. The exterior cladding installation has to be integrated with and compliment the window/door flashings, as well as any vapor barrier system on the wall.

Ed. Note: See the AAMA/CAWM references under "Window Installation & Flashing" and "Door Installation & Flashing" for more information on protection from dissimilar materials.

Storm Exposure

The performance of windows and sliding glass doors depends in large part on weather exposure. Manufacturers fabricate products for different weather performances. There are categories for performance established by AAMA. The AAMA publication 101-9: *Voluntary Specifications for Aluminum and Poly (Vinyl Chloride) (PVC) Prime Windows and Glass Doors* provides a method for selecting a performance rating for water resistance based on the location in wind zones around the country and height of the window door above ground level. There are many areas of the country which experience wind speeds up to 70 and 80 mph in conjunction with rain. This should be considered in window selection.

The weather exposure of building openings is often an important contributing cause for leaks. Wind driven rain from the predominant local storm direction can result in openings facing the weather to demonstrate leakage. Precautions in the building design, product selection and methods of installation of window and door openings facing the storm exposure should be considered.

> ## Comments
>
> Select thermal requirements for windows based on climate. Also note that government agencies, such as DOE (Department of Energy) and HUD (Department of Housing and Urban Development) and institutions responsible for other publicly-funded projects, require certain thermal ratings for windows.

Selecting Environmentally Friendly Windows & Doors

Green Building, Project Planning & Cost Estimating, **Second Edition**
(RSMeans)

Windows

The goal when selecting windows is to specify a product that will provide the climatically appropriate insulating value, while also letting in a high percentage of visible light for daylighting, and providing the appropriate solar heat gain coefficient (SHGC). Due to advances in glazing, there are many options and manufacturers to choose from, and it is possible to "tune" the glazing carefully for the particular orientation and desired conditions.

Following are several key terms that apply to windows:

- Daylight Transmittance: The percentage of visible light a glazing transmits.

- Solar Heat Gain Coefficient (SHGC): The percentage of solar energy either directly transmitted or absorbed and re-radiated into the building. SHGC ranges from 0.0 to 1.0; the lower the number, the lower the solar heat gain. (Note: SHGC has replaced the older term SC. (Shading Coefficient), SHGC=0.87 × SC.)

- U-Value: Measures the heat loss or gain due to the differences between indoor and outdoor air temperatures (Btu/hr/SF). U=1/R; the lower the U-value, the better the insulating performance.

- R-Value: Measures the insulation effectiveness of the window (R=1/U); the higher the R-value, the better the insulating performance.

- Low-Emissivity (low-E) Coatings: Applied coatings that allow short-wave energy (visible light) to be transmitted through glass, but reflect long-wave infrared radiation (heat); the lower the emissivity, the lower the resultant U-value.

In the most extreme climates (very cold), the best windows provide low-emissivity, high visible transmittance, insulating gas fill (argon or krypton), good edge seals, insulated frames (with thermal breaks if frames are metal), and airtight construction. Some window manufacturers use low-E coatings applied not to the glass as with regular low-E windows, but to a suspended plastic film in between double panes of glass. Triple-pane windows are also an option, although weight and window depth may be a serious consideration.

Newer materials on the market include innovative gels or semiconductor coatings that can be applied to glazing layers to turn a window from clear to white or tinted when it is exposed to a certain heat (thermochromic) or sunlight (photochromic) threshold or to an electric voltage (electrochromic). These could be used in skylights to provide full daylighting on cloudy days, while avoiding glare and overheating on hot sunny days. (In their light-blocking white form, they still transmit 10% of incident solar energy—potentially enough for glare-free daylighting.) Another innovative product that could become revolutionary for window technology is a silica gel, which allows over 70% visible light transmission but blocks heat transfer. (Its R-value is three to four times that of common insulation products such as rigid foam and fiberglass.)

Ordinary glass has a visible transmittance similar to its solar heat gain coefficient. Selective glass has a semiconductor coating to absorb the ultraviolet in infrared portions of the solar spectrum, but allow the visible portion to pass through, resulting in a visible transmittance of 0.70. They have a solar heat gain coefficient of only 0.37. Selective glass would be specified where the designer wants to maintain a clear appearance, but reduce solar heat gain.

Frames are available in wood (clad or unclad), metal (which need to be thermally-broken to prevent conduction through the frame), fiberglass, and vinyl. Although vinyl is a low-maintenance option, it is made from PVC, making it a less environmentally healthy option than other types of window frames.

As with many products, it is worthwhile to ask window manufacturers whether their products contain recycled materials. Even if the manufacturer does not use recycled content, knowing that customers are requesting it helps move the marketplace in this direction.

Doors

Glass (or partially glazed) doors should be designed with all the same considerations as windows. In addition, door frames should be carefully detailed, with door sweeps and weatherproofing, to prevent air infiltration. Non-glazed doors should also be insulated, preferably with non-ozone depleting EPS. In cold climates, storm doors and airlock entryways can save considerable energy.

Ed. Note: See also "Glazing Properties" and "Green Window & Entryway Strategies" at the end of this chapter.

Flashing

Comments

Most wood windows come with factory-installed flashing, metal flange, or flashing components. The jambs should have a membrane between a brick mold or stucco mold and the window jambs and should overlap the building wrap a minimum of 6". The top of the wood window should have a Z-Metal drip head flashing that extends beyond the jamb a minimum of 2" on either side.

Industry Standards

Nail-On Windows
(DTA, Inc.)

Flashing Materials

Flashing is a separate sheet of waterproof or water-resistant material used to cover or lap the edges of a window or door frame installed in a rough opening of the wall frame.

Flashing materials range from sheet metal, building paper, building felt, specialty flashing papers with asphalt cores, and recently developed self-adhering membrane flashings.

Most window leaks (which we have investigated) are attributable to a lack of flashing, poor flashing, or deteriorated flashing. The window product is often not the source of leaks observed around windows. Flashing is necessary to integrate the weather-resistant qualities of the window product with the weather-resistant functions of the exterior cladding system.

Flashings are typically concealed by the finished construction and are not intended as the primary source of water resistance around windows. However, flashings often become the only source of protection when the primary weather barrier fails. The primary weather barrier should be the exterior cladding system selected for the wall covering. The exterior surface of the wall cladding will keep out most of the water which falls against it. In time, flashings will fail if the exterior cladding system does not properly exclude most of the water from the weather-exposed cracks, crevices, joints and penetrations in the building.

Conditions Affecting Successful Flashing Assemblies

1. A solid, framed opening in which to be installed
2. Protection from physical abuse
   a. During construction
   b. During its useful life
3. Protection from environmental abuse
   a. During construction
   b. During its useful life
4. Correct sequencing of the materials
5. Correct method of attachment
6. Compatible flashing and wall cladding materials
7. Durable materials. Materials that will provide the assembly with the "expected life of that particular assembly."

Window Installation & Flashing

Comments

While the following text from AAMA/CAWM addresses aluminum windows, the basic installation requirements are the same for wood, vinyl, vinyl-clad, metal, and metal-clad windows. The installation method shown in **Figure 9.1** would include a requirement to caulk the side and top flashings to the nailing flange with butyl caulking. The building paper is then interwoven under the bottom sisalkraft flashing and over the upper flashing. The bottom tails of the sisalkraft are not caulked until the wrap is installed.

Industry Standards

Standard Practices for Installation of Windows AAMA 2400-02 (Formerly CAWM 400-95)
(American Architectural Manufacturers Association)

5. Procedure

5.1 Framing Requirements

The rough framed opening to receive the window shall be sufficiently larger in width and height than the actual frame dimensions of the window. To assure adequate clearance, the framer shall follow the manufacturer's literature for the recommended rough opening dimensions. The framing shall be plumb, square, level, and structurally adequate.

5.2 Corrosion Resistance

5.2.1 Metal products shall be isolated from dissimilar or corrosive materials with a nonconductive coating or sealant material.

5.2.2 All fasteners shall be corrosive resistant, in accordance with ASTM B 633, B 766, or B 456.

5.3 Flashing Requirements

Proper flashing and/or sealing is necessary as a barrier to prevent water from infiltrating into the building. Flashing and/or an appropriate method of sealing shall be designed as a part of an overall weather resistant barrier system. It is not the responsibility of the window manufacturer to design or recommend a flashing system appropriate to each job condition.

Note 1: The responsibility for protecting any flashing material from damage caused by weather, other trades, or vandalism, and properly integrating the flashing system into the weather resistant barrier for the entire building, is the responsibility of the general contractor or his designated agent.

5.3.1 Penetration Flashing Material—Flashing material shall be barrier coated reinforced and shall provide twenty four (24) hour minimum protection from water penetration when tested in accordance with ASTM D779. Flashing material shall carry continuous identification.

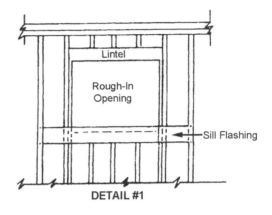

DETAIL #1

Comments

The American Architectural Manufacturers Association (AAMA) and the California Association of Window Manufacturers (CAWM) have established two acceptable methods for installing windows with an integral mounting flange. Method A puts the vertical flashing material over the flange on the vertical window jamb, while Method B places the flashing material under the flange of the vertical window jamb. It is imperative that the caulking be installed as described so that the building wrap can be properly lapped. (See **Figure 9.1**.)

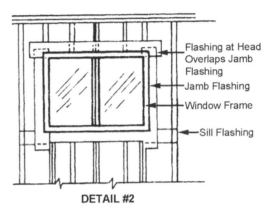

DETAIL #2

5.5 Application

5.5.1 One of the two following methods shall be selected as the application to be followed. Once a method is selected, all procedures of that method shall be performed in the described sequence. Substitution of a procedure from one method to the other is not permitted.

Method A

5.5.3.1 A strip of approved flashing material shall be at least 230 mm (9 in) wide. Flashing shall be applied in a weatherboard fashion around the full perimeter of the opening according to the following procedures:

5.5.3.2 Apply the first strip horizontally immediately below the sill, cut it sufficiently long to extend past each side of the window, so that it projects even with the vertical jamb flashing to be applied later.

5.5.3.3 Fasten the top edge of the sill flashing to the framing. Place fasteners along the edge of the rough opening where they will be covered by the mounting flange of the window later. Fasten the top edge of the sill flashing, but do not fasten the lower edge or the last 230 mm (9 in) of each end, so the weather resistant barrier applied later may be slipped up and underneath the flashing in a weatherboard fashion.

5.5.3.4 For mechanically joined frames, apply sealant at corners, the full length of the seam, where mounting flanges meet, and to the outside of the frame corner joints. Apply a continuous seal to the backside (interior) of the window mounting flange. The window shall then be installed in accordance with Section 5.6 installation procedures.

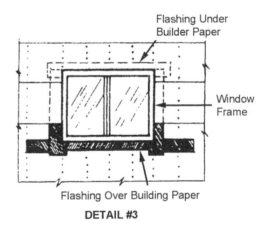

DETAIL #3

Figure 9.1   Courtesy of Western Wall and Ceiling Contractors Association, *Plaster and Drywall Systems Manual*

5.5.3.5 Next, apply a continuous seal to the exposed mounting flange at the top (head) and sides (jambs) of the installed window. Apply sealant in line with any pre-punched holes or slots on the mounting flange and over the heads of the fasteners. Continue jamb sealant vertically approximately 215 mm (8½ in) above the top of the window. The sealant applied horizontally across the head should not extend beyond the jamb sealant.

Note 2: The application of sealant to the exterior surface of the mounting flange may not be necessary if using a self-adhesive type flashing over the mounting flange. Consult the flashing manufacturer.

5.5.3.6 Starting at each jamb, embed the jamb flashing into the seal and fasten in place. Do not fasten the bottom 230 mm (9 in) of the jamb flashing, so the weather resistant barrier applied later may be slipped up and underneath the flashing in a weatherboard fashion. Extend this flashing to approximately 13 mm (½ in) less than the bottom of the sill flashing and beyond the top of the window to approximately 13 mm (½ in) less than the top of the head flashing.

5.5.3.7 Finally, embed the flashing into the sealant on the mounting flange at the window head. Cut this flashing sufficiently long so that it will extend approximately 25 mm (1 in) beyond the jamb flashing.

Comments

Figure 9.2 shows recommended flashing for window installation in wood siding. This description parallels the recommendations of the *Plaster and Drywall Systems Manual* and the California Association of Window Manufacturers (CAWM) on plaster walls, including setting the window frame in mastic against the sisalkraft. Manufacturers may specify different methods for various exterior skins.

Method B

5.5.4.1 A strip of approved flashing material shall be at least 230 mm (9 in) wide. Flashing shall be applied in a weatherboard fashion around the full perimeter of the opening according to the following procedures:

5.5.4.2 Apply the first strip horizontally immediately below the sill, cut it sufficiently long to extend past each side of the window, so that it projects even with the vertical jamb flashing to be applied later.

5.5.4.3 Fasten the top edge of the sill flashing to the framing. Place fasteners along the edge of the rough opening where they will be covered by the mounting flange of the window later. Fasten the top edge of the sill flashing, but do not fasten the lower edge or the last 230 mm (9 in) of each end, so the weather resistant barrier applied later may be slipped up and underneath the flashing in a weatherboard fashion.

5.5.4.4 Next, fasten strips of flashing along each vertical edge (jamb) of the opening. Position fasteners along the edge of the rough opening where they will be covered by the mounting flange of the window later. Extend this flashing to approximately 13 mm (½ in) less than the bottom of the sill flashing and beyond the top of the window to approximately 13 mm (½ in) less than the top of the head flashing. Do not fasten the bottom 230 mm (9 in) of the jamb flashing, so the weather resistant barrier applied later may be slipped up and underneath the flashing in a weatherboard fashion.

5.5.4.5 Apply a continuous seal to the backside (interior) of the mounting flange near the outer edge or a continuous seal to the perimeter of the opening at a point to assure contact with the backside (interior) of the mounting flange. Apply sealant in line with any prepunched holes or slots on the mounting flanges.

Note 3: Caution shall be taken to avoid disrupting the continuous seal.

5.5.4.6 For mechanically joined frames, apply sealant at corners the full length of the seam where mounting flanges meet and the outside of the frame corner joints.

5.5.4.7 The window shall be installed in accordance with Section 5.6 installation procedures.

5.5.4.8 Next, apply a continuous seal to the exterior face of the mounting flange at the window head in line with any prepunched holes or slots on the mounting flange and over the heads of the fasteners. Cut the head flashing sufficiently long so that it will extend approximately 25 mm (1 in) beyond each jamb flashing. Embed the bottom of the flashing over the sealant and the mounting flange and fasten in place.

Comments

Shims should be placed at equal distance opposite one another, top and bottom, and side to side.

Window Flashing

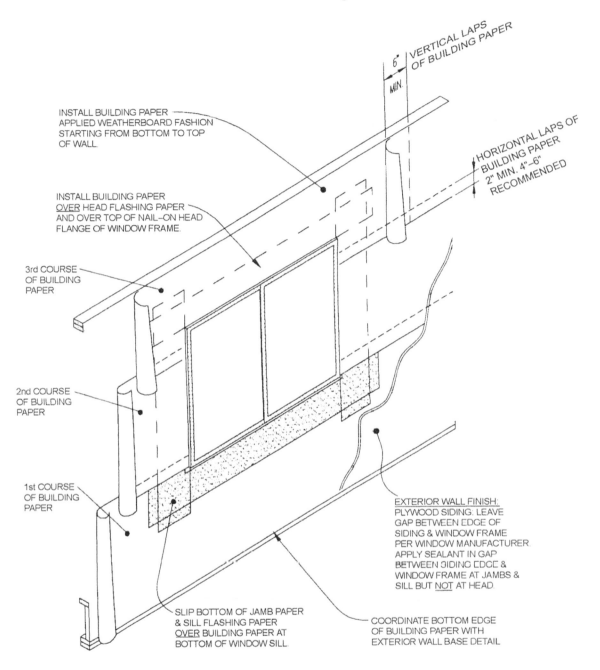

INSTALL BUILDING PAPER APPLIED WEATHERBOARD FASHION STARTING FROM BOTTOM TO TOP OF WALL.

INSTALL BUILDING PAPER OVER HEAD FLASHING PAPER AND OVER TOP OF NAIL-ON HEAD FLANGE OF WINDOW FRAME.

3rd COURSE OF BUILDING PAPER

2nd COURSE OF BUILDING PAPER

1st COURSE OF BUILDING PAPER

6" MIN. VERTICAL LAPS OF BUILDING PAPER

HORIZONTAL LAPS OF BUILDING PAPER 2" MIN. 4"-6" RECOMMENDED

EXTERIOR WALL FINISH: PLYWOOD SIDING: LEAVE GAP BETWEEN EDGE OF SIDING & WINDOW FRAME PER WINDOW MANUFACTURER. APPLY SEALANT IN GAP BETWEEN SIDING EDGE & WINDOW FRAME AT JAMBS & SILL BUT NOT AT HEAD.

SLIP BOTTOM OF JAMB PAPER & SILL FLASHING PAPER OVER BUILDING PAPER AT BOTTOM OF WINDOW SILL.

COORDINATE BOTTOM EDGE OF BUILDING PAPER WITH EXTERIOR WALL BASE DETAIL

NOTE: ATTEMPT TO KEEP FASTENER FOR TRIM & SIDING AWAY FROM WINDOW. FIN AS MUCH AS POSSIBLE, ESPECIALLY NEAR CORNERS. THE NAILS WHICH PENETRATE THE FIN CAN DISTORT THE FRAME'S CORNER JOINT SEAL.

Figure 9.2

Courtesy of DTA, Inc., *Nail-On Windows*

Aluminum Window with Wood Plant-On

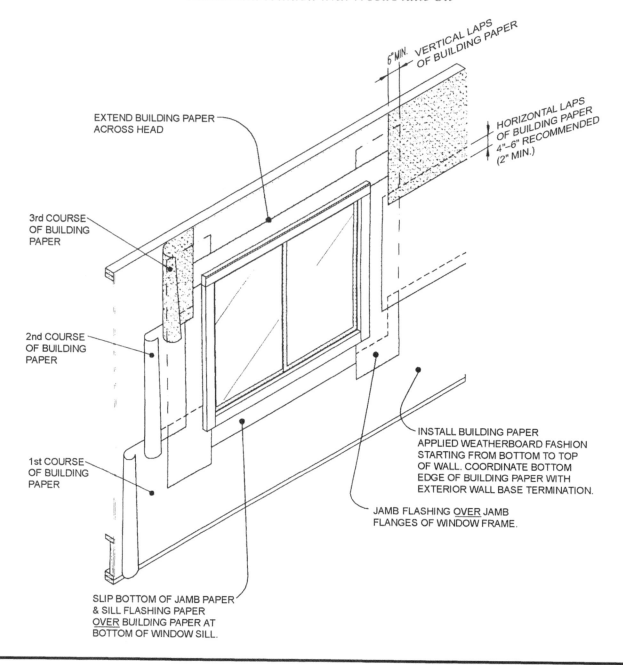

EXTEND BUILDING PAPER
ACROSS HEAD

3rd COURSE
OF BUILDING
PAPER

2nd COURSE
OF BUILDING
PAPER

1st COURSE
OF BUILDING
PAPER

SLIP BOTTOM OF JAMB PAPER
& SILL FLASHING PAPER
<u>OVER</u> BUILDING PAPER AT
BOTTOM OF WINDOW SILL.

6" MIN. VERTICAL LAPS
OF BUILDING PAPER

HORIZONTAL LAPS
OF BUILDING PAPER
4"–6" RECOMMENDED
(2" MIN.)

INSTALL BUILDING PAPER
APPLIED WEATHERBOARD FASHION
STARTING FROM BOTTOM TO TOP
OF WALL. COORDINATE BOTTOM
EDGE OF BUILDING PAPER WITH
EXTERIOR WALL BASE TERMINATION.

JAMB FLASHING <u>OVER</u> JAMB
FLANGES OF WINDOW FRAME.

Figure 9.3   Courtesy of DTA, Inc., *Nail-On Windows*

Installation Requirements

5.6 Installation

5.6.1 Shim window as necessary to insure [sic] a square, level and plumb installation. The sill must be supported in a straight and level position to prevent sagging, deflection and sill rotation.

Some manufacturers require a continuous shim under the window sill. Follow manufacturer's recommendations.

5.6.2 Close and lock the window. Shim and adjust the window as necessary to achieve a plumb, square and level condition, as well as centering the window in the frame opening. Secure the full perimeter with the minimum equivalent of 6d fasteners on a maximum of 405 mm (16 in) centers using pre-punched holes, if provided. Hinged and pivoted windows may require additional fasteners located near the hinge or pivot point. For certain windows it may be appropriate to fasten the head in a manner to allow for possible movement. In all cases follow the manufacturer's instructions for any special procedures or applications.

Comments

While these listed installation requirements apply to most windows, every manufacturer has its own specific instructions, which may include unique details essential to successful product performance.

Note 4: Avoid overdriving fasteners. Use an appropriately sized fastener to cover the width of any pre-punched hole and adequately secure the window to the structure.

5.6.3 In each direction from all corners there shall be a fastener within 250 mm (10 in) but no closer than 75 mm (3 in) to prevent frame distortion or fracture of joint seals. Note: If any damage to window frame joint seals or mounting flanges is observed during installation, the installer shall repair it or consult the manufacturer.

5.6.4 The Owner/General Contractor is responsible to ensure that the weather resistant barrier (i.e., building paper, insulating board, or other materials by other trades) is effectively integrated around the window frame in a weatherboard fashion.

5.6.5 After installation is complete, check the window for proper operation and locking.

Plant-On Trim

Comments

The following drawing recommends placement of the plant-on trim over the standard wrap. Use treated lumber for the plant-on, because exposure to moisture will cause the wood to swell. The plant-on should be made of foam or lightweight plaster that will not increase dimensionally from water absorption.

Also note the sheet metal flashing over the top of the wood plant-on header.

Radius windows with integral flange should use small pieces of paper-reinforced flashing that have been folded and set in sealant to "step flash" the radius to a keystone center piece at the top.

While the sisalkraft can perform well when it is properly installed, a self-sticking bitumen flashing is far superior to the reinforced paper products.

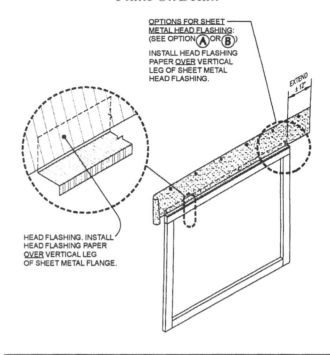

Plant-On Detail

OPTIONS FOR SHEET METAL HEAD FLASHING: (SEE OPTION (A) OR (B))

INSTALL HEAD FLASHING PAPER OVER VERTICAL LEG OF SHEET METAL HEAD FLASHING.

EXTEND ± 1/2"

HEAD FLASHING. INSTALL HEAD FLASHING PAPER OVER VERTICAL LEG OF SHEET METAL FLANGE.

Figure 9.4   Courtesy of DTA, Inc., *Nail-On Windows*

Finish & Sealant Protection

Industry Standards

Standard Practice for Installation of Windows (AAMA 2400-02)
(American Architectural Manufacturers Association-AAMA)

4.5 Finish and Sealant Protection
4.5.1 Caution shall be used to avoid damage to windows during and after installation. Prior to installation, store windows in a near vertical position in a clean area, free of circulating dirt or debris and protected from exposure to weather elements.

4.5.2 Field-applied protective coatings may damage window sealants and gaskets and may not be recommended. Contact the window manufacturer before applying any such coatings.

5.4 Sealant Requirements
5.4.1 Sealing/caulking required between the window and the flashing can be accomplished with sealant material conforming to AAMA 800. Use sealant recommended and approved by the sealant/flashing manufacturer, following their printed application procedures. ASTM E 2112 gives guidance on sealant selection and application.

5.4.2 Where sealant is required in this standard, an application of a nominal 10 mm (⅜in) diameter sealant bead or an equivalent butyl mastic sealant tape as recommended by the sealant manufacturer is intended.

Window Efficiencies

Green Building: Project Planning & Cost Estimating, Second Edition
(RSMeans)

Advances in window technology have revolutionized passive solar heating design. Excessive heat loss from large window areas used to limit the application of passive solar heating to moderate climates. The well-insulated glass assemblies available today allow large windows even in very cold climates and high elevations, albeit at higher cost.

The designer may now select glass with a wide range of optical and thermal properties. The heat loss from a glazing assembly is described by the loss coefficient, or U-value in units of (W/m2/C or Btu/SF/hour/F). The lower the U-value of a window, the less heat loss. Manufacturers construct windows with multiple layers of glass separated by gaps of air or other low-conductivity gas to reduce convective heat loss, and apply a low-emissivity (low-E) coating to reduce radiative heat loss. The U-value of a window ranges from 1.23 for single-pane with metal frame to as low as 0.24 for triple-pane with low-E coating and gas fill. Standard double-pane glass has a U-value between 0.73 and 0.49, depending on the type of frame. A low U-value is of benefit in both warm and cold climates.

Other properties to consider include the Solar Heat Gain Coefficient (SHGC), and the visible transmittance. The SHGC is the fraction of solar heat that is transmitted directly through the glass, plus the fraction absorbed in the glazing and eventually convected to the room air. SHGC varies from 0.84 for single-pane clear glass to as low as zero for insulated opaque spandrel glass. Standard double-pane clear glass has an SHGC of 0.7. A high SHGC is of benefit on the south side to admit solar heat in winter, but on east and west sides, or in warm climates, a low SHGC is best. The visible transmittance of glass is an important consideration for daylighting goals. New developments in glass technology include photochromic (changes with light level), thermochromic (changes with temperature) and electrochromic (changes with application of an electric voltage). These new glass products will offer a versatile palette to the designer when commercially available.

Vertical south-facing windows are recommended over sloped or horizontal glazing for passive solar buildings in the northern hemisphere. Sloped glazing provides more heat in the cool spring, but this benefit is negated by excessive heat gain in the warm autumn and also the additional maintenance caused by dirt accumulation and leaks. Overhangs admit the low winter sun while blocking the high summer sun, but since the ambient temperature lags behind the sun's position in the sky (cool on the spring equinox, warm on the autumnal equinox), there is no single fixed window overhang geometry that is perfect for all seasons. Therefore movable external awnings, plant trellises (which are usually fuller in autumn than in spring), or internal measures, such as drapes and blinds are often used to improve comfort.

Daylighting

Green Building: Project Planning & Cost Estimating, Second Edition
(RSMeans)

Windows are most effective for providing natural light when they introduce daylight very high into a space. Variations on windows include clerestory and roof-monitors, which are vertical windows installed in articulations in the roofline. The effectiveness of windows as daylighting apertures also depends on their orientation.

North-facing windows are good sources of daylight. The sun hits north windows only in the early morning or late evening, and then only at a very oblique angle. The diffuse, indirect sunlight coming from the north prevents the glare and heat gain of other orientations, and no overhangs, shades, or special glazing treatments are required.

South-facing windows require shades to control direct solar gain in the winter, when the sun is low in the sky. South-facing windows receive maximum sun at midday in winter, and are essential components of a passive solar heating strategy. In summer, overhangs over south-facing windows are effective at blocking direct solar gain. Specific overhang geometry is calculated using the sun angle equations.

East-facing windows receive maximum sun and very low sun angles on summer mornings. West-facing windows receive maximum sun on summer afternoons. In general, low sun angles are a source of glare and unwanted heat gain, and east- and west-facing windows would be minimized depending on the views and other program requirements. However, in some climates, such as the high desert, some heat gain in the morning mitigates the night chill, and may be acceptable.

Views can often be framed in small windows to avoid the problems that large windows or floor-to-ceiling glass would create on east or west faces. Where east or west windows are required, the most elegant way to reject the solar heat is with a highly reflective glass. Occupants would also use shades and drapes to achieve comfort.

Light shelves are used to bounce light off the ceiling, project light deeper into the space, distribute it from above, and diffuse it to produce a uniform light level below. The upper surface of the light shelf would have a high reflectivity, and may be specular (like a mirror). The ceiling in the space would also have a high reflectivity, but would be diffuse (like flat, white paint).

The sun is at its maximum on a roof during midday in summer. As a result, skylights were previously discouraged as sources of unwanted heat gain. However, new developments in glazing and shading designs have made it possible to use skylights to provide daylight above core zones in single-story buildings, or on the top floor of multi-story buildings.

Advanced solar luminaires use reflectors to increase light level and mitigate the glare and heat gain of horizontal skylights.

Getting daylight into the core of large buildings has proved challenging. Light pipes are lined with highly reflective film to reflect light down the length of the pipe from a roof aperture to a room fixture. Light pipes are becoming popular in residential construction, and have found application in industrial facilities as well. Due to the relatively small size of each pipe, they seem to be best suited for small spaces like bathrooms or hallways.

Doors: General Information

Comments

Storage & Handling of Doors

Doors should not be delivered to the site until concrete foundations and floors and plaster walls are fully dry. Doors should not be subjected to moisture, excessive

heat, or dryness (or direct sunlight). Some manufacturers indicate that if doors are stored on the site longer than five days, all surfaces should be sealed with a resin or pigmented base sealer.

Doors should be stored flat in a dry, clean, and well-ventilated indoor environment. They should be handled only by clean or clean-gloved hands.

Different types of doors, such as fire doors or decorative, may have special handling and storage requirements. Consult the manufacturer's instructions.

Grading

Industry Standards

WIC Manual of Millwork (Effective 5/1/01)
(Woodwork Institute of California, www.wicnet.org)

The following are the grades established for architectural millwork products. This referenced standards listing is not necessarily complete.

Economy

This grade establishes a standard to meet the requirements of lower cost residential and commercial construction wherein economy is the principal factor, and use in storage room and utility areas.

Custom

This grade includes all the requisites of high quality millwork and is suitable for all normal uses in high grade construction, such as higher quality residential, school, and commercial building.

Premium

This grade, as the name implies, is a superior quality of materials and craftsmanship, with a corresponding increase in cost. It is intended primarily for the best of hardwood construction, but any species of wood may be specified.

Types of Doors

Industry Standards

Fundamentals of the Construction Process
(RSMeans)

Wood Doors

Wood doors are available in two basic designs: flush and panel. Flush wood doors have two smooth faces and are manufactured as hollow core, particleboard core, or solid core. Flush facings are single sheets of lauan mahogany, birch, other hardwood veneers, or synthetic veneers created from a medium density overlay and high-pressure plastic laminate. These veneers require only a clear finish. The core materials used for flush doors depend, to a certain extent, on the quality of the interior finishes and the soundproofing provided by the denser cores. The design is the most common, having a universal appeal to commercial as well as residential owners.

Paneled-wood doors are manufactured from pine or fir. This type of door typically has a solid wood stile (vertical-edge member) and rail (cross-membrane), and one-, two-, five-, six-, or eight-panel design. Simulated six-panel doors with hollow cores and molded hardboard facings are also available. These doors are painted.

Hollow Metal Doors

The most common hollow metal (steel) doors are flush design, but residential doors are available in several decorative patterns that are embossed into or applied onto the face sheets. Metal doors can be galvanized and primed, or factory-finished with enamel in a variety of colors.

There are several grades of hardware: light duty or residential, standard duty, and heavy duty. For hinges, this is expressed in terms of usage: low, average, and high frequencies.

Most general contractors order doors, frames, and hardware from various suppliers or manufacturers and then install them with their own carpenters. The door frame schedule and supplier must be closely coordinated with the hardware schedule and supplier. For example, templates are transmitted to hollow metal suppliers immediately following approval of the door schedule. In this case, time can be a critical factor; custom hollow metal frames, doors, and hardware are long lead items.

Ed. Note: See also "Metal Doors" later in this chapter.

Door Installation

Industry Standards

Specifiers Guide to Wood Windows and Doors
(Window & Door Manufacturers Association)

The utility or structural strength of the doors must not be impaired in fitting to the opening, in applying hardware, in preparing for lights, louvers, plant-ons or other detailing.

Use two hinges for solid core doors up to 60" in height, three hinges for doors up to 90" in height and an additional hinge for every additional 30" of door height or portion thereof. Interior hollow-core doors weighing less than 50 pounds and not over 7'6" in height may be hung on two hinges. Use heavy weight hinges on doors over 175 pounds. Consult manufacturer with regard to weight and site of hinges required.

Clearances between door edges and door frame should be a minimum of $1/16$" on the hinge edge. For latch edge and top rail the clearance should be $1/8$" (+0, –$1/16$").

All hardware locations, preparations for hardware and methods of hardware attachment must be appropriate for the specific door construction. Templates for specific hardware preparation are available from hardware manufacturers or their distributors.

Comments

Hollow Core Door

If hardware is specified that is not commonly used with hollow core doors, it is possible to have inserts or stiffeners inserted during the manufacturing process that will compensate for any unusual loads or stresses that may be imposed by the hardware application.

When light or louver cutouts are made for exterior doors, they must be protected in order to prevent water from entering the door core. Metal flashing at the bottom of the cutout is one satisfactory method.

Pilot holes must be drilled for all screws that act as hardware attachments. Threaded-to-the-head screws are preferable for fastening hardware to nonrated doors and are required on fire rated doors.

In fitting for height, do not trim top or bottom edge by more than $3/4$" unless accommodated by additional blocking. Do not trim top edge of fire doors.

Doors and door frames should be installed plumb, square and level. When installed in exterior applications, doors must be properly sealed and adequately protected from the elements. Flashing should be applied at the head, jambs and sill.

Cleaning and Touchup

Inspect all wood doors prior to hanging them on the job. Repair noticeable marks or defects that may have occurred from improper storage and handling.

Field touchup shall include the filling of exposed nail or screw holes, refinishing of raw surfaces resulting from job fitting, repair of job inflicted scratches and mars, and final cleaning of finished surfaces. Field repairs and touchups are the responsibility of the installing contractor.

When cleaning door surfaces, use a nonabrasive commercial cleaner designed for cleaning wood door or paneling surfaces, that do not leave a film residue that would buildup or effect [sic] the surface gloss of the door finish.

Adjustment and Maintenance

Inspect all wood doors prior to hanging them on the job. Repair noticeable marks or defects that may have occurred from improper storage and handling.

Review with the owner/owner's representative how to periodically inspect all doors for wear, damage and natural deterioration.

Review with the owner/owner's representative how to periodically inspect and adjust all hardware to ensure that it continues to function as it was originally intended.

Wood & Plastic Laminate Doors

Industry Standards

WIC Manual of Millwork (Effective 5/1/01)

(Woodwork Institute of California, www.wicnet.org)

Ed. Note: This referenced standards listing is not necessarily complete.

Install with a maximum clearance of $\frac{1}{8}$" on the hinge side, $\frac{1}{8}$" on the lock side, $\frac{1}{8}$" between the meeting edge of doors in pairs, and $\frac{1}{8}$" between the top of the door and the frame header. The installer is not responsible for clearances in excess of these dimensions if the door supplier has erred on the prefit widths or locations for mortise hardware. Clearance at the bottom of the door will be as specified by Architect/Designer on nonrated doors and conform to NFPA 80 on fire-rated doors. Prefit and premachined doors are to be installed in accordance with manufacturers' data. Notify the contractor or owner if there is a problem before proceeding.

If not premachined, use a minimum of one hinge for each 30 inches of door height on all exterior doors and all solid core doors.

When using three or more hinges, they are to be equally spaced. Interior hollow core doors weighing less than fifty pounds and not over 7'-6" in height may be hung on two hinges.

All screws must be applied into each piece of hardware.

Comments

Framers should be made aware of any special requirements for anchoring door frames to the structure prior to laying out walls. This includes the "holding" requirements of fasteners.

Doors may not extend beyond $\frac{1}{16}$" from the face of the jamb, nor more than $\frac{1}{8}$" behind the jamb face.

Wood doors that are part of a matched paneled area must be installed by the paneling installer.

The utility or structural strength of the doors must not be impaired in fitting to the opening, in applying hardware, in preparing for lights, louvers, or plant-ons or other detailing.

All hardware locations, preparation for hardware, and methods of hardware attachment must be appropriate for the specific door construction. Templates for specific hardware preparation are available from hardware manufacturers, WDMA, or DHI.

When light or louver cutouts are made for exterior doors, they must be protected in order to prevent water from entering the door core. Metal flashing at the bottom of the cutout is one satisfactory method.

Wood doors seldom need to be replaced due to warp. Temporary distortions will usually disappear when humidity is equalized.

Extreme care must be used to prevent chipping veneer when cutting length.

The best manufactured door still requires skilled workmanship and proper care at the job site.

Installation of Doors & Jambs

The installation standard of doors and jambs shall be equal to the Premium or Custom Quality Standard of the manufactured doors and jambs being used.

Doors

In the fitting for width, trim equally from both sides. In order to preserve the label on fire-rated doors, trim per manufacturers' requirements.

If fitting for height, do not trim top or bottom rails more than $\frac{1}{4}$". Fire-rated doors shall be trimmed only from the bottom rails and shall be trimmed no more than $\frac{3}{4}$".

Threaded-to-the-head wood screws are preferable for fastening all hardware on non-rated doors and required on all rated doors. Pilot holes must be drilled for all screws.

Do not remove labels from fire-rated doors.

Door Jambs

Jambs must be set plumb.

Jambs legs must be set square with header and parallel to each other within $\frac{1}{16}$" on Premium, $\frac{1}{8}$" on Custom, $\frac{3}{16}$" on Economy.

Jambs must be securely seated directly onto floor.

Jambs must be securely anchored with concealed fasteners for Premium Grade.

Cleaning

Upon completion of the installation, the installer shall clean all items installed; pencil or ink marks shall be removed, and broom clean the area of operations, depositing his debris in containers provided by the general contractor.

Wood Doors

Industry Standards

Specifiers Guide to Wood Windows and Doors
(Window & Door Manufacturers Association)

Ed. Note: WDMA I.S.1-A is a general industry standard that provides quality levels for the construction of architectural wood flush doors.

Exterior Use

In exterior use, temperature and humidity are not controlled on both sides of the door. Care must be taken when specifying architectural wood flush doors in exterior openings. Consult individual manufacturers for specific recommendations and warranty limitations.

Wood Door Finishing

Job Site Finishing

Because of the many uncontrollable variables that exist at a site, such as temperature and moisture variation, dust and other factors, door manufacturers' warranties do not cover the appearance of finishes applied at the job site.

Finishing

Wood is hygroscopic and dimensionally influenced by changes in moisture content caused by changes within its surrounding environment. To assure uniform moisture exposure and dimensional control, all surfaces must be finished equally.

Doors may not be ready for finishing when initially received. Before finishing, remove all handling marks, raised grain, scuffs, burnishes and other undesirable blemishes by block sanding all surfaces in a horizontal position with a 120, 150 or 180 grit sandpaper. To avoid cross grain scratches, sand with the grain.

Certain species of wood, particularly oak, contain chemicals which react unfavorably with foreign materials in the finishing system. Eliminate the use of steel wool on bare wood, rusty containers or any other contaminate in the finishing system.

A thinned coat of sanding sealer should be applied prior to staining to promote a uniform appearance and avoid sharp contrasts in color or a blotchy appearance.

All exposed wood surfaces must be sealed including top and bottom rails. Cutouts for hardware in exterior doors must be sealed prior to installation of hardware and exposure to weather. Dark-colored finishes should be avoided on all surfaces if the door is exposed to direct sunlight, in order to reduce the chance of warping or veneer checking. Oil-based sealers or prime coats provide the best base coat for finishing. If a water-based primer is used it should be an exterior grade product. Note: Water-based coatings on unfinished wood may cause veneer splits, highlight joints and raise wood grain and therefore should be avoided. If a water-based primer is desired, please contact the finish supplier regarding the correct application and use of these products.

Be sure the door surface being finished is satisfactory in both smoothness and color after each coat. Allow adequate drying time between coats. Desired results are best achieved by following the finish manufactures' recommendations. Do not finish door until a sample of the finish has been approved. Finishes on exterior doors may deteriorate due to exposure to the environment. In order to protect the door, it is recommended that the condition of the exterior finish be inspected at least once a year and re-finished as needed.

Note: Certain wood fire doors have fire retardant salts impregnated into various wood components that makes the components more hygroscopic than normal wood. When exposed to high moisture conditions, these salts will concentrate on exposed surfaces and interfere with the finish. Before finishing, reduce moisture content in the treated wood below 11% and remove the salt crystals with a damp cloth followed by drying and light sanding. For further information on fire doors see WDMA publications regarding installing, handling, and finishing fire doors.

Comments

For wood entry systems, the final finish should be applied to the door as soon as it has been fit and hung (but not during periods of significant moisture). Surfaces should be clean and dry, and any dust, grease, and marks from handling removed. Any damage from handling must be repaired, and the entire door sanded lightly.

Best results are obtained if the door is lying flat when finished. All sides, including edges, should be finished. Dark-colored stain or paint is generally not recommended for surfaces that receive direct sunlight. Dark colors contribute to heat buildup, resulting in moisture loss, shrinkage, and checking.

Exterior finishes or stains should contain ultraviolet (UV) inhibitors. When painting glazed doors, apply the top coats such that they form a "bridge" between the wood and the glass. The lapping of paint onto glass by $^{1}/_{16}$" provides protection from moisture penetration.

Basic Wood Door Installation Guidelines

The following guidelines are in keeping with the general recommendations of wood door manufacturers. (Be sure to consult the specific instructions accompanying a particular door.)

- Allow $^{1}/_{8}$" clearance between frame and door.
- For doors 7' maximum height, and 3' maximum width, use 3 hinges in a straight line to prevent distortion.
- For doors over 7' high, or over 3' wide, use 4 hinges.

For more on hinge requirements, see "Door Installation," WDMA guidelines in the previous section.

Panels on stile and rail wood doors are designed to move (or "float") during climate changes. Before the door is finished, the installer should make sure the panels are properly aligned with the rails and stiles. Panels can be adjusted with a soft wood block and rubber mallet. Manufacturers do not generally consider the need for this realignment as a defect.

Wood Entry Doors

2.1 Scope

This standard provides minimum performance requirements for exterior wood door primary entry systems. Provisions are included in Section 4 for testing and identifying systems which fully comply with this standard.

3. General Requirements

3.1.1 Doors (panels). All wood doors used in exterior wood door systems shall meet the appropriate requirements of the latest revision of WDMA I.S.1 "Industry Standard for Wood Flush Doors" or WDMA 1.S.6 "Industry Standard for Wood Stile and Rail Doors."

3.1.2 Tolerances. A tolerance of plus or minus $^{1}/_{8}$ inch (3.2 mm) from the specifications of the door system tested will be permitted.

3.1.3 Weather-stripping. All exterior wood door systems shall be weather-stripped. The materials and locations of the weather-stripping shall enable the unit to meet the performance requirements of Section 4 and have the durability reasonably adequate for normal and continuous usage.

Wood Patio Doors

2.1 Scope. This standard provides minimum performance requirements for both the operating and stationary wood, prefinished wood and clad wood sliding patio doors. For purposes of this standard, a sliding patio door covers both wood, prefinished wood and clad wood sliding patio doors. Provisions are included in Section 5.6 for labeling or otherwise identifying each sliding patio door which fully complies with this standard for operating force, air infiltration, water penetration, structural performance and forced entry resistance. Provisions are also included in Section 6.2 for labeling and rating each sliding patio door for thermal performance.

3.0 General Requirements

3.1 All sliding patio doors, which are certified or otherwise indicated or represented as conforming to this standard, shall meet or exceed all the applicable requirements of this standard.

3.2 Wood. The wood parts of the sliding patio door shall be wood or wood composites that have a moisture content no greater than twelve percent (12%) at the time of fabrication.

3.2.1 All exposed wood surfaces shall be sound. Defects and discolorations are permitted provided the surface is suitable for an opaque finish.

Appearance of Individual Pieces of Veneer

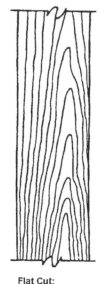
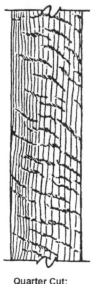
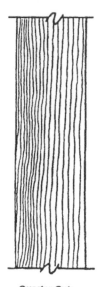
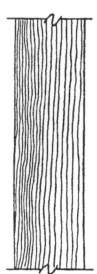
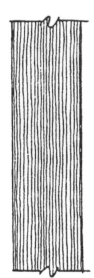

| Rotary Cut | Flat Cut:
Plain Slices | Quarter Cut:
Red & White Oak | Quarter Cut:
Other Species | Rift-Cut:
Red & White Oak | Comb Grain:
Red & White Oak |

Veneer Cuts

The way in which a log is cut, in relation to the annual growth rings, determines the appearance of veneer. The beauty of veneer is in the natural variations of texture, grain, figure, color, and the way it is assembled on a door face.

Faces will have the natural variatons in grain inherent in the species and cut. Natural variations of veneer grain and pattern will vary from these illustrations.

Rotary

This cut follows the log's annual growth rings, providing a general bold random appearance.

Flat Cut (Plain Sliced)

Slicing is done parallel to a line through the center of the log. Cathedral and straight grained patterns result. The individual pieces of veneer are kept in the order they are sliced, permitting a natural grain progression when assembled as veneer faces.

Quarter Cut

A series of stripes is produced. These stripes vary in width from species to species. Flake is a characteristic of this cut in red and white oak.

Rift-Cut (only in Red & White Oak)

The cut slices slightly across the medullary rays, accentuating the vertical grain and minimizing the "flake." Rift grain is restricted the red and white oak.

Comb Grain (only in Red & White Oak)

Limited availability. This is a rift-cut veneer distinguished by the tightness and straightness of the grain along the entire length of the veneer. Slight angle in the grain is allowed. Comb grain is restricted to red and white oak. See section G-11 for maximum grain slope. There are occasional cross bars and flake is minimal.

Figure 9.5

Courtesy of Window & Door Manufacturers Association, *Specifiers Guide to Wood Windows and Doors*

3.3 Tolerances. A tolerance of plus or minus $\frac{1}{32}$ inch (1 mm) from the specifications of the sliding patio doors tested will be permitted for all sliding patio door parts.

3.4 Adhesives. The adhesives used in the manufacture of finger jointed and/or edge bonded parts shall meet or exceed the wet use adhesive requirements as defined in the latest revision of ASTM D 5572 "Specification for Adhesives Used for Finger Joints in Nonstructural Lumber Products."

3.5 Preservative Treatment. All wood parts of sliding patio doors, except inside stops and inside trim, shall be water-repellent preservative treated, after

machining, in accordance with the latest revision of WDMA Industry Standard I.S.4 "Water Repellent Preservative Non-Pressure Treatment for Millwork."

3.6 Weather strip. All sliding patio doors shall be weather-stripped. Weather stripping shall be made, at the option of the manufacturer, with any suitable material that has the performance qualities and durability reasonably adequate for normal and continuous operation. The weather strip shall be installed in a manner which shall effectively enable the unit to meet the air and water infiltration requirements for the performance level specified.

1¾ Front Entrance Doors (Exterior)

Minimum Dimensions

Stiles & top rail	4½"
Lock rail	7½"
Intermediate rail & mullion	2⅛"
Bottom rail	8"
Panels: Raised	⁷⁄₁₆"
Bars: (2132-596)	4½"
(000-606, 000-597)	3½"

Common Door Sizes

2'6" x 6'8" x 1¾"
2'8" x 6'8" x 1¾"
3'0" x 6'8" x 1¾"
2'6" x 7'0" x 1¾"
2'8" x 7'0" x 1¾"
3'0" x 7'0" x 1¾"

4103-000   4111-000

TRADITIONAL

2005-000   2010-000   2020-600   2009-000   2035-612

2039-614   2045-000   2060-113   2130-110   2132-596   M-1073

2134-000   2031-615   2061-605   2061-606   2061-607   2061-608   2061-609   2061-610

I.S. 6-97

Figure 9.6

Courtesy of Window & Door Manufacturers Association, *Specifiers Guide to Wood Windows and Doors*

3.7.3 Exposed Exterior Hardware. All hardware exposed to the exterior side of the sliding patio door after assembly and installation shall be, when tested, in accordance with the latest revision of ASTM B 1 17 Standard Method of Salt Spray Apparatus.

3.8 Glazing Material. Glazing materials used in wood sliding patio doors must conform to the requirements of the Consumer Product Safety Commission Safety Standard for Architectural Glazing Materials (16 CFR 1201). Insulated glazing, consisting of two or more pieces of safety glazing material separated by a sealed air space, may be used.

3.8.1 Glazing Sealants. The method of glazing and the materials used shall permit the unit to meet the performance requirements of Section 5. Where glazing sealants are used, they shall be quality elastic type compounds which are designed for bedding safety glazing materials or which are specifically recommended for such use by the sealant manufacturer.

3.8.2 Insulating Glass. Sealed insulating glass shall meet or exceed the requirements of the latest revision of ASTM E 774 "Specifications for Sealed Insulating Glass Units." Each insulating glass unit shall be permanently labeled with a name or code identifying the insulating glass manufacturer.

3.9 Screen Panels. Insect screen panels shall be provided when specified or in accordance with each manufacturer's usual practice. Screen panels shall operate smoothly and shall remain in contact with the track during normal operation. Screen panels shall be equipped with a latch that does not lock automatically, i.e., when the screen panel is closed; the locking device shall not lock without a specific action by the operator. When aluminum framed insect screens are specified, they shall meet or exceed the requirements of the latest revision of ANSI/SMA 2006 "Specifications for Aluminum Sliding Screen Doors."

Wood Swinging Patio Doors

2.1 Scope. This standard provides minimum material and performance requirements for both the operating and stationary portions of all types of wood swinging patio doors. For purposes of this standard wood, prefinished wood and clad wood swinging patio doors are covered. Provisions are included in Section 5 for testing and identifying swinging patio doors which fully comply with this standard for air, water and structural performance certification. Provisions are also included in Section 6.2 for labeling and rating each swinging patio door for thermal performance.

3.2.2 Adhesives. The adhesive used in the manufacture of finger jointed and edge bonded parts shall meet or exceed the "wet use" adhesive requirements of the latest revision of ASTM D 3110 "Adhesives Used in Non-Structural Glued Lumber Products." The adhesive used in the manufacture of finger jointed parts shall meet or exceed the requirements of the latest revision of ASTM D 5572 "Adhesives Used for Finger Joints in Nonstructural Lumber Products."

3.2.3 Tolerances. Unless otherwise specified at the time the swinging patio door units are ordered, the following tolerances will apply to the overall dimensions of all doors.

3.2.3.1 Height and Width Tolerances. A plus (+)$\frac{1}{8}$ inch, minus (−) $\frac{1}{8}$ inch tolerance (+3 mm, −3 mm) is allowed in overall width and height for swinging patio door units 9 feet or less in width. For units greater than 9 feet wide, a $\frac{1}{4}$ inch (6 mm) tolerance in width, +$\frac{1}{8}$ inch (+3 mm) tolerance in height is allowed.

3.2.3.2 Thickness Tolerances. The following thickness tolerances shall apply to these swinging patio door components.

a) **Doors (panels)**—A plus (+) $\frac{1}{32}$ inch, minus (−) $\frac{3}{32}$ inch tolerance (+1 mm, − 2 mm) is allowed from the nominal thickness of a door of a unit described in this standard.

b) **Frames/Mouldings**—A plus (+) $\frac{1}{32}$ inch tolerance is allowed for the interior wood moulding of the units described in this standard.

3.2.4 Warp. The amount of bow, cup or twist in a door shall not exceed $\frac{1}{4}$ inch (6 mm) when measured by placing a straight edge, taut wire or string, on the suspected concave face of the door at any angle (i.e. horizontal, vertical, diagonal). The measurement of bow, cup or twist shall be made at the point of maximum distance between the bottom of the straight edge, taut wire or string, and the face of the door after accounting for glazing recesses.

3.2.5 Grading. All swinging patio door units shall conform to the following specifications.

3.2.5.1 Doors (panels). The doors of the units described in this standard shall meet or exceed the grading requirements in accordance with the latest revision of WDMA I.S.6 "Industry Standard for Stile and Rail Doors."

3.2.5.2 Frames/Moulding. The interior moulding of the units described in this standard shall meet or exceed the grading requirements in accordance with the latest revision of WM 1-89 "Industry Standard for Interior Wood Door Jambs."

3.2.6.1 Dimensions. The doors (panels) of the units described in this standard shall be constructed to the dimension requirements in accordance with the latest revision of WDMA 1.S.6 "Industry Standard for Stile and Rail Doors" with the following exceptions:

a) Stile and intermediate rail width must be no less than 2⅛" (54 mm).

b) Top and bottom rail width must be no less than 3½" (89 mm).

c) Stile and rail thickness must be no less than 1⅜" (35 mm).

3.3 Glazing Materials

3.3.1 Glazing Material. Glazing materials used in wood swinging patio doors must conform to the requirements of the Consumer Product Safety Commission "Safety Standard for Architectural Glazing Materials (16 CFR 1201)." Insulated glazing, consisting of two or more pieces of safety glazing material separated by a sealed air space, may be used.

3.3.2 Glazing Sealants. The method of glazing and the materials used shall permit the unit to meet the performance requirements of Section 5. Where glazing sealants are used, they shall be quality elastic type compounds which are designed for bedding safety glazing materials or which are specifically recommended for such use by the sealant manufacturer.

3.3.3 Insulating Glass. Sealed insulating glass shall meet or exceed the requirements of the latest revision of ASTM E 774 "Specifications for Sealed Insulating Glass Units." Each insulating glass unit shall be permanently labeled with a name or code identifying the insulating glass manufacturer.

Ed. Note: See "Window Installation & Flashing" earlier in this chapter for information on flashing wood windows and doors.

3.4 Hardware. When hardware is provided, the type and location of hardware installed on a wood swinging patio door shall permit the unit to meet the following requirements, and the performance requirements of Section 5.

3.5 Weather-strip. All operating units shall be weatherstripped. Weather-strip shall be made, at the option of the manufacturer, with any suitable material that has the performance qualities and durability reasonably adequate for normal and continuous operation. The weather-strip shall be installed in the swinging patio door unit so as to effectively enable the unit to meet the air and water infiltration requirements specified in Section 5.

Stile & Rail (Panel) Doors
Industry Standards
Specifiers Guide to Wood Windows and Doors
(Window & Door Manufacturers Association)

2.1 Scope. This standard covers the principal sizes, types, grades and designs of commercially available wood stile and rail doors. Included are requirements for dimensions, materials and construction. Methods of marking and labeling to indicate compliance with the standard and a glossary of trade terms are also included.

2.2 Classification. The doors covered by this standard are identified by size, species, grade and design. The illustrations in this standard are based on minimum sizes and dimensional requirements for each door design. The sizes and locations of panels, glazing and intermediate members, may vary from manufacturer to manufacturer.

3.1.3.1 Height and Width Tolerances. A plus (+)¹⁄₁₆ in., minus (–)⅛ in. tolerance (+1.6mm, –3.2mm) is allowed in overall width and/or height for all doors except bifold doors. Bifold doors are considered prefit at the time of manufacture and must conform to the tolerances listed in Section 3.3.7.

3.13.2 Thickness Tolerance. A plus (+) 0", minus (–)³⁄₃₂" tolerance (+ 0 mm, –2.4 mm) is allowed from the nominal thickness of a door or thickness of a raised panel.

3.1.4 Warp. The amount of bow, cup or twist in a door shall be measured by placing a straight edge, taut wire or string on the suspected concave face of the door at any angle (i.e., horizontal, vertical or diagonal). The measurement of bow, cup or twist shall be made at the point of maximum distance between the bottom of the straight edge, taut wire or string and the face of the door, after accounting for panel or glazing recesses. The warp for any nominal 1¾" thick by 3'6" wide by 7' high (4.4 cm x 1.07 m x 2.13 m) or smaller door, shall not exceed ¼" (6.4 mm).

3.2.1 Wood. Unless otherwise stated in this standard, all doors are to be made from wood or wood composites that have been kiln dried to a moisture content no greater than 12% at the time of fabrication. Any non-wood substrates may be used provided they meet the same performance criteria for solid wood components.

3.2.3 Adhesives. All adhesives used to assemble interior doors shall meet or exceed the requirements for "dry-use" adhesives as described in ASTM D-3110 "Adhesives Used in Non-Structural Glued Lumber

1³⁄₈ Interior Panel Doors[a]

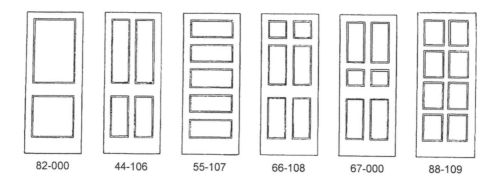

| 82-000 | 44-106 | 55-107 | 66-108 | 67-000 | 88-109 |

Minimum Dimensions

Stiles

1'0" thru 1'6"	2⅛"
1'8" thru 2'6"	3⅛"
2'8" thru 3'0"	4⅛"
over 3'0"	4½"

Rails

Top Rails	4½"
Lock Rail (44-106 & 66-108)	7½"
Intermediate Rail	3⅞"
(Except 55-107)	3¼"
Mullions	3⅞"
Bottom Rail	8"

Panels

Raised	⁷⁄₁₆"
Flat	¼"

Common Door Sizes[b]

1'6" x 6'6" x 1⅜"	2'6" x 6'6" x 1⅜"
1'6" x 6'8"	2'6" x 6'8"
1'8" x 6'8"	2'6" x 7'0"
2'0" x 6'6"	2'8" x 6'6"
2'0" x 6'8"	2'8" x 6'8"
2'0" x 7'0"	2'8" x 7'0"
2'4" x 6'6"	3'0" x 6'8"
3'4" x 6'8"	3'0" x 7'0"
2'4" x 7'0"	

a) Also for exterior use.
b) Doors 1'8" wide and narrower are made one panel wide.

1. Drawings are not to scale. Drawings show only relative position of components.

NOTE: To convert inches to millimeters, multiply by 25.4.

Figure 9.7   Courtesy of Window & Door Manufacturers Association, *Specifiers Guide to Wood Windows and Doors*

Products." Other adhesives used to assemble exterior doors shall meet or exceed the requirements for "wet-use" adhesives as described in the latest revision of ASTM D3110, unless the door manufacturer warrants that doors for exterior installation are fabricated with "dry-use" adhesives.

3.2.4 Glazing Material. All glazing materials used in doors must conform to the requirements for the Consumer Product Safety Commission, "Safety Standard for Architectural Glazing Materials (16CFR 1201)." Insulated glazing, consisting of two or more pieces of safety glazing material separated by a sealed air space, may be used.

3.2.5 Glazing Sealants. Glazing sealants shall be quality, elastic type compounds which are designed for bedding glazing materials or which are specifically recommended for such use by the sealant manufacturer.

3.2.6 Insect Screening. Metal screening shall conform to the requirements of the latest revision of Federal Specification RR-W-365, "Wire Fabric (Insect Screening)." Nonmetal screening shall conform to the requirements of the latest revision of Federal specification L-S-125a, "Screening, Insect, Non-metallic." All tacks, staples, brads or other fasteners used to attach the screen cloth or screen molding shall be of a material which is compatible with the screening being used.

3.3.4 Screening. Metal screening on screen doors or screen sections of a combination door may be rolled into a groove on the stiles and rails, or may be stapled to the stiles and rails. Screen molding on doors may be either raised or flush and shall be fastened with nails, brads or staples. A double row of fasteners shall be used on screen molding 1¾" (44.4 mm) wide and wider and shall be spaced not more than an average of 10" apart nor more than 3" from each end of the molding. Non-metal screen cloth shall be applied in a groove with a spline sufficiently pliable to engage the filaments of the screen cloth and hold it securely in the groove.

3.3.5 Glazing. All glazed exterior doors, except combination doors, shall have the safety glazing material bedded in sealants and secured in place with mitered wood glazing beads, or shall have the safety glazing material held using sealants or a glazing gasket within a channel or groove machined into the stiles and rails framing the glazed opening. For combination doors, the safety glazed insert shall be framed with wood, plastic or metal, in a manner suitable to the design of the door.

3.3.7 Prefitting. When ordered prefit, all doors shall be sized to the dimensions specified on the order. A tolerance of plus (+) or minus (–) ¹⁄₃₂" (+ or – 0.8 mm) will be allowed from the dimensions specified. The widths of stiles and rails may be reduced by the amount of prefitting.

Comments

As mentioned earlier in the "Wood Doors" section, panels on stile and rail doors are designed to move, or "float," in response to climate changes. Adjustments required to align them with the stiles and rails are not generally considered by the manufacturer to reflect any defects.

Fire Doors

Industry Standards
WIC Manual of Millwork (Effective 5/1/01)
(Woodwork Institute of California, www.wicnet.org)

General
Install fire doors as required by NFPA Pamphlet 80. All 45-, 60-, and 90-minute rated doors may be hung with either half surface or full mortise hinges. Core reinforcements can be specified to permit hardware

to be surface mounted with screws. Labels shall not be removed from fire-rated doors, 20-, 45-, 60-, and 90-minute rated doors. Preparation of fire door assemblies for locks, latches, hinges, remotely operated or monitored hardware, concealed closures, glass lights, vision panels, louvers, astragals and laminated overlays shall be performed in conformance with the manufactures inspection service procedure and under Label Service.

Exception: Preparation for surface applied hardware, function holes for mortise locks, holes for labeled viewers, a maximum ¾ inch (19 mm) wood and composite door undercutting, and protection plates may be performed at the job site. Surface applied hardware is applied to the face of a door without removing material from the door other than round holes drilled through the face of the door to receive cylinders, spindles, similar operational elements and through bolts. The holes shall not exceed a diameter of 1 inch (25.4 mm) with the exception of cylinders.

Flush Veneer Fire-Rated Doors
Wood veneered fire-rated doors are available in 90-minute label, 60-minute label, 45-minute label, and 20-minute label.

Comments

Fire Rating of Doors

The fire rating of doors applies only when doors have not been altered (for example, by adding louvers, lights, or using nonstandard hardware).

Fire Doors: Storage, Handling, Finishing, & Installation

General Recommendations:

Storage

- Store flat and level in a clean, dry, ventilated area out of sunlight.
- Do not expose doors to extreme heat and/or humidity (relative humidity not less than 30% or more than 60%).
- Store in enclosed building with operational HVAC systems.
- Seal as early as possible (edge sealing is particularly important).
- Lift or carry, but do not drag doors.
- Handle with clean hands or clean gloves. Do not walk on or place other materials on top of stacked doors.

Finishing

- Block-sand doors just before staining, sealing, and finishing. Perform sanding with doors in a horizontal

(continued)

position using no less than 150 grit sandpaper, to remove all handling marks and raised grain.

- If possible, test surface for compatibility with finish.
- Top, bottom, opening, and hardware recess edges should be sealed after fitting with at least two coats of oil-based paint, varnish, or lacquer.
- Avoid water-based stains, paints, or latex primers if possible as they can raise the grain, may cause veneer splits, or highlight veneer joints.
- Avoid dark colors on exterior doors that will be exposed to direct sunlight.
- Do not use steel wool to prepare oak-veneered or fire-rated doors.
- Apply a wash coat (thin sealer) before using a dark stain to avoid a splotchy appearance and/or sharp color contrast.
- The appearance of field-applied finishes is not covered by manufacturers' warranties.

Installation

- Acclimate doors to finished building heat and humidity before fitting and hanging.
- Be sure that applying hardware, plant-ons, or louvers will not adversely affect the door strength.
- Trim for width equally from both sides; allow $1/8$" clearance at the top and each side.
- Do not trim top edges on labeled doors. On nonrated doors, do not trim top and bottom edge more than $3/4$" unless using additional blocking.
- Threaded-to-the-head wood screws are required on all rated doors. Pilot holes must be drilled for all screws to avoid splitting. Use two hinges for doors up to 60" in height, three hinges for doors up to 90" in height, and an additional hinge for every additional 30" of door height or portion thereof.

2. Economy, Custom or Premium Grade Architectural doors used for exterior exposure shall have all lite and louver cutouts sealed at the factory with one coat of exterior sealer. The bottom edge of cutouts and top rails of doors shall have flashing, if specified, installed at the factory. The ends of the flashing shall be imbedded in caulking compound.

3. Doors intended for an exterior exposure shall be Type I Adhesive doors. Doors intended for an interior exposure may be Type 1 Adhesive or Type II Bond with choice of adhesive optional with door manufacturer.

4. Typical construction in the industry for wood faced doors is five ply (core, crossband, and face veneer) or seven ply. Typical consideration in the industry for plastic faced doors is three ply (core and plastic). If type is not specified, it shall be optional with the manufacturer.

5. For Custom and Premium Grades, stiles or edge bands shall be securely glued under pressure to the solid block core or particleboard core. Framed Block Non-Glued core is not permitted in these grades.

Cutouts for Lights and Louvers

1. In non-rated doors, combined area of cutouts for lights or louvers shall not exceed 40% of the door area or one-half of the door height. Cutouts shall be a minimum of 5" from door edges, adjacent cutouts, or hardware mortises.

2. In rated doors, combined area of cutouts for lights or louvers shall be governed by the individual manufacturer's fire approval and/or NFPA 80. Cutouts shall be a minimum of 6" from door edges, adjacent cutouts, or hardware mortises.

Solid & Hollow Core Veneered Flush Doors

Industry Standards

WIC Manual of Millwork (Effective 5/1/01)
(Woodwork Institute of California, www.wicnet.org)

1. Standards as established by Window & Door Manufacturers Association, Industry Standards I.S. 1-A Series, latest edition, for wood flush doors, are adopted as the minimum construction requirements for all WIC Grades of hollow and solid core, mineral core, acoustical, and lead lined flush veneered doors, except as hereinafter modified.

Prefinished Modular Doors

Comments

Prefinished modular doors and frames are often used in light commercial buildings. Available in a variety of textures, grains, and finishes, they are constructed of interlocking steel frame units with snap-on metal casings. These ready-to-use units offer the advantage of quick installation without the need for finishing. Follow manufacturer's instructions for installation.

Metal Doors

Hollow Metal Frames & Doors

Industry Standards

Plan Reading & Material Takeoff
(RSMeans)

> ### Comments
>
> If metal doors are combined with storm doors, painted dark colors, and exposed to direct sunlight, the temperature on the exterior face of the metal door can lead to distortion of the light inserts.

Hollow Metal Frames

Hollow metal frames are formed of 18-, 16-, and 14-gauge steel, and are made to accommodate 1⅜" and 1¾" wood or metal doors. Hollow metal frames are available in a variety of standard wall thicknesses, sometimes called throat, typically 4¾", 5¾", 6¾", and 8¾". They are available prefinished, galvanized, primed, or unfinished. Hollow metal frames can be installed in wood frame walls, masonry walls, metal stud and drywall walls, and walls that combine wood, steel, and masonry. They are available in two standard levels of fabrication: knockdown, where the frame is disassembled into the two jambs and the head piece and assembled on site, and welded assembly, where the frame is welded (at the factory) at the corners to produce a rigid, square, and true frame for site installation. Frames can be installed with the frame wrapped around the wall thickness, as in the case of interior partitions, or with the frame butted up to the jamb and the head, as in the case of metal frames installed with a masonry or concrete rough opening. Figure 9.8 illustrates some typical hollow metal door frames.

Hollow Metal Doors

Hollow metal doors are constructed of 16-, 18-, and 20-gauge face sheets, with interior metal framing for a 1⅜" or 1¾" finished thickness. Hollow metal doors are available in a variety of styles, including flush, small vision panels, full or half glass, and louvered. In accordance with most building codes, certain locations throughout the building will be required to be fire-rated. Fire rating refers to the door and frame's capacity (label) to slow the transmission of fire. Typical labels are *C Label* for a ¾-hour rating, *B Label* for a 1½ to 2-hour rating, and *A Label* for a 3-hour rating. Other restrictions and qualifications also govern label doors and frames. Carefully review the plans and specifications.

Steel Insulating Doors

Steel insulating door units for residential entrances are comprised of thin steel sheets over a wood-and-foam insulating core. They are typically provided prehung in a wood frame with an integral aluminum threshold, bored for locksets and/or deadbolts. Steel door units are available with designs either embossed in the face sheets or surface-applied, in many styles and sizes. Entry units with fiberglass face sheets and similar core construction are also available. Sizes range from 2'-8" to 3'-0" in width and 6'-6" or 6'-8" in height. Steel doors are provided primed for field-applied paint, and fiberglass units are unfinished, ready for field-applied stains or paints.

> ### Comments
>
> The ISDI (Insulated Steel Door Institute) has established criteria for air-infiltration limit as follows: Air infiltration cannot exceed .2 cfm per foot of crack length at a static pressure of 1.567 lbs./SF (approximately equal to a 25 mph wind). The ISDI has also established an index for door insulation systems to rate energy loss. The ISDI acceptable level is 5.0. The lower the number, the better the insulation value, and the greater the energy savings.

Sliding Glass Doors

> ### Comments
>
> The following excerpt from CAWM/AAMA is similar to the material in an earlier section, "Window Installation & Flashing," but it addresses doors specifically. For more information on exterior cladding and weather protection, see "Window & Door Components Defined," at the beginning of this chapter.
>
> While the following recommendations refer to aluminum doors, the same basic principles apply to other types of doors as well.

Industry Standards

Standard Practices for Installation of Sliding Glass Doors (CAWM 410-97)
(California Association of Window Manufacturers and American Architectural Manufacturers Association)

Protection from Dissimilar Materials

5.2.1 Isolate aluminum products from dissimilar or corrosive materials.

Hollow Metal Door Frames

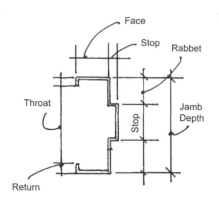

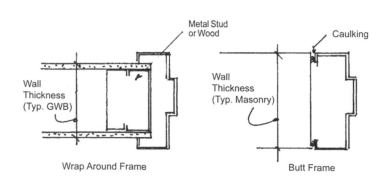

Figure 9.8

RSMeans, *Plan Reading & Material Takeoff*

5.2.2 Protect aluminum sills from direct contact with corrosive materials, e.g. concrete, steel, and stucco.

5.2.3 All fasteners shall be corrosion resistant, in accordance with ASTM B 633 or B 766.

5.3 Flashing Requirements—Proper flashing and/or sealing is necessary as a secondary barrier to prevent water from entering the wall between the door frame and the adjacent wall materials. Flashing and/or an appropriate method of sealing shall be designed as a part of an overall weather-resistive barrier system. It is not the responsibility of the door manufacturer to design or recommend a flashing system appropriate to each job condition.

Note 1—The responsibility for supporting and protecting any flashing material from sources of damage, e.g. weather, other trades, or vandalism, and properly integrating the flashing system into the weather-resistive barrier for the entire building, will be the responsibility of the owner/general contractor or his designated agent.

5.3.1 Penetration Flashing Material—Flashing material shall meet Federal Specification UU-B-790a Type I, and shall be Grade C, B or A. Flashing material shall carry continuous identification.

5.4 Application

5.4.1 One of the two following methods shall be selected as the application to be followed. Once a method is selected, all procedures of that method must be performed in the described sequence. Substitution of a procedure from one method to the other is not permitted.

Method A

5.4.1.1.1 A strip of approved flashing material should be at least nine inches wide. Flashing shall be applied in a weatherboard fashion around the top and side perimeters of the opening, as well as below the sill, when applicable.

5.4.1.1.2 Apply continuous sealant beads across the full sill length of the framed opening at a point that makes contact with the door sill or sill pan system. An equivalent of two (2) $\frac{3}{8}$" diameter beads should be used. Deposit a sufficient amount of sealant at the framed opening corners so the bottom door frame corners are embedded in sealant when door is installed.

Note 2—All surfaces contacting sealant must be clean, dry, and free of all contaminants prior to application of sealant. Sealant used must adhere and be chemically compatible with all substrates.

5.4.1.1.3 Apply a continuous seal to the backside (interior) of the sill mounting flange, if provided, near the outer edge or a continuous seal to the perimeter of the opening at a point to assure contact with the backside (interior) of the mounting flange. The door shall then be installed in accordance with Section 5.5 installation.

5.4.1.1.4 Next, apply a continuous seal to the exposed mounting flange at the top (head) and sides (jambs) of the installed door frame. For mechanically joined frames, apply seal at corners the full length of the seam where mounting flanges meet.

5.4.1.1.5 Starting at each jamb, embed the jamb flashing into the seal and fasten in place. Run this flashing beyond the bottom of the rough opening and above where the head flashing will intersect.

5.4.1.1.6 Finally, embed the head flashing into the sealant on the mounting flange at the door head. Cut this flashing sufficiently long so that it will extend beyond each jamb flashing. Fasten in place.

5.4.1.1.7 Next, go to Section 5.5 Installation.

Method B

5.4.1.2.1 A strip of approved flashing material should be at least nine inches wide. Flashing shall be applied in a weatherboard fashion around the top and side perimeters of the opening, as well as below the sill, when applicable.

5.4.1.2.2 Apply continuous sealant across the full sill length of the framed opening at a point that makes contact with the door sill or sill pan system. The equivalent of two $3/8$" diameter beads should be used. Deposit a sufficient amount of sealant at the framed opening corners so the bottom door frame corners are embedded in sealant when door is installed.

Note 3—All surfaces contacting sealant must be clean, dry, and free of all contaminants prior to application of sealant. Sealant used must adhere and be chemically compatible with all substrates.

5.4.1.2.3 Next, fasten strips of flashing at each vertical edge (jamb) of the opening. Run this flashing beyond the bottom of the rough opening and above where the head flashing will intersect.

5.4.1.2.4 Apply a continuous seal to the backside (interior) of the mounting flange near the outer edge or a continuous seal to the entire perimeter of the opening at a point to assure contact with the backside (interior) of the mounting flange.

Note 4—Caution must be taken to avoid disrupting the continuous seal.

5.4.1.2.5 The door shall then be installed in accordance with Section 5.5 installation procedures.

5.4.1.2.6 For mechanically joined frames, apply seal at corners the full length of the seam where mounting flanges meet.

5.4.1.2.7 Next, apply a continuous seal at the top (head) mounting flange and embed the bottom of the head flashing over the sealant and the mounting flange. Cut this flashing sufficiently long so that it will extend beyond each jamb flashing. Fasten in place.

5.5 Installation

5.5.1 Depending on rough opening conditions, the mounting flange, if provided on the door sill, may have to be removed. These conditions may include slab on grade that continues to the exterior; metal, plastic or flexible membrane sill pan systems; recessed installations; buildings with exterior decking. Follow door manufacturer's instructions on mounting flange removal.

5.5.2 Depending on the size and weight of the door and the opening conditions, shim blocks may be required under the sill to maintain straight and level condition and to prevent rotation. Consult manufacturer's recommendations.

5.5.3 If shims are needed at the sill, use enough to support the weight of the fixed and operable panels without causing distortion in the sill.

5.5.3.1 If a sill pan system is used, shim between the opening and the pan, not between the pan and the door sill.

5.5.3.2 Use sealant above and below the shims.

Note 5—All surfaces contacting sealant must be clean, dry and free of all contaminants prior to application of sealant.

5.5.4 If necessary, pre-drill and fill holes with sealant and seal over fasteners that penetrate door threshold.

5.5.5 Shim and adjust the door as necessary to achieve a plumb, square and level condition, as well as an even reveal around the frame opening, securing it the full perimeter with the equivalent of 6d fasteners at a maximum 16-inch center.

5.5.5.1 Some door manufacturers may require fasteners at the interior or through the frame members. Consult manufacturer's installation instructions.

Note 6—Consult door manufacturer's installation instructions regarding attachment of head flange to rough opening.

5.5.6 In each direction from all corners there must be a fastener within 10 inches, but no closer than 3 inches, to prevent frame distortion or fracture of joint.

5.5.7 In all cases consult manufacturer's instructions for any special procedures or applications.

Note 7—If any damage to door frame joint seals is observed during installation, it must be repaired by the installer.

5.5.8 Where weather-resistant building paper, insulating board, or other materials by other trades may constitute the primary weather barrier behind the exterior wall finish (i.e., stucco, masonry, siding, etc.), Owner/General Contractor is responsible to ensure that the weather barrier is continuous by effectively sealing the material to the door frame.

Threshold (Sill) Seal Application

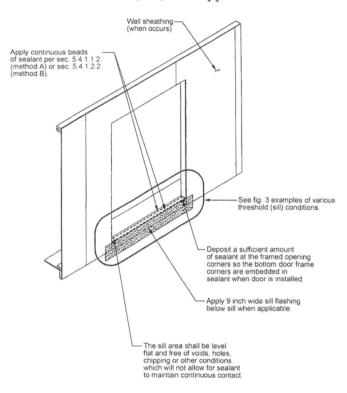

Figure 9.9   Courtesy of CAWM/AAMA, Standard Practices for Installation of
Sliding Glass Doors (CAWM 410-97)

Concrete or Wood Sub-Floor

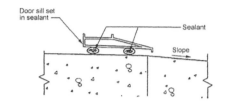

Pan Flashing

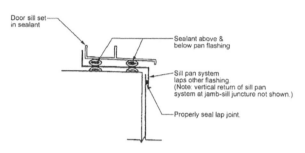

Recessed Sill

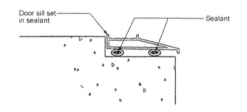

Exterior Decking

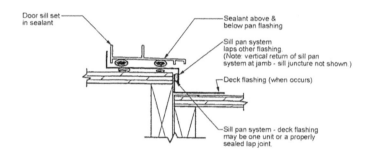

Figure 9.10   Courtesy of CAWM/AAMA, Standard Practices for Installation of
Sliding Glass Doors (CAWM 410-97)

5.6 Sealant Requirements

5.6.1 Sealing/caulking required between the door frame and the flashing can be accomplished with caulking conforming to AAMA 800 and/or ASTM C-920 and/or TT S-00230 C (Type II) Class A, or use sealant recommended and approved by the sealant manufacturer. All sealant and caulking products used must adhere and be chemically compatible with all substrates.

5.6.2 Some exterior wall finishes require additional sealing between the perimeter of the door frame and adjacent finish wall material. Owner/General Contractor is responsible for identifying the need for any additional sealant which will be applied by others. Such sealant shall be elastomeric material, compatible with door framing and adjacent wall materials. All sealant and caulking products used must adhere and be chemically compatible with all substrates.

5.7 Finish, Door and Sealant Protection

5.7.1 Caution shall be taken to avoid damage to doors during and after installation. Prior to installation, store doors in a near vertical position in a clean area, free of circulating dirt or debris and protected from exposure to weather elements.

5.7.2 Field-applied protective coatings can damage door sealants and gaskets and are not recommended. Contact the door manufacturer before applying any such coatings.

5.7.3 Caution should be used with some masking tapes as they may cause damage when they are removed from door surfaces.

5.7.4 Stucco or concrete left to cure on frames and glass will damage these surfaces. Remove and clean all such materials from surfaces before any curing action takes place.

5.7.5 Glass and frame surfaces exposed to leaching water from new concrete or stucco must be rinsed immediately with clear water to prevent permanent damage.

Doors for Disabled Users

Interior Door in Drywall Partition

Industry Standards

ADA Compliance Pricing Guide, Second Edition
(RSMeans)

ADAAG References

206.5, Doors, Doorways, and Gates

303.3, Beveled Changes in Level

309, Operable Parts

404, Doors, Doorways, and Gates

Where Applicable

All rooms along accessible routes that have walls constructed of studs and wallboard.

Design Requirements

- 32" minimum clear width measured between the door stop and the face of the door open to 90°.

- Typical maneuvering dimentions: 18" minimum clearance adjacent to the latch on the pull side of the door. If the door has closers, 12" minimum on the push side. See 404.2.4 for clearance when a turn is involved.

- Level maneuvering space on both sides of the door, depending on approach. Between 42" and 60", minimum, required in front of door, depending on approach and whether door has a closer. (Refer to ADAAG Tables 404.2.4.1 & 404.2.4.2.) Surface of required maneuvering space must be level (2% maximum slope allowed for drainage).

- Threshold: 1/2" maximum high; beveled at a 1:2 slope, (vertical to horizontal) maximum.

- Five pounds maximum pull or push weight on interior doors (no ADAAG standard for exterior doors) and other than fire doors.

- Accessible hardware (acceptable if operable with a closed fist).

- With door closer, five seconds minimum closing time to an angle of 12°. With spring hinges, 1.5 seconds minimum from 70° to closed position.

- Door surfaces: bottom 10" on push side smooth, extending full width of door.

- Vision panels: 43" maximum, to at least one vision panel.

Design Suggestions

Because the 32" clear opening is measured from the face of the door in a 90° open position to the stop on the opposite jamb, the door itself must be wider. Usually a 36" door is used.

Doors sized 2'–10' can be used, but they are not as readily available.

There are several accessible hardware options: a loop pull (allow at least 1 1/2" between inside of loop and face of door), lever handles, push plate, or panic bar. Where opening force is necessarily high or where adequate maneuvering space cannot be provided, installation of an automatic opener may be a solution.

The maneuvering space in ADAAG Tables 404.2.4.1 and .2 to make a turn from a corridor through a door are minimum, and wider dimensions are recommended to avoid banged-up walls. For instance, the new door cannot be installed if one must make a

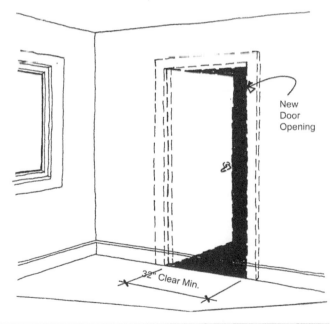

Interior Door for Disabled Users

New Door Opening

32" Clear Min.

Figure 9.11   RSMeans, *ADA Compliance Pricing Guide*, 2nd Edition

90° turn from a 36" wide corridor. Maneuvering space on each side of the door is determined by how it is approached. A 60" by 60" minimum clear space with the door off-set to the latch side is recommended, since it complies with all approaches cited in ADAAG. Where only a straight-on approach is available, a 60" deep space measured from the face of the door is required on the pull side, and a 48" deep space is required on the push side. Where only a side approach is available, the required depth of the clear area in front of the door varies from 42" to 60", and the width is affected by the latch edge clearances and presence or absence of a door opener.

Sliding Door

Industry Standards

ADA Compliance Pricing Guide, Second Edition
(RSMeans)

The installation of an accessible sliding door can create an accessible doorway where door swings might otherwise prevent access. Sliding doors can fit within the width of a standard stud wall, and can be a useful and creative method of creating an accessible route between two spaces when clearances are tight.

ADAAG References
404.2.4.2, Doorways without Doors or Gates, Sliding Doors, and Folding Doors

Where Applicable
Doors to areas on accessible routes of travel where swinging doors block required maneuvering space.

Design Requirements
- 32" minimum clear width measured between the door stop and the face of the door open to 90°.
- Typical maneuvering dimensions: 18" minimum clearance adjacent to the latch on the pull side of the door. If the door has closers, 12" minimum on the push side.
- Level maneuvering space on both sides of the door, depending on approach. Between 42" and 60", minimum, required in front of door, depending on approach and whether door has a closer. (Refer to ADAAG Tables 404.2.4.1 & 404.2.4.2.) Surface of required maneuvering space must be level (2% maximum slope allowed for drainage).
- Threshold: ½" maximum high; beveled at a 1:2 slope, (vertical to horizontal) maximum.

- Five pounds maximum pull or push weight on interior doors (no ADAAG standard for exterior doors) and other fire doors.
- Accessible hardware (acceptable if operable with a closed fist).
- With door closer, five seconds minimum closing time to an angle of 12°. With spring hinges, 1.5 seconds minimum from 70° to closed position.
- Door surfaces: bottom 10" on push side smooth, extending full width of door.
- Vision panels: 43" maximum, to at least one vision panel.

Design Suggestions
To meet the 32" clear opening requirement, expect to install a 36" door. No sliding door hardware exists that meets the regulations when the door is fully open. There are several ways to overcome this problem. One is to install blocking—either on the door or in the pocket—that keeps the door from opening all the way, leaving 2" to 3" exposed for projection hardware. Another is to apply a piece of trim the full length of the door, which serves as a ledge for a person to grab when the door is open, and, when closed, fits flush against the opposite jamb.

Exterior Entrance Door in Masonry Wall

Industry Standards

ADA Compliance Pricing Guide, Second Edition
(RSMeans)

ADAAG References
206.5, Doors, Doorways, and Gates

303.3, Beveled Changes in Level

309, Operable Parts

404, Doors, Doorways, and Gates

Where Applicable
All rooms along accessible routes that have walls constructed of brick, block, or stone.

Design Requirements
- If door is recessed, the recess cannot be greater than 8" without recessing the maneuvering spaces required by 404.2.4.3.
- 32" minimum clear width measured between the door stop and the face of the door open to 90°.

Minimum Clear Width

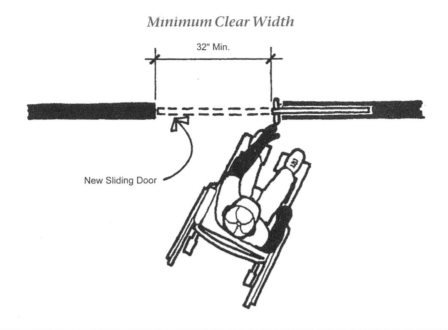

32" Min.

New Sliding Door

Figure 9.12

RSMeans, *ADA Compliance Pricing Guide*, 2nd Edition

- Typical maneuvering dimensions: 18" minimum clearance adjacent to the latch on the pull side of the door. If the door has closers, 12" minimum on the push side.

- Level maneuvering space on both sides of the door, depending on approach. Between 42" and 60", minimum, required in front of door, depending on approach and whether door has a closer. (Refer to ADAAG Tables 404.2.4.1 and 404.2.4.2.) Surface of required maneuvering space must be level (2% maximum slope allowed for drainage).

- Threshold: $\frac{1}{2}$" maximum high; beveled at a 1:2 slope, (vertical to horizontal) maximum.

- Five pounds maximum pull or push weight on interior doors (no ADAAG standard for exterior doors) and other fire doors.

- Accessible hardware (acceptable if operable with a closed fist).

- With door closer, five seconds minimum closing time to an angle of 12°. With spring hinges, 1.5 seconds minimum from 70° to closed position.

- Door surfaces: bottom 10" on push side smooth, extending full width of door.

- Vision panels: 43" maximum, to at least one vision panel.

Window Converted to Accessible Door

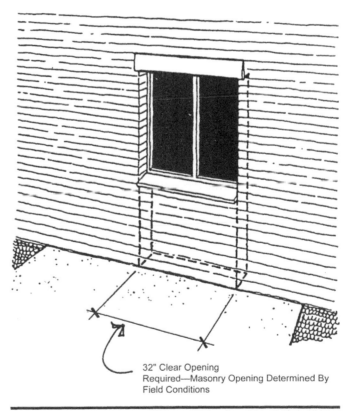

32" Clear Opening
Required—Masonry Opening Determined By
Field Conditions

Figure 9.13

RSMeans, *ADA Compliance Pricing Guide*, 2nd Edition

Design Suggestions

To address opening force, if there is a closer on the door, the closing speed can usually be adjusted. If there are hinges, oiling them is another simple way to make a door easier to open. It is almost always possible (but sometimes expensive) to install an automatic opener to compensate for insufficient latchside clearance or heavy door opening weights. However, this will require stand-by power. Some building inspectors will not allow this on egress doors.

Glass Storefront Entrance

Industry Standards

ADA Compliance Pricing Guide, **Second Edition**
(RSMeans)

Many public facilities have glass storefront façades. Although systems and materials vary widely, many storefronts are made of modules or partitions that can be removed and replaced relatively simply. This allows for the installation of an accessible door in an existing building while maintaining the building design.

ADAAG References

303.3, Beveled Changes in Level

309.4, Operable Parts

404, Doors, Doorways, and Gates

Where Applicable

Areas on accessible routes of travel that have walls constructed of metal framed glass.

Design Requirements

- 32" minimum clear width measured between the door stop and the face of the door open to 90°.

- Typical maneuvering dimensions: 18" minimum clearance adjacent to the latch on the pull side of the door. If the door has closers, 12" minimum on the push side.

- Level maneuvering space on both sides of the door, depending on approach. Between 42" and 60", minimum, required in front of door, depending on approach and whether door has a closer. (Refer to ADAAG Tables 404.2.4.1 and 404.2.4.2.) Surface of required maneuvering space must be level (2% maximum slope allowed for drainage).

- Threshold: 1/2" maximum high; beveled at a 1:2 slope, (vertical to horizontal) maximum.

- Five pounds maximum pull or push weight on interior doors (no ADAAG standard for exterior doors) and other fire doors.

- Accessible hardware (acceptable if operable with a closed fist).

- With door closer, five seconds minimum closing time to an angle of 12°. With spring hinges, 1.5 seconds minimum from 70° to closed position.

- Door surfaces: bottom 10" on push side smooth, extending full width of door.

Design Suggestions

To address opening force, if there is a closer on the door, the closing speed can usually be adjusted. If there are hinges, oiling them is another simple way to make a door easier to open. It is almost always possible (but sometimes expensive) to install an automatic opener to compensate for insufficient latchside clearance or heavy door opening weights. However, this will require stand-by power. Some building inspectors will not allow this on egress doors.

Determining Door Handing

Comments

The term **inswing** refers to a door that swings into the building, or pulls toward you if you are standing inside the building. If the door opens toward you and the doorknob is on the right-hand side, it is called a **right-hand door.** If the knob is on the left, it is a **left hand door.**

Door Tolerances

Industry Standards

WIC Manual of Millwork **(Effective 5/1/01)**
(Woodwork Institute of California, www.wicnet.org)

A. Size Tolerances (Blank Doors)

Unless otherwise specified, a height and width tolerance of plus or minus 1/16 inch (1.6 mm) will be allowed on the overall door dimensions. Thickness tolerance shall be 1/32", plus or minus.

B. Size Tolerances (Prefit Doors)
1. **Standard Prefitting:** The standard amount of prefitting of a wood flush door to be installed in a wood frame should be 3/16 inch (4.8 mm) in width with a 3-degree bevel on 1 stile only. For wood flush doors to be installed in a steel frame, the standard amount of prefitting shall be 1/4 inch (6.4 mm) in width with a 3-degree bevel

Hand of Door Is Always Determined from the Outside

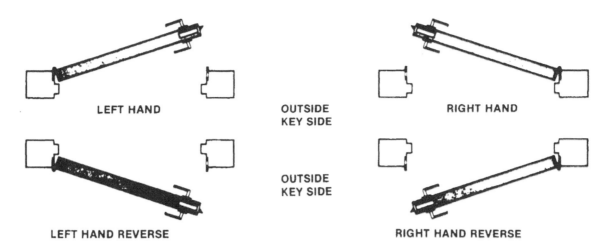

LEFT HAND   OUTSIDE   RIGHT HAND
                   KEY SIDE

                   OUTSIDE
                   KEY SIDE

LEFT HAND REVERSE   RIGHT HAND REVERSE

The diagram shown here is for wood doors. The hollow metal door industry is exactly opposite the rule for wood doors. The hollow metal door industry is exactly opposite the rule for wood doors. If you do not order doors regularly, it is suggested that you furnish a plan diagram with your confirmed order.

Figure 9.14

Courtesy of Woodwork Institute of California, *WIC Manual of Millwork*

on both stiles. A tolerance of plus or minus $\frac{1}{32}$ inch (0.8 mm) will be allowed in width only. The lock stile of a prefitted door may be reduced to a minimum $\frac{13}{16}$ inch wide (20.6 mm) after prefitting and $\frac{3}{8}$ inch wide (9.3 mm) for glued-block core doors. Wood flush doors with standard prefit are book size in height, and rail widths may not be reduced.

2. **Other Prefitting:** Prefitting other than the standard prefit may be specially ordered. However, if such prefitting is ordered, the stile and/or rail widths remaining after prefitting shall not be less than as shown in the following table. A tolerance of plus or minus $\frac{1}{32}$ inch (0.8 mm) will be allowed in width only.

C. Squareness Tolerance

All four corners of a door shall be square (right angles) when the dimensions of the door agree with size tolerances as defined above. Also, the length of the diagonal measurement on the face of the door from the upper right corner to the lower left corner shall be within $\frac{1}{8}$ inch (3.2 mm) of the length of the diagonal from the upper left corner to the lower right corner.

D. Warp Tolerance

1. **Measurement of Warp:** Warp is any distortion in the door itself, and does not refer to the relation of the door to the frame or jamb in which it is hung. The amount of bow, cup, and twist shall be measured by placing a straight edge, taut wire or string, on the suspected concave face of the door as any

angle (i.e., horizontally, vertically, diagonally). The measurement of bow, cup, or twist shall be made at the point of maximum distance between the bottom of the straight edge, taut wire or string, and the face of the door.

2. **Allowable warp, bow, cup, and twist is determined as follows:**

   a. The warp for any nominal $1\frac{3}{4}$ inches thick (44.4 mm) or thicker door shall not be more than $\frac{1}{4}$ inch (6.4mm) in any 3 feet 6 inches wide by 7 feet 0 inches high (1067 mm by 2134 mm) section of the door. The measuring section will be reduced to the actual width and/or height of the door, if the actual width and/or height is less than 3 feet 6 inches wide by 7 feet 0 inches high (1067 mm by 2134 mm).

   b. The warp for any nominal $1\frac{3}{8}$ inches thick (34.9 mm) or thinner door that is 3 feet 0 inches wide by 7 feet 0 inches high (914 mm by 2134 mm) or smaller, shall not be more than $\frac{1}{4}$ inch (6.4 mm).

3. **Limits on Warp Tolerance:** Allowable warp tolerances are not to be extended to the following doors or situations:

   a. Nominal $1\frac{3}{8}$ inches thick (34.9 mm) or thinner doors larger than 3 feet 0 inches wide by 7 feet 0 inches high (914 mm by 2134 mm).

   b. Doors with face veneers of different species.

c. Doors which are improperly hung or do not swing freely.

d. Doors with face applied paneling or siding.

e. Doors that are not sealed with two coats of paint, varnish or sealer on the top and bottom edges and around all cutouts at time of installation.

4. **Photographing stile, rail and core** showing through on hardwood veneered flush doors shall not be considered as a defect unless the faces of the door vary from a true plane in excess of $1/100"$ in any 3" span.

Ed. Note: See also "Testing for Show-Through and Warpage" in the following section.

Finishing

Prior to finishing insure that the building atmosphere is dried to a normal, interior relative humidity. Ensure that the doors have been allowed to equalize to a stable moisture content.

Windows & Doors: Testing Procedures

Door Tests

Industry Standards

Specifiers Guide to Wood Windows and Doors
(Window & Door Manufacturers Association)

Ed. Note: Following are pertinent sections of WDMA I.S.9 Industry Standard for the Performance of Exterior Wood Door Entry Systems. Contractors should refer to the full document for complete details.

4.0 Performance Requirements and Tests

4.1 All exterior wood door systems labeled or otherwise identified as complying with this standard shall conform to the requirements outlined below.

4.2 Unit Test Size. The performance tests described in this standard shall be conducted on the largest unit system size for which conformance is desired.

4.3 Performance Test Criteria

4.3.1 Air Infiltration. The unit shall be in a closed and locked position during the test. The unit shall be rested in accordance to ASTM E-283 "Standard Test Method for Rate of Air Leakage Through Exterior Windows, Curtain Walls, and Doors." The rate of air leakage through the test specimen shall not exceed 0.20 cubic feet per minute per foot of crack length when tested under a uniform static air pressure difference of 1.57 pounds per square foot (75PA).

4.3.2 Water Penetration. The unit shall be in a closed and locked position during the test. The unit shall be tested in accordance to ASTM E-547 "Standard Test Method for Water Penetration of Exterior Windows, Curtain Walls, and Doors by Cyclic Static Air Pressure Differential." The unit shall be tested for a minimum of 3 cycles, of no less than 5 minutes each, under a uniform static air pressure difference of 3.86 pounds per square foot. At the conclusion of the test, no water shall have passed beyond the interior face of the unit test specimen and overflowed into the room, or flowed into the wall area.

Note: Joints between the unit test specimen and the adjacent test apparatus shall be caulked, taped or otherwise sealed to prevent extraneous air or water leakage. Since door systems are not normally sold with lock hardware, any air or water leakage through the locking device(s) or between the locking device(s) and the door leaf is to be eliminated or contained and is not to be included in the measured performance of the unit specimen. Sealant may be used to eliminate air or water leakage between the brickmold or extensions and the door jamb; such sealant must be recorded on the test report.

Testing for Show-Through & Warpage

Industry Standards

Specifiers Guide to Wood Windows and Doors
(Window & Door Manufacturers Association)

T-1: Show-Through

Show-through (telegraphing) of vertical and horizontal edges and cores is considered a defect when the face of the door varies from a true plane in excess of 0.010 inch in any three-inch span.

The selection of high glass laminates or finishes should be avoided, because they tend to accentuate natural telegraphing.

T-2: Warp

Warp is any distortion in the door itself, and is not measured in relation to the frame in which it is hung. Warp is measured by placing a straight edge or a taut string on the concave face and determining the maximum distance from straight edge or string to door face.

Sill Track Test

Industry Standards

Nail-On Windows
(DTA, Inc.)

We recommend that the sill-jamb joints of windows be tested for weather tightness after installation. This is especially critical if the window had any apparent damage from shipping or handling that was not severe enough to have the window replaced.

To conduct the test, the sill track of the window can be filled with water after plugging and taping the weep holes. Allow the water to sit for 15 minutes to observe if the water level decreases, indicating a leak in the frame joint. This test complies with an industry report outlined in the AAMA publication 502-90, optional Test Method A. Remove weep hole plugs or tape after the test. Refer to **Figure 9.15**.

If the joints leak, then the sill-jamb joints should be cleaned and resealed according to the preparation and scaling procedures recommended by the window manufacturer.

If the flashing procedures are followed and the window sill is watertight, then the window and doors should prove successful for long-term performance.

Water Spray Tests
Section 2.3.1c notes the AAMA water spray tests that can be used to field test installations of windows and sliding glass doors. These field tests can be used to evaluate the flashings and wall claddings around the openings too.

Also effective in locating sources of leaks to windows and doors is a common garden hose used to spray water around the opening. A formalized procedure works from the bottom of the unit towards the top. Observation from inside the building can trace leaks. Removal of interior finishes and the use of a moisture meter can assist in locating leak spots and tracing water paths back to sources of entry. If there is a failure, removal of exterior finishes after water testing can help locate water entry points by following traces of moisture on the layers of building materials around the door or window opening.

Comments

Window warranties usually identify the issues that affect window performance. They also provide tolerances "not considered defects."

Many manufacturers of wood windows utilize varying versions of the Woodwork Institute of California's recommendations for warranty compliance. These warranty conditions usually include the following:

- Painting of wood windows must be accomplished on all sides of the windows within 48 hours of delivery to the construction site or immediately upon installation, and must be repainted periodically to avoid damage to the wood parts.

(continued)

Sill Track Water Test

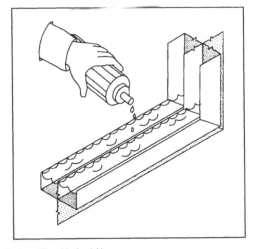
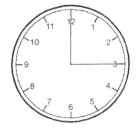

Test:
1. Plug weep holes
2. Fill sill track with water.
3. Observe water level 15 minutes.
4. There should be no leakage or reduction in the water level from sill track.
5. If failure, trace leakage. If pass, remove weep hole plugs.

(Based on AAMA 502-90 Optional Test Method A)

Courtesy of DTA. Inc., *Nail-On Windows*

Figure 9.15

- Lap the finish coat $\frac{1}{16}$" onto the glass for a proper moisture seal.
- Primers usually are not compatible with lacquer and varnishes. Primer paints must be designated to prevent the application of dissimilar products.
- Abrasive cleaners or solutions containing solvents hould not be used.

Manufacturers' Quality Certification

Industry Standards

Specifiers Guide to Wood Windows and Doors
(Window & Door Manufacturers Association)

Quality Certified Wood Windows

WDMA certifies firms which have demonstrated the ability to manufacture windows according to WDMA Industry Standard for Wood Window Units I.S. 2. Each WDMA certified manufacturer's plant is inspected by WDMA to determine if their production facilities and procedures conform to the Standard. At that time, samples of finger-joints and preservative treating solution are taken and tested.

Window units must meet all of the requirements of the Standard, including air and water infiltration, and uniform and physical loading. I.S.2 also requires that all wood window units be water-repellent preservative treated, and all adhesives used meet the requirements of a Type I "wet use" adhesive in accordance with the appropriate ASTM Standard.

Care

1. Specify that window sash and frames be treated at the factory with a WDMA approved water-repellent preservative in accordance with Industry Standard I.S.4 Water-Repellent Preservative Non-Pressure Treatment for Millwork.
2. Store in a clean, dry, well ventilated building; not in damp, moist or extremely humid environments.
3. While in storage, cover to keep clean.
4. Windows, frames and sash should be conditioned to the average prevailing moisture (humidity) of the locality before installing.
5. Deliver in clean truck and under cover in wet weather.
6. Handle with clean canvas gloves. Bare hands leave finger marks and soil stains.
7. When moving window units, carry them; do not drag them.
8. Do not drop or jar window units; any jar or shock may break the glass or glazing seal or put the window out of square.
9. In new homes, ventilate rooms thoroughly and install windows after all walls (plaster or cement) are dry.
10. Be sure frame is square before unit is installed in opening. Use a diagonal brace across corners after frame is squared. A horizontal spacer strip at midpoint of height of the frame will maintain equal width between jambs from head to sill. Remove brace and spacer strip after frame is anchored into wall opening.
11. Install and fit windows accurately in accordance with good building practice and/or with manufacturer's instructions.
12. Avoid driving nails into sash balances by marking jamb to indicate position of balance.
13. If nailing through the exterior jamb or wood brick moulding is necessary to ensure the window's structural load capabilities, the anchoring devices (nails, screws, etc.) should be countersunk and the holes puttied flush with the surface prior to coating.
14. Keep channel and weather-strip of window clean so that sash may operate freely.
15. Be sure to install proper close-fitting locks.
16. Keep woodwork clean; do not use caustic or abrasive cleaners.
17. When opening or closing windows, use handle or lift.
18. Install storm sash or insulating glass in colder climates to help prevent condensation on window glass.
19. Make certain to caulk and insulate between the window and the wall rough opening, especially around the nailing fin or brick moulding.

Finishing

1. Temperature and humidity have a major effect on drying and may affect paint film characteristics. Paint should be applied at product, surface, and air temperatures between 50°F (10°C) and 90°F (32°C) unless product label specifies differently. Relative humidity should be below 85%.

2. Use only high grade materials and follow manufacturer's instructions carefully to assure a long-lasting beautiful appearance.

3. Surfaces to be painted must be thoroughly dry and free from dust/dirt, oil, grease, wax, chalk and other contaminants. Remove dust/dirt by scrubbing or hosing. Remove oils, waxes and grease with paint thinner. If mildew is present, it must be removed prior to painting. Sand to remove any surface roughness and wipe clean.

4. Be sure that all nail holes, gouges or other surface indentations are filled before coating to ensure the performance of the top coat.

5. As soon as possible, apply a quality prime coat to the exterior of the window if not pre-primed from the factory. Apply two coats of quality trim paint to the exterior of primed units within 30 days of installation. Again, be sure to apply paint in accordance with manufacturer's directions.

6. Each coat of paint should be applied evenly. Make certain the surfaces are dry before applying the next coat.

7. Do not paint weather-strip. Remove unwanted paint from the weather-strip.

8. Be sure to overlap paint or urethane on glass to seal glazing seal joint. Do not break this seal when removing paint from glass surfaces or when cleaning.

9. To the interior of your window units, apply a quality prime coat and two or three coats of trim paint. Or, if you desire a natural finish, apply a coat of sanding sealer and two coats of urethane. Finishing done under the supervision of a reliable painting contractor is the most satisfactory.

10. When cleaning woodwork, avoid the use of caustics or abrasives which dissolve or damage the finish.

11. The exposed exterior surfaces of some wood windows are clad with aluminum or vinyl. Clad windows provide a protective, low-maintenance exterior while still giving the superior thermal performance of wood sash and frames. Clad windows do not require exterior finishing. Consult manufacturer's instructions for care and cleaning instructions.

Glazing

Industry Standards

WIC Manual of Millwork (Effective 5/1/01)
(Woodwork Institute of California, www.wicnet.org)

I. Thermal Integrity

A. Wood is a natural insulator that needs no artificial "thermal break" to retain heat in winter. ("Thermal breaks" are strips of insulating material—wood, fiberglass, etc.—inserted between layers of aluminum.)

B. Wood as a material resists conductance of cold temperatures 2,000 times better than aluminum. (Thermal conductance is the total measure of heat flow through a material from the inside surface to the outside surface.)

C. A wood window with insulating glass is approximately 30% more thermally efficient than a comparable size and style aluminum window.

D. Wood's minimal conduction of heat and cold keeps inside wood surface of windows warm in winter, cool in summer.

E. Modern, quality wood windows and wood door systems have built-in weather stripping which can reduce air infiltration to less than 0.33 cubic feet per minute.

F. Modern wood windows, and glass-paned wood patio and entry doors, are available with double and triple glazing systems, increasing thermal efficiency.

G. Some wood windows and glass-paned wood doors contain new Low-E glazing. Low-E glazing improves R-value of glass, making these windows and doors more thermally efficient.

II. Key Definitions

A. Low-E—"E" is emissivity; ability of glass to reradiate heat it absorbs. Low-E values represent better heat reradiation. The lower the emissivity ("E") of the glass, the better its insulating quality.

B. U-value—measures thermal transmission; heat flow through material or assembly from inside air to outside air. Low U-values represent greater resistance to transmission of interior heat to outside.

C. R-value—measures thermal resistance; how well material stops/resists heat flowing through it. High R-values represent greater ability to stop/resist heat absorption.

III. Types of Low-E Glazing

A. Pyrolitir—applied during manufacture of glass.

B. Sputtered—sprayed on finished glass, used on interior pane of double and triple thermal pane systems.

IV. Benefits of Low-E Glazing

A. In Insulated Glass:

1. Improves U-value (thermal transmission) from 0.49 to 0.32; increases R-value (thermal resistance) from 2.04 to 3.12.

B. In Wood Windows With Insulated Glass:

1. Improves U-value from 0.45 to 0.30; increases R-value from 2.22 to 3.33.

C. In Storm Sashes or Doors (single glazing):

1. Improves U-value from 1.04 to 0.75; increases R-value from 0.96 to 1.33.

V. Durability

A. Wood in quality windows and doors is chemically treated in the factory: to repel decay, warping, insects; protect against heat and humidity.

VI. Options

A. All quality wood windows, wood entry systems, wood patio, stile and rail doors are available as prehung units. Prehung units include the door, frames, hardware, and weather-stripping.

Multiple Glazing

Industry Standards

Construction Principles, Materials, and Methods
(John Wiley and Sons, Inc.)

8.8.4.3 Because of its thinness, a single sheet of glass is a good conductor of heat. One square foot of $\frac{1}{4}$ in. clear glass can conduct 6 to 10 times more BTUs per hour than a square foot of a typical frame wall. The rate of heat transfer through the glass is so rapid that added thickness is of almost no value. However, if layers of glass are separated by an air space, the path of conduction is interrupted, and the rate of heat flow is reduced. Heat can then pass through the air space primarily by radiation and convection and only minimally by conduction.

Storm windows can be effective in reducing conduction and infiltration with an air separation between panes of glass of as much as 6 in. However, an air space is most effective in improving thermal performance when it is between $\frac{3}{16}$ in. and $\frac{5}{8}$ in. wide. Within this range, the heat flow is reduced markedly as the width is increased from $\frac{3}{16}$ in. towards $\frac{5}{8}$ in. Increasing the air space beyond $\frac{5}{8}$ in. does not reduce heat flow to the same extent, because a wider space allows the air in it to circulate more freely and develop convection currents. These currents transport heat from the warmer glass to the colder glass. This increased convection heat loss can more than offset the slight reduction in conductive heat loss through the air. Conversely, a space of less than $\frac{3}{16}$ in. is of little value because heat is readily conducted by the air across such a short distance.

Glazing Properties

Green Building: Project Planning & Cost Estimating, Second Edition
(RSMeans)

A wide variety of window glass options are available, and careful selection of glass is an important element in any strategy to maximize natural light. Developments in glazing technology have revolutionized architecture by addressing the limitations caused by excessive heat loss, and also by controlling the amount and nature of light passing through the window. Light striking a window is reflected off the surface, absorbed by the tint in the glass, or transmitted to the other side. These properties are described by the transmittance and reflectivity of the glass. The visible transmittance (VT) is the fraction of visible light that makes it through the glass, while the total transmittance includes the infrared and ultraviolet parts of the solar spectrum. Some of the heat absorbed in the tint of the glass is convected to the room air. The parameter used to describe the sum of transmitted solar radiation plus this absorbed heat that eventually makes it into the room air, is called the Solar Heat Gain Coefficient (SHGC).

Properties of Three Different Types of Window Glazing

	Visible Transmittance	Solar Heat Gain Coefficient	U-value (heat loss)
Double-pane clear	0.82	0.78	0.46
Low-E	0.78	0.58	0.25
Selective	0.72	0.37	.27

Figure 9.16   RSMeans, *Green Building: Project Planning & Cost Estimating,* 2nd Edition

For passive solar heating applications, it may be desirable to transmit as much sunlight as possible. It is common to add a UV coating to protect occupants and items inside from ultraviolet radiation. Such coatings effectively remove 99% of ultraviolet radiation.

A reflective coating such as silver or gold rejects solar heat but adds a mirror-like appearance. A tint such as blue, green or bronze also reduces the SHGC, but affects the view out the window.

If a clear appearance is desired or required for daylighting, but solar heat is not wanted, selective glazings are available that screen out the ultraviolet and infrared, but maximize visible transmittance. Selective glazings would be specified in cases where the control of solar heat gain is important, but a clear appearance is also desired. Selective glass can have a SHGC as low as 40%, but a visible transmittance in excess of 70%. A SHGC less than 40% usually requires attenuation of the visible spectrum by tint or reflective coating. The interior and exterior appearance (reflectivity and color tint), the daylighting and passive solar heating goals, and the orientation of the window are considerations when specifying glazing properties.

Heat loss through glazing is described by the heat loss coefficient (U-value), which is multiplied by the indoor-outdoor temperature difference to calculate the heat loss rate. Multiple layers of glazing result in a lower heat loss coefficient, with air or a lower conductivity gas, like argon, used in the spaces between the layers. Low emissivity (low-E) coatings are applied to the interior surfaces to reduce the radiant heat transfer from one pane to another through the air gap. In some products, the low-E coating is applied to a thin film that serves as a third pane suspended between two glass panes. The glazing assemblies are sealed, often with a desiccant in the frame, to avoid unsightly water condensation between the panes.

Film Coatings

Comments

Sometimes homeowners have mylar film applied to their windows after the installation is complete. Some window manufacturers include disclaimers for window performance under these circumstances. Failures of dual-glazed units due to moisture condensation have been traced to the presence of tinted film on the inside face of the glass. Deflection caused by the tinted film can create heat buildup and expansion within the airspace of the

dual unit, which destroys the butyl seal. Water vapor can then be admitted, condensing between the panes. Heat buildup can also cause the decorative grids, or "muntins," within the window to detach from the butyl inside dual-glazed units.

Green Window & Entryway Strategies

 Green Building: Project Planning & Cost Estimating, Second Edition
(RSMeans)

Low-Emissivity (or Low-E) Glass

Emissivity is defined as the ability of a product to emit or receive radiant rays, thus decreasing the U-value. (U-factors represent the heat loss per unit area per degree of temperature difference, BTU/SF/°F. They are reported by the National Fenestration Rating Council, NFRC). Most non-metallic solids can emit or receive radiant rays and, therefore, have a high degree of emissivity. Fenestrations that reflect radiant rays have a low emissivity. Use of low-E glass windows allows the daylight to enter the building, but reduces the amount of thermal energy from the sun that enters the building envelope. The result is a reduction in the facility's net cooling requirements.

Heat Mirror Technology

This type of fenestration uses a low-emissivity coated film product suspended inside or between the panes of an insulating glass unit. This is a lower-cost alternative to low-E glass double-pane units.

Window Films

Films can be applied to the surface of an existing window to change the optical properties. Unlike the wavy, bubbly polyester films of the past, today's acrylic films are hardly noticeable. These films are designed to reduce the amount of solar heat transmission through window glass by increasing the solar reflection (not necessarily visible reflection) and decreasing solar absorption of the glass.

Opaque Insulated Fenestration

This composite fenestration combines controlled, usable, natural daylight with highly energy-efficient properties. This product has R-values (insulation values) from R-4 through R-12. (Typical windows have an R-value of 1.) The translucent wall panels allow for natural lighting without the thermal energy loss normally associated with windows. The panels are lightweight and shatterproof, and have impressive structural integrity.

Doors

In addition to seeking sustainable door materials made from recycled material or certified lumber, it is important to look for energy efficiency in the form of exterior door R-value and appropriate door seals. Jamb materials merit attention as they can also reduce conductive heat loss on exterior doors.

Vestibules

A vestibule is an area between two sets of doors, serving as an air lock at a building's entrance. Vestibules minimize the infiltration of exterior conditions into the space within the building envelope.

Air Doors

Air doors, sometimes called air walls, are typically used for garage- or loading dock-type doors to reduce infiltration and ex-filtration. An air door creates an invisible barrier of high-velocity air that separates different environments. Air enters the unit through the intake and is then compressed by scrolled fan housings and forced through a nozzle, which is directed at the open doorway. The system utilizes centrifugal fans mounted on direct-driven, dual-shafted motors. The result is a uniform air screen across the opening with enough force to stop winds up to 25 mph.

Plastic Curtains

Plastic curtains reduce infiltration and ex-filtration. They are an economical solution for protecting employees and goods from adverse environmental conditions. Plastic curtain or strip doors are inexpensive, easy to install, and save energy.

Fast Closing Doors

Many walk-in or drive-in refrigerated spaces are converting to "fast-closing" doors that sense the need to open for a delivery or worker, then close quickly. For refrigerated spaces, vapor migration is almost as big an energy loss as the temperature migration. Therefore a tight seal in the space is key to saving energy. A plastic curtain will help with temperature, but not moisture.

Table of Contents

Text in blue type indicates excerpted summaries from the International Building Code® (IBC) *and* International Residential Code® (IRC). *Please consult the* IBC *and* IRC *for complete coverage and specific wording. "Comments" (in solid blue boxes) were written by the editors, based on their own experience.*

 These icons will appear with references to green building practices and seismic regulations, respectively.

CHAPTER 10

DRYWALL & CERAMIC TILE

Common Defect Allegations

Drywall

Many claims in drywall construction involve issues related to facing, taping and finishing, and fire rating. Since finished drywall telegraphs imperfections through the painted surface, defects that detract from the appearance are often brought to the builder's attention upon occupancy. Even when wall covering is applied over drywall, proper taping and facing is necessary, as defects may show through.

A common defect allegation is insufficient nailing. Construction defect analysts sometimes place refrigerator magnets on each nailhead to show how a wall was undernailed.

Building codes allow drywall to be utilized as a shear panel in certain applications. When this occurs, the nailing is critical, and care must be taken to avoid breaking the paper skin while nailing. Wrinkling or beading sometimes occurs in the horizontal tape joint on walls over eight ' high, as a result of lumber shrinkage. A building can shrink vertically as much as $^3/_4$" per floor, depending on the dryness of the lumber and the lightness of the framer's assembly. Lumber shrinkage also causes nail pops, another common defect allegation. (See Chapter 5, "Wood Framing," for more on wood shrinkage and nail pops.)

Green board is a subject of defect claims. This material has great moisture resistance, but must be installed correctly for proper performance. Stacks of green board left uncovered in the rain and then measured with a moisture meter have been shown to have resisted moisture even after three weeks. On the other hand, green board used under ceramic tile with missing grout or the wrong mastic (for a shower in regular daily use) can turn to the consistency of pudding after five years.

From time to time, metal corner bead corrodes due to the use of "hot mud," or quicksetting compound. These products will not only rust the metal trim, but will bleed through light shades of paint, creating yellow blotching.

(continued)

Ceramic Tile

All installations that are determined to be defective fall under one of two definitions: observable (patent defects), or concealed (latent defects). In the defect litigation business, there are statutes of limitation to limit the time period that a builder is responsible for repairs under warranty. Patent Defects are limited to two, three, or five years, according to the type of condition and the interpretation of the owner's responsibility to observe conditions or maintain the installation. Latent defects are under warranty for ten years.

Ceramic tile allegations reflect the extremes of these rules. Homeowners often add a tile claim of variations in grout joints and water intrusion through the deck, as part of an overall defect claim, seven or eight years after moving into the house. In this case, the observable variations in the grout joints would have expired after two years, while the deck leaking could constitute a valid claim.

The most common defect claim on tile is cracking of tile and/or grout joints, usually in a sawtooth pattern. These problems generally reflect movement in the substrate. Slip sheet (also referred to as cleavage membrane) will reduce this condition when wood framing or concrete slabs crack or expand. Occasionally, cracking can result from horizontal stress even over slip sheet. If tile flooring is grouted tight in a kitchen surrounded by wood cabinets and then experiences a flood or broken pipe, the resulting swelling of the wood cabinet bases will crack the tile floor. This risk can be eliminated by grouting perimeter and key joints with sanded caulking to match the grout.

The most costly of the common tile defects is the exterior deck leak. The defect, of course, is in the underlayment. The tile was placed over the membrane; however, the membrane did not have water integrity after it was installed, or it was placed in a manner that stressed it sufficiently to tear or break. A regular cause of breaks in membrane is horizontal expansion breaking the corner where the vertical and horizontal planes meet. Use cant strips whenever possible. The use of an unreinforced flexible member with a rubberized adhesive attached slip sheet allows for membrane expansion or contraction. Vertical runs on the membrane must lap under the wall wrap by 2" and at least 2" above the overflow high-level water mark.

Another defect is caused by hand-made shower pans with "hot mop" roofing as the composite waterproofing. This material continues to be specified on drawings. Destructive testing will almost always uncover a problem using this waterproofing material for this purpose.

Installations using vinyl one-piece membrane, or vinyl that has been chemically welded, will reduce the frequency of these claims. The pan should be water-checked for 24 hours prior to floating the finishes over the vinyl.

A common complaint on natural marble floor tiles is deterioration of the marble surface, where some veins seem to "pocket out" of the surface. This usually is from excessive moisture vapor being emitted from the concrete floor below, corroding the veins of iron deposits in the marble, thereby causing oxidation or rust expansion.

Introduction   This chapter covers installation issues for gypsum wallboard, followed by a section on skim coat plaster over a gypsum composition base, and ceramic tile. Mold-resistant paperless drywall and recycled-content tile are also addressed. Note that concrete or cement board backing is covered in the ceramic tile section of the chapter.

The chapter begins with a list of common drywall installation problems. Standards for correct drywall installation are detailed in the sections that follow. Tile installation problems are addressed in the section titled, "Avoiding Failures in Ceramic Tile Installation" at the end of this chapter.

For light commercial projects, wall finish information may be provided on the room finish schedule of the architectural drawings. (See Chapter 12 for painting and wall covering standards.)

The following organizations are sources of additional information:

Association of the Wall & Ceiling Industry (AWCI)
703-534-1600
www.awci.org
AWCI's membership consists of wall and ceiling contractors, product suppliers, and manufacturers.

Ceilings & Interior Systems Construction Association (CISCA)
630-584-1919
www.cisca.org

Gypsum Association (GA)
202-289-5440
www.gypsum.org
GA has a technical staff for consultation on specific issues relating to the use of gypsum board. The association also publishes technical papers and other publications, and covers many technical issues in the "Frequently Asked Questions" area of its website. GA's evaluation reports demonstrate code compliance and acceptance of specific gypsum materials and systems.

Ceramic Tile Institute of America, Inc.
310-574-7800
www.ctioa.org

Tile Council of America, Inc. (TCA)
864-646-8453
www.tileusa.com
The TCA publishes the *2001 Handbook for Ceramic Tile Installation*, which describes in detail the methods and standards for ceramic tile installation.

Ed. Note: Comments and recommendations within this chapter are not intended as a definitive resource for construction activities. For building projects, contractors must rely on the project documents and local building codes.

Green Considerations for Drywall & Ceramic Tile

Drywall is by nature a relatively harmless substance. It's made from paper wrapped around a core made primarily from gypsum plaster (calcium sulfate), which is a mined material. It also contains fiber (usually paper and/or fiberglass) and ingredients such as plasticizers, foaming agents, potash (an accelerator), and EDTA or other chelate, and additives to prevent mildew and resist fire.

Drywall has a negative impact on the environment in several ways. Its production requires mining, which damages wildlife habitat; its processing and transport use energy and produce emissions; and its disposal creates waste that usually ends up in landfills. There are, however, green options available to reduce these impacts. Synthetic drywall is made with a by-product from the desulferization of coal at power plants, and recycled-content drywall is made with waste from drywall manufacture and also, on a limited scale, with gypsum salvaged from demolition.

Healthy indoor air quality is another tenet of green building. Paperless drywall is a plus since it reduces the opportunity for mold growth. Mold is a common source of health problems.

No matter what kind of drywall is used, waste prevention is important for a greener project. Waste can be reduced by building standard-sized walls and flat ceilings, by ordering custom-sized sheets for walls that are not standard, and by using reusable wall materials, such as modular "demountable partitions" in commercial buildings. You can also donate half- or full-size leftover sheets of drywall to Habitat for Humanity ReStores. For further guidelines on reducing drywall waste, consult Appendix C of "A Builder's Field Guide" from the National Association of Home Builders (NAHB) Research Center at 1-800-368-5242 or (202) 266-8200. Or check their website **www.nahb.com**

The manufacture, transport, and disposal of ceramic tile also affects the environment. Recycled-content ceramic tile (made from recycled glass and mining or factory waste materials) is a good option for projects calling for environmentally friendly products. It diverts waste from landfills and uses less energy than fabrication from raw materials. This helps conserve fuel and reduce environmental pollution.

Recycled tile is as durable as conventional tile and can be used for all the same applications. Although tile with a higher percentage of recycled material tends to be more expensive, most recycled-content tile is price-competitive with mid-range conventional ceramic tile. Low-toxicity grouts and adhesives are also available to reduce exposure to VOCs.

Gypsum Wallboard: Common Problems

Comments

Also see "Gypsum Base Limitations" and "Effects of Site Conditions" at the end of the Gypsum Wallboard portion of this chapter.

Common Drywall Problems

Paint and finish may show surface irregularities in certain lights. (As with most finishes it is best to judge drywall finish in sunlight or natural light.) The finished product should not show cracked corner bead, excess joint compound, blisters in tape joints, or trowel marks. Some causes for imperfections are:

- Not enough or too much compound is used to cover nails, screws, or joints.
- Not enough coats of joint compound are applied.
- Adequate time is not allowed for the various coats to dry (and shrink) thoroughly before applying the next coat.
- The person who applies the tape may be under the impression that other finishes will later cover a particular area. As a result, some nails and joints do not receive the correct amount of attention.
- Cracks may develop at corners of openings where small pieces of drywall are used. A taped joint in the board at a corner can also lead to cracking.
- Buildup of compound in corners may create a shadow line or cause poor fitting of base and other wall moldings.
- Too many drywall pieces are used instead of full sheets.
- End joints are stacked on top of each other or four-way joints are used.
- Drywall is not properly fastened.
- Drywall is used to straighten framing members, thereby creating unnecessary pressure points on the board.
- Outlets, switches, and ceiling boxes are not given careful treatment. (Solid material is always preferable to filling.)
- Improper sanding techniques are used:
  —Too little time spent on sanding.
  —Too-aggressive sanding, causing paper to become rough and porous.
- Bubbles form in tape or in compound.

Most drywall imperfections can be corrected with a relatively small investment of time and effort, unless whole walls need to be refinished. Those responsible

for quality control on a job should check finishing and hanging techniques early in the project to ensure that necessary touchup of the drywall will not have to include repainting finished walls. After the painter has applied the first coat of primer, the taper and painter should check for defects before the final coat(s) are applied.

Gypsum Wallboard Installation

Industry Standards

Plan Reading & Material Takeoff
(RSMeans)

Drywall sheets are installed on wood or metal framing systems with screws. The seams of abutting drywall sheets and screw holes are taped with a vinyl-based joint treatment compound and reinforcing tape. Joint taping is a multi-step process usually requiring three coats, including the tape coat. The tape is embedded in a coat of joint compound and allowed to dry. Subsequent coats are applied, with sanding between coats to remove the imperfections. The resulting finish conceals the joints, and should be smooth and ready for paint or other finishes.

Comments

Following are some general recommendations for drywall installation.

- Install the ceiling panels first, then the walls. Begin at a corner.
- End-to-end joints should fall at the studs or joists, except where back-blocking is used.
- On exterior walls, check to make sure adequate insulation has been installed before placing the wallboard. The vapor barrier should be facing into the room, fastened to the sides of the wall studs.
- If using adhesive on the bottom of ceiling joists, leave 6" uncovered from the wallboard sides to prevent the adhesive from oozing out at the joints between the boards.

While fiberglass tape is easier to apply and stronger than paper tape, it has no flexibility and can eventually show through where joints have come apart. Paper tape, on the other hand, contracts and expands along with the gypsum wallboard's paper facing.

Gypsum Plasterboard

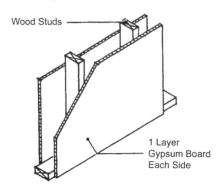

Wood Studs

1 Layer
Gypsum Board
Each Side

Staggered Stud Wall

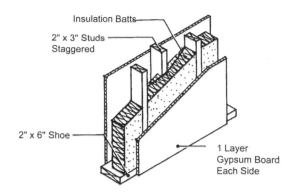

Insulation Batts

2" x 3" Studs
Staggered

2" x 6" Shoe

1 Layer
Gypsum Board
Each Side

Sound-Deadening Board

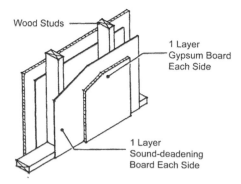

Wood Studs

1 Layer
Gypsum Board
Each Side

1 Layer
Sound-deadening
Board Each Side

Figure 10.1   RSMeans, *Means Graphic Construction Standards*

Gypsum Construction

Note: The following are summaries of the basic code requirements of the *International Building Code* and *International Residential Code*. Please consult the *IBC* and *IRC* for complete coverage and specific wording.

IBC–2006

2508.1 General: Gypsum board and plaster construction must be of the materials listed in Table 2506.2 and Table 2507.2, and must be installed according to standards listed in Tables 2508.1 and 2511.1, and Chapter 35.

2508.2 Limitations: Gypsum wallboard or plaster must not be used in any exterior surface which such construction will have direct exposure to the weather. Gypsum sheathing must be installed on exterior surfaces according to ASTM C 1280 standards.

2508.3 Single-ply application: Edges and ends of gypsum board must occur on the framing members with the exception of edges and ends that are perpendicular to the framing members. Edges and ends of gypsum board must be in moderate contact except in concealed spaces where fire-resistance-rated construction, shear resistance, or diaphragm action is not necessary.

2508.3.1 Floating angles: Fasteners at top and bottom plates of vertical assemblies, or the edges and ends of horizontal assemblies perpendicular to supports, and the wall line can be omitted except on shear resisting elements or fire-resistance-rated assemblies. Fasteners must be applied in such a way as to not fracture the face paper with the fastener head.

2508.4 Joint treatment: Gypsum board fire-resistance-rated assemblies must have joints and fasteners treated.

Exception: Joint and fastener treatment is not necessary if any of the following conditions exist:

1. Where the gypsum board will receive a decorative finish that would be the equivalent to joint treatment.

2. On single layer systems where joints exist over wood framing members.

3. With square edge or tongue-and-groove edge gypsum board, gypsum backing board or gypsum sheathing.

4. On multiplayer systems where the joints of nearby layers are offset from one another.

5. On assemblies that are tested without joint treatment.

IRC–2006

R702.3.1 Materials: Gypsum board material and accessories must conform to ASTM C 36, C 79, C 475, C514, C 630, C 931, C 960, C 1002, C 1047, C1177, C 1178, C 1278 and C 1395 and must be installed in accordance with requirements of this section. Adhesives for gypsum board installation must conform to ASTM C 557.

R702.3.2 Wood framing: Wood framing that supports gypsum board must not be less than 2 inches thick in the smallest dimension. The exception is wood furring strips that are not less than 1" x 2" can be used over solid backing or framing spaced not more than 24" on center.

R702.3.3 Steel framing: Steel framing that supports gypsum board must not be less than 1.25" wide in the smallest dimension. Non-load bearing steel framing that is light-gage must comply with ASTM C 645. Load-bearing steel framing and steel framing from 0.0333" to 0.112" must comply to ASTM C 955 standards.

R702.3.4 Insulating concrete form walls: Foam plastics for insulating concrete form walls constructed in accordance with Sections R404.4 and R611 on the interior habitable spaces must be covered in accordance with Section R318.1.2. Adhesives are allowed in conjunction with mechanical fasteners. Adhesives used for interior and exterior finishes must be compatible with insulating form materials.

R702.3.5 Application: Table R702.3.5 regulates the maximum spacing of supports and the size and spacing of fasteners used to attach gypsum board. Gypsum sheathing must be attached to exterior walls as per Table R602.3(21). Gypsum board must be applied at right angles and must be parallel to framing members. The ends and edges of gypsum board must occur on the framing members, except those that are perpendicular to the framing members. Interior gypsum board must not be installed where it can be exposed to the weather.

R702.3.6 Fastening: Screws used for attaching gypsum board to wood framing must be Type W or Type S, and must be in accordance with ASTM C 1002 and not penetrate wood less than ⅝". For attaching gypsum board to light-gage steel, screws must be Type S and in accordance to ASTM C 1002, and must not penetrate less than ⅜". Screws for attaching gypsum board to steel framing 0.033" to 0.112" must be in accordance with ASTM C 954 standards.

Industry Standards
Gypsum Construction Handbook
(United States Gypsum Company)

Drywall Construction Problems

Fastener Imperfections. A common defect, which takes on many forms. May appear as darkened, localized cracking; a depression over fastener heads; pop or protrusion of the fastener or the surface area immediately surrounding the fastener. Usually caused by improper framing or fastener application.

Joint Defects. Generally occur in a straight-line pattern and appear as ridges, depressions or blisters at the joints, or darkening over the joints or in adjacent panel areas. Imperfections may result from incorrect framing or joint treatment application, or climatic conditions if remedial action has not been taken.

Loose Panels. Board does not have tight contact with framing, rattles when impacted or moves when pressure is applied to the surface. Caused by improper application of panels, framing out of alignment or improper fastening.

Joint Cracking. Appears either directly over the long edge or butt ends of boards, or may appear along the edge of taped joints. Often caused by structural movement and/or hygrometric and thermal expansion and contraction, or by excessively fast drying of joint compounds.

Field Cracking. Usually appears as diagonal crack originating from a corner of a partition or intersection with structural elements. Also seen directly over a structural element in center of a partition. May originate from corners of doors, light fixtures and other weak areas in the surface created by penetration. Caused by movement described previously.

Angle Cracking. Appears directly in the apex of wall-ceiling or interior angles where partitions intersect. Also can appear as cracking at edge of paper reinforcing tape near surface intersections. Can be caused by structural movement, improper application of joint compound in corner angle or excessive build-up of paint.

357

Bead Cracking. Shows up along edge of flange. Caused by improper bead attachment, faulty bead or joint compound application.

Wavy Surfaces. Boards are not flat but have a bowed or undulating surface. Caused by improper board fit, misaligned framing, hygrometric or thermal expansion.

Board Sag. Occurs in ceilings, usually under high-humidity conditions. Caused by insufficient framing support for board; board too thin for span; poor job conditions; improperly installed or mislocated vapor retarder; use of unsupported insulation directly on ceiling panels; or improperly fitted panels. Refer to appropriate chapters for proper job ventilation, storage and frame spacing, particularly with waterbased texture finishes.

Surface Defects. Fractured, damaged or crushed boards after application may be caused by abuse or lumber shrinkage. Also, see Discoloration below.

Discoloration. Board surface has slight difference in color over joints, supports or fasteners. Caused by improper paint finishing, uneven soiling and darkening from aging or ultraviolet light.

Water Damage. Stains, paper bond failure, softness in board core or mildew growth are caused by sustained high humidity, standing water and improper protection from water leakage during transit and storage.

Industry Standards

Plaster and Drywall Systems Manual
(BNI Publications, Inc.)

Installation of Gypsum Board
9.1.1 Method of Cutting and Installation. Cut the gypsum board by scoring and breaking or by sawing, working from the face side. When cutting by scoring, cut the face paper with a sharp knife or other suitable tool. Break the gypsum board by snapping the gypsum board in the reverse direction, or the back paper may be cut.

9.1.2 Smooth cut edges and ends of the gypsum board where necessary to obtain neat jointing when installed. Score holes for pipes, fixtures, or other small openings on the back and the face in outline before removal or cut out with a saw or special tool designed for this purpose. Where gypsum board meets projecting surfaces, scribe and cut neatly.

9.1.3 When gypsum board is to be applied to both ceiling and walls, apply the gypsum board first to the ceiling and then to the walls.

9.1.4 Space the fasteners, when used at edges or ends, not more than 1 in. (25.4 mm) from edges and not less than ³⁄₈ in. (9.5 mm) from edges and ends of gypsum board (except where floating angles are used). Perimeter fastening into partition plate or sole at the top and bottom is not required or recommended except where the fire rating, structural performance or other special conditions require such fastening. While driving the fasteners, hold the gypsum board in firm contact with the underlying support. Application of fasteners shall proceed from the center or field of the gypsum board to the ends and edges.

9.1.5 Drive the nails with the heads slightly below the surface of the gypsum board. Avoid damage to the face and core of the board, such as breaking the paper or fracturing the core.

9.1.6 Drive the screws to provide screwhead penetration just below the gypsum board surface without breaking the surface paper of the gypsum board or stripping the framing member around the screw shank.

9.1.7 Drive the staples with the crown parallel to the framing members. Drive the staples in such a manner that the crown bears tightly against the gypsum board but does not cut into the face paper.

Note 5—Staple attachment is restricted to the base ply of the gypsum board in a two-ply system.

9.1.8 Keep the board tight against the framing.

9.1.9 Protect the external corners with a metal bead or other suitable types of corner protection that generally are attached to supporting construction with fasteners spaced nominally 6 in. (152.4 mm) on center. Corner beads may also be attached with a crimping tool.

Ed. Note: See "Selecting Appropriate Fasteners," later in this chapter, for more information.

Control Joints

Industry Standards

Gypsum Construction Handbook
(United States Gypsum Company)

Control joints are used to relieve stresses induced by expansion and contraction in large ceiling and wall expanses in drywall and veneer plaster systems. Used from door header to ceiling; from floor to ceiling in long partitions and wall furring runs; from wall to wall in large ceiling areas. Made from roll-formed zinc to resist corrosion. The control joint is covered with a roll-formed zinc trim member with a ¼" slot protected by plastic tape, which is removed after finished.

Expansion (Control) Joint

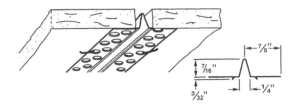

Figure 10.2

Courtesy of United States Gypsum Company,
Gypsum Construction Handbook

Green Board (Water-Resistant Gypsum Panels)

IBC–2006

Section 2509 Gypsum Board in Showers and Water Closets

2509.1 Wet areas: Showers and public toilet walls must conform to Sections 1210.2 and 1210.3.

2509.2 Base for tile: Cement, fiber-cement, or glass mat gypsum backers in accordance with ASTM C 1178, C 1288, or C 1325 must be used as a base for wall tile in tub and shower areas and wall and ceiling panels in shower areas. When installed in accordance with GA-216 or ASTM C 840, water-resistant gypsum backing is to be used for wall tile in water closet compartments. Regular gypsum wallboard is allowed under wall panels or tile in other wall and ceiling areas when installed in accordance to GA-216 and ASTM C 840.

2509.3. Limitations: Water-resistant gypsum backing board should not be used in the following areas:

1. Above a vapor retarder in a bathtub compartment or a shower.

2. In areas with constant high humidity, such as indoor pools, steam rooms, and saunas.

3. On ceilings where frame spacing goes beyond 12 inches on center for ½" thick water-resistant gypsum backing board and more than 16" on center for ⅝" thick water-resistant gypsum backing board.

IRC–2006

P2710.1 Bathtub and shower spaces: Shower walls must be finished in accordance with Section R307.2.

R702.4.2 Cement, fiber cement, and glass mat gypsum backers: These backers in compliance with ASTM C 1288, C 1325, or C 1178 shall be used for tub and shower wall tile and shower wall panels.

Comments

According to the Gypsum Association, at the "Frequently Asked Questions" area of the website, ½"-thick green board may be applied to ceilings when ceiling framing, furring, or blocking does not exceed 12" on center. Also, ⅝"-thick green board may be applied when ceiling framing, furring, or blocking does not exceed 16" on center.

Industry Standards

Gypsum Construction Handbook
(United States Gypsum Company)

Water-Resistant Gypsum Panel Application

Exposed edges and joints in areas to be tiled are treated with a coat of thinned-down ceramic tile mastic or an approved waterproof flexible sealant. Joints are treated with joint compound and joint tape.

Where water-resistant panels are used in remodeling, old wall surfaces must be removed and water-resistant panels applied to exposed studs as in new construction.

Framing—Check alignment of framing. If necessary, fur out studs around shower receptor so that inside face of lip of fixture will be flush with gypsum panel face.

Install appropriate blocking, headers, or supports for tub and other plumbing fixtures, and to receive soap dishes, grab bars, towel racks or similar items. Water-resistant gypsum panels are designed for framing 16" o.c., but not more than 24" o.c. When framing is spaced more than 16" o.c., or when ceramic tile more than ⅝₁₆" thick will be used, install suitable blocking between studs. Place blocking approximately 1" above top of tub or receptor and at midpoint between base and ceiling. Blocking is not required on studs spaced 16" o.c. or less. Vapor retarders must not be installed between water-resistant panels and framing.

Store panels in an enclosed shelter and protect from exposure to the elements.

Panels are not intended for use in areas subject to constant moisture, such as interior swimming pools, gang showers, and commercial food processing areas.

Receptors—Install receptors before panels are erected. Shower pans or receptors should have an upstanding lip or flange at least 1" higher than the water dam or threshold at the entry to the shower.

Gypsum Panels—After tub, shower pan, or receptor is installed, place temporary ¼" spacer strips around lip of fixture. Cut panels to required sizes and make necessary cut-outs. Before installing panels, apply thinned ceramic tile mastic to all cut or exposed panel edges at utility holes, joints and intersections.

Install panels perpendicular to studs with paper-bound edge abutting top of spacer strip. Fasten panels with nails 8" o.c. max. or screws 12" o.c max. Where ceramic tile more than ⁵⁄₁₆" thick will be used, space nails 4" o.c. max., and screws 8" o.c. max.

For tile ⁵⁄₁₆" thick or less, panels may be installed with stud adhesive (meeting ASTM C557) to wood or steel framing. Apply ³⁄₈" bead to stud faces, two beads on studs where panels join. Do not apply adhesive to blocking where no fasteners will be used. Position panel and drive nails or screws at 16" intervals around perimeter, ³⁄₈" from edges.

For double-layer applications, both face and base layer must consist of water-resistant Gypsum Panels.

In areas to be tiled, treat all fastener heads with Setting-Type or Lightweight Setting-Type Joint Compound rather than Ready-Mix Type Joint Compound. Fill tapered edges in gypsum panel completely with compound, embed Joint Tape firmly, and wipe off excess compound. When hardened, apply a second or skim coat over the taping coat, being careful not to crown the joint or to leave excess compound on panel (some setting-type compounds are difficult to sand and remove when dry). For butt joints and interior angles, embed joint tape with setting-type or lightweight setting-type joint compound without crowning the joints. A fill coat is not necessary. Spot fastener heads at least once with setting-type or lightweight setting-type compound.

Fill and seal all openings around pipes, fittings and fixtures with a coat of thinned-down ceramic tile mastic or an approved waterproof flexible sealant. To thin water-based mastic, add one-half pint of water per quart of mastic to make a paint-like viscosity, with a brush, apply the thinned compound onto the raw gypsum panel core at cut-outs. Allow areas to dry thoroughly prior to application of tile. Before compound dries, wipe excess material from surface of gypsum panels. Remove spacer strips but do not seal gap at bottom edge of panels. Install tile down to top edge of shower floor or tub and overlapping lip or return of tub or receptor.

For areas not to be tiled, embed tape with appropriate joint compound in the conventional manner. Finish with at least two coats of joint compound to provide a treated surface for painting and wallpapering.

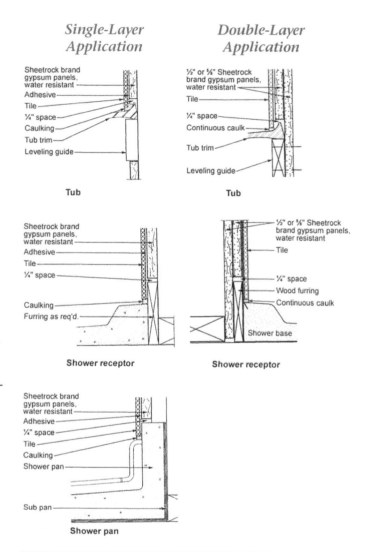

Single-Layer Application *Double-Layer Application*

Figure 10.3

Courtesy of United States Gypsum Company, *Gypsum Construction Handbook*

Comments

Ceramic tile may be applied directly over green board or cement board in a shower. However, the installation of green board requires attention to certain construction details; for example, the use of waterproof mastic (often black in color) and the priming of all open ends of board with waterproof mastic during the hanging of the board. This installation requires the site supervisor's special attention during construction.

Mold-Resistant Paperless Drywall

Comments

 Drywall can make up 70%–80% of the total interior surface area of a building. In wet conditions, traditional paper-faced drywall is susceptible to mold, which can quickly spread once established. For areas where moisture is a concern, particularly below-grade applications such as basements, paperless drywall provides a defense against mold growth and resulting air quality issues.

Paperless drywall is made of a gypsum core sheathed in fiberglass or vinyl and comes in standard 4' x 8' or 4' x 12' sheets. It is scored, cut, and fastened like traditional drywall. Finishing can be done using fiberglass or paper tape, but fiberglass tape is best for mold-resistance. Finishing and sanding should conform to the Gypsum Association's publication GA-214-07, "Recommended Levels of Gypsum Board Finish."

Refer to IBC-2006 Section 2509 for application in bathrooms, particularly around showers and tubs.

Drywall as Shear

IBC–2006

2505.1 Resistance to shear (wood framing): Wood-framed shear walls sheathed with gypsum board, lath, and plaster, will be built in accordance with Section 2306.4, and allowed to resist wind and seismic loads. Walls that resist seismic loads are subject to limitations of ASCE 7 Section 12.2.1.

2505.2 Resistance to shear (steel framing): Steel-framed shear walls sheathed with gypsum board and constructed in accordance with the materials and provisions of Section 2210.5 are allowed to resist wind loads. Walls that resist seismic loads are subject to limitations of ASCE 7 Section 12.2.1.

Comments

While the IBC allows drywall for shear bracing in all seismic zones, certain cities and counties have imposed their own code restrictions disallowing this practice. These restrictions, and others, were adopted following natural disasters. Builders need to confirm the practice followed in each locale. Building officials should be aware of this item during the plan check and inspection phases.

Selecting & Using Appropriate Fasteners

Industry Standards

Construction Principles, Materials, and Methods
(John Wiley & Sons, Inc.)

Nails

Nails for applying gypsum board can be bright coated, or chemically treated. Shanks may be either smooth or annularly threaded, with medium or long diamond points. Nail heads are flat or slightly concave, thin at the rim and not more than $5/16$ in. in diameter. Nail heads of about $1/4$-in. diameter provide adequate holding power without cutting the face paper.

Either annularly threaded nails developed for wallboard (GWB54) or smooth- or deformed-shank nails suitable for the application of gypsum board should be used. All nails should conform to ASTM C 514. Casing nails and common nails have heads that are too small in relation to the shank or too thick and should not be used.

Nails should be of the proper length for the wallboard thickness. Generally recommended penetration into supporting construction for smooth-shank nails is $7/8$ in. Annularly threaded nails provide greater withdrawal resistance, require less penetration, and generally minimize nail popping. For fire-rated construction, however, penetration of 1 in. or more usually is required and longer smooth-shank nails generally are used.

Screws

Both regular and fire-rated gypsum board can be fastened to both wood and metal supporting construction with drywall screws. The usual finish for drywall screws is a zinc phosphate coating with baked-on linseed oil. These screws typically are self-drilling and have self-tapping threads and flat Phillips recessed heads for use with a power screwdriver. Their contour head design makes a uniform depression free of ragged edges and fuzz.

Screws pull gypsum board tightly to the framing without damaging the board, minimizing fastener surface defects due to loose board attachment.

Drywall Wood Screws

Type W and similar screws are designed for fastening to wood framing or furring. Type W screws are diamond-pointed to provide efficient drilling action through both gypsum and wood and have a specially designed thread for quick penetration and increased holding power. Recommended minimum penetration into supporting construction is ⅝ in., but in two-ply application when the face layer is being screw-attached, the additional holding power developed in the base ply permits reducing the penetration into supports to ½ in.

Type W screws are available in 1¼-in. length. Drywall sheet metal screws, more readily available in longer sizes, may be substituted in two-ply construction.

Drywall Sheet Metal Screws

Type S and similar screws are designed for fastening gypsum board to 25-gauge metal studs or furring. Type S screws have a self-tapping thread and mill-slot drill point designed to penetrate sheet metal with little pressure. This is important because steel studs are flexible. The threads should be of adequate depth and turned within ¼ in. of the head to eliminate stripping. They are available in several lengths, from 1 in. to 2¼ in. Other lengths and head profiles are available for attaching wood trim, metal trim, and metal framing components. Recommended minimum penetration through sheet metal for drywall sheet metal screws is ⅜ in.

Drywall Gypsum Screws

Type G and similar screws are used for fastening gypsum board to gypsum board. Type G screws are similar to Type W screws, but have a deeper special thread design. They generally are available in 1½-in. length only. Drywall gypsum screws require penetration of at least ½ in. of the threaded portion into the supporting gypsum board. Allowing approximately ¼ in. for the point, this results in a minimum penetration of ¾ in. For this reason, drywall gypsum screws should not be used to attach wallboard to ⅜-in.-thick backing board. In two-ply construction with a ⅜ in.-thick base ply, nails or longer screws should be used to provide the necessary penetration into supporting wood or metal construction.

Staples

Staples are recommended only for attaching base ply to wood members in multi-ply construction. They should be of 16-gauge flattened galvanized wire with 1 minimum ⁷⁄₁₆-in.-wide crown and divergent sheared beveled points. Staples should be long enough to provide a minimum penetration of ⅝-in. into supporting construction.

Floating Interior Angle Application

Industry Standards

Gypsum Construction Handbook
(United States Gypsum Company)

The floating interior angle method of applying gypsum board effectively reduces angle cracking and nail pops resulting from stresses at intersections of walls and ceilings. Fasteners are eliminated on at least one surface at all interior angles, both where walls and ceilings meet and where sidewalls intersect. Follow standard framing practices for corner fastening. Conventional framing and ordinary wood backup or blocking must be provided where needed at vertical and horizontal interior angles. Apply gypsum panel to ceilings first.

Ceilings

Use conventional angle nail or screw application. Apply the first nails or screws approximately 7" from the wall and at each joist. Use conventional fastening in the remainder of the ceiling area.

Sidewalls

Apply gypsum board on walls so that its uppermost edge (or end) is in firm contact with and provides support to the perimeter of the board already installed on the ceiling. Apply the first nails or screws approx. 8" below the ceiling at each stud. At vertical angles omit corner fasteners for the first board applied at the angle. This panel edge will be overlapped and held in place by the edge of the abutting board. Nail or screw-attach the overlapping panel in the conventional manner. Use conventional fastening for remainder of sidewall area.

Double Nailing

When double nailing is used with a floating interior angle, follow above spacing on first nail from intersection and use double nailing in rest of area. Conventional framing and ordinary wood backup or blocking at vertical internal angles must be provided.

Finishing Drywall

Industry Standards

Construction Principles, Materials, and Methods
(John Wiley & Sons, Inc.)

Joint Tape

Tape used for joint reinforcement typically is a strong-fibered tape with chamfered edges. The special paper resists tensile stresses across the joint as well as longitudinally.

Joint Compounds

A topping compound is primarily a surface filler used to conceal and smooth over embedded tape, fasteners, and trim. It bonds well with joint tape and compound, gypsum board, and fasteners; it sands easily and provides a surface with sufficient "tooth" and suction for painting.

Some manufacturers make an all-purpose compound that combines the characteristics of both adhesive and filler. It is a convenient formulation available in powder or premixed form, in either a machine or handtool consistency. All-purpose compound can be used for embedding tape, topping over tape, finishing over metal trim, and concealing fasteners. It should not be used for laminating gypsum boards unless specifically recommended by its manufacturer.

Comments

It is recommended that a primer or sizing be applied to gypsum board before applications of wall coverings.

Never apply a quick-setting compound (using a chemical accelerator) directly to metal trim. The cement will react to the galvanized coating, and the item will delaminate.

Blueboard—Gypsum Base with Veneer Plaster

Industry Standard

Gypsum Construction Handbook
(United States Gypsum Company)

Gypsum Base (Lath)

Gypsum bases finished with veneer plasters are recommended for interior walls and ceilings in all types of construction. For these interiors, a veneer of specially formulated gypsum plaster is applied in one coat ($1/16$" to $3/32$" thick) or two coats (approximately $1/8$" thick) over the base. The resulting smooth or textured monolithic surfaces are preferred for hard-wear locations where durability and resistance to abrasion are required.

Gypsum Bases are available in large-size gypsum board panels (4-ft. width), rigid and fire-resistant. A gypsum core is faced with specially treated, multilayered paper (blue) designed to provide a maximum bond to veneer plaster finishes. The paper's absorbent outer layers

quickly and uniformly draw moisture from the veneer plaster finish for proper application and finishing: the moisture-resistant inner layers keep the core dry and rigid to resist sagging. The face paper is folded around the long edges. Ends are square-cut and finished smooth.

Gypsum Base Advantages

1. **Lower Cost, Lighter Weight**—Gypsum bases, in conjunction with selected veneer plaster finishes, provide the lasting beauty of plaster walls and ceilings at a lower cost and with less weight and residual moisture than conventional plaster.

2. **Rapid Installation**—Construction schedules are shortened. Walls and ceilings can be completed in 3 to 4 days, from bare framing through decorated interiors.

3. **Fire Resistance**—Ratings of up to 4 hours for partitions, 3 hours for floor-ceilings and 4 hours for column fire protection assemblies have been obtained.

4. **Sound Control**—Gypsum-base partitions faced with veneer plaster finishes on both sides have high resistance to sound transmission. Resilient attachment of base and use of appropriate insulation further improve sound isolation.

5. **Durability**—Hard, high-strength surfaces provide excellent abrasion resistance resulting in minimum maintenance, even in high-traffic areas.

6. **Easily Decorated**—Smooth-surfaced interiors accept paints, texture, fabric and wallpaper. Veneer plaster finishes also may be textured. Finish plaster can be painted with breather-type paints the day following application.

Gypsum Base Limitations

Industry Standards

Gypsum Construction Handbook
(United States Gypsum Company)

1. Maximum frame and fastener spacing is dependent on thickness and type of base used.

2. Recommended for use with basecoat and finish plaster, and basecoat and interior finish plaster. Do not apply gauged-lime putty finishes or portland cement plaster directly to base; bond failure is likely.

3. Not recommended for use in areas exposed to excessive moisture for extended periods or as a base for adhesive application of ceramic tile in wet areas (Gypsum Panels, Water-Resistant, or Cement Board are recommended for this use).

4. Gypsum base that has faded from the original light blue color from exposure to sunlight should be treated with either a plaster bonding agent or spray-applied alum solution before interior finish plaster or any veneer plaster finish containing lime is applied. Basecoat and finish plaster, or basecoat plasters, do not contain lime and are not susceptible to bond failure over faded base.

5. Joints must be treated with joint tape and setting-type joint compound when framing is spaced 24" o.c. in one-layer applications. Single-layer ½" base is not recommended with 24" o.c. spacing and one-coat veneer plaster.

Gypsum Wallboard: Effects of Site Conditions

Industry Standards

Gypsum Construction Handbook
(United States Gypsum Company)

Temperature
Install gypsum products, joint compounds and textures at comfortable working temperatures above 55°F (13°C). In cold weather, provide controlled, well-distributed heat to keep the temperature above minimum levels. For example, if gypsum board is installed at a temperature of 28°F (–2°C), it expands at the rate of ½" for every 100' when the temperature is raised to 72°F (22°C).

At lower temperatures, the working properties and performance of plasters, veneer plaster finishes, joint compounds and textures are seriously affected. They suffer loss of strength and bond if frozen after application and may have to be replaced. Ready-mixed compounds deteriorate from repeated freeze-thaw cycles, lose their workability and may not be usable. Avoid sudden changes in temperature, which may cause cracking from thermal shock.

Humidity
High humidity resulting from atmospheric conditions or from on-the-job use of such wet materials as concrete, stucco, plaster and spray fireproofing often creates situations for possible problems. In gypsum board, water vapor is absorbed, which softens the gypsum core and expands the paper. As a result, the board may sag between ceiling supports. Sustained high humidity increases chances for galvanized steel components to rust, especially in marine areas where salt air is present. High humidity can cause insufficient drying between coats of joint compounds, which can lead to delayed shrinkage and/or bond failure. Jobs may be delayed because extra time for drying is required between coats of joint compound.

Low humidity speeds drying, especially when combined with high temperatures and air circulation. These conditions may cause dryouts in veneer plaster finishes and conventional plasters. They also reduce working time and may result in edge cracking of the joint treatment. Crusting and possible contamination of fresh compound, check and edge cracking are also caused by hot and dry conditions. Under hot, dry conditions, handle gypsum board carefully to prevent cracking or core damage during erection.

Moisture
Wind-blown rain and standing water on floors increase the humidity in a structure and may cause the problems previously described. Water-soaked gypsum board and plasters have less structural strength and may sag and deform easily. Their surfaces, when damp, are extremely vulnerable to scuffing, damage and mildew.

Ventilation
Ventilation should be provided to remove excess moisture, permit proper drying of conventional gypsum plasters and joint compounds and prevent problems associated with high-humidity conditions. For veneer plaster finishes, to prevent rapid drying and possible shrinkage, poor bond, chalky surfaces and cracking, air circulation should be kept at a minimum level until the finish is set. Rapid drying also creates problems with joint compounds, gypsum plasters and finishes when they dry out before setting fully and, as a result, don't develop full strength.

Sunlight
Strong sunlight for extended periods will discolor gypsum panel face paper and make decoration difficult. The blue face paper on veneer gypsum base will fade to gray or tan from excessive exposure to sunlight or ultraviolet radiation. Applying finishes containing alkali (lime) to this degraded base may result in bond failure unless the base is treated with an alum solution or bonding agent.

Movement in Structures
Today, building frames are much lighter than former heavy masonry or massive concrete structures.

Modern structural design uses lighter but stronger materials capable of spanning greater distances and extending buildings higher than ever before. While meeting current standards of building design, these frames are more flexible and offer less resistance to structural movement. This flexibility and resulting structural movement can produce stresses within the usually non-load bearing gypsum assemblies. Unless relief joints are provided to isolate these building movements, when accumulated stresses exceed the strength of the materials in the assembly, they will seek relief by cracking, buckling or crushing the finished surface.

Structural movement and most cracking problems are caused by deflection under load, physical change in materials due to temperature and humidity changes, seismic forces or a combination of these factors.

Concrete Floor Slab Deflection

Dead and live loads cause deflection in the floor slab. If this deflection is excessive, cracks can occur in partitions at the mid-point between supports. If partition installation is delayed for about two months after slabs are completed, perhaps two-thirds of the ultimate creep deflection will have taken place, reducing chances of partition cracking. This is usually a onetime, non-cyclical movement.

 ### Wind and Seismic Forces

Wind and seismic forces cause a cyclical shearing action on the building framework, which distorts the rectangular shape to an angled parallelogram. This distortion, called racking, can result in cracking and crushing of partitions adjacent to columns, floors and structural ceilings.

Structural Movement

To resist this racking, building frames must be stiffened with shear walls and/or cross-bracing. Light steel-frame buildings are diagonally braced with steel strapping. Wood-frame structures are strengthened with let-in cross-bracing and/or shear diaphragms of structural sheathing. On larger buildings, racking is resisted by shear walls and wind-bracing without considering the strength added by finishing materials. Moreover, the partitions must be isolated from the structure to prevent cracking caused by racking movement and distortion.

Thermal Expansion

All materials expand with an increase in temperature and contract with a decrease. In tall concrete or steel-frame buildings, thermal expansion and contraction may cause cracking problems resulting from racking when exterior columns and beams are exposed or partially exposed to exterior temperatures. Since interior columns remain at a uniform temperature, they do not change in length.

Exposed exterior columns can be subjected to temperatures ranging from over 100° to 0°F (38° to –18°C), and therefore will elongate or contract in length. The amount of expansion or contraction of the exposed columns depends on the temperature difference and several other factors. (Structural movement caused by thermal differentials accumulates to the upper floors.) However, the stiffness of the structure resists the movement and usually full, unrestrained expansion is not reached.

Racking, resulting from thermal movement, is greatest in the outside bays of upper floors in winter when temperature differentials are largest. To prevent major changes, as described above, apply proper insulation to exterior structural members. The design should call for control joints to relieve stress and minimize cracking of surfaces.

Hygrometric Expansion

Many building materials absorb moisture from the surrounding air during periods of high humidity and expand; they contract during periods of low humidity. Gypsum, wood and paper products are more readily affected by hygrometric changes than are steel and reinforced concrete. Gypsum boards will expand about ½" per 100' with a relative humidity change from 13% RH to 90% RH. Unless control joints are provided, hygrometric changes create stresses within the assembly, which result in bowed or wavy walls, sag between supports in ceilings, cracking and other problems.

 ### Separation & Isolation—Relief Joints

Select gypsum assemblies to provide the best structural characteristics to resist stresses imposed on them. As described previously, these systems must resist internal stresses created by expansion and contraction of the components and external stresses caused by movement of the structure. The alternative solution is to provide control and relief joints to eliminate stress build-up and still maintain structural integrity of the assembly.

To control external stresses, partitions and other gypsum construction must be relieved from the structural framework, particularly at columns, ceilings and intersections with dissimilar materials. In long partition runs and large ceiling areas, control joints are recommended to relieve internal stress buildup. Relief joints for individual structures should be checked for adequacy by the design engineer to prevent cracking and other deformations.

As another annoyance, lumber shrinkage often results in subfloors and stair treads squeaking under foot traffic. This squeaking can be avoided by using adhesive to provide a tight bond between components and prevent adjacent surfaces from rubbing together.

Acoustical Performance Issues

Acoustical performance values (STC and MTC) are based on laboratory conditions. Such field conditions as lack of sealants, outlet boxes, back-to-back boxes, medicine cabinets, flanking paths, doors, windows and structure borne sound can diminish acoustical performance values. These individual conditions usually require the assessment of an acoustical engineer.

Separation & Isolation—Lumber Shrinkage

In wood-frame construction, one of the most expensive problems encountered is fastener pops, often caused by lumber shrinkage, in drywall surfaces. Shrinkage occurs as lumber dries. Even "kiln-dried" lumber can shrink, warp, bow and twist, causing boards to loosen and fasteners to fail. Gypsum surfaces can also crack, buckle or develop joint deformations when attached across the wide dimension of large wood framing members such as joists. Typically, this installation occurs in stairwells and high wall surfaces where the gypsum finish passes over mid-height floor framing, as in split-level houses.

Framing lumber, as commonly used, has a moisture content of 15% to 19%. After installation, the lumber loses about 10% moisture content and consequently shrinks, particularly during the first heating season. Wood shrinks most in the direction of the growth rings (flat grain), somewhat less across the growth rings (edge grain) and very little along the grain (longitudinally). Shrinkage tends to be most pronounced away from outside edges and toward the center of the member. When nails are driven toward the central axis, shrinkage leaves a space between the board and the nailing surface.

Based on experiments conducted by the Forest Products Laboratory and Purdue University, the use of shorter nails results in less space left between the board and nailing surface after shrinkage than with longer nails having more penetration. Using the shortest nail possible with adequate holding power will result in less popping due to shrinkage. Longer nails, however, usually are required for fire-rated construction, as specified by the experiments.

The annular drywall nail, with an overall length of 1¼", has equivalent holding power to a 1⅝" coated cooler-type nail, but the shorter length of the nail lessens the chances for nail popping due to lumber shrinkage.

Contractors can take several preventive measures to minimize fastener failures and structural cracking resulting from lumber shrinkage. Type W screws are even better than nails because they develop greater holding power and thus reduce possibilities for fastener pops. The floating interior angle system effectively reduces angle cracking and nail pops resulting from stresses at intersections of walls and ceilings. Gypsum boards should be floated over the side face of joists and headers and not attached. To minimize buckling and cracking in wall expanses exceeding one floor in height, either float the board over second-floor joists using resilient channels or install a horizontal control joint at this point.

Ed. Note: See "Control Joints" earlier in this chapter for further information on this topic.

Ceramic Tile

Comments

Ceramic tile continues to be a popular material for bathroom and kitchen surfaces despite the increased use of stone, stained concrete, and solid surfacing materials such as Corian®. Tile offers a range of color, size and pattern, and provides a durable surface. Ceramic tile is available in glazed, decorative, mosaic and quarry. Ceramic tile used for baths and kitchen countertops is usually glazed or mosaic. Quarry tile is generally used for flooring rather than countertops. Decorative tile is best for vertical surfaces where its painted or relief pattern is not as likely to be worn off or damaged. Non-slip tile is recommended for flooring.

The *2001 Handbook for Ceramic Tile Installation*, published by the Tile Council of America, Inc., provides detailed methods and standards for ceramic tile installation.

See the "Kitchen & Bathroom Countertops" section of Chapter 6, "Finish Carpentry & Cabinetry," for more information on types of ceramic tile and recommended applications.

See "Avoiding Failures in Ceramic Tile Installation" (at the end of this chapter) which identifies common causes of tile problems.

Wall Base for Ceramic Tile

Drywall

Comments

The base should be flat and solid and securely fastened to the framing members. If tile is to be installed over a plaster wall, inspect the wall first for holes and cracks, which must be patched with spackling or joint compound. Plaster that crumbles (when poked with a screwdriver) should be removed and replaced. The surface of the wall must be clean, dry, and free of dust before the tile is installed.

Drywall is considered an appropriate base for wall tile exposed to moisture. See "Ceramic Tile Over Green Board" in the following section, and "Green Board (Water-Resistant Gypsum Panels)" earlier in this chapter's drywall section. Basic principles of drywall installation include:

- Drywall is normally installed using nails or screws.
- Drywall sheets should be staggered from row to row to avoid having the joints line up.
- Joints should be avoided at the corners of a window or door to minimize cracking.
- At least 1/4" space should be allowed above the lip of bathtubs, shower pans, or receptors.
- Fiberglass mesh tape provides stronger joints than paper tape to support ceramic tile installation.
- After applying the joint compound, it is not necessary to provide a finish coat, though the nail or screw heads and the metal corner bead should be covered.
- Joints should be allowed to set before installing the tile.

See the Gypsum Wallboard sections in the first half of this chapter for more on correct drywall installation procedures.

Cement/Concrete Board Backing

Comments

Concrete board backing, or backerboard, is composed of a solid concrete core, faced with fiberglass on both sides. It is recommended as an underlayment for wet areas such as bathtub surrounds and shower walls.

Since backerboard can be thinner than drywall, it may be necessary to fur out the studs with felt to create a flush surface where the backerboard meets the drywalled surface. Furring should also be done in a shower with a shower pan running up the sides to make the surface even for the backerboard. (The backerboard is supported with small blocks until the mortar bed has been poured over the shower pan.)

Cement backerboard can be more effective than green board in resisting moisture effects, and does not require priming or the application of waterproof mastic. However, it can be more time-consuming to install.

Industry Standards

2001 Handbook for Ceramic Tile Installation **(From Method B 14-01)**
(Tile Council of America, Inc.)

Recommended Uses:

1. over wood or concrete subfloors.
2. in showers over dry, well-braced wood studs, furring, or metal studs.

Requirements:

- to be used in conjunction with Method W244 [of Handbook].
- form slope for waterproof membrane with portland cement mortar.
- slope waterproof membrane 1/4" per ft. to weep holes in drain.
- turn waterproof membrane up walls a minimum of 3" above shower curb (6" above floor in showers without curbs).
- fur studs with 1 1/4", or thicker, furring strips above the top of the waterproof membrane to allow the top of the membrane to be flush with the face of the furring strips.
- shower floor membrane, as required by local authority having jurisdiction.

Materials:

- cementitious backer units—ANSI A118.9 or ASTM C-1325.
- fiber cement underlayment—ASTM C-1288.
- 2"-wide glass fiber mesh tape.
- dry-set mortar—ANSI A118.1.
- latex-portland cement mortar—ANSI A118.4.
- grout—ANSI A118.6 or A118.7.
- metal studs—ASTM C-645.
- wall membrane (when required)—15 lb. roofing felt or 4-mil polyethylene film, moisture-resistant, not waterproof.

Preparation by Other Trades:

- over metal studs—see Method W244 [of Handbook].
- studs—install square and plumb.
- provide a ⅛" spacing at horizontal and vertical joints and corners of cementitious backer units and fill space solid with dry-set or latex-portland cement mortar.
- embed 2"-wide glass fiber mesh tape in a skim coat of the same mortar over joints and corners.

Preparation by Tile Trade:

- surround drain with broken pieces of tile or crushed stone to prevent mortar from blocking weep holes.

Installation Specifications:

- cementitious backer units—ANSI A108.11.
- tile—ANSI A108.5.
- grout—A108.10.

Comments

Cement board is rigid and may crack if it is installed over irregularities in the framing members. For best results, check each stud for bows or deformities, and inspect horizontally across the studs. Then, replace or shim the studs to ensure even framing.

Padding should be used in the bathtub to protect the surface from scratches or chips during backerboard installation. Use galvanized nails or screws to secure the backerboard. Nail or screw above the shower pan to avoid punctures. Center the ends of backerboard sheets over the studs, staggering the joints to avoid lining them up. ⅛" space should be allowed between the backerboard sheets.

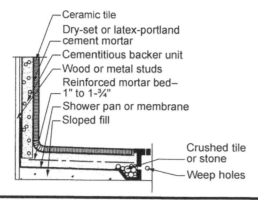

Cement Backer Board/Underlayment

- Ceramic tile
- Dry-set or latex-portland cement mortar
- Cementitious backer unit
- Wood or metal studs
- Reinforced mortar bed– 1" to 1-¾"
- Shower pan or membrane
- Sloped fill
- Crushed tile or stone
- Weep holes

Figure 10.4   Courtesy of Tile Council of America, Inc., *2001 Handbook for Ceramic Tile Installation*

Ceramic Tile over Green Board

Ed. Note: Green board is used as a base for ceramic tile and other applications where moisture will be present. Although IBC Section 2509 appears earlier (in the drywall section of this chapter), we have reprinted it here for convenient reference.

IBC–2006

Section 2509 Gypsum Board in Showers and Water Closets

2509.1 Wet areas: Showers and public toilet walls must conform to Sections 1210.2 and 1210.3.

2509.2 Base for tile: Cement, fiber-cement, or glass mat gypsum backers in accordance with ASTM C 1178, C 1288, or C 1325 must be used as a base for wall tile in tub and shower areas and wall and ceiling panels in shower areas. When installed in accordance with GA-216 or ASTM C 840, water-resistant gypsum backing is to be used for wall tile in water closet compartments. Regular gypsum wallboard is allowed under wall panels or tile in other wall and ceiling areas when installed in accordance to GA-216 and ASTM C 840.

2509.3. Limitations: Water-resistant gypsum backing board should not be used in the following areas:

1. Above a vapor retarder in a bathtub compartment or a shower.

2. In areas with constant high humidity, such as indoor pools, steam rooms, and saunas.

3. On ceilings where frame spacing goes beyond 12" on center for ½" thick water-resistant gypsum backing board and more than 16" on center for ⅝" thick water-resistant gypsum backing board.

IRC–2006

P2710.1 Bathtub and shower spaces: Shower walls must be finished in accordance with Section R307.2.

R702.4.2 Cement, fiber cement, and glass mat gypsum backers: These backers in compliance with ASTM C 1288, C 1325, or C 1178 shall be used for tub and shower wall tile and shower wall panels.

Industry Standards

2001 Handbook for Ceramic Tile Installation

(Tile Council of America, Inc.)

Ed. Note: In its publication 2001 Handbook for Ceramic Tile Installation, *the Tile Council of America, Inc. makes the following recommendations and issues a caution that should be noted.*

From Method B413-01 [from Handbook]:

- Single layer thickness shall be minimum $1/2$"-thick over studs spaced at maximum 16" o.c.

- Apply water-resistant gypsum backing board horizontally with the factory paperbound edge spaced a minimum of $1/4$" above the lip of the tub.

- All openings cut in backing board for plumbing and all cut joints between adjoining pieces seal with adhesive or other materials recommended by manufacturer of backing board.

- Gypsum backing board joints treated with tape and joint compound, bedding coat only (no finish coats). Nail heads, one coat only.

Ed. Note: See the ANSI requirement for water-resistant joint compound and tape following this excerpt.

Caution

Substrate Limitations: The performance of a properly installed thin-set ceramic tile installation is dependent upon the durability and dimensional stability of the substrate to which it is bonded. The user is cautioned that certain substrate materials used in wet areas are subject to deterioration from moisture penetration. (Reference ANSI A108, AN-2.4.) Therefore, while every effort has been made to produce accurate guidelines, they should be used only with the independent approval of technically qualified persons.

ANSI A108.1A

(American National Standards Institute/Tile Council of America, Inc.)

AN-2.5.2.1 Suitable Backings: …Water-resistant gypsum backing board is suitable backing for latex-portland cement mortars in wet areas such as tub-shower recesses, residential showers or other locations subject to similar wetting conditions.

AN-2.5.3.2 Suitable Backings: …or water-resistant gypsum backing board for walls only.

AN-3.5.2 Wet areas: Install water-resistant gypsum backing board in accordance with GA-216-89, except that joints shall be filled with water-resistant joint compound and tape.

AN-3.5.3… A $1/4$" gap shall be left between the paper edge and tub or shower receptor. The gap shall be caulked with a flexible sealant.

Wood or Metal Studs:
Gypsum Board Organic Adhesive

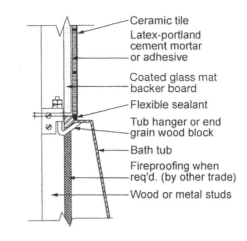

Figure 10.5

Tile over Water-Resistant Gypsum Board

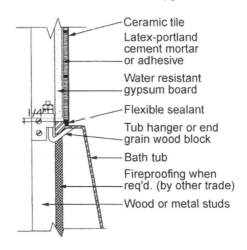

Figure 10.6

Recycled-Content Tile

Industry Recommendations
Green Home Improvement
(RSMeans)

Recycled Tile Options
Recycled-content tile can be used for floors, countertops, and walls and may be made from either recycled glass or nontoxic mine or factory wastes. Ceramic tiles may be made from factory waste generated by the production of conventional tiles, known as post-industrial waste. Some manufactures produce tiles that contain 50% to 100% in-house manufacturing waste—waste that would otherwise have ended up in landfills. Other products combine post-industrial and post-consumer recycled wastes.

Look for nontoxic thin-set mortars and adhesives. Conventional products emit volatile organic chemicals (VOCs) that could cause health problems in sensitive individuals.

Expansion Joints in Tile

Industry Standards
Gypsum Construction Handbook
(United States Gypsum Company)

Exposed edges and joints in areas to be tiled are treated with a coat of thinned down ceramic tile mastic or an approved waterproof flexible sealant. Joints are treated with joint compound and joint tape.

Industry Standards
2001 Handbook for Ceramic Tile Installation
(Tile Council of America, Inc.)

Isolation/Expansion Joint Recommendations:
- interior—24' to 36' in each direction.
- exterior—12' to 16' in each direction.
- interior tilework exposed to direct sunlight or moisture—8' to 12' in each direction.
- where tilework abuts restraining surfaces such as perimeter walls, dissimilar floors, curbs, columns, pipes, ceilings, and where changes occur in backing materials.
- all expansion, control, construction, cold, and seismic joints in the structure should continue through the tilework, including such joints at vertical surfaces.

- joints through tilework directly over structural joints must never be narrower than the structural joint.

Expansion Joint Width (Vertical and Horizontal):
- exterior (all tile)—minimum ³⁄₈" for joints 12' on center, minimum ¹⁄₂" for joints 16' on center. Minimum widths must be increased ¹⁄₁₆" for each 15°F tile surface temperature change greater than 100°F between summer high and winter low. (Decks exposed to the sky in northern U.S.A. usually require ³⁄₄"-wide joints on 12' centers.)
- interior for quarry tile and paver tile—same as grout joint, but not less than ¹⁄₄".
- interior for ceramic mosaic and glazed wall tile—preferred not less than ¹⁄₄", but never less than ¹⁄₈".

Comments
The *IBC* does not directly address expansion joints in ceramic tile.

Many instances of ceramic tile buckling up off the substrata are due to the omission of expansion joints. In its publication *2001 Handbook for Ceramic Tile Installation*, the Tile Council of America, Inc. recommends installation procedures for sealing expansion joints.

American National Standards Institute
(ANSI/Tile Council of America, Inc.)

AN–3.7 Requirements For Expansion Joints.

AN–3.7.1 It is not the intent of these specifications to make expansion joint recommendations for specific projects. Specifier must specify expansion joints and show locations.

AN–3.7.2 Exterior Work. Locate expansion joints in exterior tilework on walls and floors not more than 16 feet (5 m) on center both ways on horizontal and vertical surfaces, over all construction or expansion joints in the backing, and where backing materials change, or change directions.

AN–3.7.3 Interior Work. Locate expansion joints in the tilework over all construction or expansion joints in the backing and where backing materials change. Where tile floors abut rigid walls and at intervals of 24 to 36 feet (7 to 11 m) in large floor areas, expansion joints are mandatory for quarry

Vertical and Horizontal Movement Joint Design Essentials

Use these details for Control, Contraction, and Isolation Joints

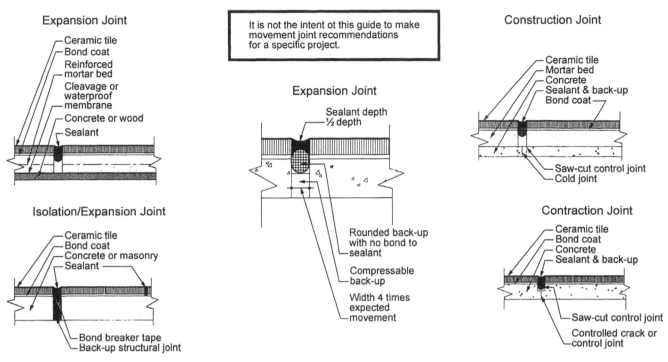

Figure 10.7

Courtesy of Tile Council of America, Inc., *2001 Handbook for Ceramic Tile Installation*

tile, and paver tile, but may be omitted in other tile on dimensionally stable backing at the discretion of the architect.

Tile Mortar

Mastic (Organic Adhesive)

Industry Standards

NKBA Kitchen and Bathroom Installation Manual, Volume 1
(National Kitchen & Bathroom Association)

In this method, tile is directly applied to the substrate material with troweled-on mastic. The countertop will only be raised the thickness of the tile. This is generally referred to as thin-set installation. Mastic manufacturers state that installation may be done over any of the following substrate surfaces: existing tile, fiberglass, wood, paneling, brick, masonry, concrete, plywood, or vinyl. Most countertop installations are done over plywood. The surface must be dry, flat, and free of dirt and grease. This installation cannot hide

any dips or bows in the substrate material, so any imperfections in the substrate will show up in the finished tile installation.

Conventional Mortar Bed (Mud)

In this method, the tile is installed on a bed of mortar ³⁄₄" to 1¹⁄₄" (1.91 cm to 3.2 cm) thick.

Thin-Set Over Backerboard

A glass mesh concrete backerboard may take the place of a conventional mortar bed. It is unaffected by moisture and has one of the lowest coefficients of expansion of all building panels. Additionally, the boards are only one-half the weight of conventional mortar installations.

A successful ceramic tile countertop installation is only as good as what is installed below the tile surface. The cabinets must be level and plumb, and the substrate set level as well. If this is not done, the backsplash grout will not be straight. A tolerance of ¹⁄₈" (.32 cm) in a 10' (304.80 cm) run of countertop is considered acceptable. A 4' to 6' (121.92 cm to 182.88 cm) level should be used to verify this. For longer runs, a 4' (121.92 cm) level and an 8' (243.84 cm) straight edge should be used.

While plywood decking is the most common substrate material for countertops, some installers prefer traditional lumber decking. Traditional decking is often used to provide flexibility under the tile. Generally, grade-one or grade-two kiln dried Douglas fir, 1" x 4" (2.54 cm x 10.16 cm) or 1" x 6" (2.54 cm x 15.24 cm) spaced ¼" (.64 cm) apart, is used. It may be installed perpendicular to the backsplash (from the front of the counter to the back) or running parallel with the cabinet space.

The decking should be delivered to the project site several days before the installation to allow the wood to reach the relative humidity of the room. The decking should overhang the cabinets and be flush with the face of the drawers.

Whenever possible, any cutout should be a minimum of 2" (5.08 cm) away from a wallboard or plastered backsplash.

Elimination of stress is critical when countertop overhangs are planned. The tile must have a solid base. If any movement occurs when pressure is placed on top, the tile and/or grout will crack. The underside of the decking should be finished to match the cabinets or correspond with other products used in the project.

Installation of Mortar Bed

Industry Standards

2001 Handbook for Ceramic Tile Installation
(Tile Council of America, Inc., TCA)

Ed. Note: In its 2001 Handbook for Ceramic Tile Installation, *the Tile Council of America, Inc., describes the installation of the mortar bed used as a substrata to which ceramic tile is adhered.*

Absorptive ceramic tile must be soaked before setting on a mortar bed that is still workable when using a neat portland cement bond coat. Under normal job conditions, a minimum of 20 hours cure at 70°F is adequate, but longer mortar bed cures of up to 10 days are desirable. When epoxy mortars, epoxy adhesives, furan, or organic adhesives are used, the mortar bed must be dry. To insure practical and satisfactory installations, the cement mortar bed to receive the tile, whether left workable or allowed to harden, is to be applied by the tile contractor who must establish all the finished dimensions at the time this bed is applied.

Cement Backer Board/Underlayment

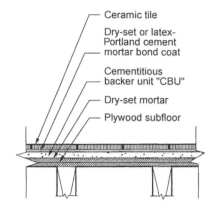

Ceramic tile
Dry-set or latex-Portland cement mortar bond coat
Cementitious backer unit "CBU"
Dry-set mortar
Plywood subfloor

Figure 10.8

Courtesy of Tile Council of America, Inc., *2001 Handbook for Ceramic Tile Installation*

Dry-Set Mortar: A mixture of Portland cement with sand and additives imparting water retentivity which is used as a bond coat for setting tile. Dry-set mortar is suitable for thin-set installations of ceramic tile over a variety of surfaces. It is used in one layer, as this as ³/₃₂" after tile are beat in, has excellent water and impact resistance, is water-cleanable, non-flammable, good for exterior work, and does not require soaking of tile.

Latex-Portland Cement Mortar: A mixture of Portland cement, sand, and special latex additive that is used as a bond coat for setting tile. The uses of latex-Portland cement mortar are similar to those of dry-set mortar. Latex additives for use in thin-set Portland cement tile setting mortars are designed to improve adhesion, reduce water absorption, and provide greater bond strength and resistance to shock and impact. These additives allow some latitude in time, working conditions, and temperatures. Therefore, latex-Portland cement mortar is required for the installation of large-unit porcelain-bodied tile.

Epoxy Mortar: A mortar system designed for chemical resistance employing epoxy resin and epoxy hardener portions. Epoxy mortar is suitable for thin-set installations of ceramic tile where chemical resistance of floors, high bond strength, and high impact resistance are important considerations. High-temperature-resistant formulas are also available. Acceptable sub-floors, when properly prepared, include concrete, wood and plywood, steel plate, and ceramic tile. Application is made in one thin layer. Pot life, adhesion, water-cleanability before cure, and chemical resistance vary with manufacturer.

Epoxy Adhesive: An adhesive system employing epoxy resin and epoxy hardener portions. Epoxy adhesive is formulated for thin-setting of tile on floors, walls, and counters. It is designed primarily for high bond strength and ease of application and not for optimum chemical resistance. However, its chemical and solvent resistance tends to be better than that of organic adhesives.

Organic Adhesive: A prepared organic material for interior use only, ready to use with no further addition of liquid or powder, which cures or sets by evaporation. Organic adhesives are suitable for thin-setting tile on floors, walls, and countertops, where surfaces are appropriate and properly prepared—in accordance with adhesive manufacturers' directions. Suitably prepared backings for dry areas include gypsum board, gypsum plaster, Portland cement mortar, formed concrete, and masonry. Suitably prepared backings for wet areas include Portland cement mortar, formed concrete, and masonry. Adhesives are applied in one thin layer with a trowel, first using the flat edge for continuous coverage and then the notched edge for uniform thickness. Where leveling or truing is required, an underlayment is used. Adhesives eliminate soaking of tile. They are not suitable for swimming pools or exteriors.

Comments

ANSI specifications A-108.1A through A-108.11, A-118.1 through A-118.9, and A-136.1 detail construction methods and recommended areas of use of each type of tile bonding agent. These specifications are detailed and parallel the recommendations of the Tile Council of America, Inc.

The word **mortar** is commonly used to describe (1) the backing substrata to which tile is adhered or (2) the material that bonds the tile to the substrata. A **mortar bed** is a layer of fresh mortar into which a structural member or flooring is set. Mortar has a Portland cement content; however, adhesives contain no Portland cement.

The *IBC* **does** provide specifications for materials needed to construct a mortar bed, to which ceramic tile is adhered. (See IBC Chapter 25, Section 2509.) However, the *IBC* **does not** provide specifications for mortar used to adhere the tile to the mortar bed.

Caution: Read and follow manufacturers' directions for installation of all tile-adhering mortars and adhesives.

Tile Grout

Industry Standards

NKBA Kitchen & Bathroom Installation Manual, Volume 1
(National Kitchen & Bathroom Association)

Generally, there are four broad categories of grout that are specified for kitchen and bathroom installations:

Epoxy Grouts are made up of an epoxy resin and hardener, and are used when superior strength and chemical resistance are necessary. New formulas produce nearly flush joints in backsplashes and cover base trim. They are not stain resistant, and are offered in a limited range of colors. Epoxy grouts are more expensive than other types of grouts, and require careful installation procedures.

Silicone Rubber Grouts, after curing are resistant to staining, moisture, mildew, cracking, crazing, and shrinking. They are used where great elasticity and moisture resistance are required. They're ideal for bathroom application (walls, floors, or vanity tops). Silicone rubber grouts are not recommended for kitchen countertops because they are unsuitable for food preparation areas.

Dry-Set Grouts, also referred to as non-sanded grouts, are suitable for grout joints that do not exceed ⅛" (.32 cm). The grout is smooth in texture, and is often used with soft glazed tiles that could be scratched by abrasive sand. While this grout is generally mixed with water, a latex additive used in place of the water improves stain resistance and bonding ability. It also reduces water absorption, making it ideal for use in wet areas such as kitchen and bathroom countertops. The latex additive also eliminates the necessity of damp curing in some installations.

Sanded Grouts are used with wider joints, up to ⅜" (.96 cm), and have a rougher texture than non-sanded grouts. The sand is added to ensure proper strength of the wider joint. Like dry-set grouts, sanded grouts may be enhanced by a latex additive. Sanded grouts are most often used for floors and ceramic mosaic tiles.

Sealers are often specified for application on grout joints once the grout has thoroughly set. Several coats are often required in heavy use areas such as countertops.

Uneven grout colors can result if the grout is allowed to dry unevenly. This is most often caused because of a nearby source of heat or cooling such as a heat duct, hot air vent, or an air conditioner. This can be prevented by shutting off the source of air or wetting the grout frequently in that area.

Ceramic tile countertops are installed directly on a deck or substrate by one of three installation methods: **mastic** (organic adhesive), **conventional mortar bed** (mud), or **thin set** over a backerboard.

Ed. Note: See also "Wall Base for Ceramic Tile" earlier in this chapter.

Comments

It is very difficult to maintain light-colored grout on floors that will be exposed to traffic entering from outside.

Waterproofing Showers & Tubs

Sloped Substrata

Industry Standards

2001 Handbook for Ceramic Tile Installation
(Tile Council of America, Inc.)

Ed. Note: In its publication 2001 Handbook for Ceramic Tile Installation, *the Tile Council of America, Inc. provides installation details for shower receptors and walls (details B414, B415, and B416). It includes other details for roof decks, tubs, fountains, and steam. Recommended installation details for all these items share a common method—placement of the waterproof membrane over substrata sloped toward the drain.*

American National Standards Institute (ANSI)

AN–3.62 Prior to applying waterproof membranes, most plumbing codes require that floors or showers and roman tubs be sloped, by means of a smooth and solidly formed sloping sub-base, to weep holes located in clamp stile drains.

Ed. Note: See **Figure 10.3** *for gypsum wallboard installation around tubs and showers.*

Examples of Typical Tile Installations

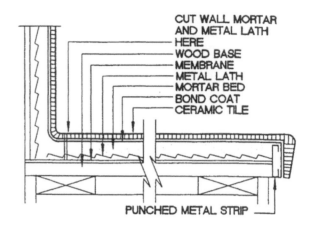

CUT WALL MORTAR AND METAL LATH HERE
WOOD BASE
MEMBRANE
METAL LATH
MORTAR BED
BOND COAT
CERAMIC TILE

PUNCHED METAL STRIP

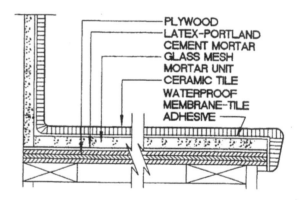

PLYWOOD
LATEX-PORTLAND CEMENT MORTAR
GLASS MESH MORTAR UNIT
CERAMIC TILE
WATERPROOF MEMBRANE-TILE ADHESIVE

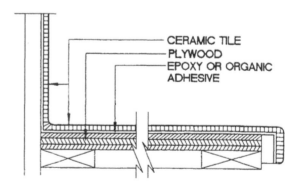

CERAMIC TILE
PLYWOOD
EPOXY OR ORGANIC ADHESIVE

Figure 10.9

Courtesy of National Kitchen & Bath Association, *Kitchen & Bathroom Installation Manual, Volume 1*

Drains

Comments

Neither the *IBC*, nor the *IRC* addresses the installation of floor drains and waterproofing.

Tile installation for floor drains should utilize a two-part drain. The lower portion of the drain should be set to accept water off the waterproof membrane, and the top section should be set to receive water off the surface of the tile. Failure to slope the substrata under the waterproofing and toward the drain is a common installation error.

Hot mop is not an acceptable membrane, because when it cools, the material tends to be brittle and inflexible. Tile suppliers sell a vinyl sheet that uses contact cement on the joints, which is an effective alternative.

The vinyl pan must be installed first and must terminate up the wall 3" above the flood level or 6" above the floor. In a shower, the vinyl pan must terminate 3" above the dam height. Then, the wall membrane is installed overlapping the vertical vinyl pan membrane.

As they work, installers have a tendency to drop nails and screws onto the vinyl pan. Care must be taken to remove and avoid stepping on dropped fasteners during the installation process in order to prevent punctures of the vinyl pan.

Ceramic Floor Tile: Over Wood

Recommended Installation

IBC–2006

2304.7.1 Structural floor sheathing: Structural floor sheathing must be designed in accordance with the provisions of the IBC and the special provisions in this section. Floor sheathing that conforms to the provisions of Table 2304.7(1), 2304.7(2), 2304.7(3), or 2304.7(4) must meet the requirements of this section.

Industry Standards

2001 Handbook for Ceramic Tile Installation
(Tile Council of America, Inc.)

Design floor areas over which tile is to be applied to have a deflection not greater than $1/360$ of the span when measured under 300 lb. concentrated load.

Comments

The *Handbook* details several alternative installations over wood subfloor. One installation includes a minimum 1¼" mortar bed, another adds a layer of plywood properly gapped between sheets and at walls, and a third method involves cementitious backer units.

American National Standards Institute

(ANSI/Tile Council of America, Inc.)

ANSI A108.4: Where ceramic tile is to be bonded directly to plywood floors with organic adhesive, include the following requirements in the carpentry section of the project specifications.

AN–3.4.1 Requirement for Carpentry for Organic Adhesive or Epoxy Adhesive.

AN–3.4.1.1 Floor Framing. Maximum spacing 16" on center with framing size and span in accordance with applicable building code provisions for floors and floor loading.

AN–3.4.1.2 Subfloor—Exposure 1 or Exterior plywood conforming to provisions of Product Standard PS 1–83 for Construction and Industrial Plywood, or plywood APA Rated Sheathing, or APA Rated Sturd-I-Floor conforming to provisions of Manufacturing and Performance Standard for APA Rated Sheathing panels, or 1" nominal boards.

Underlayment—Plywood Underlayment, Exposure 1 or C-C plugged Exterior, or sanded plywood grades

Cement Mortar

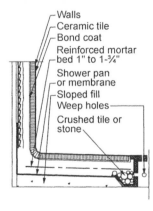

Walls
Ceramic tile
Bond coat
Reinforced mortar bed 1" to 1-¾"
Shower pan or membrane
Sloped fill
Weep holes
Crushed tile or stone

Figure 10.10

Courtesy of Tile Council of America, Inc.,
2001 Handbook for Ceramic Tile Installation

Floors (Interior): Wood Subfloor
Cement Mortar Metal Lath

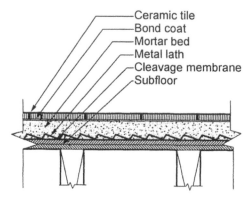

—— Ceramic tile
—— Bond coat
—— Mortar bed
—— Metal lath
—— Cleavage membrane
—— Subfloor

Figure 10.11

Courtesy of Tile Council of America, Inc.,
2001 Handbook for Ceramic Tile Installation

with special innerply construction conforming to underlayment provisions of Product Standard PS 1-83 for Construction and Industrial Plywood, or plywood APA Rated Sturd-I-Floor conforming to provisions of Manufacturing and Performance Standard for APA Rated Sturd-I-Floor panels. Each panel of subfloor and underlayment shall be identified with a trademark of the approved testing agency.

AN–3.4.1.3 Over $^{19}/_{32}$ inch (15 mm) thick structural subflooring or 1-by-6 inch (19 x 140 mm) tongue and grooved boards, or other structural subflooring, secure $^{11}/_{32}$ inch (9 mm) thick underlayment with adhesive or 3d ring shank nails; locate nails at 6 inch (152 mm) centers along panel edges and 8 inch (203 mm) centers each way throughout the panel; offset joints of subfloor and underlayment.

AN–3.4.1.4 Allow $^{1}/_{8}$ inch (3 mm) between panels and $^{1}/_{4}$ inch (6 mm) between panel and wall for expansion. Floor surfaces along adjacent edges of sheets shall not be more than $^{1}/_{32}$ inch (1 mm) above or below each other.

Comments

Means Illustrated Construction Dictionary defines **slip sheet** as "protective paper placed over the faces of prefinished plywood paneling to protect them during transport." In the ceramic tile industry, a slip sheet is known as a **cleavage membrane.** (See **Figure 10.11**.)

Installation of this type of membrane separates the minor movements of the substrate from the tile panel.

It prevents the tile sawtooth cracking of grout joints over slab cracks, as well as loosening of grout joints over plywood joints on wood decks. Tile manufacturers provide vinyl slip sheet in rolls.

We have seen installations with 15# felt slip sheets glued to the slab with a latex adhesive and the tile set in thinset over the building paper that have performed well over slab cracks.

Avoiding Failures in Ceramic Tile Installation

Comments

- The tile installer should check all corners—inside and outside—for square and plumb prior to starting a job. The surface should be flat and free of any imperfections that could cause the tile to be out of line or prevent it from laying flat.

- Exterior corners should be square to ensure the proper appearance of the finished tile surface. Wall preparation is critical in this area. Corner bead or buildup of compound and adhesive may cause the corner to be out of square.

- In laying out tile, the object is to have full tiles showing in the most visible parts of the room, and cut tiles in the less noticeable areas. Lay out each wall or section of wall separately. For expansion joints, allow approximately $^{1}/_{4}$" between the perimeter tile and the wall and right above bathtubs, floors, and fixtures. The last tile should not be less than one-half the width of a full tile.

- The wall surface should be completely free of dust, debris, and foreign substances before beginning the tile installation.

- Before grouting, all excess adhesive should be removed from the joints.

- Latex additives can be used with joint filler material to add to its flexibility and strength. It is important to fill the joints completely, leaving no gaps at the bottom. Tiles in moist areas should be grouted with mildew-resistant grout with a latex additive.

- Proper sealing of grout joints should make them stain-resistant. There are also grout formulations that include stain-inhibitors.

- Some water may contain high levels of iron or other minerals that can stain grout. Colored grout may be a consideration in these situations.

- Proper caulking when grout has cured (a few days after application) should be done at expansion joints in tile surfaces, thereby preventing cracks in areas where movement is likely (where floor tile meets cabinet toekick, where floor tile meets wall tile, or where two walls meet, as well as around faucets, valves, and sinks).

- Tile should be cut as neatly as possible around wall penetrations such as supply pipes and valves. Care should be taken to properly caulk around wall penetrations prior to installing the finish trim.

- When applying finish trim and accessories, care should be taken not to place uneven or excess pressure on tiled surfaces—this could cause cracking of tile or joints.

- Tile should be from the same run or kiln, and the color should be consistent.

- Tile with edge defects should not be used.

- Special tile (for example, bullnose or corners) should be used in lieu of cut tile whenever possible.

- Tile should lay flat on floors or walls. Causes of problems include:

  — Uneven application of adhesive mortar or mastic

  — A particle of dried adhesive, dirt, or a tile chip that has become lodged under the tile

  — A popped nail or screw

  — Sloppy flash patching

  — Placing a tile over an uneven wallboard joint **(Ceramic tile does not bend)**

- Because tile has no flexibility, it is imperative (particularly with floor tile) to provide a uniform subsurface that is free of voids. The structural support under the underlayment should be rigid and designed to support the weight of the tile flooring.

- Pre-mixed adhesives are suitable for most applications, but some of these formulas should not be used in moisture areas.

Coefficient of Friction/Slip Resistance

Industry Standards

2001 Handbook for Ceramic Tile Installation
(Tile Council of America, Inc.)

Ed. Note: The floor tiling installation section of this handbook provides the following guidance.

Consideration must also be given to (1) wear properties of surface of tile selected, (2) tile size, (3) coefficient of friction.

Unglazed Standard Grade tile will give satisfactory wear or abrasion resistance in installations listed.

Glazed tile or soft body decorative unglazed tile should have the manufacturer's approval for intended use.

Ed. Note: ANSI issues the same cautions on the use of tile. Information specific to a particular type of tile is found in the standards section referring to it. The statement in the following excerpt addresses coefficient of friction.

Universal Design Ideas for Style, Comfort & Safety
(RSMeans)

Nonslip flooring is vital in bathrooms. Look for the COF (or coefficient of friction), the measure of how slip-resistant the surface is. A COF of 0.6 or higher is best. In addition, look for flooring materials that are glare-free.

If you opt for ceramic tile in the bathroom, purchase small tiles glazed with a nonslip finish. Covering a floor with small tiles requires more grout, which further increases slip-resistance.

American National Standards Institute

(ANSI/Tile Council of America, Inc.)

ANSI A137.1—Coefficient of Friction. When coefficient of friction (COF) data are required for a specific project, testing shall conform to ASTM C 1028. However, because area of use and maintenance by the owner of installed tile directly affect coefficient of friction, the COF of the manufactured product shall be as agreed upon by manufacturer and purchaser.

Comments

The IBC does not address the slipperiness of tile shower floors. Within the industry, however there is some concern—but not much scientific data—about the required coefficient of friction for floor tile in general, and wet areas, specifically. Manufacturers provide data through their suppliers about the charactertistics of their products, including the coefficient of friction.

Occupational Safety and Health Administration

OSHA (Occupational Safety and Health Administration) has established a recognized industry standard of 0.50 (wet and dry) for slip-resistant surfaces.

Americans with Disabilities Act (ADA)

ADA recommends "a static coefficient of friction of 0.60 for accessible routes and 0.80 for ramps." ADA does not specifically state that 0.60 is both a dry and a wet requirement.

CHAPTER 11

FLOOR COVERING & ACOUSTICAL CEILINGS

Table of Contents

Text in blue type indicates excerpted summaries from the International Building Code® (IBC) *and* International Residential Code® (IRC). *Please consult the IBC and IRC for complete coverage and specific wording. "Comments" (in solid blue boxes) were written by the editors, based on their own experience.*

 These icons will appear with references to green building practices and seismic regulations, respectively.

FLOOR COVERING & ACOUSTICAL CEILINGS

Common Defect Allegations

Floor Covering

- *Imperfections in the underlayment can show through any floor covering. Sources include buildup where flash patches were not properly sanded, nails or screws that should have been set flush, and dirt/debris that should have been cleaned or removed.*

- *Floor covering is affected by extreme moisture variations. If carpet, vinyl, or wood are to be installed over a concrete slab, and there is any reason to suspect moisture problems, testing is recommended. See "Comments" under the heading "Concrete Subfloor Moisture Vapor Emission" (following the introduction to this chapter) for more on testing.*

- *Hardwood floors are very susceptible to moisture damage. Wood flooring material should be delivered to the site where it will be installed a minimum of 72 hours in advance to allow it to acclimate to the conditions in the structure. If a wood floor is to be installed over concrete, sleepers should be installed first over moisture barriers to keep the finished wood from coming in contact with the concrete.*

- *Wood flooring can fail when the edges come in contact with high, wet grade against the exterior wall, even if the floor has a good horizontal membrane. Floors can also fail from over cleaning. The side of the wood that is swelling from moisture expands more than the side that is not exposed to moisture. Therefore, if the water is coming from below, the wood will cup. Water from the top will usually cause the wood to crown. Note that when the wood expands, it shoves the outer strips away from the center, and when it dries, it shrinks, leaving gaps. If the gaps are not too large, a color caulk filler can be applied. Otherwise, the wood needs total replacement.*

- *Other installation problems that occur with hardwood flooring include:*

  - *joints staggered in a way that is not visually pleasing.*

  - *excess shrinkage, causing wider than acceptable gaps between boards or flooring strips.*

(continued)

– buckling of floorboards due to expansion from moisture penetration.

– poor layout, resulting in narrow pieces at the wall or against the base.

– uneven staining, or flashing of finish from uneven application.

– excessive chipping at cuts.

– hammer or other distress marks.

– exposed fasteners.

– excess face nailing on tongue and groove flooring (on strip next to wall).

• Vinyl and tile floor defects include joint lifts (vinyl) due to inadequate adhesive application, excess mastic oozing through joints, failure to align tiles properly for pattern, and poor layout with very narrow tile pieces around the perimeter of the room.

• Like wood, carpet will also deteriorate from moisture. Prolonged exposure to moisture can cause the latex adhesive to break down, allowing the backing to delaminate from the woven carpet.

• The majority of the claims on carpet are from improper installation, resulting in excessive stretching or seaming. Preinstallation planning should include preparation of a seaming diagram with the goal of keeping seams away from high-traffic areas. Carpet may stretch after it is installed, and may need to be re-stretched and cut to fit. Another complaint is poor fit around jambs and other protrusions.

Acoustical Ceilings

• In high seismic areas, suspended ceilings require 45 degrees play wires to stabilize the grid during earthquakes. Compression struts are also required. These are usually made from metal studs screwed to the ceiling and the grid in a predetermined pattern. The struts prevent the ceiling from shifting upwards during an earthquake.

• In airtight rooms, especially where a positive air system is in use, just opening a door will often cause the tiles to raise. This can cause loose fibers or particles of the acoustic panels to drop. To prevent this problem, install retainer clips to hold the tiles in place.

• White tiles and chrome Paracube® diffusers must also be handled with disposable gloves. Once they are contaminated, they cannot be cleaned well enough to use again.

Introduction

The first part of this chapter addresses floor coverings. There are sections on vinyl, linoleum, rubber, carpet, hardwoods and softwoods, bamboo, salvage wood, cork, parquets, and floating laminate floors, with guidelines for preparation and installation, as well as some allowable tolerances for installations. (See Chapter 10, "Drywall & Ceramic Tile," for information on ceramic tile flooring.) The kinds of problems that lead to defect claims related to floor coverings include cracks between wood floorboards or stretched or detached carpet; bubbles, ridges, or depressions in vinyl sheet flooring; and easily scratched or dented wood floors.

The second part of this chapter covers suspended ceilings. The use of a suspended acoustical ceiling system is predominantly found in commercial office and retail applications and some residential basements. One of the primary functions of a suspended acoustical ceiling is to provide a space to conceal HVAC ducting, plumbing pipe, electrical conduit, light fixtures, communications and computer cabling, insulation, and other utilities.

A suspended acoustical ceiling is also a method of providing a finished architectural surface, along with sound attenuation. A wide range of styles and colors of the metal grid system and the lay-in tiles can be used, from simple white to contrasting accents.

Inspectors will most likely look for proper fasteners and spacing of hanging wire attachments, proper number of turns of the hanging wire attachments, proper sizing of the hang wire, and proper installation of any additional seismic supports. Installers should strictly adhere to the design specifications and any local building code requirements regarding suspended ceiling systems. While elements within the support system can be changed fairly easily, any modification to the grid system itself after it has been installed is usually costly and time-consuming.

The following organizations may be helpful in providing information on floor coverings & acoustical ceilings:

Acoustical Society of America
516-576-2360
asa.aip.org

Association of the Wall & Ceiling Industry (AWCI)
703-534-8300
www.awci.org

Carpet & Rug Institute
800-882-8846
www.carpet-rug.com

Ceilings & Interior Systems Construction Association (CISCA)
630-584-1919
www.cisca.org

(continued)

Floor Covering Installation Contractors Association (FCICA)
248-661-5015
www.fcica.com

Maple Flooring Manufacturers Association, Inc.
847-480-9138
www.maplefloor.org

National Wood Flooring Association (NWFA)
800-422-4556
www.woodfloors.org

North American Laminate Flooring Association
202-785-9500
www.nalfa.org

Paint & Decorating Retailers Association (PDRA)
636-326-2636
www.pdra.org

Resilient Floor Covering Institute (RFCI)
301-340-8580
www.rfci.com

NOFMA: The Wood Flooring Manufacturers Association
901-526-5016
www.nofma.org

Western Wall & Ceiling Contractors Association (WWCCA)
714-256-1244
www.wwcca.org

World Floor Covering Association
800-624-6880
www.wfca.org

Ed. Note: Comments and recommendations within this chapter are not intended as a definitive resource for construction activities. For building projects, contractors must rely on the project documents and any applicable code requirements pertaining to their own particular locations.

Sheet Vinyl Flooring

Comments

Underlayment

It is important to use the right substrate under resilient flooring material. Manufacturers' guidelines should recommend an appropriate underlayment. Particleboard is not recommended because it can swell when exposed to moisture. Hardboard is unacceptable to many manufacturers. "Underlayment Grade" plywood at least 1/4" thick or Type 1 lauan is recommended.

Underlayment must be securely attached (1/4" plywood nailed every 4" around the edges, and every 6" within the panel). All surface holes should be filled and then smoothly sanded.

Industry Standards

Construction Principles, Materials, and Methods
(John Wiley & Sons, Inc.)

Vinyl Sheet

Vinyl sheet products are made with a vinyl wear surface bonded to a backing. The backing may be vinyl, polymer-impregnated mineral fibers, asphalt- or resin-saturated felt, nonfoam plastic, or foamed plastic. Some vinyl products have a layer of vinyl foam bonded either to the backing or between the wear surface and the backing. Backings are classified in ASTM Standard F 1303 as Class A for fibrous formulations; B for nonfoamed plastics; and C for foamed plastics.

In addition to PVC resins, the wear surface of vinyl-surfaced sheets may contain decorative vinyl chips, filler, pigments and other ingredients. Powdered vinyl resins, fillers, plasticizers, stabilizers, and pigments are mixed, rolled into sheets, and chopped to form these vinyl chips. Vinyl chips of various colors are mixed with additional resins and spread evenly over the backing and bonded to it under high heat and pressure. The vinyl resins and plasticizers together are called the *binder*.

ASTM F 1303 classifies vinyl sheet flooring as either Type I or Type II. In Type I flooring the binder constitutes at least 90% of the wear layer; in Type II, at least 34%.

ASTM Standard F 1303 designates three grades within each type, to define wear layer thickness:

- *Grade 1:* For commercial, light-commercial, and residential projects; requires a 0.020-in. wear layer in Type I and a 0.050-in. wear layer in Type II

- *Grade 2:* For light commercial and residential projects; requires a 0.014-in. wear layer in Type I and a 0.030-in. wear layer in Type II

- *Grade 3:* For residential projects only; requires a 0.010-in. wear layer in Type I and 0.020-in. wear layer in Type II

Greater thicknesses are required in Type II than in Type I, because the abrasion resistance and durability per unit of thickness of a wear layer are greater in the binder than in the fillers. The more binder, the thinner the wear layer can be for the same service.

Sheet products with vinyl backings may have a design imprinted on top of the backing or on the underside of the wear surface. They are usually printed with vinyl inks. A clear PVC wear surface is then calendered to the desired thickness and laminated to the backing with heat and pressure.

Concrete Subfloor Moisture Vapor Emission

Subfloor Moisture. Concrete subfloors and mastic underlayments mixed with water release large amounts of moisture as they cure. With lightweight-aggregate concrete (weighing less than 90 lb./cu. ft.), or under conditions that retard the curing process, moisture may be released over long periods of time. Field tests described under "Concrete Subfloors" in Section 9.11.5.2. should be used to establish that the subfloor is sufficiently dry to receive the intended product. Since it originates in the original mix of the concrete, subfloor moisture may be present in below-grade, on-grade, and suspended subfloors.

Comments

The common moisture test to determine warranty criteria is a calcium chloride test, called the Dome Test, which is designed to measure water vapor emission. A dish or tin of dry calcium chloride (premeasured by weight) is placed on the clean, exposed concrete floor. A plastic dome measuring one square foot is placed over the calcium chloride dish for 72 hours. The dome is attached to the slab with double-sided tape. When the dome is removed, the calcium chloride is weighed, and the increase is multiplied by a factor to determine the pounds per 1,000 square feet. Generally, a manufacturer will not warranty its product on concrete that tests over 5 lbs.

(continued)

Sealants are available that penetrate the concrete, creating a mechanical lock as a moisture barrier. Generally, these materials are practical only for concrete that tests under 10 lbs. (in the calcium chloride test).

Preparation for Installation

Preparation for Flooring. The effectiveness of a flooring installation greatly depends on the proper selection and preparation of the elements that make up the installation. Subfloors that are to receive flooring directly must be firm, smooth, and dense and must possess good bonding properties. When these properties are lacking, it is necessary to prepare the subfloor by grinding, sanding, or by installing underlayment. Adhesives must be compatible with all elements, including the flooring itself, and all elements must be suitable for the intended location.

Application of Flooring. The installation of sheet materials should be planned to minimize the number and total length of seams. Necessary seams should be placed in inconspicuous locations, out of the path of heavy foot traffic. In a rectangular room, running the flooring strips parallel to the side walls generally results in an economical installation with a minimum of seams. However, sheet flooring installed directly over wood strip floors should run perpendicular to the floor joints and may result in seams running the short dimension, parallel to end walls.

Installation of sheet flooring generally consists of *fitting and cutting, adhesive bonding,* and *seam treating.*

Comments

Common Problems with Vinyl Flooring

The following problems can sometimes be corrected with a repair, but may require replacement of the vinyl flooring. Exactly matching for color and pattern with material from a new lot is not always possible.

- Bubbles, ridges, or depressions in the floor surface can be caused by inadequate preparation of the subfloor, or by improper installation (e.g., irregularities in use of adhesive or failure to roll the floor). Generally, $1/8"$ is considered the maximum height or depth acceptable for raised areas or depressions in finished vinyl sheet flooring. Bubbles should not be more than $1/16"$ high. (For more information on tolerances for vinyl sheet flooring, see *Residential Construction Performance Guidelines,* published by the National Association of Home Builders.

- Lifting of the vinyl flooring (failure to adhere) is sometimes caused by moisture or the presence

of foreign material such as oil or grease between the flooring material and the subfloor, inadequate preparation of the subfloor, or a failure to apply adhesive correctly.

- Visible seams may occur where two pieces of vinyl sheet flooring are joined. A gap greater than $1/16"$ would generally be considered unacceptable. The layout should place any seams in a low traffic, less visible area.

Vinyl & Rubber Tile Flooring

Comments

Resilient vinyl tile may be used to help hide irregularities in the surface. Textured and grained surface tiles may be more durable and easier to maintain because the dirt collects in the recessed areas rather than lying on the surface where they can be ground into the tile.

Industry Standards

Construction Principles, Materials, and Methods
(John Wiley & Sons, Inc.)

Vinyl Tile. Vinyl tile may be of homogeneous solid composition or may be backed with other materials such as organic felts, mineral fibers, or scrap vinyl.

Ingredients for solid vinyl tiles are mixed at a high temperature and hydraulically pressed or calendered into homogeneous sheets of the required thickness. These sheets are then cut into tile sizes. Backed products are essentially vinyl sheet flooring cut into tile sizes. Some tiles are made with a self-adhesive back.

Rubber Tile. Natural or synthetic rubber is the basic ingredient of rubber flooring. Clay and fibrous talc or mineral fillers provide the desired degree of reinforcement; oils and resins are added as plasticizers and stiffening agents. Color is achieved by non-fading organic pigments. Chemicals are added to accelerate the curing process.

The ingredients are mixed thoroughly and rolled into sheets. The sheets are calendered to uniform thickness and vulcanized in hydraulic presses under heat and pressure into compact, flexible sheets with a smooth, glossy surface. The backs are then sanded to gauge, ensuring uniform thickness, and the sheets are cut into tiles.

Comments

Guidelines for Professional Installation

- Conduct a trial layout before any installation, placing the cuts equally on either side of the room. The layout design should discourage patterns that have less than one-half tile at the border edge. Seams should not be placed directly over a plywood joint in the subfloor.

- Properly prepare the underlayment, ensuring that there are no voids or raised irregularities. Flash-patch knotholes in plywood. Eliminate any blemishes in the concrete subsurface and ensure that there will be no moisture penetration. Thoroughly clean the underlayment using a cleaner recommended for use with tile and adhesive. Make sure to allow enough time for the flash-patching to set before adhering the tile. If the tile is applied too soon, the adhesive will not bond properly.

- Work off a center line.

- Position tiles so that smaller cut pieces are in inconspicuous locations.

- Follow manufacturer's instructions for the tile and adhesive used. (For example, use the correct size trowel notch to ensure the proper thickness of adhesive.)

- Allow for expansion and contraction of the subfloor by leaving a space of $1/4$" between the tile and the walls.

- Remove any adhesive that seeps between the joints of the tile right away.

- Protect the finished floor while the remainder of the job is completed. If an individual tile is chipped, scratched, or scuffed, it may have to be removed and replaced. Keep extra tiles for this purpose, as it may be difficult to exactly match color in a new batch of tile.

- Transition properly from one room to another where the height of the surface floor changes.

Resistance to Damage

Industry Standards

Construction Principles, Materials, and Methods
(John Wiley & Sons, Inc.)

Resilience. Resilience is a measure of the instantaneous yielding and recovery of a surface from impact. Indentation resistance, quietness, and underfoot comfort are closely related to resilience.

Indentation Resistance. In assessing indentation resistance, the momentary indentation produced by foot traffic and dropped objects is of primary importance. These impact pressures can be quite high and demanding. A 105-lb. woman in spike heels, for example, exerts a pressure on the floor of approximately 2000 psi, while a 225-lb. man with his weight spread over 3-in. by 3-in. heels exerts only 25 psi.

Permanent indentation from heavy stationary objects, such as a piano or a desk, may be minimized by using floor protectors to distribute the load. Indentation resistance of thinner flooring materials is greatly affected by the subfloor or underlayment and may be increased by selecting harder subsurface materials. Homogeneous vinyl tile and foam cushioned vinyls have the highest indentation resistance.

Permanent indentation in some flooring types and under certain conditions cannot be entirely prevented. However, these indentations may be less conspicuous in patterned, textured, and low-luster floors.

Resistance to Sunlight. The actinic rays in sunlight may cause fading, shrinking, or brittleness in some resilient floors. Linoleum and vinyl are resistant to such deterioration. Color pigments are the critical factor in fade-resistant properties. Neutral colors show the best light resistance; pastel tones, especially yellows, blues, and pinks, are least effective in retaining colors under prolonged exposure to sunlight. Cork tile has the same tendency as natural wood to fade under strong sunlight.

Slip Resistance, Mastics & Underlayment

Industry Standards

Construction Principles, Materials, and Methods
(John Wiley & Sons, Inc.)

Slip Resistance. The Americans with Disabilities Act of 1990 requires flooring materials to have a static coefficient of friction of not less than 0.60 for level surfaces and 0.80 for ramps. Some manufacturers publish these data for their flooring products, even though there is no consensus in the industry concerning the test methods needed to ensure compliance. It would be prudent to verify the current status of slip-resistance requirements before selecting a resilient flooring for any project.

Mastic. Mastic underlayments contain a chemical binder such as latex, asphalt, or polyvinyl-acetate resins and portland, gypsum, or aluminous cement. Mixtures consisting of powdered cement and sand to which only water has been added function only as crack fillers; when applied in thin coats, they break down under traffic.

Latex underlayments are most suitable for applications that require a thin layer (3/8 in. or less), for skim coating, and for patching where the fill must be feather-edged.

Skim coating smooths surface irregularities. It does not raise the elevation of the floor.

Asphaltic and polyvinyl-acetate underlayments are used where thicker (more than 3/8 in.) underlayments are needed.

Mastic underlayments must be troweled smooth and true, with not more than a 1/8 in. variation from a straight line in 10 ft. Subfloors should be free of wax, oil, and surface coatings, such as concrete curing compounds, before mastic underlayment is applied.

Linoleum

 Linoleum is one of the greenest products on the market. Made from virtually all natural and renewable ingredients, linoleum is comfortable, colorful, and durable. Although modern vinyl flooring is often referred to as "linoleum," these two products are as different as night and day. True linoleum is manufactured from wood and cork "flour," finely ground from waste products. (Wood flour is acquired from lumber mills, and cork flour is obtained from factories that manufacture products such as wine bottle corks and cork gaskets for engines.) In contrast, vinyl flooring is made from chemicals extracted from petroleum.

Linoleum also contains pine resin (extracted from the sap of pine trees) and linseed oil (from flax seed). Other linoleum ingredients include powdered limestone, which serves as filler; color pigments; and small amounts of zinc-based drying agents.

These components are mixed, then pressed onto a backing mat made from natural jute. An acrylic sealant is added as a protective topcoat. Linoleum is currently manufactured in Europe and imported to the United States. It comes in an array of colors, often in mottled patterns.

Linoleum is often installed in sheets, the edges of which can be heat-welded to hide the seams. Some types come in planks and square tiles, comprised of linoleum mounted on high-density fiberboard and cork under-layers. Like floating floor products, these tile products click in place. Because no glue is required, there is no drying time.

Linoleum is softer and warmer than ceramic tile and biodegradable (unlike vinyl). It can be ground up and composted or burned to generate energy in a waste-to-energy plant. (When incinerated, vinyl flooring products produce dioxin.) Linoleum is fire-, stain-, crack- and scratch-resistant and can be expected to last 30 to 40 years, compared to 10 to 20 years for vinyl.

Linoleum maintains a "new" look, hiding nicks, scratches, and dents because pigments run throughout the thickness of the material. (Vinyl flooring, on the other hand, has a synthetic wear layer that contains the color and pattern. When it wears away, the floor needs replacing.) It can be repaired easily if damaged— by buffing the affected area and resealing.

Possible Drawbacks

Although linoleum offers many advantages, it does have its downsides. For one, all linoleum is currently produced in Europe, and transportation to the United States consumes energy. But because less energy is used to manufacture natural linoleum, this helps offset the energy required for transportation.

Linoleum, like vinyl flooring, releases some noxious odors during and after installation. This out-gassing can last for several weeks or even months. Although both products release about the same amount of potentially toxic chemicals, there are qualitative differences. Vinyl products outgas plasticizers that act like the female hormone estrogen in the body and are therefore a risk for young girls. Linoleum gives off odors from linseed oil, including fatty acids and aldehydes. Some chemically sensitive people may react to these chemicals, but they are otherwise not harmful. When installing this product, it is a good idea to provide ample ventilation or, for new home construction, to schedule installation of linoleum floors well before move-in.

Installation

Linoleum is thicker and stiffer than vinyl and therefore more difficult to install. Linoleum is typically glued to a concrete or wood subfloor, which must be clean and flat. Voids must be filled in with a leveling compound. As noted earlier, the glue-less click-in type can requires no adhesive. Linoleum should be acclimated to the space where it will be installed for at least one week before installation. For flooring that requires adhesive, look for a low- or no-VOC type, recommended by the flooring manufacturer. Adhesives used for installing vinyl products won't work for linoleum.

Linoleum should not be installed on moist basement floors. Moisture-test the subfloor beforehand, preferably after a hard rain. If the moisture level in the concrete is too high, some installers have used an underlayment/sealant to reduce moisture penetration. These are available in low-VOC products that do not contain any known hazardous materials.

Maintenance

Linoleum should be cleaned with a damp (not wet) mop, using a mild detergent. Check with the supplier for a list of acceptable cleaning agents. If wet-mopped, manufacturers may recommend periodic application of an acrylic sealer.

Selection

Linoleum sometimes has a yellow cast on the surface. This is known as a "drying room film" and will dissipate when the floor is exposed to natural or artificial light. When selecting a product, manufacturers suggest exposing linoleum samples to the light in the area under consideration for several hours before making a final design and color choice.

Carpet

Comments

A tremendous amount of technical information has been generated on the subject of carpeting. While such coverage is beyond the scope of this book, we will focus on the basic issues that may be pertinent in an average installation application or in a claim of defect. Resolving any dispute will involve consideration of the manufacturers' specifications and installation recommendations.

Acoustic Value

Industry Standards

Construction Principles, Materials, and Methods
(John Wiley & Sons, Inc.)

Carpet. Carpet is often selected for its comfort and decorative values, but it is also effective in reducing impact sound transmission through floor and ceiling assemblies. Therefore, its acoustical performance should be a prime consideration in flooring selection. Many common installations will provide a performance considerably higher than the range of -5 to +10 on the Impact Noise Reduction (INR) scale. Specially selected combinations of carpet and cushioning may be rated as high as +17 over wood floors, and +29 over concrete slabs.

Carpet is also capable of absorbing sound and reducing sound reflection within a room, much like acoustical ceiling tile. The Noise Reduction Coefficient (NRC) of most carpet ranges between 0.35 and 0.55, which compares favorably with a range of 0.55 to 0.75 for acoustical ceiling tile. Properly selected carpet may achieve absorption coefficients equal to those of acoustical tile. However, carpet is not particularly effective in controlling the transmission of airborne sound and where this is an important consideration, special sound-isolating construction should be used.

This section describes carpet suitable for long-term wall-to-wall installation, as distinguished from rugs, which usually have bound edges and are laid loose over a finished flooring.

Carpet Construction

Carpet Construction. Most carpet consists of pile yarns, which form the wearing surface, and backing yarns, which interlock the pile yarns and hold them in place. Therefore, carpet can be identified according to its construction, which describes the method of interlocking the backing and the pile yarns. Comparative factors related to carpet construction, such as pile yarn weight and pile thickness, number of tufts per square inch, and other factors may be useful in comparing carpets of similar construction.

Its face construction is another factor by which carpet can be identified. The following terms describing face style are defined in the glossary: *level-loop pile, cut pile, level-tip shear, multilevel loop, random shear, frieze* or *twist*, and *sculptured* or *carved*. Some face styles are dictated by the method of manufacture. For example, fusion-bonded goods can only be cut pile.

Carpeting Materials

 Wool. The outstanding characteristic of wool is resilience, which, in combination with moderate fiber strength and good resistance to abrasion, produces excellent appearance retention. Wool's relatively high specific gravity contributes to greater pile density.

Comments

Wool carpet made from either 100% wool and a natural backing material is nontoxic and odor-free. It is made from a renewable resource, lasts much longer than conventional synthetic carpet materials, and is fully biodegradable.

Nylon. Nylon comprises about 85% of the commercial carpet market and a large portion of the housing market as well. The extensive use of nylon can be attributed to its lower cost, availability in many bright colors, exceptional resistance to abrasion, and high fiber strength.

Acrylics and Modacrylics. Acrylics and modacrylics (modified acrylics) are synthetic fibers that closely resemble wool in abrasion resistance and texture.

Fibers of the acrylic family are now available only in staple form and are characterized by an appearance and high durability comparable to that of wool. Acrylics often are blended with modacrylics in commercial carpet to reduce potential flammability. However, with substantial improvement in acrylic fibers, the trend is toward 100% acrylic fiber.

Polyester. Polyester is a fiber-forming thermoplastic polymer. It is made from terephthalic acid and ethylene glycol. Polyester fibers are staple fibers, and polyester yarns are spun yarns.

Polypropylene Olefin. Polypropylene has the lowest moisture absorption rate of any carpet fibers, which gives it superior stain resistance, as well as excellent wet cleanability. Its low specific gravity results in superior covering power, and high fiber strength contributes to good wear resistance.

Resistance to Damage

Selection Criteria. Carpet performance cannot be attributed to any single element of carpet construction or physical property of the pile fiber. Installed performance is the combined effect of surface texture, construction, backing, cushioning, pile thickness, weight, density, and other variables. Of these, pile weight and pile density, are the most uniformly significant, regardless of fiber type or carpet construction.

Although pile fibers differ in their physical properties, all fibers discussed here will provide adequate service when used in a carpet construction suitable for the traffic exposure. The number of variables in carpet construction is so great that it is difficult to assess their individual effects on performance and selection criteria. Therefore, in the following discussion, selection criteria are outlined for fibers only; the effects of carpet construction are described where appropriate.

Individual selection criteria may be useful in carpet selection for special conditions of traffic or exposure.

For example, alkali, acid, and stain resistance may be important in food preparation and serving areas. *Soiling resistance* and *wet cleanability* may be a factor in entry areas. Insect and fungus resistance may require consideration in potentially damp locations. Possible *static build-up* should be considered in low-humidity areas and where such build-up may affect equipment or activities, such as in computer rooms. These and other criteria have been combined into composites such as *durability, texture retention,* and *ease of maintenance* for average conditions.

Durability. Pile weight and density, backing and cushioning firmness, quality of installation, and maintenance significantly affect carpet durability. Durability is also affected by hazards that tend to destroy the pile fibers. The resistance of fibers to such hazards is shown in ratings for resistance to abrasion, alkalies, acids, insects, fungi, and burns. The rating for durability is a composite reflecting overall resistance to destruction or loss of pile fibers and is a measure of the service life of a carpet.

Abrasion Resistance. Abrasion resistance is the resistance of the fiber to wearing away due to foot traffic or other moving loads. It is measured by the actual loss of fiber when exposed to a machine that simulates the abrasive forces of foot traffic. Since loss of fiber occurs as a result of breaking, fiber strength is one of the physical properties that influences abrasion resistance. Nylon and polypropylene have superior fiber strength and hence excellent abrasion resistance.

Alkali and Acid Resistance. Foods and beverages are generally mildly alkaline or acid in nature; many soaps and detergents are strongly alkaline. If alkaline or acid solutions are not promptly removed when spilled, they may attack the pile fibers. Wool fibers are more vulnerable to such attacks because they have a higher moisture absorption rate and are less inert chemically than the synthetic fibers.

Insect and Fungus Resistance. The synthetic fibers in modern carpets contain no organic nutritive value and are, therefore, immune to attack by insects, such as carpet beetles and moths, and to fungi, such as mold and mildew. To render wool carpet resistant to these hazards, most manufacturers treat wool yarn in the dye bath with a chemical preservative that provides long-term protection from insect attack even after wet and dry cleaning. Because many carpets intended for interior use employ at least some organic fibers in the backing, some fungus hazard exists with most carpets, even those with synthetic fiber piles.

In general, the hazard of insect and fungus attack can be reduced by regular vacuuming and exposing the carpet to light and air. This is particularly important where large or heavy pieces of furniture make part of the carpet inaccessible to regular cleaning and ventilation. In such areas, greater insect protection can be provided for wool carpets by periodic spraying with mothproofing agents.

Burn Resistance. Most synthetic carpet fibers are flame resistant to some degree, but they will melt and fuse when exposed to the heat of a burning cigarette or glowing ash, which produces more than 500°F. Prolonged exposure to such concentrated heat may result in complete local loss of fiber or a slightly fused spot. The fused spot is more resistant to wear and abrasion than the surrounding area, and this causes a visible discoloration in the carpet surface.

Although wool fiber will actually burn by charring, the damage from a lit cigarette usually is less severe, and the charred spot will wear off readily or can be removed with fine sandpaper. A fused spot on synthetic carpet similarly can be snipped off if it is not too severe, and, if followed by brushing, an acceptable appearance usually will result. If the burn is severe, replacement of the burnt area may be necessary.

The behavior of a carpet in a fully developed fire is controlled by building codes and laws. All carpet manufactured in the United States must pass a methenamine "pill" test in accordance with ASTM Standard D 2859, "Test Method for Flammability of Finished Textile Floor Covering Materials."

In this test, a carpet is exposed to the burning of a methenamine tablet. The medium *flame spread index* or *critical radiant flux* must be 0.04 watts/sq. cm.

Often, carpet will be required by code to have a higher rating than the pill test minimum. The National Institute of Standards and Technology recommends that carpet used in corridors and exit ways have a radiant flux of at least 0.22 watts/sq. cm in commercial occupancies and of 0.45 in institutional occupancies.

A carpet's flame spread during a fully developed fire is usually measured by the Flooring Radiant Panel Test of ASTM E 648. This flame spread index is called the *critical radiant flux*. It represents the minimum energy necessary to sustain flame. The higher the number, the more resistant the carpet to flame propagation.

Sometimes, a carpet's flame spread index is required to be measured by the *Smoke Chamber Test* in UL 992, "Smoke Chamber Test." This test measures the length of spread and time of travel of a flame. The range is from 0 to 25.

Appearance Retention. Appearance retention depends on factors that change original carpet color, texture, or pattern, such as fading, soiling, staining, and compression and crush resistance. Other factors common to many types of fiber and carpet construction that affect appearance without impairing serviceability are pilling, shedding, sprouting, and shading. Ratings for appearance retention are composites of these factors.

Compression Resistance. The extent to which the pile will be compressed under heavy loads or by extensive foot traffic is called compression resistance. For instance, of two samples tested under the same conditions, the one that compresses less is said to have better compression resistance. With the exception of polypropylene, which is rated somewhat lower, all fibers are approximately equal in their ability to resist compression loads. Of greater importance in resisting such forces are the cushioning, the pile height, and the pile density. Looped pile construction with closely spaced tufts and tightly twisted yarns is more resistant to compression.

Crush Resistance. Crush resistance is dependent on the ability of the fibers to recover from short- and long-term compression loads. This property is measured by the extent to which the fiber springs back after a load has been removed, as a percentage of the original height. Wool and acrylic have the highest crush resistance, nylon and modacrylic moderate, and polypropylene, somewhat lower. Pile density, spacing of tufts, and tightness of yarns affect crush resistance more than the relative rating of the fibers.

Texture Retention. The ability of carpets to retain the surface texture imparted during manufacture is related to the compression and crush resistance of the fibers, as well as the density of the pile and the tightness of the yarns. Generally, all fibers have adequate texture retention, with wool rated highest and polypropylene somewhat lower than the other synthetic fibers. Within this range, special fiber types such as heat-set nylon and bicomponent acrylic (mushroom cross section) have improved texture retention.

Static Resistance & Cushioning Requirements

Static Generation. Static electricity is an annoyance in every carpeted space, but can become actually harmful in areas housing computers or other electrically sensitive equipment. Static occurs whenever two different materials come into contact with each other. People usually do not become aware of static until it

Selection Criteria for Carpet Pile Fibers[a]

Criteria	Wool	Nylon	Acrylic	Modacrylic	Polypropylene
Resistance to: Abrasion	Good	Excellent	Good	Good	Excellent
Alkalies	Fair	Good to Excellent	Good to Excellent	Good to Excellent	Good to Excellent
Acids	Fair	Good to Excellent	Good	Good	Good to Excellent
Insects and fungi	Excellent[b]	Excellent	Excellent	Excellent	Excellent
Burns	Good	Fair	Fair	Fair	Fair
Compression	Good	Good	Good	Good	Fair
Crushing	Excellent	Good	Good to Excellent	Good	Fair to Good
Staining	Good	Good to Excellent	Good to Excellent	Good to Excellent	Excellent
Soiling	Good	Fair to Good	Good to Excellent	Good to Excellent	Excellent
Static buildup	Fair to Good	Fair	Good	Good	Excellent
Texture retention	Excellent	Good to Excellent	Good to Excellent	Good	Fair to Good
Wet cleanability	Fair to Good	Good	Good to Excellent	Good to Excellent	Excellent
Durability	Good to Excellent	Excellent	Good to Excellent	Good to Excellent	Good
Appearance retention	Excellent	Good to Excellent	Good to Excellent	Good to Excellent	Good
Ease of maintenance	Good to Excellent	Good	Good to Excellent	Good to Excellent	Excellent

[a]In each case, criteria vary depending on the properties of the specific fiber type used, carpet construction, and installation procedures.

[b]When chemically treated.

Figure 11.1

Courtesy of John Wiley & Sons, Inc., *Construction Principles, Materials, and Methods*

reaches about 3.5 kilovolts (kv). The normal carpet requirements for solely human occupancies require a level of 3 kv or less. Computers require 2 kv or less.

Of the three factors regarding static electricity—static generation, static dissipation (conductivity), and static decay time—only the first is usually limited in the selection of carpets in nonsensitive locations. Static generation in carpet is measured by the American Association of Textile Colorist and Chemists' "Step Method," which simulates conditions of actual use and measures the charge generated by someone walking across the carpet.

Static dissipation may be also limited in spaces that will house computers. It is measured by a method recommended by the IBM Corporation.

Nylon is inherently high in static buildup. To fight this property, some nylon carpet manufacturers include carbon-loaded nylon fibers that carry a lifetime antistatic guarantee.

Some carpet is laced with metal wires that are in contact with a grounded backing. In very sensitive areas, it may be impossible to reduce static sufficiently using antistatic fibers or wires alone. Then, the antistatic properties of such a carpet must be supplemented with conductive shoes, furniture, mats, or other devices.

Cushioning. All broadloom carpet should be installed over cushioning to increase resilience and durability. Some carpets, especially those used in direct glue-down installations, have an integral secondary backing that serves this function. In loomed carpets, cellular (foam or sponge) rubber cushioning usually is bonded directly to the carpet at the mill. For most carpets, however, cushioning is provided in the form of a separate padding. Currently available paddings include felted hair, rubberized fibers, cellular rubber, and urethane foam.

Felted Hair. The most economical traditional type of conventional padding is made of felted animal hair. This padding has a waffle design to provide a skidproof surface and improve resiliency. It is sometimes reinforced with a jute backing or a burlap center liner. When reinforced with burlap, the hair is punched through the burlap fabric and compressed to a uniform thickness. Sizing (adhesive) sometimes is used to strengthen the bond between the fibers and the burlap core. Many manufacturers also sterilize and mothproof hair padding.

Felted padding of hair or hair and jute may mat down in time or may develop mildew, especially if the fibers become wet, as during cleaning. However, when properly cleaned, sterilized, and treated, hair padding is suitable for reasonably dry floors at all grade levels and on conventional radiant-heated floors.

Rubberized Fibers. Some padding made of jute or hair is coated with rubber on one or both sides to hold the fibers together and provide additional resilience. Sometimes this padding has an animal hair waffle top and a jute back reinforced with a patterned, rubberized application.

Sponge Rubber. In addition to cushioning bonded directly to the carpet, foam or sponge rubber is produced in sheet form with waffle, ripple, grid, or V-shaped rib designs. A scrim of burlap fabric usually is bonded to the rubber sheet to facilitate installation of the carpet. When laid with the fabric side up, this permits a taut and even stretch of the carpet.

Rubber padding is more expensive, but it retains its resilience longer than hair padding. It is highly resistant to decay and mildew and is nonallergenic. It can be used at all grade levels, but the denser cushionings are not recommended for radiant heated floors.

Polyurethane Foam. Urethane foam padding is a high-density polymeric foam available in two major types: prime and bonded. *Prime* urethane foam padding is available as either prime or densified prime. The latter is modified chemically to make it wear better.

Bonded urethane foam padding is made from heat-fused scraps of urethane, rather than being a homogeneous product as are prime and modified prime urethane padding.

The quality of urethane foam padding is defined by its density or weight per cubic foot of foam.

Environmentally Friendly Carpeting

Green Home Improvement
(RSMeans)

Wool Carpet

Wool carpet is made from either 100% wool fiber or a blend of wool and synthetics (made from petrochemicals). The most environmentally friendly and healthiest option is 100% wool made without toxic chemicals. Wool carpet is usually odor-free from the day it's installed and is great for individuals who suffer from allergies or chemical sensitivity.

One-hundred-percent wool is made from a renewable resource and lasts much longer than conventional synthetic carpet materials. The backing materials of 100% wool carpet are all-natural, such as jute. Wool carpet that comes with a natural backing material is fully biodegradable when it has reached the end of its useful life and goes to the landfill.

Wool can be a little softer than some synthetic fibers. It also captures and retains dust better than conventional carpet, which is a good thing because it holds the dust until it can be removed by a vacuum cleaner, resulting in less dust in the air than you'll experience with some synthetic carpets. All natural wool carpet is also fire-resistant.

Available in a variety of weaves and colors, wool is one of the most durable carpet fibers on the market. It cleans well and, according to retailers, is naturally stain- and soil-resistant. (Be aware though that Consumer Reports claims that wool carpet stains easily and that light colors tend to yellow in bright sunlight, so be sure to check out warranties for stain- and fade-resistance.)

Recycled-Content Carpet

Using recycled plastic to make carpet fibers is better for the environment than using virgin materials. Recycling helps reduce landfill wastes and puts a waste product produced in massive quantities to good use. According to some estimates, approximately 40 two-liter soda bottles are used to produce one square yard of carpeting.

The production of recycled carpet also results in lower emissions than manufacturing traditional carpet. Moreover, some manufacturers have implemented progressive environmental policies at their plants to recycle and reduce waste, pollution, and energy use. They've also redesigned products to eliminate hazardous materials and have replaced many solvent-based materials with water-based alternatives.

Although recycled-content carpeting is greener than most conventional carpets, carpet backings are made from a type of plastic (styrene butadiene, known as SB latex) that contains several potentially toxic chemicals, which can be outgassed into the air of the home.

Recycled-content carpeting is widely available in many colors and weaves, and is carried by many retailers. It looks, feels, and is priced the same as high-quality carpet manufactured from virgin materials (typically polyester, nylon, and olefin).

According to manufacturers, recycled carpet has greater color-fastness, resilience, and stain-resistance than virgin-fiber carpeting. It also comes with the same warranties offered for virgin-fiber carpeting (covering color-fastness, static control, and resistance to stains, crushing, and matting).

Carpet Pads

In homes, carpets are typically installed over carpet pad to provide additional cushion or "bounce." Green carpet pads are made from an assortment of natural and recycled materials. Natural materials include animal hair and jute. Carpet pad is also made from recycled materials, including PET plastic and post-industrial waste wool.

Carpet Emissions

Industry Standards

Building Materials Technology, Structural Performance & Environmental Impact
(The McGraw-Hill Companies)

Carpets. Most carpeting comes with manufacturers' specifications, including flammability and smoke-density ratings by the American Society for Testing and Materials (ASTM).

Wall-to-wall carpeting may cause health problems because of the chemicals used in the fibers, backing, pads, and adhesives. When buying new carpeting, look for the Carpet and Rug Institute indoor air quality label that indicates the product has passed tests for low emission levels of chemical pollutants. The U.S. Consumer Product Safety Commission receives many complaints of health problems after the installation of new carpeting in offices, schools, and homes because of chemicals outgassing from the carpet.

Other options to use include carpets with jute or recycled backing that is tacked down, not glued, and carpeting made from recycled plastic soda bottles.

While installation is going on, and for three days afterward, make sure there is plenty of ventilation. Then, regularly use a vacuum cleaner.

When removing old and installing new carpeting, workers should wear a dust mask and ventilate the area for at least 3 days.

In the home, instead of vacuuming throw rugs, shake them outdoors. Use doormats at entrances to prevent tracking in dirt and contaminants from outdoor soil. Dust mites, those microscopic creatures thriving in wall-to-wall carpeting, can cause allergic reactions. Since vacuuming does not eliminate them, nonslip and easily washed scatter rugs are recommended for sensitive people.

Guidelines for Avoiding Carpet Problems

Comments

Problems with installed carpet usually involve improper fit (carpet has detached or is stretched), failure to provide continuous padding under the entire carpet surface, or visible gaps at seams. None of these conditions is acceptable. Other considerations:

- The direction (knap) of the carpet should match.
- The floor should be prepped, including flash patching to eliminate bumps or depressions.
- Humidity and change in temperature can have an effect on materials during installation.
- If carpet tacks are used, they should be of correct length and color.
- Seams should be avoided in high-traffic areas.

Wood Floors

Materials Handling

Industry Standards

Construction Principles, Materials, and Methods
(John Wiley & Sons, Inc.)

Materials Handling. To maintain proper moisture content, flooring products should not be transported or unloaded in rain, snow, or excessively humid weather. Flooring should not be delivered to a construction site until the building is enclosed, concrete and plaster work has been completed, and all building materials are dry. An interior temperature of 65°F to 70°F should be maintained for at least 5 days before flooring is delivered. Flooring should be stored for several days in the rooms where it will be installed to allow it to become acclimated to local conditions.

In crawl space construction, adequate cross-ventilation should be provided under the floor. The total area of vent openings should equal 1½% of the first-floor area. A groundcover of 4- to 6-mil polyethylene film is essential as a moisture retarder. Inadequate moisture control can harm any floor installation by contributing to warping or discoloration of the flooring.

Terminology

Materials. The terms *hardwood* and *softwood*, popularly applied to the two major groups of trees cut for lumber, actually have no bearing on the degree of hardness of the wood. In fact, many softwoods are harder than some hardwoods. These terms are used primarily to distinguish the botanical characteristics of the trees. Arbitrarily, trees having broad leaves are known as hardwoods, and coniferous trees—those bearing needles and cones—are known as softwoods.

About 12 types of woods are regularly manufactured into flooring. Of these, the hardwoods account for about 80%. Their greater popularity can be attributed to their appearance and, in the species used, substantially greater hardness and wear resistance.

Industry Standards

National Wood Flooring Association
(NWFA website: **www.woodfloors.org**)

Unfinished wood flooring: A product that must be job site sanded and finished after installation.

Pre-finished wood flooring: Factory sanded and finished flooring that only needs installation.

Solid wood flooring: Completely made of lumber, it is available in unfinished and pre-finished. Solid wood flooring is produced in:

- Strip—in thicknesses of ⁵⁄₁₆" or ¾" and widths of 1½", 2", and 2¼".
- Plank—in thicknesses of ½" or ¾" and widths of 3" to 8".
- Parquet—geometrical patterns of individual wood slats held in place by mechanical fastening or an adhesive.

Solid wood flooring can be used on grade and above grade, but not below grade. Solid wood should be in a moisture controlled environment. Solid wood strip or plank is nailed down only and requires a wood

subfloor. Solid wood parquet can be glued to a variety of subfloor materials.

Engineered wood flooring: Laminate wood flooring is produced by bonding layers of veneer and lumber with an adhesive. Laminate wood flooring is available in pre-finished and unfinished. These products are more dimensionally stable and are ideal for glue-down installation or float-in installation above grade, on grade, or below grade, including basements and humid climates. Engineered wood flooring is produced in:

- Strip—thicknesses of ⁵⁄₁₆", ³⁄₈", ½" or ⁵⁄₈" and in widths of 2" and 2¼".
- Plank—thicknesses of ⁵⁄₁₆", ³⁄₈", ½" or ⁵⁄₈" and in widths of 3" to 8".
- Parquet—one-piece wood tile available in 9" x 9" or 8" x 8" and other patterns.

Acrylic impregnated wood flooring: A pre-finished wood flooring product. Through a high-pressure treatment, acrylic and color are forced into the pores throughout the thickness of the wood. The "finish" is inside the wood, creating a resistance to moisture. These materials appeal most often to commercial customers, but are also used residentially. Acrylic impregnated floors are available in the same styles as laminate floors.

Hardwoods

Industry Standards

Construction Principles, Materials, and Methods
(John Wiley & Sons, Inc.)

Hardwoods. Various commercial species of oak constitute more than 90% of all hardwood flooring produced in a year. Maple accounts for about 6%. The rest is beech, birch, pecan, and several other hardwoods in limited quantities.

Oak. There are about 20 species of oak in the United States that are considered commercially important in lumber production. Of these, about half are classed as *red oak* and half as *white oak*. As growing trees, the several species within each group are readily distinguishable, but in lumber form, the differences are fairly inconspicuous. Therefore, precise separation of the various species within each group of oaks is impractical and unnecessary in flooring manufacture.

Oak is lumbered throughout the southern, eastern, and central states, in forests of the Atlantic Plain and the Appalachian Mountains. In these regions, species of oak grow under a wide range of climatic conditions in many different kinds of soil. There is, accordingly, much variation in the color of the wood, especially the heart-wood. The sapwood shades from white to cream color in all species of oak. In the standard grading rules for oak flooring, color is entirely disregarded except in the amount of light-colored sapwood allowed. Sapwood is limited only in clear grade, the top grade of flooring.

Red oak and white oak are about equal in mechanical properties. Both make satisfactory floors when properly finished. A special feature of white oak is the prominence of large rays that make an interesting flake pattern in quartersawn flooring.

Although grading rules do not differentiate between red oak and white oak, practically all manufacturers supply either all-red or all-white oak flooring except in the lowest grades. Red oak flooring is generally higher in price and more uniform in color than white oak.

Maple. Maple flooring is made from sugar maple, logged largely in the Northeast, the Appalachians, and the lake states (Minnesota, Michigan, and Wisconsin). Sugar maple is known as *hard maple* or *rock maple*. It is extremely hard, strong, and abrasion resistant, making it particularly suitable for hard use locations, such as factories and gymnasiums, as well as residences.

The so-called soft maples (silver maple, red maple, and bigleaf maple) are not as hard, heavy, or strong as hard maple and therefore are not used commonly for flooring.

The heartwood of both sugar maple and black maple is light reddish-brown, and the sapwood, which in mature trees is several inches thick, is creamy white, slightly tinged with brown. The contrast in color between heartwood and sapwood in maple is much less pronounced than in oak, and the standard grading rules permit natural color variation in the wood.

Beech and Birch. Beech and birch are lumbered in the northeastern part of the country and around the Great Lakes. Beech and birch are used only sparingly in the manufacture of flooring. Only two of the almost 20 species of birch that grow in the United States are manufactured into flooring. Of these, *yellow birch* is by far the most abundant and the most important commercially; the other is *sweet birch*. Only one species of beech is native to the United States.

The heartwood of these species is reddish-brown, with a slight variation in color among them. There are similar slight variations in the color of their sapwood, which is of a lighter shade than the heartwood. The varying color of the natural wood is an accepted characteristic in grading beech and birch flooring.

Softwoods

Softwoods. In a typical year, more than 50% of the softwood flooring produced is southern pine, more than 40% is Douglas fir, and the balance is western hemlock, eastern white pine, ponderosa pine, western larch, eastern hemlock, redwood, spruce, cypress, and the true firs. Western larch is similar to Douglas fir in strength and is often sold in mixture with Douglas fir of the northern interior region of the western states. Ponderosa pine, eastern white pine, and redwood are softer than desirable where wear is a prime factor. However, the formidable decay resistance of redwood in the all-heartwood grade has prompted its use for porch and deck flooring.

Southern Pine. Southern pine is a commercial name applied to a group of yellow pines that grow principally in the southeastern states. They include longleaf, shortleaf, loblolly, slash pines, and several other pines of minor importance. Except in dimension lumber and structural timbers, no differentiation between the species is made in marketing the products of this group.

The wood of all southern pines is much alike in appearance. The sapwood and the heartwood often are different in color, the former being yellowish-white and the latter a reddish-brown. However, the contrast in color between sapwood and heartwood in southern pine generally is not conspicuous in a finished floor, and the standard grading rules permit sapwood in all grades of southern pine flooring.

When uniform color is desired, the standard flooring specifications can be amended to require all-sap-face stock (for a light color) or all-heart-face material (for a reddish-brown color). However, special selection of stock for color increases the cost somewhat over the established grade.

Douglas Fir. Red fir, yellow fir, coast Douglas fir, and Oregon pine are other names by which Douglas fir is known in the western parts of the United States and Canada, where it grows. Douglas fir occupies the same important position in the western and Pacific Coast states as southern pine does in the southeastern states.

The sapwood of Douglas fir is creamy white. The heartwood is reddish-brown, and, as in southern pine, the contrast in color between the two is not so pronounced as to be objectionable in a finished floor. Pieces containing both heartwood and sapwood are permitted in all grades.

West Coast Hemlock. Western hemlock grows along the Pacific coast from northern California to Alaska and as far inland as northern Idaho and northwestern Montana. The bulk of hemlock lumber being produced comes from Oregon and Washington (West Coast hemlock). Both the heartwood and the sapwood of western hemlock are almost white, with a pinkish tinge and with very little contrast, although the sapwood is sometimes lighter in color.

Western hemlock has clear color and good finishing qualities, which account for its use in moderate-wear areas, such as bedrooms, where good appearance is the principal requirement. Western hemlock flooring is relatively free from warping and is easy to cut and nail but is not as hard and wear resistant as Douglas fir or larch.

Environmentally Friendly Wood, Bamboo & Cork Flooring

Green Home Improvement
(RSMeans)

Reclaimed Lumber

Floors made from salvaged wood puts to good use waste that might otherwise end up in a landfill. It reduces wood harvesting in a world of rapidly increasing demand, which helps save energy, reduce pollution, and preserve wildlife habitat.

Extremely attractive plank reclaimed wood flooring, including tongue-and-groove, comes in widths

ranging from 3" to 24", although 4" to 10" widths are the most common. Reclaimed wood is also used to create an assortment of other useful building materials, such as siding, timbers for posts and beams, molding, paneling, wainscoting, and roof shakes.

Salvaged wood comes from numerous, sometimes unusual sources, including old barns, mills, bridges, and trees removed from urban and suburban neighborhoods, for example, after storms.

Note: Building codes may restrict the use of reclaimed wood as framing members, but there are no restrictions against its use for flooring or other nonstructural applications.

Bamboo Flooring

Bamboo flooring, somewhat of a curiosity just a few years ago, has gained in popularity and is now often installed in place of conventional wood flooring. Although bamboo is often substituted for wood, it is not wood. It is a member of the grass family. Bamboo used to make flooring comes from an extremely fast-growing species harvested in Southeast Asia.

The plant consists of hollow, round stalks, called culms, which are cut into strips, boiled and dried. The strips are then glued together to produce laminated strip flooring. The adhesive that holds the strips together is either urea-formaldehyde resin, which releases small amounts of formaldehyde, or isocyanate, a glue that, once dry, produces no toxic pollutants. In some cases, bamboo flooring is treated

Wood Flooring

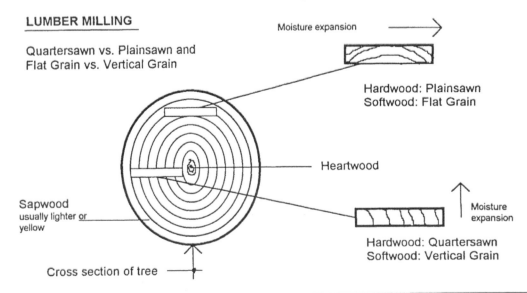

LUMBER MILLING

Quartersawn vs. Plainsawn and
Flat Grain vs. Vertical Grain

Moisture expansion

Hardwood: Plainsawn
Softwood: Flat Grain

Heartwood

Sapwood
usually lighter or yellow

Moisture expansion

Hardwood: Quartersawn
Softwood: Vertical Grain

Cross section of tree

Drawing by contributing editors

Figure 11.2

with a preservative, including the relatively nontoxic boric acid.

Bamboo flooring comes in two basic varieties: solid and engineered. The solid type consists of tongue-and-groove planks, with the bamboo strip oriented either vertically or horizontally. The horizontal product is harder and provides a more traditional look.

Solid bamboo flooring can also be made from stalks that are crushed rather than sliced. This process produces long strands, glued together lengthwise to form strand tongue-and-groove strip flooring. Denser and harder than other bamboo flooring products, stranded bamboo flooring has a totally different appearance.

Engineered flooring, the second option, consists of a top layer of horizontally or vertically oriented strips. They are glued to a backing to form veneered tiles or planks. Engineered bamboo is available in two forms: (1) tongue-and-groove planks, which are nailed or glued in place, and (2) glue-less click-in-place planks.

Bamboo is available in both light and dark shades. The light-colored product is its natural hue, while the darker color flooring is produced by heating the bamboo in the material. While the darker flooring is attractive, the heating required to produce it softens the fibers, making the flooring slightly less dense and durable.

Cork Flooring

Cork is a rapidly renewable resource, and it's also recyclable. Most of the cork used to make flooring is made from the waste from manufacturing other products, primarily wine bottle stoppers.

Cork is soft and resilient; hypo-allergenic; resistant to fire, insects, and moisture; and dampens sound. It is durable (coated with multiple layers of acrylic) when joints are properly sealed. Cork floors typically come with a 15-year warranty and can be refinished with a new acrylic surface when needed.

Like laminate flooring, cork is relatively easy to install, especially the glue-less interlocking tiles. Some products require acclimation prior to installation. Look for a low- or no-VOC adhesive for a truly green installation. Cork can be installed on any level concrete floor, wood subfloor, and over many types of finished flooring.

If you're using cork flooring in a new kitchen, it's best to install floating (click-in-place, glue-less) flooring after the cabinets are in place. Glue-down tiles and planks can be installed before or after the cabinets. In basements, floating (non-glued-down) floor products are recommended.

Flooring Grading Rules

Industry Standards

National Wood Flooring Association

(NWFA website, www.woodfloors.org)

The appearance of the wood determines its "grade." All grades are equally strong and serviceable, but each affords you a different look.

Clear

Clear wood is free of defects, though it may have minor imperfections.

Select

Select wood is almost clear, but contains some natural characteristics such as knots and color variations.

Common

Common wood (No. 1 and No. 2) has more natural characteristics such as knots and color variations than either clear or select grades, and often is chosen because of these natural features and the character they bring to a room. No. 1 Common has a variegated appearance, light and dark colors, knots, flags and wormholes. No. 2 Common is rustic in appearance and emphasize all wood characteristics of the species.

First

First grade wood has the best appearance, natural color variations and limited character marks.

Second

Second grade wood is variegated in appearance with varying sound wood characteristics of species.

Third

Third grade wood is rustic in appearance allowing all wood characteristics of the species.

Industry Standards

NOFMA: The Wood Flooring Manufacturers Association

(NOFMA website: **www.nofma.org**)

*Ed. Note: The principal function of the Wood Flooring Manufacturers Association (NOFMA) is to formulate and administer industry standards on hardwood flooring. Establishing grading rules for flooring is a major part of these standards. The following official flooring rules were published in November 2001. NOFMA updates these standards regularly and posts information on its website (**www.nofma.org**). Information is also available on grading rules for cherry, walnut, and engineered flooring.*

Oak Flooring Grading Rules

(Note: Characteristics included in a higher grade are automatically accepted in lower grades.)

NOFMA Clear Oak: A flooring product of mostly heartwood with a minimum number of character marks and discoloration, providing a uniform appearance while allowing for all heartwood natural color variations.

Will admit the following:

- $3/8$" bright sapwood entire length of strip or equivalent if not extending further than 1" for $1/3$ length of piece.
- Small burls and fine pinworm holes.
- Equivalent characters such as small tight checks.
- In the absence of these, one thin brown streak 3" long to be allowed every 6'.

NOFMA Select Oak: A flooring product with coloration variations produced by differences of natural heartwood and sapwood, along with characters described.

The face may contain:

- Unlimited sound sapwood.
- Slight imperfections in milling; a small tight knot every 3'.
- Pinworm holes.
- Burls and a reasonable amount of slightly open checks.

Brown streaks should be extended the entire length of a piece. Two flay worm holes to every 8' are permitted. Slight imperfections in face work (torn grain) admitted. An intermittent, brown burn across the face not exceeding $1/4$" width admitted. Also, a slight quantity of bark on the back or sides admitted. Will admit pieces with $1/2$ tongue. Spot filling is generally required for open characters.

NOFMA No. 1 Common Oak: A flooring product which contains prominent variations in coloration and varying characters.

The following are not admitted:

- Broken knots over $1/2$" in diameter.
- Large grub worm holes.
- Splits extending through the piece.

Open characters such as checks and knot holes are admitted, but must be sound and readily filled. Not more than 20" scant stock in thickness allowed to every 5'. Minor imperfections in machining permitted. Shall admit sticker stain; varying wood

characteristics, such as flag worm holes, heavy streaks, checks, and worm holes; and an occasional dark machine burn across the face not exceeding $1/2$" wide, $1/64$" deep and not more than two each 3'. One-quarter tongue allowed. Extremely dark pieces are not to be included.

NOFMA No. 2 Common Oak: May contain sound natural variations of the forest product and manufacturing imperfections. The purpose of this grade is to furnish a floor suitable for homes, general utility use, or where character marks and contrasting appearance is desired.

The following are not admitted:

- Shattered or rotten ends.
- Large broken knots.
- Excessive bad millwork.
- Shake.
- Advanced rot.
- Similar unsound defects.

Dark machine burns exceeding $3/64$" deep not admitted. Knot holes and open characters which will readily fill are admitted. A limited number of pieces with no tongue which may be face nailed are admitted.

Prefinished Oak Grading Rules

White Oak and Red Oak in NOFMA *Standard & Better* Grades with a natural coloration, to be separated. All other colors and grades may be mixed Red Oak and White Oak. Grades are established after the flooring has been sanded and finished.

NOFMA Prime Prefinished Oak: This is the top grade and the overall appearance shall be good. The face of strips shall be selected for appearance after finishing. This grade includes characteristics found in the unfinished grades of *Clear* and *Select* grade.

The following characters are admitted:

- Unlimited Sapwood and the natural variations of color.
- Occasional small Burls.
- Light brown streaks not more than $1/8$" in width and 6" in length or the equivalent.
- An occasional very small, tight $1/8$" knot.
- Limited $1/32$" fine pinworm holes, may be included in any one piece when properly filled.
- Will not admit pieces with less than $3/4$ full tongue.

NOFMA Standard Prefinished Oak: The face of strips may contain sound wood characteristics which are even and smooth after filling and finishing. This grade includes some characteristics found in the unfinished grades *Select, No. 1 Common,* and *No. 2 Common.*

The following characters are admitted:

- Worm holes.
- Season and Kiln Checks.
- Broken Knots up to $3/8$" in diameter, minor imperfections in machining.
- Torn Grains.
- Burns.

Other characters will be admitted if they do not impair the soundness of the floor. All larger admitted open characters are to be properly filled and finished. Limited unfinished/unfilled small open grade characters permitted.

Large Grub Worm Holes, Splits extending through the piece. Shake and similar unsound defects not admitted.

For naturally finished coloration: All the varying color characteristics of the wood admitted to include Sticker Stain, and Dark Streaks up to $3/8$" in width not to exceed 1" in length for each lineal foot.

For stained finishes: All varying colorations and streaks permitted, predominantly dark boards not permitted.

NOFMA Tavern Prefinished Oak: Should lay a serviceable floor.

A limited amount of unfilled/unfinished open characters admitted. A limited amount of pieces with finish irregularities such as bubbles, small skips, lines, stain/color variation, surface handling scratches, minor trash, and the like are allowed.

The following characters are *not* admitted:

- Mismanufactured boards.
- Shattered or rotten ends.
- Large open knots and other unsound defects of a similar nature.
- Pieces with less than $1/4$ full tongue.

Beech, Birch, & Hard Maple Grading Rules

NOFMA Select and Better—Beech, Birch, & Hard Maple: Shall have the face practically free of all defects, but the natural color of the wood shall not be considered a defect. The highest standard grade, combines appearance and durability.

Will admit the following:

- Variations in the Natural Color of the wood (with use of some finishes, slight shadows and color variation may appear).

- An occasional small, firm Pin Knot, not over $1/8$" in diameter, provided it does not occur on edges or ends of strips.
- Occasional dark Green or Black Spots or Streaks not over $1/4$" wide and 3" long (or its equivalent) which may contain a tight check not over $1/2$" long, provided it is boxed within the piece.
- Birds' Eyes and small Burls.
- Slightly Torn Grain.
- Similar defect, which can be readily removed by the ordinary method of sanding the floor after it is laid.
- A slightly Shallow Place not over 12" long on underside of the flooring if it does not extend to either end of the piece.

Pieces with $1/2$ Tongue for no more than 25% of the length are allowed. The wood must be sound and free of Shake. Bark Streaks shall not be permitted.

NOFMA No.1 Common—Beech, Birch & Hard Maple: A floor with varying wood characteristics and colors to include distinct color variations, numerous Streaks, stained Sapwood, sound Knots, and Checks. All defects must readily fill.

Will admit the following:

- Sound, tight Knots, provided they do not occur on edges or ends of strips.
- Slight Imperfections in machining.
- Distinct Color Variations.
- Sticker Stain/Shadow.
- Numerous dark Green or Black Spots or Streaks, provided they do not occur in combination with predominantly dark heartwood.
- Slight Checks not exceeding 3" in length (may be slightly open) and running parallel with and well inside the edges and ends of the strips.
- Dark Spots and Streaks with slight Checks in center.
- Small Rough Spots (Torn Grain) which cannot be wholly removed by ordinary method of sanding the floor after it is laid.
- Slightly Torn Edges.
- Short Tongue if sufficient to hold properly in the floor.
- Shallow or Waney Back, if piece has sufficient bearing of full thickness to support it in the floor.
- Small bark Streaks where bark is as sound as surrounding wood.
- Slight variation in Angle of End Matching.
- The face shall be free of Shake and wood must be sound.

NOFMA No. 2 Common—Beech, Birch & Hard Maple: Must be of such character as will lay and give a good serviceable floor. The wood must be firm, serviceable, and may contain all defects common to Maple. Pieces with 1/4 full Tongue admitted.

NOFMA No. 2 Common will not admit:

- Knot Holes over 3/8" in diameter or unsound Knots where the unsound portion is over 1" in diameter.
- Voids on Ends or Edges.
- Shake.
- Heart Checks.
- Badly Split Ends and Imperfections in Manufacture which would materially impair the serviceability of the floor.

Special Grades for Beech, Birch & Hard Maple

NOFMA Clear—Hard Maple: Special stock, selected for uniformity of color. It is almost ivory white and is the finest grade of Hard Maple flooring that can be produced. Sapwood/ Heartwood pieces must have 95% Sapwood on the face. Strips must be free from stain and Heartwood portion must be nearly white. All *Select and Better* rules apply.

Exceptions:

1. Streaks—should be light brown or light green, not over 1/4" wide and 3" long (or equivalent), one per 3'.
2. Black Spots, Sticker Stain/Shadow—not admitted.

NOFMA Clear Red—Beech & Birch: Special grades produced from all red faced stock, and are specially selected for color. The color is rich, being a soft tint which lends these two woods an individuality found in no other species. Strips must have 95% red faced characteristics. All *Select and Better* rules apply.

Exceptions:

1. Streaks—Should be light brown.
2. Black Spots, Sticker Stain/Shadow—not admitted.
3. Hickory/Pecan Grading Rules.

NOFMA Select and Better—Hickory/Pecan: Shall have the face practically free of all defects, but the natural color of the wood shall not be considered a defect. The highest standard grade, combines a nearly uniform appearance with exceptional durability.

The following characters are admitted:

- Variations in the Natural Color of the wood, Heartwood and Sapwood.
- An occasional small, firm Pin Knot or Bird Peck, not over 1/8" diameter, provided it does not occur on edges or ends of strips.
- Dark Streaks not over 1/4" wide and 3" long (or its equivalent), one for every 3' in length.
- Slight Checks not over 1/2" long, provided Check is boxed within the piece.
- Small Burls.
- Slight Torn Grain or slight intermittent Machine Burn.
- Similar defect which can be readily removed by the ordinary method of sanding the floor after it is laid.
- A slightly Shallow Place not over 12" long on underside of the flooring if it does not extend to either end of the piece.

Pieces with 1/2 tongue for no more than 25% of the length are allowed. The wood must be free of Shake. Bark Streaks shall not be permitted.

NOFMA No. 1 Common—Hickory/Pecan: A floor with varying wood characteristics and colors to include heavy Streaks, stained Sapwood, sound Knots, Checks and Small Splits. All defects must readily fill and be sound.

The following characteristics are admitted:

- Broken Knots up to 1/2" in diameter.
- Distinct Color Variations (predominantly dark, discolored pieces not allowed).
- Sticker Stain/Shadow.
- Numerous dark Streaks or black spots.
- Checks to 1/16" not exceeding 3" in length, and running parallel and well inside the strip edges.
- Small End Split 1/16" x 1/2" showing no movement.
- Bird Pecks to 1/2" where bark is sound and as hard as surrounding wood.

Minor imperfections in machining permitted:

- Torn Grain (less than 1/16" deep and 3" long for full width).
- Slightly Torn Edges.
- An occasional dark Machine Burn 1/2" in width (1 per 3).

Will admit pieces with 1/2 full Tongue entire length of piece.

NOFMA No. 2 Common—Hickory/Pecan: Must be of such character as will lay and give a good serviceable floor. The wood must be firm, and may contain defects of every character. This grade is intended to give a "rustic" appearance.

The following defects are *not* allowed:

- Knot Holes over $^3/_8$" in diameter or unsound Knots, where the unsound portion is over 1" in diameter (the unsound portion cannot extend through piece).
- Shake.
- Soft Rot.
- Splits and open defects which extend through piece or show movement.
- Torn Grain more than $^1/_4$" deep.
- Edge Splinters.
- Imperfections in Manufacture which would materially impair the serviceability of the floor.

Knot Holes, Bird Pecks, Worm Holes, and the like which will readily fill are admitted. Pieces with ¼ full tongue admitted.

Special Grades—Hickory/Pecan

NOFMA Clear Red—Hickory/Pecan: A special stock selected for its deep red/brown color with the minimal contrast of the lighter Sapwood.

Face of pieces shall be Heartwood (95%). All *NOFMA Select and Better Grade* rules apply.

NOFMA Clear White—Hickory/Pecan: Special stock selected for its creamy color with the minimal contrast of the darker Heartwood. The face of pieces shall be bright Sapwood (95%). All *Select and Better* rules apply.

Exceptions:

1. Streaks should be light brown, not over $^1/_4$" wide and 3" long (or equivalent), one per 3'.
2. Black Spots not allowed.
3. Sticker Stain/Shadow not allowed.

NOFMA No. 1 Common Red—Hickory/Pecan: Special stock selected for minimal contrasting lighter Sapwood. The face of pieces shall be Heartwood (85%). All *NOFMA No. 1 Common Grade* rules apply.

NOFMA Clear Ash Grading Rules

NOFMA Clear Ash: The face shall be practically free of defects.

The following characters are admitted:

- Small burls (less than $^1/_8$" in diameter).
- Fine pinworm holes with no discoloration (1 for every 3' in length).

In the absence of these, one (1) thin light brown streak (3" long to be allowed for every 6' of length or equivalent).

Brown Heartwood is allowed as follows: $^3/_8$" entire length or 1" for one-third the length of the strip.

NOFMA Select Ash: The face shall contain mostly Sapwood, unstained.

The following characters are admitted:

- Narrow streaks not running entire length of the strip.
- Pin worm holes (up to 3 every 3' in length)
- Imperfection in milling (Torn Grain) which will sand out.
- One (1) small tight knot ($^1/_4$" in diameter) to every 3' in length.
- Small pith fleck (less than $^1/_4$" diameter).
- An intermittent brown machine burn across the face not exceeding $^1/_4$" in width.
- Unlimited cambium miners.

Brown Heartwood is allowed as follows: $^3/_8$" entire length or 1" for one-third the length of the strip.

Will admit pieces with $^1/_2$ tongue. Most defects are lost sight of after the floor is laid and finished, giving a good appearance.

NOFMA No. 1 Common Ash: A floor with varying wood characteristics such as Heavy streaks, Stained sapwood, and Sound knots typical of this grade. All defects must readily fill and be sound.

The following characters are admitted:

- Broken knots up to $^1/_2$" in diameter.
- Pith flecks less than $^3/_{16}$" in diameter.
- Worm holes up to $^3/_{16}$".
- Checks and End splits less than $^1/_{16}$" wide and not extending through the piece.
- Sticker stain.

Minor imperfections in machining permitted; Torn grain (not over one-fourth [$^1/_4$] of the surface, less than $^1/_{26}$" in depth); One (1) dark machine burn across the face for every 3' of length, not exceeding $^1/_2$" in width, $^1/_{64}$" in depth.

Will admit pieces with ¼ tongue.

NOFMA No. 2 Common Ash: Defects of every character admitted, but should lay a serviceable floor.

The following defects are *not* allowed:

- Soft rot.
- Broken knots where the unsound portion extends through piece.

- Torn grain over ³/₁₆" in depth.
- Splits and Open defects extending through the piece.
- Shake and Pith flecks that are soft if over ¹/₄" in diameter.

Knot holes and defects which will readily fill are admitted.

A limited number of pieces with no tongue and limited number of pieces that are thin (scant) in thickness but will End Match admitted.

Wood Floor Installation

Industry Standards

Hardwood Floors: Laying, Sanding, and Finishing
(The Taunton Press)

Plywood-on-Slab and Screed Systems

As explained earlier, parquet, laminated strip and plank, and floating plank systems are the only kinds of flooring that should be applied directly to concrete slabs. Conventional strip and plank over concrete will have to be fastened to plywood underlayment or solid-wood screeds. The plywood-on-slab method is basically just another form of underlayment.

To create a vapor barrier that will protect both the underlayment and finish flooring from moisture, cover the slab with 4-mil to 6-mil polyethylene. First, lay a bed of adhesive on the slab. Then roll the poly into it. The plastic should be large enough to overlap the baseboards. The excess can be trimmed later. Next, install underlayment as described above. Regular masonry nails or concrete fasteners will do, but powder-actuated fasteners are easier and faster, even if you have to rent the tool. In any case, be certain the plastic is sealed at the seams (a 6-in. overlap should be sufficient) and that the plywood is flat.

Fasten the sheets in the center first, then work toward the edges of each sheet. If you use lead or sleeve-type concrete anchors, I suggest pouring a small amount of asphalt mastic or construction adhesive into each hole to prevent water seepage. Another vapor-barrier method (or when working over lightweight concrete) is to score the back of the underlayment with a 12-in. grid, then bed the sheets in a coat of cut-back asphalt mastic troweled onto the slab. Use an adhesive that will remain fairly elastic over time, such as a "cold-tar" mastic. By "cut back," I mean an asphalt adhesive that has been thinned somewhat with the appropriate solvent, generally paint thinner. Trowel the mastic evenly over the entire slab, then allow it to set for 12 hours or longer before laying the underlayment.

Screeds are another common way of setting a wooden floor over a slab. Screeds are basically treated 1x3s or 1x4s over which strip or plank flooring is laid. They provide a nailing surface and keep the flooring from direct contact with the slab, thereby reducing moisture exchange.

Screeds are set in a mastic bed between two layers of polyethylene vapor barrier. Fastening the screeds to the slab is optional. It's acceptable just to bed them in mastic on top of the lower vapor barrier.

If you do decide to fasten the screeds to the slab, use powder-actuated fasteners or concrete anchors. I use pressure-treated 1x3s or 1x4s for the screeds. Lay the first layer of plastic, spread the mastic and place the screeds on 9-in. centers for strip and plank flooring up to 4 in. wide. In order to have adequate nailing surface, flooring wider than 4 in. will require a subfloor over the screeds or plywood-on-slab underlayment.

Now and then, I encounter a slab with an embedded radiant-heat system, in which case I trowel mortar, Gypcrete or plasticized cement between the screeds, flush with their tops. Once set, the mortar can be sanded flush to the screeds. Besides providing additional support for the flooring, the mortar adds thermal mass for the heating system.

Partial nail schedule	Type of flooring	Fasteners	Spacing
Strip T&G	3/8 x 1 1/2 3/8 x 2	1 1/4-in. machine driven fasteners, or 4d or 5d bright casing nails or finish nails.	8 in. O.C. or closer
	1/2 x 1 1/2 1/2 x 2	1 1/2-in. to 1 3/4-in. machine driven fasteners or 5d or 6d cut-steel or finish nails.	8 in to 10 in. O.C. or closer
	3/4 up to 3 1/4 strip	2-in. machine driven fasteners or cut nails or 7d or 8d flooring nails.	8 in to 10 in. O.C. or closer
Plank T&G	3/4 up to 4	2-in. machine driven fasteners or cut nails or 7d or 8d flooring nails.	8 in. O.C. into & between joists

Figure 11.3

Courtesy of The Taunton Press, *Hardwood Floors: Laying, Sanding, and Finishing*

Another version of the screed and radiant-heat system that's a popular retrofit method consists of 2x4s installed on 9-in. to 12-in. centers on top of the slab. The radiant coils are intertwined between and around these, then covered with another layer of concrete, Gypcrete or other heavy-mass substance. The flooring is then nailed to the screeds or to ¾-in. plywood underlayment installed over the screeds.

Adhesives

The most common wood-flooring adhesives in use today can be grouped into one of three categories: cold-tar mastics or "cutback," water-based mastics, latex or emulsions, and chlorinated solvent mastics. Each of these has advantages and disadvantages, but as far as working qualities go, you're looking for an adhesive to "flash" quickly, which means that it initially cures enough to become tacky. An adhesive's open working time—specified in minutes or hours—is a measure of how long the exposed surface will remain tacky enough to work with.

Cold-tar mastic or "cutback" is the traditional adhesive for parquet and other floors and is still widely used today, especially for ¾-in. parquet. It's inexpensive and is a good choice where a polyethylene film is required as a vapor barrier. It's also flammable, smelly and messy to use and clean up, and has a tendency to bleed up between pieces or through porous wood fibers. There's also some concern over the toxicity of the solvents used to thin the mastic, so be sure to wear a respirator and gloves. Let it flash off at least four to six hours before installing over it.

I like the chlorinated solvent mastics best because they offer the most favorable combination of flash time, open working time, elasticity and longevity, even when exposed to excess moisture. They do require good ventilation and cleanup with a compatible solvent, usually paint thinner. If you happen to be using a chlorinated solvent over vinyl flooring, be sure you use a plasticizer-blocking sealer first, or the bond may be substantially weakened.

Water-based adhesives are by far the safest. They're nearly odorless, non-flammable and flash almost instantly. But, in my opinion, water-based adhesives aren't as durable as solvent-based adhesives, especially in moist conditions, such as you'd encounter over a concrete slab. One other type of adhesive, epoxy, is also occasionally used for flooring. Although it's moisture resistant, it's also messy and sets up too quickly into a brittle bond. This can cause a loose or noisy floor later on.

Whichever adhesive you pick, be sure to use the required protective equipment, especially an organic-vapor respirator with solvent and epoxy adhesives.

Epoxy is a skin irritant for many people, so use thin plastic or rubber gloves when handling it. Always extinguish gas-range and water-heater pilot lights before spreading flammable adhesives or chlorinated solvent adhesives. Arrange the ventilation so that air near the floor, where vapors tend to settle, will be kept constantly moving.

The label on the adhesive can should give specifics on how to apply the material. It should also tell what size and type of trowel to use. I spread the solvent-based adhesives with a 5/32-in. V-notch trowel. A notched trowel is more effective than a flat one because the notches automatically meter the amount of adhesive being applied and the proper ridge depth. If you spread too much, the tiles won't seat flat and the excess adhesive will ooze up between the joints, a real mess that will take forever to dry. Too little adhesive creates an inferior bond, resulting in loose tiles, another real mess since it's not easy to reset a tile later.

Wood Floor Finishes

Industry Standards

National Wood Flooring Association
(NWFA website, **www.woodfloors.org**)

Surface Finishes

Lasting beauty requires minimal care with today's wood floor finishes. These finishes are usually urethanes and remain on the surface of the wood and form a protective coating. Surface finishes are popular today because they are durable, water-resistant and require minimal maintenance. Various gloss levels are available.

Types of Surface Finishes

Oil-modified urethane is easy to apply. It is a solvent-base polyurethane that dries in about eight hours. This type of finish ambers.

Moisture-cured urethane is solvent-base polyurethane that is more durable and more moisture resistant than other surface finishes. Moisture-cure urethane comes in non-yellowing and in ambering types and is generally available in satin or gloss. These finishes are extremely difficult to apply, have a strong odor and are best left to the professional.

Conversion varnish dries clear to slight amber and is durable. These finishes have an extremely strong odor and should be applied by the highly skilled flooring professional.

Water-based urethane finishes are clear and non-yellowing. They have a milder odor and dry in about two to three hours.

Penetrating Stain and Wax - This finish soaks into the pores of the wood and hardens to form a protective penetrating seal. The wax gives a low-gloss satin sheen. It is generally maintained with solvent-based (never water-based) waxes, buffing pastes or cleaning liquids (specifically made for wax-finished wood floors and an additional thin application of wax as needed.

Wood Flooring: Moisture Effects

Comments

All wood flooring installations and/or installation failure analysis must include the proper method of testing for moisture and water migration. Most wood floor failures are the result of water intrusion above the membrane.

Industry Standards

Hardwood Floors: Laying, Sanding, and Finishing
(The Taunton Press)

Water & Wood: A Troublesome Pair
As wood cells absorb and lose moisture, a board swells and shrinks more across the grain than it does parallel to the grain. This means that with seasonal variations in moisture, a plain-sawn board will change far more in width than it will in length or thickness. In contrast, a quartersawn board swells and shrinks more in thickness than in width. Therefore, quartersawn stock is considered more moisture stable.

The width of a piece of $2\frac{1}{4}$-in. oak flooring is affected by changes in its moisture content. Here, I should explain what's meant by moisture content in wood. As I explained earlier, wood constantly absorbs and desorbs moisture from the air. However, when a dried board is not giving off or absorbing moisture from the air, it's said to be at equilibrium moisture content (EMC). EMC is expressed as a percentage of the wood's dry weight, so an EMC of 5% really means that 5% of the board's weight is water.

EMC is related to relative humidity (RH). Wood technologists have graphs that precisely tie the two together, but as a rule of thumb, a relative humidity of 25% gives an EMC of 5%, and a relative humidity of 75% gives an EMC of 14%. A 50% swing in relative humidity produces an EMC gradient of 10%. This, in turn, translates to a width variation of $\frac{1}{16}$-in. Not much in a single board but in a floor, all of the boards expand and contract, pushing against each other. Over the width of a l0-ft. wide floor, that amounts to more then 3 in. of total expansion or contraction.

In most houses, at least ones that are heated in the winter and cooled in the summer, the relative-humidity swing will be less than 50%. You will have to allow for expansion and contraction, but most of the time no moisture-related damage will occur. When it does, the results can be spectacular. Flooding caused by broken pipes or seepage through wells is the worst. I've seen swollen floors buckle like hot pavement. In extreme cases, the swelling will actually push the walls out.

The opposite extreme is wood heat, which is so dry that it tends to shrink the flooring, opening up cracks.

There are several ways to avoid moisture damage. First, buy dry flooring. Purchase a moisture meter or borrow one from your supplier (most have them) and make sure your flooring is between 6% and 9% moisture content. A $100 moisture meter is cheap insurance against the potential disaster of not recognizing and correcting moisture problems. Don't allow flooring to get rained on. You'd be surprised what even a light rain will do to flooring.

Test the moisture content of the subfloor, too, including concrete floors. The difference between subfloor and flooring shouldn't be greater than 4%. Don't bring flooring into the house until the drywall is well cured. Allow your material to acclimate uncovered in the house for three to six weeks. This should give it plenty of time to reach EMC. Finally, leave an expansion gap between the flooring and the wall, $\frac{1}{16}$-in. of expansion gap for every cross-grain running foot of flooring. The gap will be hidden by the baseboard. Very wide floors will need more of a gap than the baseboard can cover. In this case, undercut the baseboard and/or add a wider shoe molding.

Wood Floor Maintenance

Comments

Proper maintenance is required to keep wood floors looking their best over time. The following are some basic guidelines from the National Wood Flooring Association.

Industry Standards

National Wood Flooring Association
(NWFA website, www.woodfloors.org)

Regular Maintenance
With today's advances in wood flooring stains and finishes, cleaning your wood floors has never been easier. Regular maintenance requires little

more than sweeping with a soft bristle broom, and vacuuming with a soft floor attachment if your wood floor includes a beveled edge that could collect debris. You also should clean your floors periodically with a professional wood floor cleaning product recommended by a wood flooring professional. The NWFA can help you find one in your area.

Preventive Maintenance

There are other steps you can take to minimize maintenance and maintain the beauty of your wood floors as well.

- Do not use sheet vinyl or tile floor care products on wood floors. Self-polishing acrylic waxes cause wood to become slippery and appear dull quickly.

- Use throw rugs both inside and outside doorways to help prevent grit, dirt and other debris from being tracked onto your wood floors. This will prevent scratching.

- Do not wet-mop a wood floor. Standing water can dull the finish, damage the wood and leave a discoloring residue.

- Wipe up spills immediately with a slightly dampened towel.

- Do not over-wax a wood floor. If the floor dulls, try buffing instead. Avoid wax buildup under furniture and other light traffic areas by applying wax in these spots every other waxing session.

- Put soft plastic or fabric-faced glides under the legs of furniture to prevent scuffing and scratching.

- Avoid walking on your wood floors with cleats, sports shoes and high heels. A 125-pound woman walking in high heels has an impact of 2,000 pounds per square inch. An exposed heel nail can exert up to 8,000 pounds per square inch. This kind of impact can dent any floor surface.

- When moving heavy furniture, do not slide it on wood flooring. It is best to pick up the furniture completely to protect the wood flooring.

- For wood flooring in the kitchen, place an area rug in front of the kitchen sink.

- Use a humidifier throughout the winter months to keep wood movement and shrinkage to a minimum.

Allowable Tolerances in Wood Flooring

Industry Standards

Handbook of Construction Tolerances
(John Wiley & Sons, Inc.)

Wood Flooring

For strip flooring and parquet flooring, the subfloor should be level to within ¼ in. in 10 ft. with no abrupt projections or depressions.

Wood Floor Framing and Subflooring

In general, a level tolerance of ±¼ in. in 10 ft. for new construction is a reasonable expectation and is less than the maximum allowable deflection (L/240 for dead and live load) stated by the *Uniform Building Code.*

Ed. Note: See Residential Construction Performance Guidelines, *published by the National Association of Home Builders, for more information on strip oak flooring tolerances.*

Comments

This discussion on tolerances by various sources reflects the best information on this subject relating to new construction and remodeling.

 Disasters result in a broader tolerance. Building officials will sometimes loosen the minimum requirements for occupancy, as they did after the Northridge Earthquake. During that disaster, slab floors settled as much as 10" at one corner of a building, and the "mudjacking" contractors contracted to bring the floor to "Liveable Straight Line Level," which is 1" in 20'.

Mudjacking is the process of pumping a relatively stiff concrete mixture at the end of a metal pipe driven into the loose soil according to a predetermined grid (usually 6' on center each way in the horizontal plane and 2' on center in the vertical dimension), effectively compacting and raising the soil.

Pressure grouting is a similar process that uses a wet slurry-type mixture to fill cracks and voids in fractured soil or under slab voids.

Industry Standards

National Wood Flooring Association
(NWFA website: www.woodfloors.org)

Because wood is a natural product it will react to changes in its environment. Normal cracks are not uncommon if there are separations between individual flooring pieces and are uniform and general throughout the floor.

The most common causes of separations are Mother Nature and dryness. The loss of moisture results in the most frequent reason for shrinkage of individual pieces and cracks. Most cracks are seasonal—they appear in dry months, or the cold season when heating is required, and close during humid periods. This type of separation and close is considered normal. In solid $2\frac{1}{4}$" wide strip oak floors, dry time cracks may be the width of a dime's thickness ($\frac{1}{32}$"). Wider boards will have wider cracks and the reverse is true.

The cure is to minimize changes by adding moisture to the air space during dry periods. A constant Relative Humidity (RH) of 50% works in concert with the manufacture of wood floors to provide stability in the floor. You must live with normal cracks or add humidity—it's your choice.

Parquet and Block Flooring

Comments

As with other types of tile flooring, it is important to plan the layout carefully, squaring off the room and establishing a center line. Follow the manufacturer's instructions and details, such as the correct size of notched trowel and the proper solvent to use for cleaning any adhesive that seeps between the tile joints.

Industry Standards

Construction Principles, Materials, and Methods
(John Wiley & Sons, Inc.)

9.9.5 Parquet Flooring

Parquet (pattern) floors consist of individual strips of wood (*single slats*) or larger units (*blocks*) installed to form a decorative geometric pattern. Blocks may be made by laminating several hardwood veneers or by gluing a number of solid hardwood pieces into a unit to facilitate installation. Unlike strip and plank flooring, parquet flooring usually is installed with mastic.

Oak is by far the most predominant species used in all types of pattern flooring, but other species, such as

maple, walnut, cherry, and East Indian teak, also are available. Sometimes a mixture of hardwoods, such as hickory, ash, elm, pecan, sycamore, beech, and hackberry, are used at random in a single block.

9.9.5.1 Block Flooring

Block flooring is manufactured in several basic types. In *unit block* (also known as *solid unit block*), short lengths of strip flooring are joined together edgewise to form square units. In *laminated* (plywood) block, three or more plies of veneer are bonded with adhesive to obtain the desired thickness. *Slat block* (sometimes called *mosaic parquet hardwood slat*) flooring utilizes narrow slats or "fingers" of wood preassembled into larger units to facilitate installation.

Most unit and laminated block flooring is tongued on two adjoining or opposing edges and grooved on the other two to ensure alignment between adjoining blocks. Some manufacturers produce square-edged blocks, while others include grooves on all four block edges and furnish splines for insertion between adjoining blocks. Both types are designed to be installed with mastic over a wood subfloor or concrete slab. Prefinished blocks usually have eased or beveled edges.

Unit blocks typically consist of several $\frac{3}{4}$-in. T&G strips, all laid parallel or alternating in each quarter of the block checkerboard fashion. Consequently, typical block sizes are multiples of the strip width used. Common strip widths are $1\frac{1}{2}$, 2, and $2\frac{1}{4}$ in., resulting in typical block dimensions of 6, $6\frac{3}{4}$, $7\frac{1}{2}$, 8, 9, 10, and $11\frac{3}{4}$ in. The individual strips are held together with wood or metal splines embedded in the lower surface.

Laminated Block. Laminated block is made typically $\frac{15}{32}$ in. thick, in 9-in. squares, but other sizes, such as 8 in. and $8\frac{1}{2}$ in., also are available from some manufacturers. Appearance grades are Prime and Standard.

Because of its cross-laminated construction in three to five plies, shrinking and swelling of individual blocks is minimized. This type of wood flooring has good dimensional stability and is often recommended for damp locations, such as slabs on grade.

Adhesives used in the manufacture of laminated block flooring should be capable of resisting the temperature and humidity variations to which the flooring may be subjected. Melamine-urea resin adhesive gives good results at moderate cost and represents the typical adhesive used for most laminated block flooring.

Highly water-resistant adhesives such as phenols, resorcinols, and melamines may also be used if the application warrants it; however, the use of these glues adds to the cost of the product. Adhesives that create high-strength dry bonds but are adversely affected by moisture are not recommended for the manufacture of laminated-block flooring.

Slat Block. Appearance grades are based on grading rules developed by the American National Standards Institute and the American Parquet Association (APA), ANSI/APA 1-1984, "Mosaic-Parquet Hardwood Slat Flooring." APA checks compliance of these rules through periodic inspections of member plants. These products are suitable for installation in mastic over concrete surfaces, both above and on grade. The basic components of these products are solid, $5/16$ in. thick, generally square-edged slats of hardwood, $3/4$ in. to 1 $1/4$ in. wide and 4 to 7 in. long, assembled into basic squares. These in turn are factory-assembled checkerboard fashion, with the grain in each adjoining square reversed, into larger flooring blocks up to 30 in. long and wide.

Several types of slat block flooring are available. Some are assembled into panels held together with a face paper. These are 9$1/2$-in., 18-in, or 19-in. squares and are marketed unfinished. Others are made up of single 6-in. T&G squares. These are held together by mechanical attachments and are generally factory finished. Still others are assembled into panels held together with a backing material such as an asphalt-saturated felt, textile webbing, or another type of felt or non-woven interfacing. These products generally are 9$1/2$, 11, or 12 in. square; they may be square-edged or grooved and splined, and may be either unfinished or prefinished.

Floating Laminate Floors

Comments

High-pressure melamine flooring has become popular recently for its wearability, wide range of wood grain patterns and colors, low maintenance, and relatively easy installation. It comes in planks, each of which has a laminate surface bonded to a wood-based core. A "balancing layer" is bonded to the back of the plank to provide stability. Manufacturers of this type of flooring indicate that floating laminate floors can be suitable for light commercial as well as residential applications.

Installation

The major manufacturers of systems such as Pergo, Armstrong, and Wilsonart provide how-to books and telephone advice, and some rent tools to use for the installation. Distributors also offer guidance on their websites.

Floating floors can be installed over concrete or existing vinyl flooring. The floor is not anchored to the subfloor. A special underlayment (provided by the manufacturer) is placed (over polyethene film, in the case of concrete). The planks are laid in rows, with spacers inserted between the flooring and all of the walls. The manufacturer's block is used to push the planks together. They are glued, row by row, in the grooves only and not along the starting wall. Small traces of excess glue that have not been wiped away during the installation can be removed later by damp mopping or with a small amount of acetone on a cloth.

Floating floor systems can include wallbases to match or contrast with the floor, quarter round trim, end and T-moulding, stairnose, and reducer strips. Special underlayment foam is available that can even out minor surface irregularities in the subfloor, while providing sound and heat insulation. Sound reduction and comfort can also be enhanced using special underlayment boards designed by the manufacturer for this purpose.

Acoustical Ceilings: Characteristics & Use

Comments

Acoustical ceilings are often used in office and commercial space to reduce unwanted noise while providing the desired aesthetic appearance. This type of ceiling is also frequently used in residential finished basements. Use of acoustical ceilings allows access to wiring, piping, and ductwork, and makes it easier to reconfigure space in the future.

One of the biggest challenges with acoustic tile installations is coordinating all of the other trades, such as HVAC and electrical, that will be installing related items.

Acoustical ceilings can act as a support element for these items:

- fire sprinklers (supported on grid or by independent means)
- light fixtures (recessed lights within the framework or independently; check your local electrical code)
- speakers (supported on the grid system or independently)
- signs (supported on the grid or independently)

Signs, light fixtures, and speakers can all be relocated with relative ease in the event of future reconfiguration of the space.

Selecting Ceiling Tiles

The type of ceiling tile that is installed is usually predetermined by the architect, designer, or owner. Many types of ceiling tiles are manufactured, some with stringent design specifications. The room or building use will dictate whether any building code requirements apply. Some design considerations in selecting a specific ceiling tile are:

Fire Rating: There are applications where a specific fire rating is required. Standardized tests for flame spread specifications are given for each type of ceiling tile. Ceiling installers should check that the properly rated ceiling tile is received prior to installation, keeping in mind that many ceiling tile finish patterns are standardized and look the same on the surface. Installers should also check to see if hold-down clips are required in order to provide a fire-rated ceiling. These clips prevent inadvertent removal of tiles that would then cause a breech in the fire-rated ceiling.

Acoustical ceilings are rated for fire performance as follows:

- Surface burning characteristics (flame spread and smoke ratings)
- Fire resistance (may be designated in Fire-Rated Assemblies certified by Underwriters Laboratories, Inc.)
- Flash Over

Restaurant Kitchens: Commercial kitchens require a ceiling system that can be washed. The ceiling tiles are manufactured with a surface that can be cleaned without causing damage to the tile.

Light Reflectance: The use of the room or building will have different requirements for the amount of lighting that may be required. Use of tiles with high light reflectance will decrease the required number of light fixtures in a room or building.

Sound Transmission: Ceiling tiles are used for their acoustical property of reducing the amount of noise in a room or building. There are standardized tests for sound transmission specifications that are given for each type of ceiling tile. This is measured in Sound Transmission Class (STC).

Acoustical performance is also described in terms of NRC (sound absorption reduced reverberation) and CAC (Ceiling Articulation Class, or reduced sound transmission from adjacent spaces, such as the activity on the floor above or from noise from pipes and ducts, electronic devices, etc.).

Impact Resistance: Some applications may have a high probability of impact, such as a school or gym. There are ceiling tiles that are designed to withstand this type of use.

Architectural Design: Ceiling systems can be very plain and inexpensive, or can be elaborate and cost many times more than a standard fissured tile system.

Generally, the product manufacturer will be able to provide a catalog of products.

Among the more common alternatives:

Tegular Tiles: Notched at the perimeter edges so that the center drops below the grid to reveal a nice shadow effect.

Concealed Spline: Slotted so that the grid slips into the notch and the grid metal disappears. These systems do not respond well in situations in which maintenance workers randomly remove panels for access.

Fire-Rated and Clean Room Systems: Usually require retainer clips to prevent the tiles from lifting during air pressure changes.

Food Processing and Food Serving Areas: Usually require a washable surface on the tile face.

Suspended Ceilings

Industry Standards

Fundamentals of the Construction Process
(RSMeans)

Suspended ceilings consist of a ceiling board or tile and/or a suspension system. One component of the suspension system is the main runner, consisting of a 1½" channel, spaced 2' to 3' apart and hung from the supporting structure. From the main runner, cross members are supported by clips, 1' to 2' apart, to suit the modular tile size. For a concealed spline ceiling, with 1' square tiles, the spline is, in turn, supported by the cross members.

Suspended ceiling boards can be sealed in place to create an isolated air space between them and the next level, called a plenum, which acts in the heating system as a return air reservoir. This design saves on return air ductwork costs. However, most building codes require that a plenum ceiling contain fire-rated components.

On commercial projects, installation of the suspension system or ceiling grid is usually coordinated with several subcontractors whose work is related to the ceiling finishes. First, the ceiling grid must be centered within the perimeter partitions of the individual room. Next, the sprinkler heads are centered, in rows, in the individual ceiling tiles. The light fixtures are usually the same size (modular) as the ceiling tiles and the layout is as symmetrical as their positioning will allow. Finally, the diffusers for the heating system are placed in rows occupying full or half modules within the grid. Although the ceiling drawings in the plans address some of these problems, the final layout is a result of the coordination of several subcontractors' shop drawings.

Comments

Lighting

Lighting in suspended ceilings can be standard ceiling grid fixtures, fluorescent fixtures mounted on the ceiling joists (with translucent panels installed in the ceiling grid below), or a luminous ceiling comprised of fluorescent tubing with translucent panels (over the entire ceiling area). For the overall luminous ceiling, fluorescent lamps (4', 40 watt) should be spaced between 18"–24" apart.

Grid System

The grid system for a suspended acoustical ceiling must be hung from the structural ceiling surface. Galvanized wire is attached to the structural ceiling by various types of fasteners.

"Eye" lag bolts are used most often in constructing suspended ceilings for wood-framed buildings. Manufacturers have designed fastening systems that utilize a drill (with a special tip) that is secured to the end of a pole. While standing on the floor, the installer first drills the lag bolt into the ceiling joist, and then pulls the pole off the lag bolt while it is still on the hanging wire. Another quick pull of the drill trigger twists the end of the hanging wire around itself. Three to four tight turns are generally required.

There are several common methods of wire attachment for concrete ceiling surfaces. In new, multiple-story construction, the hanging wires can be installed through the sheet metal form prior to the pouring of concrete for the floor at each level. This is done early in the construction process, and the installer may still need to add hanging wires when the acoustical ceiling is installed during the finish portion of the construction project.

An efficient method in applications involving existing concrete ceilings utilizes a power-actuated pin fastener, with the hanging wire pre-attached to the fastener. There are various pole systems that allow the installer to stand on the floor to attach the hanging wire.

Another more time-consuming method requires the use of a ladder or scaffold. The installer drills a hole into the concrete, and then attaches an anchor and tie to the hanging wire.

In many regions, additional seismic support is required. This support limits the amount of buckling and sway that may occur during an earthquake, preventing possible injuries from collapsing suspended ceilings. During installation of the supplementary seismic support, additional hanging wire is attached to various points in the grid system. Wires are splayed at 45° angles to the supporting structure, and a compression strut system is installed at the central point of the splayed wires. See **Figures 11.4** and **11.5**.

The grid system layout must be carefully planned prior to the installation of the hanging wire. Within the industry, it is an accepted standard that ceiling tiles at the perimeter of the room shall not be less than $1/2$ the width or length of the tile. The hanging wire should be installed as close to perpendicular to the ceiling system as possible.

IBC–2006

2504: Vertical and Horizontal Assemblies

803.9 Acoustical ceiling systems: Metal suspension systems for acoustical tile and lay-in panel ceilings must meet this section.

803.9.1 Materials and installation: Install in accordance with manufacturers' recommendations and applicable provisions for applying interior finish.

Acoustic Tile Ceiling

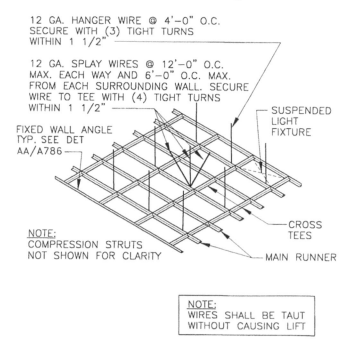

12 GA. HANGER WIRE @ 4'–0" O.C.
SECURE WITH (3) TIGHT TURNS
WITHIN 1 1/2"

12 GA. SPLAY WIRES @ 12'–0" O.C.
MAX. EACH WAY AND 6'–0" O.C. MAX.
FROM EACH SURROUNDING WALL. SECURE
WIRE TO TEE WITH (4) TIGHT TURNS
WITHIN 1 1/2"

FIXED WALL ANGLE
TYP. SEE DET
AA/A786

SUSPENDED
LIGHT
FIXTURE

CROSS
TEES

MAIN RUNNER

NOTE:
COMPRESSION STRUTS
NOT SHOWN FOR CLARITY

NOTE:
WIRES SHALL BE TAUT
WITHOUT CAUSING LIFT

Figure 11.4

Drawings by The Durrant Group, Inc.

Compression Strut

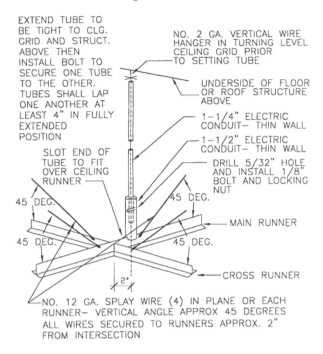

EXTEND TUBE TO BE TIGHT TO CLG. GRID AND STRUCT. ABOVE THEN INSTALL BOLT TO SECURE ONE TUBE TO THE OTHER. TUBES SHALL LAP ONE ANOTHER AT LEAST 4" IN FULLY EXTENDED POSITION

SLOT END OF TUBE TO FIT OVER CEILING RUNNER

45 DEG.

45 DEG.

NO. 2 GA. VERTICAL WIRE HANGER IN TURNING LEVEL CEILING GRID PRIOR TO SETTING TUBE

UNDERSIDE OF FLOOR OR ROOF STRUCTURE ABOVE

1-1/4" ELECTRIC CONDUIT— THIN WALL

1-1/2" ELECTRIC CONDUIT— THIN WALL

DRILL 5/32" HOLE AND INSTALL 1/8" BOLT AND LOCKING NUT

MAIN RUNNER

45 DEG.

45 DEG.

CROSS RUNNER

2'

NO. 12 GA. SPLAY WIRE (4) IN PLANE OR EACH RUNNER— VERTICAL ANGLE APPROX 45 DEGREES ALL WIRES SECURED TO RUNNERS APPROX. 2" FROM INTERSECTION

Figure 11.5

Drawings by The Durrant Group, Inc.

803.9.1.1 Suspended acoustical ceilings: These must be installed in accordance to ASTM C 635 and 636.

803.9.1.2 Fire-resistance-rated construction: These must comply with IBC Chapter 7 provisions.

2506.2 Standards: Refers to IBC Table 2506.2, Chapter 35, and (for fire protection requirements) Chapter 7.

2506.2.1 Other materials: Refers to ASTM C 635 and ASCE 7, Section 13.5.6 for high seismic areas for acoustic and lay in ceilings.

Note: The *IRC* does not specifically reference acoustical ceilings.

Comments

The wall angle and main runners are the first components of the grid system to be installed. Proper steps must be taken to be sure that the grid system is as horizontally level as possible. String levels, water levels, and lasers are the most common tools utilized to level the grid system. The hanging wire should be laid out to be directly perpendicular to the main runner locations. Once the wall angle and main runners are in place, the cross tees are

snapped in at specified intervals to fit the ceiling tiles. The most common tile sizes are 2' x 2' or 2' x 4'.

Any other items that will be installed into the grid system, such as light fixtures and HVAC registers, should be installed and connected at this time. These items will require their own seismic hanging wires, usually one at each diagonal corner.

The ceiling installer should carefully check the contract specifications to determine who is responsible for the seismic hanging wires for light fixtures, HVAC registers, and any other items that are placed in the ceiling grid.

Installation Terminology

On Center (OC): On center in suspended ceiling installations refers to the distance from the center of one tee to the center of the next.

Patterns: The two most common tee patterns or layouts are 2' x 2' and 2' x 4'. The 2' x 4' pattern is more economical, easier to plan, and faster to install.

> **2' x 4' Tee Layout:** Using 2' x 4' acoustical panels, full-length main tee sections are spaced 4' OC, with 4' cross tees at 2' OC, spanning between them.
>
> **2' x 2' Tee Layout:** Using 2' x 2' acoustical panels, 2' cross tees are added to a 2' x 4' grid, spanning between centers of the 4' cross tees.
>
> **Tees:** The metal framing members of the ceiling grid.
>
> **Main Tees:** Main tees run from wall to wall (between the wall angles) as the primary support for the ceiling's weight. They are hung by hanger wire from joists or other supports above.
>
> **Cross Tees:** Cross tees snap into main tees as secondary support members for individual ceiling panels. They come in two lengths: 4' (used for both 2' x 4' and 2' x 2' grid patterns), and 2' (used for 2' x 2' grid patterns only).

Wall Angle: An L-shaped metal strip, the continuous finished edge around the perimeter of the ceiling where it meets the wall.

Adhered Ceilings

Industry Standards

Fundamentals of the Construction Process
(RSMeans)

Ceiling tiles, 12" x 12", can also be mounted on a flat substrate with adhesive. These are usually in acoustical (sound absorbing) material made of mineral fiber, sometimes having plastic or metal facing. (See **Figure 11.6.**)

Ceiling tiles are commonly found in sizes from 1' square to 2' x 4' rectangles, almost always acoustical. The exposed face may be perforated, fissured, textured, or plastic covered. Acoustical ceiling tiles (shown in **Figure 11.6**) are available in mineral fiber in many patterns and textures.

Comments

Plan ceiling tile layout so that equal-sized tiles are used on opposing borders. Ensure a level ceiling by shimming the furring strips as necessary. Cover the gap between ceiling tile and the wall with cove molding.

Mineral Fiber Tile Applied with Adhesive

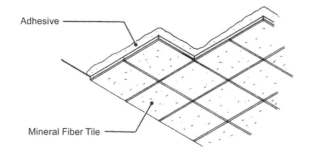

Adhesive

Mineral Fiber Tile

Fiberglass Board on Suspended Grid System

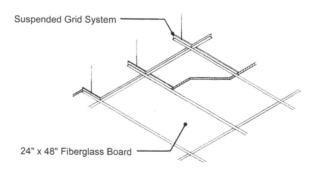

Suspended Grid System

24" x 48" Fiberglass Board

Figure 11.6

RSMeans, *Fundamentals of the Construction Process*

PAINTING & WALL COVERING

Table of Contents

Text in blue type indicates excerpted summaries from the International Building Code® (IBC) *and* International Residential Code® (IRC). *Please consult the IBC and IRC for complete coverage and specific wording. "Comments" (in solid blue boxes) were written by the editors, based on their own experience.*

 This icon will appear with references to green building practices.

CHAPTER 12

PAINTING & WALL COVERING

Common Defect Allegations

Most defect claims on painting involve the building exterior. Claims on interior painting usually relate to drywall taping and/or mud showing through the paint, which appears dull in those areas. This condition is sometimes referred to as "flashing," and may result from insufficient paint thickness or use of a quickset compound or "hot mud."

According to the National Association of Home Builders' Residential Construction Performance Guidelines, "setting nails and filling nail holes are considered part of painting and finishing." Complaints of this type are also common.

Exterior claims often result from deferred maintenance. In some regions, oil-based paints are prohibited, and exterior painting (with latex paint) is required every two years. Complaints may be raised regarding paint fading, though it is generally considered a normal occurrence. (Consult the manufacturer's product warranty information.) Paint peeling before the end of the contractor's warranty constitutes a defect.

Wood window warranties require that paint be applied with $1/16$" overlapping onto the glass pane to make a weather seal. Even when the paint is properly applied, cleaning personnel will often take a razor and cut that weather seal, allowing water to enter the assembly. (Claims are also made on scratched glass.) Many times the panes will need to be replaced, requiring painting, and the cycle starts all over again. The painter should mask the entire window, not just a border, and residual tape adhesive must be removed chemically.

Another complaint is that tops and bottoms of doors are not painted. Sealing these surfaces is an absolute must to prevent the doors from warping. Hardware should be removed, and escutcheons should fit tightly into the paint or be caulked to prevent water entry into the interior of the weather-exposed door.

Back-priming is required on all exterior carpentry, including siding. Siding shingles and boards should never be allowed to weather without some form of protection. Cedar and redwood have an inherent resistance to dry rot in the form of a natural insecticide that stops fungal growth, but this does not protect the wood from deterioration from lignin removal during the wetting/drying process.

Introduction

This chapter summarizes some common standards for painting and the installation of wall coverings. We must stress that these are guidelines, and are not a substitute for researching individual products and local customs. Read the product label and follow the manufacturer's directions regarding temperature and other requirements for storage and application.

The *International Building Code (IBC)* does not specifically address painting and wall covering. The recommendations in this chapter are from respected industry sources, with additional *Comments* from the editors based on their experience and knowledge of accepted practice in the field.

Oil-based paints are banned in some states due to air quality laws. The warranties on water-based paints tend to be of shorter duration than those on oil-based paints. It is important to be aware of the limitations of the paint product and the frequency of painting required to preserve building components.

As another resource, we recommend the *Builders Guide to Paints and Coatings*, published by the NAHB Research Center. This book, excerpts of which are included in this chapter, addresses the characteristics of paint coatings, color usage, substrate preparation, application, causes of and solutions to problems, and safety rules and regulations. It also includes a sample set of specifications. This publication is available for purchase from the NAHB Research Center (**www.nahbrc.org**).

Wall coverings are often included in the construction budget for a residential or light commercial project. It is important that the desired items are clearly specified, since the cost differences between products can be extreme. The owner or interior designer generally selects the materials, passing this information on to the architect or contractor, to be included on the finish plans. Requirements for materials and workmanship may be stated in the specifications. These may include product specification, surface preparation, method of application, workmanship, and inspection. **Figure 12.1** is a sample specification for paint and wall coverings.

Warranties should be written into the contract when using a professional paperhanger. A *Full Warranty* indicates that all faulty products will be repaired or replaced, or the fee refunded. A *Limited Warranty* may be restricted to the cost of materials only, or be limited in some other way. The warranty's duration should also be clear.

Professional paperhangers can be located through organizations such as the National Guild of Professional Paperhangers, Inc. and the Painting and Decorating Contractors of America.

The following organizations offer information on paint and wallcoverings.

Painting and Decorating Contractors of America (PDCA)
800-332-7322
www.pdca.org

National Guild of Professional Paperhangers
800-254-6477
www.ngpp.org

Paint & Decorating Retailers Association (PDRA)
636-326-2636
www.pdra.org

Window & Door Manufacturers Association (WDMA)
847-299-5200
www.wdma.com

Ed. Note: Comments and recommendations within this chapter are not intended as a definitive resource for construction activities. For building projects, contractors must rely on the project documents and any applicable code requirements pertaining to their own particular locations.

 # Green Approaches to Painting & Wall Covering

Green Building: Project Planning & Cost Estimating, **Second Edition**
(RSMeans)

Paints, Coatings & Adhesives

Paints, coatings, and adhesives for finishes, such as flooring and wall coverings, commonly off-gas VOCs, including formaldehyde, or other toxic chemicals that affect installers as well as building occupants. Therefore, it is critical to specify low- or zero-VOC products, which are readily available today. Off-gassed VOCs can be re-absorbed into soft surfaces, such as fabrics. Because most VOCs are emitted during the application and curing process, this problem can be greatly reduced by providing good ventilation and ensuring a minimum of exposed absorptive surfaces during installation.

Wall Coverings

Low- or zero-VOC paint is preferable to wall covering applied with toxic adhesive. The best wall coverings from environmental and air-quality standpoints are nontoxic textiles adhered with low or zero-VOC adhesives. Vinyl wall coverings pose environmental concerns in their production & disposal and health concerns associated with off-gassing. When vinyl decomposes (a process that is accelerated when it gets hot), it off-gasses toxic fumes. (See "Low- and No-VOC Options" later in this chapter for more on volatile organic compounds.)

Sample Wall Finishes Plan/Specification

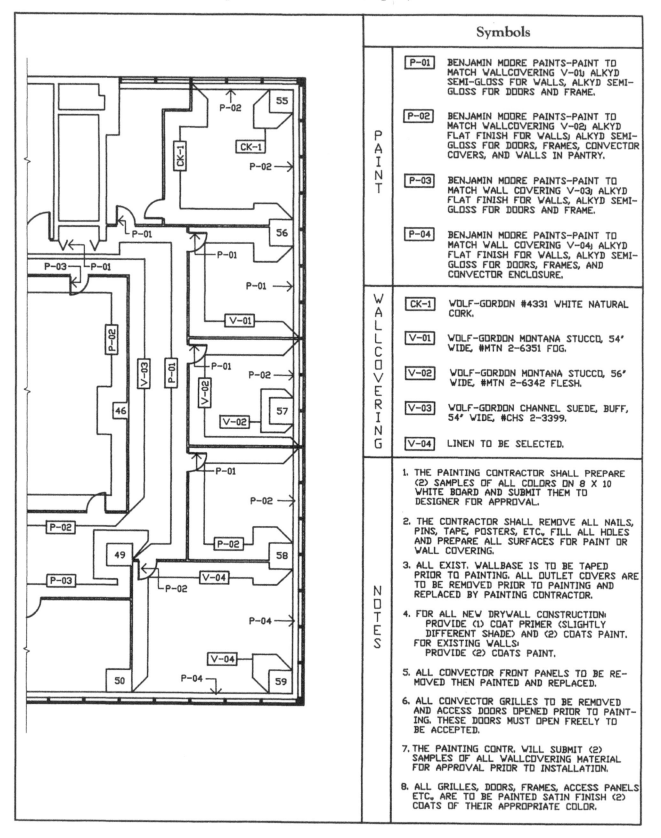

Symbols

PAINT

P-01   BENJAMIN MOORE PAINTS-PAINT TO MATCH WALLCOVERING V-01, ALKYD SEMI-GLOSS FOR WALLS, ALKYD SEMI-GLOSS FOR DOORS AND FRAME.

P-02   BENJAMIN MOORE PAINTS-PAINT TO MATCH WALLCOVERING V-02, ALKYD FLAT FINISH FOR WALLS, ALKYD SEMI-GLOSS FOR DOORS, FRAMES, CONVECTOR COVERS, AND WALLS IN PANTRY.

P-03   BENJAMIN MOORE PAINTS-PAINT TO MATCH WALL COVERING V-03, ALKYD FLAT FINISH FOR WALLS, ALKYD SEMI-GLOSS FOR DOORS AND FRAME.

P-04   BENJAMIN MOORE PAINTS-PAINT TO MATCH WALL COVERING V-04, ALKYD FLAT FINISH FOR WALLS, ALKYD SEMI-GLOSS FOR DOORS, FRAMES, AND CONVECTOR ENCLOSURE.

WALLCOVERING

CK-1   WOLF-GORDON #4331 WHITE NATURAL CORK.

V-01   WOLF-GORDON MONTANA STUCCO, 54' WIDE, #MTN 2-6351 FOG.

V-02   WOLF-GORDON MONTANA STUCCO, 56' WIDE, #MTN 2-6342 FLESH.

V-03   WOLF-GORDON CHANNEL SUEDE, BUFF, 54' WIDE, #CHS 2-3399.

V-04   LINEN TO BE SELECTED.

NOTES

1. THE PAINTING CONTRACTOR SHALL PREPARE (2) SAMPLES OF ALL COLORS ON 8 X 10 WHITE BOARD AND SUBMIT THEM TO DESIGNER FOR APPROVAL.

2. THE CONTRACTOR SHALL REMOVE ALL NAILS, PINS, TAPE, POSTERS, ETC., FILL ALL HOLES AND PREPARE ALL SURFACES FOR PAINT OR WALL COVERING.

3. ALL EXIST. WALLBASE IS TO BE TAPED PRIOR TO PAINTING. ALL OUTLET COVERS ARE TO BE REMOVED PRIOR TO PAINTING AND REPLACED BY PAINTING CONTRACTOR.

4. FOR ALL NEW DRYWALL CONSTRUCTION: PROVIDE (1) COAT PRIMER (SLIGHTLY DIFFERENT SHADE) AND (2) COATS PAINT. FOR EXISTING WALLS: PROVIDE (2) COATS PAINT.

5. ALL CONVECTOR FRONT PANELS TO BE REMOVED THEN PAINTED AND REPLACED.

6. ALL CONVECTOR GRILLES TO BE REMOVED AND ACCESS DOORS OPENED PRIOR TO PAINTING. THESE DOORS MUST OPEN FREELY TO BE ACCEPTED.

7. THE PAINTING CONTR. WILL SUBMIT (2) SAMPLES OF ALL WALLCOVERING MATERIAL FOR APPROVAL PRIOR TO INSTALLATION.

8. ALL GRILLES, DOORS, FRAMES, ACCESS PANELS ETC., ARE TO BE PAINTED SATIN FINISH (2) COATS OF THEIR APPROPRIATE COLOR.

Figure 12.1

Types of Paint

Industry Standards

Fundamentals of the Construction Process
(RSMeans)

The four main groupings for painting and coating are *transparent finishes, primers, undercoating,* and *finish coats.*

Transparent Finishes: The first group includes shellac, lacquer, and varnish, primarily to protect natural wood used in finishes such as for floors, stairs, doors, and furniture.

Primers: The two main types of primers are oil-based primer and latex. Oil-based primer is compatible with both oil (solvent) and latex-based finish paints, but latex primer can only be used with latex finish paint. A primer's functions are to seal the substrate and give the surface a uniform opacity. Other primers have been developed for highly specific substrates such as masonry, metal, or previously varnished surfaces. Concrete block surfaces must be filled, rather than primed, prior to painting.

Undercoating: Undercoating is the preferred first coat under enamel paint finish coats.

Finish Coats: The two main formulations for finish paint are latex (water) or solvent (oil) based. Latex paints are emulsions and dry through the evaporation of water. Drying is fast under normal conditions and in hot climates may be so rapid as to inhibit brushing. Latex paints do not penetrate the surface, so surface preparation is critical to a good bond. Mechanical methods such as wire brushing are employed to remove chalk, flaking paint, and loose dirt. Chemical methods such as bleach and detergents are used to remove oil, grease, and mildew.

Solvent paints dry through the solvent evaporation. Neither formulation is good for immersion in water, but solvent paints develop a tighter film than latex paints and are superior in abnormally wet environments. Solvent paint surfaces deteriorate through oxidation which a film of fresh solvent paint can arrest. A latex paint film is "breathable," and old solvent painted surfaces underneath will continue to oxidize and peel.

Paints get their color through pigments and their spreadability through the "vehicle." The vehicle component in latex paint is a man-made resin and in solvent paint is oil. Enamels are solvent-based paints in which the pigments are more finely ground and the vehicle is varnish, a combination of resins and oil. This premium finish spreads much more smoothly than paint, is self-leveling, and has considerable hiding power. The resulting film has a high gloss and retains the gloss for an extended period.

Latex vs. Alkyd Paints

Industry Standards

WIC Manual of Millwork
(Woodwork Institute of California, **www.wicnet.org**)

Note: This referenced standards listing is not necessarily complete.

Latex paint has become popular because of the environmental necessity to reduce VOCs (volatile organic compounds). Alkyd paint is a synthetic resin modified with oil and diluted with a petroleum solvent. This is very similar to the old oil based paints. Alkyd resins help enhance the flexibility of the paint. True oil based paints have almost disappeared off the market.

There is no universal correct answer as to which is best, latex or alkyd. The three P's will determine which to use. Project, what is the surface you are coating? Price, what can you afford? Preference, what look are you trying to achieve?

Each of the paints has qualities that make it appropriate for different uses. Here is a comparison of some of those qualities.

Durability—Latex has better elasticity, and alkyd has better adhesion on heavily chalked surfaces.

Versatility—Both with appropriate pre-treatment or undercoat will cover a wide range of projects.

Application —Alkyd has better hide and one coat coverage.

Color Retention —Alkyd is more likely to fade and chalk when exposed to sun.

Drying Time—Latex will dry to recoat in one to six hours while alkyd takes eight to 24 hours.

Odor—Latex wins this contest with low odor.

Low- and No-VOC Options

Green Home Improvement
(RSMeans)

Unfortunately, paints, stains, and finishes are notorious contributors to indoor air pollution. Oil-based paints, for example, release large quantities of potentially harmful volatile organic chemicals (called VOCs) as the paints dry. Their release continues for a week or two after painting. Conventional wood stains and finishes also release huge quantities of VOCs, often more than oil-based paints, and much more than water-based wall paints.

VOCs and other chemical ingredients in paints, stains, and finishes may cause short-term health effects, such as headaches, dizziness, nausea, allergic reactions, and sore throats. They may also cause serious, long-term health problems like cancer. The very old and very young are most susceptible, as are those who are ill. VOCs in paints also contribute to local air pollution, notably photochemical smog that plagues many cities in summer months.

Conventional water-based interior house paints are safer than oil paints. They release less VOCs, but also release small amounts of formaldehyde, ammonia, mildewcides, and other potentially harmful chemicals. As these paints dry, the chemicals are released into the room air, creating a distinct odor. The chemicals are inhaled by applicators as well as the home's residents—sometimes for several months afterward.

Why add chemicals if they can cause health problems? The most dangerous ones, the VOCs, are used to make the paint dry faster. Mildewcides are added to prevent mold and mildew, both in the can and when the paint is on the walls. (Generally, interior paints contain less mildewcide than exterior paints.)

Responding to these and other concerns, the paint industry has made dramatic changes in their products. They now offer many environmentally and people-friendly options. What's more, these paints don't cost any more than premium conventional paints.

What Are Your Options?

To begin with, many off-the-shelf interior paints today contain much lower VOC concentrations than in the recent past. Some manufacturers have gone a step further, producing paints with even lower levels of VOCs called "low-VOC" paints. All major paint manufacturers produce a line of low-VOC paints, including Glidden, Sherwin-Williams, Kelly-Moore, and Benjamin Moore. (See **Figure 12.2**.) They're available in paint stores, many home improvement centers, and hardware stores.

No-VOC paints are also available from many of the same companies. Lifemaster 2000, for example, is a no-VOC interior house paint manufactured by ICI paints (parent company of Glidden). It is used in hospitals, schools, and offices. Sherwin-Williams also manufactures a no-VOC paint, known as Harmony® Interior Latex. No-VOC paints are available in paint stores or can be special ordered.

No-VOC interior paints can be tinted to produce any color you want, but in many cases pigments are dissolved in solvents (VOCs). The deeper the tint (or more intense the color), the more VOCs are added. When shopping for a no-VOC paint, ask about zero-VOC colorants like those from American Pride.

While low- and no-VOC paints are safer and better for the environment than conventional paints, they often contain ammonia and antimicrobial additives (mildewcides). Another issue to be aware of is that federal regulations that apply to VOCs in paint only cover the types of VOCs that contribute to the formation of smog. VOCs that don't contribute to smog are not counted, so no- or low-VOC paints may actually contain some VOCs—chemicals that could adversely affect human health. To find out, ask the manufacturer for the Materials Data Safety Sheet.

Comments

As part of a recent trend to prevent poor air quality and illnesses associated with VOCs (volatile organic compounds), paints with low or no VOCs are now available from manufacturers. See **Figure 12.2**. Both standard oil- and latex-based paints contain VOCs as part of their chemical makeup, which readily evaporate into the air at room temperature. This can cause problems such as nausea, eye irritation, and heart or lung damage in susceptible occupants. Paints marketed as "Low-VOC," must comply with EPA regulations (no more than 250 grams per liter of VOCs for latex paint, 380 grams for oil-based). Paints marketed as "Zero VOC" or "No-VOC" must consist of less than one gram per liter.

Applications for Paint Finishes

Industry Standards

Paint & Decorating Retailers Association (PDRA)
(PDRA website: www.pdra.org)

High Gloss (70+ on a 60 degree gloss meter)

> Where to Use:
> For kitchen & bathroom walls, kitchen cabinets, banisters & railings, trim, furniture, door jambs and windowsills.

> Comments:
> More durable, stain resistant & easier to wash. However, the higher the gloss, the more likely surface imperfections will be noticed.

Low- and No-VOC Paints on the Market

Low VOC Paints

Manufacturer	Product Name
Sherwin-Williams	Duration Home® Interior Latex.
Glidden	Glidden Spread 2000
Kelley-Moore	Eviron-Cote
Duron	Genesis Odor-Free
Benjamin Moore	Eco-Spe

No-VOC paints

Manufacturer	Product Name
ICI Paints	Lifemaster 2000
Sherwin-Williams	Harmony® Interior Latex
Olympic Paint	Premium Paints (several options available)
Southern Diversified Products	American Pride paints
Pittsburgh Paints	Pure Performance
AFM	Safecoat
BioShield	Solvent-Free Wall Paint, Clay Paints, Milk Paint, and Kinder Paint

Figure 12.2

Green Home Improvement by Daniel D. Chiras, PhD

Semigloss (35 to 70 on a 60 degree gloss meter)

Where to Use:
For kitchen and bathroom walls, hallways, children's rooms, playrooms, doors, woodwork and trim.

Comments:
More stain-resistant and easier to clean than flat paints. Better than flat for high-traffic areas.

Satin or Silk (range overlapping eggshell & semigloss)

Similar characteristics to semigloss & eggshell.

Eggshell (20 to 30 on a 60 degree gloss meter)

Where to use:
Can be used in place of flat paints on wall surfaces especially in halls, bathrooms, and playrooms. Can be used in place of semigloss paints on trim for less shiny appearance.

Comments:
It resists stains better than flat paint and gives a more lustrous appearance.

Flat (less than 15 on a 60 degree gloss meter)

Where to use:
For general use on walls and ceilings.

Comments:
Hides surface imperfections. Stain removal can be difficult. Use for uniform, nonreflecting appearance. Best suited for low-traffic areas.

Matte (same characteristics as flat)

Special Paints

Industry Standards

Fundamentals of the Construction Process
(RSMeans)

Special Paints: Special paints have been developed for as many specific applications as there are surfaces or conditions, some of which bear mentioning. Paints with improved "hiding" power, that of obscuring the undercoat, are referred to as "one coat" and "high hiding." These paints can be applied in thick coats, without sagging (running), and are used for exterior, rapid interior, and acoustical repainting.

Solvents in dry fog paint are used for spraying interior walls and ceilings. These paints dry before they fall to the floor, eliminating damage caused by overspray.

Fire-retardant paints have been developed in several formulations, both latex and solvent, which

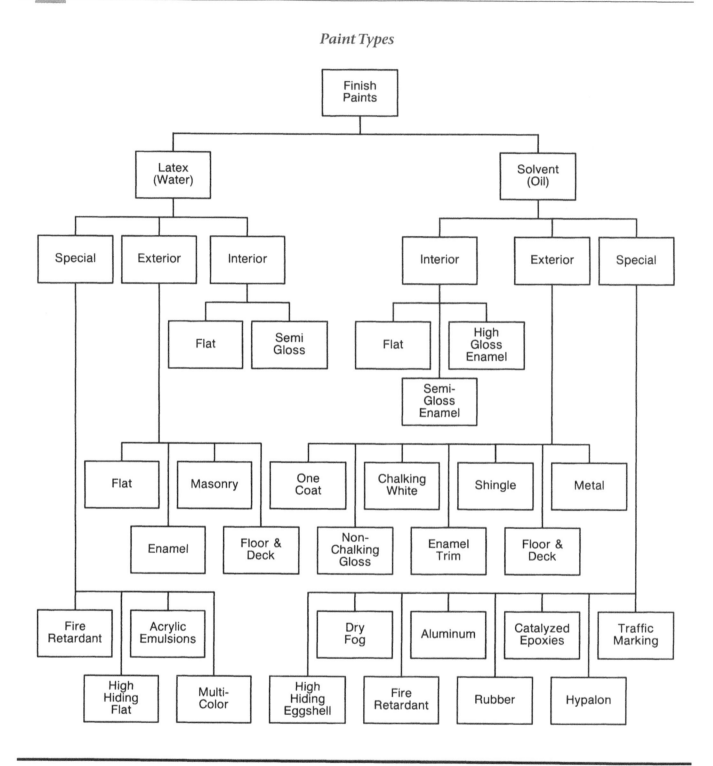

Figure 12.3

RSMeans, *Fundamentals of the Construction Process*

significantly reduce flame spread through swelling (intumescence), to form a honeycomb structure to protect the surface.

A few paints have been developed for immersion in water (for swimming pools and exterior masonry), among them cement and rubber-based types. Rubber-based paints, when used along with aluminum paints, are excellent for protecting metals in roofing, window, railing, and heating systems.

Brushwork is used for most types of painting and is the method over which the worker has the most control. It is required for narrow surfaces, accent striping, curved and irregular surfaces such as piping and millwork, and ornamental work. Some paints, like some types of machinery enamel, must be brush-applied.

Insulating Paint

Green Home Improvement
(RSMeans)

Insulating paint additives are available online from several companies, among them, Insuladd or Hy-Tech Thermal Solutions. They can be mixed with ordinary interior or exterior paints and applied to walls and ceilings. These companies also sell pre-mixed insulating paint.

How Does It Work?

Insulating paint additives consist of a fine, white powder containing hollow ceramic microspheres, developed by researchers at NASA for use in spacecraft. When mixed into paint, the microspheres form a tightly packed layer that minimizes the transfer of heat through a wall. When incorporated in exterior paints, the microspheres retard the flow of heat through exterior walls, essentially reflecting summertime heat that would otherwise make its way into a building, increasing cooling costs. In the winter, this product applied to interior ceilings and walls keeps heat from moving *out*, saving on fuel bills.

Benefits

- Reduces home energy use and cuts fuel bills
- Creates a more comfortable home
- Is easy to use
- Pays for itself in reduced utility bills, day in, day out, 365 days a year
- Is nontoxic
- Increases fire-resistance of walls
- Easier to clean paints and lasts longer than conventional paints
- Helps deaden sounds
- Resists mold and mildew

Insulating paint additives can be used in homes and businesses on interior and exterior walls, but also in attics, basements, and on roofs. It can be used on metal buildings to improve their energy performance.

Because insulating paint additives come in powder form, be sure to remove all filters from spray equipment before use. Otherwise, the filters will remove the additive from the paint during application. When applying paint with a sprayer, manufacturers recommend the use of a larger-than-normal spray tip to allow maximum coverage and boost the insulation value of your walls.

Comments

For best results, the manufacturers of insulating paints recommend two coats. Applying more than two coats results in only marginal increases in performance. When applying an insulating paint to the interior of a building, you only need to paint the interior surfaces of exterior walls and ceilings where heat losses could occur to the outside. Insulating paint can be painted over with traditional paints. However, manufacturers note that this will slightly decrease the insulating paint additive's ability to reduce heat movement through a wall.

Elastomeric Paints

Comments

New technologies in paint manufacture have solved a series of problems. Elastomeric paints are exterior acrylic latex masonry paints specifically designed for use over rough masonry substrates, stucco, and T1-11 siding. They are not, however, appropriate for all projects.

Elastomeric paint creates an elastic film over the material it covers. When walls have a high moisture emission, blisters can be created when the sun strikes the wall, causing water vapor to expand.

Plaster or wood-sided and drywall walls experience severe temperature differentials. The result is condensation in the wall cavity. If this situation is compounded by high humidity levels or minor water intrusion, the walls can absorb large quantities of water vapor.

Most building wraps are designed to allow moisture to transfer out of the wall to a point of equilibrium over extended periods. Elastomeric paint prevents that process, and all moisture must evaporate through the conditioned space. When molds develop, the air transfer will sometimes contaminate the interior space of a building.

(continued)

Another complaint is the inability of the elastomeric paint to receive an overcoat when a color change is preferred or when weathering and fading have occurred. Some paints require a sandblasting before another coat can be applied. Elastomeric wall coatings also may chalk and lighten in color. Currently, dark colors are not available for this reason.

For correct application, make sure any cracks more than 1/16" are caulked before applying elastomeric paint. If the substrate is particularly porous, be sure to first apply a quality masonry primer or paintable sealer. Do not apply elastomeric paint to areas that have poor caulking or to surfaces where water can get behind. Keep in mind that two coats of elastomeric paints are recommended. (Coverage is typically 50–60 SF per gallon.)

400, we realize that the manufacturers are recommending 4 mils of wet coat film. A manufacturer's product data on the paint can label should reveal the volume solids. If the volume solids are 25% of the product volume, the dry film thickness will be 1 mil.

Paint is applied bound up in a solvent, and when the solvent dries off, a film is left. The solids are entirely responsible for the dry film thickness and its durability. Multiple coats are preferable, as the laminated paint is more durable. A good quality undercoat is important, as this is the anchor for future coats of paint. Undercoat and topcoat of paints are better purchased from the same manufacturer, since the products are formulated to work together.

Paint Film Ingredients/Thickness

Comments

Content

Latex and solvent-based paints have similar components; however latex paint is diluted with water, and solvent paint is diluted with a petroleum product. The main constituents of paint are **pigments, surfactants**, and **dilutants**.

The primary pigment ingredient is titanium dioxide, which is white. This provides the opaque barrier that creates the "hide" ability. Deeper-color paints have reduced titanium dioxide content and rely more on the colored pigments for hiding power. They may require additional coats.

Pigment durability is an issue with paints. Yellow, orange, lavender, purple, light blue, pink, peach, and salmon are a poorer choice for exterior use because they fade faster and require more coats to cover.

Surfactants, or "surface active agents," include wetting agents, dispersants, defoamers, and emulsifiers. These chemicals help keep pigments and other ingredients in suspension until after application. As the surfactants dry off, a film is formed.

As stated above, paint is diluted with a solvent—either water or petroleum. The solvent will precipitate, or separate from the solution, leaving a dried paint film.

Film Thickness

Manufacturers offering paint warranties usually base the warranty on paint film thickness. Dry paint film thickness, which is measured in mils (1 mil = 1/1000 of an inch), is most accurately determined as follows. The liquid in 1 gallon of paint can be spread 1-mil thick to cover 1,604 SF Paint manufacturers typically recommend a gallon to square foot ratio of 400 SF per gallon. If we divide 1,604 by

Determining Paint or Coating Quality

Industry Standards

Builders Guide to Paints and Coatings
(NAHB Research Center)

*Ed. Note: This publication is available for purchase from the NAHB Research Center (**www.nahbrc.org**).*

What Is a Quality Paint or Coating?

There are a number of ways in which paints differ substantially in their performance, depending on the amount and quality of ingredients that they contain. These include:

- Durability
- Longevity of the color and freshness of the finish
- Washability
- Hiding power
- Good bonding with previous coatings
- Uniformity of color and surface finish
- For exterior finishes, elasticity to accommodate to substantial temperature and humidity changes and expansion and contraction of the substrate, and resistance to ultra-violet rays and environmental pollutants.
- Batch-to-batch consistency of color and appearance

Characteristics of a Good Coating

Qualities to look for in a good coating include the following:

- Resistance to damage by moisture
- Resistance to alkali damage

- High gloss retention
- Excellent color retention
- Good hiding capability
- Scrub resistance
- Stain and dirt resistance; washability
- Mildew resistance
- Good adhesion
- Crack resistance
- Good touch-up capability

Interior and Exterior Coatings

Exterior coatings must provide weather protection. This requirement is prominently represented in types of extenders, binder, and additives that exterior paints contain, and the ways in which they perform.

Interior finishes must be dirt and stain resistant and must have good ease of stain removal, or must be scrub resistant to allow for cleaning. A prominent cause of home buyer dissatisfaction arises from the experience of trying to scrub or clean an interior surface that has been soiled by the presence and activities of children, within months after buying the home, and discovering that the scrubbing produces undesirable and unattractive change in the appearance of the surface that has been cleaned. This problem can arise from one or both of two causes. One cause can be failure to exercise enough foresight to use a paint with a hard finish and at least some gloss, in areas where children's hands are likely to come into contact with the surfaces. A second cause can be use of a lower-quality paint, regardless of type.

Properly Painted Surface

Ed. Note: The Painting and Decorating Contractors of America (PDCA) publishes Standard PDCA P5-92, "Benchmark Sample Procedures," in order to "outline procedures for on-site demonstration of achievable quality from the specified paint and/or decorative coating systems." This document is recommended for projects whose scope makes it "advisable to establish achievable levels of quality before beginning." It involves taking and evaluating samples from a Benchmark Sample area. The following excerpt from Standard P5-94 defines "Properly Painted Surface."

Industry Standard

Standard PDCA P5-94, Benchmark Sample Procedures for Paint and Other Decorative Coating Systems

(Painting and Decorating Contractors of America)

5.6 Properly Painted Surface: One that is uniform in appearance, color and sheen. It is one that is free of foreign material, lumps, skins, runs, sags, holidays, misses, strike-throughs, or insufficient coverage. It is a surface which is free of drips, spatters, spills or overspray which were caused by the contractor's workforce. Compliance to meeting the criteria of a "properly painted surface" shall be determined when viewed without magnification at a distance of five feet or more, under normal lighting conditions and from a normal viewing position. Normal lighting conditions are described as those in place when the project is finished. This includes, but is not limited to, design lighting (e.g., wall washers, spots and floods, etc.) and natural lighting (e.g., skylights, clear view windows, window walls and window treatments, etc.).

Ed. Note: PDCA also publishes Standard P2-92, which establishes the qualifications and responsibilities of a third-party inspection, and proper inspection procedures. PDCA Standard P3-93 establishes the number and placement of paint colors prior to bidding.

Industry Standards

WIC Manual of Millwork

(Woodwork Institute of California, **www.wicnet.org**)

Note: This referenced standards listing is not necessarily complete.

Paint is the final finish product that is the first thing people see when viewing a home. It has been said that beauty is in the eye of the beholder. Disputes over the quality of a paint job are often subjective. We can offer little help with arguments over color tinting or shades of color. These problems are best handled by having the customer view a test area and approve the color and sheen before the project proceeds.

Ed. Note: See "Finishing Doors & Windows" later in this chapter for WIC's specific recommendations.

Responsibility for Touch-up & Damage Repair

Industry Standard

PDCA Standard P1-92
(Painting and Decorating Contractors of America)

Ed. Note: PDCA Standard P1-92, "Touch-Up Painting and Damage Report—Financial Responsibility," defines and categorizes the term "touch-up" and establishes financial responsibility for repair or correction of damage to finished painted surfaces by individuals other than those employed by the painting contractor.

2. Description

2.1 This standard includes the repair and repaint of finished painted surfaces which have been damaged by individuals other than those employed by the painting contractor. This type of damage is known as *damage caused by others*. The painting contractor will correct the *damage caused by others* after receiving a separate work directive from the contracting or agreement entity. A time and/or price adjustment will then be submitted by the painting contractor.

The work may be done for a lump sum or time and material depending on the most reasonable individual scenario. The painting contractor will repair and/or repaint the damaged area after receiving acceptance of his submittal and authorization to proceed.

2.2 *Latent damage* is due to conditions beyond the control of the painting contractor. They are caused by conditions not apparent at the time of initial painting or decorating. The painting contractor will correct *latent damage* after receiving a separate work directive from the contracting or agreement entity. A time and/or price adjustment will then be submitted by the painting contractor.

The work may be done for a lump sum or time and material depending on the most reasonable individual scenario. The painting contractor will repair and/or repaint the damaged area after receiving acceptance of his submittal and authorization to proceed.

2.3 The contractual work is job and item specific. In no case shall the painting contractor be responsible for *damage caused by others* or *latent damage* as herein described.

2.4 The painting contractor will produce a "properly painted surface."

Ed. Note: See the definition of "properly painted surface" in the excerpt from PDCA P5-94 in the preceding section.

Preparing the Surface for Paint

Industry Standards

Builder's Guide to Paints and Coatings
(NAHB Research Center)

Ed. Note: The full publication, Builders Guide to Paints and Coatings, *is available for purchase from the NAHB Research Center (Telephone: 800-638-8556, or on-line at* **www.nahbrc.org**).

Surface preparation is critical to the proper adhesion of coatings. Regardless of the type of substrate, all contamination must be removed prior to coating of the surface.

New Interior Wood

Sand new wood smooth with a fine sandpaper and prime with an alkyd primer. Sanding should always be done in one direction; circular motion should not be used.

Comments

Moulded urethane millwork items are available prefinished. Other finishes should be applied in accordance with manufacturer's instructions. Cut surfaces should be primed and painted within a few days of installation.

Drywall

Before a primer is applied to drywall, the surface must be clean and dry. Nail heads must be spackled, and joints must be taped and covered with joint compound. Spackled nail heads and tape joints should be sanded smooth and all dust should be removed with a damp cloth or sponge.

With drywall whose surface is made of recycled paper, the use of a high quality primer is especially important. Latex primers should be used on drywall. Solvent-based primers will penetrate the paper and raise the nap. An exception is drywall to which wallpaper is to be applied. A rough surface is desirable for adherence of the wallpaper, and an alkyd primer should therefore be used.

Existing Houses & Surfaces

For interior coating of an existing house, all surfaces should be cleaned thoroughly with a strong household detergent. Remove oil, dirt, grease, wallpaper paste, wall sizing, pencil marks, wax, chalk, and water-soluble materials before any coating is applied. Special attention should be paid to stove areas, ceilings, vent areas, bathroom areas (especially sinks and shower stalls), kitchen sink areas, fingerprints on corners, and switches.

Grease that is not removed can cause premature peeling. Test suspected areas by splashing water onto the surface. If the water beads, rewash the area. Do **not** use degreasers such as oven cleaners; they can damage the old paint film, and any degreaser that remains can attack the new top coat from underneath.

Fill all cracks and nail holes with spackling plaster and sand smooth. Cover cracks and nail holes with spackling plaster. Remove all cracking, peeling, and blistering paint with a scraper and/or sandpaper, and sand smooth.

Scruff glossy finishes with fine sandpaper. Wash with a household detergent in water to remove all dust and to dull the gloss. Do **not** use solvent-type sanding aids. Always sand in one direction. Scratches caused by circular motion can show through a topcoat and give the finish an undesired textured effect.

Either remove old wallpaper or reglue loose sections and allow to dry. Old wallpaper can be removed with steam if an alkyd primer was used as a seal coat. But if latex was used, steam will penetrate and cause the drywall to delaminate. Such wallpapered surfaces must be painted.

Before painting wallpaper, test a small area to determine if the pattern inks bleed into the paint. If so, use an alkyd primer as a seal coat.

Paint & Wood Damage

If the grain of the wood is raised as a result of water saturation or if old coats of paint are blistered or peeling, surface preparation is necessary. This involves scraping with scrapers or removal with electricity heated paint removers.

When this operation is completed, the area should be sanded smooth. Sanding should be done with the grain only. A medium grit paper should first be used, followed by finer paper as the surface becomes smoother. After sanding is completed, all dust should be removed.

Plaster

Allow bare new plaster to cure for 60 days, by which time it will be dry and hard. If a new or old plaster surface is textured, soft, porous, or powdery, wash with a mixture of one pint of vinegar in one gallon of water. Repeat until the surface is hard. Rinse thoroughly with clean water, allow to dry, and apply a wall and wood primer.

Exterior Surface Preparation

In new construction, exterior wood should be covered with coating as quickly as possible. Even relatively brief exposure of unpainted wood to sunlight will cause the lignin in the wood to degrade, creating "straw" on the surface. This can result in poorer adhesion of the coating.

Apart from this consideration, exterior wood in new construction ordinarily involves little more preparation than interior wood. Dirt must be removed, and cracks and open joints in siding should be sealed. Species and grades of wood are important in exterior paint performance.

In existing construction, it has been estimated that 80% of coating failure is the result of inadequate preparation of the surface. The most common causes of exterior paint failure are the following:

- Moisture. This is by far the biggest culprit.
- Salt build-up.
- Chalking paint.
- Dirt.
- Old cracking and peeling paint.
- Mildew.

Structural deficiencies and improper application techniques also play a role.

Concrete & Masonry

Concrete and mortar joints in concrete masonry block require 30 days to cure and dry before any coating can be applied. Coatings used over masonry must be alkali-resistant.

Repair cracks and breaks in masonry, and remove all loose stone and efflorescence with a wire brush. Efflorescence consists of highly alkali chemicals that build up on the surface in white crystalline form as water reaches the surface. These crystals can push off the topcoat. After removing efflorescence, a masonry conditioner should be applied.

Use of a primer coat is highly important to successful coating of masonry surfaces. Primers must be used that will not cause alkali activation. Special primers are made for use on masonry; these should be employed, and manufacturer's instructions should be carefully followed.

Comments

The problems arising from painting concrete products are related to moisture and alkalinity.

It is easy to understand the difficulty that can arise when moisture is trapped behind a paint film. Generally, the result is paint failure. The Plastic Sheet Method can assist the contractor in determining whether the concrete is dry enough to paint. To use this technique, tape the perimeter of a 4-mil-thick clear plastic sheet 18" square, securing it to the floor, wall, or ceiling. Allow it to remain in place for at least 16 hours. Then, make a visual check of the plastic over the concrete or masonry surface for moisture. A good time to check the test area is early morning, when the environment is cool.

Alkalinity is a common cause of paint failure on concrete products, and it is the least understood. The pH scale runs from acidic 0 to 6, 7 neutral, and alkali 8 to 14. Each number in the scale represents a tenfold change from its neighbor. A rating of 12 is 10 times more alkaline than 11. Most paint products require a pH of 10 or less before coating is applied. All manufacturers recommend that concrete be allowed to weather and cure for 30 days prior to painting. This allows the concrete to dry and also allows the alkaline level to recede. After this waiting period, it is best to test the pH level of the concrete and use an alkali-resistant primer. Concrete can be reduced in alkaline level by washing it with a clean water rinse and allowing it to dry. Repeating this cycle will reduce the alkali level.

Brick

Brick should be allowed to cure for at least one year, and should be wire brushed to remove efflorescence before being coated. Large areas may require flushing with muriatic acid and water. Glazed brick will not hold typical alkyd paint, latex paint, or enamel.

Stucco

Stucco surfaces that are to be coated must be clean and free of loose pieces. Under normal drying conditions, new stucco surfaces can be coated after about 30 days of curing time. Drying conditions vary in different locations.

Metal

Conventional finish coats are not designed for use on unprimed metal. Primers designed for use on specific metallic substrates must always be used. Iron and steel require primers that are formulated for rust inhibition. Galvanized metal requires another type of primer.

Aluminum siding is normally provided with a coating in the desired color. This coating is meant to chalk and clean itself. If painting of any portion of the siding in a different color is desired, the siding should be power-washed to remove chalking before a new coating is applied.

Inspecting Surfaces Before Painting

Industry Standards
Standard PDCA P4-94
(Painting and Decorating Contractors of America)

1. Scope

1.1 The purpose of this standard is to establish the responsibilities for inspection and approval of surfaces prior to painting and decorating.

1.2 This standard is intended for use on construction projects where the painting and decorating contractor applies paints, coatings or wallcoverings over a surface assembled, constructed and/or prepared by another contractor or trade not under the painting and decorating contractor's control.

2. Significance & Use

2.1 The owner or the owner's delegated agent, such as but not limited to the architect, is the final judge in all matters relating to the "Quality of Appearance" and acceptance of surfaces.

2.2 "Quality of Appearance" is a subjective term governed by the owner or their delegated agents, and established by specification and reference standards. It is controlled by sample review and/or mock up approval along with periodic jobsite inspections and approvals.

2.3 The painting and decorating contractor is not obligated to render any final professional opinion regarding the "Quality of Appearance" of work performed by others.

5. Standard Specification

5.1 Acceptance of Surfaces

5.1.1 The painting and decorating contractor is required to inspect surfaces to be finished only to determine, by reasonable and visible evidence, that the finish will satisfactorily adhere to surfaces provided by others and perform as specified.

5.1.2 The owner or the owner's designated agents have the responsibility to determine that a surface is complete and ready to finish painting or wallcovering.

5.1.3 When a trade has left its work without notification to the contrary; or notification to proceed has been given, such action will be construed as tacit evidence that all work has been inspected, and that it is warrantable, complete and ready for finishing.

5.1.4 If "Quality of Appearance" of a surface prior to finishing is judged marginal or unacceptable by others conducting essential inspection, such alleged defective work must be corrected prior to priming and finishing so that all surfaces are made complete and ready for finishing. If the unacceptable work is not made complete and ready for finishing, the painting contractor will be duly informed, ordered to stop work and told to proceed only as directed.

5.1.5 Once finishing has begun, as scheduled or as directed, the correction of "Defects and/or Latent Damage" is considered "Damage Repair" as per PDCA Standard P1-92, "Touch-Up Painting and Damage Repair—Financial Responsibility."

Ed. Note: See "Responsibility for Touch-up and Damage Repair" earlier in this chapter.

6. Comments

6.2 Quality of Appearance is achieved through quality control. Inspecting work in progress and taking necessary action at the appropriate time to make required corrections is imperative to ensure Quality of Appearance. This standard encourages periodic inspection and corrective actions.

Applying Coatings

Industry Standards

Builders Guide to Paints and Coatings
(NAHB Research Center)

Ed Note: The full publication is available for purchase from the NAHB Research Center (Telephone: 800-638-8556, or online at www.nahbrc.org)

Number of Coats

A primer and two topcoats are ideal for external applications. Although only one topcoat is generally employed, two topcoats will give the greatest longevity for the coatings and the greatest satisfaction to the owner.

Two coats consisting of a quality primer and topcoat should be regarded as minimum external coating protection for the home.

Weather Conditions

Most exterior coatings perform best when applied at 60–80 degrees F.

For both alkyd and latex paints, the minimum application temperature is 50 degrees F.

Certain coatings may not reach full serviceability until several days after they are applied. For example, an enamel or clear coating subjected to abrasion or pressure, such as a walking surface, should be allowed to cure for three days before being subjected to use.

Comments

Hot Weather

It is important to know what the manufacturer requires for a specific paint. There are, however, some common sense work methods that hold true for most paints. Never paint an exterior wall that has been in full sun for even a moderate period of time. Start work on the shady side of the home, and work around the home staying in the shade if possible. House paints applied to very hot surfaces will dry too quickly, which may result in application problems such as color streaking and uneven mil thickness.

Storage of paint products in direct sun will cause partially used containers to dry out, with the resulting loss of product. There is a chance overheating will cause a container to rupture.

(continued)

Cold Weather

Once again, it is important to read the product label and follow directions.

Paint application is restricted to where the surface and ambient temperatures are above 50 degrees. Do not apply paint late in the day where the overnight temperature will fall below 50 degrees. Paint manufacturers that supply the colder climates have produced paints that tolerate lower temperatures. Check with your supplier and always read the label.

Applying paints in too low temperatures can result in improper film formation. This is more likely in latex paints. The surfactants that help hold the dissimilar liquids and solids together can, in cold weather, exude them. This is most likely to occur when the temperature is low and the humidity is rising or dew has formed. This slows the drying process and allows large quantities of the surfactants to collect on the surface. The appearance of the painted surface is variations in sheen and streaking. Latex paints can be carefully washed to remove the surfactant buildup; ask your supplier or manufacturer's representative. Alkyd paint surfactant exudation is more difficult to correct. Consult the manufacturer. The paint film is not damaged by the surfactant exudation. This is only an appearance issue.

Paint that has frozen must be examined carefully. Check with the manufacturer about the specific paint to determine its resistance to damage from freezing. Inspect the paint; if it has a sour smell, the consistency of cottage cheese, or (after remixing) remains very thick, it cannot be used. If the paint will remix and return to its homogenous pre-freezing consistency, then it can be used. Many paints can survive a single freeze-thaw cycle.

Doors & Wood Windows

Ed. Note: Painting and coatings for doors and windows is a frequent subject of defect claims. It is covered here as well as in Chapter 9, "Windows & Doors."

Comments

Doors will have a manufacturer's recommendation for painting, which must be followed to maintain the warranty.

Wood Doors

Remember that a door has six sides. Most frequently missed are the top and bottom. Failure to paint these surfaces within a specified time period will result in loss of warranty. Moisture uptake from an unpainted door

bottom or top edge will frequently cause the door to warp after installation. Painting under door butts or door edge lock hardware is not required.

Metal Doors

A word of caution here about factory-primed galvanized doors. The usual primer coat is very thin, significantly less than $1/2$ mil. Carefully follow the manufacturer's recommendations for painting. Note that latex paints are generally specified. Oil-based or solvent thinned paints can strike through the factory primer. Alkyd resins can react with the zinc in the galvanized coating. The reaction is called "saponification," which is the hydrolysis of the ester in the alkyd resin by the alkali in the zinc, resulting in the formation of a soap compound. This will cause the loss of adhesion and result in peeling.

Industry Standards

Specifiers Guide to Wood Windows & Doors
(Window & Door Manufacturers Association)

Exterior Use

In exterior use, temperature and humidity are not controlled on both sides of the door. Care must be taken when specifying Architectural wood flush doors in exterior openings. Consult individual manufacturers for specific recommendations and warranty limitations.

Job Site Finishing

Because of the many uncontrollable variables that exist at a site, such as temperature and moisture variation, dust and other factors, door manufacturers' warranties do not cover the appearance of finishes applied at the job site.

For additional information, see the WDMA publication *How to Store, Handle, Finish, Install, and Maintain Wood Doors.*

Finishing

Wood is hygroscopic and dimensionally influenced by changes in moisture content caused by changes within its surrounding environment. To assure uniform moisture exposure and dimensional control all surfaces must be finished equally.

Doors may not be ready for finishing when initially received. Before finishing, remove all handling marks, raised grain, scuffs, burnishes and other undesirable blemishes by block sanding all surfaces in a horizontal position with a 120, 150 or 180 grit sandpaper. To avoid cross-grain scratches, sand with the grain.

Certain species of wood, particularly oak, contain chemicals which react unfavorably with foreign materials in the finishing system. Eliminate the use of steel wool on bare wood, rusty containers or any other contaminate in the finishing system.

A thinned coat of sanding sealer should be applied prior to staining to promote a uniform appearance and avoid sharp contrasts in color or a blotchy appearance.

All exposed wood surfaces must be sealed including top and bottom rails. Cutouts for hardware in exterior doors must be sealed prior to installation of hardware and exposure to weather. Dark-colored finishes should be avoided on all surfaces if the door is exposed to direct sunlight, in order to reduce the chance of warping or veneer checking. Oil-based sealers or prime coats provide the best base coat for finishing. If a water-based primer is used, it should be an exterior grade product.

Note: Water-based coatings on unfinished wood may cause veneer splits, highlight joints and raise wood grain and therefore should be avoided. If a water-based primer is desired, please contact the finish supplier regarding the correct application and use of these products.

Be sure the door surface being finished is satisfactory in both smoothness and color after each coat. Allow adequate drying time between coats. Desired results are best achieved by following the finish manufacturer's recommendations. Do not finish door until a sample of the finish has been approved.

Finishes on exterior doors may deteriorate due to exposure to the environment. In order to protect the door it is recommended that the condition of the exterior finish be inspected at least once a year and re-finished as needed.

Note: Certain wood fire doors have fire-retardant salts impregnated into various wood components that makes the components more hygroscopic than normal wood. When exposed to high moisture conditions, these salts will concentrate on exposed surfaces and interfere with the finish. Before finishing, reduce moisture content in the treated wood below 11% and remove the salt crystals with a damp cloth, followed by drying and light sanding. For further information on fire doors, see WDMA publications regarding installing, handling and finishing fire doors.

Finishing Doors & Windows

Industry Standards

WIC Manual of Millwork
(Woodwork Institute of California, www.wicnet.org)

Note: This referenced standards listing is not necessarily complete.

Doors—Finishing

A. Prior to finishing, make sure that the building atmosphere is dried to a normal, interior relative humidity, and that the doors have been allowed to equalize to a stable moisture content.

B. Before finishing, remove handling marks or effects of exposure to moisture with a complete, thorough, final block, sanding over all surfaces of the door, using at least 150 grit sandpaper, and clean before applying sealer or finish. Deep scratches must be steamed out before sanding. Sharp edges must be eased by sanding.

C. Certain species of wood, particularly oak, contain chemicals which react unfavorably with certain finishes causing dark stain spots. Where possible, the species/finish combination should be tested prior to finishing the doors. Notify your finish supplier or door supplier immediately if any undesirable reaction is noticed. Do not continue with the finishing until the problem is resolved.

D. In order not to induce warpage, avoid dark stains or dark colored paints on door surface exposed directly to sunlight.

E. In order to prevent blemish magnification, avoid extremely dark stains in light colored wood species.

F. Water based sealer or prime coats should not be used. Water based top coats should only be used over surfaces that have been completely sealed with a non-water based sealer or primer.

G. A first coat of a thinned clear sanding sealer, followed by light block sanding, will minimize subsequent handling marks and promote the uniformity of subsequent stain coats.

H. All exposed wood surfaces must be sealed, including top and bottom rails.

I. To achieve the desired results of color uniformity, finish build, gloss and reduce the frequency of refinishing, obtain and follow finish manufacturer's recommendations. Be sure the door surface being finished is satisfactory in both smoothness and color after each coat before applying the next coat.

J. Certain wood fire doors have edges, and possibly crossbands under the face veneer, which contain fire retardant salts. These salts are usually hygroscopic and will take on excess moisture in a damp atmosphere. The salts will concentrate at the surface and form whitish crystals that can interfere with the finish. Before finishing, remove the salt crystals with a damp cloth, followed by drying and light sanding.

Windows—Finishing

5.7.2 Field-applied protective coatings can damage window sealants and gaskets and are not recommended. Contact the window manufacturer before applying any such coatings.

5.7.3 Masking tapes shall not be used on window surfaces as they may cause damage when they are removed.

Comments

Many manufacturers of wood windows utilize varying versions of the WIC recommendations for warranty compliance.

These warranty conditions usually include the following:

1. Painting of wood windows must be accomplished on all sides of the windows within 48 hours of delivery to the construction site or immediately upon installation, and repainted periodically to avoid damage to the wood parts.

2. Lap the finish coat $1/16$" onto the glass for a proper moisture seal.

3. Primers usually are not compatible with lacquer and varnishes. Primer paints must be designated to prevent the application of dissimilar products.

4. Abrasive cleaners or solutions containing solvents should not be used.

Cabinet Finishing

Ed. Note: Wood cabinetry, which is categorized under Finishes and Furnishings in construction documents, is not usually associated with the structural integrity of a building. Therefore, standards for finishing cabinets are usually determined by professional associations and published reference books rather than by building codes. Detailed information about cabinet finishing is included in Chapter 6, "Finish Carpentry & Cabinetry," in the "Finishing of Millwork" section.

Wall Covering

Types of Wall Covering

Comments

The six basic types of wall coverings are **wallpaper** (mostly paper, with a printed design), **vinyl** (a sheet of PVC with a structural material), **fiber products** (yarn or tufted material laminated to a backing), **fabric, rigid**, and **specialties** such as acoustical and wood.

Ed. Note: Wood paneling is addressed in Chapter 6, "Finish Carpentry & Cabinetry."

Surface Preparation

Industry Standards

Fundamentals of the Construction Process
(RSMeans)

Surfaces to receive wall covering must be prepared by sizing or sealing the surface. Mildew must be treated with bleach. "Hot spots," or highly alkaline concentrations on the surface, will discolor the wallpaper and must be treated with zinc sulfate. Holes and cracks must be filled, and the surface should be left uniformly smooth. If wall covering is to be hung over paneling, be sure to apply lining paper first. This material provides a smooth surface on which to place the final wall covering.

Installation of Wall Covering

Comments

Open and inspect wall covering materials when they are delivered to the site. It is important to make sure that all rolls of wallpaper and borders are from the same dye lot. The materials should include specific instructions for hanging.

Fresh plaster should be permitted to cure for 90 days before it is primed.

Bleaching, if necessary to prevent or eliminate mold and mildew, should be done prior to the application of primer or sizing by washing walls with a solution of one part bleach to four parts water.

Material Quantities

Each room to be papered should be measured in feet, rounding off to the next highest foot or half foot. Determine the square footage of each wall, subtracting for the areas that will not be covered. This number can be divided by 25 (the square feet in one single roll of metric wall covering). The result is the number of rolls needed. Pattern requirements or other special conditions can affect this formula. The manufacturer or distributor should be able to offer guidance on any necessary adjustments.

Installation

Hanging the wallcovering begins by dropping a plumb line on each wall and correctly lining up the first strip. In planning and cutting, allow for the proper pattern match.

Air bubbles and wrinkles should be removed with a smoothing brush or soft sponge. The edges of the strips should butt and lie flat and smooth. Wallpaper should not be wrapped around an inside corner, but cut so that two pieces butt up to the corner. If the ceiling is to be covered, it should be done before the walls.

It is a good idea to inspect the wall covering strips after hanging a few, in the event that there is a manufacturer defect. While manufacturers will replace defective materials, they will not reimburse labor costs.

Pattern Matches

Patterns can be **random** (no specific points of match), **free** (separated by the trim between strips but possibly aligned for overall consistency), **drop** (a diagonal pattern where every other strip is the same at the ceiling line), or **straight across** (the same elements are repeated at an equal distance from the ceiling in each strip).

Problems

Pattern mismatches are generally not accepted in new construction. In remodeling, out of plumb walls or trim out of square may lead to some unavoidable misalignment of patterns. Wallpaper with defects in pattern should be replaced by the manufacturer.

Peeling wallpaper is a defect that should be addressed by the installing contractor. It can be reattached if the result shows no evidence of repair. Otherwise, the strip should be replaced.

Repairs

Repairs can be made to wall covering using the following method:

- Cut out a piece of wall covering (larger than the damaged area) to use for a patch.
- Paste the patch over the damaged spot, positioned to match the underlying pattern.
- Cut through both layers of wall coverings using a straight edge and safety knife.
- Remove the excess covering and place the patch exactly in the opening.

Ed. Note: Refer to the Introduction to this chapter for information on wall covering associations and resources.

Table of Contents

Text in blue type indicates excerpted summaries from the International Building Code® (IBC) *and* International Residential Code® (IRC). *Please consult the IBC and IRC for complete coverage and specific wording. "Comments" (in solid blue boxes) were written by the editors, based on their own experience.*

 This icon will appear with references to green building practices.

CHAPTER

13 SPECIALTIES

Common Defect Allegations

- *Most wall-mounted equipment, partitions, and accessories fail in their attachment due to missing or nonexistent backing. Care should be taken to measure and document the placement of this backing so that it can be located after the drywall is in place.*

- *Prefabricated metal fireplaces are a source of numerous claims including ponding water on the metal chimney cap, vertical nails in the chimney cap, and combustible debris resting on the metal draft stop support flanges and smoldering in the shaft. Another problem is a lack of air supply for the top and bottom, and fresh air to the fire box on both wood-burning and gas-fired units.*

Introduction

This chapter includes prefinished (and often preassembled) manufactured items that are installed near the end of a project when other finish work is complete. Included in this category are bathroom accessories (including shower compartments, medicine cabinets, towel and grab bars for handicapped residents or building users), partitions used for commercial applications (such as office and toilet partitions), signs and directories, bulletin and chalk boards, access panels, lockers, prefabricated fireplaces and wood stoves, cupolas, and fire extinguishers. Some distributors specialize in all or most of these items.

The project drawings must be reviewed carefully for these items, which may appear in only one reference. A general note on the drawings may describe the item, or detailed information may be given, such as the vendor's name and contact information. Substitutions may be restricted.

Contractors who are installing specialty items obtain detailed information from the manufacturer regarding installation procedures and need to plan for any special equipment that might be required. It is also important to plan for related work when installing specialties on the project. Examples include concrete bases for lockers; wood blocking for toilet partitions; anchor bolts, inserts and sleeves for equipment; pads; and box-outs for water fountains or fire extinguishers.

The items in this chapter are often supplied and installed by the distributor, or by one or more subcontractors. As a result, it is difficult to find published standards for quality installation for several of these items. In those cases, the editors have provided some general guidelines for what would be expected in a professional installation.

The following organizations may be helpful in locating further information on specialties.

For bathroom fixture and accessory standard spacing:

National Kitchen & Bath Association (NKBA)
800-843-6522
www.nkba.org

For ADA-compliant bathroom accessories, toilet partitions, grab bars, stair rails, and signage:

ADA Technical Assistance Center
800-514-0301
www.usdoj.gov/crt/ada
The ADA Technical Assistance Center provides local disability and business technical assistance and information about the *Americans with Disabilities Act—Act Guidelines.* The guidelines are available at no cost from the ADA Technical Assistance Center as well as the U.S. Department of Justice.

For fire extinguishers:

National Fire Protection Association (NFPA)
617-770-3000
www.nfpa.org

For demountable partitions:

Ceilings & Interiors Systems Construction Association (CISCA)
630-584-1919
www.cisca.org

Ed. Note: Comments and recommendations within this chapter are not intended as a definitive resource for construction activities. For building projects, contractors must rely on the project documents and any applicable code requirements pertaining to their own particular locations.

Green Approaches to Specialties

Most items in the specialty category can be found in green versions by virtue of their use of recycled materials or certified wood products—or by reusing existing units that have been removed from other facilities. For example, toilet partitions and medicine cabinets are manufactured from post-consumer recycled stainless steel, SCS/FSC certified wood, and post-industrial recycled plastic—with low-emitting adhesives. Shower stalls are available in these, plus synthetic stone materials with a substantial recycled content. Towel bars and grab bars are manufactured from recycled aluminum and plastic.

Fire extinguishers are a "green" issue in the sense of the ingredients in the foam they release when used. Some ingredients have been phased out, and new, greener (less caustic, biodegradable) options introduced for some specific applications. (Check with your local building code for details.)

Signage is available with a variety of green attributes, from recycled aluminum and plastic, to bamboo, certified wood and paper and plastic. Low- or no-VOC paints are another signage consideration. Signs from other properties or buildings can also be re-used, provided they meet ADA or other applicable requirements. Look into Energy Star® offerings for illuminated signs.

There are several ways to go green when it comes to demountable partitions. First, they can be obtained from another source, and refurbished if necessary. If new, look for partitions made from recycled (and recyclable) materials with low or no VOCs. Sturdy construction with a long expected life will also cut down on waste and energy use by reducing the need for replacement.

Lockers and locker components are available in 100% post-consumer recycled plastic (such as high-density polyethylene plastic from reused milk jugs) and recycled metals. The benefits of recycled plastic include resistance to dents, moisture, chlorine, and salt water. Used lockers are available in a variety of colors and configurations from distributors.

Cupolas can be found in several green options, from recycled plastic to certified wood, to repurposed units from salvage companies.

For all of these products, manufacture and delivery practices—to minimize energy use, waste materials, and pollution—are factors to consider.

Bathroom Accessories

Shower Stalls

Comments

The category of bathroom accessories may include prefabricated shower stalls, medicine cabinets, towel bars, and related items. We will begin with shower stalls, which can be constructed and finished with tile, or installed as prefabricated units. If a one-piece unit is to be installed, it is important to consider access to the bathroom for this large item, which may not fit through standard doorways or windows. The unit's manufacturer should provide detailed instructions, including requirements to maintain the warranty. Following are some basic guidelines.

- According to guidelines published by the National Kitchen & Bath Association in the *Kitchen & Bathroom Installation Manual, Volume 1*, shower stall interior dimensions should be a minimum of 34" x 34" (although job site limitations may make it necessary to reduce this dimension to 32" x 32"). For disabled users, shower stalls should include grab bars, a seat (17"–19" above the shower floor and at least 15" deep), and a door opening that allows adequate wheelchair entry and turning space (32"–36" depending on the interior space). Shower doors should open into the bathroom.

- The shower valve should be approximately 48" above the shower floor. The rough-in plumbing for this unit involves supplying both cold and hot water, and installing the drain, connected to a p-trap. Building codes generally require that the shower drain be a minimum of 12" from the nearest wall. If the shower drain is placed more than 6' from the main soil stack, the building code may require a separate vent.

- Prefabricated shower units are watertight and therefore do not require cement board on the surrounding walls. Once the unit has been put in place using manufacturer-recommended adhesive, it is difficult to remove in order to make plumbing adjustments. Plumbing should be carefully planned and executed to avoid leaks before attaching the shower unit.

- According to the National Kitchen & Bathroom Association's *Kitchen & Bathroom Installation Manual, Volume 1*, glass used for a shower enclosure within 18" of the floor should be safety glazed—laminated with a plastic interlayer, tempered glass, or approved plastics, such as those found in the model safety code.

- Barrier-free shower units are available with options such as shower doors, fold-up seats, hand-held shower sprays, grab bars, soap dishes, and lights, as well as custom support blocking. Following are the Americans with Disabilities Act requirements for roll-in showers in public access facilities.

Ed. Note: More information on showers can be found in Chapter 14, "Plumbing."

Roll-in Showers for ADA Compliance

Industry Standards

Means ADA Compliance Pricing Guide, Second Edition
(RSMeans)

ADAAG References

309, Operable Parts

608, Shower Compartments

609, Grab Bars

Where Applicable

Accessible public bathing facilities.

Design Requirements

- On accessible route.
- No verticle lip at entry, but $\frac{1}{2}$" threshold with a 1:2 slope is permitted.
- Standard compartment 30" minimum deep by 60" wide, with an adjacent 36" x 60" clear floor space in front. A sink may protrude into the clear floor space.
- Alternate compartment 36" by 60", with 36" wide entrance either at end or at one end of 60" side; controls mounted on end wall farthest from opening.
- Grab bars 33" to 36" a.f.f. (all grab bars the same height), $1\frac{1}{4}$" to 2" in diameter, $1\frac{1}{2}$" from wall, on three walls (omit behind seat), and extending to 6" maximum from adjacent walls.
- Grab bars to withstand 250 lbs. force applied anywhere in any direction and be tight in their fittings.
- Controls located above grab bar, 38"–48" a.f.f. If a roll-in shower has a seat, controls to be located on wall adjacent to seat and within 27" of the seat wall.

- Shower spray unit that can be either fixed or hand-held with an on/off, non-positive shut-off valve and a flexible hose at least 59" long.
- Water temperature 120° maximum and thermal shock protected.

Design Suggestions

Recessing the floor pan below floor level allows for smooth roll-in. This can be very difficult as a retrofit, since it requires strengthening the existing floor structure, but it is easier to do in new construction. Shower curtains should reach to the floor to prevent spillage. An adjustable showerhead on a 24" vertical bar can be used by both tall and short people, but if it is left in the high position, it will be out of the reach of a person in a wheelchair. If space permits, consider installing a permanent seat for people who can transfer or need sitting as a bathing option. A permanent seat (or fold-down seat) has an advantage in that it is more stable than a portable seat that might shift under a person making a transfer.

Grab Bars for ADA Compliance

Industry Standards

Means ADA Compliance Pricing Guide, **Second Edition**
(RSMeans)

ADAAG References

604.5, 604.8.1.5, and 604.8.2.3, Grab Bars (at toilets)

607.4, Grab Bars (at tubs)

608.3, Grab Bars (at showers)

609, Grab Bars

Where Applicable:
All accessible toilets, tubs, and showers.

Design Requirements
- $1\frac{1}{4}$" to $1\frac{1}{2}$" in diameter for circular cross section; 4" to 4.8" perimeter, 2" maximum diameter for non-circular cross section.
- $1\frac{1}{2}$" from wall, 12" minimum from protruding objects above except for shower controls, $1\frac{1}{2}$" minimum from protruding objects below and at ends.
- Smooth surface, free of sharp or abrasive elements behind and adjacent to grab bars.
- Capable of resisting 250 lbs. of vertical or horizontal force—tight in their fittings.

- 33" to 36" a.f.f., 36" mounting height.
- For wheelchair-accessible water closet or toilet compartment: 42" long minimum at side wall starting 12" maximum from rear wall; 36" long minimum at back wall extending 12" from center of water closet or toilet compartment in one direction and 24" in the other.
- For ambulatory-accessible water closet or toilet compartment: 42" long minimum at each side wall starting 12" maximum from rear wall.
- In transfer showers (typical, 36" deep), extend across control wall and across back wall to a point 18" from the maximum of control wall.
- In roll-in showers, on three walls to within 6" minimum of adjacent walls, but never behind seat.
- For tub with permanent seat: on foot end wall, 24" minimum grab bar at front edge of tub; on back wall, 12" maximum from foot end wall and 15" maximum from head end wall, plus an additional grab bar the same length mounted 9" above the tub rim.
- For tub without a permanent seat: on foot end wall, 24" minimum grab bar at front edge of tub; on head end wall, 12" minimum grab bar at front edge of tub; on back wall, 24" minimum grab bar 24" maximum from head end wall and 12" maximum from foot end wall, plus an additional grab bar the same length mounted 9" above the tub rim.

Design Suggestions

There are a variety of colors other than standard steel now available for grab bars. Textured grab bars provide a better gripping surface than smooth bars. In tight spaces, a fold-down grab bar allows flexibility in use, but should be used only in addition to the required fixed grab bars. Grab bars are vital for safety, and installation methods must meet strength requirements.

Comments

Even if grab bars are not necessary for the current or anticipated owners of a new or remodeled home, installation of blocking (reinforcement) in bathroom walls can still be a good idea in new construction, in the event there is a future need to add grab bars.

Roll-in Shower

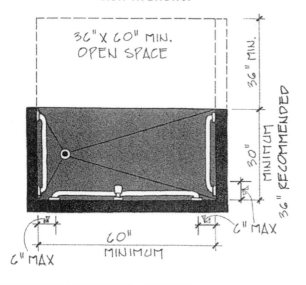

Figure 13.1   RSMeans, *Means ADA Compliance Pricing Guide*, 2nd Edition

Grab Bar Installation

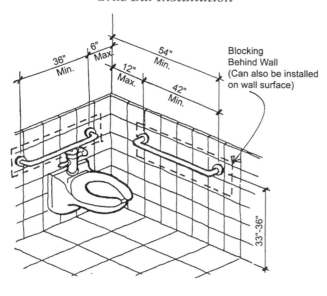

Figure 13.2   RSMeans, *Means ADA Compliance Pricing Guide*, 2nd Edition

Grab Bars for Universal Design

Universal Design Ideas for Style, Comfort & Safety

(RSMeans)

Grab bars are key for ensuring safety in the bathroom by helping people steady themselves when getting in and out of the tub or up and down from the toilet. Grab bars should meet the following guidelines:

- They should withstand a 250-pound load, which means they must be installed into the wall studs or a wall that is reinforced. To reinforce a wall, install blocking or affix ¾-inch plywood backing to the wall framing. Even if you don't plan to install grab bars immediately, building the proper reinforcement into the wall during construction makes it easier to add them later.

- Grab bars should be 1¼ to 2 inches in diameter to fit comfortable between the thumb and fingers, and should project 1½ inches from the wall for easy grasping.

- Horizontal grab bars should be installed 33 to 36 inches above the floor behind and to at least one side of the toilet.

- In the shower, horizontal grab bars should be installed on shower walls 32 to 48 inches from the floor.

- A vertical bar may be installed at the entrance to the tub; the bottom of the bar should be 32 to 38 inches above the floor.

- Grab bars placed at a 45-degree angle to the toilet or in the bathtub may be easier for people to reach. An angled 24-inch grab bar perfectly spans wall studs spaced 16 inches apart for extra support.

Medicine Cabinets

Comments

Medicine cabinets can be recessed or surface-mounted. The top of the cabinet is usually 6' above the finished floor (and the bottom no higher than 40" for public access bathrooms), although the height can be adjusted to the requirements of individual homeowners. (Mirrors in public access bathrooms can be 48" high maximum, if tilted.)

Surface-mounted cabinets should be attached (with a minimum of two screws, near each edge of the cabinet) to the wall studs. Some cabinets fit between two studs, in which case head and sill blocking is installed with L-clips. If the studs are not lined up with the desired location of the medicine cabinet, some studs will have to be cut, and new ones added.

Towel Bars, Dispensers & Storage

Comments

According to the standards for universal access in NKBA's *Kitchen & Bathroom Installation Manual, Volume 1*, there should be a minimum of 16" clearance from the center line of the toilet or bidet to any obstruction. The toilet paper holder should be 26" above the floor, within reach of a person seated on the toilet. Storage of toiletries and general bathroom supplies should be provided at a height in the range of 15"–48" above the floor.

The height of towel bars is generally in the range of 34"–48". This decision may be affected by the wall finishes and owner's preference. (For example, if the brackets are to be a ceramic material incorporated into a tiled wall, the height of the tile will affect the placement.)

Toilet Room Dispensers for ADA Compliance

Industry Standards

Means ADA Compliance Pricing Guide, **Second Edition**
(RSMeans)

ADAAG References

305, Clear Floor or Ground Space

308, Reach Ranges

309, Operable Parts

Where Applicable

At least one of each type of dispenser in accessible public toilet rooms.

Design Requirements
- Dispensers on an accessible route, 30" x 48" clear floor space in front.
- Dispensers 15" to 48" a.f.f., with 2" clearance minimum below grab bars and 12" clearance minimum above grab bars.

Toilet Room Dispensers

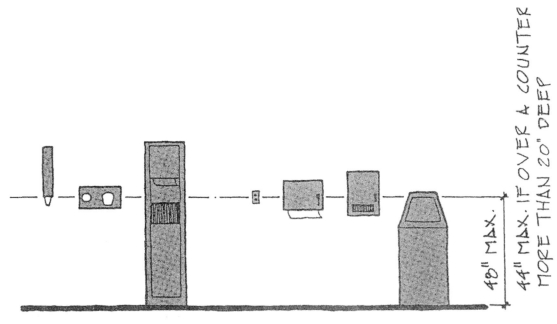

48" MAX.

44" MAX. IF OVER A COUNTER MORE THAN 20" DEEP

Figure 13.3

RSMeans, *Means ADA Compliance Pricing Guide*, 2nd Edition

- Controls operable without tight grasping, pinching, or twisting.

Design Suggestions

Specify dispensers with easy-to-operate controls. Locate all dispensers as close as possible to accessible fixtures (but still within easy reach) and at least 18" from an inside corner in a location where no one will ever put a waste basket.

Consider making the highest operating part of dispensers at 42" so they are within the reach ranges of children. Consider locating the soap dispenser lower than 48".

Carefully check all controls to make sure they do not require pinching or excessive force. One should be able to operate them with one's fist.

Toilet Partitions

Comments

Toilet partitions are available in a variety of installation configurations. The methods of vertical support include ceiling-hung, floor-anchored, overhead-braced, and floor-to-ceiling anchored.

The economy grade partitions are composed of particleboard with steel frame supports and laminated with plastic laminate. In wet applications or where a premium grade is desired, there are other options, such as a solid phenolic core with laminate cover or high density polyethylene.

Also available is a fiberglass-reinforced panel (FRP) in lieu of plastic laminate. The advantage of the FRP is that it is almost vandal-proof. The surface can be textured to discourage graffiti.

Hardware options range from chrome-plated steel to stainless steel, depending on the intended use, with available plastic or aluminum wall brackets and plastic pilaster shoes.

The phenolic core panels have a relatively high fire rating. This is critical in fire-resistive construction, especially in medical facilities.

The Americans with Disabilities Act (ADA) requires specific dimensions between the water closet and the side walls, as well as clearance between the front of the fixture and the partition door or wall. These are considerations when ordering and installing the enclosure. Many building departments now require that a percentage of the Tenant Improvement cost be applied toward ADA compliance.

Multiple-Stall Toilet Rooms for ADA Compliance

Industry Standards

Means ADA Compliance Pricing Guide, Second Edition
(RSMeans)

ADAAG References

604.5, 604.8.1.5, and 604.8.2.3, Grab Bars (at toilets)

605, Urinals

607.4, Grab Bars (at tubs)

608.3, Grab Bars (at showers)

609, Grab Bars

Where Applicable:

All public and common-use, multiple-use toilet rooms.

Design Requirements

- One accessible urinal and one fully accessible stall required. If the sum of water closets and urinals is 6 or more, an ambulatory stall is required.
- Ambulatory stall: 36" wide x 60" deep with self-closing, out-swinging door and grab bars on both sides of stall. WC centered in space.
- 9" minimum a.f.f. toe clearance extending 6" under the front and one side partitions (not required if stall is 66"+ wide and 65"+ deep).
- Accessible urinal: rim 17" a.f.f. maximum, 13½" minimum depth; accessible flush valve 44" a.f.f. maximum if hand operated; 30" wide by 48" deep space in front of urinal (29" minimum between privacy screens if they do not project beyond urinal).

(Ed. Note: Design requirements for grab bars, noted earlier in this chapter, also apply.)

Design Suggestions

Privacy partitions at entrances of toilet rooms can make it difficult to enter/exit a multi-stall toilet room, even when the clear widths comply. If possible, try to locate the entrance door so there is no need for a privacy partition, or use an entry vestibule with doors arranged so that tight turns are not necessary. But be certain to provide required maneuverability space at each door and between doors.

Often an accessible stall can be created by combining two stalls. Similarly, extra space can be created at a tight entry by removing one lavatory and shifting the privacy partition.

Multiple-Stall Toilet Room

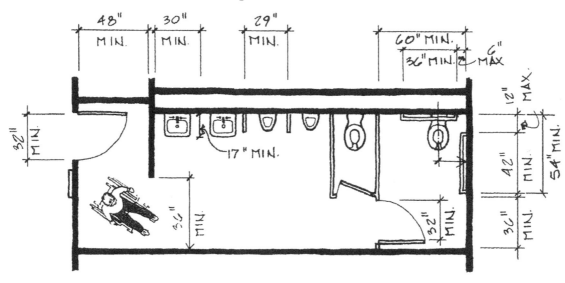

Figure 13.4

RSMeans, *Means ADA Compliance Pricing Guide*, 2nd Edition

It is possible (and preferred) to use standard sinks that are not designated "HP" if they are installed so that they meet the apron height and knee space requirements; they will be less costly, easier to install and use, and all the sinks can be the same. The same is true of tilted "HP" mirrors; if a mirror above the sink cannot be lowered, add another mirror starting at 35" a.f.f. maximum in a different location. Tilting does not always create an adjustable alternative. *Never* use an adjustable tilting mirror. If you do not install an alternate mirror, at least one mirror over the sink must be accessible with its bottom edge no more than 40" above the floor.

Be sure that grab bars are anchored to either framing or blocking, so that they meet the minimum structural strength requirements.

Stall door hardware must also be accessible. Most knobs are not; slide or flip latches are usually easier to use.

Ed. Note: Design requirements for grab bars, noted earlier in this chapter, also apply.

Fire Extinguishers

Comments

Fire extinguishers should, according to NKBA's *Kitchen & Bathroom Installation Manual, Volume 1*, be "visibly located in the kitchen, away from cooking equipment and 15"

to 48" above the floor. NFPA and most building codes recommend one fire extinguisher for each 3,000 SF of floor area. Smoke alarms should be included near the kitchen." In commercial projects, fire extinguisher cabinets are generally #18 gauge steel with metal, glass, wood or mirror doors. Cabinets may be surface-mounted, recessed, or semi-recessed. Residential fire extinguisher cabinets are generally 1'5" x 7'2".

Fire extinguishers themselves are classified by type of fire (e.g., Class A: fires of wood, paper, textile, rubbish; Class B: gasoline, oil, grease, fat; and Class C: electrical) and by occupancy (light hazard: schools, offices, public buildings; ordinary hazard: dry goods shops and warehouses; and extra hazard, such as paint shops).

There are maximum distances allowed between the fire extinguisher(s) and any point in the building, depending on the occupancy and use of the building. Consult your local building officials and/or fire department for more information.

The *IBC* does not provide specific requirements for fire extinguishers, but references the *International Fire Code*.

Ed Note: Refer to Chapter 16, "Electrical," for information on smoke detector requirements.

Signage

Exit Signs

Note: The following are summaries of the basic code requirements of the *International Building Code* and *International Residential Code*. Please consult the *IBC* and *IRC* for complete coverage and specific wording.

IBC–2006

1011.1 Where required: Exits and exit access doors must be marked with an approved exit sign that is easily visible from any direction of egress travel. Access to exits must be marked with easily visible exit signs in cases where the egress is not immediately visible to occupants. No point in an exit access corridor should be more than 100' from the nearest visible exit sign.

Exceptions:

1. Exit signs are not needed in areas or rooms that require only one exit or exit access.

2. Clearly marked main exterior doors or gates don't require exit signs.

3. Exit signs are not needed in Group U occupancies or Group R-1, R-2, or R-3 individual sleeping or dwelling units.

4. Exit signs are not needed in sleeping room areas in I-3 occupancies.

5. In A-4, A-5 occupancies that include grandstand seating arrangements, exit signs are not required on the seating side of vomitories. Egress lighting must be provided to identify each vomitory.

1011.2 Illumination: Exit signs must be illuminated internally or externally.

Exception: Section 1011.3-required tactile signs need not be illuminated.

1011.3 Tactile exit signs: A tactile sign complying with ICC A117.1 and stating EXIT must be provided adjacent to each egress access door.

1011.4 Internally illuminated exit signs: These shall be listed and labeled, and must be installed according to manufacturer's instructions and IBC-2006 Section 2702.

1101.5 Externally illuminated exit signs: These shall comply with the following:

1101.5.1 Graphics: Exit signs must have letters no less than 6" high that are plainly legible. The principal strokes of the letters must not be less than .75" wide. The letters in the word "EXIT" must not be less than 2" wide (except the "I"), and the minimum spacing between the letters must not be less than .375". Letters larger than the minimum stated here must have widths, strokes, and spacing in proportion to their heights. The word "EXIT" must be in high contrast with the background.

1101.5.2 Exit sign illumination: When the face of an exit sign is illuminated from an external source, it must have an intensity of not less than 5 foot candles.

1101.5.3 Power source: All exit signs must be illuminated at all times. To ensure continued illumination for a duration of not less than 90 minutes in case of power loss, the exit signs must also be connected to an emergency electrical system provided from storage batteries, unit equipment, or an on-site generator, and the system shall be installed in accordance with Section 2702.

Exception: Approved self-luminous signs that provide continuous illumination independent of an external power source.

Maximum Room Capacity Signs

IBC–2006

1004.3 Posting of occupant load: Any room that is used for an assembly purpose will have the occupant load of the room posted in a conspicuous place on an approved, legible, permanent sign near the main exit or exit-access doorway from the room. Such signs shall indicate the number of occupants permitted for each room use.

Live Load Signs

IBC-2006

1603.3 Live loads posted: Where the live loads for which each floor or portion thereof of a commercial or industrial building is or has been designed to exceed 50 pounds per square foot, such design live loads will be clearly posted by the owner in the part of the building where they apply, using durable signs. It will be illegal to remove or deface such notices.

Ed. Note: Live load signage requirements differ in various regions. Check your local building code.

Marquees

IBC-2006

3106.2 Thickness: The maximum height or thickness of a marquee measured vertically from its lowest to its highest point must not be more than 3' where the marquee projects more than two-thirds of the distance from the property line to the curb line, and must not extend beyond 9' where the marquee is less than two-thirds of the distance from the property line to the curb line.

3106.3 Roof construction: Where the roof or any part of a marquee is a skylight, the skylight must comply with requirements of IBC-2006 Chapter 24. Marquee roofs and skylights must be sloped to downspouts that will conduct any drainage from the marquee in such a way as to not spill over the sidewalk.

3106.5 Construction: A marquee must be supported completely from the building and must be noncombustible. Marquee design must comply with requirements of IBC-2006 Chapter 16. Structural members must be protected to keep them from deteriorating.

Signage for ADA Compliance

Industry Standards

Means ADA Compliance Pricing Guide, Second Edition
(RSMeans)

ADAAG References

216, Signs

703, Signs

Where Applicable

Building entrance signs and other signs that convey information about or directions to facilities on the site and interior spaces, including accessible elements. Follow visual specifications concerning contrast, character, height, font, and proportions.

Temporary signs (seven days or fewer), building directories, signs with building addresses, corporate logos and names, and occupant names have no access requirements.

Signs designating permanent rooms and spaces (such as restrooms, exits, room numbers, etc.). Follow visual specifications and provide tactile and Braille elements.

Transportation facilities have other special specifications in ADAAG 810.4 and 810.6.

Design Requirements

Visual characteristics:

- High contrast between characters/pictures and background (dark on light, or light on dark).
- Matte or other nonglare background and characters.
- Simple font, conventional in form. Italic, script, oblique, or highly decorative fonts not allowed.
- Character height is a function of viewing distance (see ADAAG Table 703.5.5), but as a rule of thumb, figure $1/8$" per foot. $5/8$" is the minimum.
- International symbol of accessibility at entrances if all are not accessible, with directions to the nearest accessible entrance; same for rest rooms.
- Mounted at least 40" a.f.f.

For tactile signs that are also visual:

- In addition to the visual characteristics in the previous section, characters must be raised at least $1/32$", and have a 2" maximum height.
- Characters must be in sans serif font and uppercase.

- Braille and characters must be at least ³⁄₈" from raised borders.
- Braille text must be below the corresponding text, separated by ³⁄₈".
- Braille must be Grade 2, rounded shape, and meet the spacing requirements of ADAAG Table 703.3.1.
- Signs to be located on wall adjacent to the door, on the latch side, and 60" a.f.f. to the centerline of sign. Users must be able to approach the sign, and the sign must be clear of the door swing when there are double doors with no wall beside the doors.

Design Suggestions

Regarding contrast, evidence suggests that light characters on a dark background are easier to read. Since there is no firm definition of high contrast, choose colors that leave as little doubt as possible, e.g., white characters on a dark gray or dark red background. Although room signs have been customarily placed on doors, this practice is not effective for people who must read the sign by touch or be able to approach within inches of the sign to see the letters. If a sign is on a door, adding an accessible sign adjacent to the door can be effective for both groups of users. Signs throughout the building should always be at the same height and location in relation to doors.

Informational signage also should always be the same height and in a consistent location. Raised characters and Braille are not required for informational or directional signs, but, if possible, a method of way-finding should be provided for people with severe visual impairments.

The advisories in ADAAG provide useful information on making signs as helpful as possible.

Demountable or Movable Partitions

Comments

Movable partitions, often called "operable" panels or partitions, are manufactured by office furniture and specialties companies, and are usually installed (and serviced) by those firms. Demountable partitions are used for applications such as in-plant offices, security stations and guardhouses, smoking enclosures, reception areas, hotel meeting rooms, computer and other workstations, additional/flexible office areas, mini storage buildings, and convention halls.

Partitions are available in full and partial height in a variety of finishes including vinyl-clad, gypsum panels, and fabric, in a choice of colors. They can be obtained in styles without visible fasteners for visual continuity. Some manufacturers offer wall units that incorporate power, voice and data wiring to simplify future reconfigurations of office space.

Movable walls often have available glazing, which allows light and aesthetic benefits, while providing the function of a separate area. Demountable partitions are fire rated, and also must meet seismic and sound control requirements per local building code.

Comments

While demountable partitions are usually installed by the manufacturer or distributor, the following guidelines may be helpful in ensuring a quality installation.

- Finishes must be correct as specified, and shading of fabric or other finish should match between panels.
- Existing finishes in surrounding space should be protected during the installation of demountable partition walls.
- Demountable partitions should not be fastened to ceilings or floors at any point.
- Wands used to connect to a power source in the ceiling should be carefully anchored.
- Associated cabinetry and countertops should be level and have no scratches or other damage to finishes.

Lockers

Comments

Lockers are manufactured by specialty companies, which usually offer installation if the contractor will not be responsible for this item. Lockers are available in institutional and deluxe sports club models, single-, double-, and multi-tier, and with double doors for limited swing space. The contractor on a project involving lockers will be concerned with preparation of the area where the lockers will be installed. This may involve installation of concrete, wood, or metal supports.

Supports should be in alignment with the project design requirements for the locker installation. All edges and exposed surfaces, including end units, should be finished, with no defects such as scratches or chips in the finish. Doors and hardware should operate freely, without chafing or binding. There should be no obstructions in the free swing of the locker doors (90 degrees). Consideration should be made for space allowance between benches and open locker doors.

Prefabricated Fireplaces

Comments

Prefabricated fireplaces are available from specialty woodstove and fireplace distributors. They can be installed by the distributor or by the general contractor, according to the manufacturer's instructions and with

(continued)

Prefabricated Fireplace

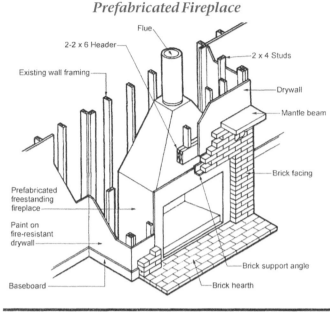

Figure 13.5

RSMeans, *Interior Home Improvement Costs*

Flue Sizes for Masonry Chimneys

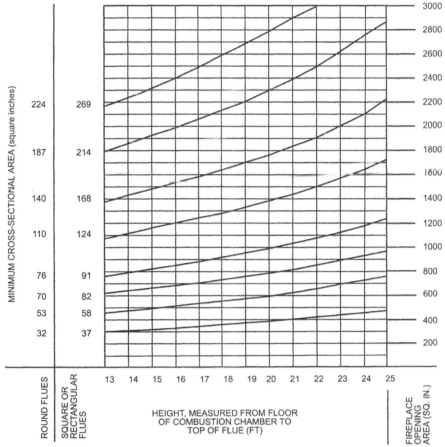

For SI: 1 inch = 25.4 mm, 1 square inch = 645 mm².

Figure 13.6   Courtesy of ICC, *IBC-2006*, [Figure 2113.16] Copyright 2006, International Code Council, Inc., Falls Church, Virginia

manufacturer-supplied or recommended fireplace and chimney materials. These units are available in gas, wood-burning, or wood pellet-burning varieties, as well as gas log-type heaters that resemble fireplaces. They can be purchased with various masonry facings including stone, brick, marble, and tile, and with prefabricated wood mantles and surrounds.

Defects related to fireplaces usually involve the ability of the fireplace to draw and exhaust smoke properly. In addition to correct installation, proper fireplace function is influenced by flue size, number of bends, height of discharge in relationship, and relationship of dimensions to roof lines, and prevailing winds.

See **Figures 13.5** and **13.6** for masonry and concrete chimney construction and correct flue sizes for the chimney height and fireplace opening area.

Cupolas & Flagpoles

Comments

Cupolas can be used as part of the calculation for venting attic space, or they can be nonfunctioning and purely decorative. If functional, cupolas must be flashed properly. Cupolas are often available at lumberyards, but can also be purchased in special and custom designs from firms that manufacture architectural sheet metal products and other specialties. Cupolas are generally made of cedar, redwood, or unfinished or painted pine, and may have copper roofs. They may come with skirt flashing and a roof template to help the contractor with the installation.

The only *IBC* reference to flagpoles is in the Penthouses and Roof Structures section (1509.2). It states that the height and other restrictions of the section "shall not prohibit the placing of wood flagpoles or similar structures on the roof of any building."

Flagpoles are also manufactured by specialty companies for attachment to buildings or installation on the ground.

Flagpoles can be fiberglass, aluminum, steel, or bronze. Electrical models offer remote switches and self-storing operation. Installation should be performed in accordance with manufacturers' instructions. Some basic guidelines follow:

Flagpoles on roofs can be braced several different ways: corner brace, side brace, three-legged tripod type brace, or four-legged brace. The flag length should be roughly $\frac{1}{3}$ the length of the pole.

Flagpoles set in the ground are usually embedded in concrete topped with dry sand, with a metal collar and caulking at the ground level. Lightning protection is embedded in the ground beneath the flagpole's foundation. The length of pole below the ground is typically 10% of the pole height. The flag length should be approximately one-fourth of the flag pole height.

Outrigger flagpoles (for building fronts) are normally at a 45° or more angle. If the pole is longer than 13', bracing is required. The flag width should be roughly $\frac{3}{8}$–$\frac{1}{2}$ the length of the outrigger flagpole.

Ed. Note: Architectural Graphic Standards, *published by John Wiley & Sons, Inc., contains further information and illustrations on flagpole heights, sizes, and placements.*

Cupola

Figure 13.7

Table of Contents

Text in blue type indicates excerpted summaries from the International Building Code® (IBC), International Residential Code® (IRC), and International Plumbing Code. *Please consult the IBC and IRC for complete coverage and specific wording. "Comments" (in solid blue boxes) were written by the editors, based on their own experience.*

These icons will appear with references to green building practices and seismic regulations, respectively.

CHAPTER

14 PLUMBING

Common Defect Allegations

Defects in plumbing work can be extensive, and corrections costly. The following items are often frequent causes of defect claims.

- *Insufficient pitch in the sewer system can cause the system to back up. Flushing of the new low-flow toilets is affected by improper pipe pitch. The flow line needs $1/4$" per foot of fall. Pipe should be set on sand beds properly prepared to achieve correct drainage after soil settlement. If the base soil is uncompacted, when the upper backfill is compacted, the pipe will settle improperly and can cause some negative flow. Investigators often run cameras down the pipe and show video tapes of the solids accumulation in the flat areas.*

- *Water heaters may not be properly strapped in seismic zones.*

- *Hot water lines should be insulated, but often they are not, or are only partially insulated.*

- *"Water hammer" occurs when you shut off the faucet suddenly and hear a clunk from the pipe reaction. Installing a water hammer arrester on each line will absorb the shock.*

- *There have been many recent claims on circulating hot water systems, which require a loop in the water system for instant hot water circulation. There are two types of water line damage on circulating systems. One is from having too large a pump where the particulates in the water wear out the insides of the fittings. The other is from galvanic action where there is a microcurrent of electricity that is actually taking particulates from the hot water pipe underground and moving them to the cold water pipe. This can result in green fuzzy growth around the valves serving the system. There are different theories on the best way to prevent this. It is suggested that dielectric fittings will solve the problem; others say that a zinc block will save the copper. It is generally agreed that the copper should be wrapped, not just through the concrete, but through the entire burial run under the soil.*

- *Second-story noise through the ceiling of the first floor when toilets are flushed is a common complaint, particularly when PVC is used instead*

(continued)

of cast iron pipe. Cast iron pipe in that area will help to reduce this noise substantially. Offsetting the vertical line in the wall slightly will cause the flow to swirl as opposed to dropping. See the "Soundproofing" section in Chapter 7 for framing and insulation approaches to the plumbing noise problem.

- Undersized pipes can cause problems, such as backed-up sewer pipes, unacceptably low volume of water from faucets or showers, and inadequate volume for outdoor sprinklers.

- Other complaints include garbage disposals that failed after several years, chips in enamel sinks, cracks in solid surface or stone sinks or counters, and deteriorated faucet finishes. Most of these items relate to the product manufacturer's warranty, rather than any defect in installation.

Introduction

While there are usually no written specifications or detailed drawings prepared for the plumbing systems of individual homes, light commercial installations typically have plans and specifications for the plumbing incorporated into the general bid or construction documents. Whether or not such documents are available at bidding time, it is understood that the installation will have to be governed by local and/or national plumbing codes.

Plumbing codes regulate the minimum number of fixtures based on use of the building and anticipated number of occupants. Codes further regulate the potable water supply and distribution, and the collection and disposal of sanitary waste and wastewater. Other code-regulated items include special laboratory wastes, gray water systems, gas piping, and fire protection systems.

There are several national plumbing codes, including the *Uniform Plumbing Code*, the *Standard Plumbing Code*, and the *International Plumbing Code*. Plumbing code requirements are also included in the *International Residential Code (IRC)* and mentioned briefly in the *International Building Code (IBC)*. There are many similarities in the requirements of these codes; all are concerned with the protection of public health, safety, and welfare.

This chapter includes excerpts from the *IRC* and the *International Plumbing Code*.

Most states have adopted one of the major codes mentioned above, and the choice of codes seems to be in large part by region of the country. All of the western states from Montana, south to New Mexico, and across to the West Coast have adopted the *Uniform Plumbing Code*, with the exception of Utah. Iowa, however, decided to go with the western states. Utah, along with most of the Northeast, Midwest, Oklahoma, and Kansas, has adopted the *International Plumbing Code*. The South, from North Carolina west to Arkansas and Texas and south along the coast, have all chosen the *Standard Plumbing Code* (an SBCCI version of the *International Plumbing Code*). North and South Dakota, New Jersey and Maryland have all selected the *National Standard Plumbing Code*. Nebraska is alone in adopting the *A40 1993 Safety Standard for Plumbing*. Kentucky, Wisconsin, Minnesota, and Massachusetts have currently not chosen a national code.

Several states, such as Massachusetts, have developed their own more stringent codes. Many cities and towns have their own specific code requirements as well. Code information in this chapter, as in Chapter 15, "HVAC," is included for easy reference to common defect problems, but it is not intended to replace your local code. For instance, it is important to determine approval and installation requirements for CPVC hot and cold water distribution systems from the appropriate local authority. Anyone who performs installations of plumbing must be qualified, experienced, licensed (in many locations), and have a full knowledge of the prevailing code and practices for their locale.

Following is a list of resources that can provide further information on plumbing codes and industry standards.

International Association of Plumbing and Mechanical Officials (IAPMO)
909-472-4100
www.iapmo.org
Note: The *Uniform Plumbing Code* is available from this organization.

Plumbing · Heating · Cooling · Contractors Association (PHCC)
703-237-8100
www.phccweb.org
Note: The *National Standard Plumbing Code* is available from this organization.

National Fire Protection Association (NFPA)
617-770-3000
www.nfpa.org

American Fire Sprinkler Association (AFSA)
214-349-5965
www.firesprinkler.org
The American Fire Sprinkler Association is a nonprofit international organization offering educational and technical information on sprinklers, and representing open shop fire sprinkler contractors.

National Fire Sprinkler Association, Inc. (NFSA)
845-878-4200
www.nfsa.org
The National Fire Sprinkler Association promotes the use of sprinklers and offers educational opportunities and technical advice. It is also involved with labor relations for sprinkler fitters.

(continued)

Note: The *International Plumbing Code* is copyrighted by and available through the International Code Council, Inc. (ICC).

Ed. Note: Comments and recommendations within this chapter are not intended as a definitive resource for construction activities. For building projects, contractors must rely on the project documents and any applicable code requirements pertaining to their own particular locations.

A Green Approach to Plumbing
Based on *Green Building: Project Planning & Cost Estimating,* Second Edition
(RSMeans)

There are several practical approaches to conserving water, including reducing the quantity used—by such measures as low-flow plumbing fixtures and reuse of gray water.

Smaller-diameter supply piping, where appropriate, is less expensive than larger diameter, and reduces waste. Instant hot water heaters can save money, depending on the application.

Relatively inexpensive carbon filters can be added to sinks to remove chemicals, heavy metals, chlorine, and many forms of bacteria and parasites.

Garbage disposals are inefficient because they require running water and deposit organic materials into septic tanks and sewage treatment plants. Composting is a better solution.

Among the cheapest and easiest water-savers are low-flow showerheads and faucet aerators. Each of these devices can cut water use by about 50%, while maintaining good water pressure. (To get an idea of the volume of water saved, a family of four can save roughly 20,000 gallons of water per year by switching to low-flow showerheads and 22,000 gallons with low-flow toilets, even more with dual-flush toilets.)

When fixtures need replacing, choose water-conserving models. Toilets older than ten years might be worth replacing even if they are still functioning, as they are major water users. Some water utilities offer rebates for water-conserving fixtures.

Energy Star® and Water Sense-qualified water heaters, washing machines, and dishwashers save water and energy. Insulating hot water heaters and piping reduces energy use. Water heater maintenance extends the unit's life and increases efficiency.

Gray water systems recycle wastewater from showers, baths, and laundries for landscape irrigation (and sometimes toilet flushing). Gray water systems must be clearly labeled and have no cross-connects to potable water systems. Check local codes for restrictions and requirements. (Another option is a rainwater collection system that stores water channeled from gutters.) Efficient landscape watering may include drip irrigation systems and rain and freeze sensors (required by law in some locations).

General Installation Requirements

Comments

Residential hot and cold water systems typically include water distribution piping, fittings, control valves, boilers and/or hot water heaters, and pumps. The cold water supply begins once it enters the building, typically through a water meter. The hot water supply system starts at the hot water generating equipment. The distribution system then delivers **potable water** throughout the building.

Potable water is suitable for human consumption and free of impurities that may cause disease. The following codes regulate the minimum number of plumbing fixtures required, based on use and building occupancy. They also regulate the potable water supply and its distribution, as well as the collection and disposal of sanitary waste and wastewater.

The following are summaries of the basic code requirements of the *International Plumbing Code* (IPC) and *International Residential Code* (IRC). Please consult the *IPC* and *IRC* for complete coverage and specific wording.

IRC–2006

P2603.2 Drilling and notching: Wood-framed structural members must not be drilled, notched, or altered in any way except as provided in Sections R502.8, R602.5, R602.6, R802.7, and R802.7.1. Holes in cold-formed, steel-framed, load-bearing members are allowed only if they conform to Sections R505.2, R603.2, and R804.2. Cutting and notching of flanges and lips of cold-formed, steel-framed, load-bearing members are not allowed.

P2603.2.1 Protection against physical damage: In concealed areas where piping is installed through notches or holes in studs, joists, rafters, or similar members that are less than 1.5" from the nearest member, the pipes must be protected by shield plates. Protective shield plates must conform to code.

P2603.3 Breakage and corrosion: Pipes that pass under and through walls must be protected. Pipes that pass through corrosive material must be protected by sheathing or wrapping that will withstand any reaction from lime and acid or concrete, cinder or corrosive material. The sheathing or wrapping must allow for expansion and contraction of piping to prevent any rubbing action.

P2603.4 Sleeves: Any annular spaces between pipes and sleeves must be filled or tightly caulked per regulations of the building official. Such spaces in fire-rated assemblies must be filled or tightly caulked according to requirements of the IRC.

P2603.5 Pipes through footings or foundation walls: Pipes that pass under footings or through foundation walls must have a relieving arch, or there must be a pipe sleeve two pipe sizes greater than the pipe built into the masonry of the wall.

P2603.6 Freezing: In areas that have a winter design temperature of 32°F or lower, a water, soil, or waste pipe must not be installed outside of a building, in attics or crawl spaces, in exterior walls, or in another place subjected to freezing temperature unless provisions are made to keep it from freezing. Water service pipes cannot be installed unless they are at least 12" deep, or 6" below the frost line.

P2604.1 Trenching and bedding: Piping must be installed in trenches so that the piping rests on a continuous and solid bearing. When over-excavated, the trench must be backfilled to proper grade with appropriate material. The piping must not be supported on rocks or blocks at any point. Rocky or unstable soil must be over-excavated by two or more pipe diameters and brought to the proper grade with appropriate compacted granular material.

International Plumbing Code–2006

704.1 Slope of horizontal drainage piping: Horizontal drainage piping must be uniformly installed by alignment and slope. The minimum slope of a horizontal drainage pipe must comply with Table 704.1 in the IPC.

704.2 Change in size: A drainage piping must not be reduced in size in the direction of flow (a 4" x 3" water closet connection is not considered a size reduction).

704.3 Connections to offsets and bases of stacks: Horizontal branches must connect to the bases of stacks at a location no less than 10 pipe diameters downstream from the stack. Except as prohibited by Section 711.2, horizontal branches must connect to horizontal stack offsets at a location no less than 10 pipe diameters downstream from the upper stack.

704.4 Future fixtures: Drainage piping for future fixtures shall terminate with an approved cap or plug.

704.5 Dead ends: In the installation or removal of any part of a drainage system, dead ends shall be prohibited. Cleanout extensions and approved future fixture drainage piping shall not be considered as dead ends.

Pipe Support

Industry Standards

Plumbing Estimating Methods, **Third Edition**
(RSMeans)

Pipe supports fasten and support piping systems to walls, ceilings, floor slabs, or structural members within a building. Some supports carry single pipelines, such as *band hangers, clevis hangers, single or double rod roll hangers,* and *riser clamps.* Other supports carry multiple pipe runs, such as *trapeze hangers* and *pipe racks.*

IRC–2006

P2605.1 General: Support for piping must be in accordance with the following criteria:

1. Piping must have support that ensures alignment and that prevents sagging, and allows expansion and contraction movement.

2. Ground piping must be laid on a firm bed for its entire length. The exception is where support is otherwise provided.

3. Hangers and anchors must have the strength to support their share of the weight of pipe and contents, and be wide enough to prevent distortion to the pipe. Hangers and strappings must be of approved material that will not promote galvanic action. Rigid support sway bracing must be provided at changes in direction greater than 45°.

4. Piping must be supported at distances not farther than those listed in Table P2605.1.

Piping Support

PIPING MATERIAL	MAXIMUM HORIZONTAL SPACING (feet)	MAXIMUM VERTICAL SPACING
ABS pipe	4	10[b]
Aluminum tubing	10	15
Brass pipe	10	10
Cast-iron pipe	5[a]	15
Copper or copper alloy pipe	12	10
Copper or copper alloy tubing ($1^1/_4$ inch diameter and smaller)	6	10
Copper or copper alloy tubing ($1^1/_2$ inch diameter and larger)	10	10
Cross-linked polyethylene (PEX) pipe	2.67 (32 inches)	10[b]
Cross-linked polyethylene/aluminum/cross-linked polyethylene (PEX-AL-PEX) pipe	2.67 (32 inches)	4[b]
CPVC pipe or tubing (1 inch in diameter and smaller)	3	10[b]
CPVC pipe or tubing ($1^1/_4$ inch in diameter and larger)	4	10[b]
Lead pipe	Continuous	4
PB pipe or tubing	2.67 (32 inches)	4
Polyethylene/aluminum/polyethylene (PE-AL-PE) pipe	2.67 (32 inches)	4[b]
Polypropylene (PP) pipe or tubing 1 inch and smaller	2.67 (32 inches)	10[b]
Polypropylene (PP) pipe or tubing, $1^1/_4$ inches and larger	4	10[b]
PVC pipe	4	10[b]
Stainless steel drainage systems	10	10[b]
Steel pipe	12	15

For SI: 1 inch = 25.4 mm, 1 foot = 304.8 mm.

a. The maximum horizontal spacing of cast-iron pipe hangers shall be increased to 10 feet where 10-foot lengths of pipe are installed.

b. Midstory guide for sizes 2 inches and smaller.

Figure 14.1

Courtesy of ICC, IRC–2006 [Table P2605.1] Copyright 2006, International Code Council, Inc., Falls Church, Virginia.

International Plumbing Code–2006

308.1 General: All plumbing piping shall be supported in accordance with this section.

 308.2 Piping seismic supports: Where earthquake loads are applicable in accordance with the building code, plumbing piping supports shall be designed and installed for the seismic forces in accordance with the IBC.

308.3 Materials: Hangers, anchors and supports shall support the piping and the contents of the piping. Hangers and strapping material shall be of approved material that will not promote galvanic action.

308.4 Structural attachment: Hangers and anchors shall be attached to the building construction in an approved manner.

308.5 Interval of support: Pipe shall be supported in accordance with IPC-2006 Table 308.5.

Plumbing Administration & Testing

Ed. Note: Drainage, waste, and vent piping (DWV) refers to the piping that routes waste to the sewer or septic system, and vents plumbing fixtures to outside air. The various waste lines contain a curved section of pipe near each fixture to trap water and prevent odors and sewer gas from entering. Waste piping from sinks, tubs, and showers is pitched to carry the waste by gravity to the soil stack. The soil stack is a large pipe, usually located in the wall behind the toilet, that vents through the roof and brings waste to the sewer.

IRC–2006

P2503.5 DWV systems testing: Testing of finished and rough plumbing installations must comply with requirements in IRC-2006 Section, P2503.5.1 and P2503.5.2

P2503.5.1 Rough plumbing: DWV systems must be tested on completion of rough pipings installation by water or air, and with no signs of leakage. Either test must be applied to the entire drainage system in its whole or its sections after rough piping has been installed. Section outlines requirements of water and air tests.

P2503.5.2 Finished plumbing: When the plumbing fixtures are set, and their traps are filled with water or gas, their connections must be tested and proven gastight/or watertight. Section outlines

tests for watertightness and gastightness (smoke test and peppermint test).

P2503.6 Water-supply system testing: When the water supply system (or a part of it) is completed, the system (or the part) must be tested and proved tight under a water pressure not less than the working pressure of the system. For nonplastic piping systems, a test by air of not less than 50 psi can be used. Potable water must be used for the test.

Comments

Alternative Air Test

Another method that may be used when performing a 5 psi air test on a DWV system (in addition to using a mercury manometer) is to use a pressure gauge calibrated in $^{1}/_{10}$ lb. increments for 15 minutes. This method provides a faster way to detect a leak.

International Plumbing Code–2006

312.1 Required tests: The permit holder must make the applicable tests prescribed in IPC-2006 Sections 312.2 through 312.9 to determine compliance with this code and must give reasonable notice to the code official when the work is ready for testing. The equipment, material, power, and labor necessary for the inspection and test must be furnished by the permit holder, and the permit holder shall be responsible for determining that the work will withstand the pressure prescribed in the tests. All plumbing system piping must be tested with water or air. After the plumbing fixtures have been set and their traps filled with water, the entire drainage system shall be submitted to final tests. The code official shall require the removal of any cleanouts if necessary to ascertain if the pressure has reached all parts of the system.

Plumbing Fixtures

IRC–2006

P2701.1 General: Fixtures, faucets, and fixture fittings must be made of approved materials and have impervious and smooth surfaces. They must be free from defects and concealed fouling surfaces and must have an adequate supply of potable water to flush and keep fixtures in a clean and sanitary condition without danger of backflow or cross connection.

ADA Requirements

Comments

The Americans with Disabilities Act requires accessible toilet facilities in buildings open to the public. Light commercial contractors should acquaint themselves with the Act. "ADAAG" stands for Americans with Disabilities Act Accessibility Guidelines. To order ADA material or ask questions about the Act, call the ADA Technical Assistance Center at 1-800-949-4232 or visit the ADA website (**www.ada.gov**).

Industry Standards

Means ADA Compliance Pricing Guide, **Second Edition**
(RSMeans)

Accessible Toilet Stalls

ADAAG Reference
604, Water Closets and Toilet Compartments

Where Applicable
All accessible toilet rooms with at least one stall.

Design requirements:

- 56" from wall behind wall-hung WC to obstruction or wall in front of WC (59" if floor-mounted WC); 60" from wall beside WC to obstruction on other side of WC.
- WC centerline 16" to 18" from the wall.
- Top of toilet seat 17" to 19" a.f.f. Seats that spring automatically to upright position are not acceptable.
- Flush valve on the approach side.
- Grab bars 33" to 36" a.f.f., 1½" from wall, 42" long minumum at side wall starting 12" maximum from rear wall, 36" long minimum at rear wall extending 12" from center of WC in one direction and 24" in other.
- 12" clearance above grab bars, 1½" clearance below from any protruding object.
- Grab bar fittings tight so grab bars will not turn.
- Toilet paper dispenser 7" to 9" in front of WC, 14" to 19" a.f.f.
- Stall door with 32" clear opening, accessible hardware, self-closing hinge if out-swinging.

- 60" wide by 56" minimum clear inside dimension for wall-mounted WC (60" x 59" for floor-mounted WC), with door swing not swinging in to these dimensions.
- 9" minimum a.f.f. toe clearance extending 6" under the front and one side partitions (not required if stall is 66"+ wide and 65"+ deep).
- Coat hook within reach range 48" a.f.f.

Design Suggestions

It is usually recommended that the end toilet be used for the accessible stall, so the door can swing in, and there is sufficient space on the latch side. Also, grab bars can be attached to the wall rather than to a partition. Be sure that grab bars are anchored to either framing or blocking, so that they meet the minimum structural strength requirements (250 lbs. minimum). If the toilet can be reused, but is too low, a raised seat can be installed. If the flush valve is on the wrong side, you may have to replace the tank or valve system.

ADA-Compliant Restroom

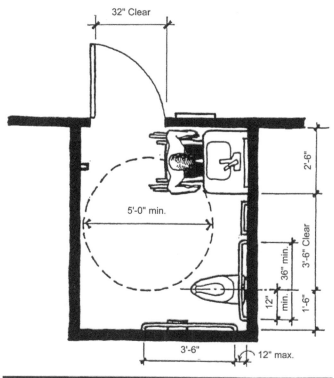

Figure 14.2   RSMeans, *Means ADA Pricing Guide*

Industry Standards
Means ADA Compliance Pricing Guide,
Second Edition
(RSMeans)

Lavatories and Mirrors
ADAAG References

213.3.4, Lavatories

305, Clear Floor or Ground Space

306, Knee and Toe Clearance

308, Reach Ranges

309, Operable Parts

603.2, Clear Floor Space

603.3, Mirrors

603.4, Coat Hooks and Shelves

606, Lavatories and Sinks

Where Applicable
At least one in all public toilet rooms.

Design Requirements:

- 30" wide by 48" front approach to sink extending 19" maximum under sink.
- 34" maximum to rim, 27" clear knee space below bowl starting at 8" from front.
- Pipes wrapped with insulation or configured to protect against contact.
- Faucets operable with closed fist (electronic sensor faucets acceptable); self-closing faucets to remain on for at least ten seconds.
- Mirrors and shelves over sink 40" a.f.f. maximum.
- Dispensers (such as soap dispensers) operable with a closed fist, 48" a.f.f. if sink protrudes no more than 20" from wall. Otherwise 44".

Design Suggestions
If a sink is located in the only accessible bathroom or in a high-use bathroom, and is not accessible due to insufficient knee clearance below, it might be cheaper to replace it than to modify it or change its height. It is possible to use standard models to meet apron height and knee space requirements. They are not only less costly, but are also easier to install and minimize the stigma and visual disruption of having one so called "handicapped" sink in a row of standard sinks. (This is also true for tilted "HP" mirrors.) At least one mirror must be installed with its bottom edge no more than

40" a.f.f., if over a counter. The accessible height mirror does not have to be above the accessible sink. If it is not above a sink, it must start at 35" a.f.f., maximum.

Since soap dispensers are almost always over the sink, they might have to be lowered.

Ed. Note: Chapter 13, "Specialties," contains more information on accessible showers, grab bars, and accessories.

Installation
IRC–2006

P2705 General: The installation of fixtures must conform to the following criteria:

1. Floor outlets or floor-mounted outlets must be secured to the drainage connection and to the floor when they are so designed, with fasteners made of brass, copper, or other corrosion-resistant material.
2. Wall-hung fixtures must be rigidly supported so that the strain is not transferred to the plumbing system.
3. Contact area must be watertight where fixtures come in contact with walls.
4. Plumbing fixtures must be accessible.
5. The centerline of bidets and water closets must be no less than 15" from adjacent walls or partitions, or no less than 30" center to center from the bidet or water closet next to it. There should be 21" clearance in front of the water closet, bidet, or lavatory to any fixture, wall, or door.
6. Piping, fixture, or equipment location must not interfere with the operation of doors or windows.
7. In flood-prone areas, plumbing fixtures must be installed according to IRC-2006 Section R323.1.5.

Comments
If the plumber purchases and installs the plumbing fixtures, the installation is much more likely to be guaranteed than if the homeowner purchases the fixtures.

P2708.1 General: Showers must have at least 900 square inches for floor area and be of sufficient size to draw a circle with a diameter of 30" or more. Hinged shower doors will open outward. The wall area above built-in tubs that have installed showerheads and in-shower compartments must be constructed according to the requirements of IRC-2006 Section R702.4. Also provides exceptions for fold-down seats and requirements for 22" unobstructed access and egress opening.

P2708.2 Water-supply riser: The riser from the shower valve to the shower head outlet must be secured to the permanent structure.

P2708.3 Shower control valves: Showers and tub/shower combinations must be equipped with control valves that meet code requirements.

P2708.4 Hand Showers: These must comply with and provide backflow protection according to ASME A112.18.1 or CSA B125.1.

P2709.1 Construction: Shower receptors must have a finished curb threshold that is no less than 1" below the sides and back of the receptor, a curb between 2" and 9" deep when measured from the top of the curb to the top of the drain, and a finished floor that must slope uniformly toward the drain meeting certain criteria. Floor drains must be flanged to provide a watertight joint in the floor.

P2709.2 Lining required: The walls and floor framing that adjoin on-site built-up shower receptors must be lined with sheet lead, copper, or a plastic liner material that complies with ASTM D 4068 or ASTM D 4551. The lining material must extend at least 3" beyond or around the rough jambs and 3" above finished thresholds.

Comments

Hot mop materials are not recommended due to their brittleness and lack of flexibility—both in showers and on exterior decks (on wood framing) where high water levels can migrate into structural components.

Prefabricated Showers & Shower Compartments

International Plumbing Code–2006

417.1 Approval: Prefabricated showers and shower compartments shall conform to ANSI Z124.2, ASME A112.19.9 or CSA B45.5. Shower valves for individual showers must conform to the requirements of IPC-2006 Section 424.3.

417.2 Water supply riser: Every water supply riser from the shower valve to the shower head outlet shall be attached to the structure in an approved manner.

417.3 Shower waste outlet: Waste outlets serving showers must be at least 1½" in diameter and have removable strainers not less than 3" in diameter with strainer openings not less than ¼". Where each shower space is not provided with an individual waste outlet, the waste outlet must be located and the floor pitched so that waste from one shower does not flow over the floor area serving another shower. Waste outlets shall be fastened to the waste pipe in an approved manner.

417.4 Shower compartments: All shower compartments shall have a minimum of 900 square inches of interior cross-sectional area. Shower compartments shall not be less than 30" in minimum dimension measured from the finished interior dimension of the compartment, exclusive of fixture valves, showerheads, soap dishes, and safety grab bars or rails. The minimum required area and dimension shall be measured from the finished interior dimension at a height equal to the top of the threshold and at a point tangent to its centerline (continued to no less than 70" high), except as required in Section 404.

417.4.1 Wall area: The wall area above built-in tubs with installed showerheads and in-shower compartments shall be of noncorrosive, smooth, waterproof materials to a height not less than 6' above the room floor level, and not less than 70" where measured from the floor at the drain. Such walls must form a watertight joint with each other and with either the tub, receptor, or shower floor.

417.4.2. Access: The access and egress opening of the shower compartment must have a minimum unobstructed width of 22".

417.5 Shower floors or receptors: Floor surfaces shall be constructed of impervious, noncorrosive, waterproof materials.

417.5.1 Support: Floors or receptors under shower compartments shall be on a smooth and structurally sound base that supports them.

417.5.2 Shower lining: Except where prefabricated receptors have been provided, floors under shower compartments must be watertight, lined by materials complying with IPC-2006 Sections 417.5.2.1 through 417.5.2.4. These liners must turn up on all sides at least 2" above the finished threshold level and must be recessed and fastened to an approved backing according to code. Liners must be pitched with a 2% slope toward the fixture drains.

Exception: Floor surfaces under showerheads provided for rinsing laid directly on the ground are not required to comply with this section.

417.6 Glazing. Windows and doors within a shower enclosure shall conform to the safety glazing requirements of the IBC-2006.

Lavatories (Bathroom Sinks)
IRC-2006

P2711 Lavatories

P2711.1 Approval: Lavatories must conform to ANSI Z124.3, ASME A112.19, or CSA B45.

P2711.2 Cultured marble lavatories: Vanity tops made of cultured marble with integral lavatories shall comply with ANSI Z124.3 or CSA B45.5.

P2711.3 Lavatory waste outlets: Lavatories must have waste outlets that are not less than 1¼" in diameter. A device must be provided to restrict the clear opening of the waste outlet.

P2711.4 Movable lavatory systems: These must comply with ASME A112.19.12.

Water Closets (Toilets)
International Plumbing Code-2006

420.1 Approval: Water closets shall conform to the water consumption requirements of Section 604.4 and shall conform to ANSI Z124.4, ASME A112.19.2M, CSA B45.1, CSA B45.4, or CSA B45.5. Water closets shall conform to the hydraulic performance requirements of ASME A112.19.6. Water closet tanks shall conform to ANSI Z124.4, ASME A112.19.2, ASME A112.19.9, CSA B45.1, CSA B45.4 or CSA B45.5. Electro-hydraulic water closets must comply with ASME 112.19.13.

420.2 Water closets for public or employee toilet facilities: These water closet bowls must be of the elongated type.

420.3 Water closet seats: Water closets shall be equipped with smooth, nonabsorbent seats. All water closet seats for public or employee facilities must be of the hinged open-front type. Integral water closet seats shall be of the same material as the fixture. Water closet seats shall be sized for the water closet bowl type.

420.4 Water closet connections: A 4" x 3" closet bend shall be acceptable, and where a 3" bend is used

on water closets, a 4" x 3" flange must be installed for the fixture horn.

IRC-2006

P2712.1 Approval: Water closets shall conform to code. Those that have an invisible seal and unventilated space or walls must be completely washed at each discharge. Water closets are not permitted to backflow contents of the bowl into the flush tank.

P2712.2 Flushing devices required: Water closets must be provided with a flush tank, flushometer tank, or flushometer valve designed to supply sufficient water flow to flush the contents of the fixture, to cleanse the fixture, and refill the fixture trap according to ASME A112.19.2 and ASME A112.19.6.

P2712.5 Overflows in flush tanks: Flush tanks must be provided with overflows discharging to the water closet that is connected to them, and such overflow must be adequate to prevent flooding the tank at the maximum rate at which tanks are supplied with water.

P2712.7 Water closet seats: Water closets must be equipped with seats that are made of smooth, nonabsorbent material. The seats must be properly sized for the water closet bowl type.

Bathtubs
IRC-2006

P2713.1 Bathtub waste outlets and overflows: Bathtubs shall have outlets and overflows at least 1½" wide, and the waste outlet must be equipped with an approved stopper.

Sinks (Kitchen)
IRC-2006

P2714.1 Sink waste outlets: Sinks must have waste outlets that are at least 1½" wide. A device must be provided to restrict the clear opening of the waste outlet.

Dishwashing Machines
IRC-2006

P2717.1 Protection of water supply: The water supply for dishwashers must be protected by an air gap or integral backflow protector.

P2717.2 Sink and dishwasher: A sink and

dishwasher are allowed to discharge through a single 1.5" trap. The discharge pipe from a dishwasher must be increased to a minimum of 0.75" wide and must be connected with a wye fitting to the sink tail piece. The dishwasher waste line must rise and be securely fastened to the underside of the counter before it connects to the sink tail pipe.

Low-Flow Showerheads & Faucet Aerators

Green Home Improvements
(RSMeans)

Water-efficient showerheads restrict water flow to 1.5 to 2.5 gallons per minute, compared to older models that consume up to 5 gallons per minute, sometimes even more. Although all models, even the most luxurious-looking showerheads on the market, are required by law to use no more than 2.5 gallons of water per minute, performance varies considerably.

New faucets come equipped with aerators, small screen-type devices that reduce water flow. By adding air into the water, aerators produce a flow/pressure sufficient for household uses, while reducing the amount of water consumed.

Aerator flow rates range from 0.7 to 2.5 gallons per minute (gpm). As a rule, bathroom sinks generally require slightly lower flow rates than kitchen sinks.

Green Plumbing Fixtures

Industry Standards

Green Building: Project Planning & Cost Estimating, Second Edition
(RSMeans)

Humans cannot live without water, but the Western world's practice of using exorbitant amounts of drinking-quality water to transport sewage is not a sustainable practice. This is becoming increasingly evident as the population grows, and water becomes increasingly scarce in the dry regions of the United States. Plumbing fixtures that use low or no water are available from a number of manufacturers. These include:

- Composting toilets, waterless urinals, and low-flow toilets (models range from 0.8–1.6 gallons per flush, including standard gravity-flush, pressure-assist models, and dual flush toilets, which can deliver either a 1.6 gallon or a 0.8 gallon flush, as needed).
- Low-flow showerheads (various models using less than 2.5 gallons per minute).

- Low-flow faucets (using less than 2.5 gallons per minute) and metered faucets (to ensure that faucets in public bathrooms will not be left on).
- Shutoff valves for kitchen faucets and showerheads that enable the temperature setting to be "saved" while the water is temporarily shut off.

Clothes Washers

IRC–2006

P2718.1 Waste connection: The discharge from a clothes washing machine must be through an air break.

Clothes Dryers

IRC–2006

G2438.1 (613.1) General: Clothes dryers must be tested in accordance with ANSI Z21.5.1 and must be installed in accordance with installation instructions from the manufacturer.

Clothes Dryer Exhaust

G2439.1 (614.1) Installation: Exhaust systems for clothes dryers must conform to manufacturer's instructions. These systems must be independent of all other systems and must convey moisture and any products of combustion to the outside of the building.

G2439.5 (614.6) Clothes dryer ducts: Exhaust ducts for domestic clothes dryers must have a smooth interior finish. The ducts must be at least 4" wide. The exhaust system must be supported and secured in place. The male end of the duct at overlapped duct joints must extend in the direction of air flow. Transition ducts used to connect the appliance to the exhaust system must be made of metal and must be no more than 8' long, and listed and labeled for the application. Transition ducts must not be concealed within construction.

G2439.5.1. (614.6.1) Maximum length: Clothes dryer exhaust ducts cannot be longer than 25' from the dryer location to the outlet terminal. The maximum length of the duct will be reduced 2.5' for each 45° bend, and 5' for each 90° bend.

Exception: The maximum length of the exhaust duct, including any transition duct, will be allowed to be in accordance with a dryer manufacturer's installation instructions, where the make and model of dryer is known.

Comments

The National Fire Protection Agency's *National Fuel Gas Code* also covers clothes dryers, including clearance, exhausting, and make-up air.

Water Heaters

IRC–2006

M2005 Water Heaters

M2005.1 General: Water heaters must be installed using manufacturer's installation instruction and code requirements. Water heaters installed in an attic must conform to the requirements of Section M1305.1.3. Gas-fired water heaters must conform to Chapter 24 requirements. Domestic electric water heaters must conform to UL 174 or UL 1453, commercial electric water heaters must conform to UL 1453, and oil-fired water heaters must conform to UL 732.

M2005.2 Prohibited locations: Fuel-fired water heaters must not be installed in a room used as a

storage closet. Water heaters located in a bathroom or bedroom must be installed in a sealed enclosure so that combustion air will not be taken from the living space. Direct-vent water heaters are not required within an enclosure.

M2005.2.1 Water heater access: Access to water heaters that are located in an attic or underfloor crawl space can be through a closet in a bathroom or sleeping room where ventilation conforms to code.

M2005.3 Electric water heaters: These must also be installed according to IRC-2006 Chapters 33–43.

M2005.4 Supplemental water-heating devices: Potable water heating devices using refrigerant-to-water heat exchangers must be approved and installed according to manufacturer's instructions.

P2801 Required: Each dwelling must have an approved automatic water heater and other type of domestic water-heating system that can supply hot water to plumbing fixtures and appliances intended for bathing, washing, or culinary purposes. Storage tanks must be built of noncorrosive metal or lined with noncorrosive material.

Hot Water Consumption Rates

Plumbing — R2240 Plumbing Fixtures

R224000-10 Hot Water Consumption Rates

Type of Building	Size Factor	Maximum Hourly Demand	Average Day Demand
Apartment Dwellings	No. of Apartments:		
	Up to 20	12.0 Gal. per apt.	42.0 Gal. per apt.
	21 to 50	10.0 Gal. per apt.	40.0 Gal. per apt.
	51 to 75	8.5 Gal. per apt.	38.0 Gal. per apt.
	76 to 100	7.0 Gal. per apt.	37.0 Gal. per apt.
	101 to 200	6.0 Gal. per apt.	36.0 Gal. per apt.
	201 up	5.0 Gal. per apt.	35.0 Gal. per apt.
Dormitories	Men	3.8 Gal. per man	13.1 Gal. per man
	Women	5.0 Gal. per woman	12.3 Gal. per woman
Hospitals	Per bed	23.0 Gal. per patient	90.0 Gal. per patient
Hotels	Single room with bath	17.0 Gal. per unit	50.0 Gal. per unit
	Double room with bath	27.0 Gal. per unit	80.0 Gal. per unit
Motels	No. of units:		
	Up to 20	6.0 Gal. per unit	20.0 Gal. per unit
	21 to 100	5.0 Gal. per unit	14.0 Gal. per unit
	101 Up	4.0 Gal. per unit	10.0 Gal. per unit
Nursing Homes		4.5 Gal. per bed	18.4 Gal. per bed
Office buildings		0.4 Gal. per person	1.0 Gal. per person
Restaurants	Full meal type	1.5 Gal./max. meals/hr.	2.4 Gal. per meal
	Drive-in snack type	0.7 Gal./max. meals/hr.	0.7 Gal. per meal
Schools	Elementary	0.6 Gal. per student	0.6 Gal. per student
	Secondary & High	1.0 Gal. per student	1.8 Gal. per student

For evaluation purposes, recovery rate and storage capacity are inversely proportional. Water heaters should be sized so that the maximum hourly demand anticipated can be met in addition to allowance for the heat loss from the pipes and storage tank.

Figure 14.3

P2801.2 Installation: Water heaters must be installed according to IRC-2006 Chapters 20, 24, and 28.

P2801.4 Prohibited locations: Water heaters must be located in accordance with IRC-2006 Chapter 20.

Installation

International Plumbing Code–2006

502.1 General: Water heaters shall be installed in accordance with the manufacturer's installation instructions. Oil-fired water heaters must comply with the IPC-2006 and the International Mechanical Code, gas-fired water heaters must comply with the International Fuel Gas Code, and electric water heaters must comply with the IPC-2006 and the ICC Electrical Code.

502.2 Rooms used as a plenum: Water heaters using solid, liquid or gas fuel shall not be installed in a room containing air-handling machinery when such room is used as a plenum.

502.3 Water heaters installed in attics: Attics containing a water heater must have an opening and unobstructed passageway, no less than 30" high and 22" wide (and not more than 20 feet long) to the water heater. The passageway shall have continuous solid flooring no less than 24" wide. At the front or service side of the water heater, a level service space at least 30" deep and 30" wide must be present. The clear access opening dimensions shall be a minimum of 20" by 30" where such dimensions are large enough to allow removal of the water heater.

502.5 Seismic supports: Where necessary according to the IBC, water heater supports shall be designed and installed for the seismic forces in accordance with the IBC.

Tankless Water Heaters

Green Home Improvement
(RSMeans)

Also known as *instantaneous* or *on-demand* water heaters, tankless water heaters (TWHs) are surprisingly compact units. Most are designed to meet the needs of either an entire household or a laundry room or bathroom. Even smaller, point-of-use models, commonly referred to as *under-the-sink* units, supply individual faucets.

Like conventional storage water heaters, TWHs are designed to provide hot water 24 hours a day, 365 days a year. However, they meet this need without the standby losses of storage tank heaters because they do not store hot water. They generate it as it's needed. When a hot water faucet is turned on, cold water begins to flow into the water heater. A flow sensor inside the TWH detects water flow and sends a signal to a tiny computer inside the unit. It, in turn, sends a signal to the gas burner or electric heating element in the water heater, turning on the heat source. As a result, water flowing through the heat exchanger in the TWH is rapidly brought up to temperature—increasing it from around 50°F to 120°F in a matter of seconds.

Although tankless water heaters offer many benefits over storage water heaters, they do have a few disadvantages worth noting. One problem is that although they produce a steady stream of hot water, they may not be able to produce enough hot water to meet everyone's needs at once when household demand is high. If hot water is being used at several locations simultaneously, water temperature at the various points of use may decline. Someone taking a shower may experience a drop in water temperature if another family member is washing dishes. (The same can occur, however, when using a traditional storage water heater.)

Comments

There are several measures that can be used to ensure enough hot water output from a TWH. Water-conserving practices, such as the installation of water-efficient showerheads and replacement of old appliances with water-efficient models, will decrease the amount of hot water needed at a given time. Purchase the highest output TWH model available or install two or more smaller tankless water heaters.

Insulating Water Heaters & Pipes

Green Home Improvement
(RSMeans)

Water Heater Blankets

The first step in making a water heater more efficient is to wrap it with an insulating water heater blanket. The most common insulation blankets are made from fiberglass with a vinyl plastic facing (on one or two sides) and are rated at R-10. Choose one with an insulating value of at least R-8. (R is a measure of resistance to heat movement; the higher the R-value, the better.)

If the insulation in the water tank's wall is less than R-15, it's generally worth adding an insulation blanket. The R-value may be posted on the water heater. If not, check with the installer or the manufacturer's customer service department.

Pipe Insulation

Insulating hot water pipes will save energy and money. Pipe insulation comes in two basic varieties, foam sleeves that fit over hot water pipes and small rolls of fiberglass that are wrapped around the pipes. Foam sleeves fit on pipes quickly and easily and are therefore the product of choice for most homeowners. They come in 6-foot sections for ¾- and ½-inch pipe, split down one side, which makes it easy to fit them around the pipes. Once you've installed a section of insulation, pull the clear plastic tape off the seam so the sides stick together. If you need to cut the insulation, use a sharp serrated knife or a pair of heavy-duty scissors. When you encounter angles in the pipes, cut a piece of insulation to fit to the corner. Cut the ends at a 45° angle so that they fit snugly against each other where pipes bend.

If the water heater has a heat trap, an S-shaped flexible copper pipe that leads from the top of the water heater to the hot water lines (to reduce convective heat loss), insulate that portion of the hot water pipe using fiberglass wrap insulation.

Water Heater Relief Valve

IRC–2006

P2803.1 Relief valves required: Appliances and equipment used for heating water or storing hot water must be protected by a separate pressure relief valve and separate temperature relief valve or a combination pressure-and-temperature-relief valve.

International Plumbing Code–2006

504.4 Relief valve: All storage water heaters operating above atmospheric pressure must have an approved, self-closing pressure relief valve and temperature relief valve or combination thereof. The relief valve must conform to ANSI Z21.22 and must not be used as a means of controlling thermal expansion.

504.4.1 Installation: Such valves must be installed in the shell of the water heater tank. Temperature relief valves must be located in the tank so they'll be triggered by the top 6" of water in the tank. For installations with separate storage tanks, the valves must be installed on the tank and there can't be any type of valve between the water heater and the storage tank. There must not be a check valve or

shutoff valve between a relief valve and the heater or tank served.

504.5 Relief valve approval: Temperature and pressure relief valves and energy cutoff devices must bear the label of an approved agency. They must have a maximum temperature setting of 210°F and a pressure setting not exceeding the tank or water heater manufacturer's rated working pressure or 150 psi, whichever is less. The relieving capacity of each relief valve shall equal or exceed the heat input to the water heater or storage tank.

504.6 Requirements for discharge piping: Lists requirements for the discharge piping serving a pressure relief valve, temperature relief valve or combination thereof.

Automatic Fire Sprinklers

Comments

Residential automatic sprinklers are not mandatory in many jurisdictions for one- and two-family residences. While sprinklers are not usually required in private residences, they are typically mandated for many light commercial buildings. Depending on local codes, buildings such as small office buildings, shops, educational, day-care or health-care buildings, taverns, restaurants, or other similar establishments may need sprinklers. The most current requirements of the *International Building Code* delineates what is required for specific usages in Section 903 (Automatic Sprinkler Systems) and 904 Alternative Automatic Fire Extinguishing Systems). Details on smoke detectors may be found in Section 907 (Fire Alarm and Detection Systems).

There are basically five types of sprinkler systems: Wet Pipe, Dry Pipe, Pre-Action, Deluge, and Firecycle.

Wet-pipe systems are by far the most common, and work by using automatic sprinklers attached to piping containing water under pressure. When the heat from a fire melts a fusible link, the water is released onto the fire. This system is used where there is no danger of freezing.

Dry-pipe systems are used in unheated areas, such as parking garages, and have automatic sprinklers with piping containing air under pressure. When the sprinkler head opens, the air is released, and water flows from the piping.

Pre-action systems are used where the accidental discharge of water would be very damaging. The piping is dry, containing low pressure air, and operates quickly

(continued)

Wet-Pipe Sprinkler System

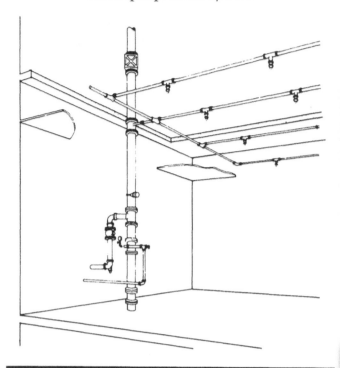

Figure 14.4

RSMeans, *Plumbing Estimating Methods*, Third Edition

Water Supply & Distribution

International Plumbing Code–2006

Section 602—Water Required

602.1 General: Every structure for human occupancy or habitation equipped with plumbing fixtures must be provided with a potable supply of water in the amounts and at the pressures specified in this chapter.

Section 603—Water Service

603.1 Size of water service pipe: The water service pipe shall be sized to supply water to the structure in the quantities and at the pressures required in this code. The minimum diameter of water service pipe shall be ¾".

Comments

Water Service Pipe

The water service pipe should not only be a minimum of ¾", but also should not be smaller than the largest portion of the water main after the outlet of the metering device (or main shut-off valve if a meter is not provided). It makes no sense to have a 1" or 1½" inside main if supply piping is only ¾".

---

to minimize fire and water damage. The water supply valve is opened by fire detection equipment, and not by a fusible link.

Deluge systems are very similar to pre-action systems in that they both use fire detection equipment and a main valve. However, deluge systems use open sprinklers instead of closed ones. They are used where flammable material can cause fire to spread quickly.

Firecycle systems cycle on and off while controlling a fire by utilizing heat detectors and an electrical control panel. Water cannot flow until the heat detector activates, so these systems are used where water damage must be kept to a minimum.

Ed. Note: Also refer to National Fire Protection Association 13D, Standard for the Installation of Sprinkler Systems in One- and Two-Family Dwellings and Manufactured Homes.

IRC–2006

P2901.1 Potable water required: Dwelling units must have supplies of potable water in the pressures and amounts listed in this chapter. In buildings with both potable and nonpotable water systems, each system must be clearly marked. A nonpotable outlet that could be confused with a drinking outlet must be posted.

P2902.1 General: A potable water supply system must be designed and installed in a way that prevents contamination into the potable water supply from nonpotable elements. Connections to the potable water supply that could compromise that supply are not allowed, neither are cross-connections between individual water supplies and potable public water supplies.

P2902.2 Plumbing fixtures: The supply lines and fittings for every fixture must be installed to prevent backflow.

P2902.3 Backflow protection: Backflow protection must be provided in accordance to IRC-2006 Sections P2902.3.1 through P2902.3.6

International Plumbing Code–2006

608 Protection of Potable Water Supply

608.1 General: A potable water supply system shall be designed, installed, and maintained in such a manner so as to prevent contamination from nonpotable liquids, solids, or gases. Backflow preventer applications shall conform to this section.

608.2 Plumbing fixtures: The supply lines and fittings for every fixture must be installed to prevent backflow. Fixture Fittings must comply with ASME A112.18.1.

608.6 Cross-connection control: Cross connections are prohibited except where approved protective devices are installed.

608.7 Stop-and-waste valves prohibited: Combination stop-and-waste valves or cocks are not to be installed underground.

608.8 Identification of potable and nonpotable water: If both potable and nonpotable water distribution systems are present in the same building, each system must be clearly marked according to this section.

Water Distribution

> ### Comments
>
> It is good engineering practice to supply each bathroom group with ¾" service and ½" to each fixture.

IRC–2006

P2903 Water-supply system

P2903.3 Minimum pressure: The minimum static pressure at the building's entrance for private or public water service will be 40 psi.

P2903.3.1 Maximum pressure: Maximum static pressure must be 80 psi. When main pressure goes beyond 80 psi, a pressure-reducing valve that conforms to ASSE 1003 must be installed on the domestic water branch main or riser at the point at which it connects to the water-service pipe.

P2903.6 Determining water-supply fixture units: Supply load in the building water-distribution system must be determined by total load on the pipe being sized in accordance with Table P2903.6.

Drainage System

IRC–2006

P3005.1 Drainage fittings and connections: Any changes in the direction of draining pipes must be made with fittings that conform to the requirements of IRC-2006 Table P3005.1.

P3005.1.4 Water closet connection between flange and pipe: One-quarter bends that are 3" wide are acceptable for water closets or like connections, as long as a 4" x 3" flange is installed to receive the closet fixture horn. A 4" x 3" elbow is allowed with a 4" flange.

P3005.2 Drainage pipe cleanouts: Drainage pipe cleanouts must be in accordance with IRC-2006 Sections P3005.2.1 through P3005.2.11.

P3005.2.2 Spacing: Cleanouts must be installed at least every 100' in horizontal drainage lines.

P3005.2.5 Accessibility: Cleanouts must be accessible and have a minimum clearance in front of 18" on 3" or larger pipes, and a 12" clearance on smaller pipes. Concealed cleanouts must have accesses large enough to allow removal of cleanout plug and system rodding. Cleanout plugs must not be concealed by permanent finishes.

P3005.2.9 Cleanout size: Cleanouts must be the same size as the pipe they serve up to 4". For pipes larger than 4", the minimum size of the cleanout must be 4".

Indirect Waste

> ### Comments
>
> Storm systems are not a plumbing concern in one- and two-family homes with pitched roofs that funnel rainwater into exterior gutters and downspouts. However, flat-roof buildings often require a system of roof drains connected by interior piping, which pipes rain water out through the foundation to a municipal or other storm system. Local code will determine if this system is kept separate from the sanitary waste disposal system.

Vents

Industry Standards
Plumbing Estimating Methods, Third Edition
(RSMeans)

The vent piping shown in **Figure 14.5** is installed as part of the sanitary system, primarily to provide:

- A flow of air to or from a drainage system
- A circulation of air within such a system to protect trap seals from siphonage and back pressure

The vent stack, also shown in **Figure 14.5**, is any vertical vent pipe extending floor to floor, connected to the vent system to provide circulation of air to and from any part of the drainage system. The vent stack ends at a minimum of two feet above the roof. This is called the *vent terminal* or *extension*. The vent terminal is flashed with lead or copper sheet flashing to make it weather-tight. In areas of the country where freezing poses a problem, vent terminals should be at least four inches in diameter to prevent frost or snow from clogging the vent opening.

Typical Waste and Vent Installation for Water Closet, Lavatory, and Bathtub

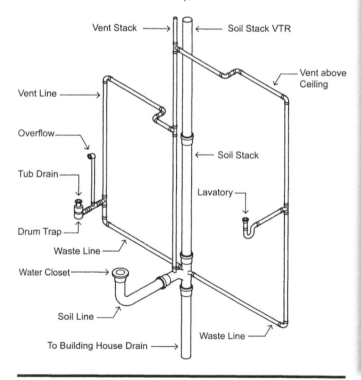

Vent Stack

Soil Stack VTR

Vent above Ceiling

Vent Line

Overflow

Tub Drain

Soil Stack

Drum Trap

Lavatory

Waste Line

Water Closet

Soil Line

Waste Line

To Building House Drain

Figure 14.5   RSMeans, *Plumbing Estimating Methods*, Third Edition

IRC–2006

Ed. Note: IRC-2006 Chapter 31, "Vents," and Chapter 32, "Traps," provide detailed requirements for the installation of vent systems and traps.

P3101 Vent systems

P3101.1 General: This chapter covers selection, piping installation, and fittings and tubings for vent systems.

P3101.2 Trap seal protection: Plumbing systems must have vent piping that allows admission or emission, so that fixture seals cannot be subjected to a pneumatic pressure differential of more than 1" of water.

P3101.2.1 Venting required: Every trap and trapped fixture must be vented according to one of the methods outlined in IRC-2006 Chapter 31.

P3101.3 Use limitations: Plumbing vent systems must not be used for purposes other than venting of the plumbing systems.

P3101.4 Extension outside a structure: Where the 97.5% value for outside design temperature is less than 0° F, vent pipes installed on the exterior of the structure must be protected against freezing. Vent terminals must be protected from frost closure in accordance with IRC-2006 Section P3103.2.

P3102 Vent stacks and stack vents

P3102.1 Required vent extension: The vent system serving each building drain must have at least one vent pipe that extends to the outdoors.

P3102.2 Installation: The required vent must be a dry vent that connects to the building drain or an extension of a drain that connects to the building drain.

P3102.3 Size: The vent must be sized according to IRC-2006 Section P3113.1.

P3103 Vent terminals

P3103.1 Roof extension: Open vent pipes that extend through a roof must be terminated at least 6" above the roof or 6" except when the roof is not being used as weather protection (in which case, the vent extensions must run at least 7' above the roof).

P3103.2 Frost closure: Where the 97.5% value for outside design temperature is less than 0°F, all vent extensions through a roof or wall must be a minimum of 3" in diameter. Any increase in the size of the vent must be made inside the structure a minimum of 1' below the roof or inside the wall.

P3103.3 Flashings and sealing: Junctures between vent pipes and roof lines must be made watertight by approved flashing. Vent extensions in walls and soffits must be rendered watertight with caulking.

P3103.4 Prohibited use: Vent terminals must not be used as supports for such items as flagpoles unless the piping has been anchored in an approved way.

P3103.5 Location of vent terminal: An open vent terminal from a drainage system must not be located less than 4' directly beneath any door, openable transom, or other air intake opening in a building. No vent terminal can be within 10' horizontally of such an opening unless it is at least 2' above the top of such opening.

P3103.6 Extension through the wall: Vent terminals extending through the wall must end at a minimum of 10' from the lot line and 10' above the highest adjacent grade within 10' horizontally of the vent terminal. Vent terminals must not terminate under the overhand of a structure with soffit vents. Side wall vent terminals must be protected to keep birds or rodents from entering or blocking the vent opening.

P3104 Vent connections and grades

P3104.1 Connection: Individual branch and circuit vents must connect to a vent stack, stack vent, or extend to the open air.

Exception: Individual, branch, and circuit vents must be allowed to end at an air admittance valve in accordance with IRC-2006 Section P3114.

P3104.2 Grade: Vent and branch vent pipes must be graded, connected, and supported so that moisture and condensate drains back to the soil or to the waste pipe by gravity.

P3104.3 Vent connection to drainage system: All dry vents connected to horizontal drains must be connected above the center line of the horizontal drain pipe.

P3104.4 Vertical rise of vent: All dry vents must rise 6" above the flood level rim of the highest trap or trapped fixture being vented.

P3104.5 Height above fixtures: A connection between a vent pipe and a vent stack vent must be at least 6" above the flood level rim of the highest

fixture served by the vent. Horizontal vent pipes forming branch vents must be at least 6" above the flood level rim of the highest fixture served.

P3104.6 Vent for future fixtures: Where the drainage piping has been roughed-in for future fixtures, a rough-in connection for the vent must be installed at a minimum of one-half the diameter of the drain. The vent rough-in must connect to the vent system or must be vented by other means as provided in this chapter of the IRC. The connection must be identified to indicate it is a vent.

P3114 Air admittance valves

P3114.1 General: Vent systems that use air admittance valves must comply with this section. Individual- and branch-type air admittance valves must conform to ASSE 1051. Stack-type air admittance valves must conform to ASSE 1050.

P3114.2 Installation: Valves must be installed according to requirements of this section and instruction of manufacturer. Air admittance valves must be installed after DWV testing required by Section P2503.5.1 or P2503.5.2 has been performed.

P3114.3 Where permitted: Individual vents, branch vents, circuit vents, and stack vents are allowed to end with a connection to an air admittance valve.

P3114.4 Location: The air admittance valve must be located a minimum of 4" above the horizontal branch drain being vented. Stack-types must be located at least 6" above the flood level rim of the highest fixture being vented. The air admittance valve must be located within the maximum developed length allowed for the vent. The air admittance valve must be installed a minimum of 6" above insulation materials when installed in attics.

P3114.5 Access and ventilation: Access must be provided to any air admittance valves. Valves must be located within ventilated spaces that allow air to enter the valves.

P3114.6 Size: Air admittance valves must be rated for the size of the vents to which they are connected.

P3114.7 Vent required: Within each plumbing system, a minimum of one stack vent or vent stack must extend outdoors to the open air.

Traps

Comments

Slip Joints

Slip Joints should not be allowed on the outlet (street side) of the trap. The packing may dry out, thus allowing the emittance of sewer gases into the building.

Trap Arms

IRC–2006

Section 3105 – Fixture Vents

P3105.1 Distance of trap from vent: Each fixture trap shall have a protecting vent located so that the slope and the developed length in the fixture drain from the trap weir to the vent fitting comply with IRC-2006 Table P3105.1. The exception is that the developed length of the fixture drain from the trap weir to the vent fitting for self-siphoning fixtures must not be limited.

P3105.2 Fixture drains: The total fall in a fixture drain due to pipe slope must not go beyond one pipe diameter, nor can the vent pipe connection to a fixture drain, except for water closets, be below the trap weir, except as provided in Section P3105.3.

P3105.3 Crown vent: A vent must not be installed within two pipe diameters of the trap weir.

Private Sewage Disposal

IRC–2006

P2602 Individual water supply and sewage disposal

P2602.1 General: Water-distribution and drainage systems of a building where plumbing fixtures are installed must be connected to the public water supply or sewer system, respectively. If a public water supply or sewer system is not available, an individual water supply or private sewage disposal system must be provided.

Comments

Requirements for private septic/sewer systems depend on local code and issues such as proximity to wetlands and site drainage.

Water Conservation

Industry Standards

 Green Building: Project Planning & Cost Estimating, Second Edition
(RSMeans)

Potable Water Reduction

The first line of defense in any green building project is conservation. Therefore, any use of water must involve conservation equipment. These devices are required by code in many areas of the country. They include:

- Water-saving, low-flow showerheads and toilets.
- Water-saving or automatic shut-off sinks.
- Waterless urinals (uses a chemical seal and highly polished surface to eliminate the need for flushing water).
- Recirculating dishwashers for commercial applications.
- Steam trap programs. (Since water is the basic component of steam, all steam trap programs inherently conserve water.) In commercial facilities that require steam for process, the steam condenses to become water. The percentage of water that is reused is a key component in water conservation.

Nonpotable Substitution Systems

These systems collect and use by-product water to replace potable water for various purposes. Sources of substitution, reclaimed water include:

- Storm water systems: rainwater collected in tanks for nonpotable water usage (can be used as potable water in some cases if properly filtered, in areas where air or other pollution does not create toxicity).
- Process water: can be recycled and collected for nonpotable systems.

Some of the uses for nonpotable reclaimed water include:

- Cooling systems heat sink
- Irrigation systems
- Toilet flushing
- Process cooling

Gray Water Systems

Treating gray water like black water is not the most efficient strategy. Once-through gray water from sinks and washing machines can often be reused directly for toilet flushing or for subsurface irrigation (depending on regional codes). Gray water can also be used on (nonedible) plantings after treatment with a commercial filter or site-built sand filter.

For showers or other hot-water fixtures, gray water waste heat recovery systems can capture the heat from the hot water as it goes down the drain and transfer it to incoming water. These systems are especially effective in high-use shower areas, such as in locker rooms.

Gas Piping Installation

Industry Standards
Plumbing Estimating Methods, Third Edition
(RSMeans)

Natural gas serves as an energy source for items such as boilers, burners, hot-water generators, unit heaters, etc. Gas is generally supplied to customers via gas mains supplied and maintained by local gas companies. In most cities, the gas service and meter to individual buildings is also provided by the gas company. However, the estimator (or contractor) should check with the local utility for a listing of the regulations for each particular project.

The gas system within a building is all the piping, valves, and devices starting from the gas meter. The plumber begins the distribution of piping within the building after the gas meter is installed, supplying a gas regulator if required. Gas regulators are usually required if the gas supply is at a pressure in excess of $\frac{1}{2}$ psi.

Comments

When gas is used as a fuel for cooking, clothes drying, water heating, gas logs, heating, cooling, or incineration, it is usually included as part of the plumbing installation. In many areas, the installing mechanic must be a licensed gas fitter rather than a plumber. Gas appliances such as water heaters, furnaces, boilers, incinerators, and the like must not only be vented to the outside air, but also must be provided with sufficient fresh make-up air to allow for combustion.

IRC-2006

G2406 Appliances

G2406 (303.1) General: Appliances must be located as required by this section, specific requirements in other locations in this code, and the conditions of the equipment and appliance listing.

G2415 (404) Piping system installation

G2415.1 Prohibited locations: Piping must not be installed in or through a circulating air duct, clothes chute, gas vent or chimney, ventilating duct, dumbwaiter or elevator shaft. Piping installed downstream of the point of delivery must not extend through any townhouse unit other than the unit it serves.

G2415.2 (404.2) Piping in solid partitions and walls: Concealed piping must not be located in solid partitions and solid walls unless they are installed in casing or in a chase.

G2415.3 (404.3) Piping in concealed locations: Parts of the piping system installed in concealed locations must not have unions, right and left couplings, tubing fittings, bushings, compression couplings and swing joints made by combinations of fittings, with the exception of fittings listed for use in concealed locations and tubing joined by brazing.

G2415.4 (404.4) Piping though foundation wall: Underground piping must be encased in a protective pipe sleeve. The annular space between the gas piping and the sleeve must be sealed.

G2415.7 (404.7) Above-ground piping outdoors: Piping that is outdoors and above ground must be elevated at least $3\frac{1}{2}$" above the ground or roof it is installed on. It must be securely supported and located where it can be guarded from physical damage. Where it passes through an outside wall, the piping must be protected against corrosion with an inert material. Where the piping is encased in a protective pipe sleeve, the annular space between the gas piping and the sleeve must be sealed.

G2415.9 (404.9) Minimum burial depth: Underground piping systems will be installed at least 12" below grade, except individual outside lines to grills, lights, and other appliances (which must be installed a minimum of 8" below finished grade).

G 2415.11 (404.11) Piping underground beneath buildings: Piping is not allowed to be installed beneath buildings unless the piping is encased in a conduit of wrought iron, steel pipe, or plastic pipe designed to withstand the superimposed loads. Conduits must extend into an occupiable section of the building. At the point where the conduit ends in the building, the space between the conduit and the gas piping must be sealed to prevent any entrance of gas leaks. Conduits must extend no less than 4" outside the building, must be vented above grade to the outdoors, and must be installed to prevent the entrance of water and insects. Conduits must be guarded against corrosion as per Section G2415.8.

G2415.12 (404.12) Outlet closures: Gas outlets that do not connect to appliances must be capped gastight.

Exception: Devices that are listed and labeled flush-mounted-type quick-disconnect and labeled gas convenience outlets must be installed in accordance with the manufacturer's installation instructions.

G2415.14 (404.14) Plastic pipe: The installation of plastic pipe must comply with IRC-2006 Sections G2415.4.1 through G2415.14.3.

Comments

To avoid any potential electrical build-up that could produce a spark, gas piping must be at ground potential. The gas piping is forbidden to be a grounding electrode, however, because it is possible for any grounding electrode to carry large currents that have a possibility of sparking if the piping should be opened for any reason. A difference of electrical potential between an ungrounded piping system and a grounded metal object could also pose an electric shock hazard to people coming into contact with the two systems.

Gas-Fired Hot Water System

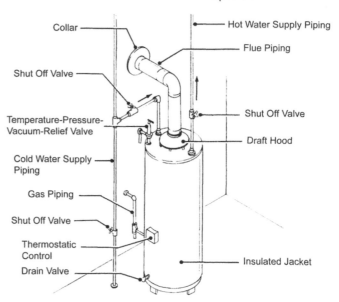

Figure 14.6

RSMeans, *Fundamentals of the Construction Process*

Table of Contents

Text in blue type indicates excerpted summaries from the International Building Code® (IBC) *and* International Residential Code® (IRC). *Please consult the IBC and IRC for complete coverage and specific wording. "Comments" (in solid blue boxes) were written by the editors, based on their own experience.*

 This icon will appear with references to green building practices.

Common Defect Allegations

- *Unsupported flexible plastic duct will kink after it settles over a few years.*

- *Sometimes condensate lines are either missing or installed too high, preventing gravity flow and causing the evaporator collector pan to overflow and stain the ceiling. The condensate overflow should be exposed to the exterior so that the owner can tell when the drain is not working. The basic condensate drain should drain into a sewer drain to prevent health hazards like Legionnaire's disease. Condensate pipe should be at least 3/4" to reduce the chance of clogging. Many building codes require condensate to drain into storm lines. Check your local code.*

- *Air flow may be insufficient due to small ducting, or heating and cooling may not have enough tonnage and Btu rating to make the building comfortable. These claims should be reviewed by a mechanical engineer who will establish calculations based on the size of the facility. Good design usually is to slightly undersize the units so that they can run without stopping for a period of time. Short starting and stopping cycles will use more energy than a continuously running system and will not properly dehumidify the air. It also creates greater temperature fluctuations and subjects the equipment to more wear and tear.*

- *Undersized exhaust fans in a shower area can cause mold buildup in bathrooms that get a lot of use. Many times a combination heat lamp/ exhaust fan provides the proper air flow without the lamp installed, but will not be adequate when the lamp is in place.*

- *Gas heaters can cause fires. However, in bench testing the heaters after a claim is made, it is usually found that the heater worked properly and was simply running during the fire. Most heaters have a series of limit switches that shut off gas and turn on the fan when the unit overheats.*

- *Other claims items include: inadequate or improperly located fresh air supplies for gas appliances in closets, inadequate working space in front of equipment, and the return air plenum partially constructed from the stairs. (On lighter shades of carpeting, the edges can turn black as the carpet acts as a filter for the return air leaking through the stringer and the wall.)*

Introduction

Usually there are no written specifications or installation drawings for the heating, cooling, or ventilation of individual homes. Notes on the architectural drawings would indicate the heating and/or cooling requirements for the occupied spaces. For light commercial properties, a more formal set of drawings and specifications is typically incorporated into the builder's plans and bid documents.

Whether or not installation plans and specifications are available at bidding time, it is understood that the installation will be sized adequately to maintain desired temperature and humidity conditions year-round.

The materials and installation will be governed by the appropriate building codes (either national or local) for the locality as set for its prevailing standards.

The type of system required will depend primarily on geographic location and use. Some buildings might require heating only, and some cooling only with an auxiliary heating backup for extraordinary weather conditions. Most locales will require a combination of heating and cooling.

Ed. Note: Refer to Chapter 14, "Plumbing," for ventilation requirements for plumbing fixtures.

The following is a list of professional organizations and other resources that establish standards for mechanical installations.

Air-Conditioning and Refrigeration Institute (ARI)
703-524-8800
www.ari.org

American Society of Mechanical Engineers (ASME)
800-843-2763
www.asme.org

American Society of Heating, Refrigerating, and Air Conditioning Engineers, Inc. (ASHRAE)
404-636-8400
www.ashrae.org
ASHRAE writes standards that set uniform methods of testing and rating equipment and establishes accepted practices for the HVAC&R industry.

American Water Works Association (AWWA)
800-926-7337
www.awwa.org

Factory Mutual
800-320-6808
www.fmglobal.com

International Association of Plumbing and Mechanical Officials (IAPMO)
909-472-4100
www.iapmo.org

National Fire Protection Association (NFPA)
617-770-3000
www.nfpa.org

Plumbing · Heating · Cooling · Contractors National Association (PHCC-NA)
703-237-8100
www.phccweb.org
Note: The *National Standard Plumbing Code* is available from this organization.

Sheet Metal & Air Conditioning Contractors' National Association (SMACNA)
703-803-2980
www.smacna.org

Solar Rating and Certification Corporation (SRCC)
321-638-1537
www.solar-rating.org

Note: The *International Plumbing Code (IPC)*, the *International Mechanical Code (IMC)*, and the *International Residential Code (IRC)* are copyrighted by and available through the International Code Council, Inc. (*ICC*). (See "Understanding Building Codes & Other Standards" at the beginning of this book for contact information.)

The *International Residential Code* excerpts in this chapter are summarized. Please consult the *IRC* for complete coverage and specific wording. The *International Building Code (IBC)* does not contain specific HVAC requirements, but references the *International Mechanical Code* and *International Fuel Gas Code*.

Ed. Note: Comments and recommendations within this chapter are not intended as a definitive resource for construction activities. For building projects, contractors must rely on the project documents and any applicable code requirements pertaining to their own particular locations.

Basic HVAC Systems

Industry Standards

HVAC: Design Criteria, Options, Selection
(RSMeans)

Heating is required in a building when the ambient temperatures are low enough to demand additional warmth for comfort. Boilers or furnaces *generate* the heat for a building; solar devices *capture, store,* and *release* heat; pipes or ducts *distribute* the heat; and convectors/radiators or diffusers are the terminal units that *deliver* the heat. A typical hydronic (hot water or steam) heating system is shown in **Figure 15.1**.

Cooling systems utilize cooler outdoor air, when available, a refrigeration cycle, or other heat rejection method to supply cool air to occupied spaces. Chilled water or cool air is distributed by pipes and ducts throughout the building to terminal units (diffusers or fan coils). These end units deliver the cooling to the desired spaces. While cooling is rarely required by code, it is almost universally expected in commercial environments. Cooling systems may be independent of heating systems (such as a simple window air conditioner) or integrated with the heating system (such as a rooftop unit).

Ventilating systems operate to provide fresh outdoor air to minimize odors and to reduce unhealthy dust or fumes. In many spaces, simple operable windows satisfy ventilation requirements. On the other hand, ventilation may be provided to a building by exhaust fans or fresh air intakes.

Air Conditioning usually combines all of the features of heating, cooling, and ventilating systems, and may also provide additional "conditioning" of the overall environment such as noise control, air cleaning (filtration), humidity control, and energy-efficient controls (free-cooling options).

The process of producing heating or cooling from generation to distribution to terminal units is common to all systems.

Basic Hydronic Heating Systems

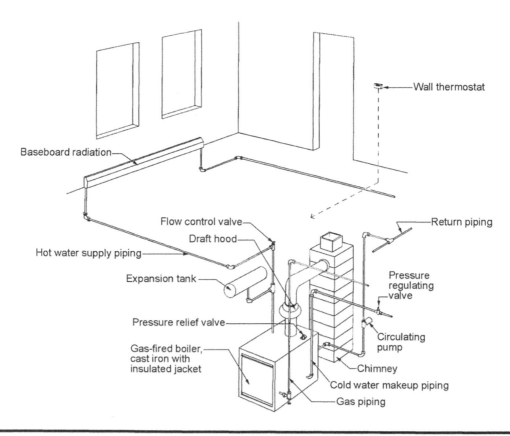

Labels: Wall thermostat, Baseboard radiation, Flow control valve, Draft hood, Hot water supply piping, Expansion tank, Pressure relief valve, Gas-fired boiler, cast iron with insulated jacket, Return piping, Pressure regulating valve, Circulating pump, Chimney, Cold water makeup piping, Gas piping

Figure 15.1

RSMeans, *HVAC: Design Criteria, Options, Selection*

Generation equipment produces heat (heating) or removes heat (cooling) to or from the building. Boilers, furnaces, or supplied steam add heat; cooling towers, chillers, or heat pumps reject heat. The equipment for generation systems is the most expensive component of the HVAC system and is generally located in the mechanical equipment room.

The warm air or cold water that the various pieces of generation equipment produce is *distributed* throughout the building. A distribution system basically consists of pipes (water or steam) or ducts (air) that take the heated or cooled medium from the equipment that generated it through the building to the terminal unit. In addition, a distribution system may have valves, dampers, and fittings.

The **terminal units**, located in the conditioned spaces, include convectors (radiators), air diffusers, and fan coil units. These units receive the air or water from the distribution system and utilize it to warm or cool the air in the space.

General Mechanical System Requirements

IRC 2006

Note: The following are summaries of the basic code requirements of the *International Residential Code*. Please consult the *IRC* for complete coverage and specific wording.

M1302.1 Listed and labeled: Appliances must be listed and labeled by an approved agency.

M1303.1 Label information: Appliances must have a permanent factory label that has either the manufacturer's name or trademark, as well as the serial and model numbers and testing seal. For electrical appliances, the electrical rating and Btu/h output must also be listed. For absorption units, the hourly rating, fuel and refrigerant type, cooling capacity, and clearances must also be listed. For fuel-burning units, the hourly rating and fuel type must be listed. For comfort heating appliances, clearances from combustible materials must additionally be listed. All labels must also include maintenance instructions and specific details on the applicable maintenance manual for further reference.

M1305.1 Appliance access for inspection service, repair, and replacement: All appliances must be accessible, without requiring the removal of permanent construction. The control side must have

30" of clearance for working space. Room heaters must have at least 18" of clearance.

M1305.1.2 Appliances in rooms: Appliances in basements, alcoves, or compartments must have an access opening and a clear passage of at least 24" wide. There must be enough room to remove the largest appliance, and at least 30" of clear area for servicing the appliance with the door open.

M1306 Clearances from combustible construction

M1306.1 Appliance clearance: Manufacturer's labeling and instructions must be followed for adequate clearance from combustible materials.

M1306.2 Clearance reduction: Clearances may be reduced according to manufacturer's instructions. There must be at least 1" of space between the type of protection and combustible wall surface.

M1307 Appliance Installation: Installation and operating instructions must remain attached to appliances. Installation must conform with label and manufacturer's instructions.

M1308.1 Mechanical systems installation—Drilling and notching: Specific IRC sections must be met for drilling or altering structural members that are wood- or steel-framed.

Vented Floor, Wall & Room Heaters

IRC 2006

M1408 Vented Floor Furnaces

M1408.1 General: Vented floor furnaces must comply with UL 729. Installation must meet UL 729, manufacturer's instructions, and these IRC requirements.

M1408.2 Clearances: Clearances must meet listing and manufacturer's requirements.

M1408.3 Location: Provides seven location requirements, including that floor registers of floor furnaces must be at least six inches away from walls. Furnace registers must be at least 12" away from doors, curtains, and other combustible items, and at least 5' away from projecting combustibles. Floor furnaces may not be installed in concrete floor construction that is built on grade.

M1408.4 Access: Access to a floor furnace must be by a foundation opening at least 18" by 24", or a trap door at least 22" by 30".

M1408.5 Installation: Provides specific installation requirement, including that thermostats are to be located in the same room as the floor furnace register. Furnaces must be at least 6" from the ground (may be reduced to 2" if sealed from water).

M1409 Vented Wall Furnaces

M1409.1 General: Wall furnaces must meet ANSI/UL 730, as well as these code requirements and manufacturer's instructions.

M1409.2 Location: Wall furnaces must not be a fire hazard to surrounding walls, doors, floors, and furnishings, and must not be located in path of door swing.

M1409.3 Installation: Wall thickness must comply with manufacturer's instructions. Ducts may not be attached. There must be a manual shut-off valve.

M1409.4 Access: There must be access for cleaning and replacement of parts.

M1410 Vented Room Heaters

M1410.1 General: Vented room heaters must comply with ASTM E 1509, UL 1482 or 896. Installation must comply with these IRC and manufacturer's requirements.

M1410.2 Floor mounting: Heaters must be installed on floors that are noncombustible or approved assemblies. Exceptions are made for heaters listed for installation on combustible floors without floor protection.

Boilers

Industry Standards

HVAC: Design Criteria, Options, Selection
(RSMeans)

Heating boilers are designed to produce steam or hot water. The water in the boilers is heated by coal, oil, gas, wood, or electricity. Some boilers have dual fuel capabilities. Boilers are manufactured from cast iron, steel, or copper.

Cast iron sectional boilers may be assembled in place or shipped to the site as a completely assembled package. These boilers can be made larger on site by adding intermediate sections. The boiler sections may be connected by push nipples, tie rods, and gaskets. Cast iron boilers are noted for their durability.

Steel boilers are usually shipped to the site completely assembled. Large steel boilers may be shipped in segments for field assembly. The components of a steel boiler consist of tubes within a shell and a combustion chamber. If the water being heated is inside the tubes, the unit is called a water tube boiler. If the water is contained in the shell and the products of combustion pass through tubes surrounded by this water, the unit is called a fire tube boiler. Water tube boilers may be manufactured with steel or copper tubes.

Electric boilers have electric resistance heating elements immersed in the water and do not fall into either category of tubular boilers. Steel boilers in the larger sizes are often slightly more efficient than cast iron and are generally constructed to be more serviceable, which with proper maintenance adds to their useful life.

IRC 2006

M2001 Boilers

M2001.1 Installation: Boiler installation must comply with manufacturer's instructions. Boilers must have nameplate, rating data, and operation instructions on them. Installers must provide control diagrams and operating instructions.

M2001.2 Clearance: Clearance must comply with the listing and label.

M2002 Operating and Safety Controls

M2002.1 Safety controls: Electrical and mechanical controls must be labeled and listed.

M2002.2 Steam boiler gauges: Boilers must have functional pressure gauges and water-gauge glass.

M2002.3 Pressure-relief valve: Boilers must have pressure-relief valves set at the maximum rate. Discharge must be by gravity to drains that are within 18".

M2003 Expansion Tanks

M2003.1 General: Boilers must have expansion tanks. Non-pressurized tanks must be attached securely and supported to handle twice the weight of the tank filled with water.

M2003.1.1 Pressurized expansion tanks: Pressurized tanks must meet the system's volume and capacity requirements.

*Ed. Note: See **Figure 15.2**, a typical boiler installation.*

Typical Boiler Installation

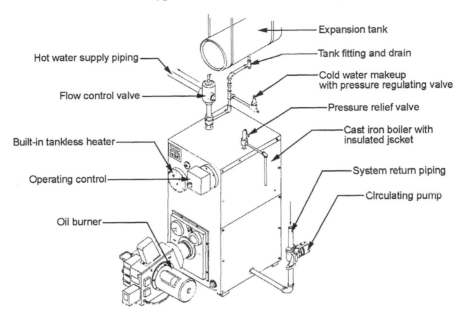

Expansion tank

Tank fitting and drain

Hot water supply piping

Cold water makeup
with pressure regulating valve

Flow control valve

Pressure relief valve

Built-in tankless heater

Cast iron boiler with
insulated jscket

Operating control

System return piping

Circulating pump

Oil burner

Figure 15.2

RSMeans, *HVAC: Design Criteria, Options, Selection*

Expansion Tanks

Industry Standards

HVAC: Design Criteria, Options, Selection
(RSMeans)

All hydronic systems undergo changes in temperature that cause the water to expand and contract. An expansion tank is always provided on each closed loop piping system, because the tank allows the water to expand into it as the water volume increases with the temperature.

Furnaces

Green Home Improvement
(RSMeans)

Conventional gas furnaces contain a combustion chamber where natural gas or propane is burned. The burner is ignited by a pilot light, a flame that burns 24 hours a day. Heat that is generated in the combustion chamber is transferred via a heat exchanger to room air that enters via the cold air return ducts. The heated air is propelled by a blower throughout the home by a warm-air duct system.

Waste gases (containing toxic pollutants) from the combustion chamber are vented to the outdoors through a flue pipe. As the hot gases rise, they create a partial vacuum in the combustion chamber. This draws room air into the fire, ensuring a continuous supply of oxygen required for proper combustion. The rise of hot air, together with the inflow of room air, is known as draft.

Conventional natural-draft furnaces are the least efficient of all furnaces. Those manufactured before 1992 have efficiencies below 78%. Many are only 55% to 65% efficient, which means that they convert only 55% to 65% of the fuel they burn into heat.

High-efficiency furnaces produce a lot more heat from the fuel they burn, saving homeowners substantially over the long haul. Most high-efficiency gas furnaces are induced-draft models—so named because they contain an energy—efficient electric fan. They draw air from outside the home into the combustion chamber and propel exhaust gases from the combustion chamber out of the house via the flue pipe.

The efficiency of induced-draft furnaces results from the use of more efficient heat exchangers, but also from an electronic ignition, which eliminates the need for a standing pilot light.

The most efficient gas furnaces on the market today are **condensing** models. These furnaces contain a second heat exchanger, which extracts additional heat from the flue gases, cooling them until the moisture they contain condenses. (Condensation of moisture releases additional heat.) Because so much

483

heat is removed by the heat exchanger, waste gases can be vented through plastic pipe, which is barely warm to the touch. The condensed moisture is often drained into a nearby floor drain, although states have different regulations on how to dispose of the condensate.

Both condensing and non-condensing furnaces are equipped with sealed combustion chambers. This feature prevents dangerous exhaust gases, such as carbon monoxide and nitrogen dioxide, from entering our homes. Replacing an old gas furnace with a highly efficient model, therefore, could also improve a home's indoor air quality.

Energy Star®-qualified models have efficiencies (listed as annual fuel utilization efficiency, or AFUE) of 83% to 97%. As a rule, the induced-draft furnaces have efficiencies in the 80% range, and induced-draft condensing furnaces are in the 90% range—with some as high as 99%. To view a list of Energy Star-qualified furnaces, log on to the Energy Star website (**www. energystar.gov**), and click on *Products*, then *Heating and Cooling* and *Furnaces*. Be sure to check out the product lists.

Oil Furnaces

Fuel oil, a product of petroleum, is burned in home furnaces in many parts of the country. It is injected into the furnace's combustion chamber through a nozzle that produces tiny droplets that mix with air to promote combustion. Many oil furnaces are designed to enhance air turbulence, which boosts combustion efficiency.

Most Energy Star-qualified oil furnaces boast efficiencies in the 83% to 86% range, with condensing oil furnaces at about 95% efficiency. All of these are much higher than oil furnaces made before 1992. (Older furnaces are typically only 50% to 60% efficient.) Although condensing models are more efficient, they're not very common. The main reason for this is that fuel oil contains many more contaminants (such as sulfur) than natural gas or propane. Condensing out of the combustion gases, these contaminants produce a fairly corrosive liquid that can damage the internal components of a furnace. For this reason, contractors often recommend against these models.

While sealed combustion chambers are widely used in high-efficiency gas furnaces, very few high-efficiency oil furnaces come with this feature. Why? Experience has shown that cold outside air drawn into the combustion chamber of an oil-fired furnace reduces combustion efficiency and may impede start-up. Because oil-furnaces are not typically sealed combustion designs,

carbon monoxide emissions can become an issue. Be sure to install carbon monoxide detectors—one on every floor of a home in areas where they can be heard, especially in or near the master bedroom.

Maintenance

According to the EPA, dirt and neglect are the main causes of heating system inefficiency and failure. To prevent problems and lower heating costs, the EPA recommends periodic professional servicing HVAC systems and cleaning or replacement of air filters in forced-air systems every month or two during the heating and cooling seasons.

Installation of Energy-Efficient Furnaces

Installing an energy-efficient furnace requires removing your old equipment. (In old houses, asbestos wrapped around boilers, furnaces, and hot water or steam pipes, or ducts, may need to be removed by a hazardous waste specialist.) Installation may also require a new flue and air intake for induced-draft models. Electrical and gas service must be temporarily disconnected and then reconnected.

Although energy-efficient furnaces are typically more expensive than less-efficient models, the higher initial cost is typically offset within a few years through lower energy bills—and provides homeowners with a hedge against rising fuel costs. State and local tax incentives or rebates from local utilities may also be available.

Water Heaters

Green Home Improvement
(RSMeans)

Although some newer models of water heaters are more efficient than in the past, older and lower-priced models waste about 20% of the energy they consume. The heat they produce escapes through the wall of the tank as the hot water sits unused for many hours at a time. (This is known as *standby loss*.)

Besides being inefficient, storage water heaters don't last very long—between 8 and 12 years. Homeowners can increase the life of their water heater by lowering the temperature to a more reasonable setting and periodically flushing sediment from the bottom of the tank and replacing the anode rod. Some of these measures also save energy.

If the water heater is more than ten years old and has not been maintained, it may be approaching the end of its useful life. If it's leaking or showing signs of rust, it definitely needs to be replaced. This might be a good opportunity to install a tankless water heater (TWH).

Gas Water Heater

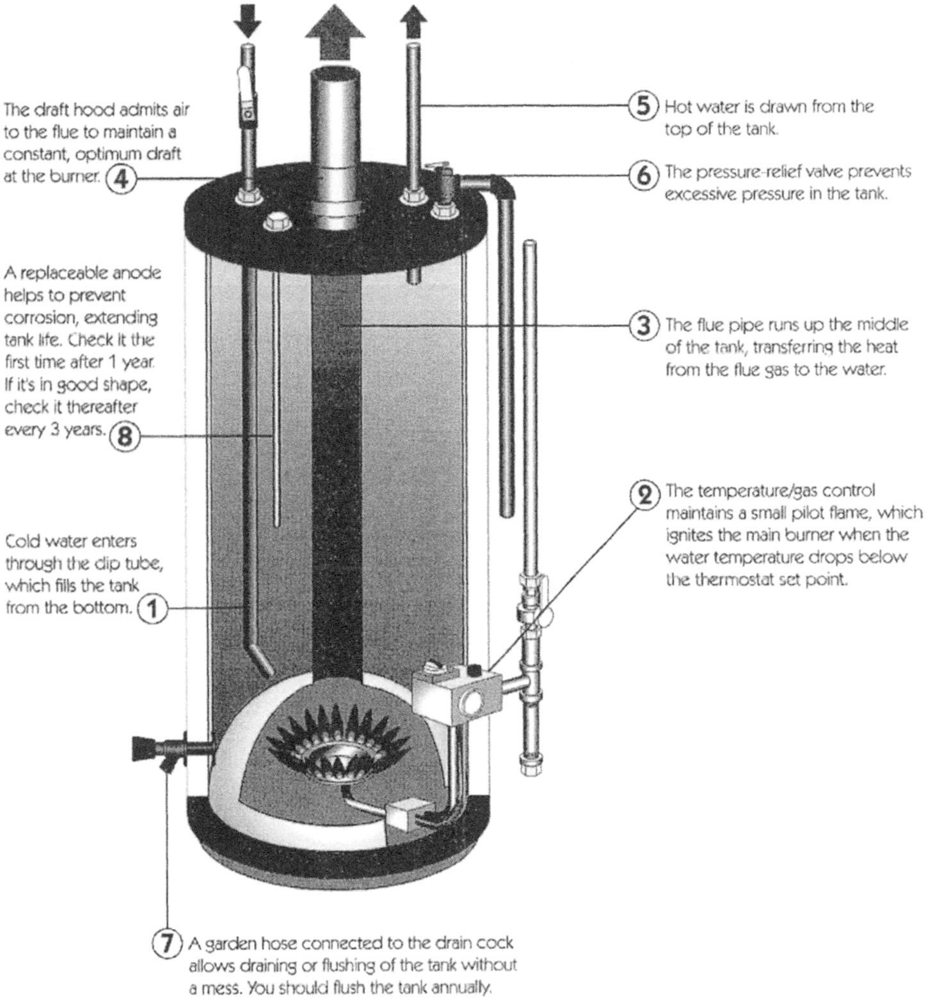

The draft hood admits air to the flue to maintain a constant, optimum draft at the burner. **(4)**

A replaceable anode helps to prevent corrosion, extending tank life. Check it the first time after 1 year. If it's in good shape, check it thereafter every 3 years. **(8)**

Cold water enters through the dip tube, which fills the tank from the bottom. **(1)**

(5) Hot water is drawn from the top of the tank.

(6) The pressure-relief valve prevents excessive pressure in the tank.

(3) The flue pipe runs up the middle of the tank, transferring the heat from the flue gas to the water.

(2) The temperature/gas control maintains a small pilot flame, which ignites the main burner when the water temperature drops below the thermostat set point.

(7) A garden hose connected to the drain cock allows draining or flushing of the tank without a mess. You should flush the tank annually.

RSMeans *How Your House Works*

Figure 15.3

Tankless Water Heater

Like conventional storage water heaters, TWHs are designed to provide hot water 24 hours a day, 365 days a year. However, they meet this need without the standby losses of storage tank heaters. (See **Figure 15.4**.) (See Chapter 14 for more coverage.)

Tankless water heaters do not suffer from standby losses because they do not store hot water; they generate it as it's needed. When a hot water faucet is turned on, cold water begins to flow into the water heater. A flow sensor inside the TWH detects water flow and sends a signal to a tiny computer inside the unit. It, in turn, sends a signal to the gas burner or electric heating element in the water heater, turning

on the heat source. As a result, water flowing through the heat exchanger in the TWH is rapidly brought up to temperature—increasing it from around 50°F to 120°F in a matter of seconds.

Because tankless water heaters eliminate standby losses, replacing an old, inefficient water heater with a sleek TWH will reduce your annual energy bills. Most sources, such as the EPA, project savings on the cost of heating water of around 20%, compared to a storage water heater.

Savings depend on several factors, primarily the efficiency of the water heater and the amount of hot water a family uses each day. For homes that use up

Tankless Electric Heater

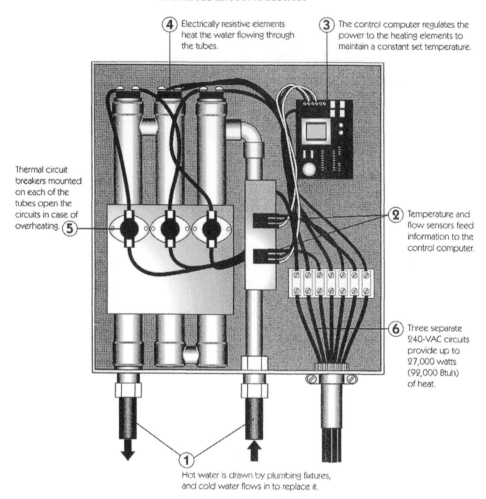

④ Electrically resistive elements heat the water flowing through the tubes.

③ The control computer regulates the power to the heating elements to maintain a constant set temperature.

Thermal circuit breakers mounted on each of the tubes open the circuits in case of overheating. **⑤**

② Temperature and flow sensors feed information to the control computer.

⑥ Three separate 240-VAC circuits provide up to 27,000 watts (92,000 Btuh) of heat.

① Hot water is drawn by plumbing fixtures, and cold water flows in to replace it.

Figure 15.4

RSMeans *How Your House Works*

Efficiency Recommendations for Electric Water Heaters from the Federal Energy Management Program (FEMP)

Electric Water Heater FEMP Efficiency Recommendation		
Storage Tank Volume)	Energy Factor[a]	Annual Energy Use[b]
Less than 60 gallons	0.93 or higher	4,721 kWh/year or less
60 gallons or more	0.91 or higher	4,825 kWh/year or less

[a] Energy Factor is an efficiency ratio of the energy supplied in heated water divided by the energy input to the water heater.

[b] Based on DOE test procedure (10 CFR 430, Sub-Part B, Appendix E). Federal Energy Management Program (FEMP) http://www.eren.doe.gov/femp/procurement/index.cfm

Figure 15.5

Courtesy of the Federal Energy Management Program (FEMP)/U.S. Department of Energy

to 41 gallons of hot water daily, the U.S. Department of Energy (DOE) estimates savings of 24%–34% on the cost of providing hot water compared to a conventional storage tank water heater. In homes that use substantially more hot water, around 86 gallons per day, the DOE estimates reduced savings, about 8%–14%. This is because there is less idle time and less standby loss with a conventional water heater when a lot of hot water is used throughout the day. For large families, then, it may make more sense to stick with an energy-efficient conventional water heater and implement other hot-water saving ideas, such as water-efficient showerheads, dishwashers, and clothes washers, to cut down the quantity of hot water used, rather than to change the way water is heated.

Even greater energy savings can be achieved by installing a tankless water heater at major points of use—for example, near the master bathroom or a washing machine or kitchen. (This reduces the length of the pipe run, which reduces the amount of hot water left in the line when the faucet is turned off.) This strategy could yield savings ranging from 27%–50%, although savings could be offset by the cost of purchasing and installing additional TWHs.

Additional economic savings also result from the long life expectancy of TWHs. According to DOE's Office of Energy Efficiency and Renewable Energy, most TWHs last at least 20 years. In addition, they are made from easy-to-replace, off-the-shelf parts, so repairing a TWH (not an option with storage water heaters) can be cheaper and could result in even longer service. In fact, a tankless water heater with periodic maintenance could outlast two or three storage water heaters.

Tankless water heaters produce a steady stream of hot water, but may not be able to produce enough hot water to meet everyone's needs at once when household demand is high.

Replacing a storage water heater with a tankless model may require rerouting or increasing the size of the exhaust (flue) pipe.

Natural gas and propane units produce fewer pollutants than electric models powered by nuclear or coal, since burning those fuels is nearly twice as efficient as making electricity. Look for a model with high energy efficiency (fuel factor) and an electronic ignition instead of a pilot light.

Ventilation & Exhaust

Ventilation

Industry Standards

HVAC: Design Criteria, Options, Selection
(RSMeans)

Building spaces must be vented for a variety of reasons. The main purpose of ventilation is to provide fresh outdoor air for the occupants. Fresh outdoor air replenishes indoor air for breathing and most noticeably reduces odors, smoke, and fumes caused by people, cooking, and manufacturing processes. All occupied rooms (apartments, offices, stores, schools, hospitals) must be properly ventilated. There are several acceptable methods of providing ventilation: operable windows, fresh outdoor air supply, exhaust air, supply air with exhaust air, and purging. These methods are illustrated in **Figure 15.6**.

The effect of ventilation on the heating and cooling system is to increase the loads that the heating and cooling system must carry, since the outside air must be treated before it is introduced into the space.

Combustion Air

IRC 2006

M1701.1 Air supply: Appliances that burn fuel (fireplaces excluded) must have means of supply air for fuel combustion and ventilation.

M1701.1.1 Buildings of unusually tight construction: Buildings with unusually tight construction must have means of getting combustion air from outside the thermal envelope. Buildings with ordinary tightness may receive combustion air from infiltration if the room is 50 cubic feet per 1,000 Btu/h input in volume.

M1701.2 Exhaust and ventilation system: To determine the space requirements for combustion air, exhaust fans, clothes dryers, and kitchen ventilation systems must be considered.

M1701.3 Volume dampers prohibited: Volume dampers may not be installed in combustion air openings.

M1701.4 Prohibited sources: Combustion air ducts and openings may not be attached to an area where a fan would affect the combustion airflow. Combustion air may not come from a source with flammable vapors or from sleeping rooms or bathrooms (with two exceptions).

Some Ventilation Methods

Types of ventilation	Diagram	Common uses	Comments
Operable windows	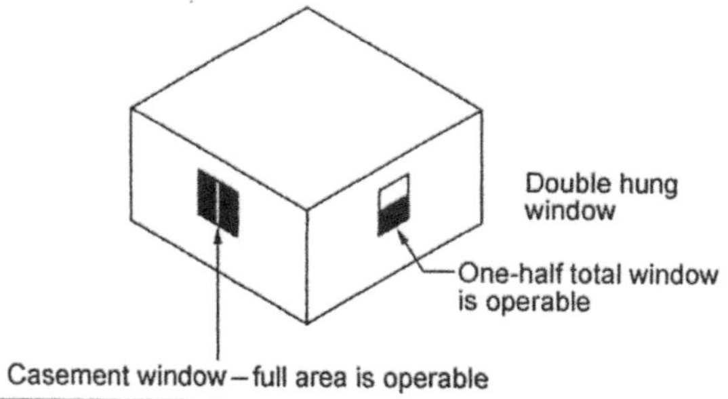 Double hung window One-half total window is operable Casement window—full area is operable	Residences, Low-rise offices	Operable window area should equal 4% of floor area.
Fresh outdoor air supply	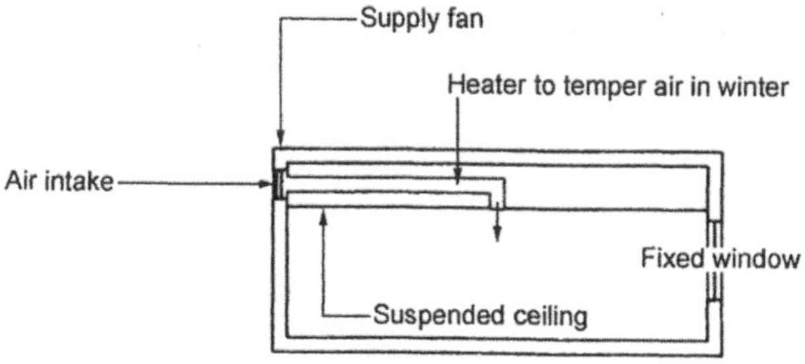 Supply fan Heater to temper air in winter Air intake Fixed window Suspended ceiling	Offices, Kitchens	15-25 cfm/person [11.8 L⅗] with reheat.
Exhaust air with no forced makeup air	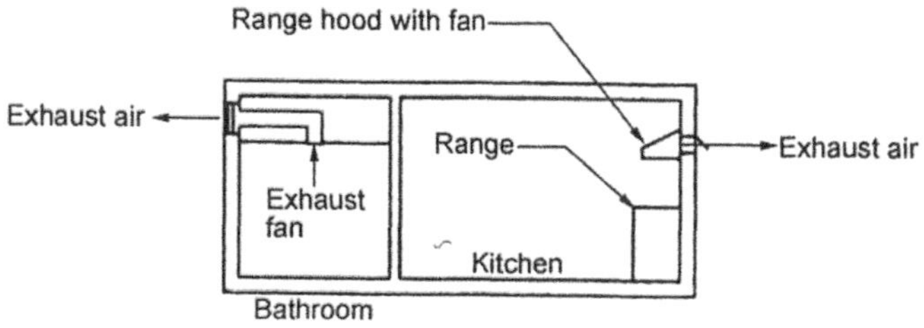 Range hood with fan Exhaust air Range Exhaust air Exhaust fan Kitchen Bathroom	Bathrooms, Kitchens	Fire protection is sometimes required in kitchens.
Supply air with forced makeup and exhaust air	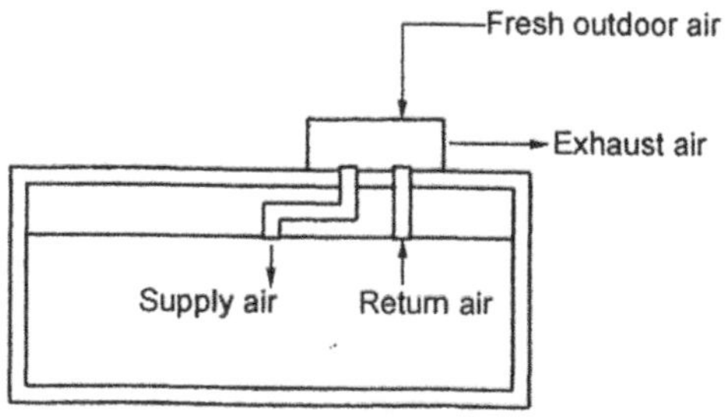 Fresh outdoor air Exhaust air Supply air Return air	Offices	Keep fresh outdoor air quantity 15-20% greater than exhaust air to "pressurize" the building.
Purging	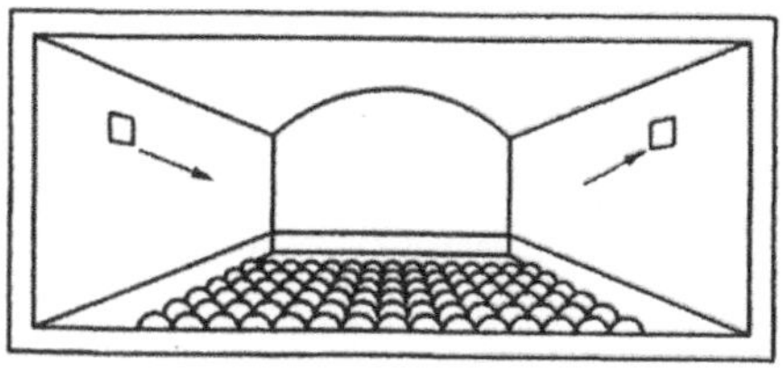	Theaters	New air is brought into the space between performances. Volume of space is large enough to provide 5 cfm/person [2.4 L⅗] over 3 hours.

Figure 15.6

RSMeans, *HVAC: Design Criteria, Options, Selection*

M1701.5 Opening area: The free area of openings must be considered (75% of the gross area for metal louvers, 25% for wood louvers) when determining combustion air requirements.

M1702 All Air from Inside the Building

M1702.1 Required volume: If the space with fuel-burning appliances exceeds 50 cubic feet per 1,000 Btu/h of input rating and the building is of ordinary tightness, normal infiltration is acceptable for combustion air.

M1702.2 Confined space: If Section M1702.1 cannot be met, there must be two openings to adjacent spaces to meet the volume requirement. These openings must be: (1) within 12" of the top, and (2) within 12" of the bottom. (See **Figure 15.7**.)

M1702.3 Unusually tight construction: If Sections M1702.1 and M1702.2 are met but building construction is too tight for proper air infiltration, then combustion air must be from outdoors.

M1703 All Air from Outdoors

M1703.1 Outdoor air: If Section M1702 cannot be met, outside air from outdoors is required to meet Sections M1703.2 and M1703.3.

M1703.2 Two openings or ducts: Openings or ducts are required for combustion air. (See **Figures 15.8** and **15.9**.) They should be located within 12" of the top of the enclosure and 12" with in the bottom, and may be attached to spaces that lead directly to the outdoors.

M1703.2.1 Size of openings: If vertical ducts are used to reach the outdoors, each opening must have free area of at least one square inch per 4,000 Btu/h of total input rating of all appliances in the space.

M1703.3 Single opening or duct: Combustion air may be supplied through one duct for appliances with minimum clearance of 1" on sides and back and 6" on front. The opening must be within 12" of the enclosure's top.

M1703.3.1 Size of opening: The opening of the single duct must have a free area of at least one square inch per 3,000 Btu/h of input rating of all appliances in the space. The opening must not be smaller than the vent flow area.

M1703.4 Attic combustion air: Combustion air from attics must have an opening with a metal sleeve that extends from the appliance enclosure to 6" or greater above ceiling joists and insulation. Provides additional specific requirements.

M1703.5 Under-floor combustion air: Combustion air from under-floor spaces (See **Figure 15.8**) must have free opening areas to the outside at least twice the required combustion air opening.

M1703.6 Opening requirements: Outside openings for combustion air must have screen covering that is resistant to corrosion with at least .25" openings.

All Air from Outdoors

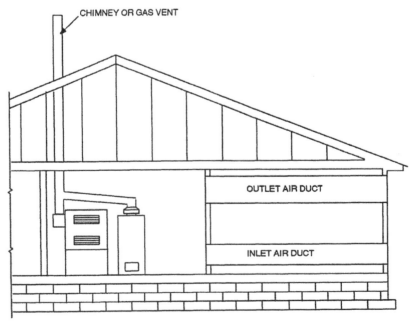

Figure 15.7

Courtesy of *ICC, IRC–2006* [Figure G2407.6.1(3)], Copyright 2006, International Code Council, Inc., Falls Church, Virginia

All Air from Outdoor—Inlet Air From Ventilated Crawl Space and Outlet Air to Ventilated Attic

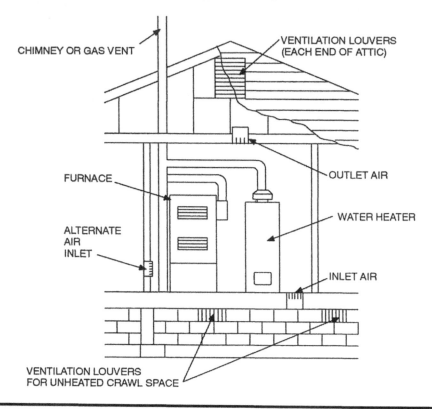

Figure 15.8

Courtesy of *ICC, IRC*–2006 [Figure G2407.6.1(3)], Copyright 2006, *International Code Council, Inc., Falls Church, Virginia*

Typical Warm Air Heating System

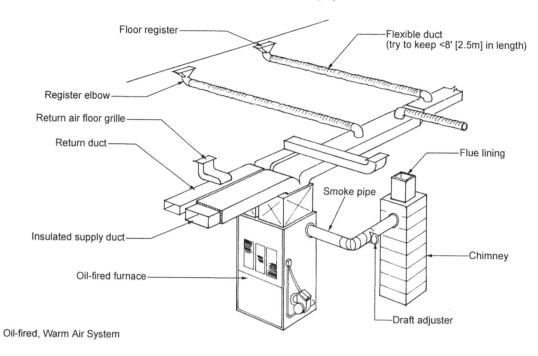

Oil-fired, Warm Air System

Figure 15.9

RSMeans, *HVAC: Design Criteria, Options, Selection*

Comments

"Tighter" houses, with less ventilation, have been built since the energy crisis in the 1970s. While they conserve energy by keeping conditioned air in and outside air out, they can, in some cases, keep moisture from evaporating, which can lead to mold and mildew. Several techniques can be used to minimize ventilation problems, including providing appropriate roof vents, installing exhaust fans in kitchens and bathrooms, and properly venting combustible appliances.

Duct Systems

Industry Standards

HVAC: Design Criteria, Options, Selection
(RSMeans)

Ductwork

The ideal size and location of the ductwork for air-supply systems is different for heating and cooling. Even when the heating and cooling loads are approximately equal, as they are in temperate climates, the cooling ductwork is always larger. Therefore, it is difficult for one system to perfectly meet heating and cooling requirements.

Because warm air rises above cooler air, heating supply ducts should be placed low and under windows. The rising heated air will stop downdrafts and cold air spill from the windows, will help to prevent condensation on the glass, and will inject the heating supply at the source of greatest heat loss. This helps to maintain overall even room temperature.

In contrast, cooling supply ducts should be located at the ceiling and slightly away from the perimeter of the room so the cool air can mix with the warm air. The cool air will drift downward over windows and over the lights and occupants, which are other sources of heat gain.

The ideal locations of air ducts are illustrated in **Figure 15.10**.

Using a system that combines heating and cooling in the same air supply ducts involves a compromise because of the inherent conflict between heating and cooling duct sizes and locations. This can be accomplished by larger duct sizes and increased fan capacity.

IRC 2006

See the *International Residential Code* Chapter 16.

Residential Ductwork

Industry Standards

Architectural Sheet Metal Manual, Fifth Edition
(Sheet Metal and Air Conditioning Contractors' National Association, Inc.)

7.2.1 Metal Gauges. Ductwork used for residential work shall not exceed 2 in. w.g. positive or negative pressures.

7.2.2 Rectangular Ducts. Minimum gauges for metal ducts not enclosed within a partition wall are listed in Table 7-1. For ducts enclosed within a partition wall, minimum gauges are listed in Table 7-2. Both tables apply to rectangular ducts.

7.2.3 Round Ducts. Minimum gauges for round ducts are listed in Table 7-3. Each joint shall be held rigidly in place by the use of mechanical fastening devices; i.e., rivets, bolts, or sheet metal screws.

Ideal Locations for Heating and Cooling Supply Ducts

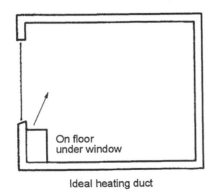

On floor under window

Ideal heating duct

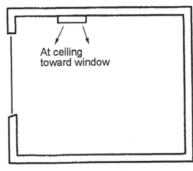

At ceiling toward window

Ideal cooling duct

RSMeans, *HVAC: Design Criteria, Options, Selection*

Figure 15.10

Mold-Resistant Guidelines

The Homeowner's Guide to Mold
(RSMeans)

To protect indoor air quality by reducing mold growth:

- Make sure the roof has appropriate vents.
- Use fans in the kitchen and baths to exhaust moist air. Choose the right size exhaust fan.
- Vent combustible appliances, such as furnaces, water heaters, and fireplaces, since they, too, produce water vapor. Make sure these appliances have air circulation by keeping doors open to the rooms they are in and ensuring their vents are properly connected, have no holes or cracks, and are not blocked.
- Route dryer vents to the outside, and keep them un-kinked and lint-free.
- Use metal ductwork—preferably without insulation.
- Insulate ductwork (on the outside of the duct) that goes through an unconditioned area like an attic, basement, or crawl space. Seal duct joints, then apply spray foam or flexible insulation around metal supply ducts, trunks, and plenums. (Flexible ductwork should not be used in crawl spaces, as vermin can gain access through them.)
- Make sure drip pans for cooling coils drain properly.
- Avoid central humidification systems. If they are used, make sure they are the type that has water flowing through with a pump, versus a reservoir that holds water.
- If using an air purifier to help reduce contaminants, including mold, consider a unit that offers more than one technology, such as HEPA filtration and ionizers.
- Consider installing radiant floor heating in a new home. Not only is it comfortable and efficient, but it helps dry floor spills.

Comments

Buildings constructed with structural insulated panels (SIPs) may have different ventilation requirements. Check with the SIP manufacturer.

Combustion Air Exhaust

Chimneys & Vents

IRC 2006

M1801.1 Venting required: Fuel-burning appliances must be vented to the outside to comply with manufacturer's instructions and their listing and label. Approved vents or chimneys are required.

M1801.2 Draft requirements: Draft requirements must be met using a venting system with positive flow to move combustion materials outdoors.

M1801.3 Existing chimneys and vents: Chimneys/vents must meet IRC Sections M1801.3.1–1801.3.4 if the appliance is disconnected from existing vent/chimney or is connected during a new installation.

M1801.3.1 Size: The chimney/vent must be resized for flue gas condensation and to meet draft requirements. NFPA 31 must be complied with for oil-fired appliances.

M1801.3.2 Flue passageways: There must be no obstructions or combustible materials in flue gas passageway. Liners and walls must be undamaged and continuous.

M1801.3.3 Cleanout: Masonry chimneys must have a cleanout opening that meets IRC Section R1001.12.

M1801.3.4 Clearances: Chimneys and vents must have clearance to combustibles that meets manufacturer's instructions. Exception made for chimneys meeting UL 1777 with tested lining system.

M1801.4 Space around lining: The space around flue lining or other vent for masonry chimney cannot be used to vent other appliances.

M1801.5 Mechanical draft systems: Mechanical draft systems may only be used with appropriately listed appliances. Fuel must be prevented from reaching the equipment when the draft system is not working.

M1801.6 Direct-vent appliances: Installation of direct-vent appliances must comply with manufacturer's instructions.

M1801.7 Support: Venting systems must support weight of materials.

M1801.8 Duct penetrations: Chimneys and vents must not extend into supply or return air ducts or plenums.

M1801.9 Fireblocking: Fireblocking is required to comply with IRC section R602.8.

M1801.10 Unused openings: Unused openings must be capped or closed.

M1801.11 Multiple-appliance venting systems: If two or more appliances are to be connected to one draft venting system, they must be on the same floor and meet other requirements for connections and inlets.

M1801.12 Multiple solid fuel prohibited: Solid-fuel-burning appliances may not share chimney passageway that is already in use to vent a separate appliance.

Air Conditioning & Refrigeration

Industry Standards

Means Mechanical Cost Data
(RSMeans)

Air Conditioning

General: The purpose of air conditioning is to control the environment of a space so that comfort is provided for the occupants and/or conditions are suitable for the processes or equipment contained therein. The several items which should be evaluated to define system objectives are:

- Temperature control
- Humidity control
- Cleanliness
- Odor, smoke, and fumes
- Ventilation

Efforts to control the above parameters must also include consideration of the degree or tolerance of variation, the noise level introduced, the velocity of air motion and the energy requirements to accomplish the desired results.

The variation in **temperature** and **humidity** is a function of the sensor and the controller. The controller reacts to a signal from the sensor and produces the appropriate suitable response in either the terminal unit, the conductor of the transporting medium (air, steam, chilled water, etc.), or the source (boiler, evaporating coils, etc.).

The **noise level** is a by-product of the energy supplied to moving components of the system. Those items which usually contribute the most noise are pumps, blowers, fans, compressors and diffusers. The level of noise can be partially controlled through use of vibration pads, isolators, proper sizing, shields, baffles and sound absorbing liners.

Some **air motion** is necessary to prevent stagnation and stratification. The maximum acceptable velocity varies with the degree of heating or cooling which is taking place. Most people feel air moving past them at velocities in excess of 25 FPM as an annoying draft. However, velocities up to 45 FPM may be acceptable in certain cases. Ventilation, expressed as air changes per hour and percentage of fresh air, is usually an item regulated by local codes.

Selection of the system to be used for a particular application is usually a trade-off. In some cases the building size, style, or room available for mechanical use limits the range of possibilities. Prime factors influencing the decision are first cost and total life (operating, maintenance and replacement costs). The accuracy with which each parameter is determined will be an important measure of the reliability of the decision and subsequent satisfactory operation of the installed system.

Heat delivery may be desired from an air conditioning system. Heating capability usually is added as follows: A gas fired burner or hot water/steam/electric coils may be added to the air handling unit directly and heat all air equally. For limited or localized heat requirements the water/steam/electric coils may be inserted into the duct branch supplying the cold areas. Gas fired duct furnaces are also available.

Note: When water or steam coils are used, the cost of the piping and boiler must also be added. For a rough estimate use the cost per square foot of the appropriate sized hydronic system with unit heaters. This will provide a cost for the boiler and piping, and the unit heaters of the system would equate to the approximate cost of the heating coils.

High-Efficiency Cooling Systems

Energy Efficient Air Conditioning

Green Home Improvement
(RSMeans)

Because of growing interest in energy efficiency, changes in federal law that require more efficient appliances, and America's Energy Star® Program, air conditioners have improved dramatically in recent years. By law, all new air conditioners must have a seasonal energy efficiency ratio (or SEER) of at least 13. (The higher the number, the more efficient

Air Conditioning Requirements

BTU's per hour per S.F. of floor area and S.F. per ton of air conditioning.

Type of Building	BTU per S.F.	S.F. per Ton	Type of Building	BTU per S.F.	S.F. per Ton	Type of Building	BTU per S.F.	S.F. per Ton
Apartments, Individual	26	450	Dormitory, Rooms	40	300	Libraries	50	240
Corridors	22	550	Corridors	30	400	Low Rise Office, Exterior	38	320
Auditoriums & Theaters	40	300/18*	Dress Shops	43	280	Interior	33	360
Banks	50	240	Drug Stores	80	150	Medical Centers	28	425
Barber Shops	48	250	Factories	40	300	Motels	28	425
Bars & Taverns	133	90	High Rise Office—Ext. Rms.	46	263	Office (small suite)	43	280
Beauty Parlors	66	180	Interior Rooms	37	325	Post Office, Individual Office	42	285
Bowling Alleys	68	175	Hospitals, Core	43	280	Central Area	46	260
Churches	36	330/20*	Perimeter	46	260	Residences	20	600
Cocktail Lounges	68	175	Hotel, Guest Rooms	44	275	Restaurants	60	200
Computer Rooms	141	85	Corridors	30	400	Schools & Colleges	46	260
Dental Offices	52	230	Public Spaces	55	220	Shoe Stores	55	220
Dept. Stores, Basement	34	350	Industrial Plants, Offices	38	320	Shop'g. Ctrs., Supermarkets	34	350
Main Floor	40	300	General Offices	34	350	Retail Stores	48	250
Upper Floor	30	400	Plant Areas	40	300	Specialty	60	200

*Persons per ton
12,000 BTU = 1 ton of air conditioning

Figure 15.11

RSMeans, *Means Mechanical Cost Data*

the unit.) Energy Star appliances have a SEER of 15 or higher. Air conditioners may also come with an energy-efficiency ratio (EER) that indicates their efficiency when operating in higher temperatures. Energy Star-qualified central air conditioners must have an EER of at least 11.5. Wall and window air conditioners have lower ratings, because they're less efficient—EER ratings range from 9.4 for larger units to 10.7 for smaller ones.

Do not oversize an air conditioner. Having too much capacity results in frequent on-and-off cycling of an air conditioner. This wastes energy. In addition, because it takes time for an air conditioner to dehumidify air, frequent cycling on and off fails to reduce humidity levels. Lower humidity makes us feel cooler and thus improves comfort.

Air conditioners are fairly noisy, so be sure to install a central air unit away from living spaces, bedrooms, porches, and patios, if possible. For optimal function, the outside components should be located in a cool, shaded area. Excess heat reduces the air conditioner's efficiency. The north side of the home is often the best location. Be sure that air can circulate around the unit, too. You may need to clear shrubs or other plants that block air flow. If not, the air conditioner won't be able to dissipate heat as effectively. Avoid rooftop installations unless the unit is shaded.

Evaporative Coolers

Green Home Improvement
(RSMeans)

Evaporative coolers have fewer moving parts than central air conditioners and, as a result, cost about half as much. Standard models require much less energy to operate—up to 75% less than an air conditioner. Evaporative coolers also provide a steady supply of fresh air, unlike central air conditioning systems, which simply circulate room air through the cooler. As an added bonus, these devices don't require ozone-depleting chemicals like those found in older model air conditioners.

Evaporative coolers are relatively simple devices that are usually mounted on the roof, although wall, window, and ground-mounted units are also available.

They come in two basic designs. The first and simpler one is the *direct evaporative cooler.* It draws outside air in through a moistened mat and then blows it into the house. As the outside air flows through the mat, it is humidified. The heat in the incoming air causes this moisture to evaporate—to enter a vapor state. Evaporation draws heat out of the incoming air, cooling it down by as much as 40°F.

The cool, slightly moistened air is then distributed throughout the house, either through ducts to individual rooms or via a single duct to a central location. The cool air circulates through the home and exits via open a windows, screen doors, or a special vent. (If you don't open window or a vent, the moist air will leak out through gaps in the building envelope, and could accumulate in insulation and cause all kinds of problems.) The house stays cool because of the continuous supply of air moving through it. Moisture levels usually aren't sufficient to cause condensation.

The second type is an *indirect evaporative cooler*, also known as a *two-stage evaporative cooler*. These units are a bit more complicated. Two-stage evaporative coolers are designed to cool incoming air, but not humidify it. To achieve this, two streams of air are drawn into the unit from the outside. One stream passes through a wet mat and is cooled. It then passes through a device known as a *heat exchanger*. The cool air cools down the heat exchanger. This air, however, does not enter the home. It's returned to the outdoors.

A second stream of outside air also flows into the cooler. It passes through the other side of the heat exchanger and is cooled. This air is then blown into the house.

Two-stage evaporative coolers cost more than direct coolers and are slightly less efficient, but they don't add moisture to room air, which can cause problems in some homes.

Installation of an evaporative cooler involves constructing and attaching a platform to support the cooler, cutting an opening to connect the cooler to the ductwork below, flashing the roof, and connecting tubing to the water supply and electrical wiring to the circuit box, by code.

Although evaporative coolers offer many advantages over air conditioners, they also consume a fairly large quantity of fresh water (between 3.5 and 10.5 gallons per hour), a resource that is often in short supply in the regions for which these systems are best suited. Systems with bleed-off valves consume the most water.

Regular maintenance includes emptying drip pans —and cleaning them if the cooler is shut off for an extended period to eliminate bacteria and mold. Drip mats should also be replaced or cleaned per manufacturer's instructions. Also worth noting: two-stage evaporative coolers force large amounts of outdoor air into a home, which can trigger reactions in people with allergies.

Direct Evaporative Cooler

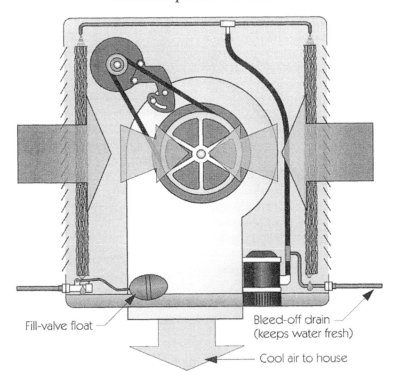

Fill-valve float

Bleed-off drain
(keeps water fresh)

Cool air to house

Figure 15.12

Commercial Cooling Systems

Green Building: Project Planning & Estimating, **Second Edition**
(RSMeans)

Air-Cooled Direct Expansion Systems (DX): In DX systems, the refrigerant expands through the TXV (thermal expansion valve), then removes heat from the air stream by way of the DX coil. For DX systems to operate, the refrigerant must be compressed from a low-temperature, low-pressure gas to a high-temperature, high-pressure gas in the compressor, where the heat is then removed by air or liquid cooling. Gas coil-to-air heat exchange is not as efficient as gas coil-to-liquid heat exchange, as the thermal conductivity is typically lower than water. Therefore, in general terms, air-cooled refrigeration systems are not as efficient as water-cooled systems. However, some manufacturers have increased the efficiency of air-cooled equipment by increasing heat surface area and using larger fans.

Evaporative-cooled condenser systems will typically drop the energy usage of any compressor system by 10%–20%, depending on weather conditions. Evaporative cooling involves the spraying of water over the condenser of a refrigeration system and allowing the water to evaporate. This evaporation increases the system's ability to remove heat.

Free Cooling Systems: Plate and frame heat exchangers, or "free cooling systems," are used when there are wide swings in outdoor conditions, and there is a building need for cooling most of the year. This system uses the evaporative cooling of the cooling tower system and a plate and frame heat exchanger to remove heat from the chilled water system directly to the condenser water system without the need for mechanical cooling.

Free cooling systems have also been described as "airside free cooling." They bring the cool outdoor air into the space and mix it with the treated air to achieve the desired conditions without mechanical cooling.

Compression-Type Refrigeration Technologies

- Electric scroll compressors: electric-powered rotary compressors for small 1–5-ton systems that use less electricity than conventional reciprocating refrigeration compressors, typically .9–1.4 kWh/ton hr.
- Electric screw compressors: electric-powered rotary compressors for larger 10–100-ton systems. These also use less electricity than

traditional reciprocating refrigeration compressors, typically .7–.95 kWh/ton hr.

Natural Gas-Fired Air-Conditioning Systems: Natural gas-fired air-conditioning systems are an option for green building designers due to their net energy savings. With any electric system there are inherent losses associated with the distribution of electricity. The average power plant has a heat rate or efficiency of 20%–35% of energy output in kWh to energy input Btus. There are also energy losses due to the transmission of electricity over wires over many miles. If a facility operates with gas-fired equipment, the heat rate for internal combustion equipment is typically 35%, with no transmission losses. Natural gas-fired units can have:

- Reciprocating compressors (used for 10–100-ton systems typically use 12–14 MBtu of natural gas per ton-hour of cooling). These are equally efficient, yet have none of the electrical transmission losses associated with conventional electric power.
- Screw compressors (used for 10–100-ton systems typically use 12–14 MBtu of natural gas per ton-hour of cooling).

Chilled Water Systems

In chilled water systems, the refrigerant expands through the TXV (thermal expansion valve), then removes heat from the chilled water medium, which is circulated through a facility and into the air stream by way of a chilled water coil. Like air-cooled DX systems, chilled water system refrigerant needs to be compressed from a low- to a high-temperature, high-pressure gas in the compressor, with the heat removed in the condenser. Again, the condenser can be air- or liquid-cooled. The system loses some efficiency due to the multiple heat exchanges; however, the heat exchange, typically liquid-to-liquid, is very efficient, as the thermal conductivity tends to be higher in water.

In general terms, water-cooled systems are more efficient than air-cooled systems. They are rated by their IPLV (integrated part load value).

IPLV Ratings
Air-Cooled Chillers:

- Chillers with Screw Compressors (25–100 tons), typical IPLV .6–.9 kWh/ton hr
- Air-Cooled Scroll Chillers (1–25 tons), typical IPLV .95–1.2 kWh/ton hr
- Evaporative-Cooled Chillers (25–100 tons), typical IPLV .65–.85 kWh/ton hr

Water-Cooled Chillers:

- Screw Chillers (25–100 tons), typical IPLV .6–.8 kWh/ton hr
- Centrifugal Chillers (100–3,000 tons), typical IPLV .45–.7 kWh/ton hr
- Centrifugal Chillers with VFDs (100–3,000 tons), typical IPLV .35–.6 kWh/ton hr

Absorption Chillers

One of the oldest artificial cooling systems available, absorption cooling is a chemical reaction type of cooling system that uses heat to separate water from lithium bromide. Once the solutions have been separated, heat is rejected through a condenser heat exchanger, which condenses the steam and cools the lithium bromide. The two chemicals are then allowed to mix in the absorber where the lithium bromide absorbs the water, and an isothermal reaction causes cooling. This isothermal reaction is similar to an ice pack where the liquid (water) is mixed with a solid (lithium bromide), causing cooling. For green building design, absorption is a perfect heat sink or way to use waste heat. Some commercially available absorbers can use waste heat (under vacuum) as low as 140° (lower than the waste heat temperature in many facilities).

BCS Building Control System: Energy-Saving Strategies

1. **Discharge Reset:** of hot water or air handling units based on the load requirements in the spaces.
2. **Static Pressure Reset:** adjusts the system static pressure set point based on the area with the greatest load.
3. **Enthalpy-Based Economizer Controls:** utilizes air with the lowest heat content for cooling, by controlling a space based on total heat, not just temperature.
4. **CO_2 Control (often called demand controlled ventilation):** Modulates the fresh air into a space above the minimum required, depending on the CO_2 level in the space. This becomes a truly dynamic control and maintains the building CO_2 level within recommended parameters. This approach is very effective in spaces that have large fluctuations in occupancy.
5. **Energy Monitoring and Trending:** The BCS system can monitor energy usage to identify large energy users or spikes. This allows a facility manager and commissioning agent to identify anomalies in a building's energy usage, saving thousands of dollars in energy costs by identifying short cycling or changes in schedules that are normally missed by the operators.
6. **VFD (Variable Frequency Drives) Modulation:** Fans and pumps can be "slowed down" by the VFD with properly located sensors. This ensures that only the volume required is delivered and not recirculated, thereby reducing wasted energy in the form of unnecessary recycling of air. VFDs are usually controlled by a combination of the above-mentioned strategies to deliver only the required volumes.
7. **Occupancy Control:** Occupancy sensors or supervisory access cards enable the fresh air louvers to open when people are in a space, a method similar to CO_2 control, but without the calculations. The outdoor air louvers are shut when there is no occupancy and opened when someone enters the space. This type of control is cost-effective when using smaller air handlers.

IRC 2006

M1411 Refrigeration Cooling Equipment

M1411.1 Approved refrigerants: Refrigerants must comply with ANSI/ASHRAE 34.

M1411.3 Condensate disposal: Condensate must be properly drained and disposed of. Discharge into the street is prohibited.

M1411.3.1 Auxiliary and secondary drain systems: A secondary drain pan is necessary for all coils and evaporators if drain overflow could cause damage to the building. Pipe size must be at least ¾".

M1411.4 Insulation of refrigerant piping: Piping for vapor lines must have insulation meeting specified thermal resistivity and external surface permeance.

M1412 Absorption Cooling Equipment

M1412.1 Approval of equipment: Installation of absorption systems must meet manufacturer's instructions.

M1412.2 Condensate disposal: Disposal of condensate from cooling coils must meet IRC Section M1411.3.

M1413 Evaporative cooling equipment:
Cooling equipment using water for cooling must meet manufacturers' installation requirements. Evaporative coolers must be installed on a secure, level platform that is at least 3" above ground. Flashing is required for all openings through exterior walls.

Comments

Where gravity flow of condensate is not possible, use of a sump pump is recommended.

Solar Systems

Solar Hot Water Used for Space Heating

Green Home Improvement
(RSMeans)

Another renewable-energy option for heating a home is a solar hot water system. These are typically installed to provide domestic hot water, but larger systems can provide space heat.

A solar hot water system consists of collectors that are typically mounted on the roof. They absorb sunlight, even on cold winter days, as long as the sun is shining. In many systems, the solar heat is drawn off by a fluid (usually propylene glycol) circulating through pipes in the collector. The heat is then transferred to a solar storage tank, typically located in the basement. Hot water from the reservoir may be circulated through the pipes in a baseboard hot-water system or in a radiant floor heating system. Or it can be extracted by a heat exchanger installed in a forced-air heating system.

Installing a Solar Hot Water System

Solar hot water systems require installation of rooftop collectors and a solar storage tank, with pipes connecting the two. The solar storage tank is coupled to the existing heating distribution system.

Active Solar Energy

Industry Standards

HVAC: Design Criteria, Options, Selection
(RSMeans)

Active solar energy systems can be used to heat or preheat domestic hot water effectively. Active solar systems also work ideally with absorption cooling systems, since the heat load in the building increases with the solar load in direct proportion to the energy captured by the solar system to run the absorber.

Active solar systems can be used with hydronic or air systems. In a hydronic system, the collectors heat water or a glycol solution and return it to a storage tank. At night the pumps will not operate, and the system may drain down. Heat exchangers are used to transfer the heat from the solar loop to the heating loop, which takes the heat from the storage tank. In this way heat collected during the day can be used at night. Air systems use the sun to heat air directly, which is then distributed to the space directly or sent over to the storage tank.

Most active solar systems (**Figure 15.14**) use either flat plate or concentrating solar collectors, which are connected to an active pumping or fan control system. They may also contain a storage tank or thermal mass.

Solar Collector Panel—Liquid

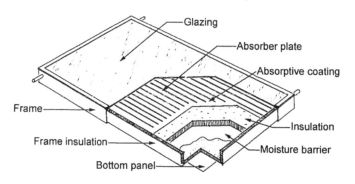

Figure 15.13   RSMeans, *Means Graphic Construction Standards*

Solar Water Heating

Green Building Project Planning
(RSMeans)

Solar water heating systems are relatively simple extensions to buildings' plumbing systems, which impart heat from the sun to preheat service hot water. Water heating accounts for a substantial portion of a building's energy use, ranging from approximately 9% of total energy use in office buildings to 40% in lodging facilities. Averaged across all buildings, hot water represents 15% of energy use in residential buildings, and 8% in commercial buildings.

Solar water heating systems are usually designed to provide about two thirds of a building's hot water needs, and more where fuel is very expensive or unavailable. Solar water heating applications include domestic water heating, pool and spa heating,

industrial processes such as laundries and cafeterias, and air conditioning reheat in hot, humid climates. Solar water heating is most effective when it serves a steady water heating load that is constant throughout the week and year (or at a maximum during the summer). For example, a residential facility that is occupied 24/7 would accrue 40% more cost savings than a school open only five days a week.

Solar water heating can be used effectively in almost any geographic location, but is especially prevalent and effective at low latitudes, where the constant solar resource matches a constant water load.

There are different types of solar water heating systems; the choice depends on the temperature required and the climate. All types have the same simple operating principle. Solar radiation is absorbed by a wide-area "solar collector," or "solar panel," which heats the water directly or heats a nonfreezing fluid

Active Solar Energy Systems

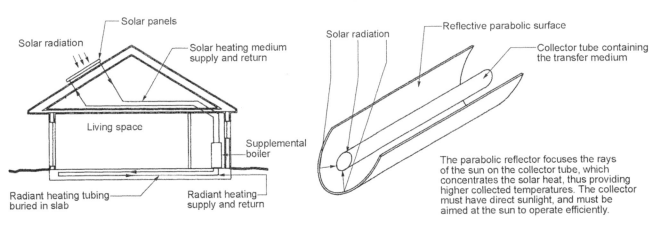

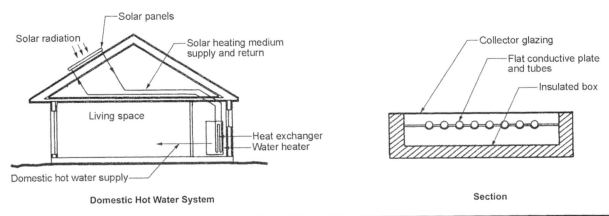

Figure 15.14

RSMeans, *HVAC: Design Criteria, Options, Selection*

which, in turn, heats the water by a heat exchanger. The heated water is stored in a tank for later use. A backup gas or electric water heater is used to provide hot water when the sun is insufficient, and to optimize the economical size of the solar system.

Solar water heating systems save the fuel otherwise required to heat the water, and avoid the associated cost and pollution. A frequently overlooked advantage of solar water heating is that the large storage volume increases the capacity to deliver hot water.

Types of Collectors for Solar Water Heating

Solar thermal collectors can be categorized by the temperature at which they efficiently deliver heat. **Low-temperature collectors** are unglazed and uninsulated. They operate at up to 18°F (10°C) above ambient temperature, and are most often used to heat swimming pools. At this low temperature, a cover glass would reflect or absorb solar heat more than it would reduce heat loss. Often, the pool water is colder than the air, and insulating the collector would be counterproductive. Low-temperature collectors are extruded from polypropylene or other polymers with UV stabilizers. Flow passages for the pool water are molded directly into the absorber plate, and pool water is circulated through the collectors with the pool filter circulation pump.

Mid-temperature systems place the absorber plate in an enclosure insulated with fiberglass or polyicocyanurate, and with a low-iron cover glass to reduce heat loss at higher temperatures. They produce water 18° to 129°F (10° to 50° C) above the outside temperature, and are most often used for heating domestic hot water (DHW). Reflection and absorption reduce the solar transparency of the glass and reduce the efficiency at low temperature differences, but the glass is required to retain heat at higher temperatures. A copper absorber plate with copper tubes welded to the fins is used. To reduce radiant losses from the collector, the absorber plate is often treated with a black nickel selective surface, which has a high absorptivity in the shortwave solar spectrum, but a low-emissivity in the long-wave thermal spectrum. Such flat plate systems cost as high as $155/SF installed for a single residential system to around $90/SF for a large commercial system.

High-temperature collectors surround the absorber tube with an evacuated borosilicate glass tube to minimize heat loss, and often utilize mirrors curved in a parabolic shape to concentrate sunlight on the tube. Evacuating the air out of the tube eliminates conduction and convection as heat loss mechanisms, and using a selective surface minimizes radiation heat loss. High-temperature systems are required for absorption cooling or electricity generation, but are used for mid-temperature applications such as commercial or institutional water heating as well. Due to the tracking mechanism required to keep the focusing mirrors facing the sun, high-temperature systems are usually very large and mounted on the ground adjacent to a facility. These collectors are usually used in very large systems and typical installed system cost is on the order of $50/SF.

Codes & Standards

The Solar Rating and Certification Corporation (SRCC) is an independent, nonprofit trade organization that implements solar equipment certification programs and rating standards. SRCC ratings are used to estimate and compare the performance of different collectors and systems submitted to SRCC by manufacturers for testing. SRCC developed a solar water heating system rating and certification program, short-titled OG 300, to improve performance and reliability of solar products.

Other standards include the following from the American Society of Heating, Refrigerating, and Air Conditioning Engineers:

- ASHRAE 90003: Active Solar Heating Design Manual
- ASHRAE 90336: Guidance for Preparing Active Solar Heating Systems Operation and Maintenance Manuals
- ASHRAE 90342: Active Solar Heating Systems Installation Manual
- ASHRAE 93: Methods of Testing to Determine the Thermal Performance of Solar Collectors

From the American Water Works Association (AWWA):

- AWWA C651 Disinfecting Water Mains
- From Factory Mutual Engineering and Research Corporation (FM):
- FM P7825 Approval Guide

From the National Fire Protection Association (NFPA):

- NFPA 70 National Electrical Code
- MIL-HDBK 1003/13A Solar Heating of Buildings and Domestic Hot Water

Solar Hot Air Collectors

Industry Standards

Green Home Improvement
(RSMeans)

Solar hot air collectors (panels) are about as simple as solar gets. Most of the collectors on the market consist of an insulated metal box containing a black metal plate, known as the *absorber plate*. It absorbs sunlight on cold winter days and, like the interior of your car, turns sunlight into heat. Solar hot air collectors are insulated, and most are covered with single- or double-pane glass (glazing). These features trap sunlight inside the collector, raising the temperature even on the coldest winter days, provided the sun is shining.

Solar hot air collectors are typically mounted on south-facing exterior walls. Air from inside the house is drawn into the collector by a small fan or blower. As the air flows through the collector over the solar-heated absorber plate, it is heated—often by 40°F to 90°F. Solar-heated air is then blown into the house via a pipe that passes through the exterior house wall. Small registers are mounted on the air intake and outtakes.

Solar hot air systems are controlled automatically. When the sun shines on the collector, and the temperature inside the collector reaches 110°F, the fan turns on, blowing warm air into the home. To prevent overheating, the fan turns on only when room temperature drops below the setting on a thermostat, which is also connected to the collector. Solar-heated air warms the room, and the thermostat shuts the unit off when the room temperature reaches the desired setting.

Installing a Solar Hot Air Collector

Installation is generally performed by a factory authorized installer. For best results, solar hot air collectors should be mounted on vertical south-facing walls to absorb the low-angled winter sun. Collectors can also be mounted on roofs or on the ground next to your home, provided the area is not shaded during the winter. Although ground and roof mounts are sometimes desirable, they're typically more complicated and expensive than wall mounts. In homes with attics, for instance, installing a collector on the roof requires the use of flexible insulated ducts to transport air to and from the collector. It also requires a much more powerful fan than a wall-mounted collector. Moreover, both roof- and ground-mounted collectors are typically exposed to sunlight year-round, which could reduce their life expectancy. Collectors can be covered though, to ensure a longer life.

IRC 2006

M2301 Solar Energy Systems

M2301.1 General: This chapter covers solar energy systems for heating and cooling, including swimming pool heating. Applies to all installation, repair, or other alterations.

M2301.2 Installation: Installation must meet IRC Sections M2301.2.1–M2301.2.9.

M2301.2.1 Access: Solar energy systems and all controls must be accessible for service and inspection.

M2301.2.2 Roof-mounted collectors: The roof where roof-mounted solar collectors are located must be able to withstand the loads. Collectors and supports must be noncombustible. If solar collectors are to serve as the roof covering, IRC Chapter 9 requirements must be met.

M2301.2.3 Pressure and temperature relief: Solar energy systems that have fluids must feature valves for pressure and temperature relief.

M2301.2.4 Vacuum relief: If the system may drop below atmospheric pressure, there must be a vacuum-relief valve.

M2301.2.5 Protection from freezing: The system must be protected from freezing of heat-transfer liquids at the winter design temperature (except where the temperature is greater than 32°F).

M2301.2.6 Expansion tanks: Expansion tanks must meet IRC Section M2003.

M2301.2.7 Roof and wall penetrations: Roof and wall penetrations must be flashed and waterproofed.

M2301.2.8 Solar loop isolation: Solar collectors must be away from the rest of the system by means of isolation valves.

M2301.2.9 Maximum temperature limitations: The maximum allowed temperature is 180°F.

M2301.3 Labeling: Labeling of solar energy systems must meet IRC Sections 2301.3.1 and M2301.3.2.

M2301.3.1 Collectors: Collectors must be listed and display the manufacturer's name, model and serial numbers, maximum temperatures and pressures, and other pertinent information.

M2301.3.2 Thermal storage units: Pressurized thermal storage units must be listed and display the manufacturer's name, model and serial numbers, maximum temperatures and pressures, and other pertinent information.

M2301.4 Prohibited heat transfer fluids: Flammable gases and liquids are prohibited as heat transfer fluids.

Special Piping, Storage & Exhaust Systems

Oil Tanks

Industry Standards

HVAC: Design Criteria, Options, Selection
(RSMeans)

Oil is normally stored in tanks which may be exposed or buried in the ground. Current laws may require containment and/or leak detection systems. Tanks may be made of single- or double-wall fiberglass or steel. Transfer pumps that supply oil to the burner reservoir or day tank are usually required on long runs.

IRC 2006

M2201 Oil Tanks

M2201.1 Materials: Supply tanks must be listed and labeled. Underground tanks must meet UL 58, and inside tanks must meet UL 80.

M2201.2 Above-ground tanks: The maximum amount of stored fuel oil is 660 gallons. Supply tanks must be properly supported by noncombustible construction.

M2201.2.1 Tanks within buildings: Supply tanks inside buildings must be capable of being installed and removed in one piece. Tanks larger than 10 gallons must be located at least five feet from flames of fuel-burning appliances.

M2201.2.2 Outside above-ground tanks: Tanks that are outdoors and above ground must be at least five feet away from property lines and protected from the elements.

M2201.3 Underground tanks: Excavation for tanks must not affect foundations. Tanks must be at least one foot away from basement walls or property lines and covered with at least one foot of earth.

M2201.4 Multiple tanks: IRC Section 2203.6 must be met for cross connection of two tanks.

M2201.5 Oil gauges: Inside tanks must have oil gauges. Glass gauges are not allowed.

Kitchen HVAC Requirements

Kitchen Appliance Installations

IRC 2006

M1503 Range Hoods

M1503.1 General: A single wall duct must be provided for range hoods to discharge to the outdoors (with exception for ductless range hoods that have natural or mechanical ventilation). Ducts must be smooth, air tight, and have a backdraft damper.

M1503.2 Duct material: Single wall ducts must be made of copper or galvanized or stainless steel. Domestic kitchen appliances with downdraft exhaust systems can have ducts made of schedule 40 PVC pipe.

M1504 Installation of Microwave Ovens

M1504.1 Installation of microwave oven over a cooking appliance: Installation must comply with microwave manufacturer's instructions when located above another cooking appliance. Both top and bottom appliances must be properly listed and labeled.

> ## Comments
> Adequate ventilation of microwave ovens is essential to proper operation.

M1505 Overhead Exhaust Hoods

M1505.1 General: Exhaust hoods must be at least 28 gage and have 0.25" of clearance between the hood and cabinet. There must be at least 24 inches between the cooking surface and cabinet.

> ## Comments
> A booster fan may be required for longer runs of range hood ductwork, or where there are two or more elbows.

M1901 Ranges and Ovens

M1901.1 Clearances: Ranges must have at least 30" of clearance over cooking surface. Clearance may be reduced for properly listed and labeled appliances.

M1901.2 Cooking appliances: Cooking appliances must be listed and labeled. Manufacturer's instructions must be followed for installation.

Commercial Kitchens

Industry Standards

HVAC: Design Criteria, Options, Selection
(RSMeans)

Commercial kitchen exhaust systems typically include the following components:

- Hood
- Grease removal device
- Exhaust duct
- Fan
- Fire extinguishing equipment

The recommended practice for these items is covered in NFPA 96—*Standard for the Installation of Equipment for the Removal of Smoke and Grease Laden Vapors from Commercial Cooking Equipment.*

Exhaust Hoods

There are two basic types of kitchen exhaust hood systems: exhaust-only systems and exhaust-plus-makeup-air systems. The *exhaust-only system* typically

consists of a hood, grease trap, filter, exhaust duct, roof curb, and fan (see **Figure 15.15**). These systems are generally used for low-intensity applications, such as delis and snack counters. They exhaust room air directly to the outside. These systems are generally less energy-efficient than make-up units because the exhaust fan removes 100% tempered air from the occupied space.

Exhaust-plus-make-up-air systems include all the features of exhaust-only systems as well as a supply air slot, supply duct, supply fan, intake extension and air-intake filter hood. (See **Figure 15.16**.)

NFPA recommends that hoods be installed in all applications that produce smoke or grease-laden vapors. It is also recommended that all solid-fuel-burning equipment be served by hoods that are separate from other kitchen ventilation equipment. Recommended clearances for hoods are as follows:

- 18" to combustible materials
- 3" to limited combustible materials
- 0" to noncombustible materials

The hood should be designed to capture a minimum amount of air. Therefore, the hood should extend at least 6" (152 mm) beyond the edge of the cooking surface on all sides and exhaust 100 cfm per square foot (508 L/s per square meter) for wall canopy hoods and 150 cfm per square foot (762 L/s per square meter) for island canopy hoods. Non-canopy applications must

Exhaust-Only Type of Kitchen Hood

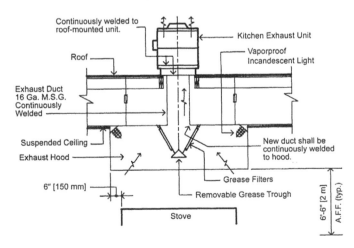

Figure 15.15

RSMeans, *HVAC: Design Criteria, Options, Selection*

Exhaust/Make-up Air Kitchen Hood

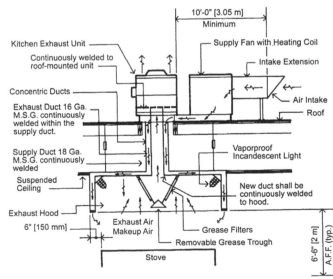

Figure 15.16

RSMeans, *HVAC: Design Criteria, Options, Selection*

have a hood set back no more than one foot from the edge of the cooking surface and exhaust 300 cfm per linear foot (142 L/s) of cooking surface.

The gauge of metal for the hood (canopy), exhaust duct, and supply air duct is also specifically controlled. The canopy or hood for kitchen exhausts should be constructed of either 18-gauge steel or 20-gauge stainless steel. All seams, joints, and penetrations of the hood should have a liquid-tight continuous weld. Interior joints and seams do not have to be continuously welded, but they should be completely sealed. Exhaust air volume for hoods should be sufficient to remove all grease-laden vapors. Since these factors are highly dependent on the size and type of equipment being used, designers should contact equipment manufacturers to determine specific requirements.

Exhaust ducts should be designed to transport the hot flue gases outside as directly as possible. Formed of 16-gauge steel or 18-gauge stainless steel, they should be installed without dips or traps that might collect grease. Ducts should not be connected with any other duct systems; all duct joints should be completely welded to provide a continuous liquid-tight seal.

Grease Removal Devices

Grease removal devices (grease traps) should be an integral part of any kitchen exhaust system. These devices generally consist of filters, baffles, or other approved devices. NFPA recommends that mesh filters not be used.

Grease filters should have a minimum area of one square inch (6.5m²) for every two cfm (1 L/s) of exhaust air from the hood.

The distance between the grease removal system and the cooking surface should be as great as possible. For charcoal or charcoal-type broilers, the minimum distance should be four feet (1.2 m). Grease removal devices should also be protected from the combustion gas outlet or from direct flame because items like deep fat fryers produce high flue gas temperatures. In cases where the minimum distance between the grease removal device and the combustion gas outlet is 18" (46 cm) or less, a steel baffle should be installed.

Cleaning and Inspection of Exhaust Systems

Access to ducts for cleaning purposes is essential to the proper design of a kitchen ventilation system. They should be accessible for cleaning and inspection purposes. There should be a sign placed on all duct access panels that reads: ACCESS PANEL—DO NOT OBSTRUCT. On *horizontal duct runs*, an opening 20" × 20" (50 cm × 50 cm) should be provided. If this is not possible, an opening large enough to allow thorough cleaning should be installed at 12' (3.654 m) on center. On *vertical duct runs*, an opening for personnel entry should be located at the top of the duct. If this is not feasible, access panels should be located at each floor. In *buildings greater than one story* in height, ducts should be enclosed in a continuous enclosure extending from the ceiling above the hood to the roof. In *buildings less than four stories*, the enclosure should have a one-hour fire rating (if it qualifies as a shaft, a two-hour enclosure is common).

Air Volumes in Exhaust Systems

Kitchen exhaust fans should provide a minimum air velocity of 1,500 feet per minute (7.6 m/s). The air volumes should be adequate to capture and remove all grease-laden cooking vapors. In the event of a fire, exhaust fans should continue to operate unless a listed component of the exhaust system requires that the fan be shut down. It is not necessary to automatically restart the exhaust fan after the extinguishing system is activated if all the cooking equipment has been shut down. Approved up-discharge fans with motors surrounded by the air flow should be hinged and supplied with flexible wiring to allow periodic cleaning.

Fire Systems for Exhaust Hoods

Approved fire extinguishing systems should be provided for all grease removal items and hoods. These extinguishing systems should encompass all duct systems and cooking equipment that could be a source of grease ignition. NFPA recommends the following methods of fire suppression for use in kitchen exhaust systems:

Dry chemical extinguishing system	NFPA 17
Wet chemical extinguishing system	NFPA 17A
Carbon dioxide extinguishing system	NFPA 12
Sprinkler system	NFPA 13
Deluge foam water sprinkler and foam spray systems	NFPA 16

In the event that a fire suppression system activates, all sources of fuel and heat to the equipment should shut down. In addition, all gas appliances not requiring ventilation but located under the same hood should be shut down. All of these systems should be tied to the central fire alarm system in the building.

Special Fuel-Burning Equipment

IRC 2006

G2433 (603) Log Lighters

G2433.1 (603.1) General: Log lighters must comply with CSA 8. Installation must follow manufacturer's instructions.

G2434 (604) Vented Gas Fireplaces (Decorative Appliances)

G2434.1 (604.1) General: Vented decorative appliances that are gas-fired must comply with ANSI Z21.50. Installation must follow manufacturer's instructions.

G2433.2 (604.2) Access: Access doors and panels for servicing must not be permanently attached to the building.

Geothermal Heat Pumps

Green Home Improvement
(RSMeans)

Heat pumps use refrigeration technology to extract heat from the outside environment —either from the air surrounding a home (air-source heat pump) or from the ground (ground-source heat pump, otherwise known as geothermal). The heat is concentrated and distributed through ducts in a forced air system or through pipes in radiant floor or hot-water baseboard systems.

In ground-source, or geothermal, heat pump systems, pipes buried in the ground (either vertically or horizontally) circulate a fluid that absorbs the Earth's heat. (The ground below the frost line remains a constant 50°F.) In air-source heat pumps, heat is drawn directly from the outside air, then transferred to the home. This works even on cold winter days because the refrigerant in the heat pump is colder than the air temperature in areas that are well suited to these systems.

The equipment in both geothermal and air-source heat pumps is powered by electricity. For every unit of electricity a ground-source heat pump consumes when in operation, it produces about four units of heat. (An electric heater produces only one unit of heat for every unit of electricity it consumes.) Air source heat pumps are slightly less efficient. They produce about three units of heat for every unit of electricity they consume.

Because they run on electricity, heat pumps require no in-home combustion of fossil fuel. This eliminates the risk of combustion gases such as carbon monoxide spilling into the rooms of a house and results in healthier indoor air. It also reduces the chances of a house fire.

Heat pumps can also be used to cool a home. Running them in reverse extracts heat from the house and deposits it into the outdoor environment—either the air or ground. In addition, some of the heat from a heat pump can be used to warm water for in-home use.

Air-source heat pumps are typically installed in milder climates, although at least two manufacturers produce them for use in cold climates. Geothermal systems (ground-source heat pumps) are typically installed in colder climates.

Ground and air-source heat pumps require electricity, which is generated by power plants, many of which burn coal or natural gas. When these fossil fuels are burned, they produce greenhouse gases and a number of other harmful pollutants. Even so, ground and air source heat pumps produce less pollution than conventional home furnaces and boilers because the main source of their heat comes from the air or ground.

While heat pumps are more efficient and cleaner than conventional furnaces and boilers, geothermal systems cost more to install—about 25% to 100% more than a high-efficiency boiler or furnace (depending on location, local labor costs, and difficulty of the installation). Even so, they can save a substantial amount of money over the long term. Air source heat pumps are fairly economical to install and provide excellent savings if the climate is suitable.

Installation

The installation of a heat pump will first require removing old heating equipment (but not the duct system or pipes). Installation of a ground-source heat pump is easiest in new home construction, as it requires extensive excavation and/or drilling to lay the heat-absorbing pipes in the ground. This can be performed while the home is being built, before the finish grading is completed. Installation in an existing yard, especially a small one, is often more difficult and considerably more expensive. Pipes may need to be installed vertically to a depth of 200 feet, which requires a drill rig. Getting a drill rig into a backyard in an urban or suburban setting may be difficult or impossible. In such cases, a solar hot water system may be more economical, provided there's sufficient sun-bathed roof area for installation of the collectors. Local building code restrictions may apply.

CHAPTER

16 ELECTRICAL

Table of Contents

Text in blue type indicates excerpted summaries from the International Building Code® (IBC) *and* International Residential Code® (IRC). *Please consult the IBC and IRC for complete coverage and specific wording. "Comments" (in solid blue boxes) were written by the editors, based on their own experience.*

 This icon will appear with references to green building practices.

CHAPTER 16

ELECTRICAL

Common Defect Allegations

- *Insufficient number of receptacles and missing GFCIs in the bathrooms, kitchens, and exterior locations.*

- *Failure to provide exterior disconnects that are weather-tight and rated for exterior application.*

- *Kitchen-dedicated circuits for heavy-load appliances wired with a 14-gauge conductor instead of 12-gauge.*

- *Improper or missing labels on the panels.*

- *Wiring within 6' of the attic access opening. This should not be allowed, in order to prevent someone from pulling themselves up using the cable as a handgrab.*

- *Failure to weatherseal exterior lighting to the wall finish, thereby allowing rainwater into the wall cavity and the wiring.*

- *Holes in the drywall of an electrical closet where electricians ran telephone and TV cables. If these holes are not patched, they can allow rodents and vermin to enter the wall cavity.*

Introduction

Each year it seems the number of electrical devices in our homes or offices increases. Because of the inherent danger of shock and fire, the installation and use of electrical power is closely regulated by numerous codes—national, state, and local. Faulty electrical systems are one of the major causes of fire, after human error.

We have included many excerpts from the *National Electrical Code Handbook®*, published by the National Fire Protection Association. The *International Residential Code* (IRC), formerly the *International One- and Two-Family Dwelling Code* (IOTFDC), covers residential construction and includes electrical.

The information in this chapter is provided as a basic reference for the general contractor, student, or building owner seeking a better understanding of the standards for electrical installation. It is not to be used as an instruction manual for the installation. An electrical contractor or installer must be experienced and licensed (where required) with full knowledge of local and applicable national codes before performing any electrical work.

The following professional organizations may be helpful in locating more information about electrical design and installation. They also provide recommendations and support.

National Electrical Contractors Association (NECA)
301-657-3110
www.necanet.org
NECA, founded in 1901, is the leading representative of a segment of the construction market comprising over 70,000 electrical contracting firms. NECA services are designed for contractors who are involved in Standard Industrial Code 1731 (electrical work—specialty contractors) and some of those involved in SIC 1623 (utility work, also referred to as "outside" or "line" work).

National Electrical Manufacturers Association (NEMA)
703-841-3200
www.nema.org
NEMA has been developing standards for the electrical manufacturing industry since 1926 and is today one of leading standards development associations. It contributes to an orderly marketplace and helps to ensure public safety.

National Fire Protection Association (NFPA)
617-770-3000
www.nfpa.org
The *National Electrical Code Handbook®* is available from the NFPA. This chapter provides excerpts from the 2002 edition.

NFPA 70: *National Electrical Code® (NEC)*—The original code document was developed in 1897 as a result of the united efforts of various insurance, electrical, architectural, and allied interests. The *NEC* code is revised and updated every three years. All electrical installations should be done in accordance with *NEC* and local ordinances.

NFPA 72: National Fire Alarm Code®—This standard covers all aspects of the installation, maintenance, and use of fire alarm systems.
NFPA 780: Installation of Lightning Protection Systems Code—This code covers lightning protection requirements for ordinary structures, miscellaneous structures, and special occupancies. It does not cover explosives-manufacturing structures and electric utility systems.

Underwriters Laboratories, Inc. (UL)
877-854-3577
www.ul.com
UL is the leading third-party certification organization in the United States and the largest in North America. As a not-for-profit product safety testing and certification organization, UL has been evaluating products in the interest of public safety since 1894.

International Electrotechnical Commission (IEC)
011 41 22 919 02 11
www.iec.ch
The IEC is a worldwide organization that prepares and publishes international standards or all electrical, electronic, and related technologies. Membership consists of more than 60 participating countries, including all the world's major nations and a growing number of industrializing countries.

The Institute of Electrical and Electronic Engineers (IEEE)
212-419-7555
www.ieeeusa.org
The IEEE is the world's largest technical professional society. Founded in 1884 by a handful of practitioners of electrical science, it now includes electronic, computer engineering, and computer science professionals. IEEE sponsors technical conferences, symposia, local chapter meetings, and educational programs.

Illuminating Engineering Society of North America (IESNA)
212-248-5000
www.iesna.org
IESNA is dedicated to the field of lighting design and application, and publishes handbooks, design guides, and recommended practices.

Ed. Note: Comments and recommendations within this chapter are not intended as a definitive resource for a given project. Contractors must rely on the project documents and any applicable code requirements pertaining to their own particular location.

Green Approaches to Electrical

This chapter includes references to solar electric power, efficient light fixtures and bulbs, and consideration of the effect of plug loads on proper sizing of an efficient HVAC system. There are many additional opportunities in electrical design for a new home or light commercial facility. Some of these include simple recommendations such as use of switch-and-receptacles and power strips to more conveniently control power use—for example, to turn off power strips that supply electronic devices, thereby eliminating phantom loads.

(continued)

Selecting from Energy Star®-qualified light fixtures, bulbs, and electrical appliances is a simple way to reduce power use. Solar landscape and other exterior lighting has greatly improved in recent years and become available in a wider variety of fixtures. LED bulbs can last virtually for the lifetime of the fixture and work well even in cold temperatures. Compact fluorescent light (CFL) flood lamps can be used for outdoor lighting, though they're not ideal for motion-sensor security lighting, since they don't come on at full power immediately. Sensors to shut lights off in unoccupied rooms are another strategy to save energy.

Stand-alone wind power systems can provide electricity in areas that are far from the nearest utility grid. Wind systems can also be connected to utility grids, provided they meet certain criteria. Suitability for a given site is determined based on factors such as available wind, property size, and local zoning codes. The systems generate AC power, which is then converted to DC, and back to AC to regulate the voltage.

Residential Service—
Underground & Overhead

Industry Standards

Means Graphic Construction Standards
(RSMeans)

Residential Service

A residential service includes all of the materials and equipment necessary to deliver electrical power from the utility supply lines to the distribution system within the residence. The electrical service may be brought to the residence by overhead or underground supply lines. Residential service equipment consists of four basic components: a service drop conductor (for overhead service) or a service lateral conductor (for underground service); metering equipment; overcurrent protection; and a distribution panel.

The service entrance, which connects the residence directly to the utility supply lines, is run either overhead or underground. (See **Figures 16.1–16.3**.) In overhead services, the connecting cable runs from the utility pole to a bracket (sometimes called a "weatherhead") installed on the building. This aerial cable, called the service drop, is installed and maintained by the utility company. In underground services, the connection between the utility pole and residence may be run from either a utility pole or a utility-owned underground supply line. Although overhead service is the most commonly used system for residential installations, underground service, or "Underground Residential Distribution," is steadily increasing in popularity.

Residential service layouts vary widely, depending on voltage and amperage rating and the type of residence being served. In most cases, residential service is 100A, but 200A systems are being installed with increasing frequency to accommodate the many convenience appliances in today's homes. The increase in installation cost of 200A service over that of 100A service is about 30%. A typical overhead service is comprised of the following components and equipment: service head; service lateral, which consists of type SE cable or PVC, EMT, or rigid steel pipe with individual conductors; meter box (sometimes supplied by the utility); LB fitting, which is used to gain entrance from outside the dwelling to the distribution panel inside; distribution panel, with a 100A, 150A, or 200A main breaker and space for 20, 30, or 42 circuits 120/240V single-phase; ground rod and bare copper cable for the grounding system; and branch circuit breakers of 15A to 60A double-pole.

The layout for a typical underground system consists of service lateral conductors made of URD (underground residential distribution) direct burial cable, PVC pipe with individual conductors made of URD direct burial cable, PVC pipe with individual cables, or galvanized steel pipe with individual cables. In cases where URD cable is used, an approved protective sleeve must be installed where the cable is exposed at each end of the service

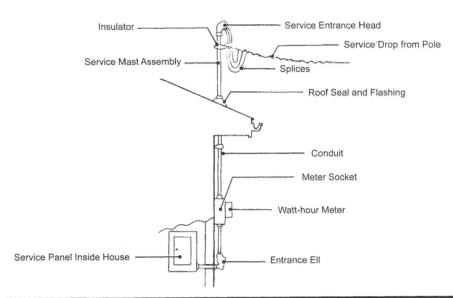

Through Roof Service Installation

Insulator — Service Entrance Head — Service Drop from Pole — Service Mast Assembly — Splices — Roof Seal and Flashing — Conduit — Meter Socket — Watt-hour Meter — Service Panel Inside House — Entrance Ell

lateral conductor (between the ground and connection to the supply line on the utility pole and between the finish grade and the meter socket on the dwelling). The layout for a typical underground system is the same as that for an overhead system in all other respects.

Comments

100A or 200A?

At the time of service installation, it is important to carefully consider whether the home or building owner may eventually require 200A service. Even though some appliances may not be anticipated at the time of construction, the owner may wish to accommodate new items such as central air, a heated swimming pool, or a hot tub in the future. It is much cheaper and easier to install the 200A service first than to have to replace 100A service later.

Underground Installation Requirements

Comments

The International Code Council has assumed responsibility for the development and maintenance of the *International Residential Code® for One- and Two-Family Dwellings* (IRC). The IRC replaces the 1998 *International One- and Two-Family Dwelling Code* (IOTFDC). Chapter 37 of the 2006 *IRC* covers wiring methods for services, feeders, and branch circuits for electrical power and distribution. It includes information about topics such as allowable applications for wiring methods, above ground/underground installation requirements, general installation and support requirements for wiring methods, and minimum cover requirements.

For underground installation of conduit and cable, refer to **Figures 16.2**, **16.3**, and **16.4**. Rigid nonmetallic conduit, such as PVC Schedule 40 conduit and fittings, should be buried at least 18" deep. Conductors under residential driveways follow the same rules (a minimum of 18" deep). If an overcurrent device is used, the burial depth can be reduced to 12". Some codes require a concrete jacket on underground installations of 220 or more volts.

Note: The following are summaries of the basic code requirements of the *International Residential Code*. Please consult the *IRC* for complete coverage and specific wording.

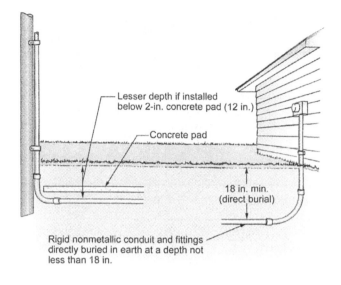

PVC rigid nonmetallic conduit buried in compliance with Table 300.5 and installed in accordance with 300.5(A).

Figure 16.2   Courtesy of NFPA, *National Electrical Code® Handbook* [Exhibit 300.6]

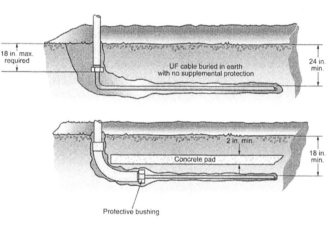

A type UF cable buried in compliance with Table 300.5.

Figure 16.3   Courtesy of NFPA, *National Electrical Code® Handbook* [Exhibit 300.10]

IRC-2006

E3703 Underground installation requirements

E3703.1 Minimum cover requirements: Buried cables or raceways must comply with IRC-2006 Table E3703.1, which specifies required depth in inches for cables, conduits, and residential branch circuits for various locations. For example, direct burial cables or conductors must be at least 18" deep if located under residential driveways.

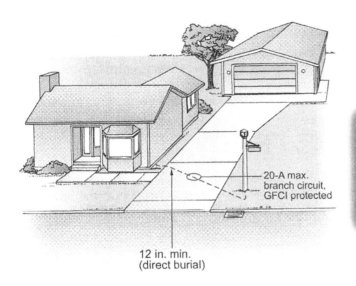

20-A max.
branch circuit,
GFCI protected

12 in. min.
(direct burial)

A 20-ampere, GFCI-protected residential branch circuit installed with a minimum burial depth of 12 in. beneath a residential driveway.

Figure 16.4   Courtesy of NFPA, *National Electrical Code® Handbook* [Exhibit 300.7]

E3703.2 Warning ribbon: Uderground service conductors that are buried 18" or more below grade and aren't encased with concrete shall have their location identified with a ribbon placed no less than 12" above them.

E3703.3 Protection from damage: Buried cables/conductors that come up from the ground must be protected by enclosures or raceways.

E3703.4 Splices and taps: Direct buried cables/conductors may be tapped or spliced without splice boxes.

E3703.5 Backfill: Backfill of materials that may damage underground installations, such as large, sharp rock or cinders, is not allowed.

E3703.6 Raceway seals: Conduits/raceways must be sealed if subject to moisture.

Overhead Service Drop

Industry Standards
Electrical Estimating Methods
(RSMeans)

Poles and *overhead routing* represent the most conventional method of distributing power and communication cables. Many cables are built and rated for aerial service. Some cables include "strength members" to carry the tensions of the stretched cables. Still other types of cable, such as service drops and telephone lines, will be supported by a steel messenger wire.

Note: Code requirements may dictate certain minimum heights for suspended cable.

Comments

Service conductors without an outer jacket must have a clearance at least 3' from windows. (See **Figures 16.5– 16.7.**) For above-roof installation, conductors must have a vertical clearance between 18" and 8' above the roof surface, depending on the slope of the roof.

The hole for a line pole is usually made with an auger machine. After the pole is set, crushed limestone or similar fill is placed and compacted around the pole. In some areas, poles will need lightning rods and grounding. Don't forget to look for these requirements on the drawings.

Comments

Chapter 35 of the 2006 *IRC* covers service conductors and equipment for the control and protection of services and their installation requirements. Section 3504 addresses overhead service-drop and service conductor installation and includes requirements for clearance from building openings and roofs, vertical clearances, point of attachment, means of attachment, and supports.

IRC–2006

E3504 Overhead service-drop and service conductor installation

E3504.1 Clearance on buildings: Clearance of at least 3' is required from doors, windows, stairs, porches, and so forth for open conductors that don't have an outer jacket.

E3504.2 Vertical clearance: Service-drop conductors must not have ready access and must comply with this Section.

E3504.3 Point of attachment: The point of attachment from the structure to the service-drop conductor must be at least 10' above finished grade.

E3504.4 Means of attachment: Approved fittings must be used for attachment.

E3504.5 Service masts as supports: Service masts used to support service-drop conductors must have braces or be of sufficient strength.

Service Conductor Requirements

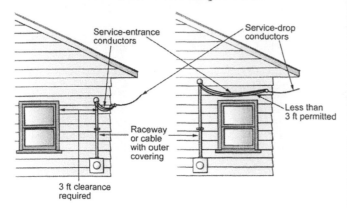

Required dimensions for service conductors located alongside a window (left) and service conductors above the top level of a window designed to be opened (right).

Figure 16.5   Courtesy of NFPA, *National Electrical Code® Handbook* [Exhibit 230.16]

E3504.6 Supports over buildings: Service-drop conductors passing over a roof shall be securely supported with supports that are independent of the building.

Clearance from Buildings

NFPA 70: National Electrical Code

230.24. Clearances

(A) Above Roofs: Conductors shall have a vertical clearance of not less than 8' above the roof surface. The vertical clearance above the roof level shall be maintained for a distance not less than 3' in all directions from the edge of the roof. (See **Figure 16.6**.)

Exception No. 1: The area above a roof surface subject to pedestrian or vehicular traffic shall have a vertical clearance from the roof surface in accordance with the clearance requirements of Section 230.24(B).

Exception No. 2: Where the voltage between conductors does not exceed 300 and the roof has a slope of 4" in 12". or greater, a reduction in clearance of 3' shall be permitted.

Exception No. 3: Where the voltage between conductors does not exceed 300, a reduction in clearance above only the overhanging portion of

the roof to not less than 18" shall be permitted if (1) not more than 6' of service drop conductors, 4' horizontally, pass above the roof overhead, and (2) they are terminated at a through-the-roof raceway or approved support.

Exception No. 4: The requirement for maintaining the vertical clearance 3' from the edge of the roof shall not apply to the final conductor span where the service-drop is attached to the side of a building.

230.9 Clearance from Building Openings: Service conductors installed as open conductors or multiconductor cable without an overall outer jacket shall have a clearance of not less than 3' from windows that are designed to be opened, doors, porches, balconies, ladders, stairs, fire escapes, or similar locations.

Exception: Conductors run above the top level of a window shall be permitted to be less than the 3' requirement.

Overhead service conductors shall not be installed beneath openings through which materials may be moved, such as openings in farm and commercial buildings, and shall not be installed where they will obstruct entrance to these building openings.

Clearance Above Roofs, Exception 2

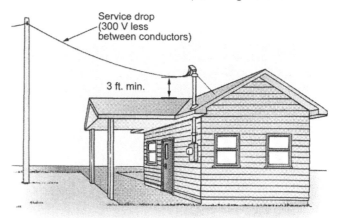

Reduction in clearance above a roof as permitted by 230.24(A), Exception No. 2.

Figure 16.6   Courtesy of NFPA, *National Electrical Code® Handbook* [Exhibit 230.19]

Clearance Above Roofs, Exception 3

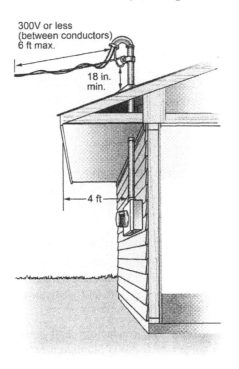

300V or less
(between conductors)
6 ft max.

18 in.
min.

4 ft

Reduction in clearance above a roof as permitted by 230.24(A), Exception No. 3.

Courtesy of NFPA, *National Electrical Code® Handbook* [Exhibit 230.20]

Figure 16.7

Green Electricity from Photovoltaic Cells & Modules

Green Building: Project Planning & Cost Estimating, Second Edition
(RSMeans)

The electric power that PV produces is DC (direct current), similar to that coming from a battery. The voltage of each cell depends on the material's band gap, or the energy required to raise an electron from the valence band (where it is bound to the atom) to the conduction band (where it is free to conduct electricity). For silicon, each cell generates a voltage of about 0.6V. The voltage decreases gradually (logarithmically) with increasing temperature. The current generated by each cell depends on its surface area and intensity of incident sunlight. Cells are wired in series to achieve the required voltage, and series strings are wired in parallel to provide the required current and power. As increasing current is drawn from the cell, the voltage drops off, leading to a combination of current and voltage which maximizes the power output of the cell. This combination, called the maximum power point (MPP), changes slightly with temperature and intensity of sunlight. Most PV systems have power conditioning electronics, called a maximum power point tracker (MPPT) to constantly adjust the voltage in order to maximize power output. Simpler systems operate at a fixed voltage close to the optimal voltage.

Each "PV cell" is a wafer as thin and as fragile as a potato chip. In order to protect it from weather and physical damage, they are encapsulated in a "glue" called ethyl vinyl acetate and sandwiched between a sheet of tempered glass on top and a layer of glass or other protective material underneath. A frame often surrounds the glass laminate to provide additional protection and mounting points. Such an assembly is called a PV module. The current and voltage of the module will reflect the size and series-parallel arrangement of the cells inside. The Rated Power of a PV module is the output of the module under standard rating conditions (1 kW/m2 light, 25°C, 1 m/s wind speed). Other standard tests conducted on PV modules include the "hi pot" test (where a high voltage is applied to the internal circuits, and the assembly dipped in electrolyte solution to detect imperfect insulation). Another test involves 1" simulated iceballs fired at 55 mph at different parts of the module to evaluate hail-resistance.

Similarly, modules are wired in series to increase the voltage, and then series strings of modules are wired in series to provide the required current and overall power output from a PV array.

For small DC systems, 12V, 24V, and 48V configurations are common to match the voltage of lead-acid batteries often used in these systems. Higher voltage results in less current and less loss in the wiring. For large systems, voltage as high as 600V is used to minimize line losses. There is a trade-off however, between line loss and reliability, since if any module in a series fails (by shading or damage), that whole series string is affected. Note that Power = Current × Voltage and power will be limited by the lowest voltage in parallel and the lowest current in series.

PV System Components

A PV system may consist of some or all of the following components, depending on the type of system and the applications:

- PV array to convert sunlight to electricity
- Array support structure and enclosure to protect other equipment
- Maximum power point tracker to match load to optimal array voltage

517

- Batteries to store charge for when it is needed
- Charge controller to protect battery from over-charging
- Low voltage disconnect to protect battery from over-discharging
- Inverter to convert direct current (DC) to alternating current (AC)
- Automatic generator starter/stopper to start a generator when battery is too low, and a battery charger to re-charge the batteries with generator power

Array Support Structures

Ground-mounted structures can be mounted on the tops of poles or on various types of truss racks with foundations. The mounting structure is 5%–7% of the system cost, depending on system size and configuration. Often, a designer determines the trade-off between the cost of more PV area and the cost and maintenance requirements of a tracker in order to decide between fixed-tilt and tracking mount.

Batteries

There is an acute need to store electrical energy for many purposes besides PV systems, and researchers are investigating alternatives. Battery manufacturers continue to implement innovations to improve performance. Battery technology is raging headlong into the 1700s, with designers specifying the same old lead-acid technology because of its low cost.

Batteries do have some dangers. They contain several toxic materials, and care must be taken to ensure that they are recycled properly. In some cases batteries are shipped dry, with the electrolyte added on-site. During installation, care must be taken to ensure that battery electrolyte (battery acid) is not ingested by an installer or an unaware bystander. Storing battery electrolyte only in well-labeled child-proof containers can reduce this risk. Finally, batteries are capable of rapidly releasing their stored energy if they are shorted; care must be taken to avoid electrocution and fires caused by sparks.

The amount of battery capacity required depends on the magnitude of the load and the required reliability. A typical battery capacity is sufficient to meet the load for 3–5 days without sun, but in applications that require high reliability, 10 days of battery storage may be recommended.

Charge Controller

The function of the battery charge controller is very important for system performance and battery longevity. The charge controller modulates the charge current into the battery to protect against overcharging and an associated loss of electrolyte. The low-voltage disconnect protects the battery from becoming excessively discharged by disconnecting the load. It seems unfortunate to disconnect the load, but doing so avoids damage to the battery, and not doing so would simply delay the inevitable, since the load would not be served by a ruined battery. The set point of the low-voltage disconnect involves a cost trade-off. For example, allowing the battery to get down to a 20% state of charge (80% discharged) would result in a short battery life. Limiting it to an 80% state of charge (20% discharged) would make the battery last considerably longer, but would also require 4 times as many batteries to provide the same storage capacity.

Inverter

Utility power in U.S. buildings is 120V or 240V AC (alternating current) of 60 Hz frequency (50 Hz in many countries overseas). Since many appliances are designed to operate with alternating current, PV systems are often furnished with power conditioning equipment called an inverter to convert the DC power from the PV array or the battery to AC power for the appliances. Inverters use power transistors to achieve the conversion electronically. Advances in inverter technology have resulted in systems that deliver a pure sine wave form and exceptional power quality. In fact, except for the PV array, the components of a PV system are the same as those of an uninterruptible power supply (UPS) system used to provide critical users of power with the highest power quality. Inverters are available with all controls and safety features built in.

Generator

For small stand-alone systems it is often cost-effective to meet the load using only solar power. However, during extended cloudy weather this approach requires a very large battery bank and solar array. To optimize cost, the PV system can incorporate a generator to run infrequently during periods when there is no sun. This hybrid PV/generator system takes advantage of the low operating cost of the PV array and the on-demand capability of a generator.

In this configuration, the PV array and battery bank would ordinarily serve the load. If the battery becomes discharged, the generator automatically starts to serve the load, but also to power a battery charger to recharge the batteries. When the batteries are fully charged, the generator automatically turns off again. This system of cyclically charging batteries is cost-effective even without PV, as it keeps a large generator from running to serve a small load. A hybrid system would be designed to minimize life cycle cost, with the PV array typically providing 70%–90% of the annual energy, and the generator providing the remainder. PV is also often combined with wind power, under the hypothesis that if the sun is not shining, the wind may be blowing.

Grid-Connected Systems

Grid-connected systems don't require batteries because the utility provides power when solar is not available. These systems consist of an array, DC disconnect, inverter, AC disconnect, and isolation transformer. Several utility and industry standards (most notably UL1741 and IEEE929) must be satisfied, and an agreement with the utility must be negotiated, before a customer's system can interact with the utility system. Photovoltaics are most cost-effective in remote applications where utility power is not available and alternatives such as diesel generators are more expensive. Historically, remote applications have been the bulk of the market. However, in 2004, for the first time, grid-interactive electricity generation became the dominant end-use of PV, with a market share of 71% (129,265 peak kilowatts), up from 39% in 2003. Grid-connected applications have averaged a compound growth rate of 64% per year during the 1999–2004 period.

Building-Integrated Photovoltaics (BIPV)

An exciting trend is building-integrated photovoltaics, or BIPV, where the photovoltaic material replaces a conventional part of the building construction. About 90% of grid-connected systems in 2004 were rooftop or building-integrated (BIPV). One-for-one replacements for shingles, standing seam metal roofing, spandrel glass, and overhead skylight glass are already on the market. The annual energy delivery of these components will be reduced if walls and roofs are not at the optimal orientation, but it has been demonstrated that PV installed within 45 degrees of the optimal tilt and orientation suffers only a slight reduction in annual performance. Tilt less than optimal will increase summer gains, but decrease the annual total, and panels facing east will increase morning gains, but decrease the daily total.

Design Tools

Design tools for PV systems are simple hand calculations and hourly simulations of PV system performance. Hand calculations are facilitated by the fact that PV systems are rated at a solar radiation level of 1 kW/m2, so a PV array can be expected to deliver its rated output for a number of hours (called sunhours) per day equal to the number of kWh/m2/day presented in the solar resource data.

Work Space in Front of Equipment

NFPA 70: National Electrical Code

110.34. Work Space and Guarding

(A) Working Space: Except as elsewhere required or permitted in this code, the minimum clear working space in the direction of access to live parts of electrical equipment shall not be less than specified in Table 110.34(A) see **Figure 16.8**. Distances shall be measured from the live parts, if such are exposed, or from the enclosure front or opening if such are enclosed.

Exception: Working space shall not be required in back of equipment such as dead-front switchboards or control assemblies where there are no renewable or adjustable parts (such as fuses or switches) on the back and where all connections are accessible from locations other than the back. Where rear access is required to work on de-energized parts on the back of enclosed equipment, a minimum working space of 30" (750 mm) horizontally shall be provided.

Where the "Conditions" are as follows:

1. Exposed live parts on one side and no live or grounded parts on the other side of the working space or exposed live parts on both sides effectively guarded by suitable wood or other insulating materials.

Minimum Depth of Clear Working Space at Electrical Equipment

Nominal Voltage to Ground	Minimum Clear Distance		
	Condition 1	Condition 2	Condition 3
601–2500 V	900 mm (3 ft)	1.2 m (4 ft)	1.5 m (5 ft)
2501–9000 V	1.2 m (4 ft)	1.5 m (5 ft)	1.8 m (6 ft)
9001–25,000 V	1.5 m (5 ft)	1.8 m (6 ft)	2.8 m (9 ft)
25,001V–75 kV	1.8 m (6 ft)	2.5 m (8 ft)	3.0 m (10 ft)
Above 75 kV	2.5 m (8 ft)	3.0 m (10 ft)	3.7 m (12 ft)

Figure 16.8 Courtesy of NFPA, *National Electrical Code® Handbook* [Table 110.34(A)]

2. Exposed live parts on one side and grounded parts on the other side. Concrete, brick, or tile walls shall be considered as grounded surfaces.

3. Exposed live parts on both sides of the working space.

Service Equipment— General

Comments

Service equipment in general includes service entrance transformers, either pad- or pole-mounted, installed near the service entrance. Fuses, circuit breakers, and panelboards are used to protect the branch circuits from short circuits or overloads.

Number of Services, Disconnects

NFPA 70: National Electrical Code

230.2 Number of Services:

A building or other structure served shall be supplied by only one service unless permitted in 230.2(A) through (D).

(E) Identification: Where a building or structure is supplied by more than one service, or any combination of branch circuits, feeders, and services, a permanent plaque or directory shall be installed at each service disconnect location denoting all other services, feeders, and branch circuits supplying that building or structure and the area served by each.

230.62 Service Equipment–Enclosed or Guarded:

Energized parts of service equipment shall be enclosed as specified in 230.62(A) or guarded as specified in 260.62(B).

(A) Enclosed: Energized parts shall be enclosed so that they will not be exposed to accidental contact or shall be guarded as in 230.62(B).

(B) Guarded: Energized parts that are not enclosed shall be installed on a switchboard, panelboard, or control board and guarded in accordance with 110.18 and 110.27. Where energized parts are guarded as provided in 110.27(A)(1) and (A)(2), a means for locking or sealing doors providing access to energized parts shall be provided.

230.66 Marking: Service equipment rated at 600 volts or less shall be marked to identify it as being suitable for use as service equipment. Individual meter socket enclosures shall not be considered service equipment.

Service Equipment—Disconnecting Means

230.70 General: Means shall be provided to disconnect all conductors in a building or other structure from the service-entrance conductors.

(A) Location: The service disconnecting means shall be installed in accordance with 230.70(A)(1), (A)(2), and (A)(3).

(1) Readily Accessible Location: The service disconnecting means shall be installed at a readily accessible location either outside of a building or structure or inside nearest the point of entrance of the service conductors.

(2) Bathrooms: Service disconnecting means shall not be installed in bathrooms.

(3) Remote Control: Where a remote control device(s) is used to actuate the service disconnecting means, the service disconnecting means shall be located in accordance with 230.70(A)(1).

(B) Marking: Each service disconnect shall be permanently marked to identify it as a service disconnect.

(C) Suitable for Use: Each service disconnecting means shall be suitable for the prevailing conditions. Service equipment installed in hazardous (classified) locations shall comply with the requirements of Articles 500 through 517.

Ed. Note: Articles 500–517 pertain to special occupancies in classified locations, including hazardous locations, commercial garages, and health care facilities.

230.71 Maximum Number of Disconnects:

(A) General: The service disconnecting means for each service permitted by 230.2, or for each set of service-entrance conductors permitted by 230.40, Exception Nos. 1, 3, 4, or 5, shall consist of not more than six switches or sets of circuit breakers, or a combination of not more than six switches and sets of circuit breakers, mounted in a single enclosure, in a group of separate enclosures, or in or on a switchboard. There shall be no more than six sets of disconnects per service grouped in any one location. For the purpose of this section, disconnecting means installed as part of listed equipment and used solely for the following shall not be considered a service disconnecting means:

(1) powering monitoring equipment

(2) surge-protected device(s)

(3) the control circuit of the ground-fault protection system or

(4) power-operable service disconnecting means

(B) Single-Pole Units: Two or three single-pole switches or breakers, capable of individual operation, shall be permitted on multi-wire circuits, one pole for each ungrounded conductor, as one multipole disconnect, provided they are equipped with identified handle ties or a master handle to disconnect all conductors of the service with no more than six operations of the hand.

(FPN): See 408.16(A) for service equipment in panelboards, and see 430.95 for service equipment in motor control centers.

Ed. Note: (FPN) denotes fine print note.

230.74 Simultaneous Opening of Poles: Each
service disconnect shall simultaneously disconnect all ungrounded service conductors that it controls from the premises wiring system.

230.82 Equipment Connected to the Supply Side of Service Disconnect: Only the following
equipment shall be connected to the supply side of the service disconnecting means.

(1) Cable limiters or other current-limiting devices.

(2) Meters, meter sockets, or meter disconnect switches nominally rated not in excess of 600 volts, provided all metal housings and service enclosures are grounded, in accordance of Article 250.

(3) Meter disconnected switches nominally rated in excees of 600 volts that have a short-circuit current rating equal to or greater than the available short-circuit current.

(4) Instrument transformers (current and voltage), high-impedance shunts, load management devices, and surge arresters.

(5) Taps used only to supply load management devices, circuits for standby power systems, fire pump equipment, and fire sprinkler alarms, if provided with service equipment and installed in accordance with requirements for service-entrance conductors.

(6) Solar photovoltaic systems, fuel cell systems, or interconnected electric power production sources.

(7) Control circuits for power-operable services disconnecting means, if suitable overcurrent protection and disconnecting means are provided.

(8) Ground-fault protection systems or type 2 surge protectors where installed as part of listed equipment, if suitable overcurrent protection and disconnecting means are provided.

Service Conductors & Grounding

Industry Standards
Plan Reading & Material Takeoff
(RSMeans)

Conductors and Grounding

A *conductor* is a wire or metal bar with a low resistance to the flow of electricity. *Grounding* is accomplished by a conductor connected between electrical equipment, or between a circuit and the earth. Wire is the most common material used to conduct current from the electrical source to electrical use. Wire is made of either copper or aluminum conductors with an insulating jacket, and is available in a variety of voltage ratings and insulating materials. Wire is installed within raceways, such as conduit or flexible metallic conduit (sometimes referred to as *Greenfield* or *flex*). *Flexible metallic conduit* is a single strip of aluminum or galvanized steel, spiral-wound and interlocked to provide a circular cross section of high strength and flexibility for the protection of the wire within. Other products similar to flex are covered with a liquid-tight plastic covering; they are used where protection from liquids is required.

Other types of conductors include armored cable (BX & MC), a fabricated assembly of cable with a metal enclosure similar in appearance to flex. Nonmetallic sheathed cable (Romex) is factory-constructed of two, three, or four insulated conductors enclosed in an outer sheath of plastic or fibrous material. It is available with or without a bare ground wire made of copper or aluminum conductors.

Special wires such as those used in low-voltage control wiring, signals, and telecommunications are also available for the performance required by the specific application.

In addition to the wire itself, special connectors or terminations at the end of each wire are required to complete the application. Various fasteners such as staples, clips, and flex fittings are also necessary.

Comments

Chapter 35 of the 2006 *IRC* covers service conductors and equipment for the control and protection of services and their installation requirements. Chapter 37 of IRC-2006 addresses wiring methods.

IRC–2006

E3501 General services

E3501.2 Number of services: Residential homes may only have one service.

E3501.4 Other conductors in raceway or cable: Except for service conductors, grounding conductors, bonding jumpers, or load management control conductors having over-current control, conductors may not be within the same service cable or raceway.

E3501.5 Raceway seal: Proper sealing is required for service raceways entering from underground distribution systems.

E3501.6 Service disconnect required: Disconnecting method is required.

E3501.7 Maximum number of disconnects: The disconnecting means must have no more than six circuit breakers/switches in each enclosure.

Deteriorating Agents

NFPA 70: National Electrical Code

110.11. Deteriorating Agents: Unless identified for use in the operating environment, no conductors or equipment shall be located in damp or wet locations; where exposed to gases, fumes, vapors, liquids, or

other agents that have a deteriorating effect on the conductors or equipment; nor where exposed to excessive temperatures.

(FPN No. 1): See 300.6 for protection against corrosion.

(FPN No. 2): Some cleaning and lubricating compounds can cause severe deterioration of many plastic materials used for insulating and structural applications in equipment.

Equipment not identified for outdoor use and equipment only identified for indoor use shall be protected against permanent damage from the weather during building construction.

Conductor Identification

Comments

The receptacles supplied by a given circuit (via the conductor) can be identified in one of two ways. The conductor can be tagged with an identifying number, or the circuit (on the panelboard) can be described using a name plate.

Chapter 33 of the 2006 *IRC* addresses general electrical requirements. Section 3307 covers ground conductor and terminal identification.

Load Centers & Panelboards

Comments

Panelboards organize circuit switching and protective devices into one metal box that accommodates bus bars, circuit protective devices, and wiring. It is covered by a trim plate and cover.

Load Centers are a special type of panelboard principally used in residential and light commercial applications. They are designed for lighter sustained loads than would be found in most commercial or industrial installations.

IRC–2006

E3606.1 Panelboard rating: Panelboards must be rated at least the minimum required feeder capacity or service entrance rating.

E3606.2 Panelboard circuit identification: Panelboard circuit usage must be clearly written on the door.

E3606.3 Panelboard overcurrent protection: The supply side must have protection consisting of no more than two main circuit breakers or sets of fuses.

E3807.2 Damp or wet locations: Cabinets/panelboards must be located so that moisture cannot reach them. In wet locations, they must be weatherproof.

E3807.3 Position in wall: Cabinets in walls of combustible materials must be positioned flush with or slightly projecting from the surface. For noncombustible walls, cabinets may be recessed up to a quarter of an inch.

NFPA 70: National Electrical Code

Panelboards

408.4 Circuit Directory or Circuit Idenfication: Every circuit or modification must be identified to show its purpose or use.

408.36 Overcurrent Protection

(A) Snap switches rated at 30 amperes or less: These must have overcurrent protection of 200 amperes or less.

(B) Supplied through a transformer: When this is the case, the overcurrent protection shall be located on the secondary side of the transformer.

(D) Back-Fed Devices: Plug-in-type overcurrent protection devices or plug-in-type main lug assemblies that are backfed and used to terminate field-installed ungrounded supply conductors shall be secured in place by an additional fastener that requires other than a pull to release the device from the mounting means on the panel.

408.38 Enclosure: Panelboards shall be mounted in cabinets, cutout boxes, or enclosures designed for the purpose and shall be dead-front.

408.40 Grounding of Panelboards: If metal, panelboard cabinet frames must be in physical contact with each other and shall be grounded. Where the panelboard is used with nonmetallic raceway or cable or where separate grounding conductors are provided, a terminal bar for the grounding conductors must be secured inside the cabinet. If it's metal, the terminal bar must be bonded to the cabinet and panelboard. If not, it must be connected to the grounding conductor that is run with the conductors feeding the panelboard.

Ed. Note: For space requirements around electrical equipment (600V, nominal, or less), see Figure 16.10. Also refer to Figure 16.8 in the section, "Work Space in Front of Equipment," earlier in this chapter.

For additional information about circuit breakers provided by Underwriters' Laboratories Inc., see "Circuit Breakers—Interchanging in Foreign Panels," later in this chapter.

Grounded Conductors of Different Systems in the Same Enclosure

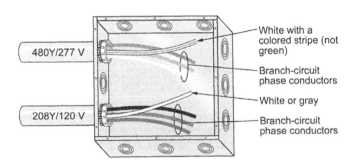

The insulation of the grounded conductors of the different systems is of a color as prescribed by 200.6(D).

Figure 16.9   Courtesy of NFPA, *National Electrical Code® Handbook* [Exhibit 200.2]

Sufficient Space for Operation and Maintenance of Equipment

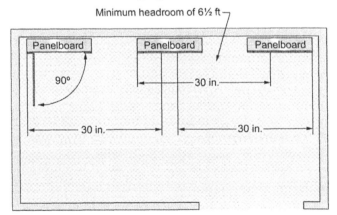

The 30 in. wide front working space not required to be directly centered on the electrical equipment if space is sufficient for safe operation and maintenance of such equipment.

Figure 16.10   Courtesy of NFPA, *National Electrical Code® Handbook* [Exhibit 110.12]

Plug Loads

Green Building: Project Planning & Cost Estimating, Second Edition
(RSMeans)

Plug loads are the electric loads drawn by all the equipment that is plugged into outlets. Computers, printers, and faxes do not draw energy at one constant rate. Energy use spikes when equipment is turned on and then falls to a much lower operating level. Rating labels on the equipment are for start-up loads (maximum energy draw) and should be used to size the wires and devices in the electrical system.

Adding up the nameplate ratings of various pieces of equipment in an office and dividing by the area will typically result in the determination of a "connected" load of 3–4 watts per square foot. This connected load is not, however, the same as the average operating, or "as-used" load, which is likely to be less than 1 watt per square foot. (A study of U.S. office buildings found it to be 0.78 watts per square foot on average.) This as-used load, rather than the connected load, should be used to calculate the sizing of mechanical systems, which must compensate for the actual heat generated by the equipment, not the amount of heat that would be generated if the equipment remained in start-up mode. The resultant downsizing of the mechanical system can have a significant impact on the first cost of the facility.

Lightning Surge Arresters

Comments

Depending on local code, lightning protection may be required for special types of facilities, such as structures that store explosives, playgrounds, and aircraft fields. Generally, lightning protection is not required for residential structures unless specified by local code or in the project documents.

Industry Standard

Electrical Estimating Methods
(RSMeans)

Lightning Protection
Lightning protection for the rooftops of buildings is achieved by a series of lightning rods or air terminals joined together by either copper or aluminum cable. The cable size is determined by the height of the building. The lightning cable system is connected

through a downlead to a ground rod that is a minimum of 2' below grade and 1½' to 3' out from the foundation wall. By code, all metal bodies on the roof that are located within six feet of a lightning conductor must be bonded to the lightning protection system.

One of the basic components of a lightning grounding system is the air terminal. These are manufactured in either copper or aluminum. The most common sizes used are ⅜" diameter copper at 10" high for roofs under 75' high. For roofs over 75', a ½" diameter by 12" high terminal is most common. For aluminum air terminals, a ½" diameter by 12" high is used for roofs under 75', and a 5/8" diameter by 12" high is used for heights over 75'. Air terminals are usually mounted in the perimeter parapet wall and include a masonry cable anchor base. A wide range of configurations is available from manufacturers for mounting air terminals to different roof surfaces. Most do not vary significantly in price.

Cable for main conductor use is calculated in pounds per 1,000'; it is available on 500' spools. Conductors are manufactured in copper and aluminum. The industry standard Class I minimum weight for copper is 187 lbs. per 1,000' when used on a roof of less than 75' high, and Class II minimum weight for copper is 375 lbs. per 1,000' for structures over 75' high. The main conductor for Class I aluminum cable is 95 lbs. per 1,000' for structures over 75' high. Connections to main grounding conductor cable are accomplished in one of three ways: clamping, heat or exothermic welding, or brazing.

National Electrical Code Handbook

Ed. Note: The following excerpt contains NFPA commentary by recognized experts in the field of safety, along with the National Electrical Code in numbered paragraphs.

280.1. Scope: This article covers general requirements, installation requirements, and connection requirements for surge arresters installed on premises wiring systems over 1 kV.

280.2. Uses not permitted: A surge arrester mustn't be installed if the rating of the arrester is less than the maximum continuous phase-to-ground power frequency voltage available at the application point.

280.3. Number required: Where used at a point on a circuit, a surge arrester shall be connected to each ungrounded conductor. A single installation of such surge arresters shall be permitted to protect a number of interconnected circuits, provided that no circuit is exposed to surges while disconnected from the surge arresters.

280.4. Surge Arrester Selection:

The surge arresters must comply with this Section.

(A) Rating: The rating of the surge arrester must be equal to or greater than the maximum continuous operating voltage available at the point of application.

(B) Silicon Carbide Types: The rating of this type of arrester must not be less that 125% of the rating specified in 280.4(A).

280.11. Location: Surge arresters shall be permitted to be located indoors or outdoors. Surge arresters shall be made inaccessible to unqualified persons, unless listed for installation in accessible locations.

280.12. Routing of Surge Arrester Connections:
The conductor used to connect the surge arrester to line, bus, or equipment and to a grounding conductor connection point must not be any longer than necessary and must avoid unnecessary bends.

NFPA commentary: Arrester conductors should be as short and be run as straight as practicable, avoiding any sharp bends and turns, which would increase the impedance. High-frequency currents, such as those common to lightning discharges, tend to reduce the effectiveness of a grounding conductor.

stabilizes the voltage with respect to ground and prevents surface potentials between equipment—which could harm both people and equipment (in a hospital, for example).

Lightning protection systems are a separate concern but are closely related to grounding in intent and practice. Lightning poses two kinds of danger. The first is the lightning strike itself. This can damage structures and distribution systems by passing a very high current for a brief time—causing heat, fire, and/or equipment failure. The second danger is from induced voltages in lines running close to the lightning's path. These pulses can be very high and can damage electrical equipment or cause injury to people.

In both systems, it is essential that a good, low-resistance ground path be provided. This can be accomplished via the use of ground rods, a ground grid, or attachment to metal pipes in contact with the earth (such as water pipes). Note: In communities where plastic water pipes are used between the street main and a building, this grounding method is not suitable—even though copper pipes may be used for the building's interior.

Connections between ground wires and pipes, conduits, or boxes are often made with cable clamps. For residential and light commercial applications, grounding is typically accomplished using the configuration shown in **Figure 16.11**.

Comments

A service surge arrester (SSA) is recommended in all geographical locations where lightning is a common occurrence.

Comments

Chapter 35 of the 2006 *IRC* addresses service conductors and equipment for the control and protection of services and their installation requirements.

Grounding Electrode

Industry Standards

Electrical Estimating Methods
(RSMeans)

Grounding
In most distribution systems, one conductor of the supply is grounded. This conductor is called the "neutral wire." In addition, the N.E.C. requires that a grounding conductor be supplied to connect non-current-carrying, conductive parts to ground. This distinction between the "grounded conductor" and the "grounding conductor" is important.

Grounding protects persons from injury in the event of an insulation failure within equipment. It also

An Application of a Listed Ground Clamp

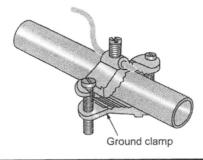

Ground clamp

Figure 16.11   Courtesy of NFPA, *National Electrical Code® Handbook* [Exhibit 250.32]

IRC-2006

E3510 Grounding electrode conductors

E3510.1 Continuous: Unspliced conductors must run to convenient available grounding electrodes in the system or to one or more grounding electrodes individually. The grounding electrode conductor must be sized for the largest required among all connected electrodes.

E3511.1 Methods of grounding conductor connection to electrodes: Electrodes must be connected to grounding conductors by one of several possible methods, including listed lugs, clamps, or pressure connectors.

NFPA 70: National Electrical Code

250.68 Grounding Electrode Conductor and Bonding Jumper Connection to Grounding Electrodes

(A) Accessibility: Mechanical elements used to terminate a grounding electrode conductor or bonding jumper to a grounding electrode shall be accessible.

(B) Effective Grounding Path: The connection of a grounding electrode conductor or bonding jumper to a grounding electrode shall be made in a manner that will ensure a permanent and effective grounding path. Where necessary to ensure the grounding path for a metal piping system used as a grounding electrode, effective bonding shall be provided around any equipment likely to be disconnected for repairs or replacement. Bonding jumpers shall be of sufficient length to permit removal of such equipment while retaining the integrity of the grounding path.

250.24 Grounding Service-Supplied Alternating Current Systems

(A) System Grounding Connections: A premises wiring system supplied by a service shall have a grounding electrode conductor connected to the grounded service conductor, at each service, in accordance with this Section.

250.66. Size of Alternating-Current Grounding Electrode Conductor: The size of the grounding electrode conductor of a grounded or ungrounded ac system shall not be less than given in Table 250.66 (See **Figure 16.12.**)

Exceptions:

(A) **Connections to Rod, Pipe, or Plate Electrode:** Where the grounding electrode connector is connected to rod, pipe, or plate electrodes as permited in 250.52 (A) (5) or 250.52 (A)(6), that portion of the grounding electrode conductor that is the sole connection to the grounding electrode shall not be required to be larger than 6 AWG copper wire or 4 AWG aluminum wire.

(B) **Connections to Concrete-Encased Electrodes:** Where the grounding electrode conductor is connected to a concrete-encased electrode as permitted in 250.52 (A) (3), that portion of the conductor that is the sole connection to the grounding electrode shall not be required to be larger than 4AWG copper wire.

(C) **Connections to Ground Rings:** Where the grounding electrode conductor is connected to a ground ring as permitted in 250.52(4) that portion of the conductor that is the sole connection to the grounding electrode shall not be required to be larger than the conductor used for the ground ring.

Switches

Comments

Switches are devices used to turn an electric circuit on and off. Circuit breakers control power to branch circuits. Snap switches are used primarily for lighting.

National Electrical Code Handbook

Ed. Note: The following excerpt contains NFPA commentary by recognized experts in the field of electrical safety, along with the National Electrical Code® in numbered paragraphs.

Installation of Switches

404.1. Scope: The provisions of this article shall apply to all switches, switching devices, and circuit breakers where used as switches.

404.2 Switch Connections

(A) Three-Way and Four-Way Switches: Three-way and four-way switches shall be wired so that all switching is done only in the ungrounded circuit conductor. Where in metal raceways or metal-armored cables, wiring between switches and outlets shall be in accordance with 300-20(A).

Exception: Switch loops shall not require a grounded conductor.

404.10. Mounting of Snap Switches

(A) Surface-Type: Snap switches used with open wiring on insulators shall be mounted on insulating material that separates the conductors at least ½ inch from the surface wired over.

(B) Box Mounted: Flush-type snap switches mounted in boxes that are set back of the wall surface as permitted in 314.20 shall be installed so that the extension plaster ears are seated against the surface of the wall. Flush-type snap switches mounted in boxes that are flush with the wall surface or project from it shall be so installed that the mounting yoke or strap of the switch is seated against the box.

Grounding Electrode Conductor for Alternating-Current Systems

Size of Largest Ungrounded Service-Entrance Conductor or Equivalent Area for Parallel Conductors[a] (AWG/kcmil)		Size of Grounding Electrode Conductor (AWG/kcmil)	
Copper	Aluminum or Copper-Clad Aluminum	Copper	Aluminum or Copper-Clad Aluminum[b]
2 or smaller	1/0 or smaller	8	6
1 or 1/0	2/0 or 3/0	6	4
2/0 or 3/0	4/0 or 250	4	2
Over 3/0 through 350	Over 250 through 500	2	1/0
Over 350 through 600	Over 500 through 900	1/0	3/0
Over 600 through 1100	Over 900 through 1750	2/0	4/0
Over 1100	Over 1750	3/0	250

Notes:
1. Where multiple sets of service-entrance conductors are used as permitted in 230.40, Exception No. 2, the equivalent size of the largest service-entrance conductor shall be determined by the largest sum of the areas of the corresponding conductors of each set.
2. Where there are no service-entrance conductors, the grounding electrode conductor size shall be determined by the equivalent size of the largest service-entrance conductor required for the load to be served.
[a]This table also applies to the derived conductors of separately derived ac systems.
[b]See installation restrictions in 250.64(A).

Figure 16.12 Courtesy of NFPA, *National Electrical Code® Handbook* [Table 250.66]

NFPA commentary: Cooperation is necessary among the building trades (carpenters, dry-wall installers, plasterers, and so on) in order for electricians to properly set device boxes flush with the finish surface, thereby ensuring a secure seating of the switch yoke and permitting the maximum projection of switch handles through the installed switch plate.

404.11: Circuit Breakers as Switches: A hand-operable circuit breaker equipped with a lever or handle, or a power-operated circuit breaker capable of being opened by hand in the event of a power failure, shall be permitted to serve as a switch if it has the required number of poles.

NFPA commentary: Circuit breakers that are capable of being hand operated must to clearly indicate whether they are in the open (off) or closed (on) position.

See Section 240-83(D) for SWD and HID marking for circuit breakers used as switches for 120V and 277V fluorescent lighting and high-intensity discharge lighting circuits.

404.12. Grounding of Enclosures: Metal enclosures for switches or circuit breakers shall be grounded as specified in Article 250. Where nonmetallic enclosures are used with metal raceways or metal-armored cables, provisions shall be made for grounding continuity. Except as covered in 404.9(B), Exception, nonmetallic boxes for switches shall be installed with a wiring method that provides or includes an equipment ground.

Ed. Note: For additional information on switches, see IRC-2006, Section 3901.

Lighting Controls for Disabled Users

Universal Design Ideas for Style, Comfort & Safety
(RSMeans)

Rocker switches are the easiest for turning lights on and off; switches with built-in illumination can be located in the dark. Light controls should be installed at an easy-to-reach height 44 to 48 inches above the floor. Switches should ideally be at least 6 feet from tubs or showers.

Wiring Devices— Receptacles and Caps

Industry Standards

Means Graphic Construction Standards
(RSMeans)

Receptacles provide a convenient means of connecting portable power equipment and electrical appliances to the electrical source. These devices are available in voltage ratings of 125, 208, 250, 277, 347, 480, and 600 volts and in amperage ratings ranging from 10 to 400 amps. Receptacles are classified as either the grounded or ungrounded type. Because of the dangers of fire and shock associated with all electrical installations, care should be exercised in determining the proper size and type of receptacle and in following installation guidelines, as well as local, state, and national codes.

In accordance with the *National Electrical Code,* all receptacles rated at 15 and 20 amps must be classified as the grounding type. The only exception to this regulation applies to the replacement of outlets that are installed in existing ungrounded systems. Installing a grounded receptacle as a replacement in such an ungrounded system may cause a false sense of safety and security. Because of the great variation of voltage and amperage combinations and the *National Electrical Code®* rule that calls for specific voltage and current ratings for all grounding-type receptacles, standard configurations have been adopted by NEMA (National Electrical Manufacturers Association). This standardization also prevents low-voltage caps (plugs) from being inserted into high-voltage receptacles. Configurations for general purpose, grounding-type receptacles and caps appear in the tables included in this section.

Receptacles are connected to the wiring leads in several ways, depending on the set-up of the particular receptacle or its amperage rating. Some receptacles with 15- and 20-amp ratings are equipped with terminal screws to which the lead wire is attached. After the end of the wire is stripped of its covering, it is wrapped clockwise around the terminal screw, which is then securely tightened to form a mechanical connection. Another common type of 15- and 20-amp receptacle provides a pressure-lock connection in place of the terminal screws. With this type of receptacle, the stripped end of the wire is pushed into a recessed pressure-locking contact that grips the wire to form a permanent locking connection. Receptacles rated at 30 amps and higher are equipped with set screws to form wire-to-device connections.

Grounding of a Metal Faceplate Through Attachment to the Grounded Yoke of a Snap Switch

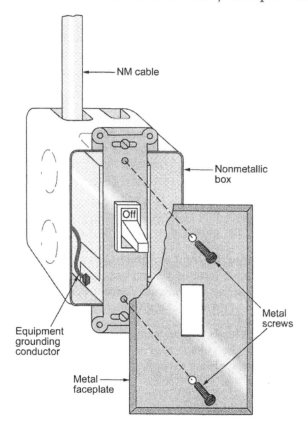

Off

NM cable

Nonmetallic box

Metal screws

Equipment grounding conductor

Metal faceplate

Figure 16.13 Courtesy of NFPA, *National Electrical Code® Handbook* [Exhibit 250.32]

Several grades of receptacles exist to assure that the proper capacity and durability requirements for their use are met. Residential-grade receptacles can be installed in structures located only in noncommercial areas; specification-grade receptacles are used in office and industrial locations. Hospital-grade receptacles, which are labeled "Hospital Grade" and contain a green dot on the face of the outlet, must be able to withstand more severe damage tests than conventional receptacles.

Another safety rating required for receptacles is the ground-fault type, or GFI, which is specified by code for installations in bathrooms, attached garages, construction sites, and outdoor locations. These receptacles are equipped with a safety switch set of 5 milliamps to prevent accidental shock and with a reset button to restore power when a ground condition has been cleared.

All receptacles must be housed in some type of specified enclosure, which is determined by the installation procedure. Outdoor installations require cast weatherproof boxes and matching weather-tight covers. Commercial and industrial receptacle enclosures often consist of a 4" square box with a raised cover. In residential and office situations, where a permanent outlet must be inconspicuous, recessed single-gang boxes may be used. The covers for all receptacle enclosures are usually manufactured from metal or plastic materials.

Receptacle Outlets

National Electrical Code Handbook

Ed. Note: The following excerpt contains NFPA commentary by recognized experts in the field of electrical safety, along with the National Electrical Code in numbered paragraphs.

Receptacles

210-52. Dwelling Unit Receptacle Outlets

(A) **General-Provisions:** In every kitchen, family room, dining room, living room , parlor, library, den, sunroom, bedroom, recreation room, or similar room, or area of dwelling units, receptacle outlets shall be installed in accordance with the general provisions specified in 210.52(A)(1) through (A)(3).

(1) **Spacing:** Receptacles shall be installed so that no point measured horizontally along the floor line in any wall space is more than 1.8 m (6') from a receptacle outlet.

NFPA commentary: Receptacles are required to be located so that no point in any wall space is more than 6' from a receptacle. This rule intends that an appliance or lamp with a flexible cord attached may be placed anywhere in the room and be within 6' of a receptacle, thus eliminating the need for extension cords.

(2) **Wall Space:** As used in this section, a wall space shall include the following:

(1) Any space 600 mm (2') or more in width (including space measured around corners) and unbroken along the floor line by doorways, fireplaces, and similar openings

(2) The space occupied by fixed panels in exterior walls, excluding sliding panels

(3) The space afforded by fixed room dividers such as freestanding bar-type counters or railings

NFPA commentary: A wallspace is a wall unbroken along the floor line by doorways, fireplaces, archways, and similar openings and may include two or more walls of a room (around corners, as illustrated in Exhibit 210-24. (See **Figure 16.15**.)

Receptacles

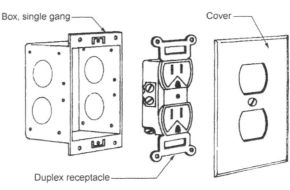

Box, single gang

Cover

Duplex receptacle

Receptacle, including box and cover

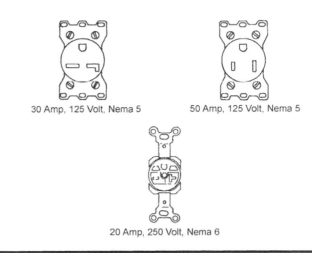

30 Amp, 125 Volt, Nema 5

50 Amp, 125 Volt, Nema 5

20 Amp, 250 Volt, Nema 6

Figure 16.14

RSMeans, *Means Graphic Construction Standards*

Fixed room dividers, such as bar-type counters and railings, are to be included in the 6-ft measurement. Fixed panels in exterior walls are counted as regular wall space, and a floor-type receptacle close to the wall can be used to meet the required spacing. Isolated, individual wall spaces 2 ft or more in width are considered usable for the location of a lamp or appliance, and a receptacle outlet is required to be provided.

(3) **Floor receptacles:** Receptacle outlets in floors shall not be counted as part of the required number of receptacle outlets unless located within 450 mm (18 in.) of the wall.

(B) **Small Appliances**

(1) **Receptacle Outlets Served:** In the kitchen, pantry, breakfast room, dining room, or similar area of a dwelling unit, the two or more 20-ampere small appliance branch circuits required by 210.11 (C) (1) shall serve all receptacle outlets, covered by 210.52

(A) and all countertop outlets covered by 210.52 (C) and receptacle outlets for refrigeration equipment.

(2) No Other Outlets. The two or more small appliance branch circuits specified in 210.52 (B) (1) above shall have no other outlets.

Exception No. 1: A receptacle installed solely for the electrical supply to and support of an electric clock in any of the rooms specified in 210.52(B)(1).

Exception No. 2: Receptacles installed to provide power for supplemental equipment and lighting on gas-fired ranges, ovens, or counter-mounted cooking units.

(3) Kitchen Receptacle Requirements: Receptacles installed in the kitchen to serve countertop surfaces shall be supplied by not less than two small appliance branch circuits, either or both of which shall also be permitted to supply receptacle outlets in the kitchen and other rooms specified in Section 210-52(B)(1). Additional small appliance branch circuits shall be permitted to supply receptacle outlets in the kitchen and other rooms specified in Section 210-52(B)(1). No small appliance branch circuit shall serve more than one kitchen.

(C) Countertops: In kitchens and dining rooms of dwelling units, receptacle outlets for counter spaces shall be installed in accordance with 210.52(C)(1) through (C)(5).

(1) Wall Counter Spaces: A receptacle outlet shall be installed at each wall counter space that is 12" or wider. Receptacle outlets shall be installed so that no point along the wall line is more than 24", measured horizontally from a receptacle outlet in that space.

(2) Island Counter Spaces: At least one receptacle outlet shall be installed at each island counter space with a long dimension of 24" or greater and a short dimension of 12" (300 mm) or greater.

(3) Peninsular Counter Spaces: At least one receptacle outlet shall be installed at each peninsular counter space with a long dimension of 24" or greater and a short dimension of 12" or greater. A peninsular countertop is measured from the connecting edge.

(4) Separate Spaces: Countertop spaces separated by range tops, refrigerators, or sinks shall be considered as separate countertop spaces in applying the requirements of 210.52(C)(1), (C)(2), and (C)(3).

(5) Receptacle Outlet Location: Receptacle outlets shall be located above the countertop (but not more than 20"). Receptacle outlets rendered not readily accessible by appliances or sinks as covered in 210.52(C)(1), Exception, or appliances occupying dedicated space are not considered as these required outlets.

Location of Receptacles

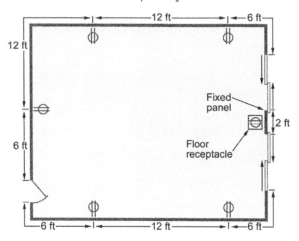

Typical room plan view of the location of dwelling unit receptacles meeting the requirements of 210.52(A).

Figure 16.15   Courtesy of NFPA, *National Electrical Code® Handbook* [Exhibit 210.25]

Exception to (5): To comply with (1) or (2), outlets are permitted to be mounted not more than 12" below the countertop. Receptacles mounted below countertop in accordance with this exception shall not be located where the countertop extends more than 6" beyond its support base.

(1) Construction for the physically impaired.

(2) On island or peninsular countertops where the countertop is flat across its entire surface (no backsplashes, dividers, etc.) and there are no means to mount a receptacle within 20" above the countertop, such as an overhead cabinet.

(D) Bathrooms: In dwelling units, at least one wall receptacle outlet shall be installed in bathrooms within 3' of the outside edge of each basin. The receptacle outlet shall be located on a wall or partition that is adjacent to the basin or basin countertop, or installed on the side or face of the basin cabinet not more than 12" below the countertop.

(E) Outdoor Outlets: For a one-family dwelling and each unit of a two-family dwelling that is at grade level, at least one receptacle outlet accessible at grade level and not more than 6½' above grade shall be installed at the front and back of the dwelling. [See 210.8(A)(3).]

(F) Laundry Areas: In dwelling units, at least one receptacle outlet shall be installed for the laundry.

Exception No. 1: In a dwelling unit that is an apartment or living area or in a multifamily building where laundry facilities are provided on the premises that are available to all building occupants, a laundry receptacle shall not be required.

Exception No. 2: In other than one-family dwellings where laundry facilities are not to be installed or permitted, a laundry receptacle shall not be required.

(G) Basement and Garages: For a one-family dwelling, the following provisions apply:

(1) At least one outlet in addition to those for specific equipment must be installed in each.

(2) Where a portion of the basement is finished into habitable space, each separate unfinished portion must have an outlet installed.

(H) Hallways: In dwelling units, hallways of 10' or more in length shall have at least one receptacle outlet.

As used in this subsection, the hall length shall be considered the length along the centerline of the hall without passing through a doorway.

NFPA commentary: The requirement in 210.52 (H) is intended to minimize strain or damage to cords and receptacles for dwelling unit receptacles. The requirement does not apply to common hallways of hotels, motels, apartment buildings, condominiums, and so on.

Comments

Consult Chapter 39 of the 2006 *IRC* for coverage of devices and lighting fixtures, including switches, receptacles, fixtures and fixture installation, and track lighting.

Grounded Receptacle Box

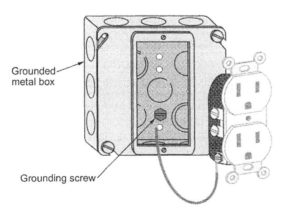

Grounded metal box

Grounding screw

Figure 16.16   Courtesy of NFPA, *National Electrical Code® Handbook* [Figure 250.2]

Ground-Fault Circuit-Interrupter (GFCI)

Comments

Any receptacle located in a potentially wet area, such as a bathroom, kitchen, laundry room, basement, or outdoors, must have a ground-fault interrupter. This type of receptacle is designed to cut power instantly when it senses a false ground, such as a wet hand.

Consult Chapter 40 of the 2006 *IRC* for installation requirements for appliances and fixed heating equipment, including disconnecting means.

IRC–2006

E3802 Ground-fault and arc-fault circuit-interrupter protection: Ground-fault circuit-interrupters are required in bathrooms, garages, crawl spaces (that are at or below grade level), unfinished basements, kitchen countertops, laundry and wet bar sink areas, outdoor areas that have 125-volt receptacles, and electrically heated floors.

NFPA 70: National Electrical Code

210.8 Ground-Fault Circuit-Interrupter Protection for Personnel

(A) Dwelling Units: All 125-volt, single-phase, 15- and 20-ampere receptacles installed in the locations specified in (1) through (8) shall have ground-fault circuit interrupter protection for personnel.

(1) Bathrooms

(2) Garages, and also accessory buildings that have a floor located at or below grade level not intended as habitable rooms and limited to storage areas, work areas, and areas of similar use.

(3) Outdoors

Exception to (3): Receptacles that are not readily accessible and are supplied by a dedicated branch circuit for electric snow-melting or deicing equipment shall be permitted to be installed in accordance with 426.28.

(4) Crawl spaces—at or below grade level.

(5) Unfinished basements—for purposes of this section, unfinished basements are defined as

portions or areas of the basement not intended as habitable rooms and limited to storage areas, work areas, and the like.

Exception to (5): A receptacle supplying only a permanently installed fire alarm or burglar alarm system shall not be required to have ground-fault circuit-interrupter protection.

(6) Kitchens—where the receptacles are installed to serve the countertop surfaces.

(7) Wet bar sinks—where the receptacles are installed to serve the countertop surfaces and are located within 6' of the outside edge of the wet bar sink.

(8) Boathouses.

GFCI and Non-GFCI

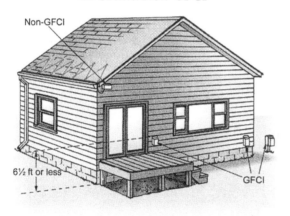

A dwelling unit with three receptacles that are required by 210.8(A)(3) to have GFCI protection, and one that is exempt because it is not readily accessible.

Figure 16.17   Courtesy of NFPA, *National Electrical Code® Handbook* [Exhibit 210.11]

GFCI-Protected Receptacles

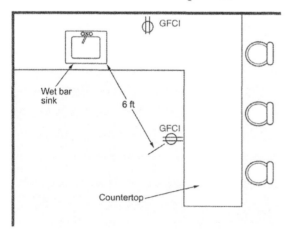

GFCI-protected receptacles that are located within six feet of a wet bar sink and serve the countertop.

Figure 16.18   Courtesy of NFPA, *National Electrical Code® Handbook* [Exhibit 210.14]

Smoke Detectors

Comments

In some locations, smoke detectors must be installed by specialty contractors, depending on the project specifications. There are also differences in local requirements for wiring and the use of battery-only smoke detectors.

Ed Note: See Chapter 13 for information on fire extinguishers, and Chapter 14 for fire protection (sprinkler) systems.

Lighting Outlets

Industry Standard

Electrical Estimating Methods
(RSMeans)

Outlet Boxes

Outlet boxes made of steel or plastic are used to hold wiring devices, such as switches and receptacles. They are also used as a mount for lighting fixtures. Some outlet boxes are ready for flush mounting; others require a plaster frame. Some have plain knockouts for pipe up to 1¼", while others have built-in brackets for Romex or BX wire. The capacity of outlet boxes ranges from one to six devices. They may have brackets for direct stud mounting or plaster ears for mounting in existing walls.

National Electrical Code Handbook

Ed. Note: The following excerpt contains NFPA commentary by recognized experts in the field of safety, along with the National Electrical Code in numbered paragraphs.

210.70 Lighting Outlets Required: Lighting outlets shall be installed where specified in 210.70(A), (B), and (C).

(A) Dwelling Units: In dwelling units, lighting outlets shall be installed in accordance with 210.70(A)(1), (A)(2), and (A)(3).

(1) Habitable Rooms: At least one wall switch-controlled lighting outlet shall be installed in every habitable room and bathroom.

Exception No. 1: In other than kitchens and bathrooms, one or more receptacles controlled by a wall switch shall be permitted in lieu of lighting outlets.

NFPA commentary: A receptacle is not permitted to be switched as a lighting outlet on a small appliance branch circuit. A receptacle can be switched as a lighting outlet (in the dining room, for example) supplied by a branch circuit other than a small appliance branch circuit.

Exception No. 2: Lighting outlets shall be permitted to be controlled by occupancy sensors that are (1) in addition to wall switches or (2) located at a customary wall switch location and equipped with a manual override that will allow the sensor to function as a wall switch.

(2) Additional Locations: Additional lighting outlets shall be installed in accordance with (A)(2)(a), (A)(2)(b), and (A)(2)(c).

(a) At least one wall switch-controlled lighting outlet shall be installed in hallways, stairways, attached garages, and detached garages with electric power.

(b) For dwelling units, attached garages, and detached garages with electric power, at least one wall switch-controlled lighting outlet shall be installed to provide illumination on the exterior side of outdoor entrances or exits with grade level access. A vehicle door in a garage shall not be considered as an outdoor entrance or exit.

(c) Where one or more lighting outlet(s) are installed for interior stairways, there shall be a wall switch at each floor level, and landing level that includes an entry way, to control the lighting outlet(s) where the stairway between floor levels has six risers or more.

Exception to (A)(2)(a), (A)(2)(b), and (A)(2)(c): In hallways, stairways, and at outdoor entrances, remote, central, or automatic control of lighting shall be permitted.

NFPA commentary: Section 210.70 points out that adequate lighting and proper control and location of switching are as essential to the safety of occupants of dwelling units, hotels, motels, and so on, as are proper wiring requirements. Proper illumination ensures safe movement for persons of all ages, thus preventing many accidents.

Although the requirement in 210.7(A)(2)(b) calls for a switched lighting outlet at outdoor entrances and exits, it does not prohibit a single lighting outlet, if suitably located, from serving more than one door.

A wall switch-controlled lighting outlet is required in the kitchen and bathroom. A receptacle outlet controlled by a wall switch is not permitted to serve as a lighting outlet in these rooms. Occupancy sensors are permitted to be used for switching these lighting outlets, provided they are equipped with a manual override or are used in addition to regular switches.

(3) Storage or Equipment Spaces: For attics, underfloor spaces, utility rooms, and basements, at least one lighting outlet containing a switch or controlled by a wall switch shall be installed where these spaces are used for storage or contain equipment requiring servicing. At least one point of control shall be at the usual point of entry to these spaces. The lighting outlet shall be provided at or near the equipment requiring servicing.

NFPA commentary: Installation of lighting outlets in attics, underfloor spaces or crawl areas, utility rooms, and basements is required when these spaces are used for storage (e.g., holiday decorations or luggage).

If such spaces contain equipment that requires servicing (e.g., air-handling units, cooling and heating equipment, water pumps, and sump pumps), 210.70 (C) requires that a lighting outlet be installed in these spaces.

(B) Guest Rooms: In hotels, motels, and similar occupancies, guest rooms must have at least one wall switch-controlled lighting outlet installed in every habitable room and bathroom.

(C) Other Than Dwelling Units: For attics and underfloor spaces containing equipment requiring servicing, such as heating, air-conditioning, and refrigeration equipment, at least one lighting outlet containing a switch or controlled by a wall switch shall be installed in such spaces. At least one point of control shall be at the usual point of entry to these spaces. The lighting outlet shall be provided at or near the equipment requiring servicing.

Lighting Fixtures

Efficient Bulbs & Fixtures

***Green Building: Project Planning & Cost Estimating,* Second Edition**
(RSMeans)

First and foremost, lighting should be designed effectively and efficiently, avoiding glare and providing light where it is needed (primarily on wall and ceiling surfaces) rather than simply assigning a set number of footcandles of light to a space. Specifying highly reflective (light-colored) interior surfaces is important to evenly distribute light and enhance occupant well being. Ambient overhead lighting should be minimal. For most applications, a direct/indirect lighting fixture will provide the most appealing and efficient ambient light source. It should be dimmable to integrate with daylighting and to afford user-flexibility.

Task lighting provides for flexibility, and accent lighting enhances visual interest. Automatic lighting controls can greatly reduce lighting energy consumption. They include occupancy sensors that turn lights off when a room is not in use (especially appropriate for infrequently used rooms) and photosensitive dimmers that dim lights when daylight is ample. Finally, lights should be easily maintainable.

Today's **fluorescent lighting** is efficient, has excellent color rendition and is appropriate for most applications. Current fluorescent technology includes T-8 and T-5 lamps with dimmable electronic ballasts. Compared to the older T-10 and T-12 lamps, the newer lamps contain less mercury and significantly improve energy efficiency. Compact fluorescent lights (CFLs) should be used instead of inefficient incandescent lamps. CFLs come in pleasant color spectrums, use 75% less energy than incandescent lights, and last ten times as long. Electronic ballasts (rather than magnetic ballasts) should be used in all linear luminaires.

LED (light emitting diode) lighting has many unique benefits that have already made it competitive in many niche applications, despite its higher cost relative to conventional sources. LEDs typically produce about 30–35 lumens per watt (though researchers have achieved 50 lumens per watt), making them much more efficient than incandescent lights (which produce 12–15 lumens per watt), but not typically as efficient as compact fluorescents (which produce at least 50 lumens per watt). *LEDs last 10 times as long as compact fluorescents* (133 times as long as incandescents), are extremely durable and emit light in one direction, providing a disadvantage for ambient lighting but an advantage for task lighting (LEDs can light the task with a smaller total lumen output than incandescents or fluorescents, which illuminate in 360 degrees). Already common in exit signs, traffic signals, pathway lighting, flashlights and other niche applications, LED technology is also available for many types of interior and exterior residential lighting.

Disposal of fluorescent, mercury vapor, metal halide, neon, and high-pressure sodium lamps is a critical issue, as they all contain mercury, direct exposure to which is toxic. Magnetic ballasts for fluorescent lights made before the late 1970s also contain highly toxic PCBs (polychlorinated biphenyls). All lamps containing mercury should be recycled with a qualified lamp recycling company and protected from breakage during transport. If lamps do break, they should be collected (with proper protection) and stored in a sealed container. Expired PCB ballasts should be stored in sealed containers and disposed of with extreme caution and scrupulous labeling, using a PCB disposal company that is registered with the Environmental Protection Agency.

Choosing & Installing Fixtures

Comments

The most important thing to remember when performing electrical work is to turn off power to the area or device you are working on. Always confirm that the power is off by testing the circuit with a neon circuit tester. Restore power only when your work is completed. Following are some additional tips:

- When choosing a light fixture, consider the weight of the fixture, height of the fixture above the floor, and location of the fixture relative to the placement of furniture in the room.
- Remember this rule of thumb: The higher the light fixture, the wider area it will illuminate.

Exact fixture placement should be established before any work begins, with sign-off from the owner, to avoid disputes and cost overruns from having to relocate fixtures, and to patch and touch up finishes. Responsibility for any related cutting, patching, and touch-up should also be determined before the electrical work begins.

IRC–2006

E3903 Fixtures

E3903.1 Energized parts: Energized parts that are exposed to contact are not permitted.

E3903.2 Luminaires near combustible material: Luminaire installation must ensure that the temperature of combustible materials will not exceed 194°F.

E3903.3 Exposed conductive parts: Grounding is required for exposed conductive parts.

E3903.5 Recessed incandescent luminaires: Thermal protection is required for recessed fixtures.

E3903.9 Lampholders in wet or damp locations: Lampholders in wet areas must be approved for such use, clearly marked that they are so approved, and must be installed in such a way as to be weatherproof.

E3903.11 Luminaires in clothes closets: Closets may only have fixtures that are surface-mounted or recessed incandescent or fluorescent.

E3904.1 Outlet box covers: All outlet boxes must have a cover.

E3904.8 Recessed fixture clearance: Recessed fixtures must be installed at least ½ inch away from combustible materials.

NFPA 70: National Electrical Code

410.10 Luminaires (Fixtures) in Specific Locations.

(A) Wet and Damp Locations: Luminaires (fixtures) installed in wet or damp locations shall be installed so that water cannot enter or accumulate in wiring compartments, lampholders, or other electrical parts. All luminaires (fixtures) installed in wet locations shall be marked, "Suitable for Wet Locations." All luminaires (fixtures) installed in damp locations shall be marked, "Suitable for Wet Locations" or "Suitable for Damp Locations."

(D) Bathtub and Shower Areas: No parts of cord-connected luminaires (fixtures), hanging luminaires (fixtures), lighting track, pendants, or ceiling-suspended (paddle) fans shall be located within a zone measured 3' horizontally and 8' vertically from the top of the bathtub rim or shower stall threshold. This zone is all encompassing and includes the zone directly over the tub or shower stall.

410.11 Luminaires (Fixtures) Near Combustible Material: Luminaires (fixtures) shall be constructed, installed, or equipped with shades or guards so that combustible material is not subjected to temperatures in excess of 90°C (195°F).

410.6 Luminaires (Fixtures) Over Combustible Material: Lampholders installed over highly combustible material shall be of the unswitched type. Unless an individual switch is provided for each luminaire (fixture), lampholders shall be located at least 8' above the floor or shall be located or guarded so that the lamps cannot be readily removed or damaged.

410.16 Luminaires (Fixtures) in Clothes Closets.

Luminaire Type Permitted

(A) Luminaire (Fixture) Types Permitted: Listed luminaires (fixtures) of the following types shall be permitted to be installed in a closet:

(1) A surface-mounted or recessed incandescent luminaire (fixture) with a completely enclosed lamp

(2) A surface-mounted or recessed fluorescent luminaire (fixture)

(B) Luminaire (Fixture) Types Not Permitted: Incandescent luminaires (fixtures) with open or partially enclosed lamps and pendant luminaires (fixtures) or lampholders shall not be permitted.

(C) Location: Luminaires (fixtures) in clothes closets shall be permitted to be installed as follows:

(1) Surface-mounted incandescent luminaires (fixtures) installed on the wall above the door or on the ceiling, provided there is a minimum clearance of 300 mm (12") between the luminaire (fixture) and the nearest point of a storage space.

(2) Surface-mounted fluorescent luminaires (fixtures) installed on the wall above the door or on the ceiling, provided there is a minimum clearance of 150 mm (6") between the luminaire (fixture) and the nearest point of a storage space.

(3) Recessed incandescent luminaires (fixtures) with a completely enclosed lamp installed in the wall or the ceiling, provided there is a minimum clearance of 150 mm (6") between the luminaire (fixture) and the nearest point of a storage space.

Luminaires, Lighting Track, and Suspended (Paddle) Fan Located Near a Bathtub

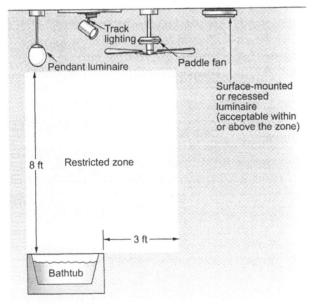

Figure 16.19 Courtesy of NFPA, *National Electrical Code® Handbook* [Exhibit 410.1]

(4) Recessed fluorescent luminaires (fixtures) installed in the wall or the ceiling, provided there is a minimum clearance of 150 mm (6") between the luminaire (fixture) and the nearest point of a storage space.

410.9 Space for Cove Lighting: Coves shall have adequate space and shall be located so that lamps and equipment can be properly installed and maintained.

410.20 Space for Conductors: Canopies and outlet boxes taken together shall provide adequate space so that luminaire (fixture) conductors and their connecting devices can be properly installed.

410.23 Covering of Combustible Material at Outlet Boxes: Any combustible wall or ceiling finish exposed between the edge of a luminaire (fixture) canopy or pan and an outlet box shall be covered with noncombustible material.

410.36 Means of Support

(A) Outlet Boxes: Outlet boxes or fittings installed as required by 314.23 shall be permitted to support luminaires (fixtures).

(B) Suspended Ceilings: Framing members of suspended ceiling systems used to support luminaires (fixtures) shall be securely fastened to each other and shall be securely attached to the building structure at appropriate intervals. Luminaires (fixtures) shall be securely fastened to the ceiling-framing member by mechanical means such as bolts, screws, or rivets. Listed clips identified for use with the type of ceiling framing member(s) and luminaires(s) [fixtures(s)] shall also be permitted.

(C) Luminaire (Fixture) Studs: Luminaire (fixture) studs that are not a part of outlet boxes, hickeys, tripods, and crowfeet shall be made of steel, malleable iron, or other material suitable for the application.

(D) Insulating Joints: Insulating joints that are not designed to be mounted with screws or bolts shall have an exterior metal casing, insulated from both screw connections.

(E) Raceway Fittings: Raceway fittings used to support a luminaire(s) [lighting fixture(s)] shall be capable of supporting the weight of the complete fixture assembly and lamp(s).

(G) Trees: Outdoor luminaires (lighting fixtures) and associated equipment shall be permitted to be supported by trees.

Exterior Lighting

***Green Building: Project Planning & Cost Estimating,* Second Edition**
(RSMeans)

Recent research has also shown harmful physiological effects that result from interrupting sleep by viewing light. Minimizing **light pollution** and **light trespass** will help protect dark skies for humans and nocturnal animals alike. Strategies include eliminating unshielded floodlighting and providing "cut-off" luminaires.

Full cut-off (FCO) luminaires considerably reduce wasteful upward lighting by directing all light down toward the intended area of illumination. (None is allowed above the horizontal plane.) Replacing defective, nonfunctioning, or non-cut-off luminaires with FCO luminaires allows for substantial lowering in the wattage of the new fixture, thereby realizing a cost and energy savings. Cut-off luminaires also enhance safety for both pedestrians and drivers by eliminating glaring light.

Uniform outdoor light distribution is important for comfort, safety, and energy efficiency. Light levels need not be high. In fact, studies have shown that about three footcandles is all that is needed for security purposes. Much brighter light (often 100 footcandles or more), which has become prevalent at all-night gas stations and other stores, is actually dangerous, because drivers (especially the elderly) can take two to five minutes to readjust their vision.

Exterior lighting controlled by motion detectors can enhance safety while reducing energy use. Some schools have reduced both energy use and vandalism by keeping the campus dark after hours. Police are informed that light seen on campus should be treated with suspicion. The security director at one San Antonio school, where vandalism dropped 75% with the dark campus approach, suggested that vandalism loses its appeal when people cannot see what they are doing.

High-pressure sodium lamps (the characteristic yellow parking lot lights) should be avoided in most applications, as they reduce peripheral vision. White light sources, such as metal halide and fluorescent, improve visibility with less light.

Supporting Ceiling Fans

National Electrical Code Handbook

422.18 Support of Ceiling-Suspended (Paddle) Fans: Ceiling-Suspended (Paddle) Fans must be supported independently of an outlet box or by listed outlet box/systems identified for the use and installed according to NEC 314.27(D)

Supporting a Ceiling (Paddle) Fan

Supporting a ceiling-suspended (paddle) fan (35 lb or less) with a box identified for such use. (Courtesy of Raco, Inc.)

Figure 16.20 Courtesy of NFPA, *National Electrical Code® Handbook* [Exhibit 422.2]

Industry Standards

Green Home Improvement
(RSMeans)

Ceiling fans can dramatically lower energy use by reducing the need for air conditioning. Attic and whole-house fans are two other excellent ways to cool a home while controlling energy costs. Energy Star®-approved ceiling fans save even more power (up to 50%, according to Energy Star) over standard models due to their efficient motors and blades. Fan-rated boxes must be attached to ceiling joists or to a support bar that attaches to joists.

When installing a ceiling fan, be sure that fan blades are at least 10" from the ceiling. If mounted closer, they will not be able to circulate air as well. Ceiling fans should be mounted so the blades are at least seven feet off the floor to avoid injury.

Conductors: Wire/Cable

Industry Standards

Means Graphic Construction Standards
(RSMeans)

Electrical conductors are the means by which current flows in an electrical distribution system. The primary elements of the distribution system are wires and cables, which are classified and rated by such variables as their diametric size, type of insulated covering, and current-carrying capacity. Basically, wires and cables are comprised of the conductor itself, either copper or aluminum, and usually some type of insulated covering. The most comprehensive source of detailed information on wire and cable material is the *National Electrical Code*, which provides guidelines and data on all aspects of wire and cable, including their characteristics, allowable operating temperatures, ampacities, and application provisions.

The only difference between wire and cable is that of size, because their function and material composition are the same. When the circular mils area of a round cross-sectional conductor is #6 AWG or larger, it is referred to as cable; when the cross-sectional area is #8 AWG or smaller, it is called wire. Confusion often arises in the size designations of small round cross-sectional conductors as established by the American Wire Gauge system (AWG), because the AWG numbers increase as the wire size decreases, and, conversely, the AWG numbers decrease as the wire size increases. For example, #6 AWG conductor is larger than #12 AWG conductor and smaller than #1 AWG conductor. This AWG numbering system is maintained to #0 AWG, more commonly designated #1/0 AWG, when a different numeric designation is employed for conductors. Beginning with #1/0 AWG, the designation numbers increase with the increase in the size of the cable to the largest AWG rating of #0000, or #4/0. For example, a cable sized at #3/0 is larger than a cable sized at #2/0. For very heavy cables larger than #4/0 AWG, the designation changes again to kcmil, or thousand circular mils. With this designation system, the kcmil number increases with the increase in cable size; for example, 500 kcmil cable is larger or heavier than cable sized at 300 kcmil. The reason for the corresponding increase of designation number and cable size is that the circular mil is an artificial area measurement which represents the square of the cable diameter measured in mils, or thousandths of an inch. For example, a solid conductor of 1/2", or 500 mils, in diameter is sized at 250,000 circular mils in area, or 250 kcmil.

Most current-carrying conductors are covered with some type of insulated covering which protects them from physical damage and provides an obvious safety function. Insulation also serves as a shield against heat and moisture and prevents arcing and short circuits. Wire and cable insulation is rated by voltage, with the most commonly used ratings of 250, 600, 1,000, 3,000, 5,000, and 15,000 volts.

The conductor or current carrying component of a wire or cable is manufactured from copper or aluminum. These two materials are used because they possess the low resistance required for efficient electrical conduction. Generally, larger aluminum conductors are necessary to meet the same ampacity needs of copper conductors. Copper, because it is less resistant than aluminum and possesses other advantageous properties, is the more commonly employed material of the two, especially for smaller wires and cables. Because aluminum costs and weighs less than copper, it is most often used in larger size cables. Difficulties may arise when aluminum is employed, however, as aluminum cold flow characteristics when under pressure may cause joints to loosen. Also, aluminum conductor is prone to rapid oxidation if exposed to the air. Because the oxide which forms on the surface of the wire or cable is not conductive, it creates high resistance to the electrical flow and must be removed and prevented from reforming. Experience and skilled craftsmanship have reduced the risk of aluminum conductor oxidation,

but many states have banned the use of aluminum conductors in branch wiring to prevent unskilled homeowners from installing them. The *National Electrical Code* provides charts and other sources of information on the ampacities of aluminum and the corresponding ampacities for copper conductors.

Conductor Sizing & Overcurrent Protection

Comments

Use of correct wire gauges for given applications is crucial to prevent overload, malfunction of current protection devices (such as fuses or circuit breakers), and risk of fire. **Figure 16.21** provides NEC's correct wire gauges for various circuit ratings, and overcurrent protection requirements, as well as maximum loads for different current ratings.

Chapter 36 of the 2006 *IRC* addresses branch circuits and feeder requirements. Section 3605 covers required overcurrent protection for branch circuits and feeders that serve less than 100 percent of the total dwelling unit load. This section includes tables for determining allowable ampacities and ambient temperature factors. Note that Chapter 35 addresses feeder circuits that serve 100 percent of the dwelling unit load.

Summary of Branch-Circuit Requirements

Table 210.24 Summary of Branch-Circuit Requirements

Circuit Rating	15 A	20 A	30 A	40 A	50 A
Conductors (min. size):					
Circuit wires[1]	14	12	10	8	6
Taps	14	14	14	12	12
Fixture wires and cords—See 240.5					
Overcurrent Protection	**15 A**	**20 A**	**30 A**	**40 A**	**50 A**
Outlet devices:					
Lampholders permitted	Any type	Any type	Heavy duty	Heavy duty	Heavy duty
Receptacle rating[2]	15 max. A	15 or 20 A	30 A	40 or 50 A	50 A
Maximum Load	**15 A**	**20 A**	**30 A**	**40 A**	**50 A**
Permissible load	See 210.23(A)	See 210.23(A)	See 210.23(B)	See 210.23(C)	See 210.23(C)

[1]These gauges are for copper conductors.
[2]For receptacle rating of cord-connected electric-discharge luminaires (lighting fixtures), see 410.30(C).

Figure 16.21

Courtesy of National Fire Protection Association, *National Electrical Code® Handbook*

Maximum Number of Wires (Insulation Noted) for Various Conduit Sizes

Table below lists maximum number of conductors for various sized conduit using THW, TW or THWN insulations.

Copper Wire Size	1/2"			3/4"			1"			1-1/4"			1-1/2"			2"			2-1/2"		
	TW	THW	THWN	TW	THW	THWN	TW	THW	THWN	TW	THW	THWN	TW	THW	THWN	TW	THW	THWN	TW	THW	THWN
#14	9	6	13	15	10	24	25	16	39	44	29	69	60	40	94	99	65	154	142	93	
#12	7	4	10	12	8	18	19	13	29	35	24	51	47	32	70	78	53	114	111	76	164
#10	5	4	6	9	6	11	15	11	18	26	19	32	36	26	44	60	43	73	85	61	104
#8	2	1	3	4	3	5	7	5	9	12	10	16	17	13	22	28	22	36	40	32	51
#6		1	1		2	4		4	6		7	11		10	15		16	26		23	37
#4		1	1		1	2		3	4		5	7		7	9		12	16		17	22
#3		1	1		1	1		2	3		4	6		6	8		10	13		15	19
#2		1	1		1	1		2	3		4	5		5	7		9	11		13	16
#1					1	1		1	1		3	3		4	5		6	8		9	12
1/0					1	1		1	1		2	3		3	4		5	7		8	10
2/0					1	1		1	1		1	2		3	3		5	6		7	8
3/0					1	1		1	1		1	1		2	3		4	5		6	7
4/0						1		1	1		1	1		1	2		3	4		5	6
250 kcmil								1	1		1	1		1	1		2	3		4	4
300								1	1		1	1		1	1		2	3		3	4
350									1		1	1		1	1		1	2		3	3

Figure 16.22

RSMeans, *Electrical Estimating Methods*

Minimum Copper and Aluminum Wire Size Allowed for Various Types of Insulation

	Minimum Wire Sizes								
	Copper		Aluminum			Copper		Aluminum	
Amperes	THW THWN or XHHW	THHN XHHW *	THW XHHW	THHN XHHW *	Amperes	THW THWN or XHHW	THHN XHHW *	THW XHHW	THHN XHHW *
15A	#14	#14	#12	#12	195	3/0	2/0	250kcmil	4/0
20	#12	#12	#10	#10	200	3/0	3/0	250kcmil	4/0
25	#10	#10	#10	#10	205	4/0	3/0	250kcmil	4/0
30	#10	#10	#8	#8	225	4/0	3/0	300kcmil	250kcmil
40	#8	#8	#8	#8	230	4/0	4/0	300kcmil	250kcmil
45	#8	#8	#6	#8	250	250kcmil	4/0	350kcmil	300kcmil
50	#8	#8	#6	#6	255	250kcmil	4/0	400kcmil	300kcmil
55	#6	#8	#4	#6	260	300kcmil	4/0	400kcmil	350kcmil
60	#6	#6	#4	#6	270	300kcmil	250kcmil	400kcmil	350kcmil
65	#6	#6	#4	#4	280	300kcmil	250kcmil	500kcmil	350kcmil
75	#4	#6	#3	#4	285	300kcmil	250kcmil	500kcmil	400kcmil
85	#4	#4	#2	#3	290	350kcmil	250kcmil	500kcmil	400kcmil
90	#3	#4	#2	#2	305	350kcmil	300kcmil	500kcmil	400kcmil
95	#3	#4	#1	#2	310	350kcmil	300kcmil	500kcmil	500kcmil
100	#3	#3	#1	#2	320	400kcmil	300kcmil	600kcmil	500kcmil
110	#2	#3	1/0	#1	335	400kcmil	350kcmil	600kcmil	500kcmil
115	#2	#2	1/0	#1	340	500kcmil	350kcmil	600kcmil	500kcmil
120	#1	#2	1/0	1/0	350	500kcmil	350kcmil	700kcmil	500kcmil
130	#1	#2	2/0	1/0	375	500kcmil	400kcmil	700kcmil	600kcmil
135	1/0	#1	2/0	1/0	380	500kcmil	400kcmil	750kcmil	600kcmil
150	1/0	#1	3/0	2/0	385	600kcmil	500kcmil	750kcmil	600kcmil
155	2/0	1/0	3/0	3/0	420	600kcmil	500kcmil		700kcmil
170	2/0	1/0	4/0	3/0	430		500kcmil		750kcmil
175	2/0	2/0	4/0	3/0	435		600kcmil		750kcmil
180	3/0	2/0	4/0	4/0	475		600kcmil		

Figure 16.23

RSMeans, *Electrical Estimating Methods*

Maximum Circuit Length (approximate) for Various Power Requirements Assuming THW, Copper Wire @ 75°C, Based Upon a 4% Voltage Drop

Maximum Circuit Length: Table R260519-91 indicates typical maximum installed length a circuit can have and still maintain an adequate voltage level at the point of use. The circuit length is similar to the conduit length.

If the circuit length for an ampere load and a copper wire size exceeds the length obtained from Table R260519-91, use the next largest wire size to compensate voltage drop.

Example: A 130 ampere load at 480 volts, 3 phase, 3 wire with No. 1 wire can be run a maximum of 555 L.F. and provide satisfactory operation. If the same load is to be wired at the end of a 625 L.F. circuit, then a larger wire must be used.

| Amperes | Wire Size | Maximum Circuit Length in Feet | | | | |
| | | 2 Wire, 1 Phase | | 3 Wire, 3 Phase | | |
		120V	240V	240V	480V	600V
15	14*	50	105	120	240	300
	14	50	100	120	235	295
20	12*	60	125	145	290	360
	12	60	120	140	280	350
30	10*	65	130	155	305	380
	10	65	130	150	300	375
50	8	60	125	145	285	355
65	6	75	150	175	345	435
85	4	90	185	210	425	530
115	2	110	215	250	500	620
130	1	120	240	275	555	690
150	1/0	130	260	305	605	760
175	2/0	140	285	330	655	820
200	3/0	155	315	360	725	904
230	4/0	170	345	395	795	990
255	250	185	365	420	845	1055
285	300	195	395	455	910	1140
310	350	210	420	485	975	1220
380	500	245	490	565	1130	1415

*Solid Conductor
Note: The circuit length is the one-way distance between the origin and the load.

Figure 16.24

RSMeans, *Electrical Cost Data*

Boxes & Fittings

Industry Standards

Plan Reading & Material Takeoff
(RSMeans)

A box is used in electrical wiring at each junction point, outlet, or switch. Boxes provide access to electrical connections and serve as a mounting for fixtures or switches. They may also be used as pull points for wire in long runs or conduits. A wiring device can be defined as a mechanism that controls but does not consume electricity, such as a switch or receptacle.

Boxes often require accessories such as plaster rings, covers, and various fasteners to support them. Boxes are constructed of galvanized or coated steel, or high-density plastic. Wiring devices, in addition to receptacles and switches, include pilot lights, relays, low-voltage transformers, and a variety of specialized controls and finish wall plates.

Figure 16.25 shows the NEC application of a grounding clip in a box.

IRC-2006

E3805.1 Box, conduit body or fitting—where required: Every conductor splice point, switch point, junction point, pull point, or outlet must have a box or conduit body (with some specific exceptions).

E3805.2 Metal boxes: Grounding is required for metal boxes.

E3805.3 Nonmetallic boxes: Nonmetallic-sheathed cable and nonmetallic raceways are required for nonmetallic boxes (with some specific exceptions).

E3805.4 Minimum depth of outlet boxes: The depth of boxes must be at least ½".

Industry Standards

Electrical Cost Data

(RSMeans)

Standard Electrical Enclosure Types: NEMA Enclosures

Ed. Note: NEMA Types 1 and 3R are used for residential and light commercial applications.

Electrical enclosures serve two basic purposes; they protect people from accidental contact with enclosed electrical devices and connections, and they protect the enclosed devices and connections from specified external conditions. The National Electrical Manufacturers Association (NEMA) has established the following standards. Because these descriptions are not intended to be complete representations of NEMA listings, consultation of NEMA literature is advised for detailed information.

The following definitions and descriptions pertain to NONHAZARDOUS locations.

NEMA Type 1: General purpose enclosures intended for use indoors, primarily to prevent accidental contact of personnel with the enclosed equipment in areas that do not involve unusual conditions.

NEMA   Type 2: Dripproof indoor enclosures intended to protect the enclosed equipment against dripping noncorrosive liquids and falling dirt.

NEMA   Type 3: Dustproof, raintight and sleet-resistant (ice-resistant) enclosures intended for use outdoors to protect the enclosed equipment against wind-blown dust, rain, sleet, and external ice formation.

NEMA   Type 3R: Rainproof and sleet-resistant (ice-resistant) enclosures which are intended for use outdoors to protect the enclosed equipment against rain. These enclosures are constructed so that the accumulation and melting of sleet (ice) will not damage the enclosure and its internal mechanisms.

NEMA   Type 3S: Enclosures intended for outdoor use to provide limited protection against wind-blown dust, rain, and sleet (ice) to allow operation of external mechanisms when ice-laden.

NEMA   Type 4: Watertight and dust-tight enclosures intended for use indoors and out—to protect the enclosed equipment against splashing water, seepage of water, falling or hose-directed water, and severe external condensation.

NEMA   Type 4X: Watertight, dust-tight, and corrosion-resistant indoor and outdoor enclosures featuring the same provisions as Type 4 enclosures, plus corrosion resistance.

NEMA   Type 5: Indoor enclosures intended primarily to provide limited protection against dust and falling dirt.

NEMA   Type 6: Enclosures intended for indoor and outdoor use—primarily to provide limited protection against the entry of water during occasional temporary submersion at a limited depth.

NEMA   Type 6R: Enclosures intended for indoor and outdoor use—primarily to provide limited protection against the entry of water during prolonged submersion at a limited depth.

NEMA   Type 11: Enclosures intended for indoor use—primarily to provide, by means of oil immersion, limited protection to enclosed equipment against the corrosive effects of liquids and gases.

NEMA   Type 12: Dust-tight and driptight indoor enclosures intended for use indoors in industrial locations to protect the enclosed equipment against fibers, flyings, lint, dust, and dirt, as well as light splashing, seepage, dripping and external condensation of noncorrosive liquids.

Use of a Grounding Clip to Attach a Grounding Conductor to a Metal Box

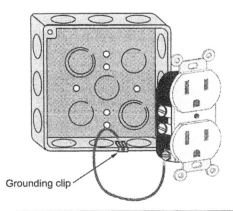

Grounding clip

Figure 16.25   Courtesy of NFPA, *National Electrical Code® Handbook* [Exhibit 250.3]

NEMA   Type 13: Oil-tight and dust-tight indoor enclosures intended primarily to house pilot devices, such as limit switches, foot switches, push buttons, selector switches, and pilot lights, and to protect these devices against lint and dust, seepage, external condensation, and sprayed water, oil, and noncorrosive coolant.

The following definitions and descriptions pertain to HAZARDOUS, or CLASSIFIED, locations:

NEMA   Type 7: Enclosures intended to use in indoor locations classified as Class 1, Groups A, B, C, or D, defined in the *National Electrical Code*.

NEMA   Type 9: Enclosures intended for use in indoor locations classified as Class 2, Groups E, F, or G, as defined in the *National Electrical Code*.

Branch Circuits

Comments

Branch circuits contain any combination of receptacles, switches, and lighting outlets.

National Electrical Code Handbook

Ed. Note: The following excerpt contains NFPA commentary by recognized experts in the field of safety, along with the National Electrical Code in numbered paragraphs.

210.19 Conductors —Minimum Ampacity and Size:

(A) Branch Circuits Not More Than 600 Volts.

(1) General. Branch-circuit conductors shall have an ampacity not less than the maximum load to be served. Where a branch circuit supplies continuous loads or any combination of continuous and noncontinuous loads, the minimum branch-circuit conductor size, before the application of any adjustment or correction factors, shall have an allowable ampacity not less than the noncontinuous load plus 125 percent of the continuous load.

FPN No. 1: See 310.15 for ampacity ratings of conductors.

FPN No. 2: See Part II of Article 430 for minimum rating of motor branch-circuit conductors.

FPN No. 3: See 310.10 for temperature limitation of conductors.

FPN No. 4: Conductors for branch circuits as defined in Article 100, sized to prevent a voltage drop exceeding 3 percent at the farthest outlet of power, heating, and lighting loads, or combinations of such loads, and where the maximum total voltage drop on both feeders and branch circuits to the farthest outlet does not exceed 5 percent, provide reasonable efficiency of operation. See 215.2(A)(3) for voltage drop on feeder conductors.

NFPA commentary: FPN No. 4 expresses a warning about improper voltage due to a voltage drop in supply conductors, a major source of trouble and inefficient operation in electrical equipment. Undervoltage conditions reduce the capability and reliability of motors, lighting sources, heaters, and solid-state equipment. Sample voltage-drop calculations are found in the commentary following 215.2(A)(4), FPN No. 3, and following Table 9 in Chapter 9.

(2) Multioutlet Branch Circuits: Conductors of branch circuits supplying more than one receptacle for cord-and-plug-connected portable loads shall have an ampacity of not less than the rating of the branch circuit.

(3) Household Ranges and Cooking Appliances: Branch-circuit conductors supplying household ranges, wall-mounted ovens, counter-mounted cooking units, and other household cooking appliances shall have an ampacity not less than the rating of the branch circuit and not less than the maximum load to be served. For ranges of $8\frac{3}{4}$ kW or more rating, the minimum branch-circuit rating shall be 40 amperes.

NFPA Commentary: A minimum 40-ampere branch-circuit rating would be, for example, 8 AWG, Type THW copper or 6 AWG, Type TXHHW aluminum conductor. See Table 310.16 for other applications.

210.20 Overcurrent Protection: Branch-circuit conductors and equipment shall be protected by overcurrent protective devices that have a rating or setting that complies with 210.20(A) through (D).

(A) Continuous and Noncontinuous Loads: Where a branch circuit supplies continuous loads or any combination of continuous and noncontinuous loads, the rating of the overcurrent device shall not be less than the noncontinuous load plus 125 percent of the continuous load.

Exception: Where the assembly, including the overcurrent devices protecting the branch circuit(s), is listed for operation at 100 percent of its rating, the ampere ratings of the overcurrent device shall be permitted to be not less than the sum of the continuous load plus the noncontinuous load.

(B) Conductor Protection: Conductors shall be protected in accordance with 240.4. Flexible cords and fixture wires shall be protected in accordance with 240.5.

(C) Equipment: The rating or setting of the overcurrent protective device shall not exceed that specified in the applicable articles referenced in 240.3 for equipment.

(D) Outlet Devices: The rating or setting shall not exceed that specified in 210.21 for outlet devices.

210.21 Outlet Devices: Outlet devices shall have an ampere rating that is not less than the load to be served and shall comply with 210.21 (A) and (B).

(A) Lampholders: Where connected to a branch circuit having a rating in excess of 20 amperes, lampholders shall be of a heavy-duty type. A heavy-duty lampholder shall have a rating of not less than 660 watts if of the admedium type and not less than 750 watts if of any other type.

(B) Receptacles.

(1) Single Receptacle on an Individual Branch Circuit: A single receptacle installed on an individual branch circuit shall have an ampere rating not less than that of the branch circuit.

Exception No. 1: A receptacle installed in accordance with 430.81(B).

Exception No. 2: A receptacle installed exclusively for the use of a cord-and-plug-connected arc welder shall be permitted to have an ampere rating not less than the minimum branch-circuit conductor ampacity determined by 630.11(A) for arch welders.

FPN: See definition of receptacle in Article 100.

(2) Total Cord-and-Plug-Connected Load: Where connected to a branch circuit supplying two or more receptacles or outlets, a receptacle shall not supply a total cord-and-plug-connected load in excess of the maximum specified in Table 210.21 (B)(2).

(3) Receptacle Ratings: Where connected to a branch circuit supplying two or more receptacles or outlets, receptacle ratings shall conform to the values listed in Table 210.21(B)(3), or where larger than 50 amperes, the receptacle rating shall not be less than the branch-circuit rating.

NFPA commentary: A single receptacle installed on an individual branch circuit must have an ampere rating not less than that of the branch circuit. For example, a single receptacle on a 20-ampere individual branch circuit must be rated at 20 amperes in accordance with 210.21(B)(1); however, two or more 15-ampere receptacles or duplex receptacles are permitted on a 20-ampere general-purpose branch circuit in accordance with 210.21(B)(3). This requirement does not apply to specific types of cord-and-plug-connected arc welders.

(4) Range Receptacle Rating: The ampere rating of a range receptacle shall be permitted to be based on a single range demand load as specified in Table 220.55.

422.10 Branch-Circuit Rating: This section specifies the ratings of branch circuits capable of carrying appliance current without overheating under the conditions specified.

NFPA commentary: Conductors that form integral parts of appliances are tested as part of the listing or labeling process.

(A) Individual Circuits: The rating of an individual branch circuit shall not be less than the marked rating of the appliance or the marked rating of an appliance having combined loads as provided in 422.62.

The rating of an individual branch circuit for motor-operated appliances not having a marked rating shall be in accordance with Part II of Article 430.

The branch-circuit rating for an appliance that is continuously loaded, other than a motor-operated appliance, shall not be less than 125 percent of the marked rating, or not less than 100 percent of the marked rating if the branch-circuit device and its assembly are listed for continuous loading at 100% of its rating.

Branch circuits and conductors for household cooking appliances shall be permitted to be in accordance with Table 220.55 and shall be sized in according with 210.19(A)(3).

422.11 Overcurrent Protection: Appliances shall be protected against overcurrent in accordance with 422.11(A) through (G) and 422.10.

(A) Branch-Circuit Overcurrent Protection: Branch circuits shall be protected in accordance with 240.4. If a protective device rating is marked on an appliance, the branch-circuit overcurrent device rating shall not exceed the protective device rating marked on the appliance.

NFPA commentary: If a labeled or listed appliance is provided with installation instructions from the manufacturer, the branch-circuit size is not permitted to be less than the minimum size stated in the installation instructions. See 110.3(B) and its related commentary regarding the installation and use of listed or labeled equipment.

Circuit Breakers—Interchanging in Foreign Panels

Industry Standards

The Code Authority
(Underwriters Laboratories Inc.)

Ed. Note: Underwriters Laboratories, Inc. publishes The Code Authority, *a newsletter for the code community. In a column called "Questions and Answers," UL engineers answer questions concerning UL and its operations, or inquiries about UL Standards and how they coincide with installation codes (such as the NEC) and various building codes. Send questions to, UL, 333 Pfingsten Rd., Northbrook, IL 60062 or visit www.ul.com.*

Q. I've seen UL Classified circuit breakers from one manufacturer used in panelboards/load centers built by other manufacturers. Is this acceptable? In other instances, UL Lists circuit breakers. When does UL Classify rather than List circuit breakers?

A. UL has a program wherein circuit breakers are Classified for use in specific listed panelboards. This program could make it possible for you to see one manufacturer's Classified circuit breaker in another manufacturer's panelboard. The appearance of the UL Classified Product marking on a circuit breaker is evidence of compliance with this UL program covering expected applications of the circuit breaker. A list of compatible panelboards, including manufacturers and model numbers is required to be issued with a Classified breaker—and the Classified breakers are to be used only with those itemized compatible panelboards. The use of the UL Classified Product marking instead of the UL Listing Mark was chosen for products in this program to draw attention to the need for the installer to check the specific instructions provided with the circuit breaker for panelboard suitability.

Following is a summary of UL's Classified circuit breaker program:

A) UL Classified molded-case circuit breakers are subjected to the identical testing and evaluation programs used for Listed molded-case circuit breakers as described in UL 489, Molded-Case Circuit Breakers and Circuit-Breaker Enclosures. The Classified breakers must have the same ratings as the breakers they may replace.

B) UL Classified molded-case circuit breakers are evaluated in specific panelboards in accordance with UL 67, Panelboards. The identical testing and evaluation requirements are used to evaluate listed molded-case circuit breakers that are identified on the listed panelboard markings.

There continue to be questions about the use of Classified circuit breakers in series-rated systems. Markings identify the limitation of Classified circuit breakers for systems having an available fault current not exceeding 10 kA—emphasizing that Classified circuit breakers are not for use in series-rated systems. Classified circuit breakers are not for installation where markings, such as those required by Section 110.22 of the *NEC*, identify the application as a series-rated system.

Requirements for Tap Conductors

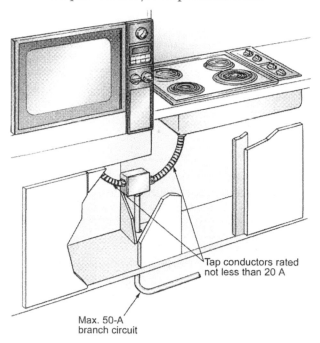

Tap conductors rated not less than 20 A

Max. 50-A branch circuit

Tap conductors are permitted by 210.19(A)(3), Exception No. 1, sized smaller than the branch-circuit conductors and not to be longer than necessary for servicing the appliances.

Figure 16.26 Courtesy of NFPA, *National Electrical Code® Handbook* [Exhibit 210.22]

Bonding

Comments

In electrical circuitry, bonding is the connecting or joining of metal parts to form an electrical conductive path. It prevents the accumulation of static electricity and ensures the safe conduction of electrical current. **Figure 16.27** shows how the bonding jumper is installed within a box. See "Service Conductors & Grounding" earlier in this chapter for more information.

IRC–2006

E3509.2 Bonding of services: Service raceways and service cable armor must be bonded, including metallic raceways and armor that enclose grounding electrode conductors. Service enclosures for service conductors must also be bonded.

E3509.3 Bonding to other systems: A method of connecting bonding and grounding conductors is required, such as using exposed, nonflexible, metallic raceways.

E3509.4 Method of bonding at the service: There are four alternatives for bonding at service equipment: using a grounded service conductor, threaded connections, threadless couplings and connectors, or approved other devices.

Bonding Jumper Installation

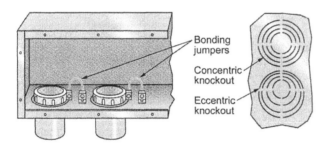

Bonding jumpers installed around concentric or eccentric knockouts.

Figure 16.27   Courtesy of NFPA, *National Electrical Code® Handbook* [Exhibit 100.3]

Safety Switches

Industry Standards

Means Graphic Construction Standards
(RSMeans)

A safety switch provides a manual method of disconnecting power from electrical equipment, which cannot be overridden by automatic controls. If the switch is fused, it provides branch circuit protection. The safety switch itself is mounted inside a sheet metal or cast iron enclosure and controlled by a handle connected to the mechanism and located on the outside of the enclosure. The switch mechanism is manufactured as either single- or double-break type, in knife-blade or butt-contact format. Because these switches usually conduct large amounts of power, the enclosure doors are designed so that they cannot be opened if the switch handle is set in the "up" or "on" position.

Safety switches are manufactured in general-duty and heavy-duty grades and in both fused and unfused types. General-duty switches are available in two-and three-pole design for up to 240 volts, with ratings of 30, 60, 100, 200, 400, and 600 amps. Heavy-duty switches are also manufactured in two- and three-pole formats, with voltage ratings of 250 and 600 volts and amperage ratings of 30, 60, 100, 200, 400, 600, 800, and 1,200 amps.

During installation, line side power is connected to the terminal lugs, which are located at the top of the switch before the blade mechanism. Power to a piece of electrical equipment is tapped off the load side of the switch before the blade mechanism. Accidental feeding of the load terminals, which would cause the blades of the switch to become "hot," even when the switch is in the open position, can be avoided by following precisely correct line and load installation rules.

The enclosures for safety switches are classified by the NEMA according to their particular interior or exterior safety function. Several of the NEMA enclosure types classified for interior use include NEMA 1, NEMA 2, NEMA 7, AND NEMA 12. The NEMA 1 enclosure type is intended for indoor use where no unusual service conditions exist. Its primary function is to protect personnel from accidental contact with live electrical equipment. NEMA 2 is designed with a drip-proof housing to protect the enclosed equipment against falling dirt and noncorrosive liquids. NEMA 7 is used to protect equipment in hazardous locations where indoor atmospheres containing volatile gas and vapors may cause explosion. This type of switch enclosure is marked to show the class and group letter designation. NEMA 12, which is designed for indoor industrial use, features dust- and drip-tight seals. Because it contains no conduit openings or knockouts, access may be gained only through field-installed holes with oil resistant gaskets. An additional safety feature of this type of enclosure is that a special tool is required to open its cover.

Two commonly used exterior NEMA enclosure classifications include NEMA 3 and NEMA 3R. NEMA 3 is a rain-tight, dust-tight, and ice-resistant enclosure that protects equipment from penetration by water, ice, and wind-blown dust. NEMA 3R is designed to protect against rain, sleet, and snow. This type of enclosure is also equipped with a conduit hub to assure weathertight connections for conduits, which are fed into the top of the unit.

Safety Switches

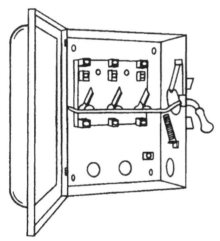

NEMA 1, non-fusible, 600 Volt

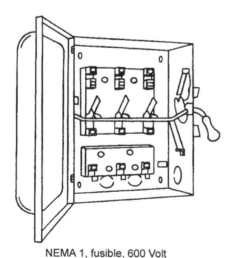

NEMA 1, fusible, 600 Volt

Figure 16.28   RSMeans, *Means Graphic Construction Standards*

Appliance Installation

Comments

Chapter 40 of the 2006 *IRC* covers installation requirements for appliances and fixed heating equipment, including disconnecting means.

Electrical clothes dryers typically require a 240-volt (30 amps), two-pole receptacle. Electric cooking ranges require a 240-volt (50 amps) receptacle.

IRC–2006

E4001.2 Installation: Installation of appliances must comply with manufacturers' requirements. Proper clearances must be met for appliances that are electrically heated.

E4001.3 Flexible cords: Flexible cords are permitted only when the appliance is listed for such use. Kitchen waste disposals, built-in dishwashers, trash compactors, and range hoods must meet minimum and maximum cord length requirements.

E4001.4 Overcurrent protection: Appliance overcurrent protection must comply with its rating and listing.

E4001.5 Disconnecting means: Appliances must have a method of disconnecting ungrounded supply conductors.

NFPA 70: National Electrical Code

Installation of Appliances

422.12 Central Heating Equipment: Central heating equipment other than fixed electric space heating equipment shall be supplied by an individual branch circuit.

Exception No. 1: Auxiliary equipment, such as a pump, valve, humidifier, or electrostatic air cleaner directly associated with the heating equipment, shall be permitted to be connected to the same branch circuit.

422.16 Flexible Cords:

(A) General. Flexible cord shall be permitted (1) for the connection of appliances to facilitate their frequent interchange or to prevent the transmission of noise or vibration or (2) to facilitate the removal or disconnection of appliances that are fastened in place, where the fastening means and mechanical connections are specifically designed to permit ready removal for maintenance or repair and the appliance in intended or identified for flexible cord connection.

(B)Specific Appliances:

(1) Electrically Operated Kitchen Waste Disposers. Electrically operated kitchen waste disposers shall be permitted to be cord-and-plug connected with a flexible cord identified as suitable for the purpose in the installation instructions of the appliance manufacturer, where all of the following conditions are met.

(1) The flexible cord shall be terminated with a grounding type attachment plug.

Exception: A listed kitchen waste disposer distinctly marked to identify it as protected by a system of double insulation, or its equivalent, shall not be required to be terminated with a grounding-type attachment plug.

(2) The length of the cord shall not be less than 450 mm (18") and not over 900 mm (36").

(3) Receptacles shall be located to avoid physical damage to the flexible cord.

(4) The receptacle shall be accessible.

(2) Built-in Dishwashers and Trash Compactors. Built-in dishwashers and trash compactors shall be permitted to be cord-and-plug connected with a flexible cord identified as suitable for the purpose in the installation instructions of the appliance manufacturer where all of the following conditions are met:

(1) The flexible cord shall be terminated with a grounding-type attachment plug.

(2) The length of the cord shall be 0.9 m to 1.2m (3' to 4') measured from the face of the attachment plug to the plane of the rear of the appliance.

(3) Receptacles shall be located to avoid physical damage to the flexible cord.

(4) The receptacle shall be located in the space occupied by the appliance or adjacent thereto.

(5) The receptacle shall be accessible.

422.43 Flexible Cords:

(A) Heater Cords: All cord-and-plug-connected smoothing irons and electrically heated appliances that are rated at more than 50 watts and produce temperatures in excess of 121°C (250°F) on surfaces with which the cord is likely to be in contact shall be provided with one of the types of approved heater cords listed in Table 400.4.

(B) Other Heating Appliances: All other cord-and-plug-connected electrically heated appliances shall be connected with one of the approved types of cord listed in Table 400.4, selected in accordance with the usage specified in that table.

422.34 Unit Switch(es) as Disconnecting Means: A unit switch(es) with a marked-off position that is a part of an appliance and disconnects all ungrounded conductors shall be permitted as the disconnecting means required by this article where other means for disconnection are provided in the following types of occupancies.

(A) Multi-family Dwellings: In multifamily dwellings, the other disconnecting means shall be within the dwelling unit, or on the same floor as the dwelling unit in which the appliance is installed, and shall be permitted to control lamps and other appliances.

(B) Two-Family Dwellings: In two-family dwellings, the other disconnecting means shall be permitted either inside or outside of the dwelling unit in which the appliance is installed. In this case, an individual switch or circuit breaker for the dwelling unit shall be permitted and shall also be permitted to control lamps and other appliances.

(C) One-Family Dwellings: In one-family dwellings, the service disconnecting means shall be permitted to be the other disconnecting means.

(D) Other Occupancies: In other occupancies, the branch circuit switch or circuit breaker, where readily accessible for servicing of the appliance, shall be permitted as the other disconnecting means.

422.11 Overcurrent Protection:

(F) Electric Heating Appliances Employing Resistance- Type Heating Elements Rated More Than 48 Amperes.

(1) Electric Heating Appliances: Electric heating appliances employing resistance-type heating elements rated more than 48 amperes, other than household appliances with surface heating elements covered by 422.11(B), and commercial-type heating appliances covered by 422311(D), shall have the heating elements subdivided. Each subdivided load shall not exceed 48 amperes and shall be protected at not more than 60 amperes.

These supplementary overcurrent protective devices shall be (1) factory-installed within or on the heater enclosure or provided as a separate assembly by the heater manufacturer; (2) accessible; and (3) suitable for branch-circuit protection.

The main conductors supplying these overcurrent protective devices shall be considered branch-circuit conductors.

424.19 Disconnecting Means:

(A) Heating Equipment with Supplementary Overcurrent Protection: The disconnecting means for fixed electric space heating equipment with supplementary overcurrent protection shall be within sight from the supplementary overcurrent protective device(s), on the supply side of these devices, if fuses, and, in addition, shall comply with either 424.19(A)(1) or (A)(2).

(1) Heater Containing No Motor Rated Over ⅛ Horsepower: The above disconnecting means or unit switches complying with 424.19(C) shall be permitted to serve as the required disconnecting means for both the motor controller(s) and heater under either of the following conditions:

(1) The disconnecting means provided is also within sight from the motor controller(s) and the heater.

(2) The disconnecting means provided shall be capable of being locked in the open position.

(2) Heater Containing a Motor(s) Rated Over ⅛ Horsepower: The above disconnecting means shall be permitted to serve as the required disconnecting means for both the motor controller(s) and heater by one of the means specified in items (1) through (4):

(1) Where the disconnecting means is also in sight from the motor controller(s) and the heater.

(2) Where the disconnecting means is not within sight from the heater, a separate disconnecting means shall be installed, or the disconnecting means shall be capable of being locked in the open position, or unit switches complying with 424.19(C) will be permitted.

(3) Where the disconnecting means is not within sight from the motor controller location, a disconnecting means complying with 430.102 shall be provided.

(4) Where the motor is not in sight from the motor controller location, 430.102(B) shall apply.

Three Correct Alternate Wiring Configurations

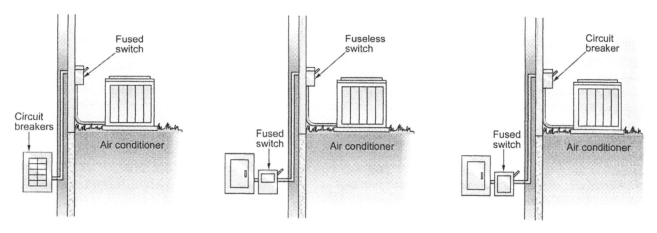

Three correct alternate wiring configurations satisfying a nameplate that specifies fuses, thus restricting the equipment to protection by fuses only. (Note that the fuse rating cannot exceed the maximum fuse size specified on the air-conditioner nameplate.)

Figure 16.29

Courtesy of NFPA, *National Electrical Code® Handbook* [Exhibit 440.2]

INDEX